CAPITAL
INVESTMENT IN AFRICA

CAPITAL INVESTMENT
IN AFRICA

ITS COURSE AND EFFECTS

BY

S. HERBERT FRANKEL

Issued by the Committee of the
African Research Survey
under the Auspices of the
Royal Institute of International Affairs

HOWARD FERTIG

NEW YORK · 1969

First published in 1938

HOWARD FERTIG, INC. EDITION 1969
Published by arrangement with Oxford University Press

Preface to the 1969 edition copyright © 1969
by S. H. Frankel

Library of Congress Catalog Card Number: 68-9593

PRINTED IN THE UNITED STATES OF AMERICA
BY NOBLE OFFSET PRINTERS, INC.

TO THE MEMORY
OF
MY FATHER

FOREWORD

AMONG the preparatory studies commissioned for the African Research Survey was a memorandum on the course of capital investment in Africa. When the suggestion of assembling material on this subject was discussed with Professor Frankel, he doubted whether it would be feasible in the short time available to secure figures on a scale which would make it possible to draw any conclusions. He eventually undertook, however, in 1935 to prepare an informative picture based on readily available material, of the form which the investment of capital from Europe has from time to time taken in Africa, of the function which it has performed in the development of the countries with which our Survey is concerned, and of the factors which may be expected in the future to influence the further supply of capital in Africa.

It will be seen from the scale and proportion of this volume how far Professor Frankel's study has outgrown its modest origin. He has devoted far more labour to his research than was originally expected, and has secured an amount of statistical data which greatly exceeds what it was originally hoped to obtain ; it will serve, I hope, as a valuable source of information to those who may wish to carry out more detailed studies of African financial development. But the scope of the work is not limited to the assembling of statistical data regarding the progress of capital investment; Professor Frankel has endeavoured at the same time to interpret the effect of modern economic forces on the structure of African society.

Owing to the extension of the scope of his work, Professor Frankel was only able to complete it in time to enable it to be used during the preparation of some of the later chapters of *An African Survey*, which embodies the report of the African Research Survey. The frequent references made in those chapters to

Professor Frankel's work testify to the value of the assistance which the authors of the report have received from the material which he has provided.   It will of course be understood that any opinions expressed by Professor Frankel in his volume are his own, and not necessarily those of the Director or Committee of the African Research Survey, and that he takes full responsibility for them.

As in the case of *An African Survey* itself the researches represented by this volume have been made possible through the generosity of the Carnegie Corporation of New York, who must, equally, be absolved from any responsibility for views expressed or statements made.

HAILEY

7th August, 1938.

CONTENTS

ERRATA

Page 28, line 5 from bottom: "iuaugurated" should read "inaugurated"

Page 151, line 16: "£1,322 millions" should read "£1,222 millions"

Page 255: in the last column of Table 61, figures for the years 1932, 1933 (b), 1934, 1935, 1936, and 1937 should read: "1,250; 2,340; 2,340; 2,340; 2,340; 2,340."

Page 329, line 2 from bottom: "demands" should read "demand"

Page 347, line 22: "capital's" should read "capital"

Page 395, line 15 of text: "£52,875" should read "£52,825"

TABLES

MAP

(at end of volume)

Principal Railways in Africa

PREFACE TO THE 1969 EDITION

The privilege is not given to many authors to write a preface to the reprint of a volume thirty years after its first appearance. I thank God for having been permitted for so long to enjoy the fruits of my labour.

It is necessary for the reader of this book to bear in mind the great contrast between the political circumstances ruling at the time at which it was written and the situation facing a new generation. The contrast can be epitomised by quoting the first line of Chapter I, and adding just eight words to it. The sentence reads: "In a single generation the European powers established sovereignty over most of Africa." The words that need to be added are: ". . . *and in a single generation they lost it.*"

When I said goodbye to General Smuts before my departure from South Africa in 1946, he said to me: "Tell your friends in England that by leaving India they have drawn out the lynch-pin on which the peace, order and good government of *Africa* depend." For him, at the very moment of victory the impending disintegration of the European empires had already begun.

What light then, can this book written under the influence of a vanished era, throw on current and future problems? It is my hope that it may bring an awareness of what the economic world of Africa was like before parts of it were laboriously brought into the twentieth century by mainly European enterprise and government, and what was involved in the process of doing so; how tenuous were the threads of economic intercourse; how meagre the resources for development; how accidental, frequently, the causes of success or failure; and above all how difficult the sociological, political, and economic tasks of stimulating worthwhile change in this vast, and for long so isolated, continent.

What I think will most astonish the reader who comes to this study for the first time is how little the fundamental problems have changed in Africa. Are the needs of Africa for capital from abroad, or the limitations on its supply, any less than they were; is order and good government more generally available than heretofore; are the risks and uncertainties which private enterprise has to face greater or smaller; has the importance of mineral exploitation diminished or increased; have governments become more successful in stimulating economic development; and are the independent nations now better able to cope with the ever-recurring challenge of population growth in Africa?

At the end of this book I concluded: "In the last resort, however, the future of capital investment, like the future of all African economic progress, will depend on freeing the African peoples from the factors which have checked their progress in the past, and the artificial restrictions which in some territories still prevent the unfolding of their abilities . . . If twentieth century experience in Africa has proved anything at all, it is that the wealth of Africa has, as yet, hardly been discovered, simply because it lies deep in the soil of Africa itself . . . The curtain has only just risen on the African scene—the drama has yet to be played."

Perhaps I was more prophetic than I knew.

S. H. Frankel

Nuffield College
Oxford
January 1968

AUTHOR'S PREFACE

THIS book is an attempt to survey the course of capital investment from abroad in Africa. It differs from other statistical studies of capital investment, not only in regard to the technique which had to be utilized owing to the difficulties involved in the collection of the statistical material, but also because it has as its object to portray the effect of the impact on the structure of African economies of the modern economic forces associated with the capital investment.

I am greatly indebted to Lord Hailey, Lord Lothian, Professor Clay and other members of the Committee of the African Research Survey for inviting me to extend my previous researches into the capitalization of the Witwatersrand Gold Mining Industry over the African field as a whole.

To Professor Henry Clay I am under a great obligation for his many suggestions based on reading the manuscript, and for his patient encouragement. Portions of a preliminary draft were also read by Professor Allan G. B. Fisher, Professor J. B. Condliffe, Mr. W. F. Crick, Mr. John Maud, Mr. I. G. Thomas, and a large part of the final manuscript by Dr. J. N. Reedman and Dr. M. Gluckman.

Without the assistance of innumerable African government departments, libraries, and very many friends, it would have been impossible to collect the statistical material on which this study is based. It is not possible to acknowledge their help individually here, but I wish to place on record the friendly assistance and advice given me by my colleagues at the University of the Witwatersrand, and in particular by the Principal, Mr. H. R. Raikes, whose personal interest enabled me to obtain many facilities for the conduct of the investigation.

ACKNOWLEDGMENTS

From members of the Staff of the Dominion and Colonial Office Library I was privileged to receive not only their personal help while I was working in London, but also a large number of duplicates of official reports which were kindly sent by them to Johannesburg. I wish also to record my appreciation of the generous assistance rendered by the Library Staff of the University of the Witwatersrand. The Railway Administrations in Africa co-operated by making available special reports, and many went to considerable trouble in extracting special information.

In conclusion, I desire to acknowledge the continuous help received from Miss Hilda Matheson, Secretary of the African Research Survey, in particular, for seeing the book through the press. I wish also to pay tribute to Mrs. E. M. White for making the Index, and to the painstaking efforts of my Statistical Assistant and my Private Secretary, without whom my task could not have been completed in the time available.

Needless to say, none of the above-mentioned are responsible for the opinions expressed in this volume.

S. HERBERT FRANKEL

University of the Witwatersrand,
    July, 1938.

CHAPTER I

THE PROBLEM AND ITS BACKGROUND

SECTION I

AFRICA AND THE WORLD ECONOMY

"Africa's modern empire builders had the habit of thinking in continental dimensions. The historian, by following them in this habit, may find the clue not only to their achievements, but also to their illusions and extravagances."—HANCOCK.[1]

I

INTRODUCTORY.

IN a single generation the European powers established sovereignty over most of Africa.[2] The rapidity of the process is illustrated by the fact that, whereas as late as 1878 only a quarter of the continent was occupied by them, to-day they control the whole of it with the exception of Liberia.

Once they had established their sovereign rights in Africa, all the colonial powers were confronted with the problem of how to finance the administration and economic development of their territories. While the hope for economic benefits was a potent factor in the scramble for Africa, the means to be adopted in realizing these hopes were not known, and the resources necessary were not mobilized.

The African continent presented the metropolitan countries with exceptional difficulties. The indigenous populations in

[1] "Problems of Nationality, 1918–1936," *Survey of British Commonwealth Affairs*, vol. i, p. 210. (London: Oxford University Press, 1937.)

[2] Throughout this book "Africa" refers to the areas of the continent south of the Sahara, Egypt and Abyssinia. African territories bordering on the Mediterranean are geographically, historically and ethnographically distinct from the territories included in this study. A detailed list of the latter is given on page 2.

general possessed primitive social and economic organizations. The very concept of production[1] for purposes of exchange was practically unknown, and accumulated wealth serving an economic purpose was almost non-existent.

Commercial access to African peoples was in itself of relatively little value to the West. Unlike the Indians or Chinese, Africans had practically nothing to offer, and as little to demand, from the traders who visited them. The only trade of real consequence which could be developed for centuries was the slave trade, the export of Africans themselves—"a trade which destroys all others".[2] In any case, the problem of the internal development of African resources could not be solved as long as the continent remained economically isolated, as most of it did until the third quarter of the nineteenth century. The modern economic history of Africa dates from the mineral discoveries in the southern portion of the continent. These inaugurated the investment of foreign resources, and therewith commenced that revolutionary process through which Africa is being incorporated in the income-creating activities of the world. The object of this investigation is to analyse that process, to examine its financial aspects, to portray its extent, and to assess its effects on the structure of African economy.

Broadly speaking, the study is confined to the territories south of the Sahara and Abyssinia,[3] which comprise nearly three-quarters

---

[1] The people subsisted on the products of a meagre hoe-culture or of pastoralism, supplemented by wild vegetable products and game. Their hoe-culture was a primitive shifting cultivation to the limit of the natural capacity of the land. When that limit was reached they proceeded elsewhere, as far as natural conditions or other groups permitted. Their activities were inhibited by great environmental and climatic obstacles, and their energies sapped by a variety of tropical diseases.

[2] This phrase is from Lionel Curtis, *Civitas Dei*, vol. ii, p. 257. (London: Macmillan, 1937.)

[3] The territories included are the following:

British—	French—
Gold Coast.	French West Africa.
Nigeria.	French Equatorial Africa.
Gambia.	*French Mandates—*
Sierra Leone.	Cameroons.
Uganda.	Togoland.
Somaliland.	*Portuguese—*
Kenya.	Angola.
Zanzibar.	Portuguese East Africa.
Nyasaland.	[*Continued at foot of p.* 3.

of the African continent. Together their area is about 8,260,000 square miles, equivalent to that of the Union of Soviet Socialist Republics in Europe and Asia, to nearly three times the area of the United States of America, and to the combined area of Canada, Australia and British India. Their population, according to the latest available calculations, is about 100,000,000, of which some 2,250,000 are whites. Barely 100,000 of the latter are to be found north of the Zambesi.[1]

II

CAPITAL AND PROGRESS.

The investigation that forms the substance of this book has been conducted on both historical and statistical lines. To present abstractly the economic facts of any situation at a given time is in itself of little value. Only when they are interpreted in relation to the background of history can they throw light on the actions of the society and serve to guide them in the future. This is particularly necessary in studies such as this, of which a large part is concerned with capital investment. For capital is an abstract term, the careless use of which is apt to hide the real meaning of the process to which it refers.

As Cannan[2] has shown so clearly, capital forms a most

[1] In the territories bordering on the Mediterranean (not included in this study) the white population numbers about 1,400,000. The total population, including that of Italian Somaliland and Abyssinia, is about 40,000,000. The total population of the African continent and its islands is not accurately known, but may be regarded as 150,000,000. Its total area is about 11,544,000 square miles.

[2] "Capital and the Heritage of Improvement," by Edwin Cannan, *Economica*, London, November, 1934, p. 381.

British (cont.)—	*Belgian*—
Northern Rhodesia.	Belgian Congo.
Southern Rhodesia.	*Belgian Mandate*—
Basutoland.	Ruanda Urundi.
Bechuanaland.	
Swaziland.	
Condominion.	
Anglo-Egyptian Sudan.	
British Mandates—	
Cameroons.	
Tanganyika Territory.	
Togoland.	
Union of South Africa—	
South-West Africa	
(South African Mandate).	

important, perhaps the most important, part of "the heritage of improvement".[1] But capital is not the whole of that man-made heritage. In common usage the term "capital" is applied to purchasable and saleable private property, and excludes things which are not openly sold for and bought with money. This concept is useful, but it suffers from two serious disadvantages. On the one hand, it excludes many things which are capital, although they cannot easily be brought into relationship with the measuring rod of money, and therefore the concept is too narrow ; on the other hand, in the attempt to give it wider meaning, it has frequently been confused with the "whole economic heritage". There is consequently a "widespread impression that the capital of society is much the same thing as the whole heritage, so that alterations in its magnitude must be regarded with the same favour and disfavour as increases and decreases of the whole heritage". But, as Cannan rightly stressed, "there are other ways of adding to the heritage of improvement besides saving and addition to capital". In fact, such other additions to or changes in the heritage often call for no increase in capital. "On the contrary" they may "wipe capital out, and are all the more beneficent for thus enabling us to discard the tools, machinery or stock rendered unnecessary", owing to newer methods of technique and production which no longer require this capital.

In this study, as will appear from the context, the term "capital" will be used both in its narrow sense, and in a wider sense to include things which are not easily valued in money or easily saleable or purchasable. This is very necessary if the importance to Africa of the resources on which it has been able to draw from Europe, and the use of those resources are to be properly assessed. There is, in fact, no hard and fast line between that which is, and that which is not capital, or between "material" and "non-material" capital. It is not helpful to restrict the use of the term "capital" by any precise definition.

The use of capital implies an indirect or "round-about" method of setting free ("economizing") labour for other tasks

---

[1] Which he has defined as "the net economic advantage which we and other generations who come late in the history of mankind possess in consequence of what has been done by mankind in the past".

than those to which it had previously been devoted. The creation of additional capital is itself part and parcel of the same process. It is a diversion of labour from tasks satisfying some relatively immediate purpose, to tasks which will create the means of more easily satisfying this and other purposes in the future.

The essence of economic progress is to be found in the change of traditional methods, occupations, and forms of economic activity. Without change, both the creation and utilization of additional capital are not possible. "Material progress," writes Professor Fisher, "is identical with a raising of the average standard of real income. Unless average real incomes rise, there is no material progress, though there may be important elements of progress of other and profounder kinds. A study of the economics of a materially progressive society must therefore include a study of the adjustments in the organization of production which are necessary in the face of a rising average income-level". What, however, is not sufficiently realized is that "the two processes, rising incomes and *changing production organization* are not independent processes. We do not increase incomes first and adapt our methods of production afterwards. . . . At the same time as we improve our production the average level of real income also rises. . . . The two processes of getting an increased income and producing new things, are for a community, identical. Unless the *new* things are produced there is no increase of income".[1]

Similarly, we cannot create capital,[2] that is, divert income-

---

[1] A. G. B. Fisher: *The Clash of Progress and Security.* (London, 1935.) p. 13. The implications of material progress and the changes necessitated thereby have been exhaustively considered by Professor Fisher in that book.

[2] If a community cannot itself create capital, it must either borrow it or receive it as a gift. Where the natural resources and skill of any community are such that labour can be made to yield a surplus over and above its immediate requirements, the surplus becomes available for the support of those engaged in creating capital in any of its multitudinous forms—it may be "invested" for the future. The surplus may, of course, be exchanged for such forms of capital as are more efficiently produced by other communities. "The field of employment which any place offers for labour and capital depends, firstly, on its natural resources; secondly, on the power of turning them to good account, derived from its progress of knowledge and of social and industrial organization; and thirdly, on the access that it has to markets in which it can sell those things of which it has a superfluity. The importance of this last condition is often under-rated; but it stands out prominently when we look at the history of new countries." (*Cf.* Alfred Marshall, *Principles of Economics*, eighth edition, 1927, p. 668.)

producing resources to activities which are to yield income in the future, nor can we, in fact, realize that future income, unless we change the production organization concomitantly. There is always a danger that this will be overlooked, and a tendency to refer to capital in abstract terms as money enhances it. The history of investment abounds in errors and wastes which might have been avoided if the fundamental realities of the process had been borne in mind. An example will serve to illustrate this. Let us suppose that some millions of pounds are spent in constructing a railway in an undeveloped area which trades with an adjoining territory, but that this commerce involves the transport of goods by head-porterage, and requires the labour of a considerable section of the working population. The construction of the line involves a diversion of the activities of a portion of the labouring population to this new effort. It will be justified on economic grounds only if, after the line has been built, the efforts of the population as a whole, including that of the porters, can be so redirected as to yield sufficient quantities of additional, or more valuable, goods, of a kind which can enter trade, and bear the cost of railway transport. To provide the line is only one step in the process of change, and the whole process—in this case the successful re-alignment of the "production organization" of the area—must be completed before the investment can yield its full economic fruits. This example is not intended to convey the impression that capital expenditure can be justified only if its direct money returns are sufficient. On the contrary, in Africa types of capital expenditure have frequently been necessary, and beneficial, whose direct economic advantages could not easily be measured. The point at issue here is the simple one that only limited advantages can accrue unless all the changes in the structure of the society, which are implied in the application of capital, are carried through.

It must, however, not be overlooked that grave errors are likely to result from concentrating attention too exclusively on investments in material equipment, and neglecting the fact that investments in what may be called personal equipment are equally important. A sound investment policy demands the maintenance of proper proportions, not only between fixed and working capital and capital invested in different directions, but also between investments in material and in personal equipment. A very large part of modern activity in Africa has taken the form of scientific research and experimentation with the object of increasing knowledge of how to foster new products, and generally to meet the obstacles of a new environment. This is part of the accumulated non-material capital which goes to form the social heritage of its inhabitants. Its counterpart is the growth in personal skill and individual knowledge, without which progress is restricted. Indeed, investments in scientific research, like those in material equipment, are only a part of the processes of change. The complementary growth of personal equipment is essential if the necessary changes, on which the increase in welfare depends, are to be carried through successfully.

Under the impact of the dynamic economic forces of the West, the indigenous peoples of Africa, like those of the East,[1] are compelled to develop a new social order to take the place of their closed, static, undifferentiated and self-sufficient economies. These must give way to those innumerable forces which increase the range of individual and social action, and which broaden the ideas and heighten the creative possibilities of the citizen in a wider society. To realize this is the key to colonial statesmanship. The difficulty always is to make isolated communities fit in with that larger society which inevitably takes shape under Western influence.

At first sight it might seem that the much less developed social structure, and the sparsity of the indigenous population in Africa, would have simplified the problem of change. This would be a most superficial view. The penetration by Western powers into large parts of Africa involved not only the contact of "higher" with "lower" civilizations, but often also conflicted with lawless and raiding peoples. It involved the suppression of the miseries of the slave trade, which laid waste large areas and ravaged their population. It involved the introduction of law, order and civilized government in territories where there were not even

[1] For an excellent account of similar changes in the East, which result from the introduction of capital, see C. F. Remer, *Foreign Investments in China* (London: Macmillan, 1933), pp. 7-10, and D. H. Buchanan, *Development of Capitalist Enterprise in India*. (London: Macmillan, 1934.)

roads. If the indigenous population had disappeared before the advance of the white man, as the Indian did in America, and if its climate had favoured European settlement, as in large parts of that continent, the problem of European colonization might indeed have been capable of the same almost automatic solution. Actually, in most parts of Africa, instead of a decadent population, rapidly tending to extinction, the intending settlers encountered a race virile, increasing and racially potent. Moreover, Europeans, unlike Asiatics, have in no part of Africa been able to engage in economic activities without utilizing, directly or indirectly, the labour of the native peoples. In fact, the absence of a sufficient and efficient labour force has frequently retarded, and still retards, European expansion, even in large areas of the temperate zone.[1] The greatest social and economic fact in the modern penetration of Africa is without doubt the universal dependence upon black labour.[2]

In large parts of the continent the basic problem of change may be said to resolve itself into the creation of such institutions,

[1] Broadly speaking, the area definitely suited to permanent settlement by black and white races may be said to be confined to "South Africa". Typically South African conditions may be said to exist as far north as the country is fit for permanent settlement of both the white and the black races. The farther north we go, the more the parts favourable (for European settlement) become isolated patches. But even in Kenya there is a region whose social and economic conditions show affinities with South Africa. "On the plateau lands to the north of the Zambesi, however, seasonal differences in temperature which contribute so much to the well-being of a white population, become small, though not negligible. . . . Life in the tropical highlands may be very pleasant to the white man whose work permits him to protect himself from the worst effects of the sunshine, but a white labour class is hardly possible there, and Europeans will always form a far smaller percentage of the population than in the Union. . . . For the present it does not seem advisable to extend the geographical concept of South Africa to the country beyond the Zambesi." (Professor P. Serton, "The Geographical Environment," *The Cambridge History of the British Empire*, vol. viii, South Africa, pp. 4–5.)

[2] Even in South Africa none of the European communities were at any time even remotely successful in segregating the natives. "Each war helped but to prove the indestructible character of native life, ready to change its form in order to preserve its being. . . . In the face of European colonization the natives neither decreased nor retreated. Each blow that fell upon them drove them not outwards into estrangement, but inwards into greater intimacy. The borders that should have excluded them, the wars that should have decimated their manhood, the alcohol and diseases that should have stricken their life in loin and womb, finally did none of these. . . . The process of white colonization pumped them into every artery and limb of South Africa's social body, until they could not be withdrawn from it safely." Professor C. W. de Kiewiet, *The Imperial Factor in South Africa—A Study in Politics and Economics*. (Cambridge University Press, 1937.) p. 2.

in place of the primitive structure of the indigenous society, as will permanently enlarge the scope and results of its efforts in relation to the environment. The economic rate of change will be that which is neither too slow nor too rapid to achieve this object. The rate of investment from abroad and the consequent introduction of modern methods of production, which is the most potent of the forces of change, must be governed by the same principle. Indeed, constructive change is the fundamental task of colonial statesmanship. It involves a dual function: that of protection, and that of calling forth the power of self-exertion. "Only when this dual function is adhered to can the life of the people, rooted as it is in ancient institutions, escape to a certain degree from disintegrating influences, until such times as it becomes capable of resistance by a new unfolding of its own vigour."[1]

III

THE NEED FOR A NEW ECONOMIC SYNTHESIS.

The introduction of capital and the application of science are essential for the development of African resources, but because they disturb the equilibrium[2] of the primitive society, they require that a new synthesis of means to ends be brought about.

The greatest asset which European powers possess for developing the resources of their African territories is the labour of the indigenous peoples themselves. The inestimable importance of

---

[1] *Cf.* the excellent study of Dr. De Kat Angelino, *Colonial Policy* (Martinus Nyhoff), The Hague, 1931, vol. i, pp. 55–6. He adds: "We must utter an emphatic warning against the views of those who attribute every kind of complication that is met with in the colonial world to the conditions obtaining therein. As soon as one takes a wider view it becomes obvious that difficulties of exactly the same nature are met with along the whole line of contact between the spirit of the twentieth century and that of former ages."

[2] But it is well to remember that, however primitive a particular economy may appear to modern eyes, when it is judged by its utility to serve other objectives than those which determined its evolution, it nevertheless will often be found on closer examination to be well adapted to the particular environment in which it originally developed. If account is taken of the people's knowledge and beliefs, on the one hand, and the obstacles to their efforts on the other, it will be seen that a balance of forces, a state of equilibrium between the ends and the means, has been achieved. It is true that the results attained appear extremely inadequate compared with those which modern techniques make possible, but the real effectiveness of the efforts of the primitive economy must not be judged without an appreciation of the technical means at its disposal, and the needs which it is endeavouring to meet.

developing its latent possibilities was not realized in the colonial policies of the past, and even at present is not realized in many parts of Africa. Yet, only when a new synthesis is achieved, can modern methods of production be utilized successfully. In the areas not permanently habitable by Europeans the whole process is bound to be slow, although this unfortunately is not always realized. For, what foreign interests in this instance consider to be only a single economic adjustment, in fact menaces the whole social fabric of native life. Moreover, a course of action which may yield considerable net returns to specific foreign activities may yield a lesser or even a negative return to the whole society; in technical economic terms, there may be very great differences between its private and social net products. It must, however, always be remembered that economic progress in Africa must be ascribed to the incentives provided by European enterprise, on which it will remain dependent for a very long time to come. The great economic revolution which is resulting from the impact of Western forces is in itself an educational process of vast importance. For, in the last resort, there is no escape from the basic fact that the limit to the progress of all African territories will be determined by the quantity, quality and efficiency of the whole of their populations.

ECONOMIC DEVELOPMENT BASED ON COMPULSION.

A striking feature of most European economic enterprise in Africa has been the constant effort of Governments, companies, and individuals, to achieve specific developments in particular directions as rapidly as possible. This objective formed and still forms the basis of all those systems of "forced labour" which are still to be found even in the modern sectors of African economies. All these attempts at rapid development necessarily rested directly or indirectly on the principle of inducing some disintegration of the indigenous economies.[1]

[1] It is when, as in Southern Africa, the direction of development is determined in the interests of a permanent European population, that the forces making for the disintegration of the indigenous society are strongest, the rate of change most rapid, the application of a variety of methods of compulsion to make native labour available most marked, the problems of controlling the pressure to which the indigenous peoples are subjected greatest, and the achievement of that new economic synthesis which is

To develop African territories at all it was essential to obtain a labour supply. It was not possible to induce that labour to offer its services voluntarily, simply because the indigenous economy of the natives fulfilled all their wants, and the European had little to offer them which would cause them to prefer to work outside it. This, of course, explains the importation of Indians for the sugar industry in Natal, the attempts to supplement native by Chinese labour on the Witwatersrand, and many similar proposals that were made, during the first decades of European penetration, in various African territories.

The methods of compulsion which are still used are many.[1] They range from directly applied force to the more refined techniques of conscripting labour or indirectly taxing natives to "go out and work". Most important and far-reaching, in its effects, has been the expropriation of native land, which has always marked European settlement, and in many parts of the continent still continues.

"When in the transition stages of a self-sufficient economy the standard of living does not have to adjust itself to ruling market values, because the natives have an alternative means of living available, there may easily be a gap between what their labour is worth to an employer and the price they set upon their time and effort."[2] But once the native's land—the basis of all his traditional economic efforts—has been taken away, the gap simply ceases to exist, and since the economic opportunities of the indigenous peoples have been drastically undermined by this, and possibly by other measures, which restrict the type of economic activity and employment open to them, their wages will remain at a very low level.

---

[1] Where there is a compulsory diversion of labour into tasks which are intended to yield future income to the indigenous society the process can perhaps be regarded as a form of "forced saving", which is brought about by direct means instead of as in advanced economies, through monetary policy.

[2] Cf. I. E. Greaves, *Modern Production among Backward Peoples*. (London: Allen and Unwin, 1935.)

---

essential throughout Africa, most difficult. For, wherever European communities have established themselves permanently, they have had to protect their civilization and their income standards; whether, in fact, the means adopted were in the long run most likely to achieve this object is another matter.

The resort to some form of compulsion was the result of historical conditions. It has brought about investment in specific directions, on the basis of labour at artificially low wage rates, and has led to a distinctive "productive and distributive scheme"[1] or "production organization". The dangers associated with it arise from that diversion of resources, which, while increasing output of some specific kind, may diminish potential activity elsewhere, and may seriously reduce the total net income of the society.

This danger exists even when there is no conflict between foreign interests and those of the indigenous society, and a benevolent authority undertakes all development purely in the interests of the indigenous society itself. The possibility of maldistribution of economic resources is increased if the main interests considered are not those of the population as a whole, but those of foreign enterprises. The investment of foreign capital in such enterprises may have taken place on the basis of calculations, which assume the continuous availability of labour at artificial wage rates. In this way vested interests will have been created which are likely to demand measures which will, in fact, ensure a supply of labour on those terms.

Moreover, policies which endeavour to maintain the value of past investments are adopted not merely on account of existing interests, but because of the desire to foster the rapid economic expansion of territories, and to encourage the further investment of resources in them. The dangers associated with the resulting diversions of resources are enhanced because they are not easily discernible. The requirements of particular enterprises, established in all good faith, and administered with great ability, are likely to cause the general economic consequences of their expansion to be overlooked.[2] As a result much apparently

[1] For an excellent discussion of the nature of this distinctive productive "scheme" see Professor W. H. Hutt, "Logical Issues in the Study of Industrial Legislation in the Union", *South African Journal of Economics*, vol. iii, No. 1, March, 1935, pp. 27–46. See also his comprehensive study, *Economists and the Public*, particularly chapter xxi, "Vested Interests and the Distributive Scheme." (London: Jonathan Cape, 1936.)

[2] Many examples of these difficulties readily spring to mind. The establishment of large-scale agricultural or mining enterprises conducted on the basis of some form of compulsory native labour has contributed to the neglect of development in native areas, which are drained of their labour supply. The appropriation of native land

valuable economic development in Africa may in the future be found to yield negligible returns from the point of view of the society as a whole, because it was premature, or otherwise failed to establish an equilibrium between the application of labour and capital and the natural resources available.

IV

INVESTMENT AND MONO-CULTURES.

In Southern Africa the establishment of a considerable European population enjoying a relatively high standard of life has resulted from the extensive foreign investments which were attracted, because exploitable resources were available to which they could be applied under a distinctive system both of the production and distribution of wealth.

It is typical of the mineral industries that production can be carried on by means of a technique which is able to utilize large numbers of relatively unskilled wage-paid labourers. Whereas in mining this type of labour can be made economic, because it is concentrated and easily supervised, it is generally not economic in those pursuits which require the intensive interest and attention of the worker. The creation of the present European economy in South Africa possibly owes as much to the surplus wealth resulting from the peculiar organization which it has been able to adopt in exploiting its mineral deposits, as to the favourable climatic conditions which distinguish it from the northern territories.

Where mineral, or relatively easily exploitable sylvan resources are lacking it has become increasingly clear that development depends on the creation of systems of peasant production, and the introduction of new products, and new economic methods.[1]

[1] For climatic and other reasons, the scope for European peasant production is limited in all but a few of the Central and East African territories, while, even where a plantation economy can be introduced, the surplus wealth which it yields is insufficient to support a large permanent European population at a high standard of life.

tends to lead to overcrowding in the remaining areas, and to conditions (such as soil erosion) which impoverish the land and its peoples. Compulsion has prevented the growth of economic systems of land tenure. Compulsion, while appearing at first to yield better results, in reality leads to a misuse of the efforts of the community, and finally destroys its most valuable asset, the personal interest and initiative of the individuals composing it.

This is a very complex task. It involves large capital expenditure on communications and public works. The returns to such investments can be reaped only in the distant future, and so Governments have had to take an active part in supplying the capital required.[1] Yet even the Governments concerned are in a dilemma. For the greater the investment from abroad, the greater becomes the need of forcing exports to create a means of meeting the debt and sinking fund charges.

Most of the European powers in Africa have attempted to foster the rapid economic development of the territories under their control. In pursuing this object they have been driven to develop particular money crops for export unless the territories were fortunate enough to possess exploitable mineral, or other indigenous, wealth.

The disadvantages of an undue expansion of export crops have, however, become increasingly apparent in recent years. It exposes the territories to particularly serious setbacks arising from industrial fluctuations in world markets. Moreover, there are definite limits to the extent to which even Governments can hasten development and can invest capital. There are limits also to the extent to which it is possible to hasten returns to capital already invested. For the attempts to do so are likely to lead, directly or indirectly, to those systems of production which involve a large measure of direct or indirect compulsion. The determination of the current rate of investment, in most African territories, therefore, provides a very difficult problem, and necessitates the most careful formulation of economic policies.

[1] Some of the factors affecting economic development in Africa have been similar to those met with in Australia. "All the primary industries (with the exception of the pastoral industry)," writes Professor D. B. Copland, "were developed partly as a result of State action and organized support of some kind. This is not a mere accident. The Australian environment differed from that of the United States in that, after the first fringe of settlement was completed, all the satisfactory areas were somewhat remote. They required transport for their development. . . . Capital was a pre-requisite, for it was not a case of hewing a home out of the forest, and settling down to a diversified agriculture with a gradually extending margin of cultivation. Whole areas had to be cleared of scrub and exploited for one crop, wheat, and this required capital. So it was not surprising that the State came in to encourage settlement by building railways, providing irrigation and supplying capital to the settlers. . . . Our settlement was, in fact, not unlike the progress of a modern army. It requires more men and more capital behind the line than it does to maintain the actual fighting force in the front line." (*Cf. W. E. Hearn, First Australian Economist*, by D. B. Copland, p. 76. Melbourne and Oxford University Press, 1935.)

Investment in Africa is thus bound up with very wide political and sociological issues. It cannot be regarded as dependent only on the normal incentives which are assumed to govern the application of capital under freely competitive conditions. African economic development is governed by numerous monopolistic and sectional interests, by particular fiscal policies and by exceptional social techniques and institutions. Diverse politico-economic policies have in the past influenced, and continue to affect, the flow of resources.

SECTION II

THE SUPPLY OF CAPITAL

"When in the stillness of some distant, uninhabited valley the
steam shovels and pneumatic drills pound out the path for steel
rails and the locomotive, a drama of new life is begun. Human
power is applying itself to an intricate creation. One world is
destroyed, another founded. Before the World War the capital of
Western Europe was impelling forward this drama of change upon
a limitless stage."—HERBERT FEIS, *Europe: The World's Banker*.

I

1870–1914.

The foregoing considerations all affect in some way or other the
demand for capital. It is necessary also to pay attention to the
special conditions which affect its supply. It is a striking fact
that the period of intensive economic development, which dates
from the mineral discoveries in South Africa in the seventies and
eighties of the nineteenth century, coincided with the commencement of a unique period in international finance. From 1870 to
1914, Europe, and in particular Great Britain, played the rôle of
the world's financier to an extent which had not been reached
previously, and may not for long be reached again. The London
financial market, which occupied pride of place in this new
development in international economic relations, derived its
power from the great wealth, diversity of experience and world
connections built up with growing momentum towards the end
of the nineteenth century. At the same time British dominance in
world commerce finally led also to direct penetration into
tropical areas, most of which had previously been connected
with the mother country only by a series of strategic outposts
and trading stations.

Up to the last decades of the century the desire to avoid
entanglements which might prove costly to the mother countries

remained the dominant feature of colonial policy.   The mid-
Victorian Empire did not seek to colonize the wilderness.   It was
an imperialism that was mainly interested in colonies and enterprises that could pay their way.[1]

At the end of the nineteenth century a new era was inaugurated
in which both new objectives of colonial policy were conceived,
and owing to the growth of wealth in Europe, fresh means of
realizing them were available.   The widespread industrialization
led to rising income levels which could find their expression only
in the development and satisfaction of new wants.   The potential
wealth of the tropics, therefore, suddenly assumed a new importance which was expressed in the political rivalry that marked
the partition of the African continent.   When the European
powers assumed control of their new African possessions, they
inaugurated colonial policies based on the deliberate economic
exploitation of the natural resources previously neglected.
Many complex factors contributed to this new development of
colonial policy.   Basically, however, it was made possible owing
to the fact that the accumulated wealth of Europe, and in
particular of Great Britain, began in the seventh decade of the
nineteenth century to grow at a rate incomparably faster than
ever before.   The new policy of "Constructive Imperialism",
enunciated by Joseph Chamberlain for the deliberate economic
development of the colonial Empire by the investment of capital,
was the product of a period in which the necessary means to
this end were growing increasingly abundant.[2]

The growth of accumulated wealth went hand in hand with,
and was in large measure due to, a unique confidence in the
maintenance of international, commercial and financial con-
tracts and obligations—whether these were entered into by
individuals or by Governments.   The post-war generation is now
labouring under the serious difficulties engendered by precisely
the opposite psychological attitude.   International distrust
predominates.   International trade and finance have to overcome

[1] For an excellent account of some aspects of mid-Victorian Imperialism see
C. W. De Kiewiet, *op. cit.*, p. 8 ff.
[2] For some striking indices of the growth of real capital per head of the population
of Great Britain see Colin Clark, *National Income and Outlay*, p. 232. (Macmillan,
1937.)

pessimism about economic intercourse across national boundaries, due to, and continuously intensified by, the restrictions and rigidities of autarchic national policies.

Very many attempts have been made to arrive at the amount of international capital investment. The task bristles with difficulties due to differences of classification and method, paucity of statistical data, diversity in the purposes for which the calculations were made, and extreme variation in the reliability and objectivity of those making them. The most comprehensive examination of all the available estimates has recently been conducted by Professor Eugene Staley.[1] He has scrutinized not only the well-known calculations of investigators such as Sir Robert Giffen, Paish, Hobson, Bowley, Feis, and Kindersley, but also a large number of special studies made by individuals or public departments in various countries and for a variety of purposes. From all these sources he has finally constructed the following table, which may serve as the best available index of the extent of international investment for the period, although the estimates from which it is compounded differ greatly in their reliability and do not in all cases measure the same thing.

TABLE I.—*Total Long-Term Foreign Investments Owned by Residents of the Principal Capital-Exporting Countries, 1855–1929.*

£(000,000)s.

Year.	Great Britain.	France.	Germany.	United States.
1855	472	205	Small	Small
1870	1,006	513	Small	Small
1885	1,602	678	390	Small
1900	2,485	1,068	986	103
1914	4,004	1,766	1,376	513
1929	3,737	719	226	3,018

At the outbreak of the Great War nearly half of all the British capital invested abroad was in the Dominions and colonies.

[1] Eugene Staley, *War and the Private Investor.* (University of Chicago Press, 1935.)

Whereas French and German investments were largely concentrated in Europe, only about 5 per cent. of British capital was so utilized.

From similar sources to those used in the table above, he arrives at the following estimate of the foreign-owned capital in the more important countries in 1929/30:

TABLE 2.—*World Total Long-Term International Investments, by Investment Areas,* 1929–30.

£(000,000)s.

Belgium	267
Japan	267
Cuba	267
South Africa	267
Malaya	328
Mexico	472
Brazil	534
India	575
Argentine	637
China	678
Australia.	780
United States	965
Canada	1,253

Again, however, attention must be drawn to the fact that such estimates are not necessarily comparable with other calculations —as, for example, those which are made later in this study in regard to the total capital investment in Africa.[1] Moreover, the amount of foreign-owned capital in 1929/30 does not indicate the *total* capital which was in fact invested in these countries from overseas.

II

THE INDUCEMENTS TO INVEST.

A remarkable complex of financial institutions was evolved to further the process of international investment. The huge British commercial banks, financing commodity movements throughout

[1] See Chapter V, where it is also shown that the above figures seriously underestimate the amount of capital invested in some countries.

the world, had long been the greatest source of short-term credit. Alongside of them there developed the banks, public, private and Imperial, of the British dominions. Around them grew up that unique security market for investment in long-term ventures which functioned through highly specialized groups of financial, promoting, underwriting, and investment companies.

Overseas investment was influenced by the spirit and institutions of the time; by the combination of sentiment, patriotism and opportunities for gain; by the large scope, often indirectly combined with national support, given to the promoters of enterprises in virgin territories; by the considerable possibilities of profit to particular individuals arising from capital windfalls due to the discovery of valuable resources; by the speculative opportunities arising from the creation of numerous enterprises, whose market valuation fluctuated considerably with the psychological propensities of the security markets and with changes in monetary policy; by the large gains that could be hoped for, and frequently accrued, through the appreciation of values in land or natural resources as a result of the movement of population to them. Only against such a background can the almost incredible financial exploits of a Rhodes be understood, or the spasmodic, and at times exaggerated, bursts of capital investment which created the mineral industries of Africa be explained.

It is true that in Great Britain, up to the outbreak of the Great War, the regulation of foreign investment was rare as compared with that exercised in continental Europe—particularly in France —where it was considerably interfered with for political and diplomatic purposes. Yet the influence of non-economic considerations on capital investment in Africa must not be underestimated. Once European powers had committed themselves to establish sovereignty over, and permanent administrations in vast territories, capital had to be diverted to them in order to make their rule effective. In British territories a considerable part of the early investment was directly financed by Government loans and grants-in-aid. Whenever this was done it was invariably because, without Government intervention, the capital could not have been made available. Apart from these loans and the powerful influence of the Colonial Stock Acts,[1] there was no direct control of investments. Nevertheless the direction it took was influenced in many ways. The diversion did not take place through definite regulation, but by the process of consciously or unconsciously influencing public opinion and the expectations of the investor.

The general atmosphere of optimism engendered by glowing descriptions of, and imperialist propaganda about the potentialities of the new African possessions had a powerful effect in making not only the loan issues of Colonial Government, but also the shares of innumerable exploration, mining and financial companies acceptable to the investor. That Rhodes could continue for years to get money from a large circle of shareholders in the Chartered Company, in spite of the fact that the payment of even a single dividend was successfully deferred for half a generation, illustrates how the direction of investment could be affected by vague and general expectations combined with patriotic and sentimental considerations.

III

THE CHARTERED COMPANIES.

In large parts of Africa capital investment for military and administrative purposes preceded every form of economic development and exercised a potent influence on subsequent economic activity. Not all European governments were able or willing to incur these expenditures. They were forced, therefore, to utilize every available method by which to influence the private *entrepreneur* to undertake tasks, the burden of which he was unprepared to assume without special advantages. This was a basic cause of the policies of large mineral and land concessions adopted in many African territories.

It was also the reason for the great revival, during the last twenty years of the nineteenth century, of the system of Chartered Companies in Great Britain, whose example was followed

[1] For an account of the events which led to, and the influence of, the Colonial Stock Acts see pp. 290 and 291 of *The British Empire: A Report on its Structure and Problems by a Study Group of Members of the Royal Institute of International Affairs*. (London: Oxford University Press, 1937.)

elsewhere. These Companies differed from their great prototypes of the sixteenth and seventeenth centuries in many fundamental respects. They were called into life for different reasons. The ideas which led to the granting of charters to the early companies and which inspired theif promoters were entirely consistent with the general principles of government and economic policy of the time. They were in essence great private monopolies, and their founders looked to the advantages of privilege and monopoly for their reward.

The later Chartered Companies were not thus privileged. Monopolistic powers were not conferred upon them; they had only limited sovereign powers, and were always subject to the control of the Home Government. They were given specific privileges, in land, in the exploitation of minerals and other natural resources, in the taxation of the native peoples, and defined rights to extend control over territories not yet under the sovereignty of European powers. These advantages, without which no capital could have been made available for their operations, were, however, coupled with corresponding administrative obligations, which first the East Africa Company, then the Niger Company, and finally the British South Africa Company found too onerous. Before the end of the century the charters of the first two companies had already been withdrawn.

None of these companies was granted a monopoly of trade, though the Niger Company did achieve a virtual monopoly. The objects of their founders were really political and patriotic, and only in a secondary degree commercial. They were supported by the British Government because, in effect, they were a convenient instrument during the transition period between the abandonment of the old, and the not yet wholehearted acceptance of the new Colonial policy. Governments were not yet prepared to assume permanent responsibilities in the interior of Africa or to find capital for long-term development purposes.

The real measure of the achievement of the Chartered Companies is the remarkable manner in which they succeeded, through the personal qualities and social position of the men who controlled them, in raising capital from the public for purposes which did not really fall within the province of the private investor at all. With what were relatively small financial means (except in the case of the British South Africa Company, which raised very large sums from the public), the companies succeeded in obtaining control over enormous new territories.

There is no doubt that the Chartered Companies achieved some noteworthy results. They built roads and railways, opened up trade, enforced order, and, at all events, laid the foundations of settled administration. But their very success in this direction finally exemplified the transitory nature of the task which they were fitted to fulfil. The fundamental economic reason for the abandonment of the Chartered Company system in British African territories lay in the fact that the companies could only continue as long as they were able to raise capital from the public. None of them was able to continue indefinitely to assume the increasing burden of long-term investment in administering and developing the vast territories under their control.

Even the Niger Company, which was financially successful owing to the expansion of the trading operations out of which it grew, and in which, in effect, it established a monopoly, was unable to bear the burden of administering the great hinterlands which it opened up. Moreover, it is significant that the German Colonial Companies,[1] which were modelled on the British Charter system, all failed in the purpose for which they were created, owing to the fact that their financial resources were inadequate.

The Chartered Company system could not finally solve the problem of supplying long-term capital for territories in which

---

[1] Bismarck commenced German colonization in Africa on the model of the British chartered companies in order to avoid political and economic responsibilities, but his plans proved a complete failure. (For an excellent account, see Mary Evelyn Townsend, *The Rise and Fall of Germany's Colonial Empire*, New York: Macmillan, 1930.) Only four such privileged companies were formed, namely the East African Company, the New Guinea Company, the South-West African Company, and the Jaluit Company. Of these, only the first two were chartered companies invested with sovereign rights; the trading companies in Togoland and Kamerun were too weak to exercise any governmental authority. Moreover of the four privileged companies which really governed in their own right, only two, the New Guinea Company and the Jaluit Company, survived after 1890. The principal reasons for their failure were that the German privileged companies "lacked money, prestige, national support and were hence unable to develop the vast resources at their disposal, to control the native people, or to deal with foreign complications. Their capital melted away because of incompetent management, lack of experience, and unscrupulous and often scandalous behaviour on the part of their governors".

opportunities for immediately profitable production were absent.[1] Those who suggest similar systems for the international development of African territories would do well to study the history of these companies[2]. Even when they were successful, their very success finally brought them into conflict with innumerable private interests (or with foreign powers), and their authority had to make way for that of a Central Government.

Inspiring all this concentrated financial activity in Africa was the belief that it was bound to be rapidly creative. Africa would be opened up; railways flung across it from Cape to Cairo and from East to West; a new America was in the making; a new continent lay at hand to be taken by millions of immigrants from Europe; new products, new wealth, new income would flow into the rapidly expanding channels of international commerce and finance.

To the generation before the war, capital was the magic key to open Africa, but at that time little was known of the many doors which it could not unlock. The present generation has learnt a little more of the realities and the inevitable gradualness of the task involved in changing the life and work of a continent. The glamour has departed from many of the methods and institutional devices which were often the only means available for Europe's new task. Even the role which capital itself can play is differently conceived. Whereas economic growth was once thought to be primarily dependent upon capital, it is now seen that the influence of capital is restricted by far-reaching institutional factors.[3] Particularly in Africa, its rate of application is likely to become

[1] The concessionaire system in many foreign territories in Africa illustrates the same principle. In most cases the concessionaires were not able to raise sufficient capital for undertaking long-term development, and, in many cases, were not interested in such activities. The retention of the concessionaire system indeed led to *relative* stagnation of economic development in many parts of the French and Portuguese territories. The system of concessions also carried with it various evils of speculation in the vendors, interests and shares of the companies. Particularly in the French, Belgian and (prior to the reversal of policy after 1908) German colonies, it was found that concessionaires were interested in immediate returns and in the opportunities of financial juggling with the shares of their concerns. Enormous opportunities for this kind of private gain were inherent in the system.

[2] For a good description of the early activities of the Chartered Companies in Africa, see an article by W. B. Duffield in vol. xxvi of the tenth edition of the *Encyclopædia Britannica*.

[3] For an interesting discussion of this point see Colin Clark, *op. cit.*

increasingly dependent on the extent to which greater skill and knowledge can be imparted to the population, and its latent powers stimulated to new activities, by more flexible economic institutions.

IV

THE CAPITAL INVESTED FROM ABROAD.

At this stage it is convenient to refer briefly to the attempt which has been made in this study to calculate the amount of capital invested in African territories from abroad. So far the only available calculations consist of one or two very rough estimates for a few special areas, such as South and West Africa. No one has previously calculated in detail the investment of capital on the basis of specifically African data.

For a complete analysis, it clearly would be desirable to measure the growth, both of income and of accumulated wealth, in each African territory, in relation to the net capital imports into it. This is, however, quite impossible. The paucity of statistical data even precludes the calculation of the balance of payments for most African territories.

Ideally, the measurement of the amount of capital absorbed from abroad by a country endeavours to arrive at the net inflow, or outflow of capital during a definite time period—for example, for each year. If the total payments due from a country for all goods and services received, are deducted from the payments due to it, for all goods and services it has supplied, the difference, negative or positive, represents the net capital either received by it from foreign territories, or invested by it in them. If these annual differences are added, the result will show, at any given moment, the net total amount of foreign capital received by the country at that date.

In Africa it is not possible to utilize this method of approach. It has, therefore, been necessary to fall back on the second available method—a direct estimate of the capital invested. This consists in examining and collating all available data about Government and other public loans, grants-in-aid, and other capital issues, as listed on the Stock Exchanges or in the financial press.

The main aim of the calculations has been to estimate the gross total of foreign capital which entered all African territories since 1870. Reliable information as to the amount of this capital which has been repaid is, except in a few cases, not available. This study, therefore, broadly speaking, confines itself to measuring all the foreign capital which was actually invested in Africa during this time.

This is justified because (1) so much of the capital required to develop African resources up to the present has been drawn from abroad, and (2) the repayments which Africa has been able to make, and the investments by African nationals in other countries, have been relatively small.

No direct calculation could be made of investments made by overseas individuals or companies, but not publicly disclosed or "listed". A tentative estimate has, however, been made of this "non-listed" capital, which includes capital brought in by settlers and colonists. There can be little doubt that the amount so introduced by settlers is of relatively small significance when compared to the total capital from other sources. Most of the Europeans who have made a permanent home in Africa came to carve out new careers for themselves. They brought skill, enterprise and enthusiasm, but not large amounts of accumulated wealth. Their numbers have been very small when compared to the great stream of migration to other lands. In certain African territories personal wealth has been invested by settlers who retired from service elsewhere, while others continue to draw on private resources abroad. Yet the total of all such investment is relatively not very large, and exaggerated estimates of it must be discounted.

The main objective of the calculations has been to provide a uniform basis for comparing the geographical direction which investment has taken and some of the purposes to which it has been applied. It is submitted that this method of calculation avoids many of the statistical pitfalls which would be involved in attempts to estimate the "outstanding capital", or the capital still "intact", in various territories at different times. The meaning to be attributed to such estimates is never very clear.[1] The method adopted in this study is relatively straightforward, and makes possible a direct comparison of the policies adopted by various territories. It is also suited to African conditions because, up to the present, the bulk of the investment of capital falls into a few well-defined categories. Of the total foreign capital supplied to Africa, amounting to £1,222 millions, nearly half has been invested by Governments or public authorities, and a large part of the remainder has been connected with mining and exploration activities.

The "listed" capital issues for commercial and industrial purposes have been relatively small, mainly for two reasons. First, the capital invested in commercial undertakings has been largely accumulated out of the proceeds of commerce itself. Secondly, industrial development is still in its infancy. Even in the Union of South Africa it became important only after the Great War.[2]

The capital invested in agriculture has mainly been accumulated in Africa itself. A distinction must, however, be drawn between private investments and the large amounts spent by Governments on public works. The modern development of African agriculture in the more advanced territories is an epic of the struggle of science with nature. The efforts of individuals have been made in conjunction with far-reaching Government action in applying capital in its countless forms. In the Union of South Africa most of this capital has been obtained from internal sources; in other territories most of it has come from abroad.

Estimates of the amount of capital invested in Africa, of course, fail to indicate the very considerable indirect benefits which have accrued to some territories from their commercial, financial and shipping connections with the metropolitan countries. For example, Nigeria owes its development very largely to a century of trading and shipping enterprise, which paved the way for the

[1] This is one of the unavoidable shortcomings of such statistics as those published annually in the *British Economic Journal*, by Sir Robert Kindersley in connection with British Overseas Investments, cf. pp. 205–6, Chapter V.

[2] The relatively rapid development of secondary industry since then has been mainly financed from internal sources. Only recently has there been a tendency to utilize overseas capital. As the size of specific industrial enterprises has increased, public issues for industrial purposes on the London market have become possible.

sovereignty subsequently established over it. The pioneering services of British, German and Dutch shipping lines along the coast of Africa provided an incalculably important stimulus to internal economic development. Similarly, the commercial credits provided by European centres and by the Imperial Banks have played a significant part in the expansion of export production.

In considering these developments in Africa, the national characteristics, traditions, and methods of the different colonizing nations must not be forgotten. Much confusion in current discussions of colonial policy arises from the fact that trade and international investment are considered abstractly. In practice, the provision of capital, the development of new products and the expansion of commerce are not processes that occur *in vacuo*. Their success inevitably depends on innumerable personal and political connections of, and on the vast store of accumulated knowledge and experience possessed by countless special groups in the metropolitan countries and their commercial or financial representatives in Africa. It is on the combined activity of these that the success and the direction of African development depends. For this reason, the economic progress of any particular African territory cannot be discussed as if it were something divorced from that whole complex of economic experience and business tradition, which has moulded the economic structure of the metropolitan country itself. Capital investment in colonial territories is, therefore, not merely a quantitative question, but also a qualitative one. Those responsible for the direction, type and application of the investment, and for creating the administrative and social structure through which alone it can be applied, must possess special individual and national qualities.

To represent the development of Africa in the last fifty years as the result merely of financial or imperialist greed is to miss the real implications of the vast changes which this period has iuaugurated. The motives of individuals and of western nations were doubtless mixed, but the main outcome was that, by the end of the nineteenth century, Europe found itself irretrievably engaged in the task of incorporating the African continent into the income-creating stream and the economy of the world. For this purpose, it was necessary to divert enormous resources to Africa in order, first, to obtain access to the interior, and, secondly, to commence the arduous task of revitalizing the habits and work of its backward peoples. That necessity continues, and with it the West remains confronted with infinitely complex problems of social and economic organization—problems which depend for their solution not only on initiating great changes in Africa, but also, in no less degree, on a continuous adaptation to the changing background of the economy of Europe itself.

Only by examining the facts of the present situation in Africa, and the phases through which it has developed, can one expect to arrive at an understanding which may indicate possible lines of development in the future. This it is hoped, to some extent, justifies the study presented in the following chapters.

CHAPTER II

A CONTINENT OF OUTPOSTS

SECTION I

THE OBSTACLES TO COLONIZATION

"The history of Africa, if we except the lower part of the valley of the Nile and the regions occupied and governed by the Greeks, the Carthaginians, the Romans, and the Arabians, is almost entirely modern. . . . Indeed until the middle of the nineteenth century, Africa was known to Europeans as a series of coastlines rather than a Continent."—E. H. WARMINGTON, "Africa in Ancient and Medieval Times", *Cambridge History of the British Empire*, vol. viii.

I

GEOGRAPHICAL FACTORS.

THE most striking feature of the opening-up of Africa to economic development by Western powers is its recent occurrence. Practically four centuries lie between its discovery and its permanent penetration by Europeans. Prior to the middle of the nineteenth century the process of development (except in the most southern portion of the continent) can hardly be said to have begun. Thus in 1835 there were only some 90,000 whites in the whole of Africa, and, of these, 66,000 were to be found in the extreme south, and 20,000 on the Mediterranean seaboard.[1]

About two-thirds of Africa lies between the tropics. Here is a barrier to European settlement which does not exist to anything like the same extent elsewhere, with the exception of South America. The surface of the African interior is marked by high plateaux, which, where the moderating effects of their altitude

[1] *Cf.* R. R. Kuczinski, *Population Movements*. (Oxford University Press, 1936.)

on temperature is sufficient,[1] and rainfall is adequate, comprise the main regions which are regarded as suitable for European settlement. Whether, however, Europeans will be able permanently to colonize the tropical plateaux of Africa is doubtful.[2]

The interior regions of the continent are separated from the oceans by high escarpments or mountain systems or by malarious or desertic coastal belts.[3]

In effect, geographical and climatic factors made the interior of most of Africa inaccessible to Europeans for centuries, and greatly assisted the indigenous population in preventing permanent settlement alike by the Arabs, the Spaniards, the Portuguese, the Dutch and the British, except in the most extreme south of the continent.

Penetration was, moreover, made difficult by the lack of navigable rivers. The rivers from the interior make their way down terraces which descend from the high plateaux. They are either broken up by cataracts and are therefore, like the Congo and the Zambesi, not navigable over any long stretches, and/or they flow through unhealthy or inhospitable valleys or coastal zones which are inimical to settlement and traffic. The continent is also characterized by a lack of natural harbours suitably situated for furthering intercourse with the interior; only after the middle of the nineteenth century did artificial harbours become financially possible.

Another drawback to the economic development of the continent has been the low rainfall over great areas and its irregularity even where annual totals would at first sight support the view that it is adequate. In addition, the biological obstacles resulting from the distribution of tropical diseases have been,

[1] This, however, raises "the important question of the influence of seasonal change of temperature upon settlers of European stock. A considerable degree of variability is necessary for maximum vigour and energy. Monotony is physically and mentally depressing. It is in this character of the tropical highland climate that a doubt is felt as to the possibility of maintaining the vigour of the European stock".

[2] Cf. J. H. Wellington, "Some Geographical Aspects of the Peopling of Africa": Presidential Address to Section B of the South African Association for the Advancement of Science, July, 1937, South African Journal of Science, July, 1937.

[3] For example, the West Coast of Southern Africa is washed by cold seas and has a cool climate, but is largely drought-stricken; from Port Nolloth to the Kunene River the coastal belt is absolute desert, and therefore as difficult a barrier to the interior as the unhealthy or dense forest belts of West and Equatorial Africa.

and remain a most serious barrier to European settlement and to economic development in general.

II

THE LACK OF TRANSPORT.

Until capital for railway and road construction was made available, it was impossible to enter most parts of Africa except on foot owing to the prevalence of diseases which made the use of animal transport impossible. "The only available beast of burden was man, the weakest and most costly of all."

Human porterage was one of the main factors (apart from the serious effects of slave raiding) which ravaged the economic powers of the indigenous populations of West, Central and East Africa until the end of the nineteenth century. Even now, it continues to take serious toll of their labour supplies and to retard development over large areas. This method of transport, if extensively adopted, eventually cripples all other forms of economic production. Mr. J. E. Holmstrom[1] has calculated that the transport of only one hundred tons of produce per month for a distance not exceeding 100 miles would require the continued labour of 2,000 men. This implies that any considerable production involving transport from the interior to the coast would require the greater part of the able-bodied population of an agricultural community[2] to engage only in carrying the crop to market. A railway train of average capacity and engine power will do the work of from 15,000 to 20,000 carriers for one-fifth to one-tenth of the cost.[3]

[1] Cf. his *Railways and Roads in Pioneer Development Overseas* (London, 1934) for a detailed analysis of the inefficiency of human porterage, and a comparison with other forms of transport.

[2] It is interesting to note that "during the War the French Government bought the whole of certain crops in West Africa. They had to organize the transport of 4,200 tons of cereals furnished by eight districts, involving the employment of 125,000 carriers, who gave altogether 2,500,000 days' work". L. C. A. Knowles, *The Economic Development of the British Overseas Empire*. (London: Routledge, 1924.) p. 144.

[3] Mr. Ormsby-Gore in his Report on West Africa (Cmd. 2744, 1926) quoted the following estimates for Northern Nigeria illustrating the cost of different forms of transport per ton mile: "Head Porterage in an area where labour is plentiful and cheap works out at 2s. 6d. per ton mile; motor transport at 1s.; camel transport at 9d. and 10d.; while the railway took baled cotton from Zaria to Lagos at 2d. per ton mile."

Whether one looks east or west, north or south, everywhere access to and production in Africa was inhibited, and, to this day, is still restricted over vast areas by this uneconomic form of transportation. Even the construction of railways was greatly retarded by it.[1]

It must, however, be remembered that, even if the obstacles of the African environment had been smaller, and the economic possibilities of the continent more attractive, Europe was in fact not ready to undertake colonization there until towards the end of the nineteenth century.

The population of Europe was too sparse, its standard of living too low, its surplus of capital resources too inadequate. It required the scientific, mechanical and medical discoveries and inventions of the nineteenth century before it became possible and worth while to open up Africa. Development was impossible without railways, and had to await their advent.[2] Railways in turn were useless without the construction of harbours, wharves and docks. Once railway construction was under way the great era of "public works" in Africa had been inaugurated, and the transformation of the African continent had commenced.

III

THE ERA OF DESPOLIATION.

Except for the settlement at the Cape, which grew into a colony gradually extending inland, Africa, until well into the third quarter of the century, remained a "continent of outposts". In no case was there any appreciable interior expansion. Under the prevailing economic conditions of Europe, the labour of the African could not be organized and applied to advantage in Africa itself; consequently the commerce of Africa remained what in effect it had for centuries been—a commerce in slaves.

---

[1] In temperate regions (as at the Cape) the economic activities of European settlers had to be restricted to a form of production which solved its own transport problems, that is to the self-conveying pastoral industry, until mineral exploitation attracted and warranted capital investment in railway construction.

[2] Even now, large areas cannot be developed because they have not been provided with railways or even with road motor services. In the Union of South Africa the native areas can generally be distinguished on a map by the fact that these are the areas which are excluded from the otherwise well-developed railway system.

It is no exaggeration to say that, until recent times, the predominant form of European—and Arab—activity can best be described by the term "Raubwirtschaft".

Both the slave trade[1] and the commerce in indigenous products involved despoliation, either by African peoples themselves[2] in the course of trade with the Arabs, Portuguese and British, or, as later, under the command of European conquerors. Indeed, the "terror economy" in the Belgian Congo and French Equatorial Africa provides one of the most terrible instances of "Raubwirtschaft" in modern history.

The first "investments of capital" in tropical Africa, if indeed they can be so described, were made to appropriate wealth and not to establish constructive activities. In fact they destroyed real economic resources. The ultimate futility of such an application of capital, based as it is on ignoring the conditions which are essential for its productive use, are well illustrated by the policies which were originally adopted in French Equatorial Africa.

In this territory, of course, climatic conditions made permanent European settlement impossible. The issue, therefore, from an economic point of view, was the straightforward one of how to exploit a vast territory sparsely peopled by a primitive native population. In 1934 the population was only about 3·3 millions, that is, about 1·5 to the square kilometre—"the lowest density . . . . . . in the non-desert regions of the continent".[3] The great majority was of debilitated Bantu stock. "What France saw was a clearly defined problem," writes Roberts.[4] "In front of her was a huge, rich, unhealthy, unorganized country, with tropical products ready for the taking, but with no roads to take them, and with a

---

[1] For an excellent account see H. A. Wyndham, *The Atlantic and Slavery—Problems of Imperial Trusteeship*. A Report in the Study Group Series of the Royal Institute of International Affairs. (Oxford University Press, 1935.)

[2] In this connection it should be borne in mind that the economic activities of most of the native peoples themselves were nomadic and predatory. During the whole period of their possession of the continent they accumulated practically no capital. They lived for the present and created little of permanent economic value for the future. Their cattle were treasured as a form of wealth; they were not really utilized for economic purposes, and it is difficult to classify them as capital.

[3] J. H. Wellington, "Possibilities of Settlement in Africa", chapter ix of *Limits of Land Settlement*, ed. I. Bowman. (New York : Council on Foreign Relations, 1937.) p. 246.

[4] S. H. Roberts, *History of French Colonial Policy*, vol. i, p. 346. (London: P. S. King, 1929.)

labour supply insufficient in number, and as low in quality as could be imagined. How, therefore, could the rubber and timber be got out of the country at the least possible expense ? That was the problem—surmount the natural difficulties, make the best of the obviously unsatisfactory native position, and drain the country of its forest resources, especially the rubber. In a way the whole matter was delightfully simple, and the only difficulty was in proportioning the means to the ends." It was decided to colonize "with capital and not with men", and the concessionaire system was adopted.[1] Between March and July of 1899, no less than forty concessionaire companies obtained privileges in the French Congo by decree. As a result, practically the whole of the exploitable area of the Congo was handed over to large companies, whose total registered capital was roughly 59 million francs. The Government, in practice, abdicated its functions and limited itself to the imposition of taxes and the collection of quit-rents.

It was not long, however, before the idea of the enormous riches to be gained began to be dissipated by the actual results of the operations of the companies. To their disappointment, investors in them discovered too late that capital had to be sunk, and returns awaited, in the usual manner. They had expected to open a treasure chest; instead, they had to develop tropical farms, and the glamour departed with the delay. Distances and marshes ruined the early companies, and would have done so even had the direction and personnel been as efficient as possible. The only gains from this frenzied activity accrued to the promoters of these ventures.[2]

Roberts estimates that, by the end of 1903, at least one-third

[1] "The Companies were to receive exclusive rights over all 'agricultural, forest and industrial exploitation' for thirty years, at the end of which time all lands which they had improved and all forests where they had regularly collected rubber were to go to them in fee-simple. In return, they were to give the State a certain sum varying with the area of their concession, to pay a quit-rent of 15 per cent. of the annual revenue, to make certain roads, and to help to maintain the customs and military services. Beyond that, there were no other limitations or obligations imposed on them, expect a general proviso that no rights were to be exercised in native villages or on lands used by the tribes. A concession virtually meant the handing-over of a given area to a private Company, with its power untrammelled within that area— in fact, the setting up of so many *enclaves* of practically independent trading kingdoms within the colony." (Roberts, i, p. 349.)

[2] For a good account of this concessions boom see E. D. Morel, *Affairs of West Africa*. (London: Heinemann, 1902.)

of the actual, and one-fifth of the nominal capital had been lost.

By 1905, the economic aspects of the matter had been submerged under the humanitarian attacks which resulted from the disclosures concerning the scandals connected with the Red Rubber *régime* in the Belgian Congo and the no less horrifying facts concerning the method of exploitation which the companies had used in French territory.

In effect, the reckless private investments in a territory of this nature could only lead to similar reckless attempts to obtain a return thereon, and this meant killing the goose for the eggs. In the French Congo, large rubber resources were completely exhausted, and replanting was almost wholly neglected.[1]

The moral is simple. When valuable mineral resources are not available, the opportunities for private investment in such territories are very limited. Development depends on the gradual opening up of the region by railways and roads, and the fostering of marketable products. The indigenous population has to be led into new forms of economic activity. If it is sparse, disease-stricken or otherwise backward, the task is extremely difficult.

In view of the nature of the territory (in addition to the usual tropical diseases, sleeping-sickness is particularly prevalent) and its previous maladministration, it is not surprising that French Equatorial Africa, despite its natural resources—it is the most richly wooded of all French Colonies—is still one of the most undeveloped regions of the continent, and the most backward of all the French Colonies. More than forty years after the commencement of French economic penetration, one finds that the total exports of this territory, whose area is nearly five times that of France, are still valued at only £2·5 millions per annum.

The early history of French Equatorial Africa and of the Congo Free State are, of course, extreme examples of the forms which the first activities of European powers in the interior of Afirca assumed. Yet it remains true to say that, until the twentieth

---

[1] As a rule the concessions, although somewhat modified, could in practice not be terminated until 1930, when the agreements entered into in 1899 became extinct, although some of them still continue. (*Cf. La Crise et Les Colonies*, Colonial International Library, Brussels, 1933.) For an account of the efforts of the State to regain control, see Roberts, *ibid.*, p. 350 ff.

century, foreign peoples were attracted to Africa by the spoils of destruction.

In this connection the evolution of economic policy in the Belgian Congo is of interest. It is usual to ascribe the cessation of the policy of despoliation, and of the ruthless extermination of the native peoples which marked King Leopold's *régime* in the Congo, to the world outcry which it finally aroused. It is possible, however, to discern a more prosaic reason—namely, the resulting serious decline of the population, which eventually made it impossible to obtain sufficient labour with which the wealth of the territory could be appropriated. Yet, even in the next stage of Congo policy, it was still assumed that one could simply appropriate the wealth of Africa by brute force; the authorities, therefore, now endeavoured to reduce the whole indigenous population to semi-slavery.

This policy, on the whole, remained in force until the Great War, when the uselessness of enslavement as a method of production in the world economy became obvious. By this time, the mere draining of indigenous produce from the Congo was no longer possible, and development had to be fostered. It came to be realized that colonization must be a constructive economic process, for which other labour policies were necessary. These were summed up in the announcement by the Belgian Minister of Colonies in 1920 when he said: "We must respect and develop native institutions and not as heretofore break them."[1]

IV

OBSTACLES TO IMMIGRATION.

An important cause of the slow evolution of constructive European effort in Africa is to be found in the relative paucity of European resources available for foreign investment. Moreover, even with the growth of European wealth, capital was first applied elsewhere, both on account of the peculiar natural

[1] The experience in the German colonies has been similar, and already in 1907 prominent Colonial experts were urging the development of native institutions. *Cf.* the writer's "Africa in the Re-making" in *Our Changing World View*, by the Rt. Hon. J. C. Smuts and others (Johannesburg: University of the Witwatersrand Press, 1932), and Roberts, *ibid.*, p. 668.

conditions in Africa and by reason of the presence of a large native population which created unusual military, administrative and economic problems. Until the end of the nineteenth century, capital could be invested with greater ease and safety in America, Canada, Australia and New Zealand than in Africa, owing to its unusual disadvantages, lack of knowledge concerning its real economic potentialities and, over most of the continent, the absence of civilized government. As with capital, so with men. Even the temperate regions of Africa did not offer a field for the immigration of the poorer populations of Europe. Unskilled labour, once the native had been subdued, was at a discount. In America, Canada, New Zealand and countries with similar conditions, from the commencement of colonization, it was at a premium. Thus, incentives to oppose the relatively greater difficulties of settlement in Africa were lacking. Skilled artisans were very scarce in Africa and they had to be attracted by very high wages. This is the origin of the prevailing high standard of pay for Europeans in skilled occupations in Southern Africa and certain other African territories. The mass of emigrants from Europe to America and Australia did not, however, belong to this class, since, in general, skilled workers have not the same incentives to migrate. For the unskilled European, Africa did not offer considerable opportunities. Large streams of emigrants consist mainly of the poor; they emigrate to seek for better opportunities; they desire to find in the country of their adoption an economic and social ladder which, beginning as labourers at the bottom, they can hope to climb so as to reach the independence it offers at the top. In Africa owing to the presence of the indigenous population there was, in general, no such ladder.[1]

[1] These considerations do not apply in the same degree to Indian immigrants owing to their lower standard of life and their greater resilience to a tropical climate. The development of East Africa and of Natal owes much to the keen commercial ability and to the labour of the Indian population. The Sanderson Commission (Cd. 5193) quoted Sir John Kirk's statement that "But for the Indians we should not be here now". Indian immigrants opened the way for the commercial penetration which led to British rule. Indian labour, no less than British capital, played an indispensable part in the construction of the Uganda Railway. Indians are still indispensable in the service of that railway and in the commercial activities radiating from Nairobi. In short, as Kirk had concluded, "Drive away the Indians and you may shut up the Protectorate". This quotation is from W. K. Hancock, ibid., p. 214, which contains what is probably the most comprehensive account so far written of

V
THE RESTRICTED AREA OF COLONIZATION.

Owing to historical accident, European settlement commenced at the most southern point of the continent. The slowness of the process was characteristic. It took nearly two centuries from the first settlement at the Cape for the European population in South Africa to reach 200,000 and to penetrate across the Vaal in the north and into Natal in the east.

Not until the closing decade of the nineteenth century did colonization commence in any other part of Africa. Until well into the new century, exports from African territories other than those now comprised in the Union largely arose out of the system of crude exploitation which has been analysed above. The following table (3) shows the trade of the territories included in this study in 1897. Not only did Southern Africa account for 66% of the total trade, but it is very significant that only five commodities—gold, diamonds, wool, rubber and palm products—together accounted for 72·4% of the total African exports.[1]

Over most of the continent the twentieth century was the first to witness efforts by European nations based on the realization of a definite responsibility for its inhabitants and some endeavour to inaugurate constructive activities for the future.

South Africa is the pioneer belt of Africa, and its history embodies a record of experience which cannot be ignored, and is likely profoundly to affect the future development of its northern neighbours. The next chapter will, therefore, examine certain fundamental aspects of the economic history of the territories now comprising the Union.

[1] The amounts and percentages for each commodity were as follows :

	Gold.	Diamonds.	Wool.	Rubber.	Palm products.
Amount £(000,000)	11	4·5	2·0	1·7	1·3
Per cent.	39·2	15·7	7·0	6·0	4·5

These figures should be compared with those given later in this study. See Chapter v, p. 207.

the Indian problem in East and South Africa. It must, however, be borne in mind that the Indians are, as the *Hilton Young Report* (Cmd. 3234, 1929) showed, "subject to competition from both sides—from Europeans who are force dinto occupations which Indians previously monopolized, and from Africans forcing their way upwards into the same occupations" (*ibid.*, p. 237).

TABLE 3.—*Trade of Africa in* 1897.

	Imports. £(000).	Exports. £(000).		Imports. £(000).	Exports. £(000).
Southern Africa(a) .	23,915	20,467	Portuguese East Africa(a) . .	4,350	273
Lagos . . .	771	811	Angola . . .	1,031(c)	1,195(c)
Niger Protectorate .	640	750	Guinea(b) . .	8	3
Gold Coast . .	911	858			
Sierra Leone . .	457	401	Total Portuguese .	5,389	1,471
Gambia . . .	140	164			
			Guinea . . .	306	269
	2,919	2,984	Senegal . . .	1,167	843
			Ivory Coast .	188	189
British Somaliland .	348	350	Dahomey . .	330	231
Egyptian Sudan .	91	66	French Congo .	143	211
British East Africa .	298	73			
Zanzibar and Pemba .	144	81	Total French .	2,134	1,743
British Central Africa	86	27			
			German East Africa	479	262
	967	597	South-West Africa .	244	62
			Togoland . .	99	39
			Cameroons . .	295	185
			Total German .	1,117	548
			Congo Free State .	950	537
			Grand totals .	37,391	28,347

(a) Including goods in transit to and from the hinterland.
(b) Trade with and *via* Portugal only.
(c) 1898.

SECTION II

THE STRUGGLING CAPE

"Virgin soil owes no debt to the past. It is as Nature has left it, hostile to man. In Europe land has been tamed from enemy into ally. To the English it is 'mother earth'—something friendly, kind, generous. In the untamed parts of the world the earth is a callous, stony-hearted mother to her children. There, it has never been subjugated to man. It is still his Master."—E. HUXLEY, *White Man's Country*.

I

FUNDAMENTAL PROBLEMS.

Colonization was not the purpose of the founders and rulers of the settlement at the Cape. "Whoever has the Cape is master of India," wrote Sir George Yonge, Governor of the Cape of Good Hope. This was also the main reason why the Dutch East India Company in 1652 established a settlement, and why the British dispossessed them temporarily in 1795 and permanently in 1806.[1] Even under British administration, "it was the colony rather than the colonist which interested the Government". Indeed, "it is an interesting speculation how and when the Cape would have become a white man's land had the Suez Canal been available in the nineteenth century".[1]

Three factors dominated the economic structure of the settlement under the Dutch East India Company, and these were destined to affect the history of European penetration in the centuries to come. The first was the rigid monopoly of the company itself. Significantly enough the history of European efforts in South Africa thus began with the clash of the privileged and the unprivileged,[2] those favoured by vested interests to own property or land or to engage in trade and skilled occupations, and those condemned to "trek elsewhere", to go where nobody was responsible for them. Persons not possessing burgher rights

---

[1] *Cf.* L. C. A. Knowles and C. M. Knowles, *The Economic Development of the British Overseas Empire—The Union of South Africa*, vol. iii, pp. 1–2. (London: Routledge, 1936.)

[2] *Cf.* Professor I. D. MacCrowe's exhaustive study, *Race Attitudes in South Africa*. (London: Oxford University Press, 1937.)

or not being past or present servants of the Company were strangers who were not allowed to own immovable property, and were obliged on the first order of the Government to leave the colony. The subsequent economic history of Southern Africa is strewn with the results of likewise ignoring the fundamental economic problems of large sections of the population, both black and white. "The condition of the Cape community at the close of the eighteenth century, if not economically static, was at any rate such that material progress was hampered in almost every sphere by monopolistic restriction on enterprise. . . . The inaccessibility of the immediate interior, the peculiarities of climate and vegetation and the aboriginal population presented a problem of effective colonization, the very enormity of which may have contributed something to the weakening of the spirit of enterprise in a small and isolated community whose resources were entirely inadequate. . . . But the Cape population suffered inevitably, too, from the absence of an identity of interest between the Government and themselves, and from the warping effect on development of rigid monopolistic institutions under the Company which prevented the prompt and full adjustment of enterprise and resources to changing conditions."[1]

History moves in cycles. The history of the nineteenth century has seen the liberation of other economic forces in South Africa, but the creation of an identity of interests, the problem of achieving a new synthesis in the economy of South Africa as a whole, still awaits solution. The poverty of a large section of the European population and the proletarization of the native can be largely attributed to the basic difficulties of remoulding traditional institutions deeply rooted in the past, (institutions) which prevent the complete utilization of the resources of the South African economy.

The second dominant factor was the lack of labour resources. The Hottentots and Bushmen could not be trained to steady work. Immigration was discouraged by the Company system. The settlement was forced to import slaves as the only available method of securing the labour required. This led

---

[1] "Economic Development 1795–1921", by Professor Arnold Plant, chapter xxix, p. 760, *The Cambridge History of the British Empire*, vol. viii, South Africa.

in time to an even more widespread dependence on native labour, which made it unnecessary for Europeans to engage in unskilled work. The need to import slaves also intensified the scarcity of capital by absorbing a considerable portion of the savings of the settlement,[1] which might otherwise have been invested in agricultural implements, livestock, wagons, roads, bridges or buildings. It also fostered the growth of idleness, ease and extravagance, and so retarded the accumulation of capital. Subsequently, as native labour became "cheap", concomitantly with the economic subjection of the Bantu which marked the path of European penetration, it was wastefully applied, and tended to retard the use of machinery and other labour-saving devices.

The third factor was the difficult environment which caused the small settlement to be faced with almost overwhelming tasks in the process of expansion. As in the rest of Africa, the physical and economic conditions were discouraging. "The Minister at the head of affairs at home, writing in 1805 to General Janssens, the Governor, remarked that the official reports of the latter 'do confirm the apprehensions that have been felt a long time since, namely, that the Cape is not such an Eldorado as it has been considered by some authors' "—a view that has since been echoed in other African territories on more than one occasion. He referred in particular to "the want of water in that immense extent of land, as also of workmen, of means of exporting its produce, of safe harbours, of different necessities of the first importance for agriculture and navigation, and even sometimes of bread . . . ", and concluded "these are certainly great obstacles to every endeavour of transforming a poor country into a rich, flourishing and happy land".[2]

These obstacles continue to determine South Africa's development. As Professor De Kiewiet has pointed out, "It cannot be stressed too often or too strongly how much the South African communities were victims of their own and of one another's problems. They were all so very poor; . . . it was poverty that had caused a handful of men to wander forth into such a wide

[1] *Cf.* M. H. De Kock, *Selected Studies in the Economic History of South Africa* (Capetown : Juta & Co., 1924.)
[2] Knowles, *ibid.*, vol. iii, p. 10.

land. Poverty brought rival groups of blacks and whites to face one another in hostility across fertile borderlands.   Poverty caused the coastal colonies to fight for trade and deny assistance to yet poorer neighbours.   To persuade such a land to yield a harvest, not in corn alone, men must be prepared to invest heavily.   That modern South Africa ranks prominently amongst the great dominions of the British Empire must not obscure the truth that for the greater part of its history it was discontented, struggling and poor. Not in its recent wealth but in two meagre and stinted centuries lie the origins of much South African political thinking and action".[1]

The Cape had no readily exploitable resources. Markets for the sale of products were extremely limited; lack of roads and navigable rivers made economic production impossible, except in areas serving harbours. Even the pastoral industry expanded slowly; its growth had to await the expansion of the textile industry in Europe. The colony possessed none of the great staples of foreign commerce which are so essential for the development of new regions. The only marked economic advantage which new communities possess over old ones lies in their rich, and relatively cheap natural resources.   In all other respects they are likely to be at a disadvantage. Their labour, considered as a separate factor of production, is not more efficient than that of older communities. The knowledge of the arts of production is likely to be less; the outfit of capital in a new country, by means of which its labour is applied to the natural resources, is inferior to that of older countries whose inhabitants are of the same grade of civilization. Thus new regions must devote their labour chiefly to those extractive industries in which they can utilize their rich natural resources. But, to do this, they must be able to find markets in other communities, where they can exchange the products of these industries for all the other forms of wealth they may require.

At the Cape the only factor of production which was easy to obtain was land. Thus the early settlers (discharged servants of the Company, sons of farmers or of men in the service of the Company, and the relatively few immigrants) had recourse

[1] De Kiewiet, *ibid.*, p. 254.

to "stock farming"—really a nomadic form of "grazing". In effect, this implied that they were forced by their environment to adopt methods of production closely approaching those of a subsistence economy.

The Bantu had been migrating south in order to obtain more land for their herds. The Europeans were soon "trekking" north and east for the same reason. Owing to the lack of markets, communications, and scientific knowledge concerning the country, a considerable portion of the European population thus found no other opportunities for economic development than that type of production from which the Bantu had failed to extricate themselves for centuries. "By the time the advancing Dutch colonists came into rivalry with the more formidable Bantu they came no longer as intensive agriculturists, but as land-hungry pastoralists and hunters."[1] Extensive and shifting exploitation of natural resources, grazing, veld-burning and hunting characterized the forms production took. In general, there was very little economic activity directed to the permanent development of the natural resources of the land. "The veeboer became the trekboer, a semi-nomadic frontiersman who was to blaze the trail of civilization far into the interior of Africa."[2]

Throughout the century the relentless process of appropriating extensive areas of native land continued. It was periodically accompanied by those characteristic outbursts of land speculation which continue to the present day. Often the purchase of land was a symptom of the lack of other opportunities for investing such resources as became available from time to time by the importation of capital and the expansion of credit facilities.

In illustration of the process of land alienation, the history of Natal is peculiarly significant. "Between 1857 and 1860 less than three hundred immigrants entered the country. Yet by a system of almost promiscuous largesse more than 1,360,000 acres were alienated. Before the Colony had been in existence a quarter of a

---

[1] Professor W. M. Macmillan, *Complex South Africa*, p. 38. (London: Faber and Faber, 1930.)

[2] Dr. H. M. Robertson in an article on "Effective Colonization" in the *South African Journal of Economics*, December, 1937, shows that private land was coming into the market in large quantities and at low prices on account of the Great Trek. "There were many causes of the Great Trek," he writes, "and not least among them the glowing reports of the land that awaited the trekkers at their journey's end."

century it had no land left sufficiently productive to encourage immigration on a scale commensurate with its needs and ambitions. . . . What Crown lands there still remained were remote from centres of population, roadless, and unsuited for occupation by inexperienced settlers. As early as 1864 the Immigration Board sorrowfully complained that immigration was handicapped by scarcity of land." By 1874, "out of an area of 12,000,000 acres two-thirds had been alienated. Of this, 2,000,000 acres had been set aside for native locations. Since fully one-half of the European population lived in the two towns of Durban and Pietermaritzburg, 6,000,000 acres were in the possession of a population of 8,000 individuals, including women and children".[1]

The position in the Transvaal was similar. Land prices were driven up, not only by speculation, but steadily through the absorption of much of the desirable land. By 1876, there were many who owned between 200,000 and 300,000 acres. Even at this early stage in the development of the territory, the inhabitants of Lydenburg were already complaining that non-occupation was "one of the greatest evils from which this district, in common with districts in this, as well as in other colonies, suffer. The land is owned in most part by men who neither cultivate nor use it in any way. Some are utter absentees".[2]

Much of the land, owing to lack of water and other environmental conditions, was economically useless for anything but grazing or primitive extensive cultivation. Nevertheless, as De Kiewiet has shown, "It is one of the most familiar paradoxes of South African life that the same process which produced an exaggerated and uneconomical sparseness of European settlement was responsible for an equally exaggerated condensation of the native population. European under-population and native over-population were phenomena with similar causes".[3]

---

[1] De Kiewiet, *ibid.*, pp. 189–190. In addition, "Even in Griqualand West, which had ostensibly been annexed in the interests of the natives, the administration proved powerless to prevent the extensive expropriation of land by Europeans. By the beginning of 1878, when Griqualand West entered upon a year of native disturbances, Europeans had possessed themselves of some 420,000 acres in that region. Less than 100,000 acres were left to the natives." (*Ibid.*, p. 185.)

[2] C. O. 179/136. Shepstone in a despatch 17th January, 1880, quoted by De Kiewiet, *ibid.*, p. 184.

[3] *Ibid.*, p. 191.

Owing to these environmental and historical conditions, no adequate system of land tenure has yet been evolved. Once the process by which land could be easily appropriated came to an end, extensive land ownership and cultivation had to give way continually to further and further subdivision of farms, until the economic use of the land was imperilled, because extensive cultivation became impossible and no other system was at hand to take its place. Once the land hunger ceased to be easily fed at native expense, the dearth of training, skill and capital of the Europeans made easy the descent to that rural poverty which forms one of the biggest problems of the Union at the present time.[1]

II

DEVELOPMENT TO 1865.

At the Cape, the arable production of vegetables, fruit, grain and wine for the limited market near the coastal towns formed the basis of permanent economic development. As shipping expanded and markets overseas became more accessible, the economic activities of the older portions of the colony were consolidated. This enabled the slow growth of public works—the building of roads, mountain passes and bridges—and the development of banking facilities.

After the middle of the nineteenth century the colony, with considerable growing-pains, achieved some measure of economic stability. The greatest progress was in the expansion of the pastoral industry. Exports of wool from Cape ports, which amounted to only 216,000 lb. in 1835, rose to 12,000,000 lb. in 1855 and 33,000,000 lb. in 1863, when, with a value of £1,680,000, they accounted for 76% of the total exports through Cape ports. Nevertheless, it is indicative of the difficulties of settlement and the lack of markets that it had taken over forty years of experimentation to bring the wool industry to this stage.[2] Other exports consisted chiefly of hides, skins, ostrich feathers and mohair. The

[1] For a valuable discussion see W. M. Macmillan, *Complex South Africa*.
[2] *Cf.* H. B. Thom, *Die Geskiedenis van die Skaap Boerdery in Suid Afrika*. (Amsterdam: Swetz en Zeitlinger, 1936.)

wine trade had declined in importance, and internal production was retarded by the slow growth of population. The foreign demand for the agricultural products of South Africa was very small, in view of the fact that other new countries were developing their agricultural resources more efficiently, and had already secured a firm footing in the markets of Europe.

In 1865 the white population was approximately 180,000. "Seventy-five per cent. of the occupied population was engaged in agriculture, only one-eighth pursued industrial occupations and less than one-sixteenth were regarded as engaged in trade and transport. There were only eighteen towns all told with more than 1,000 inhabitants each."[1] At this stage the fundamental requisites for rapid expansion were still absent. The colony did not command the necessary resources. It was in a state that distinguishes many regions of Africa at the present day.

An economy can only obtain the resources for further expansion through the creation of surplus wealth within its borders or by drawing upon the resources of other countries. At this time, European Governments (including Great Britain) were not yet prepared to invest for development purposes in new regions when private initiative could not be relied upon to do so. Without long-term loans at low rates of interest for the construction of public works and communications, the colony could not progress. Its immediate economic potentialities were not sufficient to attract appreciable amounts of private capital, and its revenues did not permit public borrowing. There were simply no activities within the colony which yielded a sufficient surplus to allow of taxation for this purpose. On the contrary, the revenue resources of the Cape, as also in later years of the Orange Free State and the Transvaal, were so meagre that the currency had frequently to be depreciated.[2] The Cape Colony's average annual revenue (including interest from the Lombard and Discount Bank) was as follows:

---

[1] Plant, *ibid.*, p. 77

[2] For example, even under the British Administration (the position was worse before) the note circulation had been increased from Rds. 283,000 in 1806 to Rds. 3,100,000 in 1814. P. Warden Grant, of the Bengal Revenue Survey Department, in an analysis of the position wrote: "There is no relief from the pernicious effects of a forced issue to aid the interests of the State", *cf.* E. H. D. Arndt, *Banking and Currency Development in South Africa*, 1652–1927. (Capetown: Juta & Co., 1928.)

	Average annual revenue.	Interest from banks.
1806–1814 . .	£101,508 .	£9,098
1815–1819 . .	124,392 .	11,042
1820–1825 . .	123,345 .	11,090
1826–1830 . .	116,216 .	9,847
1831–1835 . .	119,552 .	8,430
1852 . .	289,000 .	*
1857 . .	407,000 .	*

* The Bank was liquidated in 1842.

In the Orange Free State the total revenue for the three years 1866–1868 was only £152,000 as against an expenditure of £239,000.

Many *ad hoc* reasons were given at the time for the currency difficulties of the Cape, and there were special difficulties, such as the chaotic condition of banking. Yet the main cause was the chronic lack of public revenue and the sources from which it could be obtained. Successive Governors were compelled to make use of the printing press to finance urgent public works or the relief of distress from drought or floods, and to meet losses from native wars or raids, and the heavy military expense of the Colonial Corps and its contingent liabilities.

Symptomatic of the future was the fact that, of the first external loan granted to the Cape by the British Government in 1822, amounting to £125,000 in the form of bills, £100,000 was for the relief of farmers. The loan was granted to avoid further note issues, but it did not leave sufficient means at the disposal of the Colonial Treasury, which therefore again resorted to the printing press.[1]

The process of redeeming the depreciated currency was a gradual one. A loan of £92,775 free of interest was obtained for the purpose from the Imperial Government. Treasury loans were also obtained from this source in times of financial stringency By 1845 the Cape was entirely free of debt. In 1859 the first new loan of £80,000 was floated in London for assisting immigration.

[1] Arndt, *ibid.*, pp. 34–5.

By 1872, the Public Debt of the Cape amounted to £1,519,000, but the credit of the colony was not yet established abroad.[1]

It is of interest to note that military expenditures by the Home Government played a considerable part at times in stimulating the activity of this relatively undeveloped economy, as it has done on many other occasions in the course of the opening up of African territories. For example, in 1848 the British Government was involved in an expenditure of over £1,000,000 for war purposes in the colony. Again, in 1858 the Kaffir War cost the British taxpayer no less than £2,000,000. In times of peace, the Colonists regarded the considerable garrison as a milch cow; in time of war, with Imperial troops and money flooding the country, they enjoyed a hectic prosperity, except on the actual scene of operations.

Military activities were linked up with the policy adopted towards immigration. In fact, the immigration schemes inaugurated at the end of the first quarter of the nineteenth century were partly due to the desire to strengthen the frontier districts. Prior to this time, immigration was discouraged. After the Napoleonic wars, emigration was regarded as a definite outlet for the relief of unemployment in the United Kingdom. The British Government voted £50,000 for the encouragement of emigration to the Cape. Passages were provided at the expense of the Government, and settlers were each given a hundred-acre tract of land. Most of them were settled in the Eastern frontier of the colony, in the region between the Fish and Bushman Rivers, which received the name of Albany.[2]

This experiment was significant for its disastrous failure so long as the idea of intensive arable agriculture on the basis of free (non-slave) labour was adhered to. For some years, settlers practically existed on the Government rations issued through the commissariat of the army. It was only when, after 1825, extended

[1] The information given above in regard to the Public Debt is from De Kock, *ibid.*, pp. 392-3.

[2] A similar combination of military and economic policy accounted for the introduction, in 1857, of about 4,000 soldiers of the Anglo-German legion, who had served against Russia in the Crimean war. They were settled by Sir George Grey in British Kaffraria as a form of protection for the Cape Colony. In 1858-59 about 2,000 agricultural emigrants from North Germany were also introduced into British Kaffraria.

land grants for the adoption of extensive pastoral farming were made, and those wishing to do so were allowed to take up other occupations, that the immigrants were able to make good. The growth of the wool industry owed much to them, and through these "1820" settlers the British were established as a permanent element in the population.[1]

After the decade 1820-1830, British · emigration to South Africa "became a trickle". In 1841, when 24,000 emigrants left for Canada and 14,500 for Australia and New Zealand, only 130 went to the Cape. With the opening of the Suez Canal, eastern trade began to be developed through the Red Sea, and this gave rise to considerable apprehension as to the future of the colony. Yet, when the future looked most doubtful, a new era dawned in the history of Africa. After the diamond discoveries in 1867, Basutoland was brought under British sovereignty and Griqualand West was annexed in 1871. The indications were clear "that the British Government could no longer maintain its self-denying ordinance against expansion in Africa—the northward movement had begun".[2] Attention was diverted to the interior, and South Africa ceased to be a mere stepping-stone to the East. In 1871 Stanley entered Central Africa, and carried on the work of Livingstone in completing the exploration of the dark continent.

First diamonds and then gold "brought the nineteenth century and the Industrial Revolution to South Africa", and inaugurated the final stage of exploration of the continent as a whole. With their discovery, there began not only a new political, but also a new economic era both for the patriarchal society of the whites and for the tribal organization of the black man. The nature of the changes which followed this event is considered in the next chapter.

[1] For an excellent account see Knowles, vol. iii, pp. 14–19.

[2] De Kiewiet, *ibid.*

CHAPTER III

THE ECONOMIC REVOLUTION IN SOUTH AFRICA

SECTION I

DIAMONDS

"We have now got the country developed far, far into the centre of Africa, largely through the means supplied by this commercial company. . . . Anyone visiting these mines one hundred years hence, would, if he pushed his travels further into the interior, recognize the renewal of their life in the great European civilization of the far North, and perhaps he would feel a glow of satisfaction at the thought that the immense riches which have been taken out of the soil have not been devoted merely to the decoration of the female sex."—CECIL RHODES.[1]

I

NEW WEALTH.

"Gentlemen, this is the rock on which the future success of South Africa will be built." This was the prophetic remark of the then Colonial Secretary when, one day in 1867, he laid upon the table of the Cape House of Assembly one of the earliest of the diamonds discovered in South Africa and identified as a genuine stone.

The miracle which Europeans in South Africa needed had occurred. The most effective means for obtaining surplus wealth had been found when the size of the industry is taken into account. The wealth accruing from the production of diamonds in South Africa has probably been greater than that which has ever been obtained from any other commodity in the same time anywhere in the world.[2]

[1] Cecil Rhodes (Address at the Annual Meeting of the De Beers Shareholders, February 19th, 1900). *Cecil Rhodes—His Political Life and Speeches*, 1881–1900, by Vindex. (London: Chapman & Hall, 1900.)

[2] For a brief account of the nature, geology, mining and marketing of diamonds, see *The Story of Diamonds*, by A. C. Austin and Marion Mercer. (Chicago, 1935.)

From the date of the discovery of the fields to the end of 1936, the value of diamond production in the Union (excluding South-West Africa) exceeded £320,000,000, of which over 70% were produced in the Cape. This amount exceeds the value of minerals produced up to the present in the whole of the rest of Africa. The net dividends of diamond-producing companies over the same period have exceeded £80,000,000, excluding the profits made by individual diggers prior to the company era and subsequently on the alluvial fields.[1] Since Union the State has received over £32,000,000 in taxation of, and share of profits from, diamond mining.[2]

The total amount of foreign capital invested in the diamond industry has probably not exceeded £20,000,000. Apart from the original capital subscribed, all capital expenditure was provided for out of profits. The industry also yielded large profits to the international firms which dealt in diamonds. These had a peculiar importance, because a considerable portion of the wealth accumulated by diamond firms was later used in the development of the Rand.

[1] It is noteworthy that these dividends have been realized notwithstanding the fact that, from the establishment of the diamond monopoly in the 'eighties, relatively little new capital was made available from outside the industry.

[2] The annual receipts of the Central Government from Diamond Mining have been as follows. Their cyclical variation is significant:

TABLE 4.—*Union Government: Receipts from Diamond Mining, 11–37. Years ending 31st March.*

1911	.	.	£434,383	1924	.	.	£1,526,743
1912	.	.	808,621	1925	.	.	1,363,137
1913	.	.	866,086	1926	.	.	1,673,333
1914	.	.	1,011,164	1927	.	.	2,178,280
1915	.	.	430,704	1928	.	.	1,935,755
1916	.	.	146,679	1929	.	.	4,269,925
1917	.	.	627,190	1930	.	.	3,429,770
1918	.	.	946,732	1931	.	.	1,472,152
1919	.	.	1,126,229	1932	.	.	647,209
1920	.	.	2,640,343	1933	.	.	591,565
1921	.	.	2,149,011	1934	.	.	353,496
1922	.	.	312,341	1935	.	.	397,351
1923	.	.	536,267	1936	.	.	382,983
				1937	.	.	567,975

Total £32,825,424

The extent of the wealth which poured into the Cape as a result of the diamond discoveries can best be appreciated if it is noted that up to 1882, that is, to the commencement of amalgamation in the diamond industry, the Cape produced approximately £26,000,000 worth of diamonds, an amount greater than the whole of the exports of the Colony from 1826 to 1861. In 1882, the value of diamonds exported was approximately £4,000,000, twice the value of all goods which had been exported in the year of the diamond discoveries, and greater than the value of the combined exports of the rest of the territories in Africa included in this study. Within twenty years, that is, up to 1890, no less than £59,000,000 of diamonds had been produced in the Cape, equivalent to about £150 for each man, woman and child of the population according to the census of that date. By 1901, the output, including that of the Orange Free State, had exceeded £100,000,000.

Table 5 shows the value of exports and imports through Cape and Natal ports from 1865 to 1908, and also gives, for comparative purposes, the value of diamonds exported through Cape ports. Diamonds were not exported through Natal. These figures illustrate the very great influence of the diamond and, subsequently, of the gold discoveries on both colonies. Tables 6–9 show the growth in the Public Debt, Revenue and Expenditure, Railway Capital, Railway Revenue, Railway Mileage and Population, of the Cape, Natal, Orange Free State and the Transvaal. These should also be considered in relation to the development of the gold-mining industry on the Witwatersrand which is considered later in this chapter.

In 1886, the year of the gold discoveries on the Rand, the railway reached Kimberley; by then, no less than 1,600 miles of railway had been constructed in the Colony. Over £14,000,000 had been invested in them, equivalent to about 60% of the Public Debt, which stood at £21,000,000. The extent to which the Colony was staking its fortune on the diamond industry is further illustrated by the fact, that the Public Debt, excluding that invested in railways, increased more than seven-fold from 1874 to 1884 (from £1,000,000 to over £7,000,000), whereas general revenue (excluding railway earnings) increased only by

TABLE 5.—*Value of Imports and Exports through Cape and Natal Ports*, 1865–1908 *(excluding Specie)*. £(000).

Year.	Imports.			Exports.			Annual Value of Diamond Exports.	Diamond Exports Quinquennially.	
	Cape.	Natal.	Total.	Cape.	Natal.	Total.		Period.	Value.
1865	2,111	455	2,566	2,223	210	2,433	...	1871–75	6,532
1870	2,352	429	2,781	2,369	383	2,952	153	1876–80	11,343
1875	5,731	1,269	7,000	5,755	836	6,591	1,549	1881–85	16,208
1880	7,663	2,337	10,000	7,710	891	8,601	3,368	1886–90	20,257
1885	4,773	1,519	6,292	5,811	877	6,688	2,490	1891–95	19,691
1890	9,366	3,621	12,987	9,838	1,218	11,056	4,162	1896–00	21,237
1895	13,612	...	13,612	16,798	...	16,798	4,775	1901–05	29,011
1901	21,416	9,416	30,832	10,720	2,065	12,785	4,930	...	...
1904	21,824	10,651	32,475	27,471	2,273	29,744	6,422	...	...
1908	13,740	6,709	24,366(a)	42,011	3,625	45,881(a)	4,797	...	...

(a) The value of imports through Delagoa Bay was £3,917,000, and the value of exports was £243,000.

TABLE 6.—*Cape Colony.*

Year.	Public Debt.	Capital Invested in Railways.	Total Annual Expenditure (Inc. Railways).	Total Annual Revenue (Inc. Railways).	Railway Revenue.	Open Railway Mileage.	Population (European).
	£ (000).	£ (000).	£ (000).	£ (000).	£ (000).		
1865	1,204	...	668	537	...	...	181,592
1870	1,570	...	653	711	...	...	...
1875	2,770	1,483	1,107	1,672	111	150	236,783
1880	11,392	7,990	2,808	3,000	641	906	...
1885	21,672	13,407	3,400	3,096	1,037	1,599	...
1890	23,749	14,666	4,234	4,144	1,897	1,890	376,987(a)
1895	27,534	20,404	5,651	6,804	3,390	2,253	...
1901	31,394	22,125	8,618	9,050	3,853	2,135(b)	...
1904	39,386	26,799	9,149	8,472	4,144	2,664	579,741
1908	48,432	32,029	7,681	7,312	2,850	3,265	...

(a) 1891 Census.
(b) In 1897 the Northern System was taken over by the O.F.S.—a total mileage of 353.

Sources :
Public Debt : *Cape Statistical Register*, 1909, p. 73.
Capital Invested in Railways : ,,   ,,   ,,   p. 124 ; 1901, p. 234.
Revenue and Expenditure : ,,   ,,   ,,   p. 65.

TABLE 7.—*Natal.*

Year.	Public Debt.	Capital Invested in Railways.	Total Annual Expenditure (Inc. Railways).	Total Annual Revenue (Inc. Railways).	Railway Revenue.	Open Railway Mileage.	Population (European).
	£ (000).	£ (000).	£ (000).	£ (000).	£ (000).		
1866	160	...	126	95	...	...	16,963
1870	268	...	117	126	...	...	17,737
1877	1,232	...	284	272	...	6	22,654
1885	3,762	2,394	774	663	136	177	36,701
1891	7,170	4,528	1,394	1,319	572	335	46,788
1897	8,019	6,589	1,625	2,213	1,051	428	50,241(a)
1901	10,574	8,529	2,481	2,971	1,650	542	63,821
1904	16,019	11,170	4,071	4,160	1,934	744	97,109

(a) Including Zululand, annexed to Natal in 1897, the European population then being 1,131 persons.

TABLE 8.—*Transvaal.*

Year.	Public Debt. £(000).	Capital Invested in Railways. £(000).	Total Annual Expenditure (Exc. Railways). £(000).	Total Annual Revenue (Exc. Railways). £(000).	Railway Revenue. £(000).	Open Railway Mileage.	Population (European). (000).
1875 . . .	81	...	69	64	...	...	30
1892 . . .	...	(Private)	1,189	1,256	236	434	119
1904 . . .	35,000(b)	21,330(a)	4,539	5,333	4,588(a, c)	1,490	286
1909 . . .	39,000	25,792(a)	6,040	5,736	5,064	2,563	341

(a) Central South African Railways.
(b) Includes Loan of £30,000,000 raised for the Transvaal *and* Orange River Colony for railways and other public works and discharge of existing Transvaal debt.
(c) In 1904 the amount of the Revenue paid over by the Railway system to the Transvaal and Orange Free State treasuries amounted to £1,702,000.

TABLE 9.—*Orange Free State.*

Year.	Public Debt. £(000).	Capital Invested in Railways. £(000).	Total Annual Expenditure (Exc. Railways). £(000).	Total Annual Revenue (Exc. Railways). £(000).	Railway Revenue. £(000).	Open Railway Mileage.	Population (European). (000).
1870 . . .	105	...	53	64	...	...	40
1882 . . .	*nil*	...	200	212	...	...	64
1898 . . .	1,830	...	441	393	...	353	143
1909 . . .	8,932	...	975	991	...	...	...

30% (from £1,500,000 to £1,990,000). By the end of the century, the Cape Government had been able to borrow over £30,000,000 from abroad.

II

ITS EFFECTS.

The large new revenues and loan funds, which flowed into the Treasuries of all the South African Governments through the expansion of diamond and gold mining, were not an unmixed blessing.[1] "It is probable that during the past twenty years more money per head of the rural population has been devoted to the relief of farmers in South Africa than in any country in the world . . . .", wrote the Director of Agriculture in 1908.[2] "Not only is there little to show for this expenditure as regards advances in the theory or practice of agriculture or in other directions that make for progress, but it is to be feared that in some respects actual harm has been wrought, for instead of fostering a spirit of independence and initiative and thrift amongst the farmers, they have been induced to rely upon the Government for everything."[2] To this day it has not been possible to break down the belief of the farmers in South Africa that the State is omnipotent in determining economic conditions, and possesses unlimited resources with which to assist, relieve, or support the poor, and cure them of their poverty. To the indiscriminate relief expenditure of this period and that subsequent to the Boer War must be ascribed the tradition which has been responsible for the large, and often haphazard, assistance to agriculture since Union. A large part of the special revenues

[1] Inevitably the development of mining led to the decline of certain older agricultural industries, just as it provided markets for new ones in the interior. Thus, for example, the diamond discoveries contributed to the decline of horse-breeding, which was an important industry in the Cape in the first half of the nineteenth century. "Down to about 1860, horses were among the principal exports of the colonists and one of their chief sources of wealth. Also it was the export of horses that brought the early Cape Colonists into contact with other countries, notably India and Australia." (Knowles, *ibid.*, iii, p. 84.)

[2] F. B. Smith (Director of Agriculture, Transvaal Department of Agriculture), "Some Observations upon the Probable Effect of the Closer Union of South Africa upon Agriculture", 1908 (*South Africa, Pamphlets*, vol. iii, No. 60, in C. and D.O. Library), p. 20, quoted by Knowles, *ibid.*, vol. iii, p. 168.

from mining (which are credited to loan funds) has been absorbed in this way.[1] On the other hand, the ordinary revenues of the country have provided an excellent system of permanent and well-developed agricultural services.

Nevertheless, though so much of the assistance provided by the various Governments before Union was haphazardly distributed, the fact that it was financially possible to render it at all was of profound importance. For it enabled the farming community to withstand successive plagues, which attacked their animals and wrought havoc, until, with the coming of Union, a permanent agricultural organization for the whole country was created to combat them. It has rightly been said that "meteorological conditions alone would justify the South African farmer's complaint that he is engaged in 'a gamble with God' ". But in addition the country labours under a severe handicap as compared with the other Dominions. It is the country of animal diseases.[2] In the fight against scab disease, gall-sickness, redwater, lung-sickness, horse-sickness, rinderpest, and East Coast fever, to mention only a few, South Africa was fortunate in being in a position to draw on the steady stream of new wealth accruing from its mines. More than most countries, the Union has increasingly had to accumulate non-material capital by scientific knowledge and agricultural education, and by providing a wide network of specialized institutions such as the Divisions of Plant Industry, of Botany and Plant Pathology, and of Veterinary Science and Animal Industry, not to mention the valuable work of other Government Departments in regard to agriculture.

Not the least important of the benefits which the mineral industries have conferred on the country is that they have largely contributed to the financing of this work. Most other African territories seek anxiously for similar sources of wealth out of which to create scientific institutions and organized services to cope with the agricultural and ecological problems on the solution of which their progress so largely depends.

---

[1] This expenditure is analysed in the following chapter.

[2] For a careful account of the fight against drought, plagues and pests in the Union, see Knowles, *ibid.*, vol. iii, chapter vii, pp. 132–158.

III

THE RATIONALIZATION OF THE DIAMOND INDUSTRY.

The conditions in the diamond fields in the pioneer days are well known. The first diamond was discovered in 1867, but not until 1870 were there finds such as to attract a large population to the banks of the Vaal River. Many of the early diggers were farmers from the neighbouring districts who did digging in their spare time. Of the later arrivals some possessed good equipment and a little capital. But it is certain that only small amounts of capital were applied to the alluvial diggings. This is also true of the "dry diggings" until 1885. It was first thought that the dry diggings would soon be exhausted, but the discovery of the diamond pipes, which meant that diamonds were to be found not only near the surface but to great depths, made diamond mining a comparatively permanent industry. This raised fresh problems in the technique of mining. The workings soon became so deep that the outer claims were buried by falling reef, and those in the middle of the huge pits were under water. The method of production was primitive because the individual digger could not face the cost of purchasing and transporting plant. In 1874, a Mining Board was formed with power to levy an assessment in order to keep the claims free of water and fallen rock. In the year of its formation, the Board increased the permissible holding of a single owner from two to ten claims. The real solution, however, was to abandon open quarrying for subterranean mining. It soon became impossible to adhere to the ten-claim clause, which was at length revoked, and the way was opened for the formation of Joint Stock Companies, and eventually for the process of amalgamation, which marked the most significant stage in the evolution of the diamond industry in South Africa.

By the beginning of 1880, there were twelve companies with a total capital of some £2,500,000, the shares having been issued, in the main, to vendors and promoters who were still the holders. Of these companies, the De Beers, Kimberley Central and Compagnie Française des Mines de Diamant du Cap de Bon Esperance[1] were to play a most important part in the amalgamation which was to follow. The De Beers Mining Company was formed in 1880 with a capital of £200,000, and took over the combined claims of Rhodes, Rudd and others. "It progressed with extraordinary success, expanding its range of ownership, absorbing step by step its floundering neighbours, and finally standing out pre-eminent in March, 1885, with a capital of £841,550."

The success of the early companies inevitably inspired wild speculation. Speculative manias and booms of this type have ever since characterized the history of South Africa.[2]

In 1881, no less than fifty-nine companies were floated within six months. The total of the share capital of these companies rose to £8,000,000, the shares being subscribed for largely in the

---

[1] In 1882 Alfred Beit became the Kimberley representative of Jules Porges & Co., who started business in Paris as diamond merchants in 1869 (Paris was at this time the centre of the world diamond trade). The men who, from time to time, had been connected with M. Porges and the successors to him, Messrs. Wernher, Beit & Co., took the keenest interest in Rhodes's scheme for amalgamation, and assisted more than all others in bringing about the consolidation of the diamond interests. As early as 1871, Mr. Julius Wernher went out to Kimberley in the capacity of diamond buyer for Jules Porges & Co., and became a partner in the firm in 1878. The firm grew in importance, and became owners in some of the largest companies in the four mines. They were the founders of the Griqualand West Diamond Mining Company in the Kimberley mine which was afterwards re-formed into the "French Company". Cf. G. F. Williams, The Diamond Mines of South Africa, p. 289. (London: Macmillan, 1902.)

In 1888 Rhodes bought out the Paris shareholders in this concern; he agreed that its property should be amalgamated with that of the Kimberley Central Diamond Mining Company. The Kimberley Central Diamond Mining Company was registered in 1880, and by a steady process of amalgamation gradually extended its claim area until, in 1888, upon the absorption of the "French Company", it had an issued share capital of £1,748,190, and owned the entire Kimberley mine, a more valuable area than the De Beers.

[2] Prior to the growth in importance of the mineral industries, industrial fluctuations in economic activity were largely governed by natural causes, such as droughts or other factors affecting the yield of agriculture, prosperity and depression alternating with good and bad crops. In the later history of South Africa, the rhythm of activity is affected by the factors influencing the flow of investment from abroad, and particularly by the course of interest rates and monetary conditions in London.

colony.[1] At least half of this represented vendors' and promoters' scrip, and, of the working capital, only a small proportion was at any time subscribed.[2] The banks, by making advances against scrip, actively assisted in fanning the boom. The description of the boom, given by an eye-witness,[2] could without much alteration be applied to every mining boom in South Africa which has since occurred. The inevitable depression[3] and the fall in share values set the stage for the process of amalgamation.

[1] Of the 71 companies in existence at this date there were:

13 in the De Beers Mines with a capital of		.	.	.	.	.	£1,334,100
13 „ Kimberley Mines „ „		.	.	.	.	.	2,685,000
							4,019,100
18 „ Dutoitspan Mines „ „		.	.	.	.	.	2,220,750
16 „ Bultfontein Mines „ „		.	.	.	.	.	871,100
							7,110,950
11 „ outside mines „ „		.	.	.	.	.	923,000
							£8,033,950

[2] Mr. J. W. Mathews in his stimulating book, *Incwadi Yami* or *Twenty Years' Personal Experience in South Africa* (London: Sampson Low, etc., 1887), gives the following remarkable description of the diamond boom:

" . . . When once the idea that the joint-stock system was the most advantageous method for working the mines gained a hold upon the community, the excitement became intense, company after company was formed, and the shares in every case were eagerly taken up by the public. When the formation of a new undertaking was announced, the applications universally doubled and trebled the number of shares proposed to be allotted, and in fact a premium was invariably offered to a successful applicant for the chance he had secured of obtaining a share in any new venture. . . . It was astonishing how the mania seized on all classes in Kimberley, from the highest to the lowest, just as Law's scheme and the South Sea Bubble did during the previous century; how everyone, ... men of the pen and men of the sword, magistrates and I.D.B.'s, Englishmen and foreigners, rushed wildly into the wonderful game of speculation. . . . It was evident that it mattered very little to the general public, or the majority at all events, what the company was, what the value of the claims might be or where they were situated; so long as it was a diamond-mining company it was quite sufficient to command public favour. The public bought shares in the diamond-mining companies as to-day they are doing in the gold companies, not to obtain dividends on their capital invested, but for purposes of pure speculation." (Pp. 246-248.)

[3] The measure of the reaction can be judged from the fact that merchandise imports into the Cape, which reached the high level of £9,372,000 in 1882, had contracted to under £3,800,000 in 1886. Certain statistics made available by the Standard Bank of South Africa, Limited, are also interesting. Its Notes in Circulation, Total Deposits and Total Advances respectively were £764,586, £8,279,287 and £9,676,431 at June 30th, 1881, and by June 30th, 1886, they were respectively £308,174, £4,398,083 and £4,532,473. (*Cf.* Amphlett, *History of the Standard Bank of South Africa Limited.* London: Glasgow University Press, 1914.)

By 1885 there were only forty-two companies, and holdings were being consolidated.

The greatest danger to the continuation profitable exploitation of the diamond fields lay in over-production. Costs were rising with greater depth, but diamond prices were falling. It became clear that the control of supply was necessary, and that the only means of achieving this would be through amalgamation, as the owners of the different mines were so antagonistic that they would not agree among themselves to restrict output.

Rhodes obtained complete control of De Beers mine in 1887.

There were forty-one mines, of which the De Beers and Kimberley were the two richest. It therefore remained for Rhodes, after consolidating the various companies in the De Beers mine, to obtain control of the others. This was not possible without the support of London, where the Rothschilds in 1880, through a syndicate, and with the assistance of Lippert, bought out shareholders in the French Company. The next step[1] was the absorption of the Kimberley Central Company controlled by the Barnato interests. The shares necessary to obtain control had to be bought at considerably inflated prices.

At the time of consolidation, the total market valuation of the properties to be amalgamated was £23,434,250.[2] The shares of the De Beers and Central Companies were valued at £17,934,250. The actual cost of the other properties was £4,500,000. It was decided not to increase the capital of the corporation beyond £3,950,000. The purchases in excess of this issue were provided for by the issue of debentures.

One of the most significant facts about the growth of the diamond industry is that, until the period of amalgamation, individuals or companies outside South Africa invested a negligible amount of capital in diamond mining. Owing to the nature of

[1] At this time (1888) the capital of De Beers stood at £2,509,620. Beit, who had come to the fields in 1875 as the representative of another important group of diamond buyers (Lippert & Co., of Hamburg), and who subsequently started up in business on his own, had already combined his claims with the De Beers Company.

[2] The capital of the De Beers before consolidation was £2,009,000. The capital of the Central Company was £1,779,650. De Beers stock at the time of consolidation was selling at £50 for each £10 share, making a total valuation of £8,898,250 for the mine. At this market estimate the valuation of the two great mines was £17,934,250. In addition, De Beers bought up nearly all the companies in the Dutoitspan and Bultfontein mines.

its product, this miraculous industry could provide out of its own surplus for most of its phenomenal growth. It can be said that, during the first fifteen years, the diamond industry was financed (*a*) from within itself, and (*b*) through inflation in the Cape Colony, by means of which resources were diverted to the diamond industry through the excessive advances made by the banks on shares during the 1881 diamond boom.

The resources of the colony were increased at the time by large State borrowing for railway construction and also by the generally prosperous agricultural conditions,[1] particularly in the pastoral industry and ostrich farming.

IV

ANOTHER LUXURY INDUSTRY.

It is worthy of note that the ostrich farming industry played a role in developing farming at the Cape smaller than, but similar to that of the diamond discoveries in inaugurating mining. Here was another of those luxury industries which have so largely affected the development of the country, and which are, in considerable measure, responsible for the restlessness and speculative character of much South African economic activity.

Dr. De Kock[2] ascribed the eventual over-expansion and subsequent decline of the industry to the fact that the ostrich farmers did not learn from the lessons of experience, as the diamond industry did when it passed through a similar depression to that which assailed ostrich farming in the 'eighties.[3]   No

---

[1] The causes of recurrent credit expansion and contraction have since remained basically the same. The growth in excess funds in London of the banks, whether due to the excess of visible exports or to capital imports, leads to an expansion of credit in the Union. Eventually inflation results and usually takes the form of large increases in share, land and property values throughout the country. The process is reversed when the funds of the Banks in London decline. *Cf.* two articles by the writer on "The Situation in South Africa 1929–1932", in the *British Economic Journal*, March, 1933, and "South African Monetary Policy", in the *South African Journal of Economics*, March, 1933.

[2] M. H. De Kock, *op. cit.*, p. 234 ff., to which the author is indebted for a large part of the information given here.

[3] After the successful domestication of the ostrich in 1869 and the development of a new method of incubating ostrich eggs, the ostrich feather exports increased rapidly. Prices rose from £3 per lb. in 1870 to about double this figure in the early 'eighties.

organization was instituted with a view to limiting the production of this luxury commodity in accordance with the demand. As a result, the feather trade, and consequently the feather industry, collapsed completely after 1913. In this year, the value of the exports reached the extraordinarily high figure of about £3,000,000—nearly one-quarter of the total agricultural and pastoral exports of the Union at that time.

V

BANKING.

Prior to 1861, banking in the Colony had been in the hands of local institutions. This was followed by the advent of the so-called Imperial Banks, that is, banks having their Head Offices in London and financed by British capital. The first of these banks, the London and South African Bank, was opened in Capetown in 1861 with a capital of £400,000, and branches were established in various centres. It was followed in 1862 by the Standard Bank of South Africa.[1] The Bank was, in fact, among the earliest institutions to register with limited liability under the new English Companies Act, which also greatly influenced the subsequent development of the diamond industry. It is noteworthy that, in

---

[1] The importance of these two Imperial Banks is shown by the following comparison:

	Capital.	Paid up.
All Banks, 1861	£1,972,815 .	£1,124,021
,, ,, 1862 . . .	1,981,630 .	1,348,937
,, ,, 1863 . . .	4,117,660 .	2,018,873
2 Imperial Banks, 1863 . .	2,500,000 .	1,000,000

This state of affairs brought about a mania for ostrich farming. The value of exports reached over £1,000,000 in 1882. Soon, however, feathers of an inferior quality glutted the market, and prices drastically declined. By 1888 the value of ostrich feather exports had fallen to less than one-third of the 1882 peak. Many who had invested heavily in ostrich breeding were ruined. As a result, more scientific methods were applied to ostrich farming, and the industry again assumed large proportions in many districts of the Cape. Over-production, however, soon resulted. The weight of ostrich feathers exported advanced from 312,000 lb. in 1890 to 471,000 lb. in 1905, 741,000 lb. in 1910 and 1,023,000 lb. in 1913, when the ostrich-farming boom reached its greatest height. After 1913, ostrich feathers went out of fashion for hat decoration and prices began to fall. For a time, speculators tried to run the market, but they could not avert the collapse of the industry. In 1916 the value of exports had fallen to £486,000. By 1934, the weight of the ostrich feathers exported had fallen to 90,000 lb., valued only at £42,373. The number of ostriches declined from 314,000 in 1918 to 32,000 in 1930.

1862, no less than twenty banking companies were registered in London with an aggregate nominal capital of £25,000,000. It appears that the London and South African Bank was the last to be established under authority of a Royal Charter. Rivalry between the Standard Bank and the London and South African Bank continued until 1877, when the two were merged. The Oriental Banking Corporation had appeared on the scene in 1873, but it withdrew in 1879, some of its branches being taken over by the Bank of Africa, which started business in South Africa in that year. The last Imperial Bank was the African Banking Corporation, which was established in 1891.

By 1892, the banking business of the Cape Colony was, with one exception, in the hands of the three Imperial Banks, namely, the Standard Bank of South Africa Limited (with seventy-two branches throughout the country), the Bank of Africa (successor to the Oriental Banking Corporation, with twenty-four branches) and the African Banking Corporation (with eighteen branches). There was only one small local bank in operation, the Stellenbosch Bank.

As is, of course, well known, the Imperial Banks have rendered services to Africa the importance of which cannot be exaggerated. It is not necessary to repeat the subsequent history[1] of banking development. By 1920, the final banking amalgamation left only two big banking institutions in the Union—the Standard Bank of South Africa and the National Bank of South Africa, which latter was taken over by Barclays only a few years later, to the regret of many who would have preferred to see a different development of banking in the Union. Prior to its disappearance, however, the National Bank had in any case ceased to function effectively as a competitor to the Standard Bank, and its continuance as an independent concern would not have prevented the concentration of banking which has taken place.

The British banks operating in the Union (and in fact throughout British Central and East Africa) are typical of the English commercial banks. They follow the same conservative—perhaps

---

[1] For this the following books should be consulted. Arndt, *ibid.*; De Kock, *ibid.*; Amphlett, *History of the Standard Bank of South Africa*, 1914; *Foreign Banking Systems*, edited by Parker Willis, chapter on South Africa, by Arndt and Richards; and in particular the *Report of the Kemmerer and Vissering Commission on the Resumption of Gold Payments by the Union of South Africa*, U.G., No. 13, 1925.

ultra-conservative—banking policies which have long characterized similar institutions in London and in the other Dominions.[1]
The banking problems associated with their policies in South
Africa are, in essence, the same as those met with in other Dominions, as, for example, in Australia and New Zealand.[2] With
these technical banking questions this study is not concerned.
It must, however, be remembered that, up to the present, a large
part of the development of Africa has been bound up with the
growth of trade. When the preponderating importance of trade
in the national economy of the Union declines and, as may be the
case, production for the internal market increases, a new stage in
banking evolution is likely to commence.

VI

WORLD DIAMOND CONTROL.

The great diamond amalgamation laid the foundation for the
highly centralized control of the diamond production and diamond
trade of most of the world. Without this control, the industry
would probably have collapsed, either owing to over-production of
this extreme luxury commodity or owing to such fluctuations in
its value as would have destroyed the demand, and especially the
investment demand for it. The essential feature of the vitally
necessary policy of control on which this unique industry depends
was summarized by Sir David Harris when presiding at the De
Beers Annual Meeting in 1928. In discussing the urgent need of
the Government itself joining forces with the Conference Producers in marketing its production from the State diggings at
Namaqualand through one channel, he said: "The diamond
trade is not affected or disturbed by the known or estimated
quantity or value of diamonds existing in the mines and diggings.
The public, and especially the trade, know that South Africa has
produced in the last sixty years about £340,000,000[3] worth of

[1] Cf. the excellent book *The Imperial Banks*, by A. S. J. Baster (London: P. S. King,
1929) ; it also contains an account of the operations of the Bank of British West Africa.
[2] I have discussed some of these similar technical problems in the article, "South
African Monetary Policy", previously referred to.
[3] This general estimate by Sir David Harris apparently includes the diamond
production of South-West Africa.

diamonds, and they realize that there is at least the same amount still to be unearthed. This fact does not cause the trade and public one moment's anxiety or nervousness, but what concerns them more than anything is the quantity that will be put on the market annually. . . . For about twenty years after the discovery of diamonds in this country output and sales were uncontrolled. During this period it was difficult at times to dispose of diamonds, which realized prices far below present rates, although this Company then worked only the Kimberley and De Beers mines. Subsequently De Beers acquired possession of the Dutoitspan and Bultfontein mines; after this the Wesselton mine was discovered, which we purchased; then came the big Premier mine in the Transvaal, South-West Africa, Belgian Congo, Angola and other West African fields, all important producers, and to cap all, the recent discovery of the rich fields of Lichtenburg and Namaqualand.   Despite the production from these areas and mines, diamonds are fetching far higher prices to-day than during the first twenty years of the existence of the industry. The reason for this is not far to seek. The big producers, realizing the danger of continuing to sell in the open market, arranged to sell through one channel to feel the pulse of the demand and prevent over-production.   This brought into being the Diamond Syndicate, through whom the bulk of not only the South African diamonds, but of the world's production, has been marketed for the last thirty-five years at greatly enhanced prices in face of periods of over-production when the Syndicate, with its large financial resources, was able to hold immense stocks and just meet the world's demand.[1] If the present system were seriously disturbed, the industry would suffer a serious setback, and confidence would be shaken throughout the whole world. There is only one method of preserving this great industry for the State and all producers of diamonds—control, control, and nothing but control, it being the bounden duty of the Government to take the lead with its yield from Namaqualand.

"During the long period that De Beers practically controlled

---

[1] For the control of the diamond market before the Great War see the excellent account by Jean Demuth, *Der Diamantenmarkt* (*Volkwirtschaftliche Abhandlungen der badischen Hochsculen*, No. 13). (Karlsruhe, 1913.)

the output of diamonds, and with the intention of continuing that policy, we acquired the Wesselton, Voorspoed and Kamfersdam mines, bought nearly the whole share capital of the Premier and Koffyfontein Companies, the estate of the London and South African Exploration Company, and other concerns, involving a total cash outlay of £5,942,833—an enormous sum to stabilize the diamond trade, by which all our competitors benefited without the slightest cost to themselves."

The policy advocated by the diamond producers was adopted. The Government closed its separate selling-office. To-day, there is a new Producers' Association, which includes not only the Conference Producers (De Beers, Premier, Jagersfontein and Consolidated Diamond Mines of South-West Africa), but also the Koffyfontein Mines Limited, the Cape Coast Exploration Company Limited, the Government of the Union of South Africa and the Diamond Corporation. The last-named took over the business of the old Diamond Syndicate formed during the depression of 1892/3. Its initial capital was £5,000,000, of which half was subscribed by the producers and half by the Syndicate. The Articles of Association of the Diamond Corporation provided that the De Beers shall have the right to appoint half the Board, including the Chairman. In this way, the producers were able to direct the general sales policy of the industry, while at the same time retaining the skill and connections that the Syndicate had acquired through long experience. In this way also, the basic principles of the diamond trade, control of production and sales through one channel, have been maintained.

Since its formation, the Association has entered into an agreement for the sale of its diamonds with a new company known as the Diamond Trading Company Limited, which is now the sole channel for the sale of diamonds both in South Africa and London. The Government, like the other producers, has accepted a quota, and the Diamond Corporation has agreed to look upon its stock of diamonds, arising from necessary purchases of diamonds from alluvial diggings and outside sources in maintaining the market during the depression, as though it were a mine, and has accepted a quota on a sliding scale in respect thereof. The policy of control of the world's diamond production and trade, broadly speaking, rests first on the policy of producers stopping their production with the onset of a world depression, which is reflected in diamond sales with almost automatic promptitude, and, secondly, on the purchase of "outside diamond production" not controlled by producers' agreements, in order to keep it off the market. Furthermore, it has always been the policy of De Beers to acquire controlling holdings in other diamond companies. The Chairman, at the Annual Meeting of the De Beers Company in 1933, in referring to the acquisition by De Beers of controlling holdings in the Consolidated Diamond Mines, Jagersfontein and the Cape Coast Companies, said, "From the day your Company was formed not only has it acquired or attempted to acquire control by purchase, lease, or share acquisition of every important diamond producer in Southern Africa, but it has more than once paid large sums and/or assumed important liabilities to secure properties, not because they were of immediate value, but because in other hands they would have been of nuisance value or in years to come might be competitive." As an example, he mentioned that, after the amalgamation of the Kimberley and De Beers mines, Rhodes arranged for the lease of the Bultfontein and Dutoitspan mines, notwithstanding the fact that, at the time, these properties seemed very doubtful assets; "Too poor to work, too rich to ignore", was Rhodes's description of them. Yet, to date, the De Beers has paid over $£4\frac{1}{4}$ millions in respect of these properties and is glad to lease them at a cost of nearly $£100,000$ per annum. It is, of course, well known that, in 1917, for the same reason, the De Beers purchased a controlling holding in the Premier Diamond Mines.

The general policy outlined above has also been applied by De Beers, wholly or in part, to certain diamond companies outside the Union and South-West Africa, for example, in Angola, the Belgian Congo, and West Africa. Moreover, for many years, De Beers has held mining rights in Southern Rhodesia, and it also has a crown grant for diamonds over certain areas in Bechuanaland. It is probable that at the present time the production and sale of diamonds is controlled to an extent never before rivalled.

The production of diamonds in and outside the Union of South

TABLE 10.—*World Production of Diamonds in Metric Carats*, 1920–34.

Year.	Union of South Africa.		South-West Africa.	Belgian Congo.	Angola.	British Guiana.	Brazil.(a)	Other Countries.	Total.
	Production.	Percentage of World Total.							
	Metric Carats.	%.	Metric Carats.	Metric Carats.	Metric Carats.	Metric Carats.	Metric Carats.	Metric Carats.	Metric Carats.
1920	2,612,511	70·92	606,424	281,372	93,529	40,407	45,000	4,601	3,683,844
1921	828,036	53·51	171,331	280,655	106,719	105,325	50,000	5,389	1,547,445
1922	669,559	47·82	144,156	250,000	97,000	163,641	60,000	15,698	1,400,054
1923	2,053,094	60·74	433,229	414,954	94,478	229,162		164,083(b)	3,389,000
1924	2,449,398	62·41	492,696	548,274	113,016	190,501		120,115(b)	3,910,000
1925	2,430,128	56·91	515,860	883,903	125,000	187,745	127,364		4,270,000
1926	3,217,967	56·51	683,801	1,114,384	154,369	168,507	356,768		5,695,796
1927	4,708,038	63·77	723,877	1,041,544	200,809	178,402	530,413		7,383,083
1928	4,372,857	57·21	503,142	1,649,225	239,000	136,283	742,683		7,643,190
1929	3,661,212	49·26	507,189	1,907,765	311,903	125,799	828,885		7,432,753
1930	3,163,591	41·93	415,048	2,519,948	329,824	107,201	1,009,680		7,545,292
1931	2,119,156	29·89	71,532	3,500,000	351,495	61,840	985,929		7,089,952
1932	798,382	13·15	17,944	3,990,069	367,334	60,185	882,162		6,116,076
1933	506,553	(d)	2,374	1,931,000	374,000	48,569	898,814(c)		(d)
1934	440,313	(d)	4,126	(d)	453,000	(d)			(d)

(a) Estimated.
(b) The value of exports from Brazil in 1923 amounted to £188,605, and, in 1924, to £142,392.
(c) Brazil not available,
(d) Not available.

Africa from 1920 to 1936 is shown in Table 10. The effects of world industrial fluctuations are clearly apparent.[1]

The following statistics[2] (Table 11) of diamond sales from 1911 to 1936 also illustrate the extreme sensitiveness of the diamond market to business cycles.

The diamond industry exerted an enormous influence on the successful establishment of gold mining on the Witwatersrand, both by affecting the supply of capital and by making available skilled European labour. As that charitable and unassuming gentleman, the late Sir George Albu, than whom few were better entitled to be called pioneers of the Rand, wrote: "Kimberley was really the Alma Mater and the nursery of Johannesburg." But the permanent establishment of the diamond industry which resulted from the first great company amalgamations exerted an influence far beyond the borders of the territories comprising the Union of South Africa. A powerful financial link was created which bound first South Africa, and then Rhodesia, to London. It provided through Rhodes a stepping-stone to the period of expansion by means of the Chartered Companies, and this inevitably gave way to the next stage of expansion, during which Britain, followed by other powers, finally undertook direct financial responsibility for colonial development in Africa.

The revolutionary changes to which the discovery of diamonds led in the Cape have been parallelled in other African territories. For example, without the stimulus provided by diamonds, the economic development of South-West Africa would probably have remained insignificant. As is shown in Chapter V, of the total exports of this territory from 1906 to 1936, which amounted to £53 millions, over £41 millions represented mineral exports, of which diamonds accounted for over £30 millions. Moreover, the development of Angola since the War has been considerably assisted by its diamond industry, quite apart from the influence

---

[1] The rapid decline during depression years in the percentages which the Union output is of the world totals is due to the fact that the controlled production of the Union was usually stopped almost immediately, while that of uncontrolled producers largely continued and had to be bought up by the Diamond Syndicate or Diamond Corporation.

[2] *Cf. Report of the Government Mining Engineer*, U.G., No. 17, 1938.

exerted by the efforts of those diamond interests who have played an important part in linking up Angola with the mineral belt of Belgian Congo and Northern Rhodesia. The value of diamond exports from Angola has been about the same as from

TABLE 11.—*Total Diamond Sales, Union of South Africa,*
1911–37.

	Metric carats.		Value.		Value realized per carat.	
			£.		s.	d.
1911	5,002,499·74		8,548,821		34	2
1912	4,898,135·53		9,565,024		39	1
1913	5,684,683·43		12,088,983		42	6
1914	3,452,770·28		6,758,544		39	2
1915	566,589·29		1,459,597		51	6
1916	2,352,739·58		5,227,777		44	5
1917	2,480,287·49		6,170,906		49	9
1918	2,711,996·66		7,232,744		53	4
1919	2,719,180·66		13,379,662		98	5
1920	1,812,827·98		10,328,405		113	11
1921	544,165·12		2,161,796		79	5
1922	1,231,373·77		3,765,601		61	2
1923	2,584,269·88		7,733,368		59	10
1924	2,040,655·60		6,752,499		66	2
1925	2,598,037·43		8,665,224		66	8
1926	3,178,423·09		10,961,814		69	0
1927	4,255,774·72		11,818,987		55	7
1928	3,686,540·45		11,079,049		60	1
1929	3,084,438·24		12,453,676		80	9
1930	1,876,657·15		5,883,449		62	8
1931	1,448,530·56		2,726,778		37	8
1932	867,872·71		1,522,929		35	1
1933	646,044·67		1,859,200		57	7
1934	1,261,548·07		2,493,148		39	6
1935	2,372,990·70		2,908,789		24	6
1936	1,098,046·25		3,209,271		58	5
1937	949,113·00		3,739,260		78	10

the Gold Coast, but in view of the smaller value of Angola's export trade, they have exerted a greater influence on this colony.

The most recent and one of the most striking examples of the transformation which diamond mining can bring about in the economic situation of an African territory, the development of which has previously had to be carried out without the assistance of exploitable mineral wealth, is provided by Sierra Leone.

Since 1932 this territory has seen the growth "with almost startling rapidity" of Africa's newest diamond field,[1] whose output has increased from £20 in 1932 to over £500,000 for the year ended June, 1936. It was decided, on the advice of the Colonial Office and of the Gold Coast Government, that it would be in the interests of Sierra Leone that the diamond industry should be placed in the hands of one company. Accordingly, the Consolidated African Selection Trust Limited, which is affiliated to De Beers, was given the exclusive right to prospect for diamonds over an area of 4,120 square miles in the Eastern district of Sierra Leone. Symptomatic of the stimulus provided by diamond discoveries is the fact that, in 1935, the diamonds exported were valued at £402,000, and formed 26% of the domestic exports of Sierra Leone. In 1936 the percentage had risen to 33%, and the value of diamond exports had risen to £725,000.

Once again, therefore, diamonds have provided a new gateway through which the economic forces of the modern world can enter Africa.

[1] For an interesting account, see an article by J. D. Pollett in the *Bulletin of the Imperial Institute*, September, 1937. Mr. Pollett believes that the field is assured of a long life.

SECTION II

GOLD

"At periods when gold is available at suitable depths experience shows that the real wealth of the world increases rapidly ; and when but little of it is so available, our wealth suffers stagnation or decline. Thus gold-mines are of the greatest value and importance to civilization. Just as wars have been the only form of large-scale loan expenditure which statesmen have thought justifiable, so gold-mining is the only pretext for digging holes in the ground which has recommended itself to bankers as sound finance ; and each of these activities has played its part in progress—failing something better."—J. M. KEYNES, *The General Theory of Employment, Interest and Money*, p. 130. (London: Macmillan, 1936.)

I

THE FINANCIAL MAGNET.

For nearly fifty years[1] the gold mining industry has been the power-house of modern enterprise in the Union, and the main attraction for capital from the money markets of Europe. It promises to retain that position for a longer time than anyone would care to forecast. Nearly one-half of the private listed capital from abroad has been directly invested in the Rand gold mines. If one takes into account that large portions of the railway system and other public works, as well as a wide range of

[1] For an excellent analysis of the "Economic Effects of the Gold Discoveries upon South Africa, 1886–1910", from the point of view of the principles of international trade, and following the studies of Taussig and Viner in the United States and Canada, see D. W. Gilbert's article in *The Quarterly Journal of Economics*, August, 1933. After an exhaustive analysis of such material as he was able to obtain up to 1910 relating to the terms of trade, capital movements and immigration, he comes to the conclusion that the results of the development of the industry were as theory would lead one to expect, and that, in particular, the decline in production of other staple export industries owing to the comparative advantage of gold production was marked until 1899. In the early years of the nineteenth century, South Africa's shift to an old debtor position, in turn, produced the expected stimulant to South African exports in these directions. While the general results of Gilbert's analysis are probably accurate, their acceptance must await detailed verification of the relatively limited material on which he was able to draw.

subsidiary enterprises serve the mining industries and the urban communities in the mining areas, one can regard at least half of the total foreign capital which has entered the country as the result of the exploitation of its mineral wealth.

Most of the private listed capital from abroad has been raised by the issue of equity shares. Largely as a result of the Group System of finance on the Rand and its intimate overseas financial connections, the shares are dealt in as easily on the main capital markets of Europe as on the Johannesburg Stock Exchange, whose activities are almost wholly devoted to transactions in them. Indeed, the highly developed institutions responsible for the financing of mining enterprise continue, as in the past, to dominate the money and capital markets of the country. Credit conditions in the Union are largely determined by the fact that the flow of capital to it depends on the psychological and economic conditions which influence the attitude of that special group of investors which supplies the capital for the relatively speculative investments connected with the Union's mineral industries.

When the South African Reserve Bank, the first of the Dominion Central Banks, was established, great hopes were entertained that it would be able to exercise effective control over credit conditions and industrial activity. It has so far failed to achieve this purpose, largely because of the fluctuations in these long-term capital movements. The short-term credit situation is similarly affected. The two Imperial Banks which dominate the commercial banking system are not the only sources of short-term credit for either the Stock Exchange or commercial enterprise in the Union, both of which at times draw liberally on private sources abroad. Owing to its great dependence on the flow of capital from abroad, the Union is thus very greatly affected by financial conditions overseas, which largely determine its monetary policy.

It is not always realized that the development of the financial institutions, which for the greater part of a generation have enabled the Union's mineral industries to attract capital from abroad, has been due, to a considerable extent, to a combination of fortuitous circumstances. South Africa was able to develop means of access to the world's largest money market which were denied to Non-British African territories.   Despite the liberal granting of concessions to private *entrepreneurs*, these non-British territories (for example the Belgian Congo) have found the continued raising of capital from the home countries for colonial exploration and development a most difficult, and, in many cases, an impossible task.   Yet one must guard against the view that, simply because the Union has, in fact, created highly efficient channels of contact with the main reservoirs of overseas capital, that therefore its needs have in the past been, or will continue to be automatically fulfilled.   For, in fact, very great cyclical variations in the supply of capital have in the past conditioned, and still determine the tempo of the country's development.

II

THE CHANNELS OF INVESTMENT.

It is often not sufficiently appreciated that the class of investors which is prepared to interest itself permanently in speculative mining investment in Southern Africa has always been relatively small.   Moreover, except during booms, the type and number of shareholders in mining, financial and exploration companies both in and outside the Union has varied surprisingly little. Some years ago, the author examined the share registers of a considerable number of Rand mining companies, and followed the variations in the individual holdings of the most important investors.   The results indicated that, in general and over long periods, the investors as a body did not change.   Though they might change their investments in particular companies, they remained associated with the industry as a whole.

This is also a factor of considerable importance in the future mining development in other African territories, because of their close association with financial institutions in the Union.   The financial "Houses" responsible for the Union's mining development have also been a potent source of enterprise, technical skill and capital for mining expansion throughout Africa.

A large number of exploration, financial and mining enterprises beyond the borders of the Union are controlled by, or are connected with the companies which conduct mining on the Rand. The list of companies opposite shows the extent of some of the financial affiliations of the mining finance houses in the Union. There is little doubt that the mineral development of the territories in Africa beyond the Union is likely to be dependent to an ever-increasing degree on these specialized channels of capital investment.

If it is borne in mind that the supply of mining capital, on which the Union so greatly depends, has come from a relatively small group of investors and from the profits of mining companies themselves, one is led to attach new importance to fiscal policies which affect the amount of the dividends received by this class, and the continued increase in the taxation of gold mining in the Union assumes a new significance.[1]

The full effects of mining taxation are, as a rule, more readily appreciated when they are discussed with reference to the internal supply of capital, and the significance of the fact that mining investors abroad are. also a special class is frequently overlooked. Consequently, there is a tendency to forget that the amount of capital which the overseas investor is able to provide for new enterprise in the Union is greatly affected by the dividends which he receives from past investments, particularly as mining dividends represent not only net profits, but include also the return of the original capital subscribed.[2]

In view of these considerations the financial history of the Rand is of peculiar significance, and will be considered in the following sections.

[1] This is considered in detail in the following chapter.

[2] This point has also been stressed by Mr. R. S. G. Stokes in his recent Presidential Address on "The Economics of Rand Mining" to the Chemical, Metallurgical and Mining Society of South Africa. "As things stand to-day," he said, "shareholders in producing, developing and exploration companies are still practically the same body. Money for new ventures is provided, much more heavily and directly than is commonly supposed, from the dividend distributions of our producers. Rand share-holders to-day have to be individually persuaded to devote a portion of their mining income or of their capital increment—a waning force—to outside speculative enter-prise. Whilst their losses must be written off, their successes are to be taxed, individually to the maximum of financial endurance. It seems inevitable that a system of taxation designed to impose a maximum burden upon a group of hardy, established producers must be found, in the long run, to make inadequate allowance for the greater element of risk involved in the creation of new mines." (*Cf. The South African Mining and Engineering Journal*, August 28th, 1937, p. 847.)

RAND MINING GROUPS.

Anglo-American Corporation of South Africa Ltd.

Anglo-American Investment Trust Ltd.
Anmercosa Land and Estates, Ltd.
Brakpan Mines, Ltd.
Daggafontein Mines, Ltd.
East Daggafontein Mines, Ltd.
East Rand Gold, Coal and Estate Company, Ltd.
New Era Consolidated Ltd.
Rand Selection Corporation, Ltd.
South African Land & Exploration Company, Ltd.
Springs Mines, Ltd.
Transvaal Coal Corporation, Ltd.
West Rand Investment Trust, Ltd.
Western Reefs Exploration and Development Co. Ltd.
West Springs Ltd.

Nchanga Consolidated Copper Mines, Ltd.
Rhodesia Minerals Concession, Ltd.
Rhokana Corporation, Ltd.
The Rhodesia Broken Hill Development Company, Ltd.
Rhodesian Anglo-American Ltd.

De Beers Consolidated Mines Ltd.*

Premier (Transvaal) Diamond Mining Company, Ltd.
Consolidated Diamond Mines of South-West Africa, Ltd.
New Jagersfontein Mining and Exploration Company, Ltd.
Cape Coast Exploration Ltd.
Consolidated Company, Bultfontein Mine, Ltd.
Griqualand West Diamond Mining Company, Dutoitspan Mine Ltd.
H.L.G., Ltd.
Marmora Mines & Estates, Ltd.
The South-West Finance Corporation, Ltd.

---

* The De Beers Consolidated Mines, although not a Financial Group of The Witwatersrand, has been included for purposes of comparison.

Lewis & Marks, Ltd.

African & European Investment Company, Ltd.
Grootvlei Proprietary Mines, Ltd.
Lonely Reef Gold Mining Company, Ltd.
New Central Witwatersrand Areas, Ltd.
New Machavie Gold Mining Company, Ltd.
Palmietkuil Gold Mining Company, Ltd.
Spaarwater Gold Mining Company, Ltd.
West Spaarwater, Ltd.

African Metals Corporation, Ltd.
Amalgamated Collieries of S.A. Ltd.
Carolina Coal Mining Company, Ltd.
Chandlers Ltd.
Cobra Emeralds, Ltd.
Coronation Collieries, Ltd.
Crown Diamond Mining & Exploration Co. Ltd.
Elandsfontein Platinum, Ltd.
Largo Colliery, Ltd.
Lourenço Marques Forwarding Company Ltd.
Northern Assurance Co. Ltd.
Pretoria Portland Cement Company, Ltd.
Roberts Victor Diamonds, Ltd.
Schoongezich Collieries (Witbank) Ltd.
Schweppes (Transvaal Agency) Ltd.
S.A. Salt Union, Ltd.
S.A. Bolts & Nuts (Pty.) Ltd.
Springfield Collieries, Ltd.
Transvaal Consolidated Lands & Exploration Company, Ltd.
Union Lime Company, Ltd.
Union Steel Corporation of S.A. Limited.
Vryheid Coronation, Ltd.
Vereeniging Brick & Tile Company, Ltd.
Vereeniging Estates Ltd.

Gold.

South African Townships Mining and Finance Corporation Ltd.

African Gold and Base Metal Holdings Ltd.
Eastern Transvaal Consolidated Mines, Ltd.
Hendies Gold Mines, Ltd.
Lace Proprietary Mines, Ltd.

Johannesburg Consolidated Investment Company, Ltd.

East Champ d'or Gold Mining Company, Ltd.
Government Gold Mining Areas (Modderfontein) Consolidated, Ltd.
Langlaagte Estate and Gold Mining Company, Ltd.
New State Areas, Ltd.
Randfontein Estates Gold Mining Company, Witwatersrand, Ltd.
Van Ryn Deep, Ltd.
Witwatersrand Gold Mining Company, Ltd.

Central Mining and Investment Corporation Ltd.

Blyvooruitzicht Gold Mining Company, Ltd.
City Deep Ltd.
Consolidated Main Reef Mines & Estate, Ltd.
Crown Mines, Ltd.
Durban Roodepoort Deep Ltd.
East Rand Proprietary Mines Ltd.
Geldenhuis Deep Ltd.
Glynn's Lydenburg, Ltd.
Holtfontein (T.C.L.) Gold Mining Company Ltd.
Modderfontein B. Gold Mines Ltd.
Nourse Mines, Ltd.
Rietfontein (No. 11) Gold Mines, Ltd.
Rose Deep, Ltd.
Transvaal Consolidated Land & Exploration Company, Ltd.
Transvaal Gold Mining Estates, Ltd.
Welgedacht Exploration Company, Ltd.

Other.

New Clewer House, Ltd.
Phoenix Diamonds, Ltd.
Photo-Vision Ltd.
R. & O. Syndicate (Pty.) Ltd.
South African Alkali, Ltd.
South African Coal Estates (Witbank) Ltd.
Western Holdings Ltd.
West End Diamonds, Ltd.
Rhodesian Corporation, Ltd.

Consolidated Collieries, Ltd.
New Springs Colliery, Ltd.
Natal Cambrian Collieries, Ltd.
Phoenix Colliery, Ltd.
Potgietersrust Platinums, Ltd.
Rustenburg Platinum Mines, Ltd.
South African Carbide and By-Products Company, Ltd.
Teba Trust (Proprietary) Ltd.
Wallsend Natal Collieries, Ltd.

Ferreira Estate Ltd.
Witbank Colliery, Ltd.

Anglo-Transvaal Consolidated Investment Company, Ltd.

Consolidated Murchison (T r a n s v a a l) Goldfields and Development Company, Ltd.
Klip Nigel Estate and Gold Mining Company, Ltd.
Middle Witwatersrand (Western Areas) Ltd.
Middlewits Extensions, Ltd.
New Klerksdorp Gold Estates, Ltd.
Rand Leases (Vogelstruisfontein) Gold Mining Co., Ltd.
South and Central African Gold Mines, Ltd.
Transvaal Nigel, Ltd.
West Spaarwater, Ltd.

Union Corporation, Ltd.

East Geduld Mines, Ltd.
Geduld Proprietary Mines, Ltd.
Grootvlei Proprietary Mines, Ltd.
Modderfontein Deep Levels, Ltd.
Van Dyk Consolidated Mines, Ltd.
Withok Proprietary Company, Ltd.

Anglo-Transvaal Collieries, Ltd.
Anglo-Alpha Cement, Ltd.
Anglovaal Brick and Tile Company, Ltd.
Dunswart Iron and Steel Works Ltd.
East Rand Consolidated, Ltd. (Incorporated in England).
Gloucester Manganese Mines (Postmasburg) Ltd.
Harmony Lands and Minerals, Ltd. (Incorporated in England).
Malieveld Mining Co., Ltd.
Malieveld Mineral Concession, Ltd.
S.A. Torbanite Mining & R e fi n i n g Company, Ltd.
The Associated Manganese Mines of S.A. Ltd.
Stag Brewery Ltd.
Union Breweries, Ltd.

Haggie, Son & Love (1936), Ltd.
South African Paper and Pulp Industries, Ltd.

General Mining and Finance Corporation, Ltd.

Van Ryn Gold Mines Estate, Ltd.
West Rand Consolidated Mines, Ltd.

New Consolidated Gold Fields, Ltd.

African Land & Investment Company, Ltd.
Libanon Gold Mining Company, Ltd.
Luipaards Vlei Estate & Gold Mining Company, Ltd.
Middlevlei Estate & Gold Mining Company, Ltd.
Rietfontein Consolidated Mines, Ltd.
Robinson Deep, Ltd.
Simmer & Jack Mines, Ltd.
Spaarwater Gold Mining Co. Ltd.
The Sub Nigel, Ltd.
Venterspost Gold Mining Company, Ltd.
Vlakfontein Gold Mining Company, Ltd.
Vogelstruisbult Gold Mining Areas, Ltd.
West Vlakfontein Gold Mining Company, Ltd.
West Witwatersrand Areas, Ltd.

East Rietfontein Syndicate, Ltd.
Elandsfontein Estate Company, Ltd.
François Cementation Company (Africa) Ltd.
La Rochelle Syndicate, Ltd.
Lydenburg Platinum Areas, Ltd.
Moçambique Soap & Oil Company, Ltd.
Moray Buildings (Proprietary) Ltd.
Waterval (Rustenburg) Platinum Mining Company Ltd.

This list, in order to ensure accuracy, includes under the various Financial Groups only those companies to which they act as Secretaries, or which they have acknowledged by letter to the writer are under their administrative control, or with which they are closely associated, or in which they have a large interest. The list has been restricted in this way in order to avoid any misunderstanding, but actually the influence of the Groups is greater than this list indicates. There are connections, in some cases personal (through the same Directors), and in other cases through shareholdings or agreements, which extend the influence of some of the South African Finance Houses to other African territories, such as the Rhodesias, the Gold Coast, Sierra Leone, Angola and South-West Africa. Other Groups on the Rand have interests of a direct or indirect kind in Nigeria or East Africa. As the position is apt to change from time to time owing to changing shareholdings or for other reasons, it would be misleading to express facts such as these on a Chart, but it is, nevertheless, safe to say that the indirect influence, technically and financially, exerted by the Group system is by no means confined to the Union only.

III

THE DEVELOPMENT OF THE RAND.

The process of amalgamation in the diamond industry caused a considerable number of those whose interests had been bought out by the diamond monopoly to seek opportunities elsewhere. In addition, the class of wealthy diamond merchants and *entrepreneurs* which had emerged was soon interesting itself in the gold discovered on the Rand in 1886.

The largest proportion of the important companies and syndicates, which were formed on the Witwatersrand between 1887 and 1892, was in some way connected with well-known people in the diamond industry or trade. The international financial connections of the diamond companies were particularly important. A group of speculative investors in London, Paris and Berlin had been attracted by the increasing value of the diamond shares. The names of the leaders of the diamond industry were well known. Thus the foundation had been laid for the flotation of gold-mining companies overseas. The first company registered in England to bring the Rand goldfields before the British public was "The Gold Fields of South Africa, Limited", the predecessor of the present mining group. The capital was in 230,000 shares of £1 each, and 200 founders' shares of £100 each. The first issue was 125,000 £1 shares, 100,000 being offered in London and 25,000 in South Africa. The prospectus dated 1887 is of interest as illustrating the influence of the diamond industry. It is worth summarizing as follows:

"This Company is formed for the purpose of acquiring and dealing with certain auriferous and other mineral properties, interests and rights in South Africa, and also for carrying on general exploration with a view to making further investments of a similar nature. The work has been commenced by the promoters, Messrs. C. D. Rudd and C. J. Rhodes, who have already purchased auriferous properties to the extent of about £25,000.

"Opportunities for favourable investment of capital appear so greatly to exceed private means that the public is now invited to join in the enterprise. Nearly all the companies which have been floated up to the present time have been capitalized at an enormous increase on the original purchase price of the properties, whereas, in the case of this company, the shareholders will obtain the various properties at the original price. For many months past confidential agents have been employed in the gold centres, and prospecting in various forms has been carried on under the personal supervision of Messrs. C. D. Rudd and C. J. Rhodes. These gentlemen are prepared to superintend, and to be responsible for the management of the company, during the period necessary for complete exploration and investment of the company's capital. They have been resident in South Africa for fifteen years, and are two of the original founders and present directors of the De Beers Mining Company, the largest and most successful diamond company in the world."

After allusions to the Barberton gold companies, then at work, the prospectus states: "The promoters have so much confidence in the success of the company that for goodwill and services they ask for no direct pecuniary remuneration, contenting themselves during active management with one-third, and on retirement one-fifth only, of the net profits of the company, this latter interest being represented by founders' shares."[1]

The first period of development on the Rand was similar to that which characterizes all new mineral discoveries. Gold was worked by individuals, small companies and syndicates. On the Rand the "outcrops" of the Reef gave opportunities for this. The first boom of 1889 was also typical. It represented the usual inflation after preliminary successes, but, in the case of the Rand, it was not entirely of a local character, as mining companies were already being registered in London and appealing to the British investor directly. High dividends were for a short time paid on the relatively small capital of the companies and syndicates.[2] The

---

[1] The prospectus is accompanied by a map of the South African Republic, upon which the different goldfields are indicated by shaded lines. The town of Johannesburg does not appear. The document is interesting, as showing how the Witwatersrand fields were regarded in the year 1887 by two great experts best able to report upon them. (Cf. *Twenty-five Years of Mining*, by Edward Ashmead, reprinted from *The Mining Journal*: London, 1909.)

[2] See Table 15.

boom on the Rand gave rise to the flotation of Mining, Finance, Exploration and Land-owning companies throughout South Africa. Skinner's *Mining Manual* listed 396 of such companies operating in South Africa in 1880, and 642 in 1889. The number of companies having offices in London increased from 145 in 1888, with a nominal capital of £23,206,000 and a paid-up capital of £15,846,000, to 315 with a nominal capital of £56,565,000 and a paid-up capital of £44,331,000. These figures, of course, involve much duplication, since Investment and Exploration Companies re-invested moneys in mining and land companies. But, although the figures are of limited value for other purposes, they serve to indicate the increase in mining and financial activity and the rapidly growing connection with London. Actually at this early stage, only a portion of the capital invested was received directly from London or other European financial centres.

Once the overseas connections had been formed, every year subsequent to 1892 saw a growth in the number of companies registered in London. The next boom, in 1895, was no longer a local affair. It was due as much to financial conditions in London and Paris as to the potential development of deep level mining on the Rand. Within a few years of the 1889 boom it had become clear that, in contrast to the diamond industry which had flooded South Africa with relatively easily won wealth, the development of gold mining on the Rand implied the establishment in the interior of the country of a highly organized large-scale modern industry dependent on large supplies of capital and labour.

The successful rationalization of the diamond industry provided an example for the Rand. The most characteristic feature in its history is undoubtedly the manner in which the gold-mining industry has dealt with the problems of financial control and technical organization.

Professor Henry Clay[1] has summed up the process as follows:

"The Gold Mining Industry may claim to provide a working model of a 'rationalized' industry. Through the group system of control of the separate mining companies, and the close co-operation of the whole industry through the Chamber of Mines

[1] From the preface to *Group Administration in the Gold Mining Industry on the Witwatersrand*, by John Martin.

and its subsidiary services, it has substituted for the blind selection by competition of the fittest to survive, a conscious and deliberate choice of methods, equipment, areas and personnel on the basis of an extremely detailed comparative study of results. The experience of the industry is continuously analysed; periodic returns, which serve to measure every factor in costs that can be distinguished, are received from every unit and circulated to every unit; so that the individual mine-manager is able to check his results against those of colleagues in other mines, and the controlling authority has continuously before it the divergences of experience that point to the technical and administrative needs of the industry. Each group maintains an extensive and highly-qualified service of experts, which works on the problems so revealed; and the financial resources of the groups make it possible to give effect to any improvements—from minor process alterations to the sinking of a new shaft at the cost of half a million—which this practical research can suggest. . . ." "The English student of economic organization will be struck by the contrast between the Gold-Mining Industry and the British Coal-Mining Industry. The latter, with an annual output four or five times the value of the former, is still conducted by more than a thousand separate units, as contrasted with thirty-three on the Rand. Some grouping about outstanding personalities has always existed, and a process of amalgamation is going on; but not more than a ninth of the output is yet covered. As a consequence of the individualistic resistance to effective co-operation which these figures imply, the industry is not able to command the resources, whether of capital or technical and administrative science, which the Gold-Mining Industry enjoys. Although there are large units, the industry has not developed powerful financial and technical organizations, not themselves actually engaged in the routine work of mine operation, studying the problems of the industry, applying the results of study, providing finance for new developments, marketing the product, supplying other common services, and generally nursing the industry, as the groups nurse the gold-mining companies. This contrast may help to explain why the Gold-mining Industry has continued to expand in spite of burdens, of which a contribution of 6s. per

Table 12.—*Union Gold Mines : Selected Operating Statistics*, 1897–1937.

Year.	Total Union Output. (ozs.) (*f*)	Estimated Percentage of World Output.(*f*)	Footage Developed (*a*, *b*). All Mines.	Footage Developed (*a*, *b*). Producing Mines.	Footage Developed (*a*, *b*). Non-producing Mines.	Tonnage Milled.(*c*)	Average Grade.(*c*)	Yield per ton milled.(*c*)	Working Costs per ton.(*c*)	Working Profit per ton.(*c*)	Average Number of Employees. White.(*c*)	Average Number of Employees. Other.(*c*)	Wages. Large Mines.(*d*) European.	Wages. Large Mines.(*d*) Other.	Cost of Native Labour per shift worked.(*d*) Wages.	Cost of Native Labour per shift worked.(*d*) Food and Quarters.
	(000).	%.	(000).	(000).	(000).	(000).	Dwt.	£ s. d.	£ s. d.	s. d.	(000).	(000).	£(000).	£(000).	s. d.	
1897	2,744	24·0	...	...	...	...	...	...	1 9 6	...	...	...	...	...	...	...
1907	6,451	32·4	...	...	...	15,523	7·986	1 13 11	1 0 10	13 1	17	156	5,894	3,920	...	...
1913	8,799	39·3	878	808	70	25,628	6·533	1 7 9	17 11	9 6	23	184	7,537	5,341	...	...
1916	9,297	42·3	874	850	24	28,525	6·277	1 6 8	18 1	8 7	22	202	7,733	5,999	...	...
1921	8,129	50·9	670	631	39	23,401	6·730	1 15 2	1 5 8	9 6	21	172	10,347	5,775	...	...
1926	9,955	51·3	1,043	1,029	14	29,486	6·506	1 7 9	19 0	8 9	20	183	7,373	6,213	2 3	11¾*d.*
1930	10,716	51·4	1,290	1,241	49	31,120	6·515	1 7 10	19 5	8 5	22	200	8,191	6,664	2 3	10½*d.*
1931	10,878	47·7	1,381	1,335	46	32,016	6·432	1 7 5	19 4	8 1	22	208	8,380	6,862	2 3	10¼*d.*
1932	11,559	48·4	1,506	1,506	...	34,467	6·328	1 7 0	19 0	8 0	23	215	8,708	7,229	2 3	10*d.*
1933	11,014	44·9	1,790	1,775	15	36,384	5·685	1 15 0	19 3	15 9	25	227	9,268	7,533	2 2	10*d.*
1934	10,480	38·3	1,957	1,876	81	39,140	4·996	1 14 3	19 3	15 0	28	244	10,549	8,012	2 2	11*d.*
1935	10,774	34·8	2,094	1,975	119	44,235(*e*)	4·729(*e*)	1 13 7(*e*)	18 11(*e*)	14 8(*e*)	31	266	11,904	8,622	2 2	10*d.*
1936	11,336	32·4	2,291	2,053	238	48,221(*e*)	4·569(*e*)	1 12 0(*e*)	18 9(*e*)	13 3(*e*)	34	286	13,138	9,773	2 2	10½*d.*
1937	11,735	33·1	2,386	2,091	295	50,726(*e*)	4·462(*e*)	1 11 5(*e*)	18 11(*e*)	12 6(*e*)	35	288	14,307	9,854	2 3	11·3*d.*

Union Gold Mines : Selected Operating Statistics, 1913 = 100.

Year.	Total Union Output.	Estimated Percentage of World Output.	All Mines.	Producing Mines.	Non-producing Mines.	Tonnage Milled.	Average Grade.	Yield per ton milled.	Working Costs per ton.	Working Profit per ton.	White.	Other.	European.	Other.	Wages.	Food and Quarters.
1907	73·3	...	...	...	...	60·7	122·2	122·2	116·3	136·5	73·9	84·8	78·2	73·4	...	...
1913	100·0	...	100·0	100·0	100·0	100·0	100·0	100·0	100·0	100·0	100·0	100·0	100·0	100·0	...	...
1916	105·6	...	99·5	105·2	34·3	111·3	96·1	96·1	100·9	90·6	95·7	109·8	102·6	112·3	...	...
1921	92·4	...	76·3	78·1	55·7	91·3	103·0	126·7	143·3	100·0	91·3	93·5	137·3	108·1	...	...
1926	113·1	...	118·8	127·4	20·0	115·1	99·6	100·0	106·1	92·7	87·0	99·5	97·8	116·3	...	...
1930	121·8	...	146·9	153·6	70·0	121·4	99·7	100·3	108·4	88·5	95·7	108·7	108·7	124·8	...	...
1931	123·6	...	157·3	165·2	65·7	124·9	98·5	98·8	107·9	84·4	95·7	113·1	111·2	128·5	...	...
1932	131·4	...	171·5	186·4	0·0	134·5	96·9	97·3	106·1	83·3	100·0	116·8	115·5	135·4	...	...
1933	125·2	...	203·9	219·7	21·4	142·0	87·0	126·1	107·4	165·6	108·7	123·4	123·0	141·0	...	...
1934	119·1	...	222·9	232·2	115·7	152·7	76·5	123·4	107·4	156·3	121·7	132·6	140·0	150·0	...	...
1935	122·4	...	238·5	244·4	170·0	172·6	72·4	121·0	105·6	154·2	134·8	144·6	158·0	161·4	...	...
1936	128·8	...	260·9	254·1	340·0	188·1	69·9	115·3	104·7	138·5	147·8	155·4	174·3	183·0	...	...
1937	133·4	...	271·7	258·8	421·4	197·9	68·3	113·2	105·6	131·3	...	156·5	189·8	184·5	...	...

(*a*) Excludes Shaft-sinking.
(*b*) Statistics from Government Mining Engineer's Annual Report which cover large mines of the Transvaal only and refer to concerns other than prospecting companies, small working syndicates, or individual diggers.
(*c*) Witwatersrand mines only—Statistics from Annual Reports of the Transvaal Chamber of Mines, whose classification does not now compare strictly with that of the Government Mining Engineer.
(*d*) Government Mining Engineer's figures for Witwatersrand only.
(*e*) Includes Heidelberg.
(*f*) Extracted from Reports of the Government Mining Engineer.

shift per white miner employed to the phthisis compensation fund is only the most remarkable."

The changes in the operating conditions of the industry in the last forty years are illustrated by Table 12, which presents both the absolute figures and an index of the percentage changes from 1907 to 1937 (1913 = 100). The great lowering in the grade of ore milled, the increase in tonnage and the progressive decline of working costs should be noted. Average working costs, which were 29s. 6d. per ton milled in 1897, had been reduced to 18s. 11d. in 1937, and consequently the average grade of ore milled had fallen to 4·5 dwt.[1] An interesting feature of the table is the variation in footage developed. The present boom on the Witwatersrand is illustrated by the increase in the footage developed in particular by non-producing mines. Another point of interest is the increase in the number of employees, both European and others. It is significant that the wages of native labour per shift worked have varied extraordinarily little, notwithstanding the considerable variation in wages paid to Europeans during the period. This, of course, is due to the numerous legal and other restrictions which govern the employment of natives. "Nothing has changed so little in South Africa," an eminent South African authoress has written, "as the black man's rate of pay."

The above tables should also be compared with Table 17, which shows the growth of the net product of the industry, and compares it with the increase in the taxation which has been imposed on gold mining. The net product of the industry is shown to have risen by 96% since 1913, and the dividends paid over the same period by 103%. Taxation,[2] on the other hand, has increased by no less than 1091%.

[1] The *sources of ore supply* for the Rand as a whole in 1936 were summarized by Mr. Stokes (*ibid.*, p. 845) as follows:

Source.	Proportion %.	Grade, dwt.
Ore reserves . . .	63	5·15
Development . . .	12	2·25
Other sources . . .	25	3·00
Mine grade . .	100	4·26

With an allowance for surface sorting and a residue of 0·24 dwt., this mine grade corresponds to the Rand's declared yield of 4·5 dwt. per ton *milled*.

[2] The implications of the large increase in gold mining taxation are referred to in Chapter IV.

The writer has calculated that, whereas in 1898, of the total ore milled, 55% was attributable to individual mines which gave returns indicating that they were milling an average grade of over 9 dwt. (36% of the total ore was over 10 dwt.), the position in 1934 was that over 60% of the total ore milled was under 5 dwt., and almost 35% under 4 dwt. In 1936, owing to the increased currency price of gold and to increased efficiency, about 38·5% of the total ore milled was under 4 dwt. These changes have been accompanied by a phenomenal increase in the depth of mining. Some indication of this is given in Table 13, which classifies the dividends paid in certain areas according to mining depths reached by the corresponding companies. It will be noted that, whereas in 1898, 48·5% of the dividends came from mines working to depths of not more than 1,000 feet, and a further 43·7% from mines which had not exceeded a depth of 2,000 feet, only 7·8% were accounted for by mines which had reached 3,000 feet. In 1932 only 5·8% of the dividends were accounted for by mines working to 3,000 feet ; 37·8% came from mines working to 5,000 feet, 11% from mines working to 7,000 feet, and 2·5% from those which had already reached 8,000 feet.

It is not possible to trace the process of amalgamation in the industry in this study, but the following statistics will give some indication of the extent to which it has taken place. Out of 576 Gold-Mining Companies floated on the Rand during the period 1887–1932, 206 were amalgamated, 313 were wound up, and only 57 remained in existence in 1932. In addition, there were 160 companies which, between them, accounted for a nominal capital exceeding £5,000,000, whose operations were so short-lived that no adequate records were available for an examination of their subsequent history. The 57 Gold Mining Companies in existence in 1932 were, with some minor exceptions, controlled by six financial houses or groups. The process of amalgamation and financial concentration had taken form by 1897, and the group system can be regarded as having been firmly established by the time of Union.

By the end of the century it was already clear that gold mining on the Rand could not be compared to the working of certain rich, isolated mineral resources. The ore deposits were so

Depth.	1888. £.	1888. %.	1893. £.	1893. %.	1898. £.	1898. %.	1903. £.	1903. %.	1908. £.	1908. %.
Outcrop	...	...	...	...	137,625	2·9	3,750	0·1	96,875	1·1
0–1,000'	358,070	97·9	886,815	77·4	2,149,292	45·6	631,350	17·4	505,670	5·9
100–2,000'	7,500	2·1	241,996	21·1	2,061,818	43·7	2,209,094	61·0	4,013,188	46·8
200–3,000'	...	...	16,933	1·5	368,300	7·8	774,966	21·5	2,823,706	32·9
300–4,000'	...	...	...	...	...	...	...	...	1,134,252	13·3
400–5,000'	...	...	...	...	...	...	...	...	...	...
500–6,000'	...	...	...	...	...	...	...	...	...	...
600–7,000'	...	...	...	...	...	...	...	...	...	...
700–8,000'	...	...	...	...	...	...	...	...	...	...
	365,570	100·0	1,145,744	100·0	4,717,035	100·0	3,619,160	100·0	8,578,691	100·0

Depth.	1913. £.	1913. %.	1918. £.	1918. %.	1923. £.	1923. %.	1928. £.	1928. %.	1932. £.	1932. %.
Outcrop	184,926	2·2	...	...	...	...	...	...	17,250	0·2
0–1,000'	347,969	4·1	...	...	23,370	0·3	...	...	...	...
100–2,000'	2,684,661	31·7	1,214,758	22·4	602,823	6·6	116,945	1·4	50,000	0·6
200–3,000'	1,730,526	20·4	1,300,460	24·0	2,853,154	31·2	576,901	6·8	511,979	5·8
300–4,000'	2,545,386	30·1	2,440,478	45·0	2,775,579	30·3	4,195,901	49·2	3,359,339	37·8
400–5,000'	770,574	9·1	406,427	7·5	2,241,456	24·5	2,888,541	33·9	3,175,714	35·8
500–6,000'	204,000	2·4	39,775	0·7	551,763	6·0	136,388	1·6	546,286	6·2
600–7,000'	...	...	25,500	0·4	100,011	1·1	582,684	6·8	988,665	11·1
700–8,000'	...	...	...	...	...	...	25,002	0·3	227,930	2·5
	8,468,042	100·0	5,427,398	100·0	9,148,156	100·0	8,522,362	100·0	8,877,163	100·0

widespread in area and depth that their full extent could only be guessed. To develop the vast areas suspected of being gold-bearing, the Rand depended particularly on the supply of foreign capital on the one hand, and the supply of native labour on the other.

IV

THE RAND MINES AS A SINGLE CORPORATION.

Viewing the Rand gold mines as a single corporation, Mr. Stokes, in the paper previously referred to, outlined the operating and financial results from revenue to dividends for the year 1936 (during which 48,221,120 tons of ore were milled) as follows:

Rand gold production . . .	£77,367,000
Declared working costs . . .	45,318,000
Working profits	£32,049,000
Additional sundry revenue . .	430,000
Gross profits	£32,479,000
Capital expenditures, appropriated from profits and not provided by capital funds	1,350,000
	£31,129,000
Less taxation and Government participation in Lease Mines . . .	13,800,000
	£17,329,000
Provision on account of outstanding liability under the Miners' Phthisis Act, and miscellaneous . . .	300,000
Available for dividends . . .	£17,029,000
Rand dividend declarations . .	£16,927,000[1]

[1] "In the dividend total of £16,927,000, due allowance is made for duplication in individual declarations arising from the payment of dividends by one Rand Company to another.

"The unappropriated balance brought forward at the beginning of 1936 totalled

"The magnitude of the stake, in the fight for low working costs," he writes, "may be most clearly indicated by an analysis of the Rand's ore reserves. The total reserve in 1936 was 200,000,000 tons at 5·15 dwt. over 50 inches. In number, there are roughly 16,000 to 17,000 different blocks ranging in quantity from over 100,000 tons each, in areas of consistent payability, to small stope remnants, to fragments on faults and dykes, or development strips in patchy areas, of only 2,000 or 3,000 tons per block. Total Rand ore reserves represent an area of over 20 square miles."

He has compiled the following classification of Rand ore reserves (subject to an error of plus or minus 5% under each classification of grade):

Rand Ore Reserves, 1936.

Grade, dwt.	Tons.	%.	Average value, dwt.
2·2 to 2·9	21,000,000	10·5	2·7
3·0 ,, 3·9	54,000,000	27·0	3·4
4·0 ,, 4·9	43,000,000	21·5	4·4
5·0 ,, 5·9	28,000,000	14·0	5·4
6·0 ,, 6·9	19,000,000	9·5	6·4
7·0 ,, 7·9	13,000,000	6·5	7·4
8·0 and over	22,000,000	11·0	10·5
	200,000,000	100·0	5·15

approximately £5,030,000, and differed insignificantly from the balance carried forward at the year-end. This balance comprises net cash and investments (after deducting current liabilities), stores, materials, debtors and other miscellaneous items having little incidence upon current dividend possibilities. Declared working costs include a large sum expended on incline shafts, etc., which might be shown against capital expenditure, but it is considered advisable to follow the official returns, without attempting to introduce a measure of greater uniformity into accounting practice.

"Taxation and Government participation of profits should, more correctly, be shown apart. In view of certain adjustments due to differences of accounting period, the estimated figures for 1936 are combined for greater accuracy. The shareholder is, moreover, more closely concerned with the amount of the deductions than the exact process of their extraction.

"The assessment on the mines for the Miners' Phthisis Compensation Fund totalled £850,000, which is included in working costs. The amount due has been raised to £1,000,000 for the twelve months from 1st October, 1936."

"This analysis shows that we have, in existing ore reserves alone, 75,000,000 tons, averaging 3·2 dwt. While the losses of tonnage, due to any rise in costs and corresponding pay limit, could be broadly deduced from this tabulation, it is not possible to calculate, with mathematical precision, the total ore reserve at any particular higher average pay limit. Should the pay limit rise, thousands of blocks would be reduced in tonnage, upon re-estimation, by the exclusion of lower-grade portions, and would be retained in total reserves under a higher grade classification.

"One significant and somewhat unexpected deduction from the classification is that the ore reserves to-day, above the average pay limit for 1932, stand at a substantially higher figure than before the Union went off gold. In 1932 Rand ore reserves totalled 92,000,000 tons at 7·0 dwt., with an average pay limit of 4·3 dwt. To-day the tonnage in reserve at 4·3 dwt. and over is shown to approximate 110,000,000 tons at a value of 6·6 dwt. But if current ore reserves were fully revalued upon the 1932 basis and portions of blocks now below 4·3 dwt. taken into payable reserves upon subdivision . . . the new total, with gold at 85s. per ounce, would approximate 120,000,000 tons."

It should be noted that "the present average pay limit for the Rand is approximately 2·8 dwt. There are, in certain low-cost mines or sections, enormous tonnages in ore reserves below this average, just as in high-cost mines large tonnages between 2·8 dwt. and 3·3 dwt. or higher are necessarily excluded. Rand ore reserves would not, therefore, present a regular tonnage-grade curve in the lower values, but a curve for all the ore developed in the mines, payable or unpayable, would in all probability prove to be extremely regular for the whole Rand, as it is known to be for many individual mines".

V

THE AMOUNT OF CAPITAL INVESTED IN THE RAND.

Whereas the diamond industry, in proportion to the value of its output, utilized a small amount of capital, the Rand from

1887 to 1932 absorbed over £148,000,000[1], including cash premiums on the shares issued and paid for by the public (see Table 14 below). In addition, some £63,000,000[2] were appropriated from profits for re-investment in the industry. About two-thirds of these appropriations can be regarded as new capital expenditure (exact figures are not available), the remainder being for obsolescence and depreciation. In addition, the industry redeemed £9,000,000 of debentures out of profits. Broadly speaking, the Rand thus absorbed some £200,000,000 of capital until the end of 1932, of which roughly £120,000,000 can be regarded as having been invested from abroad. During the same period, it produced 262,116,311 oz. of gold, having a value at £4·24773 per fine oz. or £1,113,300,000, to which must be added approximately £32,000,000 for "premiums" (that is, the higher currency price of gold) realized from 1919 to 1924. The total amount realized was, therefore, £1,145,000,000. The industry distributed £248,000,000 in dividends, or £255,000,000, including the return of capital in the form of liquidation dividends, which latter amounted to £7,000,000. The greater part of the capital was supplied by overseas investors residing in Great Britain, although, before the Great War, French and also German investors were important. Paris has continued to provide some capital for the industry.[3]

It is probable that over the whole period to 1932, roughly speaking, 75% of the dividends distributed by the gold-mining industry were paid to investors residing abroad. To 1932, therefore, these overseas investors, on the one hand, probably received about £190,000,000 in dividends (including liquidation dividends), and, on the other, they invested and/or re-invested about £120,000,000 in the Rand. In addition, of course, as already

[1] An estimate of new capital invested is given on p. 98. It was not possible to continue the detailed accounting investigation on which the above calculations are based beyond 1932; a description of this investigation will be found in an article by the writer in the *Economic Journal*, London, March, 1935. See also p. 91 below.

[2] This is the amount for all Rand companies. Table 15 below shows the annual amounts of these transfers from appropriation account for the companies in existence in 1932 only.

[3] It is significant that whereas during this period the total value of gold produced on the Rand was about four times the value of diamonds exported, the gold mining industry probably attracted about £120,000,000 of overseas capital, compared with, at the most, £20,000,000 which was invested from abroad in the diamond industry.

mentioned, the industry financed itself directly by appropriation from profits, declared but not distributed.

VI

THE NET RETURN TO CAPITAL.

The growth of the industry has been continuously influenced by the interaction of many variable factors (quite apart from changes in the grade of ore) which determine the marginal yield and costs of production. Once ore bodies have been opened up, mining on the Rand can almost be described as a manufacturing process, and capital investment is pushed up to the point of marginal return. The margin, as elsewhere, depends on the rate of interest and the cost of the other factors of supply (labour, materials, etc.), with which the capital is combined. The lower the cost of capital and the other factors of supply, the lower is the grade of ore from which gold can be "manufactured".[1] The rate of production is governed by the endeavour, as far as practical mining considerations permit, to maximize the marginal net product in terms of money. The elasticity of Rand gold supplies, as has been shown above, is considerable. In view of the fact that gold mining is the main export industry of the Union, there are

---

[1] These general statements hide numerous difficulties met with in practice by individual mines. At any given time, the life of a mine is determined by the capacity of its plant in relation to the total ore which can be economically mined. There can be an increase in both the life and the scale of operations only if the grade is lowered. It must be remembered, however, that an increase in the scale of operations requiring as it does new capital investment for additional plant, etc., really involves the creation of a new mine in place of the old. Any change in the expectations which have led to such new capital investment creates a new situation—either there will have been over-investment, and capital losses will result, or the calculation will again have to be revised and further new capital investment take place, resulting in a different relation between the life, scale of operations, and the grade. Some of the complex relationships which govern gold mining on the Rand have been dealt with by Dr. Busschau in his book, *The Theory of Gold Supply* (Oxford University Press, 1936). The following should also be consulted :

Lehfeldt, R. A., *Gold, Prices, and the Witwatersrand.* (London: P. S. King, 1919.)

Idem, Restoration of the World's Currencies. (London: P. S. King, 1923.)

Sir Robert Kotze, "The Gold Mining Position", *South African Journal of Economics*, vol. i, No. 2, June, 1933.

Idem, " The Excess Profits Tax on Gold and Some of its Implications ", *ibid.*, vol. i, No. 3, September, 1933.

Ewing, J. M. M., "Witwatersrand Mining Policy", *ibid.*, vol. ii, No. 2, June, 1934.

Dalton, J. P., " On Taxation and Grade in Gold Mining ", *ibid.*, vol. v, No. 3, September, 1937.

underlying forces at work which compel the South African economy to adapt itself, from time to time, to such conditions as will enable gold mining to attract capital for expansion and to counter-balance the exhaustion of the older mines. The process of adaptation, of course, is neither immediate nor rapid, but its long-run influence cannot be doubted. So far it has been, and remains, the underlying force determining the degree of economic activity of a very great part of the South African economy.

In addition to these determining conditions allowance must be made for the inherent risks of mining, that is, that the anticipated results may be vitiated, not only by national or world economic factors, but also by unforeseen natural mining conditions. It is, then not surprising that the mean annual yield to capital invested in the Witwatersrand mining industry has been relatively low. The writer has calculated that the mean yield from 1887–1932 amounts to 4·1% per annum.[1] In other words, the sometimes very

[1] The method of calculation was described in an article by the writer on the "Return to Capital Invested in the Witwatersrand Gold Mining Industry, 1887–1932." (London: *The Economic Journal*, March, 1935.)

The calculation was made for three different series of data as follows (*cf*. p. 71 of the article):

(1) "Equating the total accumulated dividends and repayments of capital (incomings) with the total accumulated outgoings—the outgoings comprising (*a*) shares issued to the original vendors, valued at par, *plus* (*b*) shares issued for cash, and cash received from premiums on shares so issued.

(2) "Equating the total accumulated dividends and repayments of capital (incomings) with the total accumulated outgoings—the outgoings comprising (*a*) shares issued to the original vendors, valued at the price at which working capital shares (*i. e.* shares issued for cash), if any, were issued simultaneously. Where no such simultaneous issue took place, the shares issued to the original vendors were valued at par; *plus* (*b*) shares issued for cash, and cash received from premiums on shares so issued.

(3) "Equating the total accumulated dividends and repayments of capital (incomings) with the total accumulated outgoings—the outgoings comprising the total working capital shares only (that is, shares issued for cash), *plus* cash premiums received on such working capital shares, and excluding any vendors' shares whatsoever.

"The actual results of the respective calculations are given below. It should be noted that the method of calculation adopted was, in the first instance, to choose arbitrarily an anticipated rate of yield, and all the outgoings and incomings were accumulated at this rate. The actual yield was thus obtained by the actuarial method of 'trial and error'.

Method (1) The yield was found to be 4·9%
  „   (2)   „   „   „   4·1%
  „   (3)   „   „   „   10·5%".

For further details, the explanations in my article should be referred to.

It is worth drawing attention, however, to three of the factors which account for the final estimates of yield given above. These are:

large yields in particular mines have been counterbalanced by absolute losses of capital or very low yields in others.

VII

FLUCTUATIONS IN THE SUPPLY OF CAPITAL.

The large long-term investment required in Gold Mining (the amount that is to be expended in opening up a new mine to-day is not less than £2,000,000 to £3,000,000) and its "speculative"[1] nature are both main causes of the low mean annual yield. The investment is associated with a long period of development, during which no return to capital accrues. In numerous cases the normal period of development has been greatly prolonged owing to the supply of capital failing in the interim. Capital was invested in opening new mines, but owing to changes in the expectations of investors and the rate of return which they required, further capital could not be raised, and development had to be postponed until additional capital was forthcoming, that is, until investors' expectations from gold mining were such in relation to other opportunities for the investment of capital that they were prepared to direct resources to the Rand. It is for this reason that the supply of capital to the Rand has been subject to very great cyclical fluctuations closely related to changes in the rate of

[1] "Speculative" is, of course, a general term. For the purposes of this study, it is sufficient to define it as referring to a larger degree of risk than that customarily associated at the time in question with "representative" or "normal" industrial enterprises. In gold mining the greater risk is due (a) to the special risks inherently associated with mining, and (b) to the relatively long period of time that must normally elapse between the investment of capital, the first receipt of returns thereon, and its eventual amortization. The longer period of time for which the capital is "at risk" increases very considerably the degree of risk owing to possible changes in fundamental conditions. This question raises very wide issues which it is not possible to discuss here. They have been dealt with exhaustively by Dr. Busschau, *op. cit.*

(1) The very long period of time that elapses between the flotation of mining companies (and the investment of capital in them), and the payment of the first dividend.

(2) The very large influence of world economic factors (quite apart from local South African factors) which affect the supply of capital for gold mining, and which lead to the temporary closing down of developing or producing mines owing to the impossibility of raising further capital for the time being.

(3) The considerable amount of capital that is lost entirely owing to the failure to locate gold in payable quantities, or owing to inadequate methods of finance.

interest and changes in industrial activity abroad. There have inevitably been periods of considerable over-investment, that is, the application of capital on the basis of anticipated costs and returns which were not, in fact, realized. The relatively low yield shows how difficult it has been to establish a correct equilibrium between the factors of supply and demand in this industry.

As the success of the industry depends on the level of costs, all measures which artificially increase the cost of supply factors of the gold mining industry, either by taxation or owing to their artificial diversion to other uses, (for example, farming or artificially fostered manufacturing industries), decrease the opportunities for gold-mining expansion.[1] The process is, of course, similar (except for the purely natural factors) to that which affects the growth and decline of large export industries in every modern exchange economy.

Almost the whole of the capital for gold mining subscribed by the public on the Rand has been obtained by the issue of equity shares. There has been relatively little financing by debentures or other fixed interest-bearing securities. The individual mine which was not supported by the financial resources and technical organization of one of the groups (which are really a combination of Controlling and Holding Companies, Investment Trusts, and Issuing and Promoting Houses) has been almost entirely eliminated on the Rand. The financial houses are themselves controlled through London.

Since the War, a steadily increasing proportion of the shares in Gold-mining Companies have come to be held in South Africa,[2]

[1] The artificial burdens which have been imposed on gold mining in the Union have been analysed in the classic *Report of the Economic and Wage Commission,* 1925, and were again examined in the *Report of the Low Grade Ore Commission,* 1930. The present writer has analysed the transport burdens artificially imposed on the industry in *The Railway Policy of South Africa,* p. 350. (Johannesburg: Hortors Limited, 1928.)

[2] It can be assumed that before the War the percentage of the mining shares held by South Africans, apart from holdings in Investment Companies, was under $14\frac{1}{2}\%$, which was the figure calculated by the Kemmerer and Vissering Commission (U.G., No. 13, 1925). At the present time the amount is estimated to be not less than 40% (according to the statistics collected by the Census Department and published annually in the *Union Year Book*) of internal and external payments by mining companies of dividends, and debenture and loan interest. This method of arriving at an estimate of the share capital of mining companies held abroad is not very satisfactory, because a portion of the dividends which are paid in South Africa is for persons resident

but there is no reason to believe that fundamentally the importance of new investment from abroad has diminished.

The cyclical nature of the capital market for gold mining is
indicated by Table 14, which shows the amount of new capital
invested in the Rand from 1887 to 1932. It will be noted that the
greater part—£125,000,000—of the capital was invested in the
industry prior to 1913, and only about £23,000,000 from 1914 to
1932. The most important years were 1889, 1895/6, 1899, 1902
(resumption of activities after the Boer War), and 1909/10. From
1913 to 1932 there were only two very small peaks (1918, new
capital £2,435,000, and 1927, new capital £2,024,398). Prior to
1913, the average annual new capital raised was £4,628,000.
Thereafter it fell to £1,217,000.

Table 15 shows the annual transfers from appropriation
account, that is, the capital expenditure from working profits,
for the Rand Mines in existence in 1932. It is worthy of note that
most of this type of expenditure was incurred after 1913. It is
significant of the influence of the "group" system that the
industry has by this means itself supplied very large sums of new
capital during a period when interest rates were high and markets
in Europe relatively unfavourable for raising capital. The table
also shows for this special group of gold mines existing in 1932 the
annual total share capital issued (a) excluding and (b) including
capital expenditure from appropriation account. It contains also
a calculation showing (i) the annual "available profits" as a
percentage of the issued capital, including appropriations, and
(ii) the annual dividends actually declared as a percentage of
the issued capital excluding appropriations. The table clearly
indicates the cyclical fluctuations in the yield to the capital
invested, and the great importance of the amounts transferred

---

abroad. A more considerable portion is paid to Financial Houses in South Africa, but
these again pay a part of their own dividends abroad.

Apart from the statistical difficulties involved, the figure quoted is unsatisfactory
because it does not indicate the type of investment in the Union. Union investors at
certain times prefer the less speculative shares; at other times, the proportion of such
investments held within the Union may be large owing to the flotation of new mines
or prospecting companies in which the overseas investor is not yet interested. The
expansion of credit in the Union may also cause a larger proportion of shares to be
held locally, at certain times, than is normally the case.

TABLE 14.—*The Witwatersrand Gold Mining Industry*, 1887-1932.

Year.	Annual Distribution of Capital Invested.		Progressive Annual Distribution of Capital Invested.		Dividends Paid. Consolidated Statement.	
	Total Capital par Value.	Cash including Premiums.	Total Capital Par Value.	Cash including Premiums.	Annual Distribution.	Cumulative Totals.
	£.	£.	£.	£.	£.	£.
1887	1,531,117	470,546	...	...	35,775	...
1888	4,058,304	1,208,454	...	...	365,570	...
1889	12,164,533	3,568,483	...	...	398,176	...
1890	4,879,920	1,517,701	22,633,874	6,765,184	508,522	1,308,043
1891	1,032,952	707,339	...	...	571,429	...
1892	1,703,112	1,085,042	...	...	877,185	...
1893	2,730,733	1,400,391	...	...	1,145,744	...
1894	3,268,279	1,762,614	...	...	1,520,910	...
1895	10,565,678	5,608,821	41,934,628	17,329,391	2,139,480	7,562,791
1896	15,244,551	6,673,839	...	...	1,655,449	...
1897	4,479,960	3,081,560	...	...	3,051,691	...
1898	3,441,040	2,771,600	...	...	4,717,235	...
1899	9,904,314	6,085,081	...	...	2,673,668	...
1900	2,437,001	1,085,420	77,441,494	37,026,891	114,600	19,775,434
1901	1,074,576	1,074,576	...	...	522,912	...
1902	7,834,404	6,388,289	...	...	2,868,422	...
1903	7,959,441	3,992,055	...	...	3,619,160	...
1904	5,078,918	3,894,180	...	...	4,148,500	...
1905	4,948,457	3,876,918	104,337,290	56,252,909	5,271,614	36,206,042
1906	1,865,823	1,790,411	...	...	5,621,203	...
1907	984,126	816,126	...	...	7,182,660	...
1908	2,103,702	1,622,906	...	...	8,680,691	...
1909	7,422,289	5,808,632	...	...	10,520,132	...
1910	4,774,588	4,380,133	121,487,818	70,671,117	9,005,000	77,215,728
1911	715,903	701,903	...	...	7,821,760	...
1912	1,346,247	1,200,242	...	...	8,310,208	...
1913	1,280,760	1,275,760	...	...	8,468,042	...
1914	722,607	677,607	...	...	8,248,592	...
1915	648,681	573,681	126,202,011	75,100,310	7,507,838	117,572,168
1916	784,741	761,941	...	...	7,152,979	...
1917	403,918	257,998	...	...	6,704,085	...
1918	2,539,238	2,435,238	...	...	5,427,398	...
1919	1,890,530	1,765,530	...	...	6,501,163	...
1920	1,698,038	1,398,038	133,518,476	81,719,055	8,696,958	152,054,751
1921	2,029,677	1,960,135	...	...	8,062,701	...
1922	294,082	283,382	...	...	6,112,749	...
1923	989,793	605,043	...	...	9,148,156	...
1924	1,086,793	982,249	...	...	10,173,263	...
1925	519,933	457,685	138,438,754	86,007,549	8,220,264	193,771,884
1926	1,950,897	1,786,676	...	...	8,719,399	...
1927	2,137,398	2,024,398	...	...	8,439,936	...
1928	926,402	922,402	...	...	8,522,036	...
1929	1,461,311	1,461,311	...	...	8,813,697	...
1930	1,776,334	1,744,076	146,691,096	93,946,412	8,991,116	237,258,068
1931	886,757	886,757	...	...	8,747,750	...
1932	500,209	500,209	148,078,062	95,333,378	8,877,163	254,880,981

TABLE 15.—*Annual Yield to Capital Invested in Witwatersrand Gold Mining Companies existing at the end of* 1932.

Year.	1. Total "Available Profits".	2. Appropriations from Revenue.	3. Progressive Total of Appropriations from Revenue.	4. Dividends.	5. Progressive Totals of Share Capital Issued (Vendors' Shares at Par plus Shares Issued for Cash) plus Cash Premiums.	6. Progressive Totals of Share Capital Issued (as in Column 5) plus Cash premiums plus Appropriations from Revenue.	7. Percentage of "Available Profits" to Progressive Total of Capital including Appropriations from Revenue (Column 3 as a Percentage of Column 6).	8. Percentage o Dividends to Capital Invested excluding Appropriations from Revenue (Column 4 as a Percentage of Column 5).
	£.	£.	£.	£.	£.	£.	£.	£.
1887	339	339	339	...	659,661	1,387,217	...	...
1888	260,961	10,351	10,690	250,610	2,585,390	2,596,080	18·81	37·99
1889	223,539	56,808	67,498	166,731	7,724,664	7,792,162	8·61	6·45
1890	342,118	228,070	295,568	114,048	8,887,112	9,182,680	4·39	1·47
1891	371,829	165,562	461,130	206,267	9,194,580	9,655,710	4·05	2·32
1892	772,779	362,223	823,353	410,556	10,224,191	11,047,544	8·00	4·46
1893	821,946	236,781	1,060,134	585,165	12,140,069	13,200,203	7·44	6·36
1894	785,814	309,272	1,369,406	476,542	14,438,211	15,807,617	5·95	3·92
1895	1,246,659	495,520	1,864,926	751,139	18,843,077	20,708,003	7·88	5·20
1896	1,197,343	598,243	2,463,169	599,100	26,360,259	28,823,428	5·78	3·17
1897	2,308,680	819,580	3,282,749	1,489,100	28,752,917	32,035,666	8·00	5·64
1898	3,697,508	1,028,698	4,311,447	2,668,810	31,148,026	35,459,473	11·54	9·28
1899	2,306,714	648,099	4,959,546	1,658,615	37,330,966	42,290,512	6·50	5·32
1900	121,446	6,846	4,966,392	114,600	38,537,287	43,503,679	·28	·20
1901	651,490	469,890	5,436,282	181,600	39,522,290	44,958,572	1·49	·40
1902	1,954,407	347,155	5,783,437	1,607,252	42,679,076	48,462,513	4·35	4·08
1903	2,932,842	755,901	6,539,338	2,176,941	48,856,702	55,296,040	6·06	5·10
1904	3,252,154	814,977	7,354,315	2,437,177	52,764,433	59,718,748	5·87	4·98

Year								
1905	4,146,909	915,160	8,269,475	3,231,749	56,216,776	64,586,251	6·94	6·12
1906	5,264,310	1,917,875	10,187,350	3,346,435	57,121,806	67,309,156	8·15	5·95
1907	6,691,882	1,999,712	12,187,062	4,692,170	57,805,478	69,992,540	9·94	8·21
1908	6,971,888	1,216,632	13,404,694	5,754,256	59,246,549	72,651,243	9·96	9·95
1909	7,435,756	1,433,473	14,838,167	6,002,283	64,191,302	79,029,469	10·23	10·13
1910	7,434,637	1,418,605	16,256,772	6,016,032	67,882,191	84,138,963	9·40	9·37
1911	7,142,074	2,029,273	18,286,045	5,112,801	68,413,674	86,699,719	8·48	7·53
1912	6,904,201	1,149,675	19,435,720	5,754,526	69,558,273	88,993,993	7·96	8·41
1913	8,041,484	1,770,191	21,205,911	6,271,293	70,524,498	91,730,409	9·04	9·02
1914	7,510,906	1,702,305	22,908,216	5,868,601	71,158,381	93,066,597	8·19	8·23
1915	7,719,947	1,539,677	24,447,893	6,180,270	71,583,213	96,036,106	8·29	8·68
1916	8,444,796	2,523,434	26,971,327	5,921,362	72,364,181	99,335,508	8·79	8·27
1917	7,850,665	2,065,824	29,037,151	5,784,841	72,622,580	101,659,731	7·90	7·98
1918	6,315,287	1,376,274	30,413,425	4,939,013	74,997,408	105,310,833	6·21	6·80
1919	6,846,742	970,667	31,384,092	5,876,075	76,671,686	108,055,778	6·51	7·83
1920	9,071,480	1,229,721	32,613,813	7,841,759	78,355,626	110,969,439	8·39	10·23
1921	8,784,148	1,727,132	34,340,945	7,057,016	80,371,480	114,712,425	7·92	9·01
1922	6,807,335	1,093,083	35,434,028	5,714,252	80,621,744	116,055,772	5·93	7·11
1923	9,399,850	1,466,542	36,900,570	8,433,308	81,601,002	118,501,572	8·53	10·46
1924	13,302,881	3,578,008	40,478,578	9,724,873	82,438,174	122,916,752	11·22	11·82
1925	9,775,344	1,605,177	42,083,755	8,170,167	82,874,148	124,957,903	7·95	8·91
1926	9,708,401	1,613,025	43,696,780	8,095,376	84,502,789	128,199,569	7·77	9·76
1927	9,730,771	1,335,997	45,032,777	8,394,774	86,491,360	131,524,137	7·59	9·93
1928	9,682,526	1,252,435	46,285,212	8,430,091	87,401,326	133,687,038	7·37	9·74
1929	9,046,014	661,000	46,946,212	8,385,014	88,860,849	135,807,061	6·77	9·59
1930	10,258,233	1,328,191	48,274,403	8,939,042	90,630,049	138,904,452	7·27	10·04
1931	10,094,649	1,355,210	49,629,613	8,739,439	91,511,956	141,141,569	7·26	9·64
1932	9,975,764	1,098,604	50,728,217	8,877,163	92,012,165	142,740,382	7·07	9·70

N.B.—This Table deals only with the mines still existing in 1932. It is therefore not directly comparable with Table 14, which deals with *all* companies.

from profits for capital expenditure in subsequently increasing the dividends which could be declared on the issued capital.

Since 1932 (when South Africa abandoned the Gold Standard) the Rand and other gold-mining areas in the Transvaal have experienced the greatest boom in their history.

The increases in capital from the 31st December, 1932, to the 31st December, 1936, according to the statistics[1] given in the Reports of the Government Mining Engineer, were as follows:

Increases in Capital Invested in Gold Mines 31st December, 1932, to 31st December, 1936.

(000 omitted.)

	Witwatersrand.	Other areas in Transvaal.[2]	Total.
Nominal capital	£17,864	£21,678	£39,542
Issued capital	14,520	16,937	31,457
All cash (including Premiums)	22,266	21,195	43,461
Debentures	705	500	1,205
Appropriations	6,955	1,066	8,021

Most of the increase is due to the capital obtained by new mines in the developing stage.

Of the increases, including debentures, shown above, amounting to nearly £45,000,000, it is probable that a sum of about £24,000,000 was obtained directly and indirectly from investors abroad, and that about £16,000,000 was probably invested by them in the Rand. It is interesting to note that the new capital which was invested in the Rand mines in 1895/6 was about £12,000,000, while in 1909/10 it amounted to £10,000,000.

A very large portion of the capital expenditure incurred by *producing* gold mines since 1933 has again been obtained from profits. In a recent paper[3] Dr. Busschau gave the following

---

[1] These are not calculated on the same basis as the figures given in my investigation of capital investments in the Rand from 1887 to 1932. Nevertheless, owing to the short period of 3 years involved, they are sufficiently accurate.

[2] The large increase in capital for "Other Areas in the Transvaal" is accounted for by the fact that "Witwatersrand" refers to a fixed area largely equivalent to the old Rand prior to 1932. Many of the new extensions to the Rand are thus included under "Other Areas in the Transvaal".

[3] "Rand Mining Economics—the Problems," read to the Chemical, Metallurgical and Mining Society of South Africa, November, 1937.

approximate estimates of capital expenditure, including incline
shaft sinking, which illustrate the importance of the companies'
profits as a source of saving:

Producing Mines of the Witwatersrand.   Capital Expenditure (including
Incline Shaft Sinking).

	Total. £ millions.	Provided out of profits. £ millions.	Percentage out of profits.
1933	2·4	2·2	92
1934	3·7	3·0	81
1935	5·0	3·3	66
1936	3·4	1·9	56

Dr. Busschau adds: "These figures are only approximate, but,
to the extent that capital expenditure has been charged to working
costs and is not revealed by the annual accounts, the estimates err
on the side of caution.   Mr. Stokes's more comprehensive figure
for 1936 is £4·7 millions, and for the four years £17 millions.   Of
the total of £14·5 millions at least £10·4 came from profits, so on
the larger total the amount from profits was probably still
greater."

The availability of new capital for gold mining, like other
forms of long-term investment in "construction" industries, is
closely affected by the ruling long-term rate of interest.   The
periods in which capital could be obtained have mainly been
periods of very low interest rates in Europe.[1]   New capital investment, however, has not depended, by any means, only on the real
profitability of gold mining and the expectations which actual
conditions in the industry might have warranted at any given
time.   The supply of capital has also been influenced by factors
which are not clearly related to its expected long-term yield.

During periods of speculative booms, capital investment takes
place greatly in excess of the amounts warranted by the real
prospects of the industry as a whole, or even of individual mines.
In periods of quiescence in speculative capital markets, the reverse
is the case.   These cyclical variations and the psychological factors

[1] The recent boom which commenced in 1933 illustrates this.   The high rates of
interest during and subsequent to the war were unfavourable to new investment in
gold mining.   The period was, of course, also one during which the value of gold in
terms of other commodities declined.

responsible for them have led, and still lead to considerable waste in applying capital resources.

During periods of over-speculation in the directions favoured at the time (be it gold, copper, platinum, etc.), very large numbers of new companies are floated for purposes of land speculation, exploration, mining or allied activities. Some concerns are invariably considerably over-capitalized. Others succeed in obtaining resources for extremely doubtful propositions. Large sums are diverted into the pockets of vendors of relatively worthless ground alleged to be mineralized. Capital is spent in opening up areas which cannot possibly be brought to an economic stage of production at the time. Subsequently, when the boom psychology has vanished, it is not possible to obtain the additional capital required. On the other hand, in periods of quiescence in the capital markets, valuable mineral resources may have to lie fallow. It is significant that not only uneconomic, but also many relatively profitable enterprises are forced, in order to raise the capital they require, to wait for the periods of boom when investors in general are off their guard. At these times, the credit policy of the Banks and of other financial institutions causes a progressive inflation of security values which tempts the investor, and, at the same time, makes available to him the increased funds which he diverts to the security markets.

An example of the incorrect diversion of resources which can take place under such conditions is provided by the platinum boom in South Africa. Between 1923 and 1925 discoveries of what were alleged to be very valuable platinum deposits were announced in the Transvaal. The subsequent boom in platinum company flotation, which reached its peak in 1925, resulted in the issue of over £7,000,000 of capital and the investment of some £4,000,000 in cash in the platinum "industry". The shares of many of the companies reached quite ridiculous levels, and the South African public dealt very largely in them. By the end of 1926, of the 89 platinum companies which had been floated in the preceding three years, only 20 were still in existence. Of the 69 companies which had gone into liquidation, 10 were absorbed by financially stronger concerns. During 1927 only 11 companies were actually prospecting and opening up platiniferous ground.

By 1932, the total cash which had been lost amounted to £2,405,000, or 60% of the total invested. The total dividends paid by all platinum companies up to the end of 1935 amounted to only £192,750. Since 1930 no dividends at all have been paid. The average annual value of platinum produced from 1926 to 1937 amounted to £182,000. This was the result of an investment of over £7,000,000.[1]

The problem of preventing boom conditions from developing is, of course, a general one; but it has its own local complications in Africa. The mineral industries, on the development of which the Union and certain other territories in Africa so greatly depend, are, by their very nature, speculative. It is therefore peculiarly important that every method by which some measure of control could be exercised should be considered, and that a monetary policy suited to the peculiar investment problems of territories dependent in large degree on mineral development should be adopted.

VIII

SOME EFFECTS OF FLUCTUATIONS IN THE SUPPLY OF CAPITAL.

The cyclical variations in gold-mining investment greatly lengthen the time which intervenes between the flotation of companies and the actual commencement of production, and, of course, even more so, between the flotation of the company and the first payment of dividends. In the case of many now well-established mines, twenty to thirty years elapsed before the first dividend was declared, the intervening period being characterized by numerous amalgamations, reconstructions, applications for new capital, and very great fluctuations in share values. The process could, in the past, almost be described as one of drawing the shareholder into the whirl of the speculative cycle, inducing him to invest during a boom, and to wait for an opportunity to induce somebody else to relieve him of his investment during the next one.[2]

---

[1] *Cf.* M. Pelkowitz, "The Platinum Boom of 1925", *South African Journal of Economics*, vol. iv, No. 4, December, 1936.

[2] It has been mentioned above that, out of 576 companies on the Rand whose financial history was examined in detail, 206 were amalgamated. The total capital invested in the remainder, *i. e.* the non-amalgamating companies, was £29,000,000. The distribution of this capital is very significant. Nearly £13,000,000 was invested in

These conditions have invariably led to the over-capitalization of vendors' interests, accompanied by a too small proportion of "working" (*i. e.* "cash") capital. This has in the past been one of the main reasons for closing down mines or postponing their development. When the "boom" was over, the "cash" capital was frequently found to be inadequate, and could not be replenished until the peak of the next cycle. The low average yield on the capital invested in the Rand Mines is partly due to this fact. It has also been a potent factor in increasing the risk of mining investments. Very frequently the moneys obtained from investors mainly represented a transfer of resources to promoters and others.[1]

It should be noted that the Group system to some extent counteracts the misdirection of resources previously referred to. During the years following the outbreak of the Great War when the amount of new capital that could be raised for the industry showed a steady decline, the Groups "nursed" developing mines in the same way as industrial banks develop promising industrial propositions. Under the Group system there is now a smaller risk that the producing stage will not be reached owing to lack of capital. The association of most of the old Groups with a new mining venture is a guarantee of sound technical investigation. This system, however, still does not overcome excessive speculation. In fact the history of the Rand from 1913 to 1932 is somewhat misleading, because during this time the amount of capital invested in the Rand was very small compared to the pre-war period. It is likely that the South African mining boom of the last

[1] In South Africa these investment booms have also led to great fluctuations in the value of land, which has frequently risen to quite unwarranted levels. It has probably prevented the use of much land for farming. Large areas have remained in the ownership of financial companies, which hold them in order to dispose of them during boom periods, when the land may be suspected of being mineralized, or its site value may be enhanced.

companies which did not even reach the development stage. A further £10,000,000 went into companies that did not reach the producing stage. Over £4,000,000 was invested in companies that produced some gold, but could not pay any dividends. Only £2,000,000 was invested in companies which paid dividends. At first sight the sum of £29,000,000 given above may not appear unduly large in comparison to the total of £149,000,000, but it must be remembered that investments in the amalgamating companies, although generally more successful, were subject to similar long periods without dividends, and to frequent reconstructions, etc.

four years will, as usual, be found to have caused very considerable amounts of capital to have been misdirected and prematurely applied, and that many new mining areas on which development has commenced will not be brought to the production stage until another "boom" enables further capital to be raised.[1]

In these four years more new capital has been invested in the gold-mining industry than in any previous comparable period. Apart from the expansion of the mining activities of existing companies, prospecting and shaft-sinking has taken place over an area which is nearly four times as large again as the whole of the Rand in 1932. It is significant, however, that it took fifty years for the old Rand to attract a sum of not more than £149,000,000, excluding the amounts appropriated from profits. Assuming that the capital needed for a mine is not less to-day than in the past—actually the amount required is greater—it will inevitably take very long for the "new" Rand, which is probably more than three times the area of the old, to be developed[2] assuming that payable ore is discovered. Many successive periods of boom and

[1] Another factor which will hamper the completion of new development commenced during this period is the probability of a "shortage" of labour—unless new methods of organizing production are devised. The supply of labour is, as is well known, subject to considerable cyclical and seasonal fluctuations. In the past, the great activity resulting from the expansion of the industry in boom periods has inevitably been damped down, not only owing to a decline in the rate at which capital was subsequently available, but owing to the fact that the labour supply could not be increased sufficiently to allow of all development which had been commenced to be continued. To a certain extent, obviously, the decline in the rate of flow of capital into the industry is to be ascribed to this fact. "A very striking phase of the labour position is that an occupation like mining should be at the mercy of the seasons," says the *Report of the Inter-Departmental Committee on the Labour Resources of the Union*, 1930. "Yet there is, in a very real sense, a seasonal shortage of labour in mining. An analysis of the native labour employed on the larger gold mines of the Witwatersrand shows a regular seasonal movement, the peaks and troughs occurring at approximately the same points year by year. The East Coast natives, who are recruited for a comparatively lengthy period, serve as a steadying factor. . . . The trough occurs regularly in December. After that there is an upward movement, generally reaching the peak in April, but varying from February to May. . . . The economic disadvantage to an industry like mining, with heavy overhead costs, which dependence on an irregular labour supply entails, is considerable, and for the reason that this is a serious and important aspect of national economy in South Africa, your Committee has deemed it advisable to lay some stress on this aspect of the question."

[2] This is apart from such important considerations as the availability of sufficient labour and the cost of this and other factors of supply, and also, of course, the wider question of the monetary price of gold. Numerous cycles in the future development of the "new" Rand appear to be inevitable, but, during a boom, capital is applied simultaneously in innumerable directions without a realization of this.

depression will be experienced in the capital markets of Europe before all these mineral areas will reach the producing, not to speak of the dividend-paying stage.

In this connection, it should, however, be noted that one of the effects of the development of the mining lease system is to ensure that adequate working capital is available to bring mines in lease areas to the producing stage. The Mining Leases Board insists that those granted a lease shall have the funds to develop the area or, in the case of a new mine, to bring it to the production stage. Unfortunately, however, no means have yet been found of preventing undue speculation in the prospecting stage, that is, in regard to areas suspected of being mineralized, but for which mining leases have not been applied for or granted.

The South African Mining Lease system of gold areas is one of the most interesting and valuable features of the mineral policy of the Union. The system was established under the Transvaal Act No. 35 of 1908, and by Act No. 30 of 1918 the Mining Lease Board was made a Statutory Body. Its adoption is largely due to the valuable work of Sir Robert Kotze. It is, in effect, a method of leasing the right to exploit gold resources to the highest bidder. The system also ensures that areas shall be large enough, and in other ways suitable for what is in the opinion of the Government Mining Engineer "a workable mining proposition".

The Union Government, as a result of the system, has received an increasing share of the profits from gold mining enterprise. From 1910 to 1936 it received over £40,000,000 from this source.[1]

Under this system the State assumes the rights of a shareholder, but not his obligations. It makes no contribution to capital expenditure for developing new mines. It is worth pointing out that this type of State participation is possible only as long as capital for the speculative enterprises concerned is made available by private *entrepreneurs*. Should the flow of international investment at some time in the future be curtailed, Governments in African territories with mineral resources may find it necessary to

---

[1] Details of the formula applied in the case of each lease mine and of the Government share of profits, as well as of the areas leased, capital invested and other details are annually given in the Report of the Government Mining Engineer, and will also be found in the *Union Year Book*.

assume other functions than those of the fortunate recipient of profits without liabilities for potential losses.

It is in this connection of interest to note that the Union Government in the Vote of the Department of Mines in 1936, inaugurated the policy of making funds available for small struggling mines in the Union by means of loans. The assistance will be given only to mines situated outside the Witwatersrand area. A small Mines Assistance Committee has been specially appointed for the purpose by the Minister of Mines. The fund was established for the purpose of assisting all kinds of mineral development; it will, no doubt, be of particular importance in the case of base mineral deposits. What is particularly significant in the scheme is that the assistance in the form of loans is granted for development and prospecting purposes and operations in connection therewith (e. g. sampling, loan for mineral transport, etc.). The amount of the loan, it is envisaged, is not to exceed 80% of the cost of the work. Once mineral deposits have been proved, it is thought that the raising of further capital through the usual channels should not be difficult.

The Gold-mining Industry has at all times in the history of the Union been the most potent single factor determining a rise or fall in the extent of employment, saving and investment. The prosperity of, and the degree of economic activity in the country, continue to depend mainly on the sums made available for new investment in this industry.

The effects of the present high gold-mining taxation, therefore, require the most careful consideration on a basis which does not confuse the economic consequences of a check to investment in the industry with irrelevant considerations concerning taxation of individual incomes.

A serious decline in the annual increment of mining investment in the future would involve the Union in a more than proportionate decline in the income and employment of the country as a whole.[1] In this basic fact lies the key to an understanding of the economy of the Union as it is constituted at present.

[1] *Cf.* the paper by Dr. Busschau previously referred to, pp. 98–9.

CHAPTER IV

THE ECONOMIC STRUCTURE OF THE UNION

> "A development of native capacity is sometimes regarded with fear. . . . These fears are, indeed, based on the fallacy that there is a limited amount of work to be done, and that if the native does it the white man cannot do it. This fallacy, if it were true, would constitute an equal objection to the admission of any more white men to the country, for fear they should take away the work of those already in the country. It would constitute an objection to the influx of capital in the form of labour-saving machinery. In fact, there is no rigid limit to the work awaiting additional resources in labour and capital. There is no more social danger in cheap labour than in cheap capital, cheap power or cheap land. All alike, by increasing the output of the community, increase the opportunities of economic welfare ; all alike, by increasing the power to purchase of those that supply them, increase the demand for labour in the community fortunate enough to possess them.
>
> "The relation of advanced and backward labour is more complementary than competitive."—PROFESSOR HENRY CLAY, in the *Report on Industrial Relations in Southern Rhodesia*, C. S. R., 3, 1930.

I

THE IMPORTANCE OF FOREIGN TRADE.

The economy of the Union, as is shown by the comparative statistics presented in the next chapter, is the most advanced in Africa. Yet its economic structure still displays in a striking manner the characteristic feature of all African territories, that is, their relatively large dependence on a very restricted number of exportable products as the basis of their relation with the world economy. Moreover, as the late Professor Lehfeldt remarked, "South Africa is more dependent on foreign trade than most countries and is in an abnormal situation in this respect". The position is similar elsewhere in Africa. The value of the exports of all African economies is therefore an important index of their economic progress, particularly in view of the fact that estimates of the National Income in them are not available except for the Union.

Fifty years after the commencement of Rand gold-mining in

1887, over 70% of the Union's domestic exports are still represented by gold, which has formed nearly 60% of the total domestic
exports in the last thirty years (see Table 16). Indeed, mineral
products, of which diamonds are, after gold, the most important,
alone account for three-quarters of the exports during this time.
To the end of 1937, the Union has produced over £2,000 millions
of minerals, and gold production forms three-quarters of this. It is
noteworthy that even the exports of mineral products other than
gold reached £7·2 millions for 1937—equivalent to one-quarter of
the value of exports of the products of the land. In fact, agricultural and pastoral exports, whose average value for the years 1909
to 1913 was £10·2 millions and which were 18·2% of the total
exports of the Union for those years, still formed only 20·2% for
the years 1933 to 1937, their average value for these years being
£20 millions.

It is the mineral industry on which the modern economy of the
Union has been built, and largely continues to rest. In 1925 the
Economic and Wage Commission[1] made a calculation of the
National Income, on the basis of the late Professor Lehfeldt's
earlier calculation,[2] which indicated that the net income contributed by mining was £37 millions out of a total National Income
of £186 millions. But the influence of mining is much greater than

[1] *Report of the Economic and Wage Commission*, U.G., 14, 1926.
[2] R. A. Lehfeldt, *The National Resources of South Africa* (Johannesburg: University of the Witwatersrand Press. London: Longmans, Green & Co., 1922). Mr.
Per Jacobsson, in an article, "Some Foreign Trade Problems of To-day" (*Index*,
vol. v, No. 57, September, 1930), gives the following interesting table showing the
percentage ratio of imports and exports to the National Income in different countries
for the year 1928. For comparative purposes the relevant statistics for the Union
for 1923, the year in which the Economic and Wage Commission made an estimate
of the Union's National Income, have been added:

	Imports as % of National Income.		Exports as % of National Income.
United States . . .	4·9	.	6·4
Italy	20·0	.	14·2
France . . .	23·7	.	19·8
Hungary . . :	24·1	.	16·4
Germany . . .	25·0	.	19·5
Sweden . . .	26·5	.	24·3
Great Britain . .	31·5	.	22·0
Austria . . .	41·3	.	28·0
Finland . . .	44·5	.	34·6
Switzerland . .	46·0	.	36·1
South Africa . .	24·1	.	41·8

TABLE 16.—*Union of South Africa. Trade Statistics, 1909–37,(d) and Proportion per cent. of Annual Exports of Selected Commodities to Annual Value of all Domestic Produce Exported.*

| Year. | Merchandise Imports.(a) | Exports. | | Gold Exports,(b, e) | | Diamond Exports (Cut and Uncut). | | All Mineral Exports.(e) | | Wool Exports. | | Land, Agricultural and Pastoral Exports. | |
		Domestic Produce.	Re-Exports.	£(000).	%.	£(000).	%.	£(000).	%.	£(000).	%.	£(000).	%.
	£(000	£(000).	£(000).										
1909	27,356	47,782	1,122	30,753	64.4	6,389	13.4	38,611	80.8	3,721	7.8	8,958	18.7
1910	36,727	51,763	1,381	31,791	61.4	8,479	16.4	41,996	81.1	3,830	7.4	9,485	18.3
1911	36,925	54,907	1,635	35,064	63.9	8,282	15.1	45,301	82.5	3,397	7.1	9,246	16.8
1912	38,839	60,996	1,380	38,342	62.9	9,153	15.0	49,394	81.0	4,778	7.8	11,164	18.3
1913	41,829	64,565	1,455	37,589	58.2	12,017	18.6	51,857	80.3	5,715	8.9	12,240	19.0
1914	35,355	52,753	1,439	35,337	67.0	5,513	10.5	43,268	82.0	4,229	8.0	9,090	17.2
1915	31,811	52,765	1,637	38,284	72.6	1,676	3.2	42,328	80.0	5,372	10.2	9,930	18.8
1916	40,400	62,078	2,433	39,128	63.0	5,280	8.5	48,021	77.4	6,588	10.6	12,916	20.8
1917	36,476	66,072	2,893	37,956	57.4	6,097	9.2	48,466	73.4	8,782	13.3	16,291	24.7
1918	49,487	65,725	4,274	35,431	53.9	7,063	10.7	46,162	70.2	9,690	14.7	18,192	27.7
1919	50,791	88,805(c)	4,121	38,955(c)	43.9	11,547	13.0	54,280	61.1	17,886	20.1	33,064	37.2
1920	101,827	91,711(c)	5,890	46,776(c)	51.0	11,597	12.6	64,283	70.1	15,966	17.4	25,624	27.9
1921	57,800	68,812(c)	4,432	42,989(c)	62.5	1,355	2.0	49,786	72.4	8,236	12.0	17,899	26.0
1922	51,413	60,371(c)	3,316	31,841(c)	52.7	4,387	7.3	39,623	65.6	11,001	18.2	19,395	32.1
1923	57,814	76,849(c)	2,885	41,712(c)	54.3	7,207	9.4	53,147	69.2	12,374	16.1	22,613	29.4
1924	65,816	80,699(c)	2,189	44,222(c)	54.8	7,133	8.8	55,751	69.1	15,764	19.5	23,911	29.6
1925	67,929	85,551(b)	2,420	41,363	48.3	8,666	10.1	54,511	63.7	15,095	17.6	29,838	34.9
1926	73,159	80,540	2,979	42,620	52.9	10,733	13.3	58,341	72.4	12,646	15.7	21,314	26.5
1927	74,069	89,401	3,546	43,641	48.8	12,285	13.7	60,528	67.7	17,118	19.1	27,815	31.1
1928	79,088	88,991	3,600	42,832	48.1	8,888	10.0	55,934	62.9	16,851	18.9	31,816	35.8
1929	83,449	89,031	4,407	45,025	50.6	12,074	13.6	61,496	69.1	14,521	16.3	26,344	29.6
1930	64,558	76,713	3,416	46,325	60.4	5,431	7.1	55,629	72.5	8,644	11.3	19,868	25.9
1931	52,945	65,076	3,221	45,136	69.4	3,573	5.5	51,621	79.3	5,701	8.8	12,817	19.7
1932	32,673	66,176(c)	1,396	48,518(c)	73.3	1,955	3.0	52,249	79.0	6,561	9.9	13,373	20.5
1933	49,121	91,989(c)	1,580	69,923(c)	76.0	2,130	2.3	74,256	80.7	8,832	9.6	16,901	18.4
1934	66,259	78,062(c)	1,887	56,216(c)	72.0	2,816	3.6	61,429	78.7	8,084	10.4	16,108	20.6
1935	75,301	97,931(c)	2,128	71,405(c)	72.9	2,977	3.0	77,505	79.0	9,516	9.7	19,978	20.4
1936	86,282	109,318(c)	2,203	82,716(c)	75.7	3,313	3.0	89,211	81.6	9,841	9.0	19,087	17.5
1937	103,368	119,616(c)	2,832	82,878(c)	69.3	3,317	2.8	90,076	75.3	12,646	10.6	28,141	23.5

(a) Excluding specie ; including goods subsequently re-exported.   (b) From 1925, gold specie exports, previously excluded, are included in exports of domestic produce.   (c) Including gold premium.   (d) Extracted from *Union Year Book.*   (e) From 1926 the figures are less gold bullion imported, most of which comes from Rhodesia and Tanganyika for refining in the Union. The *Union Year Book* regards this as a Union product, but I have deducted it here as it is not really a domestic export. It must, nevertheless, be remembered that gold imported in any one year is not necessarily all re-exported in the same year.   Gold bullion imported has not been excluded from the first column above (Merchandise Imports).

these figures indicate, since mining and agriculture set a limit to the expansion of a large part of protected and sheltered industry. As Professor Clay has rightly stressed, "the obvious distinction between sheltered and unsheltered industries can be replaced in the study of a new and growing community by a slightly different distinction, which will throw more light on the possibilities of expansion and rising standards of remuneration. Certain industries can be classed as primary or fundamental, in the sense that they explain the presence in the country of a European population, and maintain the economic link between the settler community and the older communities from which it was drawn. The other industries, including activities not usually regarded as economic, like Government, arise to meet the needs of the population, attracted and maintained by these primary industries, and may properly be described as derivative, dependent or secondary. The demand for the services of the latter arises solely from the existence of the former, and the derivative industries can expand only as and when the primary industries develop. While the derivative industries are thus dependent on the others for their market, they may do very well out of them, and it is not uncommon in new countries, as in the case of Australia and the Union of South Africa, for the part of the population that is engaged in the secondary industries to secure a much higher average level of remuneration for their services from the primary industries than these succeed in obtaining for theirs". Much agricultural production in the Union, however, is now also dependent on protection of one kind or another, and the burden of this ultimately falls mainly on mining. The purpose of this chapter is to examine certain aspects of the economic structure and policy of the Union which have resulted from the dependence on mining. Such an examination is not only important in order to understand the Union's problems, but is also necessary for an appreciation of certain fundamental economic issues in other African territories. The next chapter will show that many African colonies are now at a stage of development which may be compared to that which existed in South Africa before the discovery of diamonds and gold. In formulating economic policies for the future, they can learn the experience of this country.

II

THE DEPENDENCE ON MINING.

During the last quarter of a century, no outside observer of the Union's development could at any time have failed to notice the unanimity with which legislature and electorate alike declared it to be their policy to develop the resources of the country in such a way that its dependence on what it has been usual to call "wasting" mineral assets could be lessened, and provision be made for the distant future when the mineral industries might no longer prove a source of income.   Yet, notwithstanding continuous legislation designed to foster other activities, the country appears to be more dependent on mining than ever before.

The notion of the "wasting" nature of mineral assets is, in any case, from an economic point of view, apt to lead to confusion. It is of course true that, once the ore has been extracted from the mine, there is nothing left—but this is a physical matter.

From an economic point of view, ore deposits differ only in degree from other natural resources, and what is, or is not exploitable ore depends on cost and price relationships, that is, on economic factors.   Mineral ores, like other natural resources, become "wealth" only when they yield income because the labour and skill of the community are applied to their extraction and to altering their natural forms.   Conservation implies that no such effort is applied for the time being.   There is no way of "replacing" natural resources, and merely to postpone the use of specific natural resources is obviously not a means of "replacing" them.   What is sometimes possible is to "replace" or substitute the income obtained by efforts applied to specific natural resources of one kind by producing the same amount of income through applying the efforts of the community to specific resources of another kind.   There is clearly no purpose in doing this, unless income can no longer be obtained from the first type of natural resources, or unless the change would increase it.

There is no need to pursue this question here.   From the point of view of the Union, the real issue involved is that of creating *new* net income *additional* to that now yielded by mining or other activities. If certain types of income are merely obtained at the expense of the income being yielded by mining, there is no addition to income. If, by taxation or other measures, resources are artificially diverted from, say, mining to other activities which are not able to make a net contribution to the national income, or whose net contribution is smaller than that which could be obtained from existing or expanded mineral or any other forms of production, then the diversion is uneconomic. Large uneconomic diversions of this kind have taken place in the Union. It is well to remember, however, that even more important than the direct consequences of this artificial shuffling and reshuffling of the country's economic activities is the fact that it prevents suitable measures for dealing with more basic problems from being considered. This chapter endeavours to indicate some of these fundamental problems.

III

THE TAXATION OF GOLD MINING.

The economic policy of successive Governments since Union has rested, and continues to rest mainly on the direct and indirect taxation of the urban communities, in order, in particular, to benefit Europeans engaged in agriculture. A large part of the burden of this taxation, as already mentioned, eventually falls on those export industries which receive no off-setting advantages and cannot pass on the tax. Of these export industries, mining, particularly gold mining, is the most important. Moreover, since 1925 the burden has grown because of the increasing protection granted to manufacturing industry. A part of the cost of this, of course, also falls in the first place on agricultural export industries, but, in many cases, these are now so organized that, by discriminating between the prices charged in local markets and those ruling in world markets, they largely succeed in shifting again the whole or part of the burden on to the urban communities. As a result of the multiplication of rigid, protected and/or sheltered markets, sectional interests are favoured at the expense of the economy and community as a whole.

The outstanding facts in the whole confused situation, however, still remain as before. First, resources are diverted elsewhere which might otherwise lead to an expansion of mining and of other unassisted primary industries. Most manufacturing and an increasing number of agricultural enterprises in the Union now have this in common—that they are, with a diminishing number of exceptions, dependent on protected or sheltered local markets, and are unable to stand on their own in the markets of the world. Secondly, most of this artificial diversion merely succeeds in hiding or intensifying certain fundamental obstacles to that increase of the national income of the country which is the really important problem.

A significant feature of the economic policy which has dominated the development of the Union is that the finances of successive Governments have come to depend, to an ever-increasing extent, not only on the indirect but also on the direct taxation of gold mining.

The extent to which gold mining is discriminated against by heavier income taxation is shown in the following statistical comparison prepared by Dr. Busschau:

Total Amounts of Tax paid by A, B, C and E, as Percentages of Amount paid by D.

Income. £	A.	B.	C.	D.	E.
500	7	4	44	100	75
2,000	19	16	44	100	75
6,000	54	54	65	100	86
10,000	62	62	69	100	86
20,000	81	81	78	100	90
24,000	87	87	82	100	91
30,000	80	80	79	100	91
60,000	80	80	79	100	91

It is not possible to enumerate here the detailed assumptions on which these figures are based. Broadly speaking, however, A represents an individual whose income is drawn entirely from sources other than companies of any kind; B also represents such an individual, but one who is married and has no children; C is an individual who has no income apart from that which accrues to him in a company other than gold or diamond mining; E's income is entirely from diamond mining; D's income is entirely from gold mining. On these broad assumptions[1] the Table then shows the total amounts of tax paid by A, B, C and E as percentages of the amount paid by D (who receives all his income from gold mining). The extent of the discrimination against D is clearly apparent.

The severity of the tax on gold-mining income in South Africa is illustrated also by the following comparison with similar taxation in other gold producing countries; the figures were submitted in evidence to the Departmental Committee on Mining Taxation (1935) by the Gold Producers' Committee of the Transvaal Chamber of Mines:[2]

Country.	Approximate rate of tax (percentage of taxable profits).
Australia	18
Canada	13 to 19
Rhodesia	23
Union of South Africa . . .	42
United States of America . . .	14 to 18
West Africa	12

It is shown in Table 17 that, whereas for the financial year ending March, 1914, the total receipts from gold mining were £1,146,000, they amounted to £13,647,000 for the financial year ending March, 1937. The table compares the value of the gold output, the net product of gold mining, the dividends declared and the Government receipts from gold mining for selected years, and also expresses these figures on a common base. Taking the figures for the financial year ending March, 1914 as 100, it will be seen that the taxation on the gold-mining industry for 1936–7 had increased to 1191, although on the same base the value of its output had grown only to 213, its net product to 196 and the dividends declared by it to 203.

[1] For further details and explanations see Chapter 7, *The Theory of Gold Supply*, by W. J. Busschau. (London: Oxford University Press, 1936.)

[2] For a further discussion see Mr. J. H. Beatty's pamphlet on *The Taxation of the Witwatersrand Gold Mines* and the articles referred to in the note on p. 90, Chapter III.

TABLE 17.—*South African Gold Mining.* £(000).

Year.	Value of Total Gold Output.(a)	Net Product of Gold Mining (i.e. value of output less stores consumed).	Dividends Declared.	Union Government Receipts from Gold Mining.(b)		
				Credited to Revenue.	Credited to Loan Account.	Total.
1913	37,376	26,743	8,597	1,049	97	1,146
1916	39,491	27,170	7,283	1,433	116	1,549
1921	43,084	28,644	7,260	2,002	96	2,098
1926	42,285	28,248	8,444	1,611	1,758	3,369
1928	43,982	29,030	8,506	1,602	1,588	3,191
1929	44,229	29,415	8,485	1,623	1,573	3,197
1930	45,520	30,474	8,716	1,648	1,670	3,318
1931	46,206	30,239	8,590	1,696	1,770	3,466
1932	49,098	32,956	9,043	2,338	1,927	4,265
1933	68,689	50,168	13,684	12,548	1,997	14,545
1934	72,312	50,199	16,038	9,206	3,999	13,205
1935	76,533	50,903	16,778	10,594	3,706	14,300
1936	79,495	52,398	17,433	10,178	3,470	13,647
1937	82,557	53,311	16,999	...	...	...

Percentage Growth of the Gold Mining Industry as compared with Increase of Gold Mining Taxation in the Union.

1913	100·0	100·0	100·0	100·0	100·0	100·0
1916	105·6	101·5	84·7	136·6	119·6	135·2
1921	115·2	107·0	84·4	190·8	99·0	183·1
1926	113·1	105·6	98·2	153·6	1812·4	294·0
1928	117·6	108·6	98·9	152·7	1637·1	278·4
1929	118·3	110·0	98·7	154·7	1621·6	279·0
1930	121·7	113·9	101·3	157·0	1721·6	289·5
1931	123·6	113·0	99·9	161·8	1824·7	302·4
1932	131·3	123·2	105·1	222·8	1986·5	372·3
1933	183·7	187·5	159·1	1195·8	2058·7	1269·2
1934	193·4	187·6	186·5	877·3	4122·6	1152·3
1935	204·7	190·3	195·1	1009·6	3820·5	1247·8
1936	212·7	195·9	202·8	970·3	3577·3	1190·8
1937	220·9	199·3	197·7	...	...	...

(a) The value of the silver and other metals produced by the gold mines is negligible.
(b) For financial year ending 31st March following that stated.

In 1930 the author prepared an estimate[1] for the Low Grade
Ore Commission, which indicated that, broadly speaking, 50%
of the Government and Provincial revenues was directly and
indirectly derived from the Witwatersrand Gold-Mining Industry.
The percentage is doubtless very much larger now. The Government receipts from gold mining consist (i) of its share of profits in
lease and other mines, which, including certain minor amounts from
other sources, are credited to loan account, and (ii) the amounts
accruing from income tax on gold-mining enterprises which,
together with a portion of the Government share of mining profits
representing the income tax which the lease mines would have
paid thereon, are credited to revenue. Table 18 shows the amounts
credited to revenue and to loan account respectively, and the
total receipts from gold mining for each of the financial years
from 1911–12 to 1936–7. The same information in regard to the
receipts from all mining and mining other than gold is given in
Table 19. The foregoing Tables should be compared with
Table 20, which shows the Ordinary Revenue and Expenditure,
Customs Revenue and the growth of the Public Debt of the Union
from 1911–12 to 1936–7. It will be noted that only gold mining
contributed to Loan Account up to 1924. From 1925 to 1927 the
amount credited to Loan Account from other mining was small.
Thereafter it increased appreciably. The fluctuations in the
receipts from mining other than gold are worthy of note.

The total amount which has been received by the State from
gold mining from the financial year ending March, 1911, to the
financial year ending March, 1937, alone amounts to over
£106,000,000. From all mining its receipts exceed £148,000,000.
The magnitude of this sum is indicated by the fact that it does
not fall far short of the capital invested from abroad in the
Witwatersrand gold-mining industry since its inception. Of the
receipts from gold mining, £31,325,000 were credited to loan
account and £74,913,000 to revenue. From all mining, the
amounts were £36,155,000 and £104,699,000 respectively.[2]

---

[1] *Cf.* evidence of the Gold Producers' Committee, Statement No. 8, *An Investigation
into the Importance of the Gold Mining Industry of the Witwatersrand in Relation to the Finances
of the Union of South Africa*, by S. Herbert Frankel.

[2] In addition, there was a sum of £7,500,000 of license and Mynpacht dues for
the whole period.

There can be no doubt that it is owing to this extremely lucrative source of income that Governments of the Union have been able to pursue with increasing liberality those policies which are intended to foster the agricultural industry. Since

TABLE 18.—*Union Government Receipts from Gold Mining.*

Year.(a)	Credited to Revenue.			Credited to Loan Account.	Total Receipts from Gold Mining.
	Taxation.	Lease Revenue.	Total.		
	£(000).	£(000).	£(000).	£(000).	£(000).
1911	1,004	...	1,004	74	1,078
1912	1,011	...	1,011	80	1,091
1913	1,049	...	1,049	97	1,146
1914	975	...	975	106	1,081
1915	1,253	...	1,253	104	1,357
1916	1,428	5	1,433	116	1,549
1917	1,291	56	1,347	268	1,615
1918	766	100	866	410	1,276
1919	943	128	1,071	631	1,702
1920	1,190	169	1,359	851	2,210
1921	1,108	894	2,002	96	2,098
1922	835	744	1,579	120	1,699
1923	1,236	810	2,046	472	2,518
1924	1,473	354	1,827	1,375	3,202
1925	1,066	388	1,454	1,457	2,911
1926	1,112	499	1,611	1,758	3,369
1927	1,105	488	1,593	1,608	3,201
1928	1,110	492	1,602	1,589	3,191
1929	1,128	495	1,623	1,574	3,197
1930	1,149	499	1,648	1,670	3,318
1931	1,182	514	1,696	1,770	3,466
1932	1,798	540	2,338	1,927	4,265
1933	9,747	2,801	12,548	1,997	14,545
1934	8,237	969	9,206	3,999	13,205
1935	9,672	922	10,594	3,706	14,300
1936	9,328	850	10,178	3,470	13,647

(a) Each year refers to the financial period ending 31st March of the following year.

1910, every possible method has been utilized not only to assist the farmers in their struggle against grave natural obstacles in the form of poor soil, recurring drought, generally irregular rainfall and plant or stock diseases, but also to divert resources to the industry as a whole by large public works and by loans to stimulate investment in it. Nearly one hundred Acts have been passed since Union to deal with permanent measures designed to aid or expand agricultural production.

TABLE 19.—*Union Government Receipts from Mining,(c) 1911–12 to 1936–37. £(000).*

Year.(a)	All Mining other than Gold.						All Mining (including Gold).		
	Credited to Revenue.			Credited to Loan Account.	Total.	Licences and Mynpacht Dues.	Credited to Revenue.	Credited to Loan Account.	Total.
	Taxation.	State Ownership.	Total.						
1911	508	350	858	...	858	304	1,862	74	2,240
1912	466	442	908	...	908	288	1,919	80	2,287
1913	568	483	1,051	...	1,051	275	2,100	97	2,472
1914	330	135	465	...	465	244	1,440	106	1,790
1915	29	143	172	...	172	241	1,425	104	1,770
1916	319	326	645	...	645	240	2,078	116	2,434
1917	667	382	1,049	...	1,049	261	2,396	268	2,925
1918	808	412	1,220	...	1,220	260	2,086	410	2,756
1919	2,021	731	2,752	...	2,752	274	3,823	631	4,728
1920	1,452	804	2,256	...	2,256	273	3,615	851	4,739
1921	374	55	429	...	429	263	2,431	96	2,790
1922	614	15	629	...	629	265	2,208	120	2,593
1923	1,012	602	1,614	...	1,614	259	3,660	472	4,391
1924	1,119	345	1,464	...	1,464	270	3,291	1,375	4,936
1925	1,279	480	1,759	12	1,771	272	3,213	1,469	4,954
1926	1,816	460	2,276	7	2,283	319	3,887	1,765	5,971
1927	1,837	206	2,043	6	2,049	317	3,636	1,614	5,567
1928	1,653	685	2,338	2,021(b)	4,359	309	3,940	3,610	7,859
1929	1,288	639	1,927	1,604	3,531	314	3,550	3,178	7,042
1930	789	248	1,037	559	1,596	305	2,685	2,229	5,219
1931	327	168	495	245	740	303	2,191	2,015	4,509
1932	206	161	367	306	673	322	2,705	2,233	5,260
1933	273	138	411	30	441	370	12,959	2,027	15,356
1934	324	147	471	22	493	336	9,677	4,021	14,034
1935	271	191	462	11	473	299	11,056	3,717	15,072
1936	590	99	698	8	697	317	10,866	3,477	14,660

(a) To 31st March of the year following that stated.
(b) Allocation as between Revenue and Loan Account as from this date made in terms of Act No. 21
(c) Extracted from the Annual Reports of the Commissioner for Inland Revenue.

TABLE 20.—*Union of South Africa. Public Finance, 1911–12 to 1936–37.*(e)

Year.(b)	Ordinary Revenue.(b)	Customs and Excise.		Ordinary Expenditure.	Gross Public Debt.			Total Receipts from Mining.(d)
		Revenue.	Customs and Excise as Percentage to Total Ordinary Revenue.		Internal.	External.	Total.	
	£(000).	£(000).	%.	£(000).	£(000).	£(000).	£(000).	£(000).
1911	14,209	4,969	35·0	13,528	14,037	103,223	117,260	2,240
1912	14,176	5,130	36·2	13,947	15,066	102,763	117,829	2,287
1913	12,606	5,354	42·5	13,294	14,488	111,809	126,297	2,472
1914	10,967	4,321	39·4	12,955	14,904	123,306	138,210	1,790
1915	13,168	5,551	42·2	12,769	18,848	131,985	150,833	1,770
1916	14,941	6,193	41·4	14,377	23,254	131,329	154,583	2,434
1917	16,011	5,644	35·3	15,313	33,497	126,939	160,437	2,925
1918	18,312	7,234	39·5	17,723	41,294	125,074	166,368	2,756
1919	23,179	7,937	34·2	20,719	50,515	123,390	173,905	4,728
1920	25,748	10,316	40·1	26,048	55,549	123,059	178,608	4,739
1921	24,551	7,004	28·5	25,757	63,063	128,722	191,785	2,790
1922	22,675	7,545	33·3	23,673	68,029	131,656	199,685	2,593
1923	24,253	8,617	35·5	24,027	74,869	133,363	208,232	4,391
1924	25,336	9,192	36·3	24,528	75,176	139,157	214,333	4,936
1925	26,987	9,944	36·8	26,315	77,799	144,157	221,956	4,954
1926	28,577	10,540	36·9	27,362	83,665	147,811	231,476	5,971
1927	30,094	10,953	33·4	28,304	87,446	151,480	238,926	5,567
1928	30,502	11,327	37·1	28,669	93,493	150,552	244,045	7,859
1929	30,486	11,272	37·0	29,998	93,655	155,996	249,651	7,042
1930	28,563	9,261	32·4	29,949	95,654	161,191	256,845	5,219
1931	27,741(a)	10,248(a)	36·9	28,742(c)	104,261	159,686	263,947	4,509
1932	28,442(a)	11,240(a)	39·5	28,452(c)	106,478	165,656	272,134	5,260
1933	37,625	10,571	28·1	33,091(c)	109,274	165,037	274,311	15,356
1934	38,730	12,319	31·8	35,456(c)	117,439	156,676	274,115	14,034
1935	39,675	11,941	30·1	36,520(c)	128,433	122,653	251,087	15,072
1936	43,087(b)	12,961(b)	30·1	37,247(b)	150,964	103,973	254,937	14,660

(a) Including primage duty collected for payment of export subsidies.
(b) To 31st March of the year following that stated.
(c) Includes export subsidies.
(d) I. e. Income Tax plus receipts credited to Loan Account, plus Licenses and Mynpacht dues.
(e) Extracted from *Union Year Books.*
(f) *Report of the Controller and Auditor-General,* 1936–7, U.G. 46, 1937.

IV

THE EXPENDITURE ON AGRICULTURE.

From 1910 to March, 1936, the State had spent over £71,000,000[1] from loan funds and over £41,000,000 from revenue for agriculture. The details of this expenditure are given in Table 21. Of the total expenditure from Loan Votes amounting to over £71,000,000 since Union, nearly £20,000,000 (a large part of which was spent on irrigation) has had to be written off, or classified as non-recoverable.[2] It is also significant that assistance to farmers, farmers' special relief measures and relief of distress account for another £20,000,000 of the expenditure from loan funds.

With the exception of investments by settlers and relatively small amounts made available by various insurance companies in the form of loans on mortgage, the agricultural industry has obtained unimportant amounts of capital from abroad. It remains greatly dependent on local long-term borrowing, of which a large part takes the form of loans on mortgage,[3] the proportion of which to the capital made available by agriculturists themselves is frequently excessive if the vicissitudes of farming in

---

[1] It will be noted that of this sum an amount of £32,678,000 was available from mining revenues which were credited to Loan Account, the balance being made up by State borrowing.

[2] Of the £71,542,911 expended from Loan Votes during the period 1910/11 to 1935/36, £12,466,418 was recovered, £6,748,508 written off, and £13,712,381 classed as "non-recoverable".

[3] The Commission on Co-operative and Agricultural Credit (1934) considered that a figure of £100,000,000 "would appear to be a fair indication of long-term farm indebtedness". The Commission found that, of this, the Land Bank holds approximately £15,000,000, the remaining and major portion being in the hands of private institutions and individuals. The more important of the former are Insurance Companies, Trust Companies, and Boards of Executors. The Land and Agricultural Bank, by obtaining its funds from the Government and being therefore dependent upon the annual, or less frequent parliamentary vote, is limited in its influence on the mortgage position of the country. The Bank commenced business on 1st October, 1912, with a capital of £2,735,000, which was transferred from the Provincial Land Banks. Further moneys authorized by Parliament from 1912/13 to 1934/5, amounted to a total of £12,333,000. The Bank was authorized in 1933 to make advances on behalf of the Government for the purpose of redeeming existing mortgages. A sum of £8,000,000 was voted by Parliament for this purpose, of which £1,798,465 was utilized in 1933, £5,959,420 in 1934, £2,879,555 in 1935, and £1,574,300 in 1936.

TABLE 21.—*Union of South Africa. Government Expenditure on Agriculture*, 1910–11 *to* 1935–36.

	From Loan Votes.		From Revenue.
Assistance to Farmers . .	£14,193,080[2]	.	£2,880,780[8]
Farmers' Special Relief and Relief of Distress	5,592,914[5]	.	...
Irrigation	12,039,382	.	4,129,364
Forestry	3,855,509	.	4,135,521
Lands and Land Settlement .	11,516,676	.	2,799,371[7]
Labour	891,309[3]	.	1,516,648[6, 9]
Land and Agricultural Bank .	21,559,499[4]	.	...
General Agricultural Votes[1] .	1,845,588	.	23,662,615
Survey	...	.	1,596,714
	£71,493,957	.	£40,721,013
Native Affairs.			
Land Purchase for Native Settlement	...	.	228,821
Fencing and Dipping Tanks, Grant to Native Development Account, Loss on Boring for Water, Soil Erosion, etc. .	48,954	.	388,068
	£71,542,911	.	£41,337,902

[1] *General Agricultural Votes.*—Including only the expenditure on permanent improvements, such as fencing and dipping tanks, etc., omitting such items as purchase of seed and fertilizer for resale to farmers.

[2] *Assistance to Farmers.*—This includes the following items: Export Subsidies, Interest Subsidies, Rebate on Railway Rates (£322,830), Maize Pool, Wheat Pool and contribution to meet deficit on Wheat Pool.

[3] *Labour.*—From the Labour Vote only the expenditure on Tenant Farmers, Irrigation Schemes, Loans to the Doornkop Sugar Estates, Limited, Forestry Stations, etc., have been included.

[4] *Land Bank.*—This includes provision for Agricultural Loan Companies and for the following items:

    (a) 1926/7 £115,000 to Ostrich Feather Industry;
    (b)   ,,   £100,000 Agricultural Credit Act, 1926;
    (c)   ,,   £30,000 Tenant Farmers;
    (d)   ,,   £50,000 Umfolozi Co-operative Sugar Planters;
    (e) 1927/8 £58,000   ,,   ,,   ,,   ,,
    (f) 1928/9 £260,000 Agricultural Loan Companies, and £20,000 Umfolozi Co-operative Sugar Planters;
    (g) 1930/1 £400,000 Agricultural Loan Companies, and £100,000 Water Supply.

[5] *Relief of Distress.*—Votes 1924/5 to 1930/1, including advances in terms of the Drought Distress Relief Act, 1927.

[6] Expenditure on Rural Unemployment.

[7] From 1918/19 to 1928/9.

[8] Export Subsidies, Interest Subsidies, and Rebates on Railway Rates.

[9] Including Grants to Farmers and Payment of Allowances, Destruction of Noxious Weeds, and Anti-Soil Erosion.

South Africa are taken into account. This, combined with the fatal ease with which long-term loans are obtained from the State for land purchase and capital improvements, has frequently led to the artificial inflation of land values. The tendency to incur long-term indebtedness is intensified owing to the lack of agricultural credit institutions for the supply of working capital. The activities of the existing co-operative associations in this connection are largely confined to the supply of credit for marketing. The considerable difficulties of farming in the Union, particularly in periods of depression when land values fall, are undoubtedly increased by the ease with which land can be acquired with money borrowed from the State and elsewhere, and the fact that much of the land so purchased subsequently remains inadequately utilized.

Table 22 from the *Report of the Carnegie Commission on the Poor White Problem*, vol. i, illustrates the ratio of farm mortgage debt to the value of farm land in the Union. But, as the *Report of the Co-operative and Agricultural Credit Commission* notes, "as land values have fallen since 1929/30 the ratio is more unfavourable at the present time".

TABLE 22.—*Ratio of Farm Mortgage Debt to the Total Value of Farm Land.*

	Total Farm area in Morgen.	Average Value per Morgen 1928/9 to 1930/1.	Total Value of Farm Land.	Mortgage Bonds on Farm Lands, 1931.	Ratio of Mortgage Indebtedness per cent.
	(000).	£.	£(000)s.	£(000)s.	%.
Cape Province	57,691	1·66	98,099	41,666	42·5
Natal	5,242	6·88	36,065	12,777	34·5
Transvaal	18,386	2·81	51,665	15,670	30·3
Orange Free State	14,417	4·69	67,616	20,562	30·4
			£253,445	£90,675	

V

THE EXCESS COST OF AGRICULTURE.

With the exception of wool, there is no longer an important agricultural commodity which is not dependent on the maintenance of an artificial internal price structure or on some other form of protection. There has grown up in the Union a system of Tariffs, Subsidies, Quotas, Price Regulating and Marketing Schemes, which is remarkable in its wide ramifications, contradictions and complexities. Nearly every important agricultural commodity for which an appreciable local market exists has now to be sold at internal prices above the corresponding world prices.[1]

Moreover, the rates structure of the railways has been mainly devised to conform with the system whereby agricultural, particularly export products, are subsidised by means of artificially low transport charges.[2] Since Union too, very large sums have been spent in the construction of unpayable branch lines in order to stimulate farming—often in quite unsuitable areas. It is significant that the annual average of all incomes subject to income taxation by the Central Government for the period 1925 to 1929 was £5,078,000. This was equivalent to 5·8% of the total taxed incomes of the Union. The corresponding figures for mining were £14,544,000, equivalent to 16·7% of the total taxed incomes. From 1930 to 1934, the average annual taxed incomes from all farming had dropped to £1,630,000 per annum. It should be noted that these figures refer to the incomes subject to tax, not to the tax collections themselves. It can be shown that, from 1930 to 1934, the taxed incomes from farming were actually less than the cost of the artificial measures (subsidies, relief expenditure, etc.) incurred by the Central Government for agriculturists. In 1933/4 farming incomes subject to tax were only 1·6% of the total taxed incomes of the Union. The low contribution made by agriculture to the direct revenues of the Central Government is due both to the special exemptions under the Income Tax Acts and to the low net incomes obtained from agricultural operations.

[1] Moreover, agricultural co-operation in the Union has been artificially fostered by the State, and has in many cases degenerated into attempts to create monopolies rather than to achieve real economies in marketing. This tendency was apparent long before the Marketing Act of 1937, which has finally established this policy, was passed. *Cf.* the author's *Co-operation and Competition in the Marketing of Maize in South Africa* (London: P. S. King, 1926). *Cf.* also C. S. Richards: "Subsidies, Quotas, Tariffs, and the Excess Cost of Agriculture in South Africa", *S.A. Journal of Economics*, vol. iii, No. 3, 1935.

[2] *Cf.* the writer's "Railway Policy of South Africa". Johannesburg: (Hortors Ltd., 1928.)

VI

THE MALAISE OF EUROPEAN AGRICULTURE.

Notwithstanding the far-reaching character of all the efforts by the State to place agriculture on a sound footing, this industry is now more dependent on the rest of the economy than ever before.

It is, therefore, not surprising that there are many who are pessimistic concerning the future of agriculture in South Africa. Indeed, an eminent authority has expressed the opinion that the Union may eventually be forced to leave the greater part of its agricultural activities to non-Europeans.

In effect, this opinion implies that the net income to be expected from agriculture is too low to maintain a considerable European population at that standard of life which European civilization and culture demand. It is doubtful whether this serious conclusion can be accepted without very considerable qualification. The present low productivity of agriculture is largely due to the existing economic structure and the traditional methods of organization in the industry itself and in the economy as a whole. As long as the established methods of farming remain unaltered, it seems premature to endeavour to forecast the natural limits to either European or to non-European productivity on the land. There are reasons for believing that the immediate limitations in South Africa, as also in other parts of the Continent, still lie in the institutions and traditions of its inhabitants rather than in the inadequacy of natural resources.[1] One cannot as yet assume that the social and economic obstacles to the creation of additional income in farming and elsewhere have been realized, still less that adequate measures have been taken to overcome them.

For the most outstanding fact in the economy of the Union is the smallness of, and the relatively restricted diversification in the existing orbit of modern economic production, and consequently the low volume of its inter-regional trade. Broadly

---

[1] The 1921 Census Report rightly stressed that "it is not a question of the capacity of the country, but of the need for closer settlement, capital and better marketing at home and abroad".

speaking, activity is concentrated in the urban areas and rests on the mineral industries and those serving or sheltered by them.[1] Here is to be found the vanguard of world economic forces, and yet, even here, the base is a huge native proletariat. These are the activities which have attracted capital from abroad, and, through them, resources have spilled over or have been diverted into agriculture and manufacturing. Outside of this small, but very advanced sector of the economy, the Union is faced with the vast task of raising the standard of life and altering the customs, traditions and occupations of a huge non-European, as well as a large section of the European population. These peoples are marginal or even sub-marginal members of the economy, as far as their present capacity for modern economic advance is concerned. The problem here, as in the rest of Africa, is that of fitting this economically less developed population into the world economy. What distinguishes and complicates the task of the Union is that here the necessary economic revolution affects not only the native peoples, but so large a section of the European population as well.[2]

[1] This is illustrated by the striking relative growth of the nine "greater" urban areas (Capetown, Durban, Johannesburg and Witwatersrand, Pretoria, Port Elizabeth, East London, Bloemfontein, Kimberley, and suburbs in each case). The following table shows the total population, according to race, in these areas, as a percentage of the corresponding total population of that race in the Union as a whole:

Greater Urban Areas, percentages of Union.

	European.	Native.	Coloured.	Asiatic.	Total.
1904	33·2	8·9	22·3	38·2	17·5
1921	37·2	12·0	26·0	48·6	20·9
1936	45·2	15·6	30·5	56·5	25·4

To-day these nine greater urban areas contain a quarter of the total population of the Union (excluding the Protectorates and Zululand) and 45% of the total European population ; over 50% of their total population is concentrated in Johannesburg, its suburbs, and in the rest of the Witwatersrand. The European population has increased threefold between 1904 and 1936 in Johannesburg and fivefold in the rest of the Witwatersrand. The increase in total population has been even greater. (*Cf.* H. A. Shannon, "Urbanization", in the *South African Journal of Economics*, vol. v, No. 2, June, 1937.)

[2] The failure of economically backward populations to adapt themselves to change in the structure of the society is one of the basic causes of poor whiteism, which is not, as is sometimes thought, a purely South African phenomenon. In some cases, there has not been sufficient time for such populations to respond successfully to the challenge of new economic, social or environmental conditions. In others, the challenge of the new environment has failed to call forth an adequate response. Professor Macmillan, in *Complex South Africa*, has made a most detailed study of these problems.

The reason, therefore, why the considerable State assistance to agriculture has not yielded better results appears to lie in the fact that it is not possible to increase the incomes and productivity of peoples organized in some form of subsistence economy, unless those sociological changes are brought about which will cause or enable them to undertake new income-creating activities.

Development, to be permanent, must rest on the growth of both material and non-material equipment; this growth depends on opening wide the doors of personal opportunity. But in South Africa those doors remain closed to a large section of the population—coloured, native and European.

VII

THE NATIVE AND THE LAND.

Non-Europeans still form not less than 70% of those occupied in farming in European areas.[1] The farm native is "at the very bottom of the scale" of efficiency, productivity and income. Broadly speaking, farm labour owing both to custom and legislation has become the most immobile in the country. It is tied to the farmers by a system of labour tenancy by means of which the services of whole families are immobilized in and out of

[1] The adult male natives engaged in agricultural labour for Europeans numbered about 376,000 in 1929 (estimated by the Inter-Departmental Committee on the Native Labour Resources of the Union, Pretoria, 1930); at the same time there were some 261,000 employed in mining and a further 325,000 in other occupations, but of the total labour force covered by these figures some 225,000 were Non-Union Natives. As there were only about 153,000 Europeans occupied in agriculture, the natives formed about 70% of the working force. This, however, excludes some 73,000 coloured workers. It is important to note, moreover, that under the existing "squatting" and labour tenancy systems the labour of women and older children is also utilized on the farms. Broadly speaking, it can be said that more than half of the Union's native population outside the Reserves is somehow utilized on, or at any rate tied to the farms.

The writer has dealt with certain aspects of this question in "Problems of Economic Inequality" in Section II of *Coming of Age—Studies in South African Citizenship and Politics*, by the Hon. J. H. Hofmeyr and others (Capetown: Maskew Miller Limited, 1930), and in an article, "Economic and Racial Problems of South Africa", in the *Journal of the Royal Institute of International Affairs*, May, 1932. The reader should consult the *Report of the Carnegie Commission on the Poor White Problem*, particularly vol. i, *Rural Impoverishment and Exodus*. (Stellenbosch, 1932.)

season.[1] The cash wages of the native farm labourer are in many parts of the country almost nominal.[2] Even if wages in kind are taken into account, the general picture of extreme poverty which characterizes this class is not altered; in any case, owing to the barriers imposed by legislation and custom, it lacks opportunity to improve its position by acquiring skill or by benefiting from increased efficiency.

Reference will later be made to the implications of a system which endeavours to curtail the movement of workers in such a way that both the inefficient and the efficient *entrepreneurs* will be assured of the use of a part of the labour resources of the community.

The difficulties of inducing economic progress are greatest in the purely native section of the Union's rural economy. Yet, even when one takes into account the magnitude of the task involved in changing "the attitude of mind of a people"[3] which economic progress in the native reserves implies, one cannot but be appalled by the extent of the potential resources which are there being destroyed under existing conditions.[4]

The literature which portrays the overcrowded, overstocked, eroded and barren conditions of the Native Reserves is large. It is, therefore, not necessary to describe these conditions here. The Native Economic Commission stated that "with the exception of a few favoured parts, a native area can be distinguished

[1] The Native Economic Commission uses the term "Labour Tenancy" to describe "the system the main feature of which, subject to innumerable differences in detail from district to district and even in the same district, is the giving of services for a certain period in the year to the farmer by the native and/or his family in return for the right to reside on the farmer's land, to cultivate a portion of land, and to graze his stock on the farm". (Par. 355, p. 51.) The Commission points out that "from the point of view of the farmer, labour tenancy is definitely an uneconomic method of securing a labour supply. . . . The only reason why it is maintained on many farms is that there is at present no satisfactory alternative. It involves waste in as much as it is generally necessary to keep more labour on the farm than the work warrants". U.G., 22, 1932.

[2] *Cf.* an excellent article by E. S. Haines, "The Economic Status of the Cape Province Farm Native", in the *South African Journal of Economics*, vol. iii, March, 1935.

[3] Native Economic Commission, p. 80.

[4] According to the calculations of the National Income made by the Economic and Wage Commission, to which reference is made below, it appears that the net product of natives occupied in agriculture in the reserves in 1923 was about £7,500,000. Assuming that the number of natives between the ages of 15 and 50 occupied in agriculture therein was 1,500,000, the average annual income per occupied native from agricultural production in these areas would have been about £5.

at sight by its bareness".   The Commission's account of the
conditions it observed is, in fact, nothing less than a picture of a
desert in the making. It could not but conclude, therefore, that
"the free resources given by nature are not so plentiful anywhere, and particularly not in the Union, that the community can
afford to leave undeveloped such a large portion as is represented
by the Reserves", and it naturally emphasized that "the cure,
the proper economic synthesis, lies in a wise, courageous policy of
development of the Reserves".   Unfortunately, however, it is
not yet generally realized that all such proposals involve widespread changes in the whole economy of the Union. Change
cannot be confined in water-tight compartments.[1]

The Native Economic Commission in emphasizing the need for
economic progress in these territories made a number of excellent
technical suggestions; but it left unanswered the fundamental
question which remains—whence the resources for the improvements it suggested were to be obtained. Instead, it expressed the
opinion that they could not be provided by the Europeans.
"Even if it were possible," they announced, "it is manifestly
undesirable for the Europeans to shoulder the burden".[2]

Thus, in effect, the position in the Reserves is on all fours
with that of other undeveloped territories in Africa, except that
artificial pressure on their populations appears to have had more
serious consequences. The basic phenomenon they represent is
but a new manifestation of a much older condition. Since the
labour of the African cannot be developed to good purposes in his

[1] There is a general belief that if the Reserves could be developed it would somehow
be possible to reverse the economic history of the Union, and reabsorb the native into
his "natural habitat", just as one can run a cinematograph film backwards. Yet, in
reality, development of the Reserves can only imply one thing, namely, a change in the
occupational structure and income stream of their populations. These areas can at
present be distinguished from the European economy simply because they are
undeveloped. Development in them implies the creation of a modern, in place of a
primitive economy.   If this were to be achieved, they would tend to become economically indistinguishable from the European economy itself and, what is more, would be
inseparable from it. It is impossible to visualize the Reserves as an economic *imperium
in imperio* with agricultural, mineral, manufacturing and other income-creating
activities segregated from the larger economy of the Union.

[2] This view appears to be in keeping with the policy of the State in the past;
whereas, according to Table 21, over £112 millions were spent on agriculture since
Union, the amount made available directly for native agricultural needs was less than
£750,000.

own areas, he has no alternative but to export it and, therefore, himself.[1]

VIII

THE NEED FOR PROGRESSIVE CHANGE IN THE WHOLE ECONOMY.

Permanent migration from rural areas is but a symptom of change in a progressive economy. Moreover, if the society as a whole is progressive, one should expect an economic backwash which revitalizes rural activity and supplies it with capital, skill and experience. The movement of workers from backward economic areas is a means of raising the economic condition of those remaining in them; migration from native areas to European areas should have similar effects. For, apart from loans or gifts of capital, the only way in which resources for new development can be obtained is by increased productivity, that is, by progressive change in the income-creating structure of the economy as a whole.

The projects envisaged by the Native Land and Trust Act of 1937, which makes provision for land purchase and for the expenditure of considerable sums on re-settling natives and increasing their productivity in both the new and old native areas,[2] may do something to stem the present disastrous deterioration in native areas. State action of this nature, however, while of importance in itself, particularly in view of the fact that it has been neglected in the past, cannot be a substitute for the necessary

[1] E. A. G. Robinson, dealing with the economic problems of the African economy in Northern Rhodesia, stressed the part which has been played by the movement of labour: "Having nothing else to sell the native has sold himself. The need of finding money to pay his taxes, his mission and education dues and to buy the products of the store has led him to seek work in the towns, on the farms and mines . . ." (*Cf.* J. Merle Davis, *Modern Industry and the African.* London: Macmillan, 1933.) See also Chapter I above.

The *Report of the Native Economic Commission* also bears witness to the evils of excessive migration of able-bodied male adults from native areas. The situation in many other African territories is similar. The *Report of the Nyasaland Committee on Emigrant Labour* gives a classic account of the serious effect on native areas of this exodus. The Committee concluded that if migration is allowed to continue unchecked and uncontrolled, "large tracts of land will be rendered unfit for habitation, and in consequence the economic life of the whole country will suffer as a result".

[2] Everything will depend on the practical application of the policy. Moreover, very little will be achieved if natives are saddled with a burden of debt out of proportion to their incomes.

wider changes in the economy as a whole. For without them an appreciable increase in the productivity and income of the native population cannot be achieved.

Throughout Africa there is always the danger that the problem of land be viewed too exclusively in terms of area. For example, to say that natives require more land at first sight appears so obvious as not to require further consideration. But there are certain implicit assumptions on which alone such a statement can have meaning; namely, that on the land already occupied no change is possible either in the uses to which it can be put, or in the availability of the other factors of production, capital and labour, and in knowledge and efficiency, as well as in markets and suitable crops. In short, that it can only continue to be used in the same manner, for the same purposes, and with the same intensity as in the past, and that, therefore, any increase in population requires a proportionate increase in the supply of land.

Now it is true that in many regions some or even all of these assumptions hold good. Land may be so "poor" that it can only carry a very sparse population, and can only continue to be very extensively utilized. But, even when this is the case, a moment's reflection will show that the problems of agriculture cannot continue to be solved indefinitely by the mere allocation of more land to all and sundry.

The real problem which will have to be faced sooner or later throughout Africa is how to utilize more effectively those types of land which are capable of more intensive cultivation. It is in fact just because so far little has been done to enable a more effective use of the occupied land that it is so readily assumed that the needs of a growing population can be met only by providing still more land for it. It is indeed significant that, notwithstanding the large expropriation of native land of the past, the European land-hunger in the Union still continues. It continues because changes which would enable the more intensive use of the land by Europeans are taking place very slowly.[1] Yet it must surely be

---

[1] A. P. Van der Post in his excellent book on *The Economics of Agriculture* (South Africa, Central News Agency Limited, 1937) has shown that in 1933/4 European occupied farms numbered 98,930 and had a total area of 97,352,709 morgen. Of the farms only 21,481 (*i. e.* 21·7%) were 100 morgen (211·65 acres) or less in size, and these accounted for only ·66% of the total occupied area. A further 51·86% of the

obvious that no society can indefinitely continue to obtain more land, and that productive methods which depend on the continued availability of additional land cannot generally solve the population problem. "The population capacity of the land depends, not on its degree of vacancy, but on the total available resources that land, people, science, technology and market demand plus transport facilities, make possible."[1]

The habit of thinking about land in terms of area without sufficient attention to its real economic value is apt to lead to serious waste. If, for example, natives are provided with land which is distant from markets, drought-stricken, or otherwise not suited for the economic production of marketable crops, this not only fails to meet the difficulties of the landless native; it also results in a loss to the economy as a whole because it represents a misuse of the efforts of the population. The labour of the native population in such areas is less productive than it would be if it were applied elsewhere, or in other occupations. The waste which results from the misuse of the efforts of the community in this way is considerable in the Union. Moreover, it is not confined to natives. Much of the permanent expenditure on agriculture for Europeans has had the fallacious objective that land should almost everywhere be made available for Europeans irrespective of its real suitability for economic production. As a result, people are attracted to poor areas, or are prevented from moving to areas where their efforts will be more productive to themselves and to the community. Similarly, capital is applied in attempts to improve relatively poor land instead of being invested where its returns would be higher.

The ultimate problem in Africa is not one of dividing up the

[1] *The Limits of Land Settlement. A Preliminary Report on Present-day Possibilities prepared under the direction of Isaiah Bowman, Council of Foreign Relations, New York.* Royal Institute of International Affairs, 1937.

---

farms were 101 to 1000 morgen in size, and these accounted for 24·6% of the total occupied area. Thus about 75% of the occupied land in European ownership was divided into farms of over 1000 morgen (2116 acres) in extent. Van der Post rightly stresses that the problem of more intensive cultivation is partly a problem of the density of population and the intensity of demand for agricultural products. It is my opinion that the effective demand of the existing population of the Union, small though it is in relation to the area of the country, is lower than it need be, and lower than it would be if the efforts of the population were given free scope and its national income increased.

land between different races—however necessary this may appear to be on social grounds, or as a stage in economic development—but of increasing the effective use which is made of it. This great problem bristles with psychological, ecological and economic difficulties. It cannot be solved quickly or by any one method. Nevertheless a successful approach to it is impossible unless the fundamental fact is realized that the whole of the existing population—be it black or white—cannot remain on the land in agricultural occupations if income standards are to be raised. A large proportion must do other things or move to other places.

Unfortunately, in the Union, this occupational diversification is proceeding with extreme slowness. The migrants from the Reserves do not find permanent opportunities in European areas for appreciably increasing their net earnings or engaging in all the activities for which they may be fitted, and through which they could help to increase the income of the society as a whole. Moreover, the forms which new income can take are correspondingly limited, and thus inhibit the inauguration of new productive activity. Policies which retard the development of educational, medical and social services, and which prevent an improvement in the existing primitive diet, housing or consumption standards of the poorer population, in short, policies which bind it to a narrow and limited horizon of wants, imply the suppression of the ability to produce.

The economic organization of the European economy is such that it interposes a rigid and at times insurmountable barrier to the efforts of large numbers of those who wish to enter it. Quite apart from the numerous laws which prevent the native from entering skilled occupations, from purchasing land in urban areas, or even from residing in them except under licence, the industrial wage structure tends, as is shown in detail below, to curtail entry even for Europeans into any but the low paid unskilled occupations, not to mention the great handicaps under which the growing coloured population labours.[1] Indeed, as Professor Clay has remarked, "a large part of the so-called poor

[1] For an account of these see the *Report of the Cape Coloured Commission* and Prof. W. H. Hutt's article thereon in the *S.A. Journal of Economics*, June, 1938.

white problem may be merely the problem referred to as unemployment in other countries, due to requiring the payment of rates of wages which these workers are not worth" as a result of Industrial Wage Legislation.   Thus the landless European is prevented from "making good" in the towns by less onerous but in many respects essentially similar obstacles to those which confront the native.   On European farms, on the other hand, the absence of any system whereby either a black or white tenantry might be established reduces the workers, and by no means only the native workers, to an amorphous wage-paid proletariat or to a type of labour tenant dependent on customarily circumscribed remuneration in kind; and the landless European seeks in vain for that ladder of opportunity which would enable him to recapture an independent status on the land.[1]   If the artificial restrictions which now check potential native efforts both in and outside the reserves were to be removed, it is likely that the expenditure on capital works and development which the Native Economic Commission concluded would constitute "an undesirable burden" on the European community, but which the State is now undertaking because of its urgent necessity, will become a justifiable and economic investment.   Again there is a parallel with the European sector of the economy.   For capital expenditure is always a "burden" when it takes place unaccompanied by changes which are necessary in the other factors of production.   Much of the expenditure by the State on European agriculture has been ineffectual precisely because these concomitant changes have been prevented.   As a result, much of the capital has been wasted and the proletarization of the European has continued.

The fact of the matter is that much thinking on economic problems throughout Africa is based on the fallacious belief that the whole population, every member of it and every part of it, could somehow, by a sudden miracle, have its income raised if only the proper formula could be discovered.   There is no justification for this kind of catastrophic interpretation of economic history or economic processes.   Halting changes and the adaptations required therefore by the more progressive members

[1] Van der Post, p. 105.

of the society finally raise them and others to new income levels. If the opportunities of the progressively inclined are inhibited, the possibility of progress for the mass does not exist.

IX

MANUFACTURING INDUSTRY.

It is necessary now to examine the effects of the existing productive and distributive organization on the industrial section of the Union's economy.

Table 23[1] shows the growth in manufacturing production in the Union from 1924/5 to 1934/5, and gives indices of the prices of Industrial Products and the Volume of Output for the same years. A considerable part of this growth has been in sheltered and/or protected industry.

The Customs Tariff Commission[2] arrived at the following estimates of the size of secondary industries dependent on protection for the industrial census year 1933, but excluding industries processing agricultural products:

Value of output £19,305,000
Employment: Europeans   .   .   26,000 to 28,000 persons
　　　　　　 Non-Europeans .   .   21,000 to 23,000 persons
Salaries and wages paid £5,120,000

The Commission stated that "While the sheltered and non-protected industries developed with the general development of the country, it is clear that a great deal of the industrial development which took place after 1925 is directly due to the stimulus given by the protectionist policy inaugurated in that year. . . . Protected industries show a much greater increase in employment than sheltered industries". Seven protected industries alone accounted for just over 50% of the total increased employment of Europeans in all private industries.

The most striking facts about manufacturing industry in the Union are (i) the low average productivity per worker employed and (ii) the artificial wage structure according to which this low

[1] The table is from the *Union Year Book*, No. 18.
[2] *Report of the Customs Tariff Commission*, 1934/5, U.G., No. 5, 1936.

TABLE 23.—*Manufacturing Production in the Union—General Summary, 1924–25 to 1934–35.*

Year.	Number of Establishments.	Number of Employees.		Salaries and Wages paid to		Engines and Motors.(a)		Materials Used.	Value of Gross Output.	Value Added by Process of Manufacture.	Net Output.
		European.	Other.	Europeans.	Others.	Prime Movers. H.P.	Net Total. H.P.				
				£(ooo).	£(ooo).			£(ooo).	£(ooo).	£(ooo).	£(ooo).
All Undertakings :											
1924–25	7,206	71,004	120,594	15,661	5,844	665,406	161,635	42,293	84,160	41,867	38,406
1925–26	7,085	75,987	117,435	16,766	5,933	706,243	167,100	47,071	91,537	44,466	40,933
1926–27	7,170	80,745	121,919	17,850	6,281	823,927	191,128	50,536	97,867	47,331	43,816
1927–28	7,338	84,368	122,690	18,758	6,512	860,018	251,649	55,760	106,770	51,010	47,460
1928–29	7,433	89,141	128,345	19,606	6,914	944,332	275,625	59,243	113,182	53,939	50,549
1929–30	7,695	90,858	127,440	20,507	7,019	1,032,910	264,129	56,802	111,799	54,997	51,533
1932–33	7,669	87,173	105,310	16,823	5,052	1,234,061	302,990	43,738	90,948	47,210	43,899
1933–34	8,530	102,232	127,270	20,298	6,102	1,385,117	367,425	55,723	111,392	55,669	51,699
1934–35	9,042	115,971	149,877	24,350	7,325	1,467,416	416,067	66,021	131,332	65,311	60,949
Private Undertakings only :											
1924–25	6,866	53,450	99,297	10,838	4,829	468,996	149,566	35,878	69,976	34,098	31,062
1925–26	6,829	57,405	104,457	11,764	5,258	500,940	148,578	40,995	77,581	36,586	33,482
1926–27	6,916	61,412	109,000	12,605	5,584	585,814	163,216	42,938	81,964	39,026	35,990
1927–28	7,073	64,916	111,248	13,554	5,906	677,968	222,272	49,028	91,687	42,659	39,579
1928–29	7,148	68,382	116,463	14,296	6,283	762,556	244,801	51,960	97,032	45,072	42,175
1929–30	7,383	69,736	115,680	15,042	6,430	811,667	229,176	49,505	95,503	45,998	43,048
1932–33	7,321	68,981	95,809	12,846	4,607	976,407	260,988	40,329	80,439	40,109	37,298
1933–34	8,180	83,461	117,700	15,910	5,668	1,132,430	322,607	51,741	99,508	47,766	44,321
1934–35	8,689	95,592	138,703	19,299	6,801	1,202,501	370,228	59,866	116,267	56,401	52,592

Index Numbers of Prices of Products and Volume of Output, 1924–25 to 1934–35.
(Based on the Particulars of all Industrial Establishments.)

Year	Individual Products for which Particulars regarding Quantity and Value of Output are available.			Total Output of all Classes of Industry.	
	Total recorded Value of Output at each Census.	Output at each Census Revalued at 1920–21 Prices.	Index of Prices 1920–21 = 1000.	Index of Volume of Output (excluding Repair Work) 1920–21 = 1000.	Index of Gross Value of Output (including Repair Work) 1920–21 = 1000.
1924–25	38,814	53,290	728	1149	856
1925–26	42,672	60,301	708	1294	931
1926–27	44,601	62,522	713	1344	996
1927–28	48,749	68,250	714	1476	1086
1928–29	50,276	71,768	701	1590	1151
1929–30	47,716	72,633	657	1707	1137
1932–33	42,204	73,567	574	1594	925
1933–34	47,025	81,576	576	1970	1133
1934–35	50,336	89,207	564	2292	1336

(a) Not strictly comparable

net product is divided among different classes of employees. The following comparison of factory returns in New Zealand,

TABLE 24.—*International Comparison of Factory Returns.*[1]

Heading.	New Zealand (1934–35).	Common-wealth of Australia (1934–35).	Union of S. Africa. (1934–35).	Canada (1934).
Value of Land and Buildings £(000)	23,160	110,841	31,686	} 966,592
Value of Machinery and Plant £(000)	44,109	122,641	47,499	
Motive power, prime movers :				
Steam . . 1,000 h.p.	145	983	1,409	1,244
Water . . ,,	387	134	9	7,158
Other · . ,,	39	147	49(c)	124
Total . . ,,	571	1,264	1,467	8,526
Electric Motors . 1,000 h.p.	150	731	355	3,330
Cost of Fuel and Light £(000)	1,107	12,338	4,315	16,406
Employees—Male . . No.	59,874	322,465	232,823	416,674
,, Female . . ,,	19,484	127,133	33,025	128,488
Total No. . . .	79,358	449,598	265,848	545,162
Total Wages Paid £(000)	13,244	72,825	31,675	109,646
Average Wage per Employee £	166	169	122	201(a)
Value of Material Used £(000)	52,085	209,047	66,021	252,949
Value (Gross) of Production £(000)	79,325	364,912	131,332	520,653
Value Added in Process of Manu- facture . . . £(000)	27,240	155,865(b)	65,311	267,704
Net Output . . £(000)	26,133	143,527	60,949	251,298
Value of Production per head of Employees . . . £	1,000	812	494	955
Value of Production per head of mean European Population £	54	54	67	48
Net Output per head of Employees £	329	319	229	461
Net Output per head of Mean European Population £	18	21	31	23

(a) Includes working proprietors.
(b) Now includes fuel.
(c) Excludes horse-power of windmills and air-compressors.

Australia, Canada and the Union of South Africa illustrates the latter's relatively low industrial productivity.

In 1934/35, 41% of the workers employed in private industrial

1 Extracted from the *Union Year Book*, No. 18.

undertakings were Europeans. They took 74% of the wages and salaries paid—equivalent to £202 per head. The remaining 59% of the workers were non-Europeans who obtained 26% of the wages and salaries equivalent to £49 per head.

It has been an essential part of the protective policy to attempt to induce employers to use more European labour. As a result, the Tariff Commission found that "for 1933 the ratio of employment of Europeans is higher in protected than in economic secondary industry. In 1933 the ratio of European to total employees in all industries covered by the Industrial Census was 42%, while in a number of fully protected secondary industries, for which special data are available, the ratio was 57%." The policy of insisting on the employment of Europeans is carried furthest in Government undertakings, where in 1934/5 European employees represented 66·3% of the total, and took no less than 91% of the total wages and salaries paid—equivalent to the surprisingly high figure, when compared with private industrial undertakings, of £233·7 per head. Non-Europeans formed approximately 36% of those employed, but obtained only 9% of the wages and salaries. They received on the average £47 per head.

The essential character of manufacturing industry in South Africa is epitomized in one of the conclusions of the Tariff Commission. "The evidence which we have received," it reported, "is nearly unanimous on the point that the wage rates payable to European labour in South Africa are much higher than those paid in countries which compete in the South African market, and that for this reason protection is an essential condition for the continued existence of local industry." They summed up the situation as follows: "The greatest competitive drawback of South African industry is the high cost of European labour (which it is expected to use in as large a measure as possible), and the protection which exists is to a large extent the protection of the wage rates payable to Europeans in industry in South Africa. . . . The net economic efficiency of South African industry is low. Combined with this the next most important

---

[1] That the policy of employing Europeans has been intensified is indicated by the fact that in 1927/8 the proportion of European employees was 63·55%, these Europeans taking 89·58% of the total wages and salaries paid.

disadvantage is the limited size of the local market (the high cost of manufacturing rules out the export market), which makes it impossible to take the fullest advantage of the economy of large-scale production."

The "limited size of the local market" is, of course, but another way of expressing the low net income of the South African economy as a whole. South African manufacturing industry is, in many respects, a further extension of that rigid organization of South African economic life which endeavours to maintain particular income levels for certain groups at the expense of the standard of life and the potential economic development of other sections and of the economy as a whole.[1]

X

THE UNEQUAL DIVISION OF THE NATIONAL INCOME.

In an economy such as that of the Union, burdened with so large a population living at subsistence levels, it is not surprising that the National Income is very low. In 1923 the total National Income, as calculated by the Economic and Wage Commission,[2] was estimated to be £186,000,000. This gave a figure of £26 per head of the total population, and £43 per occupied person.

If, for convenience of statistical comparison, the purely native production in the native areas is excluded, the National Income becomes £178,000,000, giving £96 per annum per occupied person. It is the figure of £26—the total net income per head of

[1] It is not possible to examine this matter here. Numerous commissions have discussed special aspects of it. *Cf. Report of the Economic and Wage Commission, Report of the Low-Grade Ore Commission*, and also the writer's *Railway Policy of South Africa* (Johannesburg: Hortors Limited, 1928), and his chapter, "A National Economic Policy", in *Coming of Age, ibid.*

[2] These estimates were made on the basis of Professor R. A. Lehfeldt's calculations in *The National Resources of South Africa*. (Johannesburg: University of the Witwatersrand Press, 1918.)   The total given above was made up as follows:

	£ Million.
Agriculture	47
Mining	37
Manufactures	31
Transport	16
Commerce and Finance	12
Services	27
Rent	16
Total	£186

the population—which indicates the results of the efforts of the whole society. This low figure throws into relief the extent to which a large part of the Union's economy is still based on methods of production which yield only a very meagre subsistence to its inhabitants.[1]

The unequal manner in which the National Income is divided formed the subject of comment in a classic chapter by the Economic and Wage Commission. It found that, "taken in connection with the capacity to pay of industry in the different countries, the rates of wages in South Africa are relatively far higher than in any other country" and concluded that " the explanation . . . is to be found in the characteristic of South African wages that we noted first—the wide spread, a spread several times as great as in any other country, between the highest and the lowest rates of wages. The rates of mechanics, building artisans, miners and printers are the rates of a small skilled class of urban white labour. . . ."

In 1935 the Industrial Legislation Commission gave certain statistics of current wages under existing wage regulations and agreements in selected individual occupations. It classified these according to three categories—skilled, semi-skilled and unskilled. Table 25 gives some of these figures in order to illustrate the wide spread between the different wage rates. The Commission showed that this is due to the fact that "in reality every wage-earner has

[1] In this connection the Industrial Legislation Commission gives the following interesting *per capita* estimates for various countries:

Country.				Year.		£
United States .	.	.	.	1928	.	154·1
Canada .	.	.	.	1928	.	124·2
United Kingdom	.	.	.	1928	.	84·5
Germany	.	.	.	1928	.	57·4
France .	.	.	.	1928	.	39·5
Belgium .	.	.	.	1924	.	38·4
Italy .	.	.	.	1928	.	24·9
Switzerland	.	.	.	1924	.	59·4
Austria .	.	.	.	1927	.	29·0
Hungary	.	.	.	1929	.	17·9
Spain .	.	.	.	1923	.	33·3
Russia .	.	.	.	1929	.	22·0
Japan .	.	.	.	1925	.	18·3
India .	.	.	.	1921/2	.	4·1
Australia	.	.	.	1927/8	.	103·7
South Africa .	.	.	.	1923	.	24·9

TABLE 25.—*Selected Wage Rates in the Union.*

Industry or Trade.	Area.	Skilled.	Semi-skilled.	Unskilled.	Skilled. (%.)	Semi-skilled. (%.)	Unskilled. (%.)
Baking and confectionery	Durban, Pietermaritzburg and certain other centres in Natal	£3–£5 p.w.	£2–£3 p.w.	£1 4s. p.w.	100	66–60	30–27
Building	Witwatersrand Cape Peninsula	£4 10s. p.w. 2s. 2d.–2s. 10d. p.h. 3s. 4d.–3s. 6d. p.h.	... ... 1s. p.h.	£1 p.w. 8d. p.h. 4¼d. p.h.	100 100 100	 30–29	25 31–24 11–10
Furniture	Witwatersrand and Pretoria	2s. 5⅜–2s. 9⅜d. p.h.	8⅞d.–1s. 10⅞d. p.h.	6d. p.h.	100	28–65	24–18
	Principal industrial centres	2s. 3d. p.h.	8¼d.–1s. 3d. p.h.	6d. p.h.	100	30–56	22
Motor engineering	Witwatersrand and Pretoria	2s. 8¼d.–2s. 9¾d. p.h.	1s. 3d.–2s. p.h.	4½d.–10d. p.h.	100	47–73	14–30
Printing and newspaper(a)	Capetown Witwatersrand and Pretoria.	£5 19s p.w.(b) £6 19s. p.w.(b)	£1 15s. p.w.(c) £2 10s. p.w.(c)	... ...	100 100	29 36	... ...

(a) Industrial Council Agreement applies to Union which is divided into various areas for wage purposes; three specimen areas only have been taken.

(b) Journeymen on day work.

(c) Wage rates after three years' experience of Printers' Assistants, who form the bulk of the employees in the semi-skilled class. There are, however, other classes of semi-skilled employees who are paid considerably above the rates quoted, thus increasing the average for such labour and reducing the gap between it and skilled labour.

not an equal opportunity of entering any occupation. . . . An upward movement from certain groups to certain others is usually hampered by various factors, so that the higher grades have to all intents and purposes become "non-competing groups", that is, "groups in which the supply is limited owing to the restrictions placed upon outsiders wishing to enter them".

The whole situation cannot be better summed up than in the words of the *Economic and Wage Commission Report of* 1926,[1] which stated: "The high level of European wages and the low level of native and other wages originated in a time of rapidly developing industry in which there was a constant scarcity of competent European and relatively a more adequate supply of native unskilled labour. . . . But it is very doubtful whether (to-day) there are sufficient posts at the high level obtainable to absorb the whole European population. . . . *With a given* net product in any industry it will be possible to employ only a limited number of workers at a rate of pay above the average product per head.[2] . . .

[1] 1925.   U.G., No. 14, p. 88.

[2] "If the average revenue of the industry is considerably less than a pound a day per person occupied in the industry, a rate of a pound a day and upwards will be restricted to a small minority of special workers; and if, owing to public opinion or trade union action, European labour cannot be obtained for less, the tendency will be to organize production on a basis of a small number of highly skilled or responsible men and a large mass of cheap unskilled labour. This tendency would appear to have been realized in South Africa. At the rates of pay customary for Europeans, industry can employ only Europeans of high economic character and efficiency; *there are not enough posts at these rates for the whole European population seeking employment in industry.* Those Europeans who are unable to qualify for such posts have a difficulty in fitting themselves into industry, since the very *productive organization* that makes it possible to pay one section of its employees a pound a day or more out of a total revenue of only £96 per annum per person occupied, is dependent on large numbers of unskilled workers, and can only pay rates so low that Europeans find it difficult to live on them. A wage-rate that is enforced, whether by law, trade union action, or custom, always has a selective effect on employment, largely restricting employment to those workers whose output, having regard to the price obtainable for the industry's product in the market, will cover that wage-rate and rejecting all others. The workers who are not, with the commercial return to industry what it is, worth employing at the relatively higher rate exacted for skilled European labour have no alternative but to swell the ranks of unskilled labour and handymen; in other words, to put themselves into competition with the native. By greater efficiency they may command higher earnings than the native; but industry cannot pay them wages higher than in proportion to their higher efficiency, and a wage of double the ordinary native rate is very low for a European. . . . Consistent with this analysis was the evidence put before us in many centres that while European youths and adults find a difficulty in finding employment, a universal shortage of native labour is experienced." (*Economic and Wage Commission, ibid.,* p. 89. Italics are mine.)

The amount of employment at any place and time is generally a function of the rate of wages; the shortage of employment for European labour is a shortage of posts in which industry can afford to pay the customary standard of European wages; the shortage of native labour merely means that, at the rates at which native labour can be secured, it would pay industry to employ more."

In the meanwhile the situation has become more complex. "European labour, once a great scarcity, is now available in increased numbers in urban areas. Moreover, these increased numbers do not consist of artisans, capable managers, or supervisors only, but of every grade of labour," for "in every race the existence of grades of labour and of differences in ability must be admitted.[1] The same applies to the Europeans in South Africa." "The labour supply no longer consists of a small skilled European labour force superimposed upon a mass of non-European unskilled labour with a low standard of living. Economic forces have now drawn Europeans into the unskilled labour group, while some of the non-Europeans have elevated themselves into the semi-skilled and skilled groups. But notwithstanding this radical change in the structure of the labour supply, the South African wage structure has in the meantime remained essentially unaltered."[1]

XI

THE "SHORTAGE" OF NATIVE LABOUR.

One of the most serious consequences of this customary wage structure is the very uneconomic utilization of the nation's resources to which it necessarily leads. This shows itself in the constant complaint by certain classes of employers that there is a "shortage" of labour. What this really implies is simply that certain employers would like more labour at the same price and obviously à fortiori at a lower price, but that they are unwilling or unable to pay higher prices. In fact, they are asking for more labour to be made available to them at the expense of other

[1] Report of the Industrial Legislation Commission, U.G., No. 37, 1935, p. 14.

industries or other avenues of employment in which the labour is really worth higher prices, that is, in which its productivity is higher. For, if its productivity were not higher elsewhere, labour would offer itself at the price which those very people, who complain of the "shortage", are willing to pay. The reader will have no difficulty in picturing to himself why there is a "shortage" if he will think of the demand there would be for native labour if it was declared that nothing at all had to be paid for it. It is clear that the "shortage" would be colossal, simply because labour would be used for innumerable uneconomic purposes at the expense of tasks which are more important. This analogy will perhaps assist to illustrate the uneconomic nature of the restrictions on the movement of natives such as that contained in the Masters and Servants Act, which, as is well known, ties very large numbers of native workers to particular employers by artificial and non-economic expedients.[1]

It is no exaggeration to say that a basic cause of the low average income of the inhabitants of the Union is the lack of "economic mobility" of its workers—both black and white. We are back again at the starting-point of this study —progress involves change; inhibit change and you inhibit progress.

The customary organization of farming and also of mining in the Union prefers to ration the labour supply artificially rather than to compete for it by higher wages. This involves the elimination of the function of price as an indicator of productivity. It implies that labour is not to move into those avenues where it is more productive, but that, instead, its supply is to be divided between all existing avenues of employment in such a way that both the uneconomic and the economic employments shall continue to function at the same time. In farming, in particular, the cause of the demand for legislative and other restrictions which are intended to make labour available at customary prices is simply that much farming is so uneconomic that it cannot afford to pay a higher wage or to pay cash wages at all. To

---

[1] The question of the labour tenancy or squatting system which is so indicative of primitive farm conditions and lack of capital cannot be discussed in detail here. The writer has analysed the position in "Problems of Economic Inequality", in *Coming of Age, ibid.*

continue to force labour in uneconomic directions is to continue to use it uneconomically.[1]

This situation is epitomized in the observation of the Native Economic Commission that it was "satisfied that where farmers are poor, natives are poor, and generally speaking the remuneration is better where agricultural conditions are more favourable". The Commission was here face to face with the fundamental cause of the unsatisfactory condition of the agricultural industry, namely, that "poor farmers" can continue to tie up labour in occupations which keep both them and their employees in a state of poverty. To continue by artificial expedients to ensure to uneconomic producers a supply of labour at an artificially low price is to penalize those farmers who do possess the necessary capital, skill and suitable natural resources for economic production—just as to ensure labour to relatively uneconomic mines or to uneconomic industries is to penalize potential expansion of richer mines or more profitable industries.[2]

[1] In this connection it must be borne in mind that the point at which some natives cease to offer their labour voluntarily in response to the inducement of higher wages is not necessarily the same as in the case of Europeans. Higher wages may cause them to work for a shorter time. This failure of wage inducements to attract workers was, as we have seen, one of the causes which brought about the introduction of methods of compulsion. There are now, however, an increasing number of natives who are compelled to seek work owing to the economic devastation of the native reserves and the growth of an urban or detribalized native population. In any case, the fact that some natives do, under certain conditions, withdraw their services earlier than Europeans is not a reason for the wasteful use of non-European labour in general. The assumption that a section of a particular population is not working as the society believes it should is not a reason for retarding the opportunities of work open to that population as a whole, and of the wages it can command. It may be a reason for measures designed to limit that section's undue preference for leisure, if it exists—a fact which is far too readily assumed in view of the innumerable other factors which may account for the unwillingness of natives to enter wage-paid employment under the existing, frequently unattractive conditions.

[2] This state of affairs is partly due to a common fallacy which confuses the absolute number of workers who can be forced to enter the labour market with the supply of labour, i. e. the amount of effort made available to the society by them. Nothing is more characteristic of the South African economy than the inefficient manner in which it utilizes the efforts of non-Europeans and even of large numbers of Europeans. This is due to the absence of incentives to greater efficiency on the part of both employees and employers. The circumscribed level of earnings restricts the efforts of the former, and the apparent low cost of native labour reduces the incentives to the more efficient organization of production by the latter.

Thus, Van der Post has stressed that, in farming, the labourer's efficiency "would also to a large extent seem to be determined by his opportunity some day to become a farmer himself, and even an owner of land", but in South Africa, for various reasons,

The counterpart to this system is the widespread reliance on a growing class of casual labour which, restricted in its economic opportunities and standards of remuneration, moves continually from one industry to another, from town to country, and from the native reserves to the European economy and *vice versa*.   This implies that the Union's economy is denied those benefits of specialization which are so important in modern production. Instead of a working population growing in skill and specialized abilities, and well adapted to specific tasks, all enterprise is burdened by a high labour turnover which elsewhere has been long recognized as a basic cause of inefficiency and industrial unrest.   What in South Africa is still regarded, fallaciously, as a great advantage, namely the possibility of substituting any one native worker by any other at a moment's notice, is the result of reducing the labour force to a uniform level, whose common denominator is inefficiency and whose effects are a low national income.

The aspects of the economic structure of the Union discussed in this chapter can be summed up in the words which Professor Clay has applied so tellingly to Southern Rhodesia: "The

---

he has no prospect of becoming independent, and therefore " *the supreme economic motive is entirely absent*".

Under-nourishment is a further factor which affects certain classes of both native and European workers. The mines have to "feed up" the natives recruited by them for weeks before they are fit to work. This struggle against the evils of malnutrition and the diseases resulting therefrom exists throughout Africa. The alleged laziness of the native is in many cases simply due to an inadequate diet. The poorer Europeans frequently suffer in the same way. This malnutrition cannot be remedied (a) as long as those policies continue which prevent, through artificial price maintenance, the sale of essential foods, *e. g.* butter, cheese, milk, wheat and vegetables, at low prices because they stop economic agricultural producers ousting less efficient producers, and (b) as long as agricultural methods in the reserves remain as they are. "At successive International conferences M. de Wildemann," says the *Report of a Special Study Group of the Royal Institute of International Affairs on "The Colonial Problem"* (Oxford University Press, 1937), "has defended with great force a thesis he laid down in 1923: that the development of cultivation by and for the native definitely assists the formation of a more efficient labour force, the stabilization of the native family, the health and consequently the increase of the population." "It is a common error to regard the encouragement of native farming and the provision of labour for other purposes as antithetical ; they are complementary. In communities which are allowed to stagnate and to be content with a subsistence standard of living, there will be no natural incentive to wage-earning. A flourishing and progressive native community, with increasing wants, will find in wage-earning a welcome additional source of income." (p. 139.)

country is in the position of a firm with heavy overhead expenses and an inadequate turnover." In other words, the effective population must be increased and the efforts of the community utilized more fully and to better purpose.

The weakest feature of South African economic life is, however, not only the failure to utilize much potential effort, but also the misdirection of the efforts of those who are occupied in certain enterprises which can obtain command over their services too easily, and can utilize them for purposes which, from the point of view of the economy as a whole, are relatively uneconomic—in fact, third- and fourth-rate activities. Stated in economic terms, there is an extremely wide gap between the individual and the social net product of such labour. This gap is increased because there is little incentive to provide for the training, education and social improvement of the workers, so that, while the utility of their labour to the individual employers may at times be large, its value to the society is often low. Significant of this gap is the belief that native education is a luxury which the Union cannot afford,[1] whereas, in fact, it is of course the *sine qua non* of the increased productivity of the society as a whole. There is, moreover, no reason for the belief that the gap between the individual and the social net product of labour exists only among non-Europeans. On the contrary, its existence in their case necessarily implies wrong diversions of the efforts of the European section of the economy as well, since the National Income results from the co-operant efforts of all sections of the society.

XII

THE OBSTACLES TO INVESTMENT.

As is to be expected, the fundamental obstacles to increased productivity which have been discussed in this chapter greatly influence the direction and opportunities for new investment.

Investment from abroad depends on the capacity of economies to receive resources and to utilize them; investment from internal resources depends on the size of the National Income

---

[1] I have discussed this question in *Our Changing World-view: Africa in the Re-making.* (University of the Witwatersrand Press, 1932.)

stream, and therefore on the success with which the economy utilizes the efforts of its population in conjunction with its natural resources. Eventually a debtor country, if it makes good use of the resources borrowed or otherwise obtained by it from abroad, so increases its own National Income that it no longer requires to obtain capital from abroad, and may in fact become a creditor instead of a debtor country.

That the Union is still so dependent on the supply of capital from abroad is but another aspect of its low National Income, due to the fact that the efforts of its whole population are not being fully and effectively utilized.

In fact, investment in the Union from abroad is inevitably restricted by the barriers which in general prevent the broadening of economic activity. The growth of the National Income is consequently retarded, and so also is the rate at which the economy can itself create or accumulate capital.

Significant of this situation is the fact that probably three-quarters of the total capital invested in the Union from abroad in the past has been utilized in the mineral industries and the urban communities directly and indirectly serving them. The rest has flowed mainly into those rural areas in which the State has undertaken public works such as the construction of railways, or in which there has been protected or subsidized production of one kind or another. Even recently, during the largest boom in South Africa's history, private capital investment has taken place along established channels. The large sums of capital which have flowed to South Africa have again been directed into gold mining, or, to a lesser extent, into protected and sheltered industrial enterprises directly or indirectly connected with it. Capital which could not find opportunities in these directions has been utilized to inflate the values of land and urban property and of securities in the Stock Markets. The Union provides an example of a country in which the "marginal efficiency" of capital is exceptionally low in most enterprises not in some way connected with mining.

The great progress which has been achieved in the past on the basis of mineral exploitation and through the investment of capital from abroad tends to hide the poverty of the great mass, not only of the native and coloured, but also of the European population. That is why the basic and most urgent problem which faces the Union is to increase the productivity of its population. "The greatest flexibility, elasticity and freedom in the fitting of workers into jobs and the arrangement of terms of employment is called for if the economic growth of the country is not to be retarded."[1]   Indeed, if the necessary changes by which this can be achieved are not inaugurated, there is reason to believe that the rate of economic progress in the Union will be seriously retarded.   The lesson which other African territories can learn from the economic history of the Union is that, in the last resort, economic progress depends on the aptitude effectively to organize the efforts of the population and to educate and train its backward members, and that there is no real substitute for this slow and difficult task.

This is one of the conclusions of Professor Clay's *Report on Southern Rhodesia* (p. 43). It is equally applicable to the Union.

CHAPTER V

AFRICA JOINS THE WORLD ECONOMY

SECTION I

FOREIGN INVESTMENT IN AFRICA

"Zahlen regieren die Welt nicht aber sie Zeigen wie sie regiert werden muss."—GOETHE.

I

PREVIOUS ESTIMATES.

THE only comprehensive estimate of the amount of foreign capital in Africa which has been undertaken previously is that which forms part of the well-known calculations by Sir George Paish in papers published in the *Journal of the Royal Statistical Society* (in 1909 and 1911[1]) and subsequently in the *Statist*,[2] which brought his calculations up to the end of 1913. He estimated that, to the end of 1910, the British capital invested in the whole of Africa amounted to £455 millions, but this figure included an amount of £44 millions invested in Egypt which falls outside the purview of this study. The total of £455 millions did not include an allowance for capital invested privately, but referred only to what I have defined as "listed capital". The *Economist's* statistics of new capital issues were separately extracted for Africa as a whole, from 1900 onwards (see Table 26). From that date to 1910 an amount of £176 millions of new capital was subscribed for Africa; probably, therefore, the amount of British "listed capital"[3] in Africa about 1900 was roughly £235 millions.

[1] Vol. lxxii, part 3, 1909, and vol. lxxiv, part 2, 1911.
[2] February, 1914.
[3] The reader is reminded that "Africa" refers only to the territories listed on p. 2 of Chapter I ; Paish's figures for Egypt have, therefore, been deducted.

At this time the amount of non-British capital invested in Africa was very small as development, beyond the borders of the territories now comprised in the Union of South Africa, the Rhodesias and British West Africa, had hardly begun. It is probable that the total foreign, including private investments in Africa at the turn of the century did not exceed £275 millions.

From the figures published by Paish in the *Statist* and from other information, it is possible to arrive at a rough estimate of the position at the end of 1913. The listed capital for South Africa, including Rhodesia, according to Paish was £370 millions, and the investment in West Africa £37 millions.[1] Making allowance for non-listed capital, the total for South and West Africa can be regarded as £430 millions, but this does not include grants-in-aid. To this may be added roughly £40 millions for capital invested in the Belgian Congo and £85 millions, which includes an allowance for non-listed capital, for the German colonies. The investment from abroad in French possessions may be regarded as amounting to £25 millions, and roughly a further £30 millions must be added for the investments in British East and Central Africa, the Anglo-Egyptian Sudan, and the remaining non-British territories. It remains to make an allowance for the grants-in-aid to British territories, which may be regarded as amounting to some £20 millions, including those made to West African colonies. The total of these sums amounts to £610 millions and may be regarded as a maximum.

An interesting point arises from Paish's estimates for the Union, which include Rhodesia. A separate calculation made by me indicates that the amount of listed capital invested in Rhodesia to the end of 1913 was roughly £50 millions. If this is subtracted from Paish's figures for South Africa, the amount of British capital in the Union at the end of 1913 would appear to have been approximately £320 millions. To this must be added an allowance for non-listed and for non-British capital, which can be taken as £30 millions, which brings the total foreign investment in the Union to £350 millions. This figure must,

---

[1] An incidental point that is worthy of note in Paish's calculation is the considerable amount of capital which was subscribed for Africa in London between 1907 and 1913. According to his figures the total is some £71 millions, which is higher than that of the *Economist* new issues.

however, be used with caution; it cannot be regarded as more than a rough approximation.

Paish's estimates have not been arrived at on the same basis as my own calculations presented below. Nevertheless, the figure of £350 millions, when compared with my own estimate of £523 millions as the total investment in the Union to the end of 1936, is of some interest. It suggests that, broadly speaking, the average rate of capital investment for the whole of the two periods from 1870 to 1913 and from 1914 to 1936 has been approximately the same. In the first period, the average annual amount of capital, if we take the capital invested to have been £350 millions, is seen to be £8 millions. In the second period, on the basis of £173 millions as the total capital invested, the average is £7·8 millions. This comparison is, of course, a general one.

The total foreign investment in Africa to the end of 1936, according to my calculations, amounted to £1,322 millions, so that, without considering repayments and capital wastage, it would appear that a larger sum than that invested in Africa before the War was made available from 1914 to 1936. In the Union of South Africa, however, the total amount invested during and after the War has been smaller than before 1913, so that the greater part of the foreign investment in Africa since that date has found its way into the other territories included in this study.

This conclusion is supported by Table 26, which shows the annual amount of new issues of listed capital for (a) South Africa, and (b) for all African territories in London as registered by the *Economist*, and kindly extracted for me from its files from 1900 onwards. The percentage which the South African issues are of the total issues in Africa for each year is also given.

It is noteworthy that, since the War, the percentage which the new capital issues[1] for Africa have formed of the total new Overseas capital issues in London has been considerably higher than it was before 1913. This is indicated by Table 27.

The exceptionally high percentage for the quinquennium 1900–04 is due to the large loans raised for reconstruction after the Boer War. The rise in the percentage of African issues to all

[1] As listed by the *Economist*.

TABLE 26.—*Economist Issues.*

Year.	Total African £000.	Total South African £000.	South African as Percentage of Total African.
1900 . . .	4,939	3,563	72·1
1901 . . .	6,059	2,621	43·3
1902 . . .	22,867	20,205	88·4
1903 . . .	39,088	36,562	93·5
1904 . . .	22,294	21,696	97·3
1905 . . .	20,565	15,265	74·2
1906 . . .	5,077	2,722	53·6
1907 . . .	4,053	3,576	88·2
1908 . . .	8,034	7,269	90·5
1909 . . .	13,043	10,166	77·9
1900–09 .	146,019	123,645	84·7
1910 . . .	8,848	2,677	30·3
1911 . . .	12,362	4,895	39·6
1912 . . .	5,691	3,706	65·1
1913 . . .	7,767	5,793	74·6
1914 . . .	7,532	5,080	67·4
1915 . . .	3,690	3,412	92·5
1916 . . .	...	...	...
1917 . . .	...	...	...
1918 . . .	136	136	100·0
1919 . . .	15,123	3,300	21·8
1910–19 .	61,149	28,999	47·4
1920 . . .	13,037	458	3·5
1921 . . .	20,589	12,641	61·4
1922 . . .	3,298	1,460	44·3
1923 . . .	15,772	5,544	35·2
1924 . . .	14,785	9,508	64·3
1920–24 .	67,481	29,611	43·9
1925 . . .	14,616	5,471	37·4
1926 . . .	6,261	4,792	76·5
1927 . . .	28,180	8,673	30·8
1928 . . .	15,225	4,242	27·9
1929 . . .	10,767	2,239	20·8
1925–29 .	75,049	25,417	33·9
1930 . . .	24,381	13,147	53·9
1931 . . .	8,924	397	4·4
1932 . . .	4,498	...	...
1933 . . .	6,073	1,651	27·2
1934 . . .	16,999	8,317	48·9
1930–34 .	60,875	23,512	38·6
1935 . . .	5,934	3,508	59·1
1936 . . .	18,656	15,095	80·9

TABLE 27.—*New Capital Issues for Africa as a Percentage of Total New Overseas Issues in London.*

				Total Overseas Issues. £(000).	Total African Issues. £(000).	Percentage of African to Total Issues.
1900–4	.	.	.	48·0(a)	19·0	39·6
1905–9	.	.	.	106·1(a)	10·2	9·6
1907	.	.	.	79·3(a)	4·0	5·0
1908	.	.	.	132·2	8·0	6·1
1909	.	.	.	163·7	13·0	7·9
1910	.	.	.	207·1	8·8	4·2
1911	.	.	.	165·6	12·4	7·5
1912	.	.	.	165·5	5·7	3·4
1913	.	.	.	160·6	7·8	4·9
1914	.	.	.	148·1	7·5	5·1
1910–4	.	.	.	169·4	8·4	5·0
1915	.	.	.	(b)		
1915–9	.	.	.	(b)		
1919	.	.	.	49·9	15·1	30·3
1920–4	.	.	.	106·2	13·5	12·7
1925–9	.	.	.	115·3	15·0	13·0
1930–4	.	.	.	53·1	12·2	23·0
1935–6	.	.	.	47·3	12·3	26·0

(a) C. K. Hobson's estimate. *Cf. The Export of Capital.* (London, 1914.)
(b) Unavailable.

issues is partly due to the well-known fact that, since the War, new capital issues in London for the Empire have greatly increased in importance, whereas those for foreign countries have declined.

II

THE METHOD OF CALCULATION.

As has been stated in Section II of Chapter I, my calculations are based on a direct estimate of the capital from abroad invested in Africa from 1870 to 1936. As no reliable information exists as to the amount of capital that has been repaid or lost, I decided to ignore this problem of capital wastage, and not to attempt a calculation of the "outstanding" capital in African territories at any particular dates. In certain cases, particularly in regard to Government borrowing, fairly exact information as to capital repayments is available, but for the sake of consistency such repayments have not been deducted from my estimates of the total capital, since I am endeavouring to show the total amount which was in fact invested during the whole of the period. Of course, loans specifically raised for repayments or conversions have not been included, as this would have led to duplication.

My estimates have been arrived at by examining separately all the investments of capital (*a*) according to geographical area, and (*b*) broadly speaking, according to the purposes for which it was raised. All capital raised by or with the assistance of Governments or Public Authorities was traced from the published accounts. Special calculations of all Government operations, Municipal borrowing and railway loans were made for each territory for which sufficiently detailed information was available. It was possible to do this in detail for British, Belgian and the ex-German colonies, but in less detail and with a smaller degree of accuracy in the case of French and Portuguese possessions, for which many of the figures are only approximate. Moreover, the revenue, expenditure, public debt, grants-in-aid and loan grants for each British territory were extracted from 1900 onwards. The same calculations were made for the Belgian Congo since the War and for part of the pre-war period.

As regards private listed capital, the same procedure was adopted wherever possible, and a large number of company reports or summaries thereof published in the financial press were examined and tabulated. In doing this, my detailed studies of the capital invested in the Witwatersrand gold-mining industry were largely drawn upon, and were used as a basis for similar calculations for other mining enterprises in Africa wherever the material available permitted. Where detailed calculations were not possible, the information provided by the *Economist* issues of overseas capital were used as a basis for further estimates.[1]

It should be specifically noted that, as is shown below, no *direct estimates* have been possible for (*a*) the capital brought in by settlers or immigrants, and (*b*) such investments by private persons in private ventures or such loans by private persons to other private persons as are not disclosed to the general public in published accounts or in the financial press. Moreover, no estimate has been made of the investments abroad of capital by persons resident in African territories.

[1] These were also supplemented by information from the considerable range of special studies and reports of official commissions and committees of inquiry, and from special memoranda dealing with the industries concerned.

The estimates represent the total amount of capital actually subscribed abroad and can be classified as follows:

1. *Government Capital.*—This includes the net amounts of capital (*i. e.* excluding conversions) obtained through loans, grants-in-aid, and grants from the Colonial Development Fund, including loans and securities of municipalities and other local authorities.[1]

2. *Private Listed Capital.*—This includes the net amounts of capital subscribed for non-government enterprises listed on the Stock Exchange or in the financial press. It comprises both equity and loan capital.

A considerable part of the capital invested in African territories from abroad in mining, financial and exploration companies resulted from the purchase by overseas investors of what were, in fact, vendors' and promoters' shares. Where the sales of vendors' shares abroad were important, as in the gold-mining industry, they have been included, but an endeavour has been made to eliminate vendors' shares which did not give rise to the inflow of capital from abroad. The total capital raised abroad under the headings of 1 and 2 are referred to in this study as "Listed Capital".

3. *Non-Listed Capital.*—It has not been possible to make similar direct calculations for investments made by private persons abroad in private enterprises in Africa of a kind not disclosed to the general public in prospectuses or published accounts, nor has any direct calculation been possible of capital brought in by settlers and/or immigrants. Nevertheless, in view of the fact (*a*) that immigration has been relatively small, and (*b*) that private capital for commerce, industry and agriculture has been mainly accumulated from local sources, and (*c*) that all such non-listed investment has been largely conditioned by the development of specific kinds of enterprises, *e. g.* mining, communications, public utilities, etc., the writer is of the opinion that the

---

[1] War expenditures by European powers in African territories have been excluded where possible as, for example, the expenditure by Great Britain on the Boer War and by Germany on the Native wars in South-West Africa in 1907 and 1909, and the Ashanti wars, where the expenditure was charged to the Gold Coast and was subsequently repaid by it. Recurring subsidies and grants-in-aid were included, although these were often necessitated by expenditures on permanent military establishments.

amount of this non-listed investment may (except in a few special cases) be regarded as amounting to between 10% and 15% of the total capital raised abroad in the form of listed capital. All such undisclosed investments are referred to in this study as "non-listed capital".

III

THE AMOUNT OF FOREIGN CAPITAL.

The amount of foreign capital invested in each African territory from 1870 or from the commencement of colonization to 1936 is shown in Table 28, and the proportion per cent. which the various types of foreign capital in each territory are of the total amounts so invested from abroad in Africa[1] as a whole is shown in Table 29. These two tables are largely self-explanatory, but the following special features should be noted:

Union of South Africa.—Of the total private listed capital, amounting to roughly £251 millions, invested in the Union of South Africa, roughly two-thirds found its way into mining, and, as was shown in Chapter IV, gold mines absorbed by far the largest part. My estimates indicate that of the balance about two-fifths was invested in commerce, agriculture and industry, and three-fifths in land-owning, financial (including banking and insurance) and investment companies. It should be mentioned that the duplication involved owing to the re-investment by financial companies in mining or other ventures has been eliminated as far as possible.

South-West Africa.—In South-West Africa, of the private listed capital by far the largest part has been invested in mining and in exploration work connected therewith. Mention should be made of an interesting calculation by Professor Th. Marx[2] of the *value* of the private enterprise in all German colonies. The basis of the calculations used by him is different from that required in my investigations, but the material presented by him has been found to be of considerable value.

---

[1] The reader is reminded that Africa refers to the territories south of the Sahara and the Anglo-Egyptian Sudan, and includes only those territories referred to on p. 2, Chapter I.

Cf. Koloniale Rundschau, 1930, Nos. 4/5/6.

Southern and Northern Rhodesia.—The relatively large amount of private listed capital for Northern and Southern Rhodesia is partly due to the fact that, for over twenty-five years, the territories were administered by the British South Africa Company. The capital raised by it for the Rhodesian Railway System[1] (mainly by debentures guaranteed by the B.S.A. Company) has been included under the heading of public listed capital, of which it forms the largest part. From 1891 to 1918, the British South Africa Company claimed to have spent over £20 millions in Southern Rhodesia ; this expenditure was alleged to have been in excess of receipts by £7,238,000. The Chartered Company was awarded £4,435,000 by the Southern Rhodesia Commission which reported on its administration. In my calculation of the capital in Southern Rhodesia allowance has been made for the amount invested under the Chartered Company's *régime*.

Of the total private listed capital, 90% (approximately £48 millions) has been invested in mining, but this includes a certain amount of capital of financial, land and exploration companies. The balance of the private listed capital has found its way into commerce, agriculture and, to a very small extent, into industry. It is of interest to note[2] that, prior to 1904, some £44½ millions of nominal capital had been registered for mining and exploration companies in *Southern* Rhodesia (excluding approximately £6 millions of British South Africa Company capital). At least one-third of this nominal capital was registered before 1896, and, up to 1904, at least £10 millions of cash was invested in mining in the territory. It is therefore significant that, as late as 1909, the dividends paid on the whole of the nominal capital (£44½ millions) did not exceed £500,000 per annum; in the earlier years the dividends were even less. The bulk of the listed capital for gold mining was invested prior to 1913. Thereafter, re-investments from profits, and, even more so, the capital invested by large numbers of private individuals operating small mines, became important. In Northern Rhodesia, of course, base metal

[1] The capital invested in the Beira Railway in Portuguese territory has been included under that of the Rhodesian Railway System.

[2] On the basis of figures given in "Twenty-Five Years of Mining," by Edward Ashmead (reprinted from the *Mining Journal*, London, 1909), and certain other information.

TABLE 28.—*The Amount of the Capital Invested in Africa from Abroad by Individual Territories, 1870–1936.*
(a) British Territories.

	Listed Capital.			Non-Listed Capital.		Total Capital.
	Public Listed Capital.(a)	Private Listed Capital.	Total Listed Capital.	Estimated Percentage to Total Listed Capital.	Amount.	Listed + Non-Listed.
	£(000).	£(000).	£(000).	%.	£(000).	£(000).
Union of South Africa	(aa)224,089 }546	250,835	475,470	10	47,547	523,017
Basutoland and Swaziland						
South-West Africa	21,557 }886	7,228	28,785(b)	10	2,879	31,664
Bechuanaland						
Southern Rhodesia	(c)35,993 }2,731	53,484	93,094	10	9,309	102,403
Northern Rhodesia						
Total	285,802	311,547	597,349	...	59,735	657,084
Nigeria	34,721	36,790(d)	71,511(d)	5	3,576	75,087
Gold Coast	13,462	20,160	33,622	5	1,681	35,303
Sierra Leone	2,454(e)	750 (j)	3,204	5	160	3,364
Gambia	234	(j)	234	5	12	246
Sundry West African Issues	...	2,730	2,730	...	...	2,730
Total West Africa	50,871	60,430	111,301	...	5,429	116,730
Anglo-Egyptian Sudan	36,143(f)	5,145 (f)	41,288	5	2,064	43,352
British Somaliland	2,840(g)	(j)	2,840	5	142	2,982
Kenya and Uganda	31,542	8,583	49,125	15	6,019	46,144
Tanganyika	31,211 }129	15,841	47,181(h)	10	4,718	51,899
Zanzibar	129					
Nyasaland	10,298(i)	1,000	11,298	7½	848	12,146
Total	112,163	30,569	142,732	...	13,791	156,523
Miscellaneous	...	10,970	10,970	...	...	10,970
Total all British Territories	448,836	413,516	862,352	...	78,955	941,307

(b) Non-British Territories.

French:							
French Equatorial Africa .	15,248	5,000	20,248	...	5	1,012	21,260
French West Africa .	16,477	12,500	28,977	...	5	1,449	30,426
Togo and Cameroons .	11,306	6,431	17,737(k)	...	5	887	18,624
Total French .	43,031	23,931	66,962	...	...	3,348	70,310
Portuguese: (l)							
Angola .	10,188	19,553(m)	29,741	...	7½	2,230	31,971
Mozambique .	8,444	23,157	31,601(n)	...	10	3,160	34,761
Total Portuguese .	18,632	42,710	61,342	...	...	5,390	66,732
Belgian:							
Belgian Congo including Ruanda Urundi .	35,846	100,670	136,516	...	5	6,821	143,337
Total Belgian .	35,846	100,670	136,516	...	...	6,821	143,337
Total Non-British .	97,509	167,311	264,820	...	...	15,559	280,379
Grand Total (Total British and Non-British Territories) .	546,345	580,827	1,127,172	...	...	94,514	1,221,686

(a) Up to the end of 1935 only. (aa) Includes £29,165(000) raised abroad by municipalities and private Public Utility Companies.
(b) Includes £26,557(000) German investment. Excludes the Public Debt and the accumulated railway loss owing to the Union of South Africa.
(c) Includes £25,930(000) of capital invested in the Rhodesian Railway System which extends into Bechuanaland and Portuguese East Africa. Includes also capital raised abroad by sundry Public Utility Companies—£897(000).
(d) Includes capital invested not only in Nigeria, but in other West African territories by such companies as the African and Eastern Trading Corporation and the United Africa Company.
(e) Excludes domestic loans which are assumed to have been subscribed for within the colony.
(f) Includes the capital and debenture issues of companies controlled by the Sudan Government, and the loans and grants made to the Sudan Government by the Egyptian Treasury.
(g) 1900 to 1936 only.
(h) Includes £33,576(000) capital invested in German East Africa.
(i) Includes approximately £4,000(000) of private railway capital after making allowance for duplication, and after including Trans-Zambesi Railway.
(j) Negligible.
(k) Includes £15,827(000) capital invested in German Togoland and Cameroons. The post-war figures are for the French Mandates only.
(l) Portuguese Guinea has been omitted. Capital investment therein is unimportant.
(m) Includes approximately £16,000(000) of British capital, the great bulk of which is in the Benguella Railway.
(n) Includes approximately £20,000(000) British capital. The capital invested in Portuguese East Africa by the Rhodesia and Nyasaland Railway systems has been included under Rhodesia and Nyasaland respectively.

TABLE 29.—Classes of Investment as Percentage of the Total Capital Invested from Abroad in Africa by Individual Territories.

	"Public Listed" Capital in each Territory as Percentage of "Public Listed" Capital in all Territories.	"Private Listed" Capital in each Territory as Percentage of "Private Listed" Capital in all Territories.	Total "Listed" Capital in each Territory as Percentage of Total "Listed" Capital in all Territories.	Total Capital in each Territory as Percentage of Total Capital in all Territories.	Total Capital in each British Territory as Percentage of Total British Capital in all Territories.	"Public Listed" Capital as Percentage of Total Capital in each Territory.
Union of South Africa	41·01 }	43·17	42·17	42·81	55·54	42·85
Basutoland and Swaziland	·10 }					
South-West Africa	3·94	1·24	2·55	2·59	3·37	68·08
Bechuanaland	·16 }					
Southern Rhodesia	6·59 }	9·22	8·25	8·38	10·88	38·68
Northern Rhodesia	·51 }					
Total	52·31	53·63	52·97	53·78	69·79	43·50
Nigeria	6·35	6·34	6·35	6·15	7·97	46·24
Gold Coast	2·45	3·47	2·98	2·89	3·75	38·13
Sierra Leone	·46	·14	·28	·28	·36	72·95
Gambia	·04	...	·03	·02	·03	...
Sundry West Africa	...	·47	·24	·22	·29	...
Total West Africa	9·30	10·42	9·88	9·56	12·40	43·58

Anglo-Egyptian Sudan	6·62	·89	3·65	3·55	4·60	83·37
British Somaliland	·53	...	·26	·24	·32	...
Kenya and Uganda	5·77	1·48	3·57	3·78	4·91	68·36
Tanganyika	5·71 }	2·72	4·18	4·25	5·52	60·14
Zanzibar	·02 }	·17	1·01	·99	1·29	84·79
Nyasaland	1·89					
Total	20·54	5·26	12·68	12·81	16·64	71·66
Miscellaneous Issues	...	1·88	·97	·90	1·17	...
Total British Territories	82·15	71·19	76·50	77·05	100·00	47·68
French Equatorial Africa	2·79	·87	1·80	1·74	...	71·72
French West Africa	3·01	2·15	2·57	2·49	...	54·15
Togo and Cameroons	2·08	1·11	1·57	1·53	...	60·71
Total French	7·88	4·13	5·94	5·76	...	61·20
Angola	1·87	3·37	2·64	2·62	...	31·87
Mozambique	1·54	3·99	2·81	2·84	...	24·29
Total Portuguese	3·41	7·36	5·45	5·46	...	27·92
Belgian Congo, Ruanda Urundi	6·56	17·33	12·11	11·73	...	25·01
Total Non-British	17·85	28·81	23·50	22·95	...	34·78
Grand Total (British and Non-British)	100·00	100·00	100·00	100·00	...	44·72

mining is the basis of all economic development. Nearly £25 millions of capital from abroad was made available for the copper industry during the past decade.

Nigeria.—The amounts given for the public and private listed capital in Nigeria are roughly equal. Of the private listed capital, by far the largest part has been invested through the activities of the trading companies, whose gradual amalgamation into the present large concerns, among which the United Africa Company stands pre-eminent, has been so characteristic a feature of economic development in Nigeria in particular, and West Africa in general. An exact calculation of the investment in the companies now controlled by the United Africa Company is not possible, but from certain private information it is clear that the amount is not less than £25 millions. If all the earlier companies, which were subsequently amalgamated, had been taken into account, the amount would have been considerably larger. Of course, a considerable part of this capital was not invested in the West African colonies themselves, and no doubt much of it was accumulated out of profits of the West African trade. The capital invested in the mining industry, mainly tin mining, has been appreciable though relatively not as important.

Gold Coast.—In this territory the private listed capital invested in gold mining and more recently in manganese production has been the most important. It is of some interest to note that Ashmead[1] listed a very large number of companies, commencing with 7 in 1881, which were registered for gold mining and exploration ventures in the Gold Coast and also for operations along the West Coast in general. In 1900, he listed 82 and, in 1901, some 220 new mining exploration companies for West African activities, and there was also a considerable number of new companies in 1902 and 1903, although a decline had by then set in. In fact, Ashmead listed altogether 476 companies as having been registered from 1880 to 1904 for West Africa, the Gold Coast and the Ivory Coast; the nominal capital of these companies amounted to nearly £43 millions. There is no clear indication of the exact purpose for which, or the exact geographical

[1] "Twenty-five Years of Mining", by Edward Ashmead. London, *The Mining Journal*, 1909, p. 62 ff.

area in which these companies were intended to, or did in fact operate. There is no doubt that much of the nominal capital was not issued, and that much of the issued capital was never spent anywhere near West Africa in general or the Gold Coast in particular. In fact, notwithstanding the repeated West African mining booms and the considerable speculation in the shares of these companies, it is highly significant that in 1904 there were only some 13 companies which could report any gold production at all, and, of these 13, there were only 4 who returned an output worth more than £10,000. These four producing companies were the predecessors of the existing mines in the Gold Coast. In 1905 gold production in the Gold Coast amounted to only 167,000 ounces. Notwithstanding the early West Coast mining booms, I regard the estimates of private listed capital for the Gold Coast as too low. It must not be forgotten that we are concerned in this study with capital actually invested in the territories.

Kenya and Uganda.—Of the private listed capital in Kenya, the figure for which given in Table 28 is relatively small, by far the largest part has been invested in agricultural estates, particularly sisal and coffee plantations. The private listed capital so invested must be supplemented by a considerable amount, probably at least £4 millions, of private non-listed capital brought in by settlers themselves and not raised by land and agricultural companies. It is difficult to be certain that this estimate of private listed capital and private non-listed capital is adequate. Dr. Salvadori, who has an intimate knowledge of Kenya, and has conducted a large number of investigations of conditions in that territory, expressed the opinion to me[1] that probably £20 millions was invested from abroad in agriculture. He based this estimate partly on his belief that very large amounts of capital had been wasted in the early years after the War by settlers with considerable means. I have preferred to estimate the actual capital invested from abroad on a more conservative basis, but Dr. Salvadori's figures should be borne in mind.

[1] I also had the benefit of receiving his interesting Memorandum, *An Approximate Evaluation of the Amount of Capital required for the Mise en Valeur of the European Farms in Kenya.* This evaluation was made for a different purpose than that of calculating the amount of capital invested in Kenya from abroad.

Tanganyika.—A very large part of the total listed capital in Tanganyika was made available before the War while the territory belonged to Germany.[1] Of the private listed capital which has been invested since the War, by far the most important part has found its way into agriculture and plantation activities. In recent years, of course, mineral exploration and mining have grown in importance.

It was not always possible to follow the general method of calculation previously described owing to the paucity of the information available, while for the Non-British territories the *Economist* figures of new capital issues in London did not provide a satisfactory basis.

Belgian Congo.—For the Belgian Congo a considerable amount of statistical data was available both for Government and for non-Government economic activities, but it was difficult to piece this together owing (*a*) to the fluctuations in the value of the Belgian currency and (*b*) to the scattered nature of much of the data, particularly those relating to development before the War.

The amount of capital invested in the Belgian Congo has been arrived at (i) by a detailed examination of the official accounts of the territory and of numerous company reports or abstracts, in particular, those of mining, railway and exploration enterprises ; (ii) by utilizing the data published in the Belgian Senate Commission reports relating to the capital invested in all enterprises in the Belgian Congo since the War; and (iii) from some very interesting estimates given by Professor M. W. van der Velde in his book, *Economique Belge et Congo Belge.*[2]

The official estimate[3] by the Belgian Senate Commission of the capital invested in the Belgian Congo up to 1932 in unstabilized

---

[1] For this territory the estimates of Th. Marx, previously referred to, are also of considerable interest and have been drawn upon by me. Marx estimated that, before the War, there were some 270 commercial and industrial undertakings, 8 cotton plantations, 60 coffee plantations and about 440 plantations and farms for mixed agricultural products. There were 6 mining companies, but no success had as yet followed their activities.

[2] Antwerp, 1936. Editions des "Lloyd Anversois".

[3] Slightly revised ; original estimate is given in Report No. 85, Belgian Senate Session February 13th, 1934. It is possible that some of the estimates include 1933 as well, but most of the figures appear to be to the end of 1932 only. Railway figures have been estimated to 1934.

francs, *i. e.* by addition of pre-war gold francs and post-war paper francs, is as follows:

TABLE 30.—*Official Estimate of Capital Invested in the Belgian Congo to* 1932.

	Francs (000,000) Unstabilised.	Percentage to Total.
Railway[1] . . .	3,821 .	39·7
Other Transport . .	168 .	1·7
Mining . . .	1,891 .	19·7
Agriculture . . .	919 .	9·6
Commerce . . .	795 .	8·3
Real Estate . . .	378 .	3·9
Finance. . . .	289 .	3·0
Building . . .	140 .	1·5
Sundry Industries . .	1,213 .	12·6
Total .	9,614 .	100·0

This estimate is useful, because it shows the purposes for which the capital was utilized.

It will be noted that railways, transport and mining enterprises account for 61% of the capital invested in the Congo, excluding the Colonial Debt. It must not be forgotten, however, that a considerable portion of the capital which is listed under commerce, real estate, finance and sundry industries is, of course, due to secondary enterprises connected with mining and railway expansion, while a considerable portion of the railway system has been built to serve mineral exploitation. The amount invested in agriculture is only 9·6% of the total. The Government, however, has supported agricultural development both from loan funds and from ordinary revenue.[2]

The following table gives the total of new issues of capital invested in the Belgian Congo (excluding Government borrowing) from 1919-35 as estimated by Van der Velde. The amounts are stated both in paper and in gold francs, and the co-efficients used by Van der Velde for purposes of converting paper francs into gold francs have been added.

It should be noted that Van der Velde's figures do not agree in all cases with certain other estimates of new issues which are

---

[1] Railway figures have been estimated to 1934.

[2] The amount invested from loan funds for this purpose was approximately £765,000 from 1909–32, while the amount spent from revenue was approximately £1,500,000 over the same period.

TABLE 31.—*New Issues of Capital for the Belgian Congo*, 1919–35.

	Unstabilised Francs (Millions).		Value of Franc as Percentage of Pre-War Parity.		Value of Issues in Pre-War Gold Francs.
1919 . . .	29	.	65·5	.	19
1920 . . .	82	.	38	.	31
1921 . . .	23	.	38	.	9
1922 . . .	225	.	40	.	90
1923 . . .	61	.	27	.	17
1924 . . .	170	.	24	.	41
1925 . . .	367	.	25	.	92
1926 . . .	473	.	16	.	76
1927 . . .	1,293	.	14·5	.	187
1928 . . .	1,574	.	14·5	.	227
1929 . . .	1,406	.	14·5	.	201
1930 . . .	1,046	.	14·5	.	152
1931 . . .	1,623	.	14·5	.	235
1932 . . .	276	.	14·5	.	40
Total 1919/35 .	*8,648*				*1,417*
1933 . . .	118	.	14·5	.	17
1934 . . .	353	.	14·5	.	51
1935 . . .	105	.	10·4[1]	.	11
Total 1919/35 .	9,224				1.496

available, but they have been used by me because they present the general position most satisfactorily.[2]

If Van der Velde's total for the new issues from 1919 to 1932 is deducted from the total investment as estimated by the Senate Commission, with which my own calculations have been found to agree broadly, it will be seen that an amount of approximately 966 million Gold Francs of private listed capital was invested in the Belgian Congo up to 1919.

[1] New parity, as from March 30th, 1935.

[2] Gaston Eyskens in a very comprehensive article, "Les indices de la conjoncture économique du Congo Belge depuis la guerre (de 1919 à 1933)" (*Bulletin de l'Institut des Sciences Économiques*, Louvain, August, 1933) gives the following estimates:

Emissions de Valeurs Coloniales à Bruxelles, Apports en Nature Déduits, de 1919 à 1932 (milliers de francs).

1919:	29,806	.	1926:	473,549
1920:	81,437	.	1927:	944,455
1921:	23,139	.	1928:	1,514,455
1922:	225,040	.	1929:	1,330,490
1923:	60,651	.	1930:	739,060
1924:	170,217	.	1931:	421,155
1925:	367,488	.	1932:	101,304

After examining other data concerning the operations of Belgian Companies before the War, I have come to the conclusion that of this sum of 966,000,000 Gold Francs, equivalent to about £38 millions, approximately 483 million Gold Francs (about £19 millions) was invested in railways, and some 333 million Gold Francs (£13 millions) in mining, financial and exploration companies, and the balance of £6 millions was absorbed in other activities such as commerce, agriculture, real estate and sundry industries. My figures for this pre-war investment are higher than those arrived at by Van der Velde, and also exceed the estimates published in *L'Essor Economique Belge*[1], but as they are based on the analysis of Belgian Company reports I regard them as more accurate.

As far as Government capital invested in the Belgian Congo is concerned, it should be noted that the Public Debt stood at 249·5 million Francs (£10 millions) in 1909. Prior to 1921 there was practically no change in that figure, but since then it has been increased by nearly 3,500 million paper Francs, equivalent to about 600 million Gold Francs, *i. e.* £24 millions. There was a considerable rise in the Public Debt subsequent to 1928, as is shown by the following figures:

	1928. Francs.		1934. Francs.
Dette consolidée	1,767,440,883	.	2,367,639,883
Dette flottante	61,139,900	.	1,407,572,100
	1,828,580,783	.	3,775,211,983
Capitaux garantis (actions, obligations) .	711,361,000	.	2,646,466,250
Total .	2,539,941,783	.	6,421,678,233

The investment in the Belgian Congo from abroad can now be summarized as follows:

The total Private Listed[2] capital invested in the Belgian Congo to the end of 1935 amounts to	£100·7	(millions)
The Public Listed[3] capital (including an allowance for grants and subsidies by Belgium to the Colony during the last depression, but excluding issues guaranteed by the State for private companies)	35·8	,,
Total . .	136·5	,,

[1] Brussels, 1932.

[2] Including capital invested in railways which, in other territories, is included under Public Listed capital; an allowance has been made for duplications arising from the fact that some part of the Government loans was invested in private companies.

[3] For the years 1933–5 there was a subvention of 165 million francs per annum from Belgium. For 1936 the subvention was 155 million francs.

The Government of the Congo has guaranteed interest or dividends on portions of the capital of a considerable number of companies engaged in mining, exploration, transport and industrial or agricultural activities. In addition, as is well known, the Government has participated to a large extent in a considerable number of railway, mining and exploration companies, but actually, apart from obligations under its guarantees, the State did not invest large amounts of cash in these enterprises. To the 31st December, 1934, the Government had made itself responsible by guarantees of interest, dividends, etc., for an amount exceeding 2,600 million Francs, and the payments under these guarantees in 1934 amounted to 110 million Francs. The system of attracting private capital by means of concessions accounts for the relatively small proportion of the Government (Public Listed) capital actually invested in the Congo.

French Colonies.—It is very difficult to arrive at an estimate of foreign investment in the French dependencies both on account of the paucity of data, particularly in regard to the non-listed capital, and owing to the changes in the value of the franc. Some general estimates of the investment in the French Colonial Empire are available, but they are of relatively little value.[1] Others, as, for example, the well-known studies of Moulton and Lewis, *The French Debt Problem*, H. D. White, *The French International Accounts*, and G. Martin, *La Situation financiére de la France*, 1914–24, either do not deal specifically with the French Colonial Empire, or do not classify the investment according to geographical areas.

As the largest part of the investment in the French African colonies has taken place since the War, some of the excellent pre-war calculations of French capital abroad, such as those by Neymarck[2] and Yves Guyot,[3] were of restricted value for this study.

---

[1] For example, Southworth's *The French Colonial Venture* contains calculations which are frequently quoted, but they were not suitable for this study; they also suffer from a considerable number of inaccuracies and contradictions. On the other hand, an estimate in *l'Europe Nouvelle* of January 11th, 1930, is of interest, although it is of a very general nature.

[2] A. Neymarck, *Bulletin de l'Institut International de Statistique*, vol. xx, Part II, 1915, p. 1406.

[3] *Annals of the American Academy of Political and Social Science*, vol. lxviii, November, 1916.

The estimate given in Table 28 is based on an examination of all French loans for African Colonies, and also on an analysis of the nominal capital of companies operating in Africa. In making these calculations, I had the assistance of a well-known French economist, who kindly obtained a great deal of the material, available in Paris, for me. Although every effort has been made to make these estimates as comprehensive as possible, the fact that the data available are very inaccurate makes it necessary to regard the figures given as rough approximations. These remarks apply also to the Portuguese Colonies. Owing to the poverty of Portugal, the total amount invested by it in its African Colonies has been small, while the nationalistic policies adopted by it since the War have restricted foreign enterprise.

More than half of the capital invested in these territories is British and has been raised in London. Most of the British, and a portion of the Portuguese capital has been invested in railway and harbour works, and, of the Portuguese private capital, a large portion has gone into the development of the plantations which characterize the economy of Mozambique.

Although population estimates in Africa are very crude,[1] and all calculations utilizing them must be regarded largely as informed guesses, it is, nevertheless, of some interest to supplement the preceding tables by the following figures of the total overseas capital per head of the population of each territory. The figures are a useful index of the difference in the degree of development, and also show how relatively small is the amount of capital so far invested in Africa: the average for all the territory listed in Table 32 is less than £12·7 per head of the population.

The most striking facts which emerge from the tables of capital investment so far presented, are (a) the large preponderance of investment which has taken place under the ægis of Government; (b) the preponderance of capital invested in British territories; (c) the comparative importance of the Union of South Africa as a field of investment; and (d) the great role which mining has played in attracting capital to Africa.

It will be convenient at this stage to examine the first of these.

[1] Cf. R. R. Kuczinski, *Colonial Population*, Oxford, 1936.

TABLE 32.—*Total Overseas Capital per head of the Population of each African Territory.*

	Total Capital Invested. £(000).	Estimated Total Population. (000,000).	Capital per Head of the Population.
Union of South Africa } South-West Africa . }	554,681 .	9·9 .	55·8
Northern Rhodesia . } Southern Rhodesia . }	102,403 .	2·7 .	38·4
Nigeria	75,087 .	19·1 .	3·9
British West Africa . .	116,730 .	24·4 .	4·8
Anglo-Egyptian Sudan .	43,352 .	5·8 .	...
Kenya and Uganda . .	46,144 .	6·7 .	6·8
Total Kenya, Uganda, Tan- ganyika and Nyasaland .	110,189 .	13·5 .	8·1
French West Africa . .	30,426 .	14·7 .	2·1
French Equatorial Africa } Togo and Cameroons }	39,884 .	6·5 .	6·1
Total French Colonies .	70,310 .	21·2 .	3·3
Belgian Congo . . .	143,337 .	11·0 .	13·0
Angola and Mozambique .	66,732 .	6·8 .	9·8

IV

INVESTMENT BY GOVERNMENT.

The large proportion of capital investment under the ægis of Governments in Africa deserves special attention, because capital borrowed by or under the guarantees of Colonial Governments is obtained on terms which involve the payment of fixed interest, and Sinking Fund charges. This implies that a very large portion of African activities financed from abroad is conducted on a basis which involves regular payments outside the country, whether the capital invested in the territory is in fact yielding sufficient for these or not.

The percentage ratio of the public listed capital to all capital invested from abroad in each African territory, is shown in Table 29. It will be noted that the ratio ranges from 24% for Mozambique to 85% for Nyasaland; for British Southern Africa it is 43·5%, for British West Africa 43·6%, and for British East and Central Africa 71·7%. For all British territories in Africa taken together the ratio is 48%, while for the combined French possessions it is 61%. The ratio is only 25% for the Belgian Congo, largely owing to the concession and guarantee system, which has characterized the development of that territory.

A detailed statement of the Public Listed capital invested in each African territory is given in Table 33. This shows the total

TABLE 33.—*Detailed Statement of the " Public Listed Capital "(a) Invested in British African Territories, showing the Amount of Loans and Grants respectively.* £(000).

	Loans.(c)	Grants-in-Aid.(f)	Grants by Colonial Development Fund : Loan and Free Grants.(f)	Total Public Listed Capital.
Union of South Africa	224,089	...	...	224,089
Basutoland and Swaziland	55	309	182	546
South-West Africa	3,670	17,887(b)	...	21,557
Bechuanaland	...	797	89	886
Southern Rhodesia	35,993	...	...	35,993
Northern Rhodesia	2,347	...	384	2,731
Total	266,154	18,993	655	285,802
Nigeria	28,813	5,737(d)	171	34,721
Gold Coast	12,961	401	100	13,462
Sierra Leone	1,881	33	540	2,454
Gambia	200	9	25	234
Total	43,855	6,180	836	50,871
Anglo-Egyptian Sudan	25,391	10,752(e)	...	36,143
British Somaliland	256	2,539	45	2,840
Kenya	} 25,876 {	2,843	256	} 31,542
Uganda		2,548	19	
Tanganyika	22,905	7,870(b)	436	31,211
Zanzibar	100	...	29	129
Nyasaland	8,972	603	723	10,298
Total	83,500	27,155	1,508	112,163
Total all British Territories	393,509	52,328	2,999	448,836

(a) As shown in Table 28.
(b) In the case of South-West Africa this represents German Imperial Grants; in the case of Tanganyika the amount, to all intents and purposes, consists of German Imperial Grants.
(c) For explanatory notes, see Table 28.
(d) Includes £865,000 for appropriation of Niger Company.
(e) From the Egyptian Treasury.
(f) It should be noted that these figures are approximate. The method of classification of receipts into grants-in-aid, loan, and free grants has varied greatly in different territories and from time to time, while exact information has not been available in all cases.

amount of the public loans raised (excluding conversion loans), the total of the grants-in-aid, and, in the case of British territories, the loan and free grants given from the Colonial Development Fund.[1]

A point of great importance emerges from this table: if the grants-in-aid by the German Imperial Government to the German colonies before 1914 are excluded, the total grants-in-aid[2] to the British colonies in Africa for the whole of the period under review amount to less than £27 millions. Even including the loans and free grants from the Colonial Development Fund in recent years, the amount is still under £30 millions.

While this is, no doubt, a tribute to the rapidity and success with which the colonies were made financially independent of the mother country, yet, taking a wider point of view, it must be regarded as regrettable that only such a small sum could be spared in order to enable African territories to further developments for which they were unable to borrow. The relatively negative policy of forcing the territories to curtail development when they could not afford to increase the burden of their public debt appears to have held the field, and insufficient attention has been given to the need of devising other methods for fostering important developments requiring capital at low or even nominal rates of interest.

It is noteworthy that over half of the public listed capital in British territories has been invested in railways. Owing to its special importance, railway finance is considered in detail in a separate section of this chapter.

V

RESTRICTED DEVELOPMENT BEFORE 1913.

In considering investments in Africa, a point that must be stressed at the outset is the fact that, with the exception of the

---

[1] The figures in the table are approximate and also involve a small amount of duplication, owing to the fact that some of the African territories invested their Sinking Funds in the securities of other African States. A list of such holdings compiled for 1935 shows that the duplication involved does not exceed £25 millions. It should be noted that the public accounts do not always distinguish clearly between loan and free grants; moreover, what was originally a free grant may later be converted to a loan grant or *vice versa*.

[2] In regard also to grants-in-aid it should be noted that it was not always clear whether these were loan grants or free grants; sometimes what was a grant-in-aid was subsequently repaid or converted to a loan grant.

Union, and some of the West African colonies, economic development can be said to have got fully under way only during the quinquennium before the World War. It is not usually realized that most of these African territories were, as late as 1907, even less developed than Cape Colony more than thirty years before; even in 1935, the value of the export trade of Kenya, Uganda, Tanganyika, Nyasaland, South-West Africa, Northern Rhodesia and the Anglo-Egyptian Sudan was still below that of the Cape in 1875. The same considerations apply to Sierra Leone, Gambia, the Portuguese possessions, French Equatorial Africa, Togo and to the Cameroons.[1]

In 1880 the ordinary annual revenue of the Cape Colony, including the earnings of its railways, had reached £3 millions. Nigeria attained a similar total revenue only as late as 1913. Before the war there was no other colony in Africa which was able to show a revenue even approximating this figure. Moreover, most of the territories whose exports in 1935 were below those of Cape Colony fifty years ago fail even now to produce an annual revenue equal to that of Cape Colony at the earlier date.[2]

VI

THE RETARDING EFFECT OF THE GREAT WAR.

Economic progress in African territories, other than the Union, was retarded by the Great War, not only owing to the resulting setback to trade and settlement, but also because the supply of

---

[1] The value of all exports from Cape ports in 1875 amounted to nearly £6 millions (see Table 5, Chapter III). As late as 1907 the value of the domestic exports from Nigeria was £3·6 millions, and for all British West African territories taken together the figure was £7 millions. The only other British territory (excluding those now forming the Union) for which the exports reached a total of some importance at this time was Southern Rhodesia, for which they amounted to £2·3 millions. The whole of the French West African exports were valued at £3 millions, while the only other Non-British territory of importance was the Belgian Congo which, like French West Africa, was still in the stage of despoliation and yielded domestic exports valued at £2.3 millions. Statistics of the domestic exports and net imports (i.e. imports less re-exports) of each African territory for selected years from 1907 to 1935 are given in Tables 43 and 44, and of the total net trade of each territory in Table 45.

[2] A comparison of the annual revenues of each British African territory for selected years from 1907 to 1935 is given in Table 38, and of the annual expenditures in Table 40. Attention should be drawn to the "Note on African Statistics" in the Appendix.

TABLE 34.—*Amount and Proportion of Funded Debt in each British Territory in Africa for Selected Years.*

Rate of Interest %	Nigeria £(000)	Nigeria Per Cent of Total	Gold Coast £(000)	Gold Coast Per Cent	Sierra Leone £(000)	Sierra Leone Per Cent	West Africa £(000)	West Africa Per Cent	Anglo-Egyptian Sudan £(000)	A.-E. Sudan Per Cent	Kenya £(000)	Kenya Per Cent	Uganda £(000)	Uganda Per Cent	Nyasaland £(000)	Nyasaland Per Cent	Tanganyika £(000)	Tanganyika Per Cent	Northern Rhodesia £(000)	N. Rhodesia Per Cent	Southern Rhodesia £(000)	S. Rhodesia Per Cent	Total all other than Union of S.A. £(000)	Total Per Cent
1913.																								
3	…	…	1,098	51·6	…	…	1,098	9·1	…	…	…	…	…	…	…	…	…	…	…	…	…	…	1,098	8·8
3¼	…	…	…	…	…	…	…	…	…	…	…	…	…	…	…	…	…	…	…	…	…	…	…	…
3½	8,268	100·0	1,030	48·4	730	42·2	10,028	82·7	…	…	…	…	(T)296	100·0	(T)115	100·0	…	…	…	…	…	…	10,439	83·3
3¾	…	…	…	…	…	…	…	…	…	…	…	…	…	…	…	…	…	…	…	…	…	…	…	…
4	…	…	…	…	1,000	57·8	1,000	8·2	…	…	…	…	…	…	…	…	…	…	…	…	…	…	1,000	7·9
4½	…	…	…	…	…	…	…	…	…	…	…	…	…	…	…	…	…	…	…	…	…	…	…	…
5	…	…	…	…	…	…	…	…	…	…	…	…	…	…	…	…	…	…	…	…	…	…	…	…
5½	…	…	…	…	…	…	…	…	…	…	…	…	…	…	…	…	…	…	…	…	…	…	…	…
6	…	…	…	…	…	…	…	…	…	…	…	…	…	…	…	…	…	…	…	…	…	…	…	…
Total	8,268	100·0	(d) 2,128	100·0	1,730	100·0	12,126	100·0	(f)	…	(f)	…	296	100·0	(a) 115	100·0	…	…	…	…	…	…	12,537	100·0
Average Rate of Interest	3·5%	…	3·24%	…	3·79%	…	3·50%	…	…	…	…	…	3·5%	…	3·5%	…	…	…	…	…	…	…	3·5%	…
1925.																								
3	…	…	1,098	9·3	…	…	1,098	3·3	…	…	…	…	…	…	…	…	…	…	…	…	…	…	1,098	1·7
3¼	…	…	…	…	…	…	…	…	…	…	…	…	…	…	…	…	…	…	…	…	…	…	…	…
3½	4,046	21·0	1,030	8·7	730	42·2	5,806	17·7	…	…	(T)3,500	41·2	(T)226	20·5	155	23·6	…	…	…	…	…	…	9,687	15·2
3¾	…	…	…	…	…	…	…	…	…	…	…	…	…	…	…	…	…	…	…	…	…	…	…	…
4	5,700	29·5	1,035	8·8	1,000	57·8	7,735	23·6	1,500	11·1	…	…	(T)329	29·8	11	1·7	…	…	…	…	…	…	9,575	15·0
4½	…	…	4,628	39·3	…	…	4,628	14·1	5,693	41·5	…	…	…	…	…	…	…	…	…	…	…	…	10,221	16·1
5	…	…	…	…	…	…	…	…	…	…	…	…	(T)550	49·7	463	70·6	(T)3,135	100·0	…	…	4,000	100·0	8,148	12·8
5½	…	…	…	…	…	…	…	…	6,380	47·4	…	…	…	…	…	…	…	…	…	…	…	…	6,380	10·0
6	9,563	49·5	4,000	33·9	…	…	13,563	41·3	…	…	5,000	58·8	…	…	27	4·1	…	…	…	…	…	…	18,590	29·2
Total	19,309	100·0	11,791	100·0	1,730	100·0	32,830	100·0	13,573	100·0	8,500	100·0	1,105	100·0	656	100·0	3,135	100·0	…	…	4,000	100·0	63,699	100·0
Average Rate of Interest	4·88%	…	4·74%	…	3·79%	…	4·78%	…	4·92%	…	4·97%	…	4·39%	…	4·67%	…	5%	…	…	…	5%	…	4·84%	…

1932.

3	...	...	1,098	8·5	...	...	1,098	2·6	...	...	...	...	...	...	...	...	...	...	...	...	...	...	1,098	1·1
3¼	...	...	...	...	...	...	...	...	...	...	...	...	...	...	...	...	...	...	...	...	...	...	...	...
3½	4,046	14·5	1,030	7·9	730	34·1	5,806	13·5	...	...	...	...	...	...	134	4·3	...	...	...	...	...	...	5,940	6·2
3¾	...	...	...	...	...	...	...	...	...	...	...	...	...	...	...	...	...	...	...	...	...	...	...	...
4	5,700	20·5	1,035	8·0	1,000	46·7	7,735	18·0	1,500	9·8	...	...	...	...	9	0·3	3,500	40·3	...	...	...	...	12,744	13·3
4½	...	...	5,798	44·7	411	19·2	6,209	14·5	5,659	37·1	6,900	40·8	...	...	2,000	64·3	2,070	23·8	...	...	1,955	34·1	24,793	25·9
5	8,513	30·6	...	...	...	...	8,513	19·8	2,097	13·8	5,000	29·6	2,000	100·0	939	30·2	(T)3,121	35·9	1,250	100·0	3,776	65·9	26,696	27·9
5½	...	...	...	...	...	...	...	...	5,986	39·3	...	...	...	...	...	...	...	...	...	...	...	...	5,986	6·2
6	9,563	34·4	4,000	30·9	...	...	13,563	31·6	...	...	5,000	29·6	...	...	30	0·9	...	...	...	...	...	...	18,593	19·4
Total	27,822	100·0	12,961	100·0	2,141	100·0	42,924	100·0	15,242	100·0	16,900	100·0	2,000	100·0	3,112	100·0	8,691	100·0	1,250	100·0	5,731 (e)	100·0	95,850	100·0
Average Rate of Interest	4·92%	...	4·72%	...	3·92%	...	4·81%	...	4·91%	...	5·09%	...	5·0%	...	4·62%	...	4·48%	...	5%	...	4·83%	...	4·85%	...

1935.

3	4,188	15·0	...	...	307	17·9	4,495	10·8	...	...	...	...	...	...	1,570	32·7	...	...	...	...	...	...	6,065	6·1
3¼	...	...	...	...	...	...	...	...	...	...	...	...	...	...	...	...	...	...	...	...	2,750	34·6	2,750	2·8
3½	...	...	1,030	8·7	...	...	1,030	2·5	...	...	305	1·8	(T) 236	10·6	(T) 127	2·7	...	...	1,097	46·7	2,250	28·3	5,045	5·1
3¾	...	...	...	...	...	...	...	...	...	...	...	...	...	...	...	...	...	...	...	...	...	...	...	...
4	5,700	20·4	1,035	8·7	1,000	58·2	7,735	18·6	1,500	10·3	...	...	...	...	9	0·2	3,500	40·3	...	...	...	...	12,744	12·8
4½	...	...	5,798	48·9	411	23·9	6,209	14·9	5,419	37·3	6,900	40·0	...	...	2,000	41·7	2,070	23·8	...	...	1,955	24·6	24,553	24·7
5	8,513	30·4	...	...	...	...	8,513	20·5	1,991	13·7	5,000	29·1	2,000	89·4	1,062	22·1	(T)3,121	35·9	1,250	53·3	1,000	12·5	23,937	24·1
5½	...	...	...	...	...	...	...	...	5,633	38·7	...	...	...	...	...	...	...	...	...	...	...	...	5,633	5·7
6	9,563	34·2	4,000	33·7	...	...	13,563	32·7	...	...	5,000	29·1	...	...	30	0·6	...	...	...	...	...	...	18,593	18·7
Total	27,964	100·0	11,863 (h)	100·0	1,718	100·0	41,545	100·0	14,543	100·0	17,205	100·0	2,236	100·0	4,798 (b)	100·0	8,691 (c)	100·0	2,347	100·0	7,955 (e)(g)	100·0	99,320	100·0
Average Rate of Interest	4·83%	...	4·88%	...	3·94%	...	4·81%	...	4·90%	...	5·06%	...	4·84%	...	4·10%	...	4·48%	...	4·30%	...	3·85%	...	4·72%	...

The rates of interest shown in these Tables are the nominal rates at which each stock was issued. No allowance has been made for the various discounts at which issues were made. Most of the stocks included in these Tables were issued at a discount, and the actual burden of interest payments is somewhat higher than that shown. No allowance has been made for any expenses of issue. Where the financial year does not coincide with the calendar year the figures were taken as at 31st March of the year following that stated.

(T) Treasury loans.
(a) A small Treasury advance had been made, but there had been no public borrowing.
(b) Excluding non-interest bearing loans in aid of interest.
(c) Excludes the Colonial Development Fund loan of £26,000, on which the rate of interest has not been fixed.
(d) Excludes the net sum of £321,000 due to the Imperial Government in respect of the Ashanti disturbances.
(e) Excludes floating debt.
(f) Advances had been made by the Treasury, the rates of interest being unknown There had been no public borrowing.
(g) To March 1935 only.
(h) Part of this only was included in the Public Debt in 1914.

Overseas capital virtually ceased. Moreover, after the War the level of interest rates ruled high. It had been rising steadily for some years before the War. In fact, economic development of large parts of Africa has taken place for the most part during a period in which interest rates have been exceptionally high, as compared to the last quarter of the nineteenth century, when large sums of capital were made available for colonial development elsewhere. It was during this earlier period that the Cape, Natal, the Transvaal and the Orange Free State were able to borrow extensively abroad at low rates of interest, and could therefore undertake considerable development. The other African territories entered the world economy later, and were not able to borrow as cheaply. Their economic expansion was thus greatly curtailed.

The importance of this factor is shown by Table 34, which classifies, for each British territory in Africa, the Government loans comprising its funded debt at the end of the years 1913, 1925, 1932 and 1935. The loans are classified according to the specific nominal rates of interest[1] at which they were raised. The amounts raised at each rate are also shown as a percentage of the total funded debt for each year.

These figures are reclassified in Table 35, which gives the same information for the Union of South Africa on the one hand, and for all the British African territories combined on the other. For the Union the amounts of the internal and the external debt have been separated. This is not necessary for the British African colonies, as the internal debt is negligible. Both Tables show the average rate of interest on the whole of the funded debt for the different periods.

In 1913, the total funded debt in British Africa was £131 millions; in 1935, it had nearly trebled and stood at £347 millions. But, of the total in 1913, only £12 millions was accounted for by British territories other than the Union, and 97% of this sum was made up by the debt of British West Africa alone.[2] The loans

---

[1] The nominal rates of interest at which each stock was issued had to be used because insufficient information was available to enable an allowance to be made for the expenses of issue, or for any discounts at which the loans were raised. The nominal rates used, therefore, understate the real interest burden.

[2] Over 90% of this West African debt had been raised at or below 3½%.

raised by non-British territories to 1913, of which no exact tabulation was possible, were very small.

By 1935 the funded debt of the British territories other than the Union had risen to over 800% of the amount in 1913; it had increased by £87 millions and had reached a total of £99 millions. On the other hand, the Union's external debt in 1935 stood at £122·6 millions, an increase of only £14·8 millions on 1913; the external debt had, however, reached a higher figure during the intervening period, but repayments subsequently again reduced it.

At the end of 1913 the Union of South Africa's total funded debt (90% of which was external debt) amounted to £119 millions and formed 90% of the refunded debt of all British territories. The Union's external debt had been raised at an average rate of interest of 3·39%, and nearly 50% of it had been borrowed at or under 3%.

The general rise in interest rates after the War is illustrated by the debt situation at the end of 1925. At that date the Union's external debt had grown to £144 millions, as compared with £108 millions in 1913, and of this 52·3% had been borrowed at or under 3½%, 65·4% at or under 4%, and 29% had been borrowed at 4½% or over.[1] On the other hand, the funded debt of all other British territories had risen from £12 millions to £64 millions, but these territories did not have the advantage, like the Union, of being able to borrow internally. Practically all the loans carried a high rate of interest. In 1925, only 16·9% of their funded debt had been raised at 3½% or under; 52% had been borrowed at 5% or over, and 29·2% carried a rate of interest of 6%. The average rate of interest on the funded debt of these territories in 1925 was 4·84%.

By 1932, the funded debt of these British colonies had risen to £96 millions, on which the average rate of interest was 4·85%, which can be compared with the average of 3·97% on the Union's external debt at that time.[2] No less than 53·5% had been borrowed at or over 5% (19·4% at 6%).

[1] The internal debt had risen from £11 millions to £65 millions, and over 63% of the total in 1925 had been borrowed at or over 4½%.

[2] The average rate on the Union's internal debt was 4·57%. Of the total debt of the Union, 64% had been raised externally at this date.

TABLE 35.—*Amount and Proportion of Funded Debt in British Africa at each Rate of Interest for Selected Years.*

Rate of Interest. %	Union of South Africa Internal Debt (a) £(000).	Proportion to Total Internal Debt (a) %.	Union of South Africa External Debt (a) £(000).	Proportion to Total External Debt %.	Union of South Africa Total Debt (a) £(000).	Proportion to Total Debt %.	All other British Territories. £(000).	Proportion to Total %.	British Africa. £(000).	Proportion to Total %.
1913.										
3	627	5·6	53,485	49·6	54,112	45·5	1,098	8·8	55,210	42·0
3¼	...	...	...	...	...	...	...	...	...	...
3½	2,295	20·5	24,831	23·0	27,126	22·8	10,439	83·3	37,565	28·6
3¾	3,000	26·8	...	...	3,000	2·5	...	...	3,000	2·3
4	4,756	42·5	28,323	26·3	33,079	27·8	1,000	7·9	34,079	25·9
4½	82	0·8	1,169	1·1	1,251	1·1	...	...	1,251	0·9
5	420	3·8	...	...	420	0·3	...	...	420	0·3
5½	...	...	...	...	...	...	...	...	...	...
6	...	...	...	...	...	...	...	...	...	...
Total	11,180	100·0	107,808	100·0	118,988	100·0	12,537	100·0	131,525	100·0
Average Rate of Interest	3·82%	...	3·39%	...	3·43%	...	3·5%	...	3·44%	...
1925.										
3	2,634	4·0	51,465	35·7	54,099	25·9	1,098	1·7	55,197	20·2
3¼	...	...	...	...	...	...	...	...	...	...
3½	4,661	7·2	23,870	16·6	28,531	13·6	9,687	15·2	38,218	14·0
3¾	3,000	4·6	...	...	3,000	1·4	...	...	3,000	1·1
4	13,733	21·1	18,952	13·1	32,685	15·6	9,575	15·0	42,260	15·5
4½	1,704	2·6	8,384	5·8	10,088	4·8	10,221	16·1	20,309	7·4
5	34,783	53·4	30,500	21·2	65,283	31·2	8,148	12·8	73,431	26·9
5½	...	...	...	...	...	...	6,380	10·0	6,380	2·3
6	4,638	7·1	10,986	7·6	15,624	7·5	18,590	29·2	34,214	12·6
Total	65,153	100·0	144,157	100·0	209,310	100·0	63,699	100·0	273,009	100·0
Average Rate of Interest	4·60%	...	3·95%	...	4·15%	...	4·84%	...	4·32%	...

1932.

Rate	Amount	%	Amount	%	Amount	%	Amount	%	Amount	%
3	3,223	3·5	50,874	30·7	54,097	21·0	1,098	1·1	55,195	15·6
3¼	...	...	...	...	...	...	...	...	...	...
3½	4,996	5·4	29,535	17·8	34,531	13·4	5,940	6·2	40,471	11·4
3¾	3,000	3·2	...	...	3,000	1·2	...	...	3,000	0·8
4	14,385	15·5	18,508	11·2	32,893	12·7	12,744	13·3	45,637	12·9
4½	15,558	16·8	12,359	7·5	27,917	10·8	24,793	25·9	52,710	14·9
5	51,409	55·6	54,380	32·8	105,789	40·9	26,696	27·9	132,485	37·4
5½	...	...	...	...	...	...	5,986	6·2	5,986	1·7
6	...	...	...	...	...	...	18,593	19·4	18,593	5·3
Total	92,571	100·0	165,656	100·0	258,227	100·0	95,850	100·0	354,077	100·0
Average Rate of Interest	4·57%		3·97%		4·19%		4·85%		4·37%	

1935.

Rate	Amount	%	Amount	%	Amount	%	Amount	%	Amount	%
3	13,667	10·9	26,431	21·6	40,098	16·2	6,065	6·1	46,163	13·3
3¼	...	...	...	...	...	...	2,750	2·8	2,750	0·8
3½	38,336	30·7	32,027	26·1	70,363	28·4	5,045	5·1	75,408	21·7
3¾	23,421	18·8	...	...	23,421	9·5	...	...	23,421	6·8
4	14,603	11·7	18,406	15·0	33,009	13·3	12,744	12·8	45,753	13·2
4½	15,557	12·5	4,410	3·6	19,967	8·1	24,553	24·7	44,520	12·8
5	19,201	15·4	41,380	33·7	60,581	24·5	23,937	24·1	84,518	24·4
5½	...	...	...	...	...	...	5,633	5·7	5,633	1·6
6	...	...	...	...	...	...	18,593	18·7	18,593	5·4
Total	124,785	100·0	122,654	100·0	247,439	100·0	99,320	100·0	346,759	100·0
Average Rate of Interest	3·91%		4·01%		3·96%		4·72%		4·18%	

(a) Excludes floating debt.

The 1935 figures show that the British colonies in general were at a disadvantage in that they were not able to convert or repay their loans as readily as the Union, which reduced its external debt from £166 millions in 1932 to £123 millions in 1935, and increased its internal debt from £92 millions in 1932 to £125 millions in 1935. It succeeded also in reducing the average rate of interest on the internal debt from 4·57% in 1932 to 3·91% in 1935. At this date the external debt formed 50% of the total, and, on the whole debt, the average rate of interest stood at 3·96%, which should be compared with the average for the British African colonies, which stood at 4·72%.

The position may be summed up by saying that the territories now comprising the Union of South Africa managed before 1913 to borrow, at or below 3½%, as much as all the other British African colonies together had to borrow subsequent to the War at rates ranging from 4½% to 6%.

Some interesting facts emerge when the situation in individual territories is examined. Before the War all of Nigeria's debt had been raised at or below 3½%, but this territory borrowed so heavily after the War that, by 1935, the average rate of interest on its total debt was 4·83%.

Kenya shows the highest rate of interest—5·06% in 1935—of all the British territories in Africa. At that date 29·1% of its debt was carrying an interest rate of 6%. The Anglo-Egyptian Sudan has also had to borrow at high rates, the average in 1935 being 4·9%. Southern Rhodesia, which at the end of 1925 had a funded debt of only £4 millions (at 5%), had ten years later increased this to £8 millions, on which the average rate of interest stood at only 3·85%, the lowest rate for all the British colonies at that time.

As the interest burden of the different territories has been so greatly influenced by the period during which borrowing took place, the following figures, which express the funded debt of each territory in 1935 on the basis of the respective debt in 1925 as 100, will be of interest.

Between 1925 and 1935 the greatest absolute increase in the debt took place in Kenya and Nigeria, while practically no change took place in the debt of the Gold Coast, Sierra Leone and the

TABLE 36.—*Funded Debt of British African Territories*, 1925 = 100.

	1925.	1935.	1925 = 100.
Nigeria	19,309	27,964	144·8
Gold Coast	11,791	11,863	100·6
Sierra Leone . . .	1,730	1,718	99·3
West Africa	32,830	41,545	126·5
Anglo-Egyptian Sudan . .	13,473	14,543	107·9
Kenya	8,500	17,205	202·4
Uganda	1,105	2,236	202·4
Nyasaland	656	4,798	731·4
Tanganyika	3,135	8,691	277·2
Northern Rhodesia . .	(a)	2,347	...
Southern Rhodesia . . .	4,000	7,955	198·9
Total all other than Union of			
South Africa . . .	63,699	99,320	155·9

(a) No Public Debt.

Anglo-Egyptian Sudan. Relative to the economic development of Nyasaland, the large growth in its public debt is particularly striking.

VII

ECONOMIC EFFECTS OF EXTERNAL DEBT CHARGES.

The economic consequences of heavy external debt charges are well known. The difficulties which arise are greatest in those countries which, like the African territories, are dependent on the export of raw materials and foodstuffs, which are subject to considerable price fluctuations in world markets.

The effect of these charges on an economy, when its productivity is reduced, is to place a relatively increased burden on its immediately available resources, because an increased proportion of its curtailed income has to be sent abroad. When capital is provided by overseas investors through subscription for equity shares, the amount of the territory's external payments depends on the earnings of the undertakings, and if in periods of depression these earnings are reduced, the payment of dividends on the capital is *pro tanto* reduced also. In the case of fixed interest-bearing debt, however, this is not so; the debt charges remain whether the capital is yielding a corresponding return or not.

Some developing territories are fortunate in that the bulk of the capital they have received from abroad has taken the form of investment in equity shares. For example, it has been estimated[1] that the total British investment in Malayan rubber and tin companies (which account for a very large portion of the exports of that territory) amounts to approximately £100 millions.

Practically the whole of this is of the "equity" type. Of the entire external investment in Malaya, only a small fraction involves contractual payments for debt service; for the rest, remittances for dividends vary in amount, roughly speaking, with the prosperity or adversity of the companies. When, in the depth of the slump, world prices of rubber and tin fell precipitately, very few of the companies were able to conduct their business profitably and little was paid in dividends on their share capital. Sir Robert Kindersley has estimated that the income from the British capital invested in all rubber-producing companies, registered in the United Kingdom, fell from £7 millions in 1929 to half a million in 1933; these figures give some indication of the fluctuations in the productivity of the externally owned capital in Malaya. Since 1933, in consequence of an improvement in world demand, and the operation of schemes of regulating output, the prices of tin and rubber have recovered sharply, dividend payments have been resumed or increased, and the total yield on the capital invested has risen far above the low point at which the investment was, for the time being, in terms of finance, almost barren; in 1936 rubber company dividends had risen to £3·8 millions. The characteristic of equity investment, therefore, is that the trend of the yield of capital corresponds to the movements of trade. Thus, when as a consequence of adversity almost entirely beyond Malaya's control, the export surplus dwindled to a very small amount, the same circumstance reduced almost to vanishing point the sum to be remitted abroad in payment of dividends on the externally owned capital.

In Africa, however, more particularly in those territories in which little of the capital from abroad is invested in mining and allied activities, the situation is in general the opposite one, owing

[1] *Cf. The Midland Bank Review,* June, 1936.

to the relatively very large investment of fixed interest-bearing capital in railways and public works.

Where mining plays a predominating role in the economy these difficulties are lessened, owing to the fact that mining capital is very largely of the equity type. It is of some interest to note that, of the non-Government capital issues in London for Africa as a whole (as listed by the *Economist* from 1900 to 1936), approximately 60% took the form of ordinary shares, and a further 7% consisted of preferred shares, so that the equity share capital formed 67% of the total. Moreover, mining and exploration companies accounted for 66% of all capital issues.

The Union and Southern Rhodesia have also been greatly assisted, during periods of depression, by the stabilizing influence and relative profitability of their gold production, particularly owing to the high currency price of gold in recent years. Northern Rhodesia and the Belgian Congo, on the other hand, suffered during the depression from the large fluctuations in the value of their chief mineral product, copper. Although a large amount of equity capital in those territories which exploit considerable mineral wealth is an advantage, it must not be forgotten that it is accompanied by the construction of extensive railway systems and public works which give rise to considerable fixed interest charges abroad.

The extent of the external debt burden in Africa is also indicated by Table 37, which shows the proportion which the debt charges of selected territories formed of the total value of the domestic exports on the one hand, and of gross revenue on the other. The increase of the burden during the depression years is clearly discernible.

In Nigeria, in which, as was shown in Table 29, the public listed capital formed 46% of the total capital invested, it is not surprising to find that the ratio of the debt charges to the total value of domestic exports, which was approximately 7·8% in 1928, rose to 19·1% in 1934. In Kenya the ratio rose from 11·8% in 1927 to the extremely high figure of 53·7% in 1934, while, in Tanganyika, it increased from 4·1% in 1928 to 6·1% in 1934.

On the other hand the ratio of the debt charges to the

TABLE 37.—*Percentage of Debt Charges to Revenue and to Domestic Exports, 1928–35, for Gold Coast, Tanganyika, Kenya and Nigeria.*

Year.	Debt Charges.	Domestic Exports.	Percentage of Debt Charges to Domestic Exports.	Percentage of Debt Charges to Revenue.
Gold Coast :				
1928	694	13,694	5·1	17·7
1929	694	12,401	5·6	20·42
1930	701	9,911	7·1	20·03
1931	673	7,574	8·9	29·5
1932	699	8,022	8·7	26·2
1933	717	7,800	9·2	26·7
1934	724	7,850	9·2	27·5
1935	692	9,241	7·5	21·8
Tanganyika :				
1928	158	3,873	4·1	8·0
1929	214	3,722	5·7	10·7
1930	227	2,636	8·6	13·0
1931	311	1,645	18·9	20·4
1932(a)	189	2,190	8·6	14·6
1933	385	2,543	15·1	24·6
1934	425	2,646	16·1	24·7
1935	431	3,445	12·5	21·8
Kenya :				
1928	542	3,266	16·6	17·9
1929	772	2,746	28·1	23·2
1930	772	3,423	22·6	23·9
1931	891	2,344	38·0	29·3
1932	1,010	2,281	44·3	33·6
1933	995	2,247	44·3	31·9
1934	1,026	1,910	53·7	32·3
1935	1,043	2,978	35·0	31·9
Nigeria :				
1928	1,326	16,927	7·8	22·5
1929	1,329	17,581	7·6	22·0
1930	1,566	14,778	10·6	27·9
1931	1,566	8,552	18·3	32·2
1932	1,566	9,267	16·9	31·4
1933	1,608	8,460	19·0	32·9
1934	1,626	8,500	19·1	32·8
1935	1,613	11,197	14·4	26·9

(a) For nine months.

gross revenue of Nigeria rose from 13·7% in 1926 to 32·8% in 1934. In Kenya the ratio was 17·9% in 1928, but 33·6% in 1932, while in Tanganyika it rose from 8% in 1928 to 24·7% in 1934. These ratios have not changed to the same extent in all territories. This is due to the fact that, on the one hand, certain territories have borrowed much less than others during the period under review (as was shown in Table 36 above), and, on the other hand, some territories have been less affected than others by the fall in world prices for their exports.

Thus the contrast between the relatively normal debt burden of the Gold Coast and Southern Rhodesia, as compared with Tanganyika and Kenya, is most striking. Indeed, in both the Gold Coast and Southern Rhodesia, the ratio of debt charges to domestic exports has never exceeded 10%.

Table 37 should be compared with Table 38, which shows the percentage change in the ordinary revenue of British territories for selected years from 1907 to 1935, with the revenue for 1913 taken as 100. The absolute figures of ordinary revenue, customs revenue, and ordinary expenditure are given in Tables[1] 38, 39 and 40. As these tables indicate, there have been considerable differences in the rate of growth of the revenue and expenditure of various territories, and this fact should be taken into account in considering the relative burden of debt charges. Some territories, moreover, have a fiscal system in which the proportion of customs revenues to total ordinary revenue is small, and the amount obtained by direct taxation (in the form of poll taxes or similar imposts on the indigenous population) relatively large.

The figures in Table 41, p. 188, show the proportion of customs revenue to ordinary revenue in selected territories.

It is noteworthy that, in some of the territories where the proportion of customs revenue is small, the depression did not lead to as serious a decline in total ordinary revenue as was generally experienced elsewhere, for the reason that there was a more stringent collection of, or even an increase in direct taxes on the indigenous peoples. In this way, the external debt burden was passed directly on to the taxpayer.

[1] See "Note on African Statistics" in the Appendix.

TABLE 38.—Revenue of British Territories in Africa for Selected Years 1907–35.(b) £(000).

	1907.	1909.	1913.	1924.	1928.	1929.	1930.	1931.	1932.	1933.	1934.	1935.
Gambia	66	73	125	208	255	235	216	185	206	232	222	245
Sierra Leone	359	361	618	886	826	741	743	804	872	656	599	679
Gold Coast	704	779	1,302	3,971	3,914	3,397	3,499	2,284	2,671	2,685	2,636	3,169
Nigeria	1,673	1,645	3,327	6,944	5,895	6,045	5,622	4,858	4,935	4,887	4,961	5,996
Total West Africa	2,802	2,858	5,372	12,009	10,890	10,418	10,080	8,211	8,734	8,460	8,418	10,089
Anglo-Egyptian Sudan	948	1,008	1,609	4,409	6,048	6,391	6,179	5,288	4,584	4,278	4,698	5,455
Somaliland	29	31	29	83	157	106	101	93	99	109	105	105
Kenya	475	503	1,124	2,112	3,021	3,334	3,226	3,036	3,007	3,116	3,178	3,274
Uganda	112	165	257	1,240	1,519	1,683	1,412	1,400	1,399	1,350	1,528	1,567
Nyasaland	75	77	125	293	375	373	385	371	383	369	363	422
Tanganyika	395	543	688	1,559	1,973	1,993	1,749	1,522	1,291(a)	1,565	1,720	1,974
Zanzibar	248	205	275	554	472	514	494	536	456	475	451	457
Total East Africa	2,282	2,532	4,107	10,250	13,565	14,394	13,546	12,246	11,219	11,262	12,043	13,254
Northern Rhodesia	82	101	138	310	542	672	830	856	617	646(a)	693	833
Southern Rhodesia	554	620	777	1,599	2,333	2,487	2,449	2,110	2,269	2,465	2,722	2,821
Total Northern and Southern Rhodesia	636	721	915	1,909	2,875	3,159	3,279	2,966	2,886	3,111	3,415	3,654
Total excluding the Union of South Africa and South-West Africa	5,720	6,111	10,394	24,168	27,330	27,971	26,905	23,423	22,839	22,833	23,876	26,991
Union of South Africa	…	…	12,606	25,336	30,502	30,486	28,563	27,741	28,442	37,625	38,730	39,675
South-West Africa	…	…	(c)794	652	834	868	632	529	387	474	522	620
Total all British territories	…	…	23,794	50,156	58,666	59,325	56,100	51,693	51,668	60,932	63,128	67,292

Gambia	58·4	52·8	100·0	166·4	204·0	183·0	172·8	148·0	164·8	185·6	177·6	196·0
Sierra Leone	58·4	58·1	100·0	143·4	133·7	119·9	120·2	143·0	141·1	106·1	96·9	109·9
Gold Coast	59·8	54·1	100·0	305·0	300·6	260·9	268·7	175·4	205·1	206·2	202·5	243·4
Nigeria	49·4	50·3	100·0	208·7	177·2	181·7	169·0	146·0	149·8	146·9	149·1	180·2
Total West Africa	53·2	52·2	100·0	223·5	202·7	193·9	187·6	152·8	162·6	160·5	156·7	187·8
Anglo-Egyptian Sudan	62·6	58·9	100·0	274·0	375·9	397·2	384·0	328·7	284·9	265·9	292·0	339·0
Somaliland	106·9	100·0	100·0	286·2	541·4	365·5	348·3	320·7	341·4	375·9	362·1	362·1
Kenya	44·8	44·3	100·0	187·9	268·8	296·6	287·0	270·1	267·5	277·2	282·7	291·3
Uganda	64·2	43·6	100·0	482·5	591·1	654·9	549·4	544·7	544·4	525·3	594·6	609·7
Nyasaland	61·6	60·0	100·0	234·4	300·0	298·4	308·0	296·8	306·4	295·2	290·4	337·6
Tanganyika	78·9	57·4	100·0	226·6	286·8	289·7	254·2	221·2	187·6	227·5	250·0	286·9
Zanzibar	74·5	90·2	100·0	201·5	171·6	186·9	179·6	194·9	165·8	172·7	164·0	166·2
Total East Africa	61·7	55·6	100·0	249·6	330·3	350·5	329·8	298·2	273·2	274·2	293·2	322·7
Northern Rhodesia	73·2	59·4	100·0	224·6	392·8	487·0	601·4	620·3	447·1	468·1	502·2	603·6
Southern Rhodesia	79·8	71·3	100·0	205·8	300·3	320·1	315·2	271·6	292·0	317·2	350·3	363·1
Total Northern and Southern Rhodesia	78·8	69·5	100·0	208·6	314·2	345·2	358·4	324·2	315·4	340·0	373·2	399·3
Total excluding the Union of South Africa and South-West Africa	53·8	55·0	100·0	232·5	262·9	269·1	258·9	225·4	219·7	219·7	229·7	259·7
Union of South Africa	...	...	100·0	201·0	242·0	241·8	226·6	220·1	225·6	298·3	307·2	314·7
South-West Africa	...	...	100·0	82·1	105·0	109·3	79·6	66·6	48·7	59·7	65·7	78·1
Total all territories	...	...	100·0	210·8	246·6	249·3	235·8	217·3	217·1	256·1	265·3	282·7

(a) For nine months only.

(b) This table is based on the finance statistics given in the tables relating to individual territories, to which reference should be made for later figures and in notes. Revenue in most cases is gross revenue. (Cf. "Note on African Statistics" in the Appendix.)

(c) Estimated.

TABLE 39.—*Customs Revenue of British African Territories for Selected Years 1907–35.(b)* £(000).

	1907.	1909.	1913.	1924.	1928.	1929.	1930.	1931.	1932.	1933.	1934.	1935.
Gambia	52	55	98	133	177	124	140	122	100	157	142	174
Sierra Leone . .	198	189	317	481	558	507	427	339	452	370	313	441
Gold Coast . .	415	459	780	2,283	2,603	2,490	1,735	1,474	1,648	1,823	1,906	2,435
Nigeria . . .	1,262	1,076	1,773	2,935	3,438	3,360	2,981	2,077	2,377	2,133	2,069	2,912
Total West Africa .	1,927	1,779	2,968	5,832	6,776	6,481	5,283	4,012	4,577	4,483	4,430	5,962
Anglo-Egyptian Sudan	90	66	192	524	687	748	681	467	395	401	504	623
Somaliland . .	23	26	23	69	122	80	73	63	64	73	71	72
Kenya . . .	79	64	159	590	915	950	815	699	597	582	612	690
Uganda . . .	11	37	52	427	432	439	325	304	285	309	394	437
Nyasaland . .	14	11	17	69	104	106	113	107	119	123	128	166
Tanganyika . .	136	161	221	427	698	740	566	411	300(a)	405	476	613
Zanzibar . .	153	128	167	328	256	290	268	295	224	257	239	245
Total East Africa .	506	493	831	2,434	3,214	3,353	2,841	2,346	1,984	2,150	2,424	2,846
Northern Rhodesia .	13	20	30	68	163	234	321	316	178	204(a)	271	292
Southern Rhodesia .	162	208	254	462	681	705	740	543	644	719	791	792
Total Northern and Southern Rhodesia .	175	228	284	530	844	939	1,061	859	822	923	1,062	1,084
Total British territories excluding the Union of South Africa and South-West Africa	2,608	2,500	4,083	8,796	10,834	10,773	9,185	7,217	7,383	7,556	7,916	9,892
Union of South Africa . .	...	...	5,354	9,192	11,327	11,272	9,261	9,548	10,076	10,571	12,319	11,941
South-West Africa .	...	...	117	121	295	291	218	110	90	90	145	148
Total British territories .	...	...	9,554	18,109	22,456	22,336	18,664	17,575	18,713	18,217	20,380	21,981

(a) For nine months only.
(b) Figures for later years will be found in the tables of finance statistics of individual territories, to which reference should now be made for notes.

TABLE 40.—*Expenditure of British African Territories for Selected Years 1907–35.*(c) £(000).

	1907.	1909.	1913.	1924.	1928.	1929.	1930.	1931.	1932.	1933.	1934.	1935.
Gambia	58	56	95	203	251	290	253	227	196	180	175	195
Sierra Leone	346	337	562	778	815	871	806	884	832	692	603	586
Gold Coast	602	709	1,238	3,828	4,109	3,861	3,721	2,824	2,673	2,313	2,554	3,128
Nigeria	1,716	2,215	2,916	5,769	6,861	6,290	6,330	6,188	4,984	5,036	4,837	5,757
Total West Africa	2,722	3,317	4,811	10,578	12,036	11,312	11,110	10,123	8,685	8,221	8,169	9,666
Anglo-Egyptian Sudan	986	1,129	1,572	3,542	5,392	5,968	6,152	5,666	4,896	4,637	5,009	5,696
Somaliland	105	193	69	169	199	207	193	179	152	151	164	177
Kenya	692	669	1,116	1,862	2,835	3,505	3,423	3,185	3,116	3,162	3,173	3,218
Uganda	196	240	290	919	1,368	1,607	1,640	1,452	1,299	1,276	1,362	1,440
Tanganyika	690	679	1,025	1,384	1,873	2,085	2,103	1,821	1,255(a)	1,651	1,871	1,750
Nyasaland	106	109	133	295	384	411	414	428	402	403	424	475
Zanzibar	189	189	248	508	599	562	508	581	459	449	441	434
Total East Africa	2,964	3,208	4,453	8,679	12,650	14,345	14,433	13,312	11,579	11,729	12,444	13,190
Northern Rhodesia	138	143	186	340	525	555	705	820	794	779(a)	713	806
Southern Rhodesia	544	614	836	1,592	2,274	2,411	2,453	2,229	2,177	2,500	2,637	2,915
Total Northern and Southern Rhodesia	682	757	1,022	1,932	2,799	2,966	3,158	3,049	2,971	3,279	3,350	3,721
Total British territories excluding the Union of South Africa and South-West Africa	6,368	7,282	10,286	21,189	27,485	28,623	28,701	26,484	23,235	23,229	23,963	26,577
Union of South Africa	...	...	13,294	24,528	28,669	29,998	29,949	28,742	28,452	33,091	35,456	36,520
South-West Africa	...	...	752(b)	713	737	827	767	753	603	613	685	731
Total British territories	...	...	24,332	46,430	56,891	59,448	59,417	55,979	52,290	56,933	60,104	63,828

(a) For nine months only.
(b) Estimated.
(c) This table is based on the finance statistics given in the tables relating to individual territories, to which reference should be made for later figures. Expenditure in most cases is *gross* expenditure. (*Cf.* "Note on African Statistics" in the Appendix.)

TABLE 41.—*Percentage of Customs Revenue to Revenue for Selected British African Territories, 1928 and 1935.*

	1928.	1935.
Gambia	69·4	71·0
Sierra Leone	67·6	64·9
Gold Coast	66·5	76·8
Nigeria	58·3	48·6
Anglo-Egyptian Sudan	11·4	11·4
Kenya	30·3	21·1
Uganda	28·4	27·9
Nyasaland	27·7	39·3
Tanganyika	35·4	31·1
Northern Rhodesia	30·1	35·1
Southern Rhodesia	29·2	28·1
Union of South Africa	37·1	30·1

VIII

THE INDIRECT BURDEN OF EXTERNAL DEBT CHARGES.

The various statistics which have been quoted so far do not indicate the whole of the burden resulting from the fixed interest charges. It is well known that during periods of depression debtor countries have, as a rule, to export a greater volume of their products, in order to obtain the same absolute monetary return. It has been estimated that in the case of Australia, which provides a good example of the difficulties which arise from large external debt charges, the catastrophic fall which took place in the sterling values of export commodities was such that the index number thereof, with the 1928 average as 100, dropped well below 50 in the period 1931–33. For the year ending June, 1935, Australia's exports realized £88 millions sterling, out of which about one-third was required for interest. In 1929, Australia's exports were valued at nearly £140 millions sterling, and only one-fifth of that sum was required to meet interest payments on external debt. The volume of. goods which Australia had to export to meet her interest charges in 1935 was roughly twice as much as in 1928/29. It is in this way that extraneous and uncontrollable circumstances may add grievously to the weight of fixed debt charges.

It is significant that the value of the total domestic exports of all African territories (see Table 43), which amounted to nearly

£179 millions in 1929, declined to £117 millions in 1931, and then they exceeded the 1913 value of the total exports only by some £12 millions. But the volume of goods which had to be exported to realize that value was much greater than in 1913 and in 1929. By 1935 the total had again reached £179 millions.

The difficulties of African territories, as a result of the fall in export values, are well illustrated by the experiences of the Belgian Congo. The disastrous decline in the price of its limited range of exportable products is given by the following indices[1] of the minimum prices ruling during the depression, calculated on the basis 1927–29 equals 100. The indices for March, 1935 and February, 1936 have been added, and indicate the effects of the devaluation of the Belga.

Minima Des Prix Coloniaux Depuis La Crise et Indices De Mars, 1935 et De Février, 1936. (Base: moyenne de 1927–29=100.)

Produits.		Minima.		Indices.		% de hausse depuis la dévaluation.
	Dates.	Indices.	Mars 1935.	Février 1936.	
Huile de palme	.	août 1934	. 18·5	. 29·2	. 37·5	. 28
Noix palmistes	.	juillet 1934	. 19·0	. 28·4	. 49·5	. 74
Sésames	.	juillet 1934	. 26·4	. 36·6	. 51·4	. 40
Cacao .	.	novembre 1934	. 26·7	. 29·8	. 40	. 34
Coton .	.	juin 1932	. 33	. 40·7	. 55	. 35
Café .	.	mars 1935	. 37·9	. 37·9	. 38·4	. 1
Copal .	.	mars 1935	. 38·7	. 38·7	. 63·2	. 63
Caoutchouc .	.	juin 1932	. 10·4	. 32·2	. 46·3	. 44
Ivoire .	.	octobre 1933	. 27·1	. 34·1	. 35·7	. 5
Peaux .	.	mai 1932	. 19·2	. 28·5	. 53·7	. 88
Cuivre .	.	octobre 1934	. 22·5	. 23·5	. 42	. 79
Étain .	.	avril 1932	. 33·8	. 52·1	. 70·8	. 36
Or .	.	septembre 1934	. 99·9	. 100·2	. 139·2	. 39

As a result, the value of the exports of the Belgian Congo declined from 1,511 million Francs in 1930 to 658 million Francs in 1933 (see Table 42). Unfortunately, the Belgian Congo had been borrowing heavily during the years before the depression, and debt charges increased nearly four-fold between 1927 and 1934. In fact, the large external debt charges which this colony has to meet still present one of its most difficult problems. Table 42 shows the growth in the percentage ratio of these debt charges

[1] Extracted from an article by M. Gaston Eyskens, *Bulletin de l'Institut des Sciences Économiques de l'Université de Louvain*, February, 1936.

TABLE 42.—*Belgian Congo : Percentage Ratio of Debt Charges to Revenue and to the Value of Domestic Exports.*

Year.	Debt Charge (Millions of Unstabilized Francs).	Ordinary Revenue (a). (Millions of Unstabilized Francs.)	Ordinary Expenditure (Millions of Unstabilized Francs). (b)	Debt Charge as Percentage of Ordinary Revenue.	Domestic Exports (000,000).	Debt Charge as Percentage of Domestic Exports.	Imports (000,000).
1924	...	188	178	...	477	...	490
1925	...	266	234	...	629	...	876
1926	...	322	325	...	729	...	1,293
1927	89	525	462	17·0	1,055	8·4	1,496
1928	122	591	564	20·6	1,288	9·5	1,624
1929	...	690	636	...	1,444	...	1,943
1930	126	634	584	19·9	1,511	8·3	1,581
1931	141	542	564	26·0	1,104	12·8	962
1932	177	375	419	47·2	668	26·5	465
1933	298	339(c)	397	87·9	658	45·3	389
1934	316	365(d)	374	86·6	843	37·5	378
1935	322	406(e)	362	79·3	1,203	26·8	525

(a) Excluding subsidy from Home Government.
(b) Including pensions but excluding debt charge.
(c) Final result.
(d) Provisional estimate.
(e) Provisional result.

to the internal revenue (excluding the subsidy received during the depression years from Belgium), and to the value of domestic exports. It will be seen that the ratio of debt charges to internal revenue rose from 7% in 1927 to 88% in 1933 (86% in 1934), after which it has declined; in 1936 the debt charges still formed nearly 45% of the ordinary expenditure. The ratio of debt charges to the domestic exports of the Belgian Congo rose from 5% in 1927 (8% in 1930) to 45% in 1933. The devaluation of the Belga, and also the rise in world prices, brought about relief, so that, by 1935, the ratio had declined to 27%.

IX

EFFECTS OF CYCLICAL FLUCTUATIONS IN CAPITAL IMPORTS.

The economic difficulties of African territories are intensified by cyclical fluctuations in the flow of external capital to them. The supply of capital increases during periods of relative prosperity, and fans that prosperity; it improves the revenues of the Government from its public undertakings, and it leads naturally to a large increase in imports and therefore in customs revenues. As a consequence of the flourishing condition of the budgets of the territories, there is further borrowing by Governments and further private investment. When the depression sets in, the inward flow of capital, on which so much of the previous activity depended, ceases abruptly, and thus causes the burden of debt charges to rest even more heavily upon the economic structure. The difficulties of meeting the increased fixed interest burden, which has to be paid abroad, are intensified by the decline in customs revenues owing to the lower volume and value of imports; budget deficits result and expenditure has to be curtailed wherever possible. The population of the territory as a whole has to reduce its standard of life by importing less and exporting more.

Moreover, in some African territories, these industrial fluctuations are particularly serious, because they also affect the cash earnings of the native population, and make it difficult to collect poll taxes and other direct imposts from them.

It is noteworthy that, whereas in 1928 the value of the total net imports into all British territories was £138 millions, by

1931 it had declined to £85 millions; customs revenues declined from £22 millions to £17 millions. By 1935, total imports had again risen to £113 millions and customs revenues to £22 millions.

A particularly striking example of the extent to which capital imports can be suddenly curtailed is provided by the experience of the Belgian Congo. Between 1928 and 1932 the import of capital[1] into the Congo was estimated to have been approximately 6 milliards of paper Francs. Of this sum, roughly Frs. 1,900 millions represented a rise in the consolidated and floating debt; approximately Frs. 1,900 millions arose from capital borrowed, under guarantees of the State, by various companies; Frs. 1,600 millions was the amount of capital[1] in new colonial companies; and Frs. 2,500 millions represented the increase in the capital[2] of existing companies. The suddenness with which this large inflow of capital was stopped is indicated by the fact that, whereas in 1929 new capital underwritten by Belgian companies amounted to Frs. 1,406 millions, in 1932 the amount was only Frs. 276 millions.[3] The Belgian Senate Commission in one of its Reports expressed the view, after an analysis of new capital issues, that up to 1930 half of the budget (and half of the economic activity of the Colony) was based upon capital imports. It concluded that the subsequent crisis in the budget of the colony was due in greater degree to the reduction in the inflow of capital than to the decline in the value of the exports of the Congo owing to the fall in world prices—a conclusion which would have been applicable, but to a lesser extent, to the situation in many other African territories at this time.

X

INVESTMENT AND TRADE.

In order to compare the amount of foreign investment with the economic progress of each territory, the following data concerning the trade of Africa have been tabulated: the total value of domestic

---

[1] Cf. p. 166 for a discussion of the large growth in imports which resulted from this.

[2] Nominal capital, of which a portion was held in reserve.

[3] As already mentioned (cf. p. 166), there are various estimates relating to the new issues of capital for the Belgian Congo, and they do not always agree. The above figures are given by Van der Velde. The Senate Commission's Reports give slightly different figures for some of the years, but the discrepancies are not large. For 1932 the Senate Commission's estimate is only Frs. 96 millions.

£(000).(j)

	1907.	1909.	1913.	1924.	1928.	1929.	1930.	1931.	1932.	1933.	1934.	1935.
Gambia	280	341	655	856	1,113	783	878	517	400	506	394	376
Sierra Leone	676	760	1,376	1,510	1,609	1,319	1,046	616	878	754	832	1,556
Gold Coast	2,502	2,452	5,014	9,590	13,629	12,401	9,911	7,574	8,022	7,800	7,850	9,241
Nigeria	3,612	3,829	6,779	14,384	16,927	17,581	14,778	8,552	9,267	8,460	8,500	11,197
Total West Africa	7,070	7,382	13,824	26,340	33,278	32,084	26,613	17,259	18,567	17,520	17,576	22,370
Anglo-Egyptian Sudan	461	691	1,215	3,633	5,778	6,692	5,079	1,777	3,894	2,672	3,947	4,684
Somaliland	212	213	209	255	564	239	193	150	121	146	437	127
Kenya	157	191	444	2,240	3,266	2,746	3,423	2,344	2,281	2,247	1,910	2,978
Uganda	140	212	554	3,897	3,395	4,275	2,060	1,978	2,225	3,465	3,774	3,631
Nyasaland	54	98	201	564	676	589	663	502	656	514	753	736
Tanganyika	625	656(a)	1,778	2,611	3,873	3,722	2,636	1,645	2,190	2,543	2,646	3,445
Zanzibar	548(a)	462(a)	604	1,406	1,099	1,269	1,017	933	668	638	591	655
Total East Africa	2,197	2,523	5,016	14,606	18,651	19,532	15,071	9,329	12,035	12,225	13,758	16,256
Northern Rhodesia	96	81	195	406	784	819	769	989	2,436	3,589	4,400	4,668
Southern Rhodesia	2,319	2,806	3,297	5,120	6,576	6,609	5,634	4,437	5,339	5,906	7,502	8,077
Total Northern and Southern Rhodesia	2,415	2,887	3,492	5,526	7,360	7,428	6,403	5,426	7,775	9,495	11,902	12,745
Total all British territories excluding the Union of South Africa and South-West Africa	11,682	12,792	22,332	46,472	59,289	59,044	48,087	32,014	38,377	39,240	43,236	51,371
Union of South Africa	45,485	47,782	64,565	80,699	88,991	89,031	76,713	65,076	66,176	91,989	78,062	97,931
South-West Africa	81	1,104	3,515	2,851	3,296	3,524	2,550	1,339	1,041	1,347	1,099	2,473
Total all British Territories	57,243	61,678	90,412	130,022	151,576	154,599	127,350	98,429	105,594	132,576	122,397	151,775
French West Africa	3,174	4,393	5,000	7,649	9,232	9,396	8,841	5,661	5,022	5,404	7,052	9,432
French Equatorial Africa	739	698	1,468	514	1,208	1,223	1,594	1,078	1,348	1,678	2,182	2,351
Togo(b)	296	368	457	713	692	678	670	426	314	321	351	487
Cameroons(b)	793	772	1,103	783	1,280	1,370	1,100	713	933	929	948	1,338
Total French Colonies	5,002	6,231	8,028	9,659	12,412	12,667	12,205	7,878	7,617	8,332	10,533	13,608
Angola	961(c)	1,193	1,068	1,471	2,279	2,610	2,166	1,877	1,818	2,244	2,149	2,018
Mozambique	935	1,482	1,678	2,617(d)	3,181	3,089	2,682	1,989	1,863	1,814	1,820	1,753
Guinea	122(e)	93(f)	310	416(i)	400	458	362	289	343	...	198	...
Total Portuguese	2,038	2,768	3,056	4,504	5,860	6,157	5,210	4,155	4,024	4,058	4,167	3,771
Belgian Congo	2,340	2,224	2,190	4,970	7,017	8,250	8,634	6,773	5,143	5,529	7,806	9,045
Ruanda Urundi	...	...	...	...	103	76	61	40	50	99	221	291
Total all Non-British Territories	9,380	11,223	13,274	19,133(h)	25,392	27,150	26,110	18,846	16,834	18,018(g)	22,727	26,715(g)

(a) Domestic Exports plus total imports (including goods subsequently re-exported). In 1913 merchandise re-exported amounted to £386,000.
(b) The post-war area here included is, of course, smaller than the pre-war.
(c) 1905 figures.
(d) 1906 figures.
(e) 1906 figures.
(f) 1908 figures.
(g) Excluding Guinea.
(h) Excluding Ruanda Urundi.
(i) Estimated.
(j) This table is based on the trade statistics given in the tables relating to individual territories, to which reference should be made for later figures and notes. (Cf. also "Note on African Statistics" in the Appendix.)

produce exported is given in Table 43, the total net value of the imports in Table 44, and the total value of the trade in Table 45; in each case the statistics refer to selected years from 1907 to 1935,[1] and are given for each African territory. These figures have also been expressed as percentages; Tables 46 and 47 show the proportion per cent. which the domestic exports and the total net trade in each territory bear to the respective totals for Africa.

For purposes of convenience, Table 48 summarizes some of the most important information given in the previous Tables, and also shows the percentage territorial distribution of the populations of Africa, and the percentage of the total area of Africa which is occupied by each territory.

All these tables should be considered in conjunction with the detailed statistics of the trade and finances of each individual territory, and with Tables 38, 39 and 40, relating to the revenue, customs revenue, and expenditure.

XI

IMPORTANCE OF BRITISH INVESTMENTS.

The most striking fact which emerges from the various statistics referred to above is the preponderance of the amount of overseas capital invested in, and the trade of British territories. Of the £1,222 millions invested in Africa, £941 millions, i. e. 77%, is in British territories, including the Union, the Mandates and the Protectorates.

No information is available on which to base a formal estimate of the amount of capital actually subscribed by British and non-British investors respectively. This question raises the very well-known difficulties of tracing the ownership of internationally traded securities. I see no reason, however, to suppose that the percentage of capital originally supplied by British investors is less than 75% of the total.

It is true that, of the £941 millions of capital in what are now British territories, some £84 millions were invested before the

[1] Statistics for later years will be found in the detailed tables relating to the trade and finances of each individual territory. See also "Note on African Statistics" in the Appendix.

TABLE 44.—*Total Value of Imports of each African Territory for Selected Years 1907–35.(a)* £(000).

	1907.	1909.	1913.	1924.	1928.	1929.	1930.	1931.	1932.	1933.	1934.	1935.
Gambia	285	395	611	533	968	539	509	240	286	427	319	466
Sierra Leone . .	806	700	1,324	1,649	1,734	1,558	1,285	969	1,199	799	761	1,113
Gold Coast . .	1,917	1,998	3,500	7,116	11,191	9,530	8,353	4,316	5,269	5,016	4,293	7,274
Nigeria . . .	3,587	4,245	6,006	10,805	15,613	13,040	12,363	6,291	6,996	6,172	5,224	7,662
Total West Africa .	6,595	7,338	11,441	20,103	29,506	24,667	22,510	11,816	13,750	12,414	10,597	16,515
Anglo-Egyptian Sudan	1,596	1,759	2,069	5,294	6,310	6,742	6,026	3,552	2,761	2,955	3,772	5,074
Somaliland . .	262	290	244	374	618	471	308	262	264	283	268	271
Kenya ⎫ Uganda ⎬ .	897	847	2,742	6,255	8,496	8,208	6,600	4,540	3,567	3,464	4,087	4,577
Nyasaland . .	166	107	192	543	875	735	756	745	712	607	499	609
Tanganyika . .	1,190	1,697	2,668	1,974	3,560	4,021	3,720	2,251	1,705	1,764	2,132	2,711
Zanzibar . .	1,082	898	717	1,164	1,016	1,138	991	833	704	626	559	721
Total East Africa .	5,193	5,598	8,632	15,604	20,875	21,315	18,401	12,183	9,713	9,699	11,317	13,963
Northern Rhodesia .	115	337	247	622	2,339	3,551	4,825	5,166	1,695	1,846	2,796	2,854
Southern Rhodesia .	1,282	1,723	2,782	3,521	6,995	6,783	5,675	4,154	3,158	3,743	4,427	5,482
Total Northern and Southern Rhodesia .	1,397	2,060	3,029	4,143	9,334	10,334	10,500	9,320	4,853	5,589	7,223	8,336
Total all British Territories excluding the Union of South Africa and South-West Africa .	13,185	14,996	23,102	39,850	59,715	56,316	51,411	33,319	28,316	27,702	29,137	38,814
Union of South Africa .	25,691	26,234	40,374	63,627	75,488	79,042	61,142	49,724	31,277	47,541	64,372	73,173
South-West Africa .	1,620	1,736	2,171	1,746	2,803	2,993	2,024	1,481	774	946	1,203	1,428
Total all British Territories .	40,496	42,966	65,647	105,223	138,006	138,351	114,577	84,524	60,367	76,189	94,712	113,415

French West Africa	3,770	4,742	6,030	8,935	11,416	10,676	11,159	6,156	6,461	7,000	7,091	8,946
French Equatorial Africa	606	445	834	550	1,824	2,238	2,737	2,365	2,489	2,132	2,091	2,271
Togo	334	562	532	643	725	822	810	609	742	501	402	418
Cameroons	865	386	1,629	854	1,659	1,565	1,400	904	820	892	752	864
Total French Colonies	5,575	6,635	9,025	10,982	15,624	15,301	16,116	10,034	10,512	10,525	10,336	12,499
Angola	1,366	1,170	1,697	1,776	2,258	2,909	2,274	1,348	1,740	1,600	1,519	1,495
Mozambique	1,514	1,374	2,341	3,146	4,365	4,537	5,038	4,232	2,736	2,868	2,629	2,763
Guinea	187	162	323	513	400	401	401	180	250	...	178	...
Total Portuguese	3,067	2,706	4,361	5,435	7,023	7,847	7,713	5,760	4,726	4,468	4,326	4,258
Belgian Congo	993	866	2,850	5,103	9,280	11,104	9,036	5,902	3,857	3,271	3,500	3,948
Ruanda Urundi	...	...	...	...	267	324	306	327	166	196	246	256
Total all Non-British Territories	9,635	10,207	16,236	21,520	32,194	34,576	33,161	22,023	19,261	18,460	18,408	20,961

(a) This table is based on the trade statistics given in the tables relating to individual territories, to which reference should be made for later figures and notes. Imports are less re-exports. (Cf. "Note on African Statistics" in the Appendix.)

TABLE 45.—*Total Value of the Trade of each African Territory for Selected Years 1907–35.*(*j*) £(000).

	1907.	1909.	1913.	1924.	1928.	1929.	1930.	1931.	1932.	1933.	1934.	1935.
Gambia	565	736	1,266	1,389	2,081	1,322	1,387	757	686	933	713	842
Sierra Leone	1,482	1,460	2,700	3,159	3,343	2,877	2,331	1,585	2,077	1,553	1,593	2,669
Gold Coast	4,419	4,450	8,514	16,706	24,820	21,931	18,264	11,890	13,291	12,816	12,143	16,515
Nigeria	7,199	8,074	12,785	25,189	32,540	30,621	27,141	14,843	16,263	14,632	13,724	18,859
Total West Africa	13,665	14,720	25,265	46,443	62,784	56,751	49,123	29,075	32,317	29,934	28,173	38,885
Anglo-Egyptian Sudan	2,057	2,450	3,285	8,927	12,088	13,434	11,105	5,329	6,655	5,627	7,719	9,758
Somaliland	474	503	453	629	1,182	710	501	412	385	429	405	398
Kenya and Uganda	1,194	1,250	3,750	12,392	15,157	15,229	12,083	8,862	8,073	9,176	9,771	11,186
Tanganyika	1,815	2,353	4,446	4,585	7,433	7,743	6,356	3,896	3,895	4,307	4,778	6,156
Nyasaland	220	205	393	1,107	1,551	1,324	1,419	1,247	1,368	1,121	1,252	1,345
Zanzibar	(a)1,630	(a)1,360	1,321	2,570	2,115	2,497	2,008	1,766	1,372	1,264	1,150	1,376
Total East Africa	7,390	8,121	13,648	30,210	39,526	40,847	33,472	21,512	21,748	21,924	25,075	30,219
Northern Rhodesia	211	418	442	1,028	3,123	4,370	5,594	6,155	4,131	5,435	7,196	7,522
Southern Rhodesia	3,601	4,529	6,079	8,641	13,571	13,392	11,309	8,591	8,497	9,649	11,929	13,559
Total Northern and Southern Rhodesia	3,812	4,947	6,521	9,669	16,694	17,762	16,903	14,746	12,628	15,084	19,125	21,081
Total all British Territories excluding the Union of South Africa and South-West Africa	24,867	27,788	45,434	86,322	119,004	115,360	99,498	65,333	66,693	66,942	72,373	90,185

Union of South Africa	71,176	74,016	104,939	144,326	164,479	168,073	137,855	114,800	97,453	139,530	142,434	171,104
South-West Africa	1,701	2,840	5,686	4,536	6,099	6,517	4,574	2,820	1,815	2,293	2,302	3,901
Total all British Territories	97,744	104,644	156,059	235,184	289,582	289,950	241,927	182,953	165,961	208,765	217,109	265,190
French West Africa	6,944	9,135	11,030	16,584	20,648	20,072	20,000	11,817	11,483	12,404	14,143	18,378
French Equatorial Africa	1,345	1,143	2,302	1,064	3,032	3,461	4,331	3,443	3,837	3,810	4,273	4,622
Togo (b)	630	930	989	1,356	1,417	1,500	1,480	1,035	1,056	822	753	905
Cameroons (b)	1,658	1,658	2,732	1,637	2,939	2,935	2,500	1,617	1,753	1,821	1,700	2,202
Total French Colonies	10,577	12,866	17,053	20,641	28,036	27,968	28,311	17,912	18,129	18,857	20,869	26,107
Angola	(d)2,327	2,363	2,765	3,247	4,537	5,519	4,440	3,225	3,558	3,844	3,668	3,513
Mozambique	2,469	2,856	4,019	(c)5,763	7,546	7,626	7,720	6,221	4,599	4,682	4,449	4,516
Guinea	(e)309	(f)255	633	929	(i)800	859	763	469	593	...	376	...
Total Portuguese Colonies	5,105	5,474	7,417	9,939	12,883	14,004	12,923	9,915	8,750	(h)8,526	8,493	(h)8,029
Belgian Congo	3,333	3,090	5,040	10,073	16,297	19,354	17,670	12,675	9,000	8,800	11,306	12,993
Ruanda Urundi	...	...	...	...	370	400	367	367	216	295	467	547
Total all Non-British Territories	19,015	21,430	29,510	(g)40,653	57,586	61,726	59,271	40,869	36,095	36,478	41,135	47,676

(a) Domestic exports plus total imports (including goods subsequently re-exported).
In 1913 merchandise re-exports amounted to £386,000.
(b) The post-war area here included is, of course, smaller than the pre-war.
(c) 1926 figures.
(d) 1905 figures.

(e) 1906 figures.
(f) 1908 figures.
(g) Excluding Ruanda Urundi.
(h) Excluding Portuguese Guinea.
(i) Estimated.
(j) Cf. "Note on African Statistics" in the Appendix.

TABLE 46.—*Value of the Domestic Exports of each African Territory as a Percentage of the Total Value of Domestic Exports of Africa for Selected Years 1907–35.*

	1907.	1909.	1913.	1924.	1928.	1929.	1930.	1931.	1932.	1933.	1934.	1935.
Gambia	·42	·47	·63	·57	·63	·43	·57	·44	·33	·34	·27	·21
Sierra Leone	1·01	1·04	1·33	1·01	·91	·74	·68	·53	·72	·50	·57	·87
Gold Coast	3·75	3·37	4·84	6·43	7·70	6·94	6·46	6·46	6·55	5·18	5·41	5·18
Nigeria	5·43	5·25	6·54	9·66	9·56	9·84	9·63	7·29	7·57	5·62	5·86	6·27
Total West Africa	10·61	10·13	13·34	17·67	18·80	17·95	17·34	14·72	15·17	11·64	12·11	12·53
Anglo-Egyptian Sudan	·69	·95	1·17	2·44	3·27	3·74	3·31	1·52	3·18	1·77	2·72	2·62
Somaliland	·32	·29	·20	·17	·32	·13	·13	·12	·10	·10	·09	·07
Kenya	·24	·26	·43	1·50	1·84	1·54	2·23	2·00	1·86	1·49	1·32	1·67
Uganda	·21	·29	·54	2·61	1·92	2·39	1·34	1·69	1·82	2·30	2·60	2·03
Nyasaland	·08	·14	·19	·38	·38	·33	·43	·43	·54	·34	·52	·41
Tanganyika	·94	·90	1·71	1·75	2·19	2·08	1·72	1·40	1·79	1·69	1·82	1·93
Zanzibar	·82	·63	·58	·94	·62	·71	·66	·80	·55	·42	·41	·37
Total East Africa	3·30	3·46	4·82	9·79	10·54	10·92	9·82	7·96	9·84	8·11	9·48	9·10
Northern Rhodesia	·14	·11	·19	·27	·44	·46	·50	·84	1·99	2·38	3·03	2·62
Southern Rhodesia	3·48	3·85	3·18	3·43	3·72	3·70	3·68	3·78	4·36	3·93	5·17	4·53
Total Northern and Southern Rhodesia	3·62	3·96	3·37	3·70	4·16	4·16	4·18	4·62	6·35	6·31	8·20	7·15
Total all British Territories excluding the Union of South Africa and South-West Africa	17·53	17·55	21·53	31·16	33·50	33·03	31·34	27·30	31·36	26·06	29·79	28·78

Union of South Africa	68·28	65·55	62·28	54·10	50·29	49·81	49·99	55·49	54·05	61·09	53·79	54·87
South-West Africa	·12	1·50	3·39	1·91	1·86	1·97	1·66	1·14	·85	·89	·76	1·39
Total all British Territories	85·93	84·60	87·20	87·17	85·65	84·81	82·99	83·93	86·26	88·04	84·34	85·04
French West Africa	4·76	6·03	4·82	5·13	5·22	5·26	5·75	4·83	4·10	3·59	4·87	5·28
French Equatorial Africa	1·11	·96	1·42	·34	·68	·68	1·04	·92	1·10	1·11	1·50	1·32
Togo	·44	·50	·44	·48	·39	·38	·44	·36	·26	·21	·24	·27
Cameroons	1·19	1·06	1·06	·53	·72	·77	·72	·61	·76	·62	·65	·75
Total French Colonies	7·50	8·55	7·74	6·48	7·01	7·09	7·95	6·72	6·22	5·53	7·26	7·62
Angola	1·44	1·64	1·03	·99	1·29	1·46	1·41	1·60	1·48	1·49	1·48	1·13
Mozambique	1·43	2·03	1·62	1·75	1·80	1·73	1·75	1·70	1·52	1·20	1·25	·98
Guinea	·18	·13	·30	·28	·23	·25	·23	·24	·28	...	·14	...
Total Portuguese Colonies	3·05	3·80	2·95	3·02	3·32	3·44	3·39	3·54	3·28	2·69	2·87	2·11
Belgian Congo	3·52	3·05	2·11	3·33	3·96	4·62	5·63	5·78	4·20	3·67	5·38	5·07
Ruanda Urundi	...	...	...	...	·06	·04	·04	·03	·04	·07	·15	·16
Total all Non-British Territories	14·07	15·40	12·80	12·83	14·35	15·19	17·01	16·07	13·74	11·96	15·66	14·96

TABLE 47.—*Value of Trade of each African Territory as a Percentage of the Total Value of the Trade of Africa for Selected Years 1907–35.*

	1907.	1909.	1913.	1924.	1928.	1929.	1930.	1931.	1932.	1933.	1934.	1935.
Gambia	·48	·58	·68	·50	·60	·37	·46	·34	·34	·38	·28	·27
Sierra Leone	1·27	1·16	1·46	1·15	·96	·82	·77	·71	1·03	·63	·62	·85
Gold Coast	3·79	3·53	4·59	6·05	7·15	6·24	6·07	5·31	6·58	5·23	4·70	5·28
Nigeria	6·17	6·41	6·89	9·13	9·37	8·71	9·01	6·63	8·05	5·97	5·31	6·03
Total West Africa	11·71	11·68	13·62	16·83	18·08	16·14	16·31	12·99	16·00	12·21	10·91	12·43
Anglo-Egyptian Sudan	1·76	1·94	1·77	3·24	3·48	3·82	3·69	2·38	3·29	2·29	2·99	3·12
Somaliland	·41	·40	·24	·23	·34	·20	·17	·18	·19	·17	·16	·13
Kenya and Uganda	1·02	·99	2·02	4·49	4·37	4·33	4·01	3·96	3·99	3·74	3·78	3·58
Nyasaland	·19	·16	·21	·40	·45	·37	·47	·56	·68	·46	·48	·43
Tanganyika	1·55	1·87	2·40	1·66	2·14	2·20	2·11	1·74	1·93	1·76	1·85	1·96
Zanzibar	1·40	1·08	·71	·93	·61	·69	·66	·79	·68	·52	·45	·44
Total East Africa	6·33	6·44	7·35	10·95	11·39	11·61	11·11	9·61	10·76	8·94	9·71	9·66
Northern Rhodesia	·18	·33	·24	·37	·90	1·24	1·86	2·75	2·04	2·22	2·78	2·40
Southern Rhodesia	3·08	3·59	3·28	3·14	3·91	3·81	3·75	3·84	4·21	3·93	4·62	4·34
Total Northern and Southern Rhodesia	3·26	3·92	3·52	3·51	4·81	5·05	5·61	6·59	6·25	6·15	7·40	6·74
Total all British Territories excluding Union of South Africa and South-West Africa	21·30	22·04	24·49	31·29	34·28	32·80	33·03	29·19	33·01	27·30	28·02	28·83

Union of South Africa	60·96	58·71	56·55	52·32	47·38	47·80	45·78	51·29	48·23	56·89	55·16	54·69
South-West Africa	1·46	2·25	3·06	1·65	1·76	1·85	1·52	1·26	·90	·93	·89	1·24
Total all British Territories	83·72	83·00	84·10	85·26	83·42	82·45	80·33	81·74	82·14	85·12	84·07	84·76
French Equatorial Africa	1·15	·91	1·24	·39	·87	·98	1·44	1·54	1·90	1·55	1·65	1·48
French West Africa	5·95	7·25	5·94	6·02	5·95	5·71	6·64	5·28	5·68	5·06	5·48	5·87
Togo	·54	·74	·53	·49	·41	·43	·49	·46	·52	·34	·29	·29
Cameroons	1·42	1·31	1·47	·59	·85	·83	·83	·72	·87	·74	·66	·70
Total French Colonies	9·06	10·21	9·18	7·49	8·08	7·95	9·40	8·00	8·97	7·69	8·08	8·34
Angola	1·99	1·87	1·49	1·18	1·31	1·57	1·47	1·44	1·76	1·57	1·42	1·12
Mozambique	2·12	2·27	2·17	2·09	2·17	2·17	2·56	2·78	2·28	1·91	1·72	1·45
Guinea	·26	·20	·34	·33	·23	·25	·25	·21	·29	...	·15	...
Total Portuguese Colonies	4·37	4·34	4·00	3·60	3·71	3·99	4·28	4·43	4·33	3·48	3·29	2·57
Belgian Congo	2·85	2·45	2·72	3·65	4·69	5·50	5·87	5·67	4·45	3·59	4·38	4·15
Ruanda Urundi	...	...	...	...	·10	·11	·12	·16	·11	·12	·18	·18
Total all Non-British Territories	16·28	17·00	15·90	14·74	16·58	17·55	19·67	18·26	17·86	14·88	15·93	15·24

TABLE 48.—*Summary Percentage Table.*

	Capital Invested in each African Territory as Percentage of Total Capital Invested in Africa.	Trade of each African Territory as Percentage of Total Trade of Africa.		Domestic Exports of each African Territory as Percentage of Total Domestic Exports of Africa.		Area of each African Territory as Percentage of Total Area of Africa.	White Population(a) of each African Territory as Percentage of Total White Population of Africa.	Total Population(a) of each African Territory as Percentage of Total Population of Africa.
		1928.	1935.	1928.	1935.			
All British Territories	77·05	83·42	84·76	85·65	85·04	43·68	96·02	57·71
All Non-British Territories	22·95	16·58	15·24	14·35	14·96	56·32	3·78	42·29
All British Territories excluding the Union of South Africa and South-West Africa	34·24	34·28	28·83	33·50	28·78	33·66	5·19	48·75
Union of South Africa	42·81	47·38	54·69	50·29	54·87	5·95	89·51	8·61
Southern Rhodesia / Northern Rhodesia	8·38	4·81(d)	6·74(d)	4·16(d)	7·15(d)	8·94	2·99	2·91
Bechuanaland								
British West Africa(b)	9·56	18·08	12·43	18·80	12·53	5·66	·38	24·29
British East Africa(c)	12·81	11·39	9·66	10·54	9·10	22·48	1·63	19·72
French West Africa	2·49	5·95	5·87	5·22	5·28	22·88	·85	14·63
French Equatorial Africa	1·74	·87	1·48	·68	1·32	10·98	·19	3·37
All French Territories	5·76	8·08	8·34	7·01	7·62	34·54	1·15	21·08

Individual Territories:								
Gambia	·02	·60	·27	·63	·21	·05	·00	·19
Sierra Leone	·28	·96	·85	·91	·87	·35	·03	1·88
Gold Coast	2·89	7·15	5·28	7·70	5·18	·99	·12	3·21
Nigeria	6·15	9·37	6·03	9·56	6·27	4·27	·23	19·01
Anglo-Egyptian Sudan	3·55	3·48	3·12	3·27	2·62	12·27	·30	5·74
Kenya	3·78	4·37	3·58	1·84	1·67	2·84	·80	3·07
Uganda				1·92	2·03	1·19	·08	3·64
Somaliland	·24	·34	·13	·32	·07	·86	·00	·34
Tanganyika	4·25	2·14	1·96	2·19	1·93	4·72	·37	5·11
Zanzibar		·61	·44	·62	·37	·01	·01	·23
Nyasaland	·99	·45	·43	·38	·41	·60	·07	1·59
Southern Rhodesia	8·38	3·91	4·34	3·72	4·53	1·89	2·47	1·28
Northern Rhodesia	·90	·90	2·40	·44	2·62	3·63	·44	1·37
Union of South Africa	42·81	47·38	54·69	50·29	54·87	5·95	89·51	8·61
South-West Africa	2·59	1·76	1·24	1·86	1·39	4·06	1·32	·35
French West Africa	2·49	5·95	5·87	5·22	5·28	22·88	·85	14·63
French Equatorial Africa	1·74	·87	1·48	·68	1·32	10·98	·19	3·37
Togo	1·53	·41	·29	·39	·27	·25	·01	·75
Cameroons		·85	·70	·72	·75	·43	·10	2·33
Angola	2·62	1·31	1·12	1·29	1·13	6·15	1·34	2·70
Mozambique	2·84	2·17	1·45	1·80	·98	3·75	·44	4·08
Guinea		·23		·23				...
Belgian Congo	11·73	4·69	4·15	3·96	5·07	11·61	·82	10·94
Ruanda Urundi	·10	·10	·18	1·06	·16	·27	·03	3·37

(a) The total populations on which these percentages are calculated are made up of the populations of all the territories included in this study, although all the territories are not included in the above Table. The date is approximately the end of 1935, and the figures are based on these.

(b) Gambia, Sierra Leone, Gold Coast and Nigeria.

(c) Nyasaland, Tanganyika, Kenya, Uganda, Anglo-Egyptian Sudan, Somaliland and Zanzibar.

(d) Southern Rhodesia and Northern Rhodesia only.

War in the German colonies, but by no means all of this was German capital. Considerable sums were raised through British financial channels and were subscribed for by English investors. Paish was of the opinion that the participation of continental investors in the issues in London for South Africa (including Rhodesia) did not amount to more than 8% of the total. This figure has been challenged by various writers as being too low. After considering all the available evidence, I am of the opinion that Paish's view is well founded, and Gilbert, in the article previously referred to,[1] supports this conclusion. It is true that there was considerable German enterprise associated with the foundation of the Witwatersrand Gold Mining Industry, and an important German and French holding of South African mining shares, but to regard the capital supplied by continental investors as more than 8% of all the new capital subscribed for South Africa does not appear warranted. On the other side of the account, it must be remembered that there is no doubt that a very large part of the capital invested in the Portuguese colonies was supplied by British investors. The figures given in the footnotes to Table 28[2] probably underestimate the amount and, as previously stated, at least half of the capital drawn from abroad for the development of Portuguese territories came from English sources. A part of the capital in the Belgian Congo, and even some of the capital, particularly the non-listed capital, invested in the French possessions, also came from London.

After the War, the new capital supplied from foreign sources for British territories (including the ex-German colonies and the Union of South Africa) can be regarded as unimportant, while, as is well known, German interests were liquidated, both in the Union and in the German colonies. The view is sometimes held that American capital has played an important part in some of the African territories since the War, but this appears to be fallacious. American capital has been associated in the development of a restricted number of special mining areas, and special types of commerce, but the total amount of capital invested by American interests is relatively unimportant. Professor Staley puts the total of such investments in the whole continent, including

[1] *Ibid., Quarterly Journal of Economics*, August, 1933, p. 561.   [2] *Vide supra*, p. 159.

Egypt and the Mediterranean countries, at roughly £24 millions[1] at the end of 1930.

XII
THE " OUTSTANDING " CAPITAL.

At this point, one is again brought up against the lack of information on the one hand, and clarity of definition on the other, in regard to the question of the amount of capital now actually held by British and other investors in Africa.

This question of the outstanding capital at a particular time bristles with difficulties.[2] The only estimates which attempt to break through some of these are the series of articles on "British Oversea Investments" by Sir Robert Kindersley in the *Economic Journal*. Unfortunately, however, his method appears to me to lead to considerable under-estimation[3] so that the results are of limited value for purposes of this study, although they may be a good index of the trend of British overseas investment as a whole. In the *Economic Journal*, in December, 1937, Sir Robert Kindersley arrives at the following totals in regard to British investments in Africa, at the end of 1936. In a table which he calls British Oversea Government and Municipal Investments, of which he gives two series, for 1936 and 1930, as follows:[4]

	1936.	1930.
South Africa and Rhodesia . ·	103	118
British East Africa . . .	15	18
West Africa	20	28
Other British African territories[5] (say)	20	13
	158	177

[1] *Ibid.*, p. 509.

[2] Some of these have been referred to in Section 2 of Chapter I, and Section 1 of this chapter.

[3] That Sir Robert Kindersley's calculations under-estimate the amount of capital invested has also been stressed by Staley, *ibid.*, p. 535, who states that Kindersley's result (for 1930) "drastically understates investments in the United States, and to a less extent, investments in South America, India, Canada and China".

[4] *Cf. ibid.*, p. 660.

[5] The table does not distinguish between African and non-African territories, but I have taken two-thirds of the amount given as applying to African territories in order not to under-estimate.

In another table he gives the total of all nominal British capital invested abroad at the end of 1936, from which the following figures have been taken[1]:

South Africa and Rhodesia	248
British East Africa · · · · ·	31
British West Africa · · · · ·	37
Other (two-thirds of the sum given) . . .	33
	———
	349

If the Government capital above is subtracted from this total, it would appear, according to his figures, that the total non-Government capital in British African territories at the present time is £191 millions. Sir Robert Kindersley states that his estimates refer to 85% of the total, but, even so, the figure quoted for Africa as a whole appears to me too small.[2] For the purposes of this study, as stated previously, I did not regard the statistical data available to me as warranting a calculation for Africa on the lines adopted by Kindersley.

XIII

FURTHER ANALYSIS OF AFRICAN TRADE.

There is reason to believe that investment in British territories has led to greater development than has resulted from investment elsewhere. It is difficult to verify such an impression statistically, but it is significant that the percentage which the total trade of British territories forms of all African trade is larger than might have been expected by considering the proportion which the capital invested from abroad in British territories bears to the total capital invested in Africa. In 1935 the total trade of British territories formed 85% of the whole, and for none of the years for which statistics are given in the above tables has the proportion

---

[1] Cf. ibid., p. 657.

[2] One source of error may be due to the fact that the figures refer to the Nominal Capital, and that this leads to very considerable under-estimates, particularly in the case of mining investments. In the Witwatersrand Gold Mining Industry, for example, and also in the Copper Industry of Northern Rhodesia, a very large part of the share capital was issued at a premium, and these premiums were invested in the industry.

fallen below 80%. In 1907 it was actually 84%, and, during the whole of the period since then, British territories have maintained their preponderating importance in this respect. On the other hand, in some territories the investments of capital from abroad have resulted in a lesser proportionate development. For example, the Belgian Congo accounts for 11·7% of the capital invested in Africa, but its trade has in these selected years never exceeded 5·9% of the total, and formed only 4·2% in 1935.

The Portuguese colonies account for only 5·6% of the total capital from abroad in Africa, and in 1935 their trade was only 2·6% of the whole; it had, however, reached 4·4% in 1931.

The fluctuations in the percentages which the trade or exports of individual territories form of the total trade or exports of the continent make it clear that these statistics must not be too strictly interpreted. As a broad index of relative economic development they are, nevertheless, significant.

Apart from the more rapid development of some territories, the fluctuations in the percentages are largely due to that characteristic feature of African economic development to which reference has already been made, namely, their dependence on mono-culture, or on a few important exportable products. Indeed, as is shown in Table 49,[1] only 8 products accounted for 76·6% of the total domestic exports of Africa. The products were gold (46·7%), diamonds (3·3%), copper (3·5%), wool (5·4%), cotton and cotton seed (5·0%), palm products (3·7%), cocoa (4·5%), and ground nuts (4·5%).[2]

[1] The statistics given in this Table are approximate.

[2] The figures in the table should be compared with those given in Table 3, Chapter II, and the footnote on page 39, where it was shown that in 1897, five commodities accounted for 72·4% of the total exports. The five commodities were gold (39·2%), diamonds (15·7%), wool (7·0%), rubber (6·0%), and palm products (4·5%). Rubber has greatly declined in importance, and in 1935 accounted for only 0·04% of the total domestic exports of Africa. The growth in cotton and cotton seed, cocoa and ground nut exports is significant. The figures for 1935 understate the importance of diamonds. It will be seen that in 1929 these accounted for 8·7% of the total African exports. It is significant that gold occupied a more important position in 1935 than in either 1913 or in 1897. In 1929, however, it formed only 27·5% of the total domestic exports of Africa owing to the relative decline of the value of gold in terms of commodities. For this reason also in 1929 all the other products listed in the table, with the exception of copper, occupied a more important place than they did in 1935. It will be noted that gold plays a more important part in British than in non-British territories.

TABLE 49.—*Value (a) of Exports of Selected African Products, and as Percentage of Total Domestic Exports of Africa, 1913, 1929, 1935. £(000).*

	Total British Territories excluding the Union of South Africa.			Total all British Territories.			Total all Non-British Territories.			Total all Territories.			Percentage of Total Domestic Exports of Africa.		
	1913.	1929.	1935.	1913.	1929.	1935.	1913.	1929.	1935.	1913.	1929.	1935.	1913.	1929.	1935.
Gold	4,588	3,650	9,134	42,177	48,675	80,706	240	490	2,779	42,417	49,165	83,485	40·9	27·5	46·7
Diamonds	2,669	2,149	1,536	14,716	14,223	4,513	20	1,394	1,315	14,736	15,617	5,828	14·2	8·7	3·3
Copper	52(b)	940	4,029	501	1,560	4,369	370	3,370	1,842	871	4,930	6,211	0·8	2·8	3·5
Wool	(b)	175	120	5,715	14,696	9,636	(b)	(b)	60	5,715	14,696	9,696	5·5	8·2	5·4
Maize and Maize Meal	105	760	408	189	3,585	3,399	(b)	385	229	189	3,970	3,628	0·2	2·2	2·0
Cotton and Cotton Seed	895	10,077	7,271	895	10,237	7,300	29	1,193	1,661	924	11,430	8,961	0·9	6·4	5·0
Palm Products	6,309	9,113	4,602	6,309	9,113	4,602	682	3,673	1,979	6,991	12,786	6,581	6·7	7·2	3·7
Cocoa	3,006	12,010	6,788	3,006	12,010	6,788	253	1,381	1,251	3,259	13,391	8,039	3·1	7·5	4·5
Rubber	598	221	82	598	221	82	2,399	130	...	2,997	351	82	2·9	0·2	0·04
Ground Nuts	861	3,394	2,728	861	3,394	2,728	80	4,811	5,334	941	8,205	8,062	0·9	4·6	4·5
Total	19,083	42,489	36,698	74,967	117,714	124,123	4,073	16,827	16,450	79,040	134,541	140,573	76·2	75·3	78·7

(a) The statistics given in this table are approximate.
(b) Information not available.

As a consequence, some territories gain relative to others at times when the world prices for their particular products are exceptionally favourable. For example, when the prices of mineral products rise more than those of agricultural or sylvan products, the mineral territories gain proportionately in their share of African trade.

It should also be borne in mind that the nature of the chief products in some territories, as for example West Africa, is such that they are produced under relatively primitive conditions by the indigenous population. In fact that process is often largely one of collecting natural products. The capital invested in these territories from abroad has, therefore, been utilized largely to provide public works, communications and commercial facilities, and their trade thus forms a larger proportion of the total trade of Africa than their share of the capital invested from abroad would lead one to expect. For example, in British West Africa, the capital invested forms 9·6% of the whole, but in 1935 the percentage ratio of its trade was 12·4%, and in 1928, when the prices obtained abroad for its main exports were particularly favourable, the ratio was as high as 18·1%. The situation in the Gold Coast illustrates the same point. The percentage of capital invested in this territory is 2·9%, but in 1935 its trade formed 5·3% of all African trade, while in 1924 it was as high as 6·1%. Similarly, French West Africa accounts for 2·5% of all capital invested in Africa from abroad, but its trade was 5·9% of the trade of Africa in 1935. This ratio, incidentally, is the same as in 1907; it reached its highest point in 1930, when it stood at 6·6%.

The Anglo-Egyptian Sudan, on the other hand, provides an example of a territory where production has been fostered by very large capital expenditure on irrigation and communications, as a result largely of Government enterprise. The capital invested in the Sudan forms 3·6% of all the capital invested in Africa, and it is therefore interesting to note that its trade accounted for 3·1% of all African trade in 1935, and 3·8% in 1929; the progress of the territory is indicated by the fact that before the War the corresponding percentage was only 1·8%.

When considering the preponderating economic position of

British territories in Africa, it is well to bear in mind that in 1935 about 55% of the total population, 96% of the European population and 44% of the area of the territories included in this survey was under the British flag. The relatively advanced economic position of the British territories, including in that term the Union of South Africa and the British Mandates, is, however, largely but by no means entirely due to the progress of the Union. The latter accounts for no less than 42·8% of the total capital invested in Africa, while its share of African trade in 1935 was 54·7%. The trade percentage has fluctuated considerably owing to the Union's large dependence on gold production. Consequently the country has enjoyed greater stability in periods of depression than most other territories, and this has shown itself in a rise in its share of trade at such times, followed by a fall when the other territories were favoured by relatively high prices for their special products. In 1907 the Union's share of African trade was nearly 61%, whereas in 1928, owing to the progress in other African territories and the favourable conditions in world markets for their products, the Union's trade percentage had fallen to 47·3%. Since then, however, it has again risen considerably.

If the Union and South-West Africa are excluded, it will be found that the remaining British territories account for 34·24% of the capital invested in Africa, and 28·8% (34·28% in 1928, the peak year) of African trade. On the other hand, the non-British territories taken together account for 22·9% of the capital, but only 15·23% of the trade (the ratio being 19·7% in 1930, which was the peak year). It thus appears that the trade of British territories, even excluding the Union and South-West Africa, had developed further than that of non-British territories.

XIV

THE IMPORTANCE OF MINING.

Mining has been the touchstone of economic development in most of Africa, and the areas most advanced economically are those whose main activities rest on mineral exploitation. In fact, the large part which mineral products form of African trade is, as a rule, not sufficiently stressed. Table 50 presents statistics for

TABLE 50.—*Value of Mineral Exports of Selected African Territories, 1907–35.   £(000,000).*

	1907.	1909	1913.	1924.	1929.	1930.	1931.	1932.	1933.	1934.	1935.
Sierra Leone	(a)	(a)	(a)	(a)	(a)	(a)	(a)	(a)	·2	·4	·8
Nigeria	(a)	(c)	·6	1·6	2·3	1·4	·9	·6	·8	1·5	1·8
Gold Coast	1·2	1·0	1·7	1·5	2·2	2·5	1·9	1·9	2·7	3·7	3·8
Total West Africa	1·2	1·0	2·3	3·1	4·5	3·9	2·8	2·5	3·7	5·6	6·4
Kenya and Uganda	(a)	(a)	(a)	·2	·3	·3	·2	·3	·3	·3	·4
Tanganyika	(a)	(a)	(a)	(a)	(a)	·1	(a)	(a)	·2	·3	·4
Southern Rhodesia	2·2	2·6	3·1	3·8	4·4	3·7	3·1	3·9	4·7	5·9	6·5
Northern Rhodesia	(a)	(a)	(a)	·2	·6	·6	·8	2·3	3·4	4·2	4·5
South-West Africa	(a)	3·3	1·0	1·8	2·7	1·8	·6	·2	(a)	·1	·8
Union of South Africa	39·2	38·6	51·9	55·8	61·5	55·6	51·6	52·3	74·3	61·4	77·5
Total all British Territories	42·6	45·5	58·3	64·9	74·0	66·0	59·1	61·5	86·6	77·8	96·5
% of Domestic Exports of above Territories	76·6%	76·2%	66·5%	52·5%	52·1%	55·3%	62·6%	61·6%	67·6%	66·7%	66·3%
% of Total Domestic Exports of British Territories	74·5%	73·9%	64·4%	49·1%	48·8%	51·1%	60·1%	58·3%	65·3%	63·5%	63·5%
Belgian Congo	(a)	(a)	(a)	3·0	4·8	5·8	4·8	3·2	3·0	4·6	5·6
Angola	(a)	(a)	(a)	·2	·6	·7	·6	·4	·6	·6	·6
Total Non-British Territories	(a)	(a)	(a)	3·2	5·4	6·5	5·4	3·6	3·6	5·2	6·2
% of Domestic Exports of above Non-British Territories	…	…	…	50·4%	50·0%	59·8%	62·0%	50·4%	46·9%	52·3%	56·7%
% of Total Domestic Exports	…	…	…	16·9%	20·0%	24·7%	28·0%	20·8%	20·2%	22·0%	23·5%
Total all Territories £(000)	42,644	45,628	58,216	67,958	79,496	72,576	64,575	65,017	90,243	82,993	102,723
% of Total Domestic Exports of all African Territories	64·0%	62·6%	56·1%	48·9%	44·5%	47·3%	55·1%	53·1%	59·9%	57·2%	57·5%
% of Domestic Exports of all above Territories	72·3%	72·1%	64·1%	52·4%	52·0%	55·7%	62·6%	60·9%	66·4%	65·6%	65·7%

(a) Negligible, or small, exact statistics not available.

selected years from 1907 to 1935[1] of the mineral exports of those British and foreign territories in which mining is of some importance. A comparison of the value of the mineral, with the value of the non-mineral, exports of the same territories for the years 1913, 1929, and 1935 is made in Table 51.

TABLE 51.—*Value of Mineral and Non-Mineral Exports of Selected African Territories*, 1913, 1929, 1935. £(000).

	1913.		1929.		1935.	
	Mineral.	Non-Mineral.	Mineral.	Non-Mineral.	Mineral.	Non-Mineral.
Sierra Leone . . .	(a)	1,376	(a)	1,319	810	746
Nigeria . . .	568	6,211	2,300	15,281	1,753	9,444
Gold Coast . . .	1,656	3,358	2,203	10,198	3,793	5,448
Kenya and Uganda .	(a)	1,008	345	6,676	419	6,190
Tanganyika . .	(a)	1,777	95	3,627	404	3,041
Southern Rhodesia .	3,077	220	4,359	2,250	6,457	1,620
Northern Rhodesia .	52	143	557	262	4,492	176
South-West Africa .	1,005	2,510	2,709	815	812	1,661
Union of South Africa .	51,857	12,708	61,496	27,535	77,505	20,426
Total British Territories	58,216	29,311	74,064	67,963	96,445	48,752
Belgian Congo . .	(b)	(b)	4,806	3,444	5,647	3,398
Angola . . .	(b)	(b)	626	1,984	631	1,387

(a) Negligible, or small.
(b) Not available.

It will be seen from Table 50 that the territories there listed together exported over £100 millions of minerals in 1935, and that this was equivalent to 66% of the value of the total domestic exports of the same territories. In 1907 the respective amount was £42·6 millions, equivalent to 72·3% of the value of the domestic exports of the same territories, although many of the territories in fact had no mineral production at all at that time. In 1935, the value of the mineral exports of the Union of South Africa, amounting to £77·5 millions, was three times the value of all the mineral exports of the remaining African territories. In fact, the

[1] Statistics for later years will be found in the detailed tables relating to the trade of each individual territory.

gold production of the Union in 1935 was in itself of greater value than all the non-mineral exports of the remaining territories in Africa taken together.

The great importance of gold in the economy of Africa as a whole is apparent from the fact that it formed roughly 47% of the total domestic exports of Africa in 1935.

In the detailed tables which have been prepared for most of the African territories, in order to illustrate the growth of their trade, statistics are given which show the percentage of their mineral exports. From these it will be seen that, in 1935, copper accounted for 29% of the domestic exports of the Belgian Congo and 72% of those of Northern Rhodesia. Diamonds formed 24% of the domestic exports of South-West Africa and 32% of the general exports of Angola, and were also important in the Belgian Congo. Moreover, gold is important not only in the Union, but formed 63% of the exports of Southern Rhodesia. On the other hand, the tin production of Nigeria, although appreciable in itself, accounted for only 13% of its exports.

It is further noteworthy that of the capital invested from abroad in Africa, no less than 66% has found its way into a special group of territories which, for convenience, may be regarded as the "special mineral territories". In this group it is convenient to include the Union of South Africa, South-West Africa, Southern Rhodesia, Northern Rhodesia and the Belgian Congo. Together, these territories in 1935 accounted for 92% of the value of minerals exported by the territories listed in Table 50; their trade formed 67% of the trade of Africa, and minerals accounted for 78% of their domestic exports. Certain other territories, however, also directly or indirectly owe much of their progress to mining. Thus, in 1935, 41% of the domestic exports of the Gold Coast were composed of minerals, mainly gold and diamonds, while in Nigeria the percentage was 15%—mainly tin. An example of the indirect stimulus of mining is provided by economic development in Portuguese East Africa which has been greatly influenced by the mineral expansion on the Rand and in the Rhodesias. Moreover, much of the capital invested in this territory, as has already been stated, was made available to facilitate economic, and particularly mining, development in the

Rhodesias. A good example of this is provided by the Beira Railway and the Beira Junction Railway and the harbour works undertaken by these companies. In Angola, also, economic development has been greatly dependent on the production of diamonds. Moreover, its main railway, the Benguella line, was built largely with British capital, and was intended to serve the copper belts of the Belgian Congo and Northern Rhodesia.

The special group of mineral territories accounts for a particularly large proportion of the capital made available for private enterprise in Africa, that is, all capital other than that which falls under the heading of Public Listed capital in Table 28.[1] The total of this private capital invested in Africa amounts to £675 millions of which no less than £479 millions, or 71%, was invested in these mineral territories. The remainder, invested elsewhere, amounts to £196 millions, but this latter sum still includes the private capital invested in territories such as Nigeria, the Gold Coast, and the Portuguese colonies, which have also been indirectly dependent on mineral development.

It is also not surprising to find that the ratio of public listed capital to total capital in the special group is 40%, while in the combined other territories it is 53%. This is due to the fact that, in the special group, Government enterprise did not have to play such a prominent role as elsewhere. Of course, the absolute amount of public listed capital in the mineral territories is larger than in the others, but this is simply due to the greater extent of their general economic development.

The analysis conducted in this chapter shows that, broadly speaking, capital investment in Africa falls into two large groups, of which the first and most important, is the large investment by Government, and the second the supply of equity capital for mining and exploration. The extent of the investment which falls under the first heading has involved most African territories in the difficult problem of fostering a sufficient export trade in order to meet their obligations abroad. On the whole, that problem has not yet been adequately solved, although its urgency has, in some territories, already tended to lead to the relative neglect of economic development in other directions.

[1] *Vide supra*, pp. 158–9.

It is probable that, in future, the rate of investment by, or under the ægis of Governments will be slower than in the past. In some territories such public investment has proceeded at a greater rate than the general internal development warranted, and leeway will have to be made up before further large Government expenditure will be justified.

The investment of equity capital will, at first, depend mainly on the possibility of further mineral expansion, but, taking a wider view, it is bound up with the general development of new income-creating activities, and, therefore, with the rate at which African populations can be induced, in some territories, and will be permitted, in others, to change their present economic outlook, to enter new occupations, and to engage in new forms of production.

THE ECONOMIC PROGRESS OF INDIVIDUAL AFRICAN DEPENDENCIES

"The running of a tropical colony is, of all tests, the most searching as to the development of the nation that attempts it. To see helpless people and not oppress them, to see great wealth and not confiscate it, to have absolute power and not abuse it, to raise the natives instead of sinking yourself, these are the supreme trials of a nation's spirit."—A. CONAN DOYLE.

THIS section surveys some special features of the economic progress of individual African territories. It is not intended in any way to be an economic history of those colonies, but confines itself to matters which illustrate some of the general issues considered in the earlier chapters of this study.

I

THE MANDATED TERRITORY OF SOUTH-WEST AFRICA.

The characteristic features of this country are its extent, its relative poverty, and the importance of diamonds in its economic development up to the present. It covers an area of 317,725 square miles, slightly more than two-thirds of that of the Union. In this vast territory it is estimated that there is a population of only 359,000, of whom 31,000 are Europeans, 65,000 are coloured, and 263,000 are natives.[1] Large tracts of the territory are uninhabited, and the inhabited portions may be said to be wedged in between two deserts—the Namib in the West and the Kalahari in the East. The Namib, which varies in width from 50 to 90 miles, stretches from the Kunene River in the north down the whole length of the territory. It is an arid region, where rain seldom falls, and it is almost devoid of vegetation. Except for the coastal towns, this portion of the country, covering an area of over 40,000 square miles, is uninhabited and practically uninhabitable.

[1] Preliminary 1936 Census figures.

The southern part of the country, from the Orange River to about 70 miles south of Windhoek, is mainly suitable for small stock-farming, but owing to the low annual rainfall, the severe droughts to which it is periodically subject and the great heat in summer, farming is often accompanied by such hardship and privation that only people of a certain type, such as "the trekboer", are willing, and able, to undertake it.

The central portion of the territory is suited for cattle-farming, particularly of the ranching type. But, in general, a large farm is required to afford a family a living, with the result that the population is thinly scattered over a large area, and the farms are far removed from the nearest railway station or village.[1]

"According to our evidence," says the *Report of the South-West Africa Commission*,[2] "the present surveyed farming area is 126,900 square miles, divided into some 3,980 farms. This means that on the average a farm comprises nearly 32 square miles (approximately 9,700 morgen). Yet, even on such huge farms, it is frequently difficult to make a living, and, in a great drought, the carrying capacity of the veld is reduced to practically *nil*."

The extreme north of the territory comprises the tracts of land known as the Kaokoveld (in the West), Ovamboland, the Okavango Area and the Caprivi Zipfel (in the East). These parts all lie outside the area known as the police zone, and, except for a few Europeans connected with the Government service or missionary work, are inhabited exclusively by natives numbering nearly 150,000, and comprise, roughly, three-fifths of the total non-European population of the territory.

The density of the population on the basis of the preliminary 1936 figures is 1·13 persons to the square mile, of which 0·096 are Europeans. "Outside the few urban centres," wrote the Commission, "a European was almost as difficult to find as the proverbial needle in a haystack."

The colonization of German South-West Africa may be said to have begun with the founding of the German Company for

[1] The above description is taken from the *South-West Africa Commission Report*, which contains an excellent account of the territory, and of its historical and economic development. U.G., No. 26, 1936.

[2] U.G., No. 26, p. 7.

South-West Africa, which was one of the " Chartered " type of companies by which Bismarck hoped to commence German colonization in Africa. It was registered in April, 1885, with a capital of £40,000, and received all rights to the lands which Luderitz had acquired, with the exception of those immediately adjoining Angra Pequana. By 1892 the company's political and administrative functions had ceased, and Germany had extended her imperial sway over the entire protectorate. The company then continued as a privileged commercial concern, with monopoly rights over large mining areas. In the early days of the Protectorate concession-hunting characterized economic activity. Eventually the mining rights over practically the whole country and the ownership of large tracts of land were vested in the following companies (apart from those vested in the Government):

The Deutsche Kolonial Gesellschaft.
The South-West Africa Company.
The South African Territories Company.
Siedlungsgesellschaft für D.S.W. Afrika.
The Kaoko Land und Minen Gesellschaft.
The Gibeon Schürff und Handels Gesellschaft.
The Anglo-German Territories Limited.

The keynote of the economic history of South-West Africa, until the years immediately preceding the Great War, was the difficulty of finding capital for its development and the burden it proved to be on the German Imperial Exchequer, owing to its limited possibilities. Even before the War, a considerable part of the private capital had to be obtained from British investors, and numerous British companies took part in exploring the economic possibilities of the territory. For example, the South-West Africa Company Limited, which was a Company with both British and German shareholders and directors, was registered in London with an issued capital of £1,750,000. It owned various areas in Demaraland and Great Namaqualand which it acquired from the Government in 1892. This Company constructed a branch railway line from Otavi to Grootfontein to serve the copper mines; the line was later acquired by the German Government. The South African Territories Limited was another company registered in London. It had an issued capital of £482,328.

There was also the Anglo-German Territories Limited, which was registered in London in 1891 with an issued capital of £251,527. The South-West Africa Company Limited floated various other companies for mineral exploration from time to time.

The large cost of the colony to the German Imperial Government is indicated by the fact that, up to 1906, nearly £5 millions had been paid to the territory in the form of annual imperial subsidies; in addition, about £23 millions had been spent on the 1904–1907 Native War. Thereafter, up to 1915, the expenditure of a further sum of nearly £14 millions in imperial subsidies of one kind or another was necessary. During the last five years before the South African occupation, the subsidies paid by the German Imperial Government amounted to nearly £3,500,000, or an average of some £700,000 per annum.[1]

Actually the colony was saved from stagnation only by the discovery of diamonds and by the exploitation of the copper mines which had begun in 1902, but was of secondary importance. The history of the Cape and the Orange Free State after the diamond discoveries, was repeated on a miniature scale in South-West Africa. This is illustrated by the following Table of the imports and exports[2] of the colony from 1900 to 1913:

German South-West Africa.

	Imports. £(000).	Exports. £(000).
1900	348	45
1901	504	62
1902	423	111
1903	397	172
1904	503	15
1905	1,182	11
1906	3,431(a)	19
1907	1,620	81
1908	1,659	390
1909	1,736	1,104
1910	2,217	1,735
1911	2,655	1,429
1912	1,625	1,952
1913	2,171	3,515

(a) Includes an unusually large amount in respect of Government stores.

[1] *South-West Africa Commission Report*, p. 64.
[2] The large excess of imports over exports, particularly in the earlier years, is an indication of the large expenditure on the territory from external sources.

The growth of the diamond output since the discovery of the fields was as follows:

Before Formation of Regie.

1908	.	.	.	.	.	39,375 carats
1909 (part)	.	.	.	.	.	5,303 ,,

Particulars of Regie Operations.

				Carats.		Value.
1909/10 .	.	.	.	560,977	.	£ 836,000
1910/11 .	.	.	.	798,865	.	1,069,000
1911/12 .	.	.	.	816,296	.	1,045,000
1912/13 .	.	.	.	902,157	.	1,324,500
1913	.	.	.	1,284,727	.	2,698,500
				285,273 unsold.		

Thus, from the commencement of diamond mining to the end of 1913, approximately 4,693,000 carats were extracted and exported, realizing over £7 millions.

The effect of the diamond production on the exports of the colony is indicated by the following statistics.   As will be seen, fluctuations in exports closely corresponded with the yearly increase or decrease in the export of diamonds.

Difference between	Total exports.		Exports of diamonds.	
	Increase.	Decrease.	Increase.	Decrease.
1910 and 1909 . 631	.	...	.	572	.	...
1911 ,, 1910	.	306	.	...	.	192
1912 ,, 1911 . 523	.	...	.	369	.	...
1913 ,, 1912 . 1,563	.	...	.	1,425	.	...

£(000).

As a result of diamond mining the ordinary revenue of the colony greatly improved.

The Imperial Government also sanctioned the raising of a loan of about £5 millions for the territory.   A large proportion of this, in addition to the surplus revenues of the years 1904–14, was expended in carrying out an extensive policy of development —the construction and acquisition of railways, improvements to harbours, land settlement, the establishment of an agricultural department, experimental farms, surveys, irrigation projects, water boring, and the provision of credit facilities for those engaged in farming.

In 1915 the railway mileage of the territory was 1,310 miles, and the capital invested in the State railways was nearly £7 millions. The white civilian population on January 1st, 1913, was about 13,000. After the outbreak of hostilities during the Great War, the South African Railway System was extended from Prieska to Upington, and connected with the German System at Kalkfontein South. A line was also constructed from Walvis Bay to Swakopmund.

The most significant feature of the railway system of South-West Africa is that, mainly owing to military exigencies, it has been overbuilt. Since the Union took over the territory there have been no profits on the railways, and the South African Railways and Harbours Administration has borne all the losses. From 1920 to 1936 they amounted to nearly £3 millions. There is insufficient traffic, particularly of a type able to bear high railway rates, and the population is far too small to support the existing railway system. These conditions, as the Commission on the Economic and Financial Conditions of the Mandated Territory has shown, are not likely to be altered unless new minerals are discovered, or existing mining operations greatly extended.

From 1926 until the depression considerable sums were spent on settlement, and in assisting farmers. Boring took place on a large scale, and considerable efforts were made to hasten agricultural development in the territory. The sanguine expectations of the sponsors of this policy were shattered by the world depression and by the prolonged and severe drought, which, with the exception of one season, continued for seven years.

The South-West Africa Commission has shown that, starting with a credit balance of nearly £1,000,000 in 1920, the Mandated Territory nevertheless had a debt of £2,360,900 after fourteen years. What really happened was that the Administration had to borrow from the mandatory power the money to pay for its interest and guarantees, thus steadily increasing the interest burden. "It is clear," says the *Report of the South-West Africa Commission*, "that unless revenue improves considerably, there is no prospect of the territory being able to meet the annual charge for the service of the debt, while the practice of borrowing for this purpose only makes the position worse from year to year. Without a reversal of the present trend, the situation must resolve itself in the not too distant future in absolute bankruptcy."

The Commission showed that, if to the existing debt of the territory (amounting to £2,360,900) there is added the capital expenditure which was incurred on the South-West Africa Railways by the South African Railways, the total amounts to £3,671,900.. It compared the net debt per head of the population in the Union and in the mandated territory as follows:

	Net debt per head of—					
	White population.			Total population.		
	£	s.	d.	£	s.	d.
Union . . .	131	4	6	29	13	6
South-West Africa .	116	4	0	15	12	0

Taking into account the fact that "the natives in the territory can hardly be said to contribute towards the service of the debt", it concluded that "the mandated territory, starting with free use of considerable capital assets, including nearly £1,000,000 in cash, accumulated in fourteen years a debt per head of the white population almost equal to that which the Union has accumulated during the whole period of its existence, including that taken over from the colonies which now constitute its provinces".

Moreover, the Commission found that there was little prospect of establishing the territory on a sound financial footing unless mining revenue were to increase considerably. The average annual mining revenue has been as follows:

1924/5–1926/7	.	.	.	.	.	£290,000
1927/8–1929/30	.	.	.	.	.	86,000
1930/1–1932/3	.	.	.	.	.	43,000
1933/4–1935/6	.	.	.	.	.	37,000
1936/7	.	.	.	.	.	123,257

Mining has for many years been one of the chief sources of revenue of the territory, but unfortunately the receipts from this source fluctuate widely, as is well illustrated by the fact that in 1925/6 they were £352,000, while in 1932/3 they fell to £10,000. In fact, the fluctuations in mining revenue make it difficult to draw up the budgets of the territory on the customary annual basis.

At the 31st March, 1936, the total indebtedness of the territory to the Union Government (apart from the latter's expenditure on the South-West Africa Railway System) stood at £2,606,000. Of this amount £1,059,000 had been utilized to meet deficits incurred on ordinary revenue and expenditure. The decline in the ordinary revenue is significant; it amounted to £439,764, £478,329 and £551,796 for the three years up to March, 1936,[1] as compared with an average of £739,000 for the three years 1927/8 to 1929/30, and an average of £870,000 for the years 1920 to 1930. In 1937 revenue recovered to £669,140, and extraordinary revenue to £198,976. At the 31st March, 1937, the Public Debt was £2,570,266.

The percentages of the territory's revenues absorbed by interest and redemption charges on loans, and by the payment of losses incurred in the operating of Walvis Bay harbour and of the Gobabis Railway (but not including the losses of the rest of the railway system), were as follows:

Year.	Percentage of Revenue paid in Interest and Redemption of Loans.	Percentage of Revenue paid in Losses on Walvis Bay Harbour and Gobabis Railway.	Total Percentage.
1926/7	nil	2·2	2·2
1927/8	·6	1·9	2·5
1928/9	1·4	4·0	5·4
1929/30 (a)	2·4	3·6	6·0
1930/1	7·5	6·9	14·4
1931/2	15·9	9·9	25·8
1932/3 (unaudited)	28·5	11·0	39·5
1933/4 (estimated)	40·0	14·0	54·0

(a) Excluding repayment of a temporary advance of about £41,000.

There is no doubt that the future of the territory is largely bound up with its mineral prospects. Dr. W. P. de Kock, who was until recently in charge of the mining affairs in the territory, gave evidence to the South-West Africa Commission to the effect that, apart from diamonds and copper, the known minerals were found only in small quantities and were widely dispersed.

[1] As given in the Union's Report to the League of Nations for the year 1937 (U.G. No. 25, 1938), and excluding extraordinary revenue for the above years as follows: £34,229, £43,910, £90,422.

In addition, exploitation was rendered difficult by transport over long distances and lack of water and fuel. He considered that there were good prospects for the small miner in regard to gold, lithium, flourspar, vanadium, etc. As small miners were, however, not in a position to pay for scientific exploration and technical advice, he thought this should be undertaken by the Administration.

The following figures illustrate the percentages of the principal exports of the territory which fall under the headings of—

(a) Minerals, including precious and semi-precious stones, precious and base metals, ores and concentrates of base metals and non-metals;

(b) Animals, agricultural products and foodstuffs:

Year.	Amount.	Percentage of total.
1928 (a)	2,033,870	61
(b)	1,144,819	34
1929 (a)	2,587,931	72
(b)	825,157	23
1930 (a)	1,835,790	72
(b)	604,763	24
1931 (a)	587,672	40
(b)	697,714	48
1932 (a)	195,113	18·7
(b)	784,244	75·3
1933 (a)	90,629	6·22
(b)	1,195,446	82·12
1934 (a)	121,404	10·63
(b)	924,715	82·24
1935 (a)	844,134	33·55
(b)	1,566,047	62·80
1936 (a)	1,194,005	38·43
(b)	1,796,925	57·83
1937 (a)	1,421,784	38.52
(b)	2,134,792	57.84

The improvement in the economic conditions of the territory since the depression is reflected not only in the general revival of trade, but also in the increase in the percentage which minerals form of the total exports, which rose from 6% in 1933 to 58% in 1936. The value of diamonds sold increased from approximately £58,000 in 1933 to £916,000 in 1936, as compared with £1,618,000 in 1929. Owing, however, to the accumulated unabsorbed losses of the diamond mines, which at the end of the financial year 1935/6 amounted to £1,050,000, no profit tax on diamonds accrued to the Administration during the financial year, which, incidentally, closed with a deficit of £177,000. In 1937 the total value of diamonds sold amounted to £1,100,492.

Table 52 shows the development of the trade and finances of the territory to 1937. The rise in the total imports and exports in the last few years, as a result of the general world recovery and, in particular, the revival of the diamond trade, is noteworthy. The very important role which mining has played in this territory is indicated by the fact that of its total exports from 1906 to 1936, amounting to £53 millions, over £41 millions represented minerals, of which diamonds alone accounted for over £30 millions. The farming industry of South-West Africa remains predominantly pastoral. It produced 7,137,509 lb. of butter in 1937, of which 56·6% was exported to South Africa, and the remainder overseas. The Karakul sheep industry has continued to grow in importance. The value of exports of Karakul pelts is estimated to have increased from approximately £68,000 in 1931 to approximately £1,222,629 in 1937.

In 1937 cattle, including sheep and goats, to the estimated value of £226,000 was exported to the Union from South-West Africa, from which its total imports in the same year were valued at £935,330. It is worth noting that, with the exception of its trade with the Union, with which it forms an economic unit, South-West Africa has no trade of importance with any other African territories. The exports to the Union were of particular importance for the territory during the depression, when its mineral exports greatly declined. In 1936 exports to the Union amounted to £604,607.

Broadly speaking, South-West Africa provides an example of a territory which, except in particularly favourable years, cannot as yet pay its own way. It still requires the support of a colonial power able and willing to spend considerable sums on development, in the form of subsidies or grants-in-aid. Indeed, some of the recommendations of the South-West Africa Commission, supporting the conclusions of a previous inquiry,[1] envisaged the

[1] Commission on the Economic and Financial Relations between the Union of South Africa and the Mandated Territory of South-West Africa, 1935, U.G. No. 16, 1935, which should also be consulted for an excellent analysis of the economic development of the country.

TABLE 52.—*South-West Africa. Trade and Finance Statistics,(a) 1920–37, and Proportion per cent. of Annual Exports of Selected Commodities to the Domestic Produce Exported.(a)*

Year. (g)	Imports.(e) (000).	Exports. Domestic. £(000).	Exports. Re-exports. £(000).	Copper Exports. £(000).(b)	Copper Exports. %.	Diamond Exports. £(000).	Diamond Exports. %.	All Mineral Exports. £(000).	All Mineral Exports. %.	Ordinary Revenue. £(000).	Ordinary Expenditure. £(000).	Customs and Excise. £(000).	Percentage of Ordinary Revenue.
1920	2,180	5,401	...	...	...	1,600	29·62	...	...	1,601	929(c)	127	7·93
1921	1,211	1,537	...	...	...	493	31·06	...	...	871	678	75	8·61
1922	1,148	1,247	...	...	...	791	63·43	...	...	854	626	78	9·13
1923	1,301	2,672	...	...	...	1,657	62·01	...	...	849	629	155	18·26
1924	1,777	2,851	...	...	...	1,113	39·04	2,147	75·31	652	713	121	18·56
1925	2,176	2,769	66	555	20·04	1,387	50·09	2,148	77·57	753	715	131	17·40
1926	2,478	3,227	71	502	15·56	1,864	57·76	2,526	78·28	889	638	358	40·27
1927	2,497	3,533	66	425	12·03	1,872	52·99	2,504	70·87	691	694	273	39·51
1928	2,872	3,296	69	525	15·93	1,216	36·89	2,034	61·71	754	737	295	39·12
1929	3,071	3,525	78	703	19·94	1,564	44·37	2,588	73·42	773	827	291	37·65
1930	2,099	2,550	75	425	16·67	1,184	46·43	1,836	72·00	628	767	218	34·71
1931	1,590	1,340	109	170	12·69	227	16·94	588	43·88	531	753	110	20·72
1932	883	1,041	109	(f)	...	85	8·17	195	18·73	357	603	90	25·21
1933	1,037	1,347	91	(f)	...	10	0·74	91	6·76	440	613	108	24·55
1934	1,256	1,099	53	(f)	...	25	2·27	121	11·01	476	685	145	30·46
1935	1,486	2,473(d)	58	(f)	...	588	23·78	844	34·13	552	732	148	26·86
1936	1,941	3,055(d)	52	(f)	...	896	29·22	1,194	38·94	669	804	197	29·45
1937	2,421(h)	3,691(h)	47(h)	187(i)	5·07	917	24·84	1,446	39·18	...	...	...	...

(a) Extracted from the Reports by the Mandatory Power to the League, and from the *Union Year Books.*
(b) From 1924 copper exports include copper-lead matte and pig lead.
(c) This figure includes £22,748, being the expenditure on military establishment.
(d) In these years gold bullion was valued at the prices ruling on the day of export.
(e) After 1925 import figures excluded value of specie; domestic produce exported excludes value of specie, and re-exports; prior to 1925 these items appear to be included.
(f) Negligible.
(g) Finance statistics refer to the year ended 31st March following that stated.
(h) Includes value of specie.
(i) Estimated.

establishment of a system whereby development would be financed by the mandatory power from a separate account, and interest would not accrue on the amounts so spent, unless in the future the territory should be fortunate enough to develop in such a way as to be able to meet the interest burden involved.

II

BASUTOLAND, BECHUANALAND AND SWAZILAND.

The political future of the High Commission territories, as is well known, has been subject to much dispute in recent years, and as a result, a considerable literature[1] on the conditions in these territories is now available. It is, therefore, not necessary to give a description of them here.

Basutoland covers an area of approximately 11,716 square miles and is entirely a Native Reserve. Its population, according to the 1936 Census, numbered 562,311, of whom 1,434 were Europeans, 1,263 Coloureds, 341 Asiatics and the rest Bantu. The density of population per square mile in 1936 was 47·99.

Bechuanaland covers an area which has been estimated at 275,000 square miles, and its population, according to the 1936 Census, amounted to 265,756, of whom 3,737 were Coloured and 1,889 were European.

Swaziland is the smallest of the territories, and has an area of only 6,705 square miles. Its population, according to the 1936 Census, amounted to 153,270, of whom 2,740 were Europeans. At the time of the Census 9,561 Bantu were absent at labour centres outside Swaziland, but were included in the total population.

From an economic point of view the outstanding feature of the territories is their lack of economic development, but Basutoland appears to have shown relatively greater progress than the other two territories. Capital investment from abroad in the territories, in none of which mineral resources of

[1] *Cf.* Bibliography.

importance have yet been developed, and none of which possess any valuable natural products, has been absolutely negligible. The railway which traverses Bechuanaland was not built to serve that territory at all.

The three territories now exist in greater or in lesser degree as economic appendages to the Union of South Africa. Their commodity exports consist mainly of cattle, hides and skins, and, in the case of Basutoland, also of wheat and maize, and depend for their market on the Union. Their main export is the labour of their peoples, who obtain work in the Union ; the absence of so large a part of their populations from home involves the usual disadvantages.

It is difficult to envisage the successful development of any of these territories as separate economic entities. Their economic future is bound up with the fortunes and policies of the sur- rounding countries, and it is only as a part of a larger economic whole that their potentialities are likely to be developed.

Unfortunately, at present, their political status has made them dependent on fortuitous economic circumstances, such as the trade policies adopted by their neighbours. They are not assured of continually open markets for some of their main products, while the political uncertainties about their future have obviously prevented the inauguration of large development schemes which might otherwise have been adopted. The fear of losing more than they might gain, economically or otherwise, by union with their neighbours has kept the territories in a state of uncertainty which has been most detrimental to their economic progress. From the point of view of the economic welfare of their popula- tions, the sooner this uncertainty can be terminated, and definite guarantees for the future economic status of the populations obtained, the better.

Table 53 gives the trade statistics and the gross revenue and expenditure of the territories in recent years. These figures strikingly illustrate the small degree of development that has taken place. In view of the special circumstances which have prevented the economic progress of these territories, their present trade and finances are not an indication of their real potentialities.

TABLE 53.—*Trade Statistics for Basutoland and Bechuanaland Protectorate, and Finance Statistics for Basutoland, Bechuanaland Protectorate, and Swaziland.*

Basutoland. (a)   Trade Statistics.

Date.	Total Imports. (b)	Total Exports. (b)	Wool Exports.	Cattle Exports.	Maize Exports.	Wheat and Wheat Meal Exports.	Mohair Exports.
	£(000).	£(000).	£(000).	£(000).	£(000).	£(000).	£(000).
1906	242	185	...	...	...	...	...
1907	239	249	...	...	...	...	...
1908	240	193	...	...	...	...	...
1909	259	350	139	...	75	...	...
1916	667	840	331	79	91	99	157
1917	901	812	389	89	58	106	127
1918	882	1,008	466	115	27	199	163
1919	1,137	1,380	594	99	45	357	213
1920	1,219	937	419	106	21	218	112
1921	556	510	212	45	17	153	64
1922	702	669	377	8	11	139	105
1923	827	804	514	7	41	72	120
1924	942	959	716	1	7	32	183
1925	851	756	469	4	35	106	119
1926	710	697	427	12	3	112	121
1927	894	839	509	10	18	115	139
1928	972	1,013	611	7	59	131	139
1929	761	695	436	7	42	64	94
1930	533	318	157	14	2	105	22
1931	463(c)	251	98	28	(d)	91	22
1932	455(c)	308	105	16	1	168	10
1933	611(c)	330	196	42	(d)	45	27
1934	567(c)	285	119	54	1	89	13
1935	588(c)	331	131	15	3	152	23
1936	712(c)	302	154	34	(d)	66	42

(a) Source : *Colonial Reports* 1909 and 1916–36.
(b) These statistics appear to be general trade, excluding specie and including goods for re-export.
(c) Excluding Government Imports (£62,660 in 1934, £33,095 in 1935 and £38,236 in 1936).
(d) Negligible.

Bechuanaland Protectorate. (e)   Trade Statistics.

Date.	Total Imports.	Total Exports.	Butter Exports.	Cattle Exports.
	£(000).	£(000).	£(000).	£(000).
1929	288	282	34	141
1932	175	169	25	94
1933	151	28	...	3
1934	179	139	32	(f)
1935	311	260	10	62
1936	363	348	11	105

(e) Sources : *Union Year Book*, 1937 ; *Colonial Report*, 1931.   (f) Negligible

Swaziland.
No Trade Statistics for Swaziland are obtainable

Finance Statistics.   £(000).

Date.	Basutoland.(g)		Bechuanaland Protectorate. (g)		Swaziland.(g)	
	Gross Revenue.	Gross Expenditure.	Gross Revenue.	Gross Expenditure.	Gross Revenue.	Gross Expenditure.
1928–29	340	317	142	144	96	131
1929–30	327	334	146	156	111	119
1930–31	282	322	149	155	103	128
1931–32	267	280	107	156	112	119
1932–33	275	264	102	143	115	113
1933–34	246	292	78	187	128	123
1934–35	302	295	109	184	174	138
1935–36	322	299	133	210	158	135

(g) Sources : *Union Year Books*, 1931–37.

TABLE 54.—*Southern Rhodesia. Trade Statistics, 1900–37, and Proportion per cent. of Annual Exports of Selected Commodities to Annual Value of all Domestic Produce Exported.(f)*

Year.	Merchandise Imports.(a) £(000).	Exports.(b) Domestic Produce. £(000).	Re-exports. £(000).	Gold Exports. £(000).	Gold Exports. %.	Asbestos Exports. (Raw.) £(000).	Asbestos Exports. (Raw.) %.	Chrome Iron Ore Exports. £(000).	Chrome Iron Ore Exports. %.	All Mineral Exports. £(000).	All Mineral Exports. %.	Tobacco Exports (Unmanufactured.) £(000).	Tobacco Exports (Unmanufactured.) %.
1900	1,222(d)	(c)	...	...	...	...	...	...	...	...	...	...	...
1901	1,443(d)	(c)	...	...	...	...	...	...	...	...	...	...	...
1902	1,859(d)	(c)	...	...	...	...	...	...	...	...	...	...	...
1903	1,540	(c)	...	...	...	...	...	...	...	...	...	...	...
1904	942	(c)	...	...	...	...	...	...	...	...	...	...	...
1905	1,214(d)	1,982(d)	...	...	...	...	...	...	...	...	...	...	...
1906	1,249	1,961(g)	116(g)	...	...	...	...	...	...	...	...	...	...
1907	1,363	2,319(g)	81(g)	...	...	...	...	...	...	...	...	...	...
1908	1,662	2,614(g)	82(g)	...	...	...	...	...	...	...	...	...	...
1909	2,022	2,806(g)	299(g)	2,551	90·9	3	0·1	72	2·6	2,628	93·7	11	0·4
1910	2,329	2,812	166	2,531	90·0	2	0·1	101	3·6	2,637	93·8	27	1·0
1911	2,746	2,851	225	2,544	89·2	3	0·1	118	4·1	2,669	93·6	30	1·1
1912	2,766	2,975	177	2,627	88·3	...	...	155	5·2	2,801	94·2	33	1·1
1913	2,939	3,297	157	2,887	87·6	2	0·1	141	4·3	3,077	93·3	51	1·5
1914	2,539	2,760	147	2,180	79·0	2	0·1	115	4·2	2,410	87·3	104	3·8
1915	2,065	4,801	174	2,974	61·9	27	0·6	144	3·0	3,520	73·3	37	0·8
1916	2,340	4,311	264	3,014	69·9	89	2·1	336	7·8	3,984	92·4	36	0·8
1917	2,418	4,487	318	2,855	63·6	167	3·7	265	5·9	3,886	86·6	55	1·2
1918	2,957	3,802	396	2,043	53·7	200	5·3	130	3·4	3,104	81·6	68	1·8
1919	3,207	4,116	322	2,181	53·0	240	5·8	58	1·4	3,098	75·3	76	1·8
1920	5,200	5,159	576	2,428	47·1	356	6·9	201	3·9	3,561	69·0	143	2·8
1921	5,183	4,299	503	2,299	53·5	431	10·0	81	1·9	3,415	79·4	189	4·4

Year					%		%		%		%		%
1922	3,853	4,269	357	2,605	61·0	288	6·7	195	4·6	3,678	86·2	161	3·8
1923	3,506	4,916	365	2,586	52·6	469	9·5	249	5·1	3,925	79·8	186	3·8
1924	3,956	5,120	435	2,395	46·8	499	9·7	362	7·1	3,813	74·5	277	5·4
1925	4,783	5,184	947	2,056	39·7	636	12·3	316	6·1	3,530	68·1	148	2·9
1926	6,282	5,445 (h)	1,060	2,536	46·6	580	10·7	389	7·1	3,887	71·4	329	6·0
1927	7,480	6,300	1,038	2,479	39·3	537	8·5	424	6·7	3,771	59·9	1,254	19·9
1928	8,332	6,576	1,337	2,421	36·8	733	11·1	392	6·0	4,047	61·5	838	12·7
1929	8,734 (e)	6,609	1,951	2,396	36·3	891	13·5	639	9·7	4,359	66·0	470	7·1
1930	7,472 (e)	5,634 (i)	1,797 (e)	2,223	39·5	620	11·0	441	7·8	3,693	65·5	306	5·4
1931	5,493	4,437	1,339	2,165	48·8	455	10·3	218	4·9	3,072	69·2	375	8·3
1932	4,028	5,339 (j)	870	(j)3,404	63·8	249	4·7	85	1·6	3,887	72·8	548	10·6
1933	4,434	5,906 (j)	691	(j)3,910	66·2	512	8·7	82	1·4	4,676	79·2	447	7·3
1934	5,271	7,502 (j)	844	(j)4,888	65·2	578	7·7	174	2·3	5,868	78·2	769	10·5
1935	6,374	8,077 (j)	892	(j)5,123	63·4	793	9·8	289	3·6	6,457	79·9	652	8·1
1936	6,859	9,268 (j)	847	(j)5,639	60·8	959	10·3	465	5·0	...	...	652	7·0
1937	8,497	...	...	...	...	1,230	...	673	...	...	...	935	...

(a) Excluding bullion and coin, including goods subsequently re-exported. To 1904, inclusive, for twelve months ended 31st March of the year following that stated.

(b) Excluding coin only. To 1904, inclusive, for twelve months ended 31st March of the year following that stated.

(c) Not available.

(d) Including bullion and Coin.

(e) As from this year Goods in Transit via Beira to Northern Rhodesia, formerly included in Imports and Exports, were excluded. The value of such Goods in Transit in 1930 amounted to £761,000.

(f) Extracted from the *Statistical Abstracts for the British Empire*. There are slight differences between the figures as given in the 1935 and 1936 volumes. Figures for "All Mineral Exports" are from Southern Rhodesia Reports.

(g) Includes goods in transit.

(h) Estimated.

(i) Prior to 1930 the figures for exports of domestic produce are inclusive of the produce of other South African countries exported from Southern Rhodesia. These are subsequently included as re-exports.

(j) Includes estimated value of gold premium.

III

SOUTHERN RHODESIA.

Southern Rhodesia is at present the most important mineral territory in Africa north of the Union. But, in general, mining is not conducted on such a large scale as in the Union, Northern Rhodesia, and the Belgian Congo. About one-third of the occupied population is engaged in mining and agriculture. Up to 1920 nearly the whole of the exports of the country consisted of minerals, as is still the case at present.

Table 54 traces the growth of the imports and exports of Southern Rhodesia from 1900 to 1937, and shows the percentage which the most important exports formed of the total domestic exports in each year. It is significant that the only non-mineral export of importance is tobacco. This table should be compared with Table 55, which shows the growth of the revenue, expenditure and Public Debt of the territory.

Professor Clay's Report on *Industrial Relations in Southern Rhodesia*, gives the following bird's-eye view of the economic structure of the country: "In Southern Rhodesia there would appear to be four industries, or branches of economic activity, that can be placed in the primary or fundamental class. There is first the trade with the indigenous native population. The natives, although largely self-sufficing in their economy, produce certain commodities in excess of their own needs for which there is a demand elsewhere, and have acquired a taste for commodities of European manufacture which they can obtain in exchange for their surplus. The initiative in this trade naturally comes from the European side; it provided perhaps the earliest economic opening for Europeans in the country, and offers a growing field not only for European traders, but for local manufacturers, as the native's habit of life approximates to European standards, and his ability to satisfy these growing wants by his economic production increases. Second is the mining industry, historically much the most important, the most exclusively export in the direction of its activities, and still, by its large local purchases of stores and foodstuffs and its large distribution of wages, the chief support of the derivative industries. There is, thirdly, that

TABLE 55.—*Southern Rhodesia. Finance*, 1900–36.(c) £(000).

Year. (b)	Gross Revenue.	Customs and Excise Revenue.	Percentage to Total.	Gross Expenditure.	Public Debt.
1900	406	91(a)	22·4	639	...
1901	435	121	27·8	711	...
1902	498	128	25·7	770	...
1903	435	127	29·2	737	...
1904	453	106	23·4	590	...
1905	524	129	24·6	500	...
1906	545	157	28·8	501	...
1907	554	162	29·2	544	...
1908	564	194	34·4	535	...
1909	620	208	33·5	614	...
1910	773	274	35·4	752	...
1911	809	298	36·8	838	...
1912	758	255	33·6	885	...
1913	777	254	32·7	836	...
1914	718	224	31·2	849	...
1915	745	266	35·7	769	...
1916	736	254	34·5	751	...
1917	737	224	30·4	790	...
1918	888	298	33·6	889	...
1919	1,053	316	30·0	1,082	...
1920	1,368	417	30·5	1,350	...
1921	1,489	437	29·3	1,335	...
1922	1,326	403	30·4	1,357	...
1923	1,522	432	28·4	1,356	...
1924	1,599	462	28·9	1,592	3,034
1925	1,842	487	26·4	1,752	4,114
1926	2,010	570	28·4	2,007	4,119
1927	2,165	686	31·7	2,169	4,280
1928	2,333	681	29·2	2,274	6,146
1929	2,487	705	28·3	2,411	6,142
1930	2,449	740	30·2	2,453	6,149
1931	2,110	543	25·7	2,229	6,382
1932	2,269	644	28·4	2,177	6,559
1933	2,465	719	29·2	2,500	8,969
1934	2,722	791	29·1	2,637	9,214
1935	2,821	792	28·1	2,915	10,160
1936	3,060	809	26·4	3,018	10,898

(a) Customs Duties were first imposed on 1st August, 1899.
(b) For twelve months ended 31st March of the years following that stated.
(c) Extracted from the *Southern Rhodesian Year Books*, the *Statistical Abstracts for the British Empire*, and the *Reports of the Auditor-General*.

part of agriculture—more than a quarter of the whole—which is carried on for export. So far as agriculture has developed to meet the needs of the mining population and the other workers who were drawn into the country, either by the needs of the mining industry or the opportunities of native trade, it is derivative and dependent on these; but in so far as it is working for export, it is exploiting special advantages of the Rhodesian soil and situation, and would continue, even if there were no local market to supply. Similarly, a fourth opening for European economic activity is that part of the work of transport done by the Railways which is done for territories outside Rhodesia.[1] On these four primary industries the other economic activities of the community all depend; in the extent of their development lies the limit to the employment that these derivative industries can give, in the state of prosperity they enjoy the limit to the prices, and therefore wages and profits, that these others can secure."

From the commencement of production to the end of 1936, the total value of all minerals and precious stones produced in Southern Rhodesia has been estimated to amount to £131,535,680 made up as follows:

TABLE 56.—*Southern Rhodesia. Total Value of All Minerals and Precious Stones Produced from the Commencement of Mining to December 31st, 1936.*

Gold	£100,170,430
Silver	602,590
Antimony Ore	5,201
Asbestos	12,535,843
Arsenic	124,567
Barytes	1,277
Chrome Ore	7,197,313
Coal (raised)	7,265,063
Corundum	1,285
Copper	2,873,880
Iron Ore	9,388
Iron Pyrites	50,609
Ironstone	4,196
Lead	96,719
Lepidolite	48
Limestone	9,427
Magnesite	19
Mica	387,339
Nickel Ore	1,403
Ochre	300
Sulphur	843
Tantalum	71
Tin	37,538
Tungsten Ores	72,198
Zinc	4,725
Diamonds	75,343
Other Precious Stones . . .	8,065
	£131,535,680

[1] Some aspects of Rhodesian railway finance are dealt with in a separate section of this chapter. It is noteworthy that in 1936 the gross earnings of the Rhodesian railways arising from the transport of copper for export (from the Northern Rhodesian and Union Miniere Copper Mines) amounted to over £730,000, and the earnings on stores for Northern Rhodesia and the Congo copper mines to over £110,000.

The great importance of gold is apparent from these figures. Gold accounted for no less than 79% of the mineral production of the territory in 1936, as compared with 81% in 1935. In 1937 the total value of gold, asbestos and chrome ore produced was respectively £5,656,693, £840,026 and £367,386.

A very important feature of gold mining in Southern Rhodesia is the number of small mines, many of which are worked by individuals; these accounted for no less than 79% of the gold produced in the territory in 1936. The share of the large mines in the total gold output has been steadily declining. This is shown in Table 57, which gives certain statistics of the gold mining industry in Southern Rhodesia from 1915 to 1937; the statistics also show the great expansion of the industry, and the lowering of the grade of ore milled, as a result of the increased currency price of gold.

In 1936 there were 1,707 gold producers,[1] but only 10 of these had an output exceeding 10,000 oz. There were no less than 1,583 with an output of less than 1,000 oz. The following figures illustrate the position:

		1936. Producers.		1936. Ounces.		% of total output.
(a)	Over 10,000	10	.	296,445	.	37·19
(b)	5,000–10,000	8	.	58,786	.	7·38
(c)	2,000–5,000	35	.	100,528	.	12·61
(d)	1,000–2,000	71	.	98,718	.	12·38
(e)	Under 1,000	1,583	.	242,584	.	30·44
		1,707	.	797,061	.	100·00

The percentage of the total output produced by large mines has declined from 75% in 1930 (68% in 1919) to 37% in 1936. It is of interest to note that the various classes of producers obtained their highest proportionate share of the total output recorded in

[1] The number for 1937 is shown in Table 57.

TABLE 57.—*Southern Rhodesia. Gold Mining.*

Year.	Value of Total Gold Output.	Gold Mining.			Tonnage Milled.	Recovery dwts.	All Mining.	
		Total Number of Contributors to Output.	Large Producers.				Employees.	
			Number.	Percentage Contribution to Total Output.			Native.	European.
	£(ooo)				(ooo).		(ooo).	(ooo).
1915	3,823	508	8	45·2	2,845	6·34	38	1·8
1919	2,499	314	10	67·8	1,769	6·59	30	1·4
1928	2,438	...	..8	77·3	1,665	6·92	...	...
1929	2,374	290	8	73·6	1,636	6·86	...	...
1930	2,317	332	9	74·8	1,389	7·88	45	1·6
1931	2,274	454	9	69·0	1,390	7·65	35	1·4
1932	3,366	782	10	61·4	1,750	6·56	36	1·7
1933	4,014	1,188	11	52·3	2,381	5·4	48	2·2
1934	4,696	1,636	11	43·7	3,050	4·53	62	2·6
1935	5,090	1,754	9	38·1	3,734	3·89	76	2·9
1936	5,632 (a)	1,707	10	37·2	4,350	3·66	84	3·1
1937	5,657	1,572	11	39·1	4,397	3·66	90	3·1 (b)

(a) Add balance of premiums amounting to £408,731.   (Cf. *Annual Report of the Department of Mines*, 1937, C.S.R. 10, 1938).
(b) Estimated

the years specified below. (The classification, (a)–(e), is the same as that shown above):

		Producers.	Ounces.	%.
(a) Year 1916	. .	17 .	568,139 .	61·07
(b) „ 1912	. .	16 .	114,622 .	17·83
(c) „ 1914	. .	41 .	130,771 .	15·30
(d) „ 1936	. .	71 .	98,718 .	12·38
(e) „ 1936	. .	1,583 .	242,584 .	30·44

"Prior to 1904," says the 1932 *Report of the Secretary for Mines and Public Works*, "the small worker was practically unknown, and the prospector was the advance agent for locating mining properties; development companies acquired the properties from prospectors and carried out the work of opening up the mines, and they in turn eventually disposed of the ground to mining companies. In those days the average prospector directed his efforts chiefly to finding old workings, and disposing of these to development companies. With the advent of the small worker, who is the prospector of to-day, and who might truly be termed the saviour of the mining industry in Rhodesia, conditions began to alter, and milling plants were erected on many propositions which were too small to interest mining companies, but which proved remunerative to small workers. If the history of some of the large mines of to-day were traced, it will be found that the small worker did most of the spade work in the early stages, and to the small workers the country owes a debt of some magnitude".

The Government has adopted a progressive policy towards the mining industry, both in regard to assistance to small workers by way of loans, and, since 1924, by the carrying out of a diamond-drilling programme in an endeavour to locate ore bodies at depth. No small worker is refused assistance by the Government if, in the opinion of the Government Mining Engineer, his property warrants it, and if the owner is considered a person capable of operating his property on proper and economic lines.[1]

---

[1] *Cf. Report of the Secretary, Department of Mines and Public Works, 1934.*

It is still apparent, however, that there is insufficient capital in the colony for the successful development of the mining industry, and whilst leading local mining companies have expended quite considerable sums of money on exploratory work on small properties under option, there is, generally speaking, a lack of funds for development purposes, which has given rise to some concern. It is not the present policy of the Government to find the large sums of money which are necessary for the expansion of the mining industry on a large scale. "That there are in Southern Rhodesia a large number of promising prospects which should attract capital and which would, properly developed and handled, repay the investor handsomely, is undoubted," says the 1935 *Report of the Secretary for Mines*, "and it is hoped that the signs which are already evident that some of the financial houses in South Africa and elsewhere are turning their attention to the mining fields of Southern Rhodesia, will materialize during 1936".

It is noteworthy that the number of Europeans employed in mining in 1935 was 2,899, while in agriculture the number was 4,305, of which 2,733 were farm owners.

Considerable efforts have been made in the past by the Chartered Company, by other large companies, among which De Beers may be mentioned, and by the Rhodesian Government, to develop farming and assist the strenuous efforts of private settlers to find suitable export crops, but great difficulties have to be overcome if agricultural production for export is to become a more important and an independent part of Rhodesia's economy.[1] The farming industry of Rhodesia is handicapped owing to the distance of the territory from the coast, and the resultant high transport costs for export products.

The most important export crops are maize and tobacco. The value of maize is really too low in relation to its bulk to enable a considerable expansion of this industry, as far as the European farmer is concerned. With maize production an important factor is transport; it rarely pays to grow maize further than

---

[1] From 1923/4 to 1933/4 there has been spent on agriculture about £1,609,000 from Loan Votes, and £2,250,000 from revenue.

TABLE 58.—*Southern Rhodesia.   Maize and its Relation to the Aggregate Value of the Agricultural Output of the Colony.*

Period.	European Farming.							Native Crops and Live Stock.	Estimated gross Output from European and Native Farming.	Proportion of European Maize Crop to Aggregate Value of Agricultural Output.
	Field Husbandry.				Animal Husbandry, Dairying, etc.	Total Value of European Agricultural Output.	Proportion of Maize Crop to Total estimated Output.			
	Estimated Value of Maize Crop.	Proportion of Maize Crop to Total Crops.	Value of other Crops.	Value of all Crops.						
	£(000).	%.	£(000).	£(000).	£(000).	£(000).	%.	£(000).	£(000).	%.
Annual Average.										
1920–22	474	52	443	917	1,312	2,229	21	1,303	3,532	13·5
1923–25	547	52	510	1,057	869	1,926	28	1,273	3,199	17
1926–28	724	39	1,119	1,843	1,264	3,107	23	1,282	4,389	16·5
1929	885	55	730	1,615	1,316	2,931	30	1,353	4,284	21

about twenty miles from the railway, and, at thirty miles from the railway, transport costs are absolutely prohibitive.

The conditions of land occupation at the present time appear to be that almost all cultivable land within fifteen miles of the railway line is occupied; new settlers will have to buy land already alienated, or else take up land near the transport limit of profitable grain production.[1]   In 1929/30 2,261 farmers were growing maize. The area planted to European grown maize was 318,000 acres, as compared with an average of 177,000 acres for the three years from 1918/19 to 1920/21; by 1936/37 the acreage had been reduced to 278,000 ; the total production was 2,039,341 bags. Unfortunately the local supplies, in years when there is no drought, usually exceed the local demand by 40% or more, and this has involved the territory in all the difficulties of over-production, and has led to various attempts to discriminate between local and export prices.

A useful analysis of the agricultural output of the country and of the importance of maize is given in Table 58, compiled by the Maize Enquiry Committee in 1930.   An indication of the

TABLE 59.—*Value of the Total Output and Exports of the Principal Agricultural Products of Southern Rhodesia, 1930 and 1931.*

	Value of Production.		Value of Exports.	
	1930. £(000).	1931. £(000).	1930. £(000).	1931. £(000).
Cattle for slaughter	775	325	340	49
Meat, fresh	329	200	18	6
Hides, cattle, dry	85	50	79	44
Tobacco, cigarettes	221	242	68	79
Tobacco, leaf	450	378	306	375
Maize, grain	719	570	254	170
Maize, meal	521	450	91	24
Citrus fruit	90	97	82	78
Butter	116	100	72	45
Eggs	64	61	40	32
Flour and meal, wheaten	190	165	39	42
Pigs	60	40	13	4
Bacon and hams	32	24	5	14
Ground nuts	22	21	11	10
Cotton, lint	13	18	9	19
Cheese	10	8	2	1
Total less duplications	2,509	1,783	1,429	982

[1] *Cf.* Wellington, "Possibilities of Settlement in Africa", *ibid.*, p. 278.

difficulties of agriculture in the territory is given by the Committee's conclusion that "in the present circumstances the main object must be to produce as small a surplus as possible". The same problem of over-production has also been met with in regard to dairy products and certain other commodities.

The value of the total output and exports of the sixteen principal agricultural products in 1930 and 1931 was estimated by a Government Committee[1] (see Table 59).

An estimate of the value of the gross output of the agricultural and livestock industry of Southern Rhodesia from 1920–30 is given in the *Southern Rhodesia Year Book*, No. 3, 1930.[2] The figures for selected years are as follows:

Year.	European Agriculture.			Native Crops.	Grand Total.
	Field Husbandry.	Animal Husbandry and Dairying, etc.	Total.		
	£(000).	£(000).	£(000).	£(000).	£(000).
1920	1,070	1,670	2,740	1,560(a)	4,300
1925	970(b)	1,010(c)	1,980	1,010	2,990
1927	2,140(d)	1,250	3,390	990	4,380
1929	1,590	1,560	3,150	1,090	4,240
1930	1,470(e)	1,500	2,970	930	3,900

(a) Large crops at good prices.

(b) Maize "pay-out" only 10s. per bag. Poor year for tobacco. Good year for cotton.

(c) Cattle prices low.

(d) Good maize crop, "pay-out" 10s. 9d. per bag. Good tobacco crop, but difficult to sell. Unsold portion of tobacco crop valued at only 7½d. per lb.

(e) Low export price for maize. Reduced tobacco crop.

The fall in the value of native production is significant.

The total value of the domestic exports of animal, agricultural and pastoral products, foodstuffs and tobacco in 1936 was £1,170,000, of which tobacco (including cigarettes) accounted for over £700,000. In 1935/6 tobacco was grown on 41,507 acres and the yield was 22,401,000 lb. The size and value of this crop have fluctuated greatly both on account of the changes in world prices, and also owing to climatic factors, which cause the

[1] *Southern Rhodesia: Ottawa Conference Report*, C.S.R. 1, 1933.
[2] Unfortunately, no later edition of the *Year Book* has appeared.

yield of tobacco to be very irregular.[1] Although new markets
are being investigated, and an agreement has been arrived at
with Northern Rhodesia and Nyasaland, it would seem that the
expansion of this industry has almost reached its limit for the
present.[2]

The economy of Southern Rhodesia exhibits, in a smaller but
nevertheless marked degree, some of the difficulties of the Union.
The income of a considerable part of its European population is,
to a large extent, drawn from sheltered or derivative activities, as,
for example, railways, government services and agricultural
production for the local market.   These activities cannot be
expanded unless there is an expansion of the primary industries
serving export markets, or unless there is an expansion in the
market provided by, and therefore in the productivity of the
native population. "In every case except that of native trade,"
Professor Henry Clay wrote in his valuable Report on Southern
Rhodesia in 1930, "the limiting factor is costs. This is most
clearly the case with gold mining, which supplies 30 per cent.
(in 1936 about 61 per cent.) of the country's exports. . . . Output
can be increased so long as costs do not exceed the yield in
gold; any increase in costs will throw out of payability so much
ore and thereby reduce the volume of output. . . . The railway

---

[1] The growth and fluctuations in the yield of this crop are shown by the following
figures:

Year.						Yield in lb.
1913/14	.	.	.	.	.	3,061,750
1914/15	.	.	.	.	.	426,423
1923/4	.	.	.	.	.	3,878,460
1926/7	.	.	.	.	.	19,264,532
1927/8	.	.	.	.	.	24,943,044
1928/9	.	.	.	.	.	7,042,414
1929/30	.	.	.	.	.	5.844,203
1930/31	.	.	.	.	.	8,644,390
1931/2	.	.	.	.	.	15,026,166
1932/3	.	.	.	.	.	14,170,642
1933/4	.	.	.	.	.	26,792,092
1934/5	.	.	.	.	.	21,205,924
1935/6	.	.	.	.	.	22,401,707
1936/7	.	.	.	.	.	22,044,000

(*Southern Rhodesia Year Book*, No. 3, p. 282, and *Reports of Agricultural Department;*
figures for 1937 are estimates.)
[2] Wellington, *ibid.*, p. 277.

services performed for other territories are at present in a peculiar position, since the Rhodesian Railways have an advantage of alternative routes almost amounting to monopoly. In a few years' time, however, . . . the Rhodesian Railways will secure a share of the traffic only by carrying it at competitive rates. . . . To sum up: the secondary industries are dependent for their markets on the primary industries and can expand only if these expand; and the expansion of the primary industries is limited by their costs, which are intimately affected by the charges which the secondary industries make."[1]

A reduction in the cost of maintaining the existing standards of living, however, is difficult. "The country has to maintain all the services that are required in a civilized community, without being able to utilize these services to the full extent that would make them cheap. The railway system, the merchanting and retailing organization, the banks, could all handle a much greater volume of trade than they can get. Government has to be provided for an extensive territory, and would cost little more if that territory carried double its present white population. The industries that from their nature must be carried on in the locality that constitutes their market, such as building, can be carried on only on a relatively small scale, and other industries that in larger communities would be carried on locally have no scope. The country is in the position of a firm with heavy overhead expenses and an inadequate turn-over. . . ." An analogy which can indeed be applied to most territories throughout Africa.

The turn-over of Southern Rhodesia can be increased only by an increase in population from abroad—or by increasing the productive population at home, that is, by increasing the productivity of both the native and the European population.

The importance of the native trade is that its expansion has not

[1] He added: "There is at present a considerable inequality in the return which the different industries of the country bring to the persons working in them, on the whole the return being higher in the more sheltered industries and lower in unsheltered agriculture. It follows that any further advance in the money wages of the sheltered industries would tend either to restrict employment in them or reduce their already unsatisfactory returns. Further improvement in the position of workers in these industries should be sought rather, therefore, in a raising of real wages by a reduction in the cost of living than in a raising of money wages, which would probably indeed defeat the end in view by either restricting employment or raising the cost of living."

to wait on the necessarily gradual process of immigration and settlement. "If all the natives lived on the European standard, the population of the country would no longer be 45,000 Europeans and 850,000 natives, with an aggregate spending power equivalent to that of perhaps 80,000 Europeans, but 900,000 persons with a combined spending power perhaps ten times that of the present population. That state of things may never arrive, and at best must take generations; but every increase in the native's economic capacity, every extension of his economic range, by increasing his output, increases in the same degree his power to purchase. If the Europeanization of the native population must be slow, so far as it goes, it is equivalent economically to the immigration of more Europeans, and has the same effect of spreading the burden of the necessary costs of government, trade and transport."

Native development is taking place at a slow rate. In 1936 the total indigenous Native population was estimated to be 1,088,000, of whom 719,000 were in the Native Reserves, 55,000 in the Native purchase area, 137,000 on land in the European area, 100,000 on privately owned land, 5,000 in Native occupational areas, and 3,270 on mines and in towns.

In 1936 the estimated acreage cultivated by the indigenous population was 1,389,000, as compared with 534,000 in 1902, and 1,186,261 in 1924, but the yield in 1936 was estimated at 2,991,000 bags of maize as compared with 1,676,000 in 1902.

Apart from the large growth in the number of native-owned cattle, it appears that the increase of the productivity per head has been very small.[1] Attempts to improve native methods of agriculture and to combat soil erosion are still necessarily on a small scale.

Southern Rhodesia has given an indication of her desire to

---

[1] It is true that a sign of change is the steady growth in the number of ploughs in use. In 1926 the number was 28,000, which it was estimated had grown to 97,000 ten years later. But whether, under present conditions, the use of the plough is always an advantage is another matter. For it is now being realized in many African territories that "modern methods" of production without a clear appreciation of ecological conditions may do more harm than good. As the Secretary for Agriculture in Rhodesia reported in 1930/31, "No attempt should be made to induce changes in systems of native agriculture until the soundness of the improvement has been abundantly proved under the conditions in which the native farmer himself works".

"find the best way in which the native people may safely go forward in their own progress and in the advancement of the colony",[1] by setting aside relatively large areas of land for future development by them. The following table shows the distribution, between Europeans and natives, of the total land available in Southern Rhodesia[2]:

	Acres.	Acres.
Forests, National Parks, Towns, etc. (approximate)		2,000,000
Area alienated to Europeans up to 31.xii.1933	32,100,000	
Unalienated Crown Land available for European settlement . .	15,076,700	
Total European area . .		47,176,700
Native Reserves as defined by the 1920 Order in Council . . .	21,595,000	
Lands already acquired by Government which may become native reserves or native area . . .	82,000	
An undetermined area which natives are expected to take . . .	88,540	
Area scheduled by Act of 1930 as land open to native purchase . .	7,464,560	
Total native area . . ,		29,230,100
Unassigned area . . .		17,793,300
Total area of Southern Rhodesia . .		96,200,100

How development is to be fostered in these large areas, and how it is to be related to the Rhodesian economy, as a whole, is a problem that has not yet been clarified.

There is in Southern Rhodesia the usual migration of the able-bodied workers from the native to the European areas, to take up

[1] Report of the Chief Native Commissioner for 1936.
[2] A. C. Jennings, "Land Apportionment in Southern Rhodesia", *Journal of the Royal African Society*, vol. xxxiv, 1935, pp. 296–312.

paid employment,[1] and this has, of course, retarded the development of the native areas. The number of Southern Rhodesian natives engaged in industrial employment has increased from 37,000 in 1912 to 94,646 in 1937, a relatively high figure considering the small native population of the country. In 1937 the non-indigenous natives in industrial employment numbered 149,040, of whom 66,700 were employed in mining.

So far, however, the great problem arising from the increasing absorption of the native into the European economy has not been seriously faced. That a clear policy has not yet emerged is not surprising. For it must be borne in mind that the future economic possibilities of Southern Rhodesia are not clear. The development of export crops, as has been remarked above, has been hampered by the geographical situation of the territory; moreover, considerable parts of Southern Rhodesia are malarious, and others are not suited for agricultural activities other than ranching. Altitude is an important factor in settlement, and the lower limit of the land with a "temperate" climate is estimated to be about 4,000 feet. Only some 24% of the area of the colony lies above this altitude, and approximately 89% of the European inhabitants are settled on the "plateau" districts above or near the 4,000-ft. contour.[2]

Rhodesia can, in fact, profit greatly by the experience of its southern neighbour. It can see there the effects of the uneconomic diversion of resources owing to compulsion; it can also take note of the artificial rigidities in the economic structure of the Union which prevent the reduction of costs of production, and therefore decrease the opportunities for expanding the National Income. The difficulties of agriculture in recent years have led naturally to special measures of a kind similar to those adopted elsewhere. But, again, Southern Rhodesia can learn from the experience of others not to regard measures of price control, subsidies, quotas and other policies which increase rigidity as a final solution of its real economic difficulties. The permanent solution must depend on increasing the National Income. It must endeavour to avoid the adoption of all measures which will retard that objective. As Professor Clay has

[1] It is, however, significant that the number of natives following independent vocations such as barbers, blacksmiths, bakers, carpenters, cycle repairers, etc., is now about 3,000 and has been steadily growing.

[2] Wellington, ibid., p. 275.

concluded, "There is every reason for confidence in the future. The growth in the effective economic strength of the community proceeds steadily, both by the advance of the native population and the immigration of Europeans.[1] There are great natural resources waiting to be developed, and the disadvantages of the commercial situation are being lessened by the development of adjoining territories".

Nothing would be to the greater detriment of the Rhodesian people than unnecessary restrictions on production and unnecessary interference in the free flow of resources and activity.

IV

NORTHERN RHODESIA.

Within less than a decade Northern Rhodesia has developed into one of the most important mineral territories in Africa. In 1936 it exported over £5,629,000 of minerals, of which copper was valued at £4,994,716. The value of the mineral exports of Northern Rhodesia now exceeds that of the Belgian Congo, and is nearly equal to that of Southern Rhodesia.

The extraordinary development of the copper field, the great new copper region of the world, has revolutionized the economic structure of the territory. In 1924 this land-locked country, covering an area of 290,000 square miles in the heart of Africa, produced only £400,000 of exportable commodities; the only copper mine was the Bwana M'Kubwa, which was worked intermittently. About this time there was a revival of interest in copper production,

---

[1] Professor Clay added: "Expressions of disappointment are not uncommon that immigration is not greater. It does not seem to me that such expressions are justified. There is a limit to the rate at which a country can at any time absorb additional population, a limit set chiefly by the size of the existing economic organization into which the immigrants are to be fitted. They have to be housed and fed, equipped with the capital needed to set them at work, and their work co-ordinated with that of the rest of the community. Rhodesia, having a small population, cannot absorb a large number of immigrants at present; but in proportion to its population it is absorbing them at a high rate. In the last five years the average annual immigration has been 3,350, which is about 8·2% of the 1926 population. This may be compared with Australia, which has added ½% per annum to its population by immigration on the average of the last 70 years; or the United States of America, which at a period of great immigration (1910–14) added only 0·8% per annum to its population by immigration. There are few countries, if any, in which population is increasing at a greater rate than in Southern Rhodesia."

although the possibilities of the Northern Rhodesia copper area were still highly nebulous. The surface deposits were of the same general ore character as in Haut Katanga, but of much lower grade and in narrow bands. It was impossible to work 3% oxide ore at a profit, and the fact that the much richer, oxidized, surface ores of the Congo changed to low-grade and worthless ores at depth discouraged further attention.[1]

Conditions from the first encouraged large-scale methods, as the British South Africa Company, owner of all the mineral rights, granted exclusive mineral rights over large areas for stated periods of years. This permitted deliberate and systematic prospecting. The Rhodesia Congo Border Concessions was granted a concession over an area equal in size to England, and, if we add the Rhodesia Minerals, Loangwa, Serenje and Kasempa Concessions, the total area being explored was 150,000 square miles. These groups were controlled by Minerals Separation Limited, Chester Beatty, Edmund Davis, the Anglo-American Corporation of South Africa and their associates, who invested about £1,000,000 for preliminary exploration.

The real possibilities of the field began with the search for sulphides below the oxidized outcrops. A rich zone of sulphides was found by drilling on the N'Changa property and, more conclusively, by shaft-sinking on the Roan Antelope. A giant new copper field was in the making. It proved to be a field ideally suited for rapid and large-scale development, as great masses of ore could be proved by a relatively small number of drill-holes when the geology of the area was understood. American mass-mining experience was invaluable for the rapid and successful development of the area, and the technical development was almost entirely American-controlled. At the end of 1926 only a few men believed that the field contained any real ore; at the end of 1927 some 40,000,000 tons of 3·5% ore were reported; and, by the end of 1930, over 500,000,000 tons of ore containing twenty odd million tons of copper were established.[2] Nevertheless

[1] *Cf. International Control in the Non-Ferrous Metals*, by W. Y. Elliott, E. S. May, J. W. F. Rowe, Alex Skelton and Donald Wallace, p. 446. (New York : The Macmillan Company, 1937.)

[2] This information is from *International Control in the Non-Ferrous Metals*, *ibid*.

it is significant that, as late as 1928, scepticism concerning the possibilities of Northern Rhodesia copper was still so great that the major members of the International Copper Cartel ignored the field.

The Rhodesian copper belt is the Central African Rand of the future, the expansion of which will possibly have an influence on the development of the neighbouring territories, particularly Southern Rhodesia, comparable to that exerted on the Transvaal and the other provinces of the Union by the Witwatersrand Gold Mining Industry.

The lure of minerals has resulted in Northern Rhodesia's being provided, like the Rand during its early development, with railways which traverse enormous distances to reach their objective, notwithstanding the paucity of traffic in the regions which they have to cross. There is now direct railway connection with Beira on the East, the Union *viâ* Southern Rhodesia on the South, and with Lobito Bay *viâ* the Rhodesia and Benguella Railways on the West. Capital amounting to nearly £25 millions has been invested from abroad in the copper belt during the last decade. The mines have been equipped with the most up-to-date machinery, and can produce copper at a profit when the price of copper is as low as £20 per ton. The European population of Northern Rhodesia increased from approximately 3,600 in 1921 to nearly 14,000 in 1931. As a result of the depression, it declined to 11,000 in 1933, and has not increased appreciably since then. The African population was estimated to be 1,366,000 in 1934. Not the least remarkable feature of this enclave of modern large-scale industry in the centre of the African bush is the attention which has been devoted to the welfare of the European and the native population by the well-planned housing, medical and social services which have been provided. The impression I formed during a visit to the copper belt in 1936, was that in many respects those responsible for this development are succeeding in creating a model industrial system for tropical areas. Many mining fields in other countries can already learn much from this pioneer achievement of a relatively small number of men and women, and the efficient and excellent personnel relations which have been established by them. The situation in the copper belt has indeed rightly been described as being "as unlike the development of other important mining areas in olden days as could be imagined"—to the great advantage of Northern Rhodesia.

A comparison with the early history of the Rand must, however, not be pushed too far. Certain factors in particular deserve special attention. The first is the fact that copper is a metal subject to very large price fluctuations resulting from periods of over- and under-production in relation to rapidly changing world demand. Northern Rhodesia has already had one experience of the serious results of these fluctuations. As a result of the curtailment of world copper production from 1932, development was for the time being stopped, and the copper belt was subject to all the strains and stresses of modern large-scale industrial unemployment. The average number of natives employed by the mines[1] declined from 16,726 in 1930 to 6,664 in 1932, and the number of European employees fell from 1,903 to 1,066, while the total paid native labour forces in Northern Rhodesia declined from about 70,000 to about 54,000. A distressed area in a highly industrialized country with diversified economic activities is bad enough, but a distressed area in the centre of Africa, thousands of miles from opportunities for other avenues of activity for its European and non-European population alike, gives rise to very serious additional problems of its own. With industrial recovery, employment has, of course, increased. The figures for 1936 were: Europeans 1,767, natives 14,521, and total natives' employed in Northern Rhodesia 53,000.

Notwithstanding the curtailment of development expenditure, the output of copper rose steadily throughout the depression; its phenomenal growth is shown by the following figures: (p. 251).

Apart from mining, economic development is in its infancy in Northern Rhodesia. The territory is faced with the necessity of avoiding the production of more than can be absorbed by the local demand of any agricultural commodity which does not have a high value in relation to its bulk. The territory is so far

---

[1] These figures refer to the four mines, Roan Antelope, Mufuliva, N'kana and Broken Hill. (*Cf. Report of the Commission on the Financial and Economic Position of Northern Rhodesia*, Colonial No. 145, 1938.)

		Copper (fire refined). (Tons.)		Electrolytic. (Tons.)
1930	.	6,269	.	...
1931	.	36,521 (a)	.	...
1932	.	67,887	.	...
1933	.	104,204	.	...
1934	.	137,295	.	602
1935	.	119,927	.	23,574
1936	.	113,903 (b)	.	...

(a) Of which 24,110 tons were copper concentrate.
(b) Estimated.

from the sea and from world markets that it is not likely to develop a large agricultural export industry. The opportunities for European agriculture are limited by climatic factors. For Northern Rhodesia is a typical Central African territory. The portions of the territory at an altitude greater than 5,000 feet are relatively small. The little colony of about 150 Europeans at Abercorn in the extreme north of the Eastern province of Northern Rhodesia is the only European settlement of any size which is situated at an altitude above 5,000 feet. Settlement in Northern Rhodesia is concentrated along the railway, and the bulk of the population lives at altitudes varying from 3,160 feet at Livingstone in the Zambesi Valley, to over 4,000 feet in the North. Whatever one may think of the uplands, the valleys below about 3,500 feet are hot and enervating, and by general agreement are not areas in which the vigour of the European races can be maintained.[1]

Moreover, production is not profitable for other than high-priced crops such as coffee, tobacco and cotton, beyond the 30-mile haul to the railway line, but in this railway belt, "some 97% must, under present conditions, be considered as pastoral land".

Northern Rhodesia has an area of about 290,323 square miles

[1] Cf. Wellington, ibid., p. 263. He remarks : "The fact is that white settlement has not been planned as it has been to some extent in Tanganyika and Kenya, but it has followed the railway line, grouping itself within easy access to markets. The factor of communication has outweighed climatic factors. This is apparently the reason why Abercorn is as yet the only European settlement of more than one hundred souls in the North-East of the Colony."

(185,807,100 acres). Professor Wellington has calculated that in this almost "empty" country the land is divided as follows:

	Million acres.
Total area	185·81
Barotseland Reserve · · · ·	36·82
Other Native Reserves · · ·	34·71
Forest, Game and Archæologic Reserves.	5·01
Companies Concessions (less Native areas)	6·25
Alienated to European settlers . .	2·58
Townships	0·12
Total reserved or alienated . . .	85·49
Land unalienated	100·32
Lowlands, Swamps, etc. . . .	13·00
Fly-infested (outside Native Reserves) .	29·00
Available for occupation . . .	58·32

From this last figure, however, "a deduction would have to be made for rough ground, lack of water, malarious valleys and other conditions (particularly the fly-infested areas), which would leave, perhaps, at most 50 million acres available for new settlement. Under present conditions this would be ranch land, and, estimating 10,000 acres as the minimum for each ranch, the total available land would provide about 5,000 holdings".

The 1931 Census showed that only 544 male Europeans were occupied in agriculture. European crop production is confined mainly to the supply of the internal market. The demand of the Katanga province in the Belgian Congo has declined in importance. The only important agricultural export product is tobacco. Coffee production is developing slowly; it increased from 120 cwt. in 1931 to 627 cwt. in 1935, but declined to 430 cwt. in 1936. Cotton production is still in the experimental stage. To all intents and purposes, both native and European agriculture are thus dependent on the development and prosperity of the mining industry. The following statistics show the acreage and production of European-grown crops, and illustrate the restricted nature of European agriculture. Information in regard to native production is unreliable.

		Acreage.	Production.
1929/30	Maize	47,085	18,014 (tons)
	Tobacco	3,585	1,318 (1,000 lb.)
	Wheat	2,095	856 (tons)
	Ground nuts	2,213	448 ,,
1934/5	Maize	40,018	16,040 ,,
	Tobacco	3,411	1,580 (1,000 lb.)
	Wheat	3,234	1,823 (tons)
	Ground nuts	702	70 ,,
1935/6	Maize	41,203	29,375 (a) (tons)
	Tobacco	3,441	1,225 (1,000 lb.)
	Wheat	4,249	11,121 (tons)

(a) Estimated.

The development of the trade of the territory is shown in Table 60, and the finance statistics for the same period, 1900–36, are given in Table 61. Mineral exports now account for about 95% of the domestic exports; this fact furnishes a strikng commentary on the character of Northern Rhodesia's economic development up to the present.

V

EAST AFRICA.

Northern Rhodesia, Nyasaland, Tanganyika, Kenya and Uganda are physically connected with no great barrier dividing them. The political boundaries are to a large extent the results of historical accident or administrative convenience, and have no natural justification. The natural links of a large part of North-East Rhodesia are with Nyasaland. The high plateau which forms the backbone of Central Africa runs through all the territories. Lake Victoria links the three northern territories by a single inland coast. The type of agricultural production is throughout the same. There are, of course, large

TABLE 60.—*Northern Rhodesia. Trade Statistics,* 1906–36.(*c*)

Year.	Merchandise Imports. (*b*), (*d*)	Exports.		Copper Exports.	
		Domestic Produce. (*a*), (*d*), (*e*)	Re-exports.(*d*)	£(000).	Percentage of Total Exports of Domestic Produce.
	£(000).	£(000).	£(000).		
1906	188(*b*)	109(*a*)	...	...	...
1907	115(*b*)	96(*a*)	...	...	...
1908	120(*b*)	118(*a*)	...	...	...
1909	337(*f*)	(*a*), (*f*)81	...	...	...
1910	213(*f*)	26	4	8	30·8
1911	154	90	19	42	46·7
1912	197	70	5	16	22·9
1913	255	195	8	52	26·7
1914	207	153	6	31	20·3
1915	171	118	3	30	25·4
1916	284	141	7	34(*g*)	24·1
1917	297	200	15	74(*g*)	37·0
1918	356	322	21	23	7·1
1919	434	435	19	27	6·2
1920	650	508	28	5	1·0
1921	725	546	20	2	0·4
1922	498	574	24	25	4·4
1923	522	428	25	12	2·8
1924	670	406	48	9	2·2
1925	1,299	383	49	1	0·3
1926	1,694	428	55	24	5·6
1927	1,988	684	62	133	19·4
1928	2,398	784	59	240	30·6
1929	3,627	819	76	237	28·9
1930	4,933	769	108	226	29·4
1931	5,357	989	191	506	51·2
1932	1,934	2,436	239	2,088	85·7
1933	1,973	3,589	127	3,115	86·8
1934	2,927	4,400	131	3,706	84·2
1935	2,961	4,668	107	3,361	72·0
1936	2,335	5,960	101	3,939	66·1

(*a*) Includes merchandise re-exports in 1909, and in addition bullion and coin in preceding years (includes bullion only thereafter).
(*b*) Includes bullion and coin in 1908 and preceding years, but excludes them thereafter.
(*c*) Extracted from the *Statistical Abstracts for the British Empire.*
(*d*) Zambesi Basin only, 1909 to 1936.
(*e*) Includes South African produce, *i.e.* produce of the Union, S.W. Africa, S. Rhodesia, and the Zambesi Basin, 1909 to 1936.
(*f*) Inclusive of goods in transit other than raw gold.
(*g*) Inclusive of brass.

variations in the crops produced, due to differences in altitude, climate and rainfall. Contact with the outside world and all the deep-seated changes that it is bringing have come to all

TABLE 61.—*Northern Rhodesia.(c) Finance*, 1900–37.(d)

Year.(a)	Gross Revenue. (e), (f)	Customs Revenue.	Percentage to Total.	Gross Expenditure.	Public Debt.
	£(000).	£(000).		£(000).	£(000).
1900	3	1	33·3	75	...
1901	11	1	9·0	70	...
1902	19	2	10·5	92	...
1903	20	3	15·0	111	...
1904	48	4	8·3	150	...
1905	59	9	15·3	140	...
1906	89	16	18·0	150	...
1907	82	13	15·9	138	...
1908	87	14	16·1	136	...
1909	101	20	19·8	143	...
1910	97	19	19·6	149	...
1911	117	21	17·9	165	...
1912	126	23	18·3	178	...
1913	138	30	21·7	186	...
1914	135	27	20·0	193	...
1915	122	27	22·1	167	...
1916	144	32	22·2	184	...
1917	139	33	23·7	188	...
1918	152	36	23·7	199	...
1919	170	45	26·5	260	...
1920	235	67	28·6	332	...
1921	279	67	24·0	341	...
1922	259	61	23·6	330	...
1923	279	65	23·3	323	...
1924	310	68	21·9	340	...
1925	371	77	20·8	394	...
1926	421	100	23·8	455	...
1927	475	136	28·6	519	...
1928	542	163	30·1	525	...
1929	672	234	34·8	555	...
1930	830(g)	321	38·8	705(g)	...
1931	856	316	36·9	820	...
1932	617	178(h)	28·8	792	1,250
1933(b)	646(b)	159(b)	28·8	779(b)	2,34
1934	693	271	39·1	713	2,34
1935	833	292	35·1	806	2,34
1936	863	267	30·9	857	2,34
1937	982	332	33·8	909	...

(a) For twelve months to 31st March of the year following that stated up to 1932 and to 31st December thereafter.
(b) Nine months to 31st December.
(c) For the years prior to 1911 the figures for North-Eastern and North-Western Rhodesia have been combined.
(d) Extracted from the *Statistical Abstracts for the British Empire*, and the *Report of the Commission on the Economic and Financial Position of Northern Rhodesia*, Colonial No. 145, 1938.
(e) Excluding Head-Office Revenue and Expenditure of the B.S.A. Co., up to and including 1923.
(f) Excluding receipts from Mines, Land, etc., in South Africa prior to 1909, excluding grants-in-aid throughout.
(g) Including ordinary receipts from Colonial Development Fund but not extraordinary receipts, and similarly in the case of gross expenditure, from 1930 onwards.
(h) Customs plus excise, from 1932 onwards.

the territories through the same channels, and at the same periods.[1]

For the purpose of this study Northern Rhodesia has been considered separately owing to its close connection and joint railway system with Southern Rhodesia and its recent large mineral developments, but many of the considerations discussed below apply to it.

The problems confronting all the territories of East Africa are similar. At present we have in all of them the absence, on the one hand, of any considerable mineral exploitation, and, on the other, the striking paucity of indigenous products of a kind which, for example, have made possible economic progress in West African territories. There are no natural products of economic importance other than timber, gum and resin. As a result, East Africa has not been able to offer the same attractions for private capital as South Africa, nor the opportunities for commercial enterprise provided by West Africa.

It is noteworthy that the bulk of the trade which has been developed with the natives of East Africa is in the hands of Asiatics, who have played a most important *rôle* in the development of commerce with the indigenous peoples, and are also responsible for considerable capital investment in agriculture. Indians form roughly 57% of the non-native population in Tanganyika, over 80% in Uganda, nearly 60% in Nyasaland, and some 50% in Kenya, according to the population censuses or estimates in or about 1931. Altogether there are now about 100,000 Asiatics, about 50,000 Europeans, and roughly 14,000,000 Africans in Kenya, Uganda, Tanganyika and Nyasaland. The European population is, in the main, composed of Government officials, missionaries, and the higher professional and commercial classes.

East Africa provides the most striking example, apart from the Anglo-Egyptian Sudan, of a region where private enterprise has been greatly dependent on Government activity, which has had to pave the way, by extensive public works and administrative

---

[1] For an excellent account of the channels of European influence see the *Report of the Commission on Closer Union of the Dependencies of Eastern and Central Africa*, Cmd. 3234, 1929.

services, not only for European settlement, but also for all modern economic activity. By far the most important task of the Government has been the construction of railways. Even now, the development of large parts of East Africa is impossible owing to the lack of modern means of transport. Except in Uganda, where road material is readily available, and an excellent system of roads has been built, the roads of East Africa, generally speaking, provide only dry-weather transport. Consequently, large areas are unable to produce crops for export owing to the distance from the railway. In some parts, human porterage still takes an enormous toll of the efforts of the indigenous population. The exports from North-Eastern Rhodesia and the southern third of Tanganyika have remained negligible owing to the distance from the railway. One Commission after another has stressed that the most urgent requirement is further railway development. It is, however, one thing to draw attention to the great changes that railways would bring about, but quite another to envisage how, with their main traffic consisting of one or two seasonal bulky export crops, and with relatively little high-rated or local traffic, they are to be made to pay their way, unless the capital required for their construction is made available free of interest charges. The provision of railways for a primitive indigenous population which has to be taught new methods of production, and which even then can only provide traffic for part of the year, presents a most difficult financial problem.[1]

The importance of Government enterprise in East Africa has been illustrated by the percentage ratio of "Public Listed" capital to all capital (see Table 29), which is much higher for East and Central Africa than for other regions. For Kenya and Uganda the percentage is 68%, for Tanganyika 60%, and for Nyasaland of 85%, the ratio highest for all African territories.

All the territories of East Africa offer opportunities, on the high plateaux which link them together, for some European settlement, but its character must be distinguished from that in Southern Africa. It has been argued by the Commission on Closer Union that "in South Africa, if the black population

[1] This question is dealt with below in the section on railway finance, pp. 374 to 420.

were to disappear, the white population could with great difficulty adjust itself to the change". Whether this view is correct is open to doubt, but there can be no doubt about the second part of the Commission's statement, that "in the tropics, at whatever altitude, non-native enterprise is in a far more fundamental way dependent on native labour . . . a colour bar in Eastern and Central Africa is for climatic reasons impossible, and a far larger portion of the general activities of the country than in South Africa will be undertaken by natives. The material prosperity of the white community is inseparably, and permanently, bound up with that of the black; and white settlement and enterprise can be maintained only through the co-operation of the native races."[1]

The European requires the services of the native peoples to an even greater extent in East Africa than elsewhere, if he is to be enabled to create a permanent home in these tropical regions. For the white man's struggle with climatic conditions is here more severe, and to withstand the environment he requires a standard of life even higher than that which is necessary in the Union or Southern Rhodesia.

Throughout East Africa men and domestic animals are engaged in a perpetual struggle with insect-borne infections ; very nearly half of Tanganyika, and very considerable parts of North-East Rhodesia and Nyasaland, are depopulated on account of the tsetse fly alone, and large parts of all the territories are malarious. It is for these reasons that absolute figures of the areas of these territories are misleading if they are used to indicate the possibilities of economic development. For example, Tanganyika is the largest East African territory, with a total area of about 360,000 square miles, of which the land surface is roughly 339,000 square miles (about 218 million acres). But it is estimated that some two-thirds of this area is uninhabited on account of the insufficiency of water. Out of a total of 222,960 square miles, the land area of Kenya is 219,730 square miles and the water area 3,230 square miles, but again one finds that some three-fifths of the territory is arid and comparatively waterless. The estimated

[1] Report of the Commission on the Closer Union of the Dependencies of Eastern and Central Africa, Cmd. 3234, 1929, pp. 32-3.

area of Uganda is 93,981 square miles (roughly 60 million acres), but of this, 13,610 square miles are water. The smallest of the East African territories is Nyasaland, with a total area of approximately 37,596 square miles, and approximately 10,353 square miles of water.

It is worth noting here that only approximately 4,000,000 acres of the land surface in Nyasaland, some 2,700,000 acres in Tanganyika, 6,700,000 acres in Kenya and 6,400,000 acres in Uganda have been alienated. Indeed, the characteristic feature of the economy of the greater part of East Africa is the preponderance of primitive native subsistence production, based on varying types of communal tenure, and returning to the indigenous populations a most meagre income, very frequently an insufficiency of essential foods, and at all times leaving little or no surplus over and above what is required for a hand-to-mouth existence.

In large parts of East Africa the absence of mineral resources and of indigenous products has compelled Europeans to base their economy on the development of new agricultural products for export. For example, in Kenya, measures have been adopted which give the Europeans (a) the most suitable land, (b) a labour supply to work it, and (c) every assistance possible in the form of public works, communications and special railway rates for export crops. But there are very considerable differences between the various territories in this regard.

There is a great gulf between Uganda, where the conflict between European and native interests is least, and economic progress is largely the result of individual native enterprise benefiting from European guidance, and Kenya, where there has been considerable interference with native development in the interest of Europeans. In Tanganyika independent native production plays a far more important part than in Kenya, but the future may well see considerable changes in this respect, particularly in view of the possibility that mining development may show rapid expansion. In Nyasaland native production predominates, but it already owes much to European example and Asiatic settlement and, as in Kenya, to the impetus provided by Asiatic commercial enterprise in providing contact with outside markets. In this colony the indirect influence of developments in surrounding territories has been of considerable importance. As the Committee on Emigrant Labour from Nyasaland has shown, the chief export of the territory is the labour of its inhabitants. This fact illustrates both the general unity of economic problems in East Africa and the important fact that, if development in one area, for climatic, ecological or other reasons lags behind that of others, it is inevitable that migration must result from the poorer to the more developed areas. These migrations are part and parcel of the great economic revolution through which Africa is passing.

VI

THE COLONY AND PROTECTORATE OF KENYA.

One of the most important factors in the economy of Kenya is the relatively large amount of overseas capital which has been invested in it, and through which there has been established that selected but small European population which occupies most of the 12,750 square miles which the Kenya Land Commission has included under the term "European Highlands", and which is, apart from the unhealthy coastal belt, the land of greatest value for arable purposes. Up to the present, however, only about 6% of this alienated land has been cultivated.[1]

The opinion has been expressed earlier in this chapter that my estimate of the private capital invested in Kenya probably understates the true position. Even so, the large amount raised by the Government of Kenya is sufficiently striking.

Borrowing from abroad, however, is a two-edged weapon, and Kenya has suffered in a greater degree than any other British territory from its vulnerability as a result of its heavy debt burden, its limited number of exportable products, and the fall in their prices on world markets during the depression. Three agricultural

[1] For an excellent account of the settlement of these highlands by Europeans, of the movement of natives to other areas, and of the construction of railways to serve the sparsely populated "European" areas, see the comprehensive article by Dr. Ernst Weigt, "Die Kolonisation Kenias", in *Mitteilungen der Gesellschaft für Erdkunde*, vol. li, 1930/31, pp. 25-120. The article is a geographical and historical study and includes 14 maps.

products, coffee, sisal and maize, alone account for over 50% of the value of Kenya's domestic exports. The official statistics do not separate the trade of Kenya and Uganda. Table 62 has been prepared from the official returns, and shows the development of the trade of the two territories from 1900 to 1936, and the percentage of the chief commodities to the total domestic exports. Sir Allen Pim, however, in his recent Report,[1] made estimates which separate the Kenya and Uganda trade. The average percentage contribution of the main commodities to the total domestic exports of Kenya from 1932 to 1935 was as follows:

Average Percentage Contribution to Total Exports.[2]

	1932. (%.)	1933. (%.)	1934. (%.)	1935. (%.)
European settled areas production—				
Coffee	53	37	26	31
Sisal	8	11	16	14
Sodium bicarbonate . .	8	9	7	6
Tea	1	3	6	7
Gold Bullion . . .	3	3	4	6
Dairy Products . .	2	2	3	2
Sugar	1	3	3	2
Native areas production—				
Hides and skins . .	5	7	10	6
Wattle Bark and Extract .	4	3	4	4
Raw Cotton . . .	...	1	2	3
European and Native production—				
Maize	5	9	5	6
Miscellaneous . . .	10	12	14	13

Detailed statistics from 1908 to 1937 showing the quantity and value of Kenya's domestic exports and the percentage of the exports of each commodity to the total are given in Table 64.[3]

[1] *Report of the Commission Appointed to Enquire into and Report on the Financial Position and System of Taxation of Kenya*, Colonial No. 116, 1936.

[2] Extracted from the above Report.

[3] This table is from Sir Allen Pim's Report, *ibid.*, Appendix II. It has, as far as possible, been brought up to date from the *Annual Trade Reports of Kenya and Uganda*.

TABLE 62.—Kenya and Uganda. Trade Statistics 1900–37, and Proportion per cent. of Annual Exports of Selected Commodities to Annual Value of all Domestic Produce Exported.(i)

Year.(c)	Kenya and Uganda Merchandise Imports.(a) £(000).	Domestic Exports.(b)			Kenya and Uganda Re-exports.(d) £(000).	Cotton Exports.		Cotton Seed Exports.		Coffee Exports (Raw).		Sisal Exports (Fibre & Tow).	
		Kenya. £(000).	Uganda. £(000).	Total.(d) £(000).		£(000).	%.	£(000).	%.	£(000).	%.	£(000).	%.
1900	450(g)	...	...	71	...	...	...	...	...	...	...	...	...
1901	787	...	...	96	...	...	...	...	...	...	...	...	...
1902	621	...	...	135	...	...	...	...	...	...	...	...	...
1903	507	...	...	134	...	...	...	...	...	...	...	...	...
1904	585	123	61	184	...	...	...	...	...	...	...	...	...
1905	743	125	107	232	...	1	0·4	...	...	...	...	...	...
1906	940	164	126	290	47	6	2·1	...	...	...	...	...	...
1907	937	157	140	297	40	25	8·4	...	...	...	...	...	...
1908	965	140	140	280	27	36	12·9	3	1·1	...	...	...	...
1909	881	191	212	403	34	79	19·6	1	0·2	...	...	...	...
1910	1,132	276	372	648	70	211	32·6	3	0·5	4	0·6	...	...
1911	1,658	334	377	711	135	241	33·9	6	0·8	10	1·4	1	0·1
1912	2,317	421	427	848	150	289	34·1	11	1·3	21	2·5	4	0·5
1913	2,939	444	564	1,008	197	359	35·6	13	1·3	47	4·7	13	1·3
1914	1,954	315	507	822	113	347	42·2	18	2·2	63	7·7	36	4·4
1915	1,884	330	357	687	36	213	31·0	10	1·5	52	7·6	75	10·9
1916	3,147	587	700	1,287	243	432	33·6	10	0·8	172	13·4	126	9·8

Year													
1917	2,985	758	785	1,543	548	703	45·6	7	0·5	124	8·0	197	12·8
1918	3,821	984	1,247	2,231	726	1,064	47·7	6	0·3	328	14·7	224	10·0
1919	5,411	(h)	(h)	4,510	755	2,139	47·4	26	0·6	636	14·1	184	4·1
1920(f)	9,564	1,833	2,867	4,700	685	3,195	68·0	9	0·2	575	12·2	184	3·9
1921(f,c)	3,267	(h)	(h)	2,111	507	1,235	58·5	...	...	263	12·5	140	7·0
1922	3,667	1,085	1,696	2,781	315	1,196	43·0	10	0·4	379	13·6	259	9·3
1923	5,193	1,565	2,431	3,996	914	2,094	52·4	53	1·3	621	15·5	236	5·9
1924	7,485	2,240	3,897	6,137	1,230	3,489	56·9	106	1·7	803	13·1	397	6·5
1925	10,146	2,725	5,097	7,822	1,478	4,694	60·0	123	1·6	964	12·3	531	6·8
1926	8,946	2,414	3,596	6,010	1,592	3,057	50·9	195	3·2	895	14·9	579	9·6
1927	8,809	3,987	2,310	5,397	1,462	1,693	31·4	170	3·1	1,310	24·3	469	8·7
1928	10,327	3,266	3,395	6,661	1,830	2,486	37·3	323	4·8	1,284	19·3	496	7·4
1929	10,093	2,746	4,275	7,021	1,885	3,315	47·2	424	6·0	880	12·5	554	7·9
1930	7,991	3,423	2,060	5,483	1,391	1,570	28·6	138	2·5	1,582	28·9	437	8·0
1931	5,676	2,344	1,978	4,322	1,136	1,510	34·9	149	3·4	1,148	26·6	233	5·4
1932	4,819	2,281	2,225	4,506	1,252	1,593	35·4	169	3·8	1,437	31·9	187	4·2
1933	4,835	2,247	3,465	5,712	1,371	2,706	47·4	263	4·6	1,042	18·2	250	4·4
1934	5,613	1,910	3,774	5,684	1,526	2,956	52·0	87	1·5	785	13·8	311	5·5
1935	6,549	2,978	3,631	6,609	1,972	2,899	43·9	139	2·1	1,161	17·6	432	6·5
1936	7,180	3,888	4,467	8,355	1,956	3,477	41·6	266	3·2	1,349	16·1	720	8·6
1937	10,054	3,554	5,703	9,657	2,235	4,461	46·2	395	4·1	1,153	11·9	692	7·2

(a) Excluding specie, including goods subsequently re-exported; including Government imports but excluding Government specie and Government imports from 1933 onwards.
(b) Excluding specie.
(c) For nine months only.
(d) Exports include re-exports up to 1905.
(e) To 31st March of the year following that stated up to 1920, and for the calendar year thereafter.
(f) 1919/20 and 1921 figures are inflated by conversion at Rs. 10 per £ instead of Rs. 15, as previously.
(g) Excludes imports on behalf of the administrations and for construction of railway, which amounted to £367,000 in 1901.
(h) Details are not available.
(i) *Sources*: (1) *Statistical Abstracts for the British Empire.* (2) *Annual Trade Reports of Kenya and Uganda.* (3) *Pim Report*, Colonial No. 116, 1936. (Re-exports from *Pim Report* only, except 1926 and 1937.)

"The financial history of the colony from 1921 to the present time," wrote Sir Allen Pim, "may be summarized as including three periods. The first of economy from 1922 to 1924, then of general expansion and lavish expenditure from 1925 to 1929, followed by a steadily increasing depression and enforced economies from 1930 onwards. Since 1935 there has been a recovery in the position of the territory, as a result of the rise in world prices of raw materials." From 1921 to 1933 Kenya incurred nearly £17,200,000 of Public Debt, roughly three-quarters of which was for railways and harbours. Table 63 shows the financial development of the colony, and gives statistics of revenue, expenditure and public debt from 1900 to 1936. Reference has been made previously to the increase in the debt charges of the territory since the War.

The extent of the burden of the external debt can be fully appreciated only if we consider the extent to which the volume of exports had to be increased during the depression to combat the fall in export prices. Thus, the quantity of coffee exported rose from 212,000 cwt. in 1928 to 257,000 cwt. in 1933, but its value declined from £1,120,000 to £832,000. During the same period the quantity of sisal exported rose from 16,516 tons to 19,850 tons, but the value fell from £496,000 to £250,000. The quantity of maize and maize meal exported has fluctuated greatly, but in 1928, 892,000 cwt. were exported, valued at £306,000, while in 1933 1,132,000 cwt. realized only £213,000. Sodium bicarbonate exports fell from some 78,000 tons in 1928 to 43,000 tons in 1933, but the value fell from £403,000 to £194,000. The value of the domestic exports of the colony as a whole, it will be seen from Table 64, declined from £3,266,000 in 1928 to £1,910,000 in 1934 ; it reached £3,954,000 in 1937.

The depression was naturally accompanied and intensified by the almost complete cessation of private investment and Government borrowing from abroad, and consequently by a marked decline in imports, which in turn was further intensified by the fall in the value of the exports, and the need to cover the territory's obligations abroad. Sir Allen Pim's figures for Kenya show that imports fell from £6,506,000 in 1928 to £2,210,000 in 1933 ; they had partially recovered to £2,960,000 in 1935. The revenue from

TABLE 63.—*Kenya. Finance*, 1900–37.

Year.(c)	Gross Revenue. (b), (g)	Customs Revenue.	Percentage of Customs to Total Revenue.	Grant-in-Aid.(e)	Gross Expenditure. (b), (g)	Public Debt.
	£(000).	£(000).		£(000).	£(000).	£(000).
1900	64	29	45·3	...	193	...
1901	68	27	39·7	...	278	...
1902	95	31	32·6	...	311	...
1903	109	33	30·3	256	419	...
1904	155	60	38·7	251	303	...
1905	270(a)	74	27·4	214	419(a)	...
1906	461	81	17·6	164	616	...
1907	475	79	16·6	193	692	...
1908	486	82	16·9	138	703	...
1909	503	64	12·7	134	669	...
1910	610	78	12·8	130	682	...
1911	729	101	13·9	190	772	47
1912	953	146	15·3	23	961	422
1913	1,124	159	14·1	...	1,116	422
1914	985	86	8·7	...	1,152	568
1915	1,166	145	12·4	...	1,073	567
1916	1,534	244	15·9	...	1,197	560
1917	1,368	171	12·5	...	1,491	553
1918	1,549	181	11·7	...	1,571	544
1919	2,590	279	10·8	...	3,037	1,121
1920	2,979	400	13·4	...	2,977	1,148
1921	1,291(d)	230(d)	17·8	...	1,667(d)	5,000
1922	1,649	377	22·9	...	1,972	5,000
1923	1,839	486	26·4	...	2,138	5,000
1924	2,112	590	27·9	...	1,862	8,500
1925	2,431	679	27·9	...	2,340	8,500
1926	2,627	741	28·2	...	2,415	8,500
1927	2,846	831	29·2	...	2,515	10,000
1928	3,021	915	30·3	...	2,835	13,500
1929	3,334	950	28·5	...	3,505	13,500
1930	3,226	815	25·3	...	3,423	16,900
1931	3,036	699	23·0	...	3,185	16,900
1932	3,007	597	19·9	...	3,116	16,900
1933	3,116	582	18·7	...	3,162	17,205
1934	3,178	612	19·3	...	3,173	17,205
1935	3,274	690	21·1	...	3,218	17,205
1936	3,450	775	22·5	...	3,286	17,581
1937	3,667	898	24·5	...	3,566	17,581

(a) Only the *profit* on the railway was included in the figures for 1905–6.
(b) Excludes Imperial Grants, and Grants from the Colonial Development Fund.
(c) To 31st March of the year following that stated up to 1920, and to 31st December thereafter.
(d) For nine months only.
(e) The amount of the annual grant prior to 1903–4 is not available. There were Parliamentary Grants for special purposes, in 1935 (£15,470); 1936 (£9,424) and 1937 (£16,710).
(f) Extracted from the *Statistical Abstracts for the British Empire.*
(g) Net figures are obtained by deducting approximately 33⅓% to allow for re-imbursements from neighbouring territories in regard to joint services. (*Cf. Annual Colonial Report*, No. 1806, 1936.) 1936 and 1937 figures include Imperial Grants.

customs duties in Kenya fell from £1,913,000 in 1928 to £595,000 in 1932. Had it not been for the more stringent collection of native hut and poll taxes, which brought in no less than £558,000 in 1933 (only £16,000 less than in 1928), the budget deficits would have been very much greater than they were.

The situation in regard to the large Public Debt of Kenya is really a symptom of more deep-seated difficulties. For the territory finds itself at that stage of development in which capital investment, utilized to create the frame-work of civilized administration, to supply communications, and to foster particular types of economic expansion, has proceeded at a faster rate than the economic development of the population as a whole warranted.

Sir Allen Pim has summed up the position in a striking passage which can be summarized as follows: The circumstances in Kenya illustrate the difficulties arising from the presence of three communities at three different levels of civilization. First there is the European community of some 17,000 persons, including over 2,000 farmers of a very individualistic type, controlling very large areas in proportion to their numbers and growing a large variety of crops, some of them of a very special type, needing the best available scientific advice. The agricultural progress of the colony is mainly due to their efforts, and they obtain all the assistance that can be given them, either to secure the welfare of the industries in which they are interested, or to secure amenities for themselves and their families to which they have been accustomed. Their requirements include the organization of adequate scientific services to deal with the many problems arising out of their special industries, both agricultural and pastoral, and, what is even more costly, the development of communications on lines in advance of what is customary in rural Africa. The expenditure on roads has been substantially increased by the small, isolated blocks of European settlers. The cost of constructing and maintaining roads bears little relation to the numbers served. Last, but by no means least, they require educational facilities for their children, and on account of the scattered character of settlements, this must be given in boarding-schools. The commercial community has special needs of its own connected mainly with communications and the townships. The Indian community

Export statistics for Kenya, 1908–1937 (values in £; quantities as noted).

Year	Coffee Qty (Cwt.)	Coffee Value (£)	Coffee %	Sisal Qty (Tons)	Sisal Value (£)	Sisal %	Hides & Skins Value (£)	H&S %	Sodium Carbonate Qty (Tons)	Value (£)	%	Maize Qty (Cwt.)	Value (£)	%	Tea Qty (Cwt.)	Value (£)	%
1908	69	226	..				27,312	18									
1909	630	1,088	..				15,261	11									
1910	1,230	2,995	1				44,724	23	36	596	..	35,621	11,899	8			
1911	2,089	5,765	1				42,258	23	65	1,016	..	119,972	5,995	8			
1912	3,032	11,071	3				73,250	22	21	361	..	181,788	21,297	8			
1913	5,501	18,502	4				87,673	17	15	803	..	226,438	43,270	13			
1914	2,784	21,738	7	1,652	35,537	11	147,474	33	16	1,200	..	189,355	53,920	13			
1915	6,708	17,297	7	2,300	74,669	23	106,392	34	256	13,712	4	59,843	34,715	8			
1916	16,552	47,028	8	3,105	136,258	23	104,764	32	77	1,724	..	8,421	13,665	..			
1917	..	..	..	4,517	197,473	26	156,056	26	2,153	45,056	8	10,672	1,855	4			
1918	..	..	..	..	..	..	..	..	4,588	117,332	..	1,339	2,748	..			
1919	71,545	244,468	25	5,600	224,025	23	156,547	16	12,207	269,348	15	55,776	21,437	2			
1920	106,396	392,507	33	4,196	122,558	10	141,086	12	10,544	146,709	27	145,554	51,491	4			
1921	93,987	379,100	26	5,702	139,683	10	41,552	12	12,329	107,166	12	270,555	177,300	7			
1922	77,902	279,722	26	8,970	239,344	24	49,429	5	48,710	260,410	6	393,769	148,910	14			
1923	139,928	401,181	28	8,820	230,044	16	118,413	8	31,752	142,917	4	874,701	249,545	16			
1924	148,411	635,618	28	11,416	299,277	13	161,104	6	34,396	154,606	9	811,144	381,144	16			
1925	147,257	823,901	39	14,369	531,139	20	325,145	12	48,430	140,076	7	416,064	316,044	15	8	71	..
1926	140,920	747,195	31	14,928	579,499	24	239,795	10	19,427	87,426	4	929,178	280,596	12	90	728	..
1927	209,805	1,140,293	37	15,899	468,974	15	246,228	8	56,375	263,129	8	1,707,665	505,892	16	71	798	..
1928	211,608	1,119,448	32½	16,516	495,958	16	347,825	11	78,235	403,131	12	892,660	306,078	9	1,434	8,193	1
1929	133,091	1,022,760	26	15,647	533,572	20	353,448	13	55,437	277,294	10	905,892	305,892	11	6,252	16,785	1
1930	310,088	1,426,869	44	15,947	437,269	13	188,104	20	49,270	222,305	7	2,222,528	505,517	17	17,462	29,261	3
1931	245,993	986,429	42	15,994	293,504	12	109,458	5	44,171	199,389	8	1,859,517	419,399	18	22,115	76,660	5
1932	275,916	1,213,715	55	15,385	186,574	8	117,124	5	37,473	199,972	8	117,677	117,677	9	45,108	112,062	6
1933	256,972	831,197	37	19,850	249,863	11	159,324	7	43,031	194,193	9	1,731,549	212,699	9	67,099	217,047	7
1934	186,759	491,759	26	24,016	311,371	16	195,915	5	30,832	140,564	4	439,958	104,754	6	81,835	335,690	9
1935	358,072	929,796	31	34,136	423,112	14	180,915	10	38,723	175,899	6	1,198,605	184,965	6	..	466,872	12
1936	..	(d)968,000	..	34,746	690,459	18	(d)191,000	6	..	(d)211,000	5	..	(d)233,000	5			
1937	..	(d)733,000	19	31,275	673,719	17	(d)202,000	8	..	(d)187,000	5	..	(d)199,000	5			

Year	Wattle Bark & Extract (a) Qty (Cwt.)	Value (£)	%	Sugar Qty (Cwt.)	Value (£)	%	Dairy Produce Value (£)	%	Raw Cotton Qty	Value (£)	%	Gold Bullion Qty (Troy Oz.)	Value (£)	%	Miscellaneous Value (£)	%	Total (£)	Kenya Produce to Uganda (£)
1908							2,501	2	2,725	1,843	1				127,942	81	157,997	
1909							2,259	1	2,344	5,997	4				104,614	75	104,478	
1910									1,266	4,443	2				131,586	70	199,668	
1911	200	47	..				4,829	2	1,632	7,477	2				176,561	64	276,480	
1912	860	333	..				9,355	3	1,660	6,313	2				195,023	53	333,670	
1913	1,036	509	..				10,638	3	1,831	11,831	3				244,639	53	421,084	
1914	4,040	1,917	..				5,063	1	1,349	5,475	2				229,277	53	443,624	
1915	540	237	..				3,137	1	175	614	..				119,772	39	314,804	
1916							6,901	2		2,920	..				119,389	37	329,519	
1917							5,746	1		2,423	..				202,727	35	587,044	
1918	120	10	..				9,180	1	200	1,473	..				447,714	59	758,411	
1919	9,025	31	..				6,756	1	337	3,284	..				65,320	7	984,370	
1920	9,414	6,780	..				14,693	1	645	6,343	..				310,891	27	1,178,460	
1921	71,843	2,708	2	1,926	2,754	..	3,640	1	1,615	18,738	1				976,086	53	1,832,805	
1922	72,020	5,386	2	2,675	6,092	..	8,281	1	677	3,086	..				77,311	20	1,084,590	
1923	84,858	18,023	2	5,271	9,417	..	7,028	1	677	8,347	..				399,594	18	504,935	
1924	95,313	24,832	3	21,932	29,254	1	20,438	1	1,696	5,149	..				412,327	16	239,614	
1925	124,993	36,506	2	21,619	32,055	1	60,865	2	1,261	1,731	..				367,574	15	2,724,639	130,118
1926	133,458	61,990	3	13,070	18,790	..	42,344	2	570	10,714	..	1,078	3,700	..	408,588	15	2,414,341	236,255
1927	147,871	55,847	3	15,343	24,647	1	49,709	2	2,527	2,435	..	712	2,444	..	382,548	18	3,086,916	169,938
1928	198,441	63,080	4	15,045	15,247	..	36,572	2	4,693	6,586	..	1,999	9,553	..	486,148	12	3,666,403	189,296
1929	246,354	72,231	4	21,196	24,344	1	51,865	2	4,920	8,586	..	1,039	3,575	..	466,182	12	2,745,910	146,166
1930	308,311	66,784	3	15,568	17,617	..	74,608	2	3,131	23,582	1	4,652	7,835	..	408,865	12	3,429,571	144,979
1931		60,309	4	89,214	66,735	2			4,516	28,485	2	14,344	19,565	1	212,265	10	2,343,874	121,291
1932				22,735	57,511	3			10,660			14,111	61,375	3	223,503	12	2,280,982	151,648
1933									11,748			14,759	63,100	3	286,296	14	2,246,999	
1934													69,442	4	265,796	13	1,909,371	
1935	325,026	(d)103,562	4	83,923	58,017	2			58,419	76,326	3	27,556	164,997	6	395,063		2,928,307	167,356
1936		(d)113,000	3	125,656	74,594	2			58,452	149,765	7	45,459	278,396	7			(d)3,888,000	213,108
1937		(d)121,000	3	74,136	43,899	1			71,189	191,516	10	69,286	415,967	10			(d)3,954,000	278,698

(a) Includes Mangrove Bark to 1924.
(b) Extracted from the *Report of the Commission on the Financial Position and Taxation of Kenya*, Colonial No. 116, 1936.
(c) Figures prior to 1923 should be accepted with reserve.
(d) To the nearest £000.

of some 36,000 persons is mainly engaged in marketing, distribution and transport, and in these directions they require facilities similar to the European community, while the education of their children is a rapidly-growing problem. Finally, as the basis of all activities, there are 3,000,000 natives with growing desires and wants, and an increasing appreciation of both the amenities of the European type and of the advantages of education and medical facilities, but living on an income which provides little margin either for satisfying these wants, which are fast becoming necessities, or for paying taxes. There is also the general tendency to insist on using European agencies mainly from overseas, and therefore as permanent and pensionable employees for work which in the Eastern colonies would be carried out by indigenous agencies.

What is, therefore, of prime importance in Kenya is that the National Income as a whole, that is, the productivity of the economy in general, must be greatly increased in order to justify

TABLE 65.—*Inter-Territorial Trade* : *Kenya, Uganda, Tanganyika,*
1927–37.

Year.	Imports of Produce from Tanganyika Territory to Kenya and Uganda. (£.)	Re-Exports from Kenya and Uganda to Tanganyika Territory. (£.)	Kenya and Uganda Domestic Exports to Tanganyika Territory. (£.)	Domestic Exports from Kenya to Uganda. (£.)	Domestic Exports from Uganda to Kenya. (£.)
1927	929,650	522,864	146,617	130,118	(a)
1928	1,120,419	642,191	129,709	236,255	(a)
1929	757,724	678,143	192,353	189,938	(a)
1930	599,193	592,977	191,388	182,026	(a)
1931	377,109	384,921	182,878	146,166	(a)
1932	597,719	385,116	165,317	144,979	98,605
1933	642,824	413,127	200,083	121,291	74,692
1934	832,626	480,237	266,012	151,648	88,666
1935	833,061	641,842	276,321	167,356	96,274
1936	724,500	700,093	275,430	213,108	63,379
1937	942,515	864,373	353,241	278,368	99,949

(a) Reliable figures not available.

the heavy capital investments and the expensive administrative and scientific services that have been established. This economic expansion will depend (a) on an increase in the "effective" population, either by new immigration or by the development of the economic efforts of the existing and, therefore, mainly of the large native population; and (b) on the progress of the "effective" population in the surrounding territories, for Kenya draws a considerable part of its National Income from the relatively large trans-shipment, re-export and general entrepôt trade which it does for its neighbours.

The port of Mombasa is the main collecting and distributing centre for the trade of East Africa, and the commercial agencies situated here are East African in character. It is not possible to assess the actual value of the commercial services rendered by Kenya to the neighbouring territories, or of the indirect benefits which accrue to the colony as a result of the transportation undertakings of the Kenya and Uganda Railway, but they are by no means negligible. The movements of goods through Kenya, which provide a source of income to the colony, include (i) imports on behalf of Uganda; (ii) Uganda domestic exports; (iii) Kenya re-exports; (iv) transit and trans-shipment traffic. Table 65 gives a detailed analysis of this trade.[1]

In view of the obvious need of stimulating production, it is significant that in Kenya in 1935, as is shown by the figures on p. 261, the main products from native areas accounted for only 13% of the total exports of the colony. The total value of native domestic exports in 1928 was estimated to be some £472,000. It dropped in 1931 to £222,000, while in 1933 it was £355,000, of which hides and skins accounted for £155,000, wattle bark and extract for £66,000, maize for £36,000, and cotton for £24,000.

It is true, as the Report of the Economic Development Committee stated, that figures of this kind are not an adequate index of the non-native production in the colony. A comparison of agricultural exports, of native origin, with other exports, overlooks the fact "that practically all the manual labour necessary to the production of any part of the colony's exports is performed by natives, who earn large sums as wages in the effort to produce non-native exports, and that large quantities of produce, of native origin, are consumed in the Colony, outside the reserves, and,

---

[1] Cf. Sir Allen Pim's Report, ibid., p. 9 ; Table 65 has been extracted from Appendix IV of the Report, and from the Annual Trade Reports of Kenya and Uganda.

though not themselves reaching the export market, liberate non-native products to do so."[1] Nevertheless, the relatively low production of natives in the reserves is symptomatic of the danger that purely native production may be retarded by the requirements of European producers for wage-paid labour. Some critics have expressed very decided views concerning this question.[2]

It is not possible to enter into a further discussion of this complex problem here. The experience of the Union and of other African territories, which has already been examined, is sufficient to indicate the factors involved, while the heavy external obligations of Kenya give point to the need for every possible elasticity in its economic policy.

The main technical factors which have influenced the establishment of Kenya's agricultural export industries were the construction of the Kenya and Uganda Railway, and the expansion of European colonization. The latter has played a predominating part in determining the character of development and the direction of policy. The lack of important mineral development,[3] or, as in West Africa, of other valuable natural products, has caused the European population to invest large amounts of capital in developing special crops.

The real task which now faces Kenya is that of considering objectively whether the types of production it has fostered are best suited to the advancement of the country, and therefore of both the European and the non-European populations. For, in the long run, the policies adopted will either advance or retard the welfare of both these sections of the population; the progress of the one without that of the other will eventually be found to be impossible.

For proof that the income of the African can be increased, and his economic horizon widened, Kenya need only look to her neighbour, Uganda, and note that the exports of that small country, with an almost negligible European population, already almost equal her own.

[1] Nairobi : Government Printer, 1935, p. 104.
[2] As, for example, Norman Leys in his well-known book, *Kenya*, London : Hogarth Press, 1926.
[3] The value of gold production has increased steadily from £67,665 in 1933 to £379,626 in 1937.

VII
UGANDA PROTECTORATE.

It was not possible to divide the estimate of capital investment from abroad between Kenya and Uganda; the figures given in Table 28 refer to both territories together. The investment in Uganda, however, has been relatively small, and has been mainly composed of grants-in-aid, which amounted to roughly £2·5 millions up to 1915, of recent grants from the Colonial Development Fund, and of the public debt incurred by the territory. The money has been spent on public works, and partly on the construction of railways by the Kenya and Uganda Railways.

The Public Debt at the end of 1936 amounted to £2,236,000.[1] The development of the trade is shown in Table 62, and that of the finances of the territory in Table 66. The economic progress of Uganda can indeed be described as remarkable, particularly if it is borne in mind that the territory lacks indigenous products of commercial value, that its mineral wealth is conjectural, that the European population is less than 2,000, and that the investments from abroad have been so small.

In order to appreciate its rapid progress, which is well illustrated on Chart "E", it is perhaps well to visualize Uganda as it was in the last days of the nineteenth century. Mr. H. B. Thomas and Mr. Robert Scott in their excellent book *Uganda*[2] give the following description : "In a territory extending from Naivasha and Lake Rudolf to Ruwenzori, and from the Kagera River to Gondokoro, there were but a few score British civil and military officers, and vast areas remained unadministered and even unexplored. Concentrated for the most part in Uganda was a strong contingent of missionaries, both Protestant and Roman

[1] There is a contingent liability in respect of the services of the loan of £3,393,000 raised by the Government of Kenya for the Kenya and Uganda Railways and Harbours.

[2] *Uganda*, by H. B. Thomas and Robert Scott (of the Uganda Protectorate Service). (London : Oxford University Press, 1935, pp. 560.) In my opinion, this is the best book of its kind yet written on any African territory, and is an example of what a very superior type of handbook can be.

TABLE 66.—Uganda. Finance, 1900–36.(e)

Year.(b)	Gross Revenue.(c)	Customs Revenue.(a)	Percentage of Customs to Total Revenue.	Grant-in-Aid.	Gross Expenditure. (f)	Public Debt.
	£(000).	£(000).		£(000).	£(000).	£(000).
1900	82	9	11·0	204	252	...
1901	73	10	13·7	172	229	...
1902	41	6	14·6	135	204	...
1903	51	7	13·7	130	187	...
1904	60	8	13·3	140	173	...
1905	78	13	16·7	103	191	...
1906	97	13	13·4	112	192	...
1907	112	11	9·8	85	196	...
1908	103	13	12·6	95	256	...
1909	165	37	22·4	103	240	...
1910	191	40	20·9	96	252	120
1911	203	35	17·2	65	284	170
1912	239	40	16·7	45	292	295
1913	257	52	20·2	35	290	293
1914	283	70	24·7	10	289	297
1915	287	52	18·1	...	285	295
1916	315	80	25·4	...	289	291
1917	326	79	24·2	...	285	332
1918	352	84	23·9	...	324	283
1919	743	136	18·3	...	698	411
1920	777(d)	161(d)	20·7	...	593(d)	406
1921	803	158	19·7	...	786	700
1922	820	190	23·2	...	920	845
1923	1,000	272	27·2	...	939	888
1924	1,240	427	34·4	...	919	1,052
1925	1,479	514	34·8	...	1,108	1,105
1926	1,390	409	29·4	...	1,296	1,114
1927	1,292	348	26·9	...	1,431	1,108
1928	1,519	432	28·4	...	1,368	1,099
1929	1,683	439	26·1	...	1,607	1,088
1930	1,412	325	23·0	...	1,640	1,077
1931	1,400	304	21·7	...	1,452	1,066
1932	1,399	285	20·4	...	1,299	2,000
1933	1,350	309	22·9	...	1,276	2,236
1934	1,528	394	25·8	...	1,362	2,236
1935	1,567	437	27·9	...	1,440	2,236
1936	1,713	497	29·0	...	1,624	2,236

(a) Prior to 1909–10, all customs revenue collected at Mombasa on Uganda imports was retained by the British East Africa Protectorate (Kenya). From that year such moneys were handed over to Uganda.
(b) To 31st March of the year following that stated up to 1919, and to 31st December thereafter.
(c) Excluding Imperial Grants.
(d) For nine months only.
(e) Extracted from the *Statistical Abstracts for the British Empire*, 1936, figures are from the *Colonial Report*.
(f) Including payments to Reserve Fund except in 1936.

Catholic. There were as yet no non-native planters, and no agricultural production for export, and a handful of European and Indian merchants and a few Arabs sufficed for the external trade of the country, from which the only export was ivory. The Uganda Railway did not reach Port Florence (Kisumu) until 20th December, 1901, and beyond the railway zone there were no real roads and no wheeled transport. A European mail, seldom less than three months old, was received once a month."

By 1928 the domestic exports of this territory nearly equalled, and in 1929 they exceeded those of Tanganyika. From 1930 to 1935, the total domestic exports of Uganda were £17,132,000, while those of Tanganyika amounted to only £15,105,000.

It is particularly significant that Uganda's progress has been brought about by European science and government which have developed successfully the high innate capacity of the African population. Uganda, with considerable areas of generally fertile soil, combined with an evenly distributed rainfall, has been well suited for development on the basis of small native holdings, while cotton, the mainstay of the territory, is one of the crops which best lends itself for cultivation in this way.

Production in the hands of non-natives is relatively small. Prior to 1911, European planting was confined to what was little more than experimental work on a handful of estates. Between 1911 and 1914, however, great interest was evinced in the possibilities of plantation rubber, coffee and cocoa, and at the outbreak of the War a miniature boom in the acquisition of land was in progress. This resulted in an increase of production during the first years of the war, but expansion was naturally checked, and a certain number of projects were abandoned or postponed. The cultivation of cocoa ceased altogether, and has not since been resumed. High prices following the War stimulated planting activity, but the reviving industry was seriously affected by the slump of 1921, and many estates were finally closed. Later, improving markets for primary products led to an influx of new settlers, who took up land for coffee-planting in the Toro district in 1926/7; but they were unfortunate enough to encounter the subsequent world-wide economic depression, and only a small proportion were able to establish themselves. There is now no tendency towards any material addition to the ranks of European planters, whose numbers have remained constant for some years, as is instanced by the following census figures relating to non-native agriculture[1]:

Numbers Engaged in Agriculture.

				Europeans.	Other non-natives.
1921	.	.	.	106	23
1931	.	.	.	103	26

The prospects of the non-native who wishes to take up agricultural land in Uganda are small. "Before the War there seemed to be few bounds to the possible developments of agriculture by European capital under European control. But a greater knowledge of the limitations of Uganda as a 'plantation' country, and the adoption of the policy of development by native agency to which the Protectorate is now deliberately committed, have inevitably restricted the openings for agricultural enterprise by non-natives. No fortunes have ever been made by European planters in Uganda, and though a number who have shown adaptability and courage have gained, and are gaining, a fair livelihood in far from unattractive surroundings, it would nevertheless be unwise to assume that there is likely to be room for more than a limited expansion in the ranks of this small but vigorous section of the community."[2]

The economy of Uganda has been developed with cotton as the mainstay, although a very considerable number of other products have been tried, and some are now well established. In the main cotton-growing areas there is a network of all-weather roads, and this has permitted the economic production of cotton in practically all parts of the Protectorate which are suitable for this crop. Statistics of the annual exports of cotton from 1902 to 1937 are given in Table 67.

The great dependence of the country on this one product is of course associated with obvious disadvantages, but they are counterbalanced by the important fact that Uganda has only a small foreign debt charge to meet. In 1936 this amounted to £137,598, *i. e.* 8% of the ordinary revenue. The development of

[1] The above information has been extracted from Thomas and Scott, *ibid.*, p. 143.
[2] *Ibid.*, p. 107.

Uganda's public works has to no small extent been paid for out of revenue. In other words, the necessary saving has been undertaken by the population itself.

TABLE 67.—*Uganda. Cotton Exports from* 1902.(*a*)

Year.(b)	Equivalent Number of Bales of 400 lb. Lint Cotton Exported.	Value of Lint Cotton Exported.	Value of Cotton Seed Exported.	Percentage of Value of Cotton Lint and Cotton Seed to Total of Domestic Exports.
		£.	£.	%.
1902–3	...	...	...	...
1903–4	...	...	...	...
1904–5	54	236	...	0·39
1905–6	241	1,089	...	1·21
1906–7	980	11,411	2	9·84
1907–8	3,973	51,594	263	35·27
1908–9	3,945	41,232	2,910	34·71
1909–10	6,209	59,596	849	34·36
1910–11	13,378	165,412	3,208	55·00
1911–12	20,433	230,850	5,909	64·41
1912–13	25,841	254,379	11,335	60·82
1913–14	27,568	317,687	13,499	64·73
1914–15	32,535	351,146	18,172	70·59
1915–16	26,226	245,426	9,753	50·66
1916–17	21,832	348,914	10,220	56·31
1917–18	27,854	537,631	7,402	69·46
1918–19	27,492	965,951	6,149	77·93
1919–20	36,530	1,209,663	25,783	67·56
1920 (9 mths. to 31st Dec.)	47,695	3,778,931	8,990	91·63
1921	81,366	1,281,357	22,113	84·67
1922	48,290	877,625	9,532	72·97
1923	88,046	2,026,820	52,964	86·89
1924	128,604	3,486,565	106,280	92·19
1925	196,038	4,685,992	122,790	94·34
1926	180,860	3,051,791	194,887	90·28
1927	131,728	1,690,837	170,303	80·56
1928	138,486	2,475,328	323,110	82·42
1929	204,057	3,312,668	423,999	87·41
1930	129,122	1,555,344	137,387	82·15
1931	188,920	1,503,307	149,224	83·53
1932	207,326	1,584,172	168,366	78·77
1933	294,828	2,682,210	262,539	85·00
1934	285,642	2,927,796	85,947	79·86
1935	253,242	2,822,739	135,779	...
1936	321,348	3,326,879	263,180	...

(*a*) Compiled from a table in Appendix IV of *Uganda* (Thomas and Scott), p. 505.
(*b*) Year ending 31st March (Calendar Year from 1921).

Moreover, the expenses of Uganda's administration have not been inflated beyond the economic capacity of the country by the cost of an expanded European personnel. On the contrary the administrative services of Uganda are well proportioned to the National Income of its people. In fact, at the end of 1936 Uganda possessed a reserve fund of no less than £534,000 and surplus balances of £1,162,000. Throughout the depression there were no deficits. Indeed, it is significant that the index number of the ordinary revenue of Uganda was 609·7 for 1935 on the basis 1913 = 100—a larger increase than that of any other African territory. (See Table 38.)

One of the striking lessons to be learnt from the economic development of the Protectorate is the value of capital creation and accumulation by the population itself through its own efforts. No one can doubt that this slower, but surer, path of development by avoiding heavy borrowing abroad will be a source of strength to the territory in the future.

The development of the main exports of the country, other than cotton, is shown by the following statistics:

Values.[1]

Year.	Coffee. (£.)	Sugar. (£.)	Timber. (£.)	Tin Ore. (£.)	Gold Bullion.[2] (£.)
1925	140,019	7,441	75	...	...
1928	164,188	4,435	609	50,673	...
1931	161,389	46,576	725	24,436	(401)
1932	223,162	45,012	2,245	47,168	(3,275)
1933	210,638	128,802	3,438	57,503	(7,365)
1934	293,313	240,593	8,204	63,320	(40,126)
1935	230,976	168,358	4,556	86,027	(39,978)
1936	381,244	90,127	4,637	85,844	(92,709)
1937	420,000	123,516	6,247	...	124,713

Quantities.[1]

Year.	Coffee. (Cwt.)	Sugar. (Cwt.)	Timber. (Cubic ft.)	Tin Ore. (Tons.)	Gold Bullion. (Ozs. Troy.)
1925	29,884	4,053	497	...	...
1928	40,348	2,749	1,913	261	...
1931	69,990	44,995	3,697	150	71
1932	87,077	41,049	9,738	365	586
1933	100,444	144,229	15,433	389	1,261
1934	154,298	294,685	31,611	437	6,373
1935	125,706	253,951	17,816	552	6,329
1936	228,783	180,652	23,578	575	14,906
1937	...	226,843	37,522	...	19,590

[1] Compiled from Table in Appendix V, *Uganda* (Thomas and Scott), pp. 506/7, and from the Annual Colonial Reports for Uganda.

[2] In order that these figures shall remain consistent with those contained in the *Annual Blue Book*, the values obtained from the Customs returns are shown in principal and the ascertained values on sale are given in brackets.

VIII

TANGANYIKA TERRITORY.

Tanganyika provides another example of a territory which suffers from the disadvantages of being still dependent on a relatively small number of export products, the world prices of which are subject to great fluctuations, and of having to meet considerable debt charges abroad. The total Public Debt, including loans from the Imperial Treasury, amounts to nearly £9 millions, of which about two-thirds has been spent on railway construction.[1]

Tanganyika, moreover, entered the last depression with heavy administrative charges on account of the expansion of government and social services. The development of the finances of the territory is shown in Table 68.

The prosperity of the territory has in the past been intimately bound up with fortunes of the sisal producers. Table 69 analyses the trade of the territory from 1900–36, and shows that sisal exports have steadily increased in relative importance since the War, until in 1929 they amounted to £1,486,000 and formed 40% of the total domestic exports (44·5% in 1930 and 43·0% in 1931). Thereafter the catastrophic fall in sisal prices set in, with the result that, notwithstanding a very considerable fall in the value of the domestic exports of the territory as a whole, sisal

---

[1] Sir Armitage Smith in his *Report on a Financial Mission to Tanganyika* (Cmd. 4182, 1932), observed that "In view of the moderate agricultural wealth of the territory, the entirely conjectural value of its mineral resources (the position has now been altered by recent gold mining developments), such a debt charge (then amounting to about 25% of the annual revenue) is a very serious burden, and it is obviously imperative to avoid all recourse to further borrowing until the financial outlook improves very considerably." In fact, since he reported, there has been no increase in the Public Debt. He added : "it is unwise in a new and untried territory, relying for its economy on one or two main export crops, and for its revenue on one or two large heads of taxation, to budget up to the hilt on the hypothesis of continued and unbroken prosperity. It is unwise, more particularly, to do so in the absence of a substantial liquid reserve fund. Further, it is unwise to provide in a territory which is not actually rich, but rather of moderate resources, a scale of social services, however desirable in themselves, such as might be appropriate to an established and prosperous community. Slow and continuous progress is better than alternating extravagance and retrenchment, and any progress is conditional on recognizing the limitations imposed by circumstances." (*Ibid.*, pp. 39/40.)

TABLE 68.—*Tanganyika. Finance*, 1900–36.(*e*)

Year.(*b*)	Gross Revenue. (*a, d*)	Customs Revenue.	Percentage of Customs to Total Revenue.	Grant-in-Aid.	Gross Expenditure. (*a*)	Public Debt.
	£(000).	£(000).		£(000).	£(000).	£(000).
1900	...	...	...	...	...	...
1901	...	...	...	...	...	...
1902	...	...	...	...	...	...
1903	...	...	...	...	...	...
1904	296	85	28·7	309	522	...
1905	347	100	28·8	348	672	...
1906	361	134	37·1	298	631	...
1907	395	136	34·4	293	690	...
1908	381	136	35·7	224	595	...
1909	543	161	29·7	178	679	...
1910	658	202	30·7	179	694	...
1911	689	219	31·8	177	733	...
1912	623	205	32·9	180	966	...
1913	688	221	32·1	180	1,025	...
1914	823	277	33·7	165	1,187	...
1915	...	...	...	...	...	...
1916	...	...	...	...	...	...
1917	336	117	34·8	...	157	...
1918	462	119	25·8	...	383	...
1919	1,004	211	21·0	...	1,185	...
1920	947	188	19·9	...	1,389	14
1921	978	210	21·5	...	1,808	836
1922	1,228	268	21·8	...	1,618	1,636
1923	1,315	326	24·8	...	1,406	2,386
1924	1,559	427	27·4	...	1,384	2,736
1925	1,975	501	25·4	...	1,631	3,135
1926	1,716	563	32·8	...	1,578	3,135
1927	1,904	632	33·2	...	1,741	3,135
1928	1,973	698	35·4	...	1,873	5,205
1929	1,993	740	37·1	...	2,085	5,205
1930	1,749	566	32·4	...	2,103	5,196
1931	1,522	411	27·0	...	1,821	5,196
1932(*c*)	1,291(*c*)	300(*c*)	23·2	...	1,255(*c*)	8,717(*c*)
1933	1,565	405	25·9	...	1,651	8,717
1934	1,720	476	27·7	...	1,871	8,717
1935	1,974	613	31·1	...	1,750	8,717
1936	2,206	697(*f*)	31·6	...	2,030(*f*)	8,717

(*a*) In 1925 and preceding years gross railway revenue and expenditure were included. In 1926 and 1927 net railway revenue only is included. From 1928 all railway figures are excluded, except for an accumulated railway deficit of £200,000 charged in 1934 figures, and £11,000 in 1935. In 1936 a small net profit was included.

(*b*) The precise financial year during the period of German administration is not known. From 1917 to 1931 the figures are to 31st March of the year following that stated. Thereafter they are to 31st December of each year.

(*c*) For nine months only.

(*d*) Excluding grants-in-aid.

(*e*) Extracted from the *Statistical Abstracts for the British Empire.*

(*f*) Revised estimate.

TABLE 69.—*Tanganyika.   Trade Statistics, 1900–37, and Proportion per cent. of Annual Exports of Selected Commodities to Annual Value of all Domestic Produce Exported.(g)*

Year.(a)	Merchandise Imports.(b),(e),(f)	Exports.(b),(c)		Sisal Exports.		Coffee Exports.		Cotton Exports.	
		Domestic Produce.(e)	Re-exports.	£(000).	%.	£(000).	%.	£(000).	%.
	£(000).	£(000).	£(000).						
1900	601	214	...	(d)	...	(d)	...	(d)	...
1901	476	231	...	(d)	...	(d)	...	(d)	...
1902	442	264	...	(d)	...	(d)	...	(d)	...
1903	559	352	...	(d)	...	(d)	...	(d)	...
1904	716	447	...	(d)	...	(d)	...	(d)	...
1905	882	497	...	(d)	...	(d)	...	(p)	...
1906	1,207	549	...	(d)	...	(d)	...	(d)	...
1907	1,190	625	...	(d)	...	(d)	...	(d)	...
1908	1,289	543	...	(d)	...	(d)	...	(d)	...
1909	1,697	655	...	(d)	...	(d)	...	(d)	...
1910	1,932	1,040	...	151	14·5	42	4·0	38	3·7
1911	2,294	1,121	...	227	20·5	63	5·6	66	5·9
1912	2,515	1,570	...	368	23·4	95	6·1	105	6·7
1913	2,667	1,777	...	(d)	(d)	(d)	...	(d)	...
1914	(d)	(d)	...	(d)	...	(d)	...	(d)	...
1915	(d)	(d)	...	(d)	...	(d)	...	(d)	...
1916	(d)	(d)	...	(d)	...	(d)	...	(d)	...

Year			(d)	(d)		(d)		(d)		(d)	
1917	1,110	634	...	...	...	...	...	...	...	...	...
1918	1,008	701	...	...	...	...	...	...	...	...	...
1919	1,738	1,994	98	654	32·8	281	14·1	94	4·7		
1920	1,729	1,282	133	364	28·4	89	6·9	119	9·3		
1921	1,426	1,090	157	238	21·8	138	12·7	119	10·9		
1922	1,392	1,300	144	289	22·2	204	15·7	141	10·8		
1923	1,839	1,657	76	367	22·1	205	12·4	178	10·7		
1924	2,081	2,611	107	645	24·7	353	13·5	374	14·3		
1925	2,864	2,902	107	688	23·7	481	16·6	540	18·6		
1926	3,152	3,026	103	911	30·1	495	16·4	427	14·1		
1927	3,672	3,295	145	1,161	35·2	463	14·1	362	11·0		
1928	3,737	3,873	177	1,111	28·7	740	19·1	495	12·8		
1929	4,286	3,722	265	1,486	39·9	589	15·8	488	13·1		
1930	3,982	2,636	262	1,172	44·5	397	15·1	247	9·4		
1931	2,496	1,645	245	707	43·0	247	15·0	120	7·3		
1932	1,872	2,190	167	698	31·9	464	21·2	184	8·4		
1933	1,947	2,543	183	882	34·7	430	16·9	277	10·9		
1934	2,343	2,646	211	848	32·0	495	18·7	327	12·4		
1935	2,990	3,445	279	1,135	32·9	487	14·1	570	16·5		
1936	3,357	4,516	290	1,873	41·5	343	7·6	641	14·2		
1937	3,924	4,959	...	342	41·8	430	8·7	604	12·2		

(a) The figures for 1917–20 are up to 31st March of the following years, and those for 1921 and subsequent years are for calendar years. There is, therefore, some element of duplication in 1921.
(b) The pre-war and post-war statistics are not strictly comparable owing to the change in area.
(c) Minerals constitute a relatively small proportion of total exports. Gold is the only such product of any importance, the value exported in 1935 being £370,000, and £499,000 in 1936. Rubber, which was the most important single export in 1910–12, is no longer of any significance in the trade of Tanganyika.
(d) Details not available.
(e) Excluding bullion and coin from 1917, in the case of imports and re-exports but including gold bullion in exports.
(f) Including goods subsequently re-exported.
(g) Extracted from the Statistical Abstracts for the British Empire.

exports formed only 32% of the total in 1932, and were valued at only £698,000, although the quantity exported increased continuously from 36,186 tons in 1928 to 60,554 tons in 1932. The fall in world prices also affected the other main exports of the territory, of which cotton (71,888 centals valued at £184,000 in 1932, as compared with 109,607 centals, valued at £495,000 in 1928) and coffee (11,362 tons in 1932, valued at £464,000 as compared with 10,431 tons, valued at £740,000 in 1928) were the most important.

The recent improvement in the economic position of the territory is, in turn, to be ascribed largely to the recovery of sisal exports, which reached 80,559 tons and a record value of £1,873,000 in 1936, and in that year again accounted for 41·5% of the total domestic exports. Cotton exports also established a new record in 1936 (252,534 centals compared with 110,000 in 1928) and were valued at £641,000. Coffee exports declined from 18,588 tons in 1935 to 12,146 in 1936.

However, the most important development of recent years has been the increase in gold production. Gold now takes second place in the exports of the territory. The value of gold exports rose from £60,000 in 1931 to £296,000 in 1934 and to £490,000 in 1936, when gold accounted for 10·8% of the total domestic exports, as compared with only 3·7% five years earlier. The importance of the recent development of gold mining is illustrated by the fact that, for the ten years ending December, 1932, the value of all mineral exports from Tanganyika had amounted to only about £1,136,000; diamonds, the production of which was very irregular, contributed nearly one-half of this sum. In 1936, sisal, cotton, coffee and gold accounted for 74·1% of the domestic exports of the country. Ground nuts, cocoa, sesame, beeswax, ghee, tobacco, grain, hides and skins made up the remainder.

If the production of gold continues to increase, Tanganyika may be far less seriously affected by the next depression than she was by the last one.

Nevertheless, the prosperity of its sisal, coffee and cotton industries when world markets are favourable, as they are now, must not blind one to the fact that, apart from mining potentialities, Tanganyika is a poorly developed territory. This is due not only to geographical and climatic factors, but also to the fact that it is mainly a "native African territory not merely in the sense of the mandate, but still more in the sense that the economy of the territory is predominantly Native African". Its progress, therefore, both from an economic and from a sociological point of view, will be determined by this fact.

Tanganyika, although the largest and most populous of the British East African territories (according to the 1931 census the native population was 5,022,640, and there were 23,422 Asiatics), is, in fact, relatively the least developed, if we except Nyasaland, and it has to contend with a wide range of exceptional disadvantages. Its population is very unevenly distributed, and the health of the native population is poor owing to the prevalence of tropical diseases.

"Over 62%, or nearly two-thirds of Tanganyika Territory is uninhabited," writes Gillman.[1] "Most of these 214,000 square miles form large continuous blocks especially in the centre and in the West, and the rest dovetails into the various occupation types, none of which is entirely without areas unfit or undesirable for human settlement."

From an analysis of his population table Gillman concludes that the well-watered parts of the country, although comprising only one-tenth of the area, contain two-thirds of the whole population, the fairly well-watered areas contain one-sixth of the population on one-twelfth of the total area, and the poorly watered parts of the country contain another one-sixth of the population on one-fifth of the total area. Stated in another form, the one-fifth of the country which possesses good or fairly adequate domestic water supplies holds five-sixths of the people, while the remaining one-sixth of the population occupies another one-fifth of precariously watered land.

The vast uninhabited or only sparsely inhabited regions, which cover 70% of the surface but harbour only 18% of the population, have an average density of only 1·4 people per square kilometre (3·6 per square mile).

[1] In his remarkable report, "A Population Map of Tanganyika Territory", reprinted in the *Report by His Majesty's Government in the United Kingdom on the Administration of Tanganyika Territory for the year 1935.* Colonial No. 113, 1936, Appendix IX, p. 197 ff.

In the population map of Tanganyika is also to be found the key to the absence of railway communication over large parts of the country. The extreme difficulty of providing such communications is readily understandable when the sparsity of the possible traffic is borne in mind.

The European population in Tanganyika is now only about 9,000; the number of male adults engaged in agriculture is less than 2,000. The number of natives in paid employment in 1935 was about 220,000, of whom 112,000 were employed in agriculture and 24,000 in mining.

The natural difficulties with which Tanganyika has to cope have not always been fully realized, and, as a result, there has at times been much misunderstanding and unnecessary criticism of the efforts made by the administration to develop the territory. This is unfortunate, because, taking all the circumstances into account, and bearing in mind, too, the effect of political uncertainty on settlement and capital investment in the territory, its progress does not compare unfavourably with that of other African colonies. Tanganyika provides an example of a territory which, so far, has not had the benefit of possessing "fruits ready for the plucking", and in which only slow, expensive and laborious development can lead to progress.

IX

NYASALAND PROTECTORATE.

The territory comprised in the Nyasaland Protectorate is a strip of land about 520 miles in length and varying from 50–100 miles in width. The area is roughly 40,000 square miles, of which about 10,353 square miles are water. The most southern part of the Protectorate is about 130 miles from the sea.

To the west lies Northern Rhodesia, to the north and north-east Tanganyika, and to the south and east, Portuguese East Africa. Of the total land surface of about 25,000,000 acres, only about 4,000,000 have been alienated. There are nearly 3,000,000 acres of forest areas, of which 20,000 are estimated to be under commercial timber. The dominant feature of the physiography of the country is the deep trough-like depression forming part of the great Rift Valley which traverses it from end to end; the greater part of this trough is occupied by Lake Nyasa and the remaining part by the Shire River Valley.

In its essential features the climate, with local variations, is similar to that of the rest of East Africa and is predominantly of the tropical monsoon type, modified by the numerous mountain ranges and barren plateaux. The territory is subject to the usual disadvantages of these tropical areas.

The population consists of about 1,800 Europeans, 1,400 Asiatics and 1,600,000 natives. Both the native and the European populations are unevenly distributed. 76% of the former reside in the five districts, Blantyre, Zomba, Cholo, Mlanje and Lilongwe, *i. e.* in the healthy highlands. The male adult European population is mainly engaged in the tobacco industry, government services, Christian missions, commerce, and to a small extent in other primary production. In 1935 about 81,000 natives were engaged in growing cotton for sale, and nearly 50,000 were registered as tobacco growers.

Reference has been made previously to the large emigration of native labour from the territory. In 1935 the Nyasaland Committee which inquired into emigrant labour made the conservative estimate that there were 120,000 natives absent from the Protectorate. Of this number, some 75,000 were in Southern Rhodesia, and 25,000 in the Union of South Africa. The Committee was of the opinion that this constituted more than 25% of the male adult population of Nyasaland. The causes of the exodus, they found, lay in economic pressure consisting of taxation, communal obligations, and the desire for a higher standard of living than could be obtained by working for wages in the Protectorate, or by selling surplus produce. Particularly in the north of the Protectorate, there are large areas of undeveloped land, and the inhabitants cannot even meet the tax obligations unless they emigrate to seek other work. The love of travel and adventure is a further cause of the exodus.[1]

---

[1] The Committee found that a further cause lay in the devastation of this comparatively thickly populated country by deforestation, soil erosion, and soil exhaustion, caused by bad methods of cultivation.

TABLE 70.—*Nyasaland. Trade Statistics, 1900–36, and Proportion per cent. of Annual Exports of Selected Commodities to Annual Value of all Domestic Produce Exported. (d)*

Year.(e)	Merchandise Imports.(a) £(000).	Exports. Domestic Produce.(c) £(000).	Exports. Re-exports.(c) £(000).	Tobacco Exports. £(000).	Tobacco Exports. %.	Tea Exports. £(000).	Tea Exports. %.	Cotton Exports. £(000).	Cotton Exports. %.
1900	134	37	...	(b)	...	(b)	...	(b)	(b)
1901	129	22	...	(b)	...	(b)	...	(b)	(b)
1902	144	35	...	(b)	...	(b)	...	(b)	(b)
1903	207	27	...		...	(b)	...	2	7·4
1904	228	66	...	1	1·5	(b)	...	6	9·1
1905	248	87	...	3	3·4	(b)	...	16	18·4
1906	257	72	...	7	9·7	(b)	...	15	20·8
1907	189	54	23	9	16·7	(b)	...	14	25·9
1908	153	82	20	14	17·1	1	1·2	28	34·1
1909	127	98	20	27	27·6	1	1·0	26	26·5
1910	224	148	21	43	29·1	1	0·7	59	39·9
1911	281	152	33	54	35·5	1	0·7	44	28·9
1912	318	175	20	57	32·6	2	1·1	81	46·3
1913	208	201	16	94	46·8	3	1·5	65	32·3
1914	201	182	11	83	45·6	4	2·2	72	39·6
1915	249	198	15	93	47·0	9	4·5	69	34·8
1916	402	289	13	112	38·8	14	4·8	127	43·9
1917	354	145	12	68	46·9	5	3·4	40	27·6
1918	677	511	21	280	54·8	28	5·5	156	30·5
1919	591	430	55	271	63·0	33	7·7	55	12·8
1920	508	613	57	482	78·6	23	3·8	86	14·0
1921	638	378	39	297	78·6	4	1·1	67	17·7
1922	522	425	17	317	74·6	20	4·7	73	17·2
1923	493	410	15	258	62·9	40	9·8	86	21·0

1924	563	564	20	352	62·4	57	10·1	121	21·5
1925	615	542	22	346	63·8	64	11·8	96	17·7
1926	816	647	25	457	70·6	63	9·7	93	14·4
1927	963	930	31	781	84·0	57	6·1	46	4·9
1928	906	676	31	497	73·5	74	10·9	58	8·6
1929	771	589	36	405	68·6	74	12·6	63	10·7
1930	784	663	28	485	73·2	57	8·6	73	11·0
1931	781	502	36	401	79·9	49	9·8	38	7·6
1932	735	656	23	566	86·3	43	6·6	35	5·3
1933	629	514	22	390	75·9	60	11·7	50	9·7
1934	518	753	19	470	62·4	171	22·7	103	13·7
1935	628	736	19	297	40·4	224	30·4	205	27·9
1936	674	797	9	391	49·1	257	32·2	133	16·7

(a) Excludes transit trade from 1904 to 1919. Excludes bullion and coin; apparently includes goods subsequently re-exported, to 1922. After this figures represent imports for "Home Consumption".
(b) Insignificant.
(c) Includes re-export trade prior to 1907 and transit trade from 1904 to 1919. Excludes bullion and coin.
(d) Extracted from the *Statistical Abstracts for the British Empire*.
(e) Year ended 31st March following that stated, to 1919.

The Committee, as has been mentioned previously, uttered a warning, couched in most emphatic terms, against the effects of the export of this labour on the future of the territory. However, they found it impossible to recommend in practice, and undesirable in principle, that the exodus should be prohibited altogether, (a) because they feared it would not be possible to obtain the whole-hearted co-operation of those countries which depend on Nyasaland labour, and, very significantly, (b) because it would not be possible at the moment "to find any economic alternative to wage-earning abroad for some 120,000 of our natives".

This is not surprising, for, as is shown by Table 70, relating to the Trade, and Table 71, to the Finances of the territory, economic development in Nyasaland is still in its infancy. Its total trade in 1936 was valued at only £1,611,758. Moreover, it would seem that more natives obtain paid employment outside the territory than within it.

Apart from the general difficulties met with in East Africa, development of Nyasaland has been retarded by its geographical situation, the lack of rail communications,[1] which until recent years served only roughly one-third of the territory, and by the absence, so far, of mining activity.

The year 1935 will be memorable in the history of Nyasaland as the year in which the Protectorate first had direct railway communication with the sea, by reason of the completion of the Zambesi bridge. The Trans-Zambesi Railway connects Beira with the south bank of the river (200 miles), and the Nyasaland

---

[1] At the opening of the session of the Legislative Council in October, 1935, His Excellency the Governor, made the following statement: "I have, in the course of my year's residence visited every district in the Protectorate. From Port Herald to Dowa there is activity and production, but Dowa is to all intents and purposes 'farthest north' so far as production is concerned. And yet it is a lamentable and at the same time most instructive thought that Dowa is still geographically in the southern half of the Protectorate. This means that more than half of the country is practically dead ground. We cannot afford to allow this state of things to continue if a remedy can be found. It is not as if this northern half of the Protectorate were inaccessible. Owing to the configuration of the country it should be possible to get produce down to the cheap water transport on the Lake at comparatively frequent intervals. This will require the construction of additional feeder roads, but I consider that the first step is a much closer investigation of the agricultural possibilities of the Northern half of the Protectorate." (*Report of the Committee appointed by His Excellency the Governor to enquire into Emigrant Labour, 1935*. Zomba: Government Printer, 1936.)

Railways continue from the north bank to Port Herald (65 miles), Blantyre (164 miles), and Salima (334 miles). The Shire High-

TABLE 71.—*Nyasaland. Finance*, 1900–36.(*d*)

Year.(*a*)	Gross Revenue.(*b*)	Customs Revenue.	Percentage of Customs to Total Revenue.	Gross Expenditure.	Public Debt.
	£(000).	£(000).		£(000).	£(000).
1900	49	8	16·3	78	...
1901	54	7	13·0	107	...
1902	70	12	17·1	107	...
1903	76	19	25·0	103	...
1904	68	14	20·6	123	...
1905	77	18	23·4	109	...
1906	82	21	25·6	112	...
1907	75	14	18·7	106	...
1908	80	14	17·5	103	...
1909	77	11	14·3	109	...
1910	95	20	21·1	112	...
1911	97	22	22·7	118	...
1912	128	26	20·3	116	50
1913	125	17	13·6	133	115
1914	119	16	13·4	143	193(*e*)
1915	138	21	15·2	126	193
1916	148	34	23·0	128	193
1917	144	30	20·8	144	193
1918	188	62	33·0	150	193
1919	187	52	27·8	218	221
1920	268	87	32·5	262	209
1921	259	74	28·6	305	306
1922	247	71	28·7	312	380
1923	281	75	26·7	283	430
1924	293	69	23·5	295	511
1925	322	84	26·1	302	611
1926	348	93	26·7	313	777
1927(*c*)	346(*c*)	85(*c*)	24·6	240(*c*)	827
1928	375	104	27·7	384	790
1929	373	106	28·4	411	823
1930	385	113	29·4	414	932
1931	371	107	28·8	428	1,109
1932	383	119	31·1	402	3,228
1933	369	123	33·3	403	3,309
1934	363	128	35·3	424	4,980
1935	422	166	39·3	475	5,119
1936	...	160	...	...	5,198

(*a*) For year ended 31st March following that stated up to 1926. Thereafter to 31st December of each year.
(*b*) Excludes grants. The total of all grants from 1897–17 amounted to £603,000.
(*c*) For nine months to 31st December.
(*d*) Extracted from the *Statistical Abstracts for the British Empire.*
(*e*) Excluding Nyasaland's share of campaign in German East Africa.

land Railway from Port Herald to Blantyre was opened to traffic in 1905, the Central African Railway (Chindio to Port Herald) in 1915, and Trans-Zambesia Railway in 1922, and the northern extension (Blantyre to Salima) in 1935. Almost all the productive areas of Nyasaland have now been brought within reasonably direct railway communication with the Port of Beira, the third most important harbour in the African sub-continent.

The very high percentage, nearly 85%, which the public listed capital forms of the total overseas investment in Nyasaland, is largely due to the railway development outlined above, and the construction of the Zambesi bridge. The private overseas investment has been mainly confined to tea and tobacco plantations, to the relatively small amounts invested in commerce, and to capital brought in by settlers. The construction of the Trans-Zambesi Railway was possible only owing to the assistance received from the Imperial Treasury, in the form of non-interest-bearing loans, to enable Nyasaland to meet the payments under its guarantee to the Railway Company. Over £1,150,000 was received by Nyasaland from 1921/2 to 1935/6 in the form of these loan grants. Including the above non-interest bearing loans, the Public Debt of the territory at the 31st December, 1935, amounted to £5,118,500. The very rapid rise in the debt in recent years is illustrated in Table 36. Interest on the public issued loans is met up to £500,000 from Colonial Development Fund Grants.

It is, of course, obvious that Nyasaland is at present not financially self-supporting. Moreover, so far, no dividend has been paid on the share capital of the Nyasaland Railways Limited.[1] It is hoped that the Trans-Zambesi Railway, the Zambesi Bridge, and the other railway extensions will greatly expedite economic development. But whether these large investments will achieve that object in the near future is still highly problematical. Indeed, if the development is not to be retarded, the territory will have to be relieved, for a long time to come, of the considerable debt charges involved.

As is shown in Table 70, tobacco formed 73·5% of the total domestic exports of the country in 1929, 86·3% in 1933, but only 49·1% in 1936. In 1936 tea accounted for 32·2%, and cotton for

---

[1] The Nyasaland Railways Limited was registered in 1930 to acquire the debenture stock and shares of the Shire Highlands Railway, and to acquire the greater part of the issued share capital of the Central African Railway Company.

16·7%, of the total domestic exports. The European contribution to the total quantity of tobacco exported (which amounted to 13,391,541 lb. in 1936) was 19%, and the native contribution 81%.

The production of tea is entirely in the hands of Europeans. The acreage planted has increased continuously from 1931, when it was 11,414, to 16,346 acres in 1936. The quantity of tea exported increased from nearly 2,000,000 lb. in 1931 to over 8,000,000 lb. in 1936.

The Empire Cotton-growing Corporation began work in Nyasaland in 1923. The recent increase in cotton production is due largely to its encouragement and to that of the British Cotton-growing Association. European, as compared with native, cotton production is, however, very small. The record weight exported (8,194,036 lb.) was reached in 1935, but in 1936 the total was only 5,320,279 lb. owing to unfavourable climatic conditions.

X

THE BELGIAN CONGO.

The Belgian Congo covers an area of 2,385,000 square kilometres (920,848 square miles); it is nearly half the size of Europe, roughly twice the size of the Union of South Africa, and, after French Equatorial Africa, it is the largest of the territories considered in this study. Many of its basic economic problems are, in essence, similar to those already discussed in relation to East Africa. There are the usual obstacles—tropical diseases, particularly sleeping-sickness and malaria, the large areas not served by adequate transport facilities, and the great distances from world markets. The lowest limit of possible settlement in the Congo is recognized to be at altitudes of about 1,500 metres (5,000 feet), and this restricts settlement mainly to the highland rim of the Congo basin from the Katanga along the eastern border of the territory.

The Report of the Commission for National Colonization in the Congo[1] states that, as a whole, it is not a colony suitable for

[1] *La Colonisation Nationale du Congo Belge*, Congo II, 1936 (quoted by Wellington, *ibid.*)

settlement, at least in its present state. Up to the present, there is no place in any of the regions of the Congo for the small peasant class.

These views coincide with opinions which have been regularly expressed for some years by the Colonial Commission of the Belgian Senate. In its 1936 Report[1] the Commission again refutes the idle dreams of those who would like to see millions of Belgians migrating to settle in the colony. It sums up its previous conclusions on this question in the following striking terms:

"S'imaginer par ailleurs que l'immigration massive soit possible dans une colonie tropicale serait folie: *le Congo n'est pas une colonie de peuplement dans la majorité de ses régions et rien ne peut modifier cet état de choses.* Les lois naturelles ne se laissent pas violer impunément; là où les conditions essentielles de la vie humaine imposent une colonisation lente et progressive, nul peuple n'aurait mieux réussi que le nôtre à s'implanter.

"Ceci dit, faut-il en conclure qu'il n'y a pas, au Congo, de place pour de nombreux Belges? *L'affirmer serait nier l'évidence et méconnaître nos propres intérêts.*

"Mais, aux règles de prudence et de mesure déjà mentionnées, il convient d'ajouter les principes doctrinaux exposés l'an dernier et que nous résumerons comme suit.

"1. Rien de ce qui peut être fait par un noir ne doit être confié au blanc. Le Congo est un pays qu'il faut développer avec le noir et par le noir et nous n'entendons pas y admettre l'establissement d'une barrière de couleur. Cette vérité, déjà énoncée par l'honorable Ministre Franck, reste d'ordre primordial; elle implique toutes les mesures qui s'imposent pour prévenir la création d'un proletariat blanc;

"2. Aucun auxiliaire noir ne pourra être recruté en faveur du colonat blanc si ce n'est conformément aux règles prescrites par la Commission de la main-d'oeuvre.

"3. Il importe que l'Etat assure au colon une intervention loyale et soutenue; qu'il le guide et lui procure les conseils d'ordre scientifique ou expérimental, indispensables pour promouvoir son activité; qu'il lui facilite les moyens de transport à bon marché de façon à lui permettre d'écouler

---

[1] *Rapport de la Commission des Colonies, chargée d'examiner le projet de Loi contenant le Budget Ordinaire du Congo Belge et du Vice-gouvernement général du Ruanda-Urundi pour l'exercice 1936*, No. 87, February, 1936.

ses produits tant à l'intérieur de la Colonie, qu'à l'exportation; que l'Etat surveille et réglemente la production des matières précieuses;

"4. L'État ne peut assumer aucun risque de nature à déséquilibrer son budget; ceci implique qu'il ne peut prendre a charge aucune intervention nouvelle sans contrepartie budgétaire assurée et notamment que toutes les institutions de crédits *indispensables*, telles que les Caisses Centrales de Crédit, les Fonds de colonisation ou autres, les Sociétés de prévoyance, de secours et de prêts mutuels agricoles ou toute autre société similaire relèveront en ordre principal de l'initiative privée judicieusement subventionnée, ou en tous cas d'organismes autonomes.

"5. Le but fondamental de notre entreprise africaine reste donc, non point d'installer au Congo le plus grand nombre possible d'Européens, mais de créer entre la population de la Métropole et celle de la Colonie, considérées toutes deux dans leur ensemble, des relations économiques aussi étendues, aussi intenses et aussi profondes que possible."

The European population of the Congo has never been large, and it declined still further during the depression. The following classification is of interest (*ibid.*, p. 15):

	1930.	1931.	1932.	1933.	1934.
Belges	17,676	17,432	15,034	...	...
Étrangers	8,003	7,747	7,448	...	...
Population totale . .	25,679	25,179	22,482	18,471	17,593
Missionaires (hommes) .	1,222	1,260	1,377	1,464	1,511
Fonctionnaires . . .	2,383	2,588	2,443	2,129	1,882
			Sur 1930: diminution de 21%.		
Femmes	6,234	6,616	6,124	5,254	4,726
			Sur 1930: diminution de 24%.		
Enfants	2,725	2,870	2,856	2,483	2,502
	12,564	13,334	12,800	11,330	10,621

From the above figures, and assuming that most of the women and children are members of the families of the civil servants, the Commission concluded that Belgian Nationals were not in the majority—a fact which it deplored.

The total number of Europeans occupied in commerce, industry (including mining), and agriculture was only about 7,000 in 1934, of which some 1,500 were engaged in mining. Some 120,000 natives were in paid employment in industry, 21,000 in commerce, and 112,000 in agriculture, giving a total of 253,000; in addition there were some 15,000 natives working for other natives, or on their own account. Of the Europeans about 1,500 were engaged in managerial or executive posts, 4,400 were employees, and 1,100 were artisans, and this European population employed a further 11,000 to 12,000 natives in domestic or similar occupations.

The two most significant characteristics of the economic development of the Belgian Congo are (a) the predominating importance of mining, and (b) the system of large financial companies through which the economic activities of the colony are controlled.

As is shown in Table 72, which gives statistics of the trade of the Congo and the percentage which the main commodities formed of its domestic exports, mineral products have accounted for over 60% of the total value of the domestic exports of the colony for many years. In 1931 the percentage rose to 70%. As the Belgian Senate summarized the matter, "It is useless to dispute the economic facts with idle theories; mine production does and will for a long time account for the riches of the Congo".

In 1932, it has been estimated, there were approximately 200 companies in the Belgian Congo whose capital amounted to roughly 9 milliards of Francs. Of these companies 71, controlled by four financial groups, accounted directly for 6 milliards of Francs, and, if account is taken of the fact that, indirectly, these four groups exercised an influence over a considerable number of smaller concerns, it can be said that another milliard of capital came under their influence, so that roughly 75% of the capital of the companies in the Colony was directly controlled or dependent upon them.[1] The great extent of this ownership and control

[1] The groups are as follows :

Groupes.	Nombre de Sociétiés.	Capitaux.
1. Société Générale	41	4,852,000,000 Frs.
2. Groupe Empain	5	448,000,000 Frs.
3. „ Cominière	9	437,000,000 Frs.
4. Banque de Bruxelles	16	392,000,000 Frs.
Total	71	6,129,000,000 Frs.

TABLE 72.—*Belgian Congo.   Trade Statistics*, 1900–36.

(Millions of Belgian Francs.)

Year.	Imports, "Special."	Exports, "Special."	Copper Exports.	Precious Stones Exports.	All Mineral Exports.	Percentage of Total Special Exports.	Palm Nuts and Palm Oil Exports.	Percentage of Total Special Exports.	Cotton Exports.	Percentage of Total Special Exports.	Ordinary Revenue.	Ordinary Expenditure.
1900	25	47	...	...	...	...	...	...	...	...	...	...
1905	20	53	...	...	...	...	...	...	...	...	...	...
1909	22	56	...	...	...	...	...	...	...	...	...	...
1913	72	55	...	...	...	...	...	...	...	...	340	...
1919	86	204	...	...	...	...	...	...	...	...	...	...
1920	238	315	...	...	...	...	...	...	...	...	92	77
1924	490	477	...	...	...	...	...	...	...	...	188	178
1925	876	629	...	...	...	...	...	...	...	...	266	234
1926	1,293	729	...	...	...	...	...	...	...	...	322	325
1927	1,496	1,055	436	114	649	61	216	20	52	5	525	462
1928	1,624	1,228	539	103	747	61	235	19	102	8	591	564
1929	1,943	1,444	623	131	874	60	253	17	135	9	690	636
1930	1,581	1,511	739	137	1,012	67	211	14	120	8	634	584
1931	962	1,104	474	173	778	70	123	11	90	8	542	564
1932	465	668	102	130	397	60	112	17	57	8	375	419
1933	389	658	...	...	358	54	...	...	...	...	339	397
1934	379	843	...	...	499	59	...	...	...	...	365	374
1935	525	1,203	345	91	751	62	148	12	143	11	406	362
1936	725	1,489	...	...	...	...	...	...	...	...	...	...

will be more fully realized if it is noted that, of the total capital under the control of the financial groups, more than 50% fell under the power of the Société Générale in which the Government is a shareholder. This group alone controlled 3 railways, 3 general companies, 2 banks, 12 mining companies, 6 plantations, 3 financial companies, 11 industrial and commercial companies, and 1 real estate company. In 1932 these 41 companies had a total capital, including loan capital, of over 4,800 million Francs. From 1920 to 1932 they paid 2,138 million Francs in dividends and placed 1,736 million Francs to reserves. Through its companies the Société Générale controlled practically the whole production of copper, diamonds, radium, cement, and a considerable portion of the gold production of the Congo. The company owned the most important electricity systems of the country, and in addition, without having control, it had a large shareholding in seven other companies and held shares in, and had representatives on the Boards of 15 others.[1]

The most significant fact which emerges from the operations of this enormous concern is that, with the exception of its agricultural and plantation interests, all its companies are in a healthy financial condition. The Report of the Belgian Senate Commission summed up the position in the following highly significant words: "In comparison with the reports of other companies one can say that without the group of the Société

[1] The following table shows the operations of the companies controlled by the Société Générale from 1920 to 1932:

Sociétés.	Capital.	Immobilisé.	Bénéfices.	Pertes.	Amortisse-ments.	Réserves.	Dividendes.
	000 Frs.	000 Frs.	000 Frs.	000 Frs.	000 Frs.	000 Frs.	000 Frs.
Trans. et Entrep. .	2,698,063	2,824,263	573,695	18,792	30,048	42,402	312,748
Industries diverses	411,500	549,203	114,051	20,137	76,917	11,282	49,254
Batim. et Matér. .	49,250	60,446	151,953	...	54,642	39,609	64,226
Minières . . .	1,143,111	1,584,266	2,489,138	...	680,839	308,701	1,459,145
Commerciales . .	285,200	266,528	428,492	5,727	72,424	198,930	186,950
Agriculture et Elev.	143,400	91,535	53,228	7,277	58,759	37,332	18,087
Immobilières . .	25,000	3,500	2,642	...	5,879	32	...
Financ. et Banq. .	45,000	13,250	338,015	...	64,860	53,300	47,615
Totaux .	4,800,524	5,392,991	4,151,214	51,993	1,044,368	691,588	2,139,025

Générale, economic Congo can be said not to exist." It added
that neither the shareholders of the companies controlled by the
Société Générale nor the State could have any complaints against
the methods of the company, and that the company had in no
way abused the rights given to it by the State.

The Commission, in examining the operations of various other
financial groups, found their results very unsatisfactory when
compared with those of the Société Générale, and it was not
satisfied that the interests of the State had not been abused in
various ways. For example, it alleged that some of the companies
tended to batten on their State guarantees, and profited privately
without the State sharing proportionately in any measure of
success that they achieved.[1]

Apart from the general difficulties associated with the concession system, one is led to the conclusion that one of the main
causes of the relative success of the Société Générale, as compared
with most of the other financial groups, lies in the fact that the
Société Générale controls, and has succeeded in bringing to the
productive stage, large mineral assets, whereas, in the case of
most of the other companies, their mineral wealth, even where
existent, has not yet been very successfully developed.

The system of large concessions in vogue in the Congo has had
other unsatisfactory consequences. Year after year the Colonial
Commission of the Senate has ascribed the lack of greater mining
development in the Congo to the relative inactivity of the large
concessionaires whose rights block the way to those who would
be willing to engage in prospecting and development, if the
mining laws of the Colony were altered to make this possible.
The Commission has frequently suggested that new mining laws
should be modelled on those in operation in British African
territories, in order that greater freedom of prospecting should be
brought about.

It appears that many of the concessionaires have not had, or
have not been able to raise sufficient capital for exploiting the
large areas under their control. Belgium has, moreover, not had
the advantage of those large resources which British exploration
and financial companies were able to tap in London, and the

[1] Cf. Sénat de Belgique, No. 85, February, 1934.

existing laws of the territory have not assisted foreign *entrepreneurs* to take an active part in opening up the vast mineral resources of the territory—particularly since the War.

The large growth, before the depression, of the Public Debt of the Belgian Congo, and consequently in the burden of debt charges, has been discussed previously. The Senate Commission concluded that the increase in expenditure which caused this was ascribable, not to the necessity for it, but to the unnecessary ease with which funds were made available to the Government of the territory.

Extraordinary expenditure[1] rose from an average for the five years 1923–1926 of 391 million Francs to 590 million Francs, the average of the four years 1927–1930. By 1931 the amount had fallen to 292 million Francs, and in 1932 it was only 62 million Francs. The striking effect on the imports into the Congo of these fluctuations in the extraordinary expenditure is shown in Table 73. The figures indicate the value of imports for "public works" and compare them with the annual amounts of the extraordinary expenditure, from 1920 to 1932[2]:

TABLE 73.—*Belgian Congo: Imports for Public Works and Extraordinary Expenditure, 1920–32.*

Year.	Extraordinary Expenditure. Actual Frs.	Imports for Public Works. Actual Frs.	Extraordinary Expenditure. Stabilized Frs.	Imports for Public Works. Stabilized Frs.
1920	124,394,787·56	48,740,630	433,992,825	170,045,750
1921	73,586,158·67	64,526,539	247,954,290	217,574,000
1922	124,537,678·44	57,732,786	373,186,625	173,000,625
1923	93,133,527·68	76,863,241	184,162,300	151,989,250
1924	115,255,001·86	95,316,691	269,907,250	113,582,000
1925	307,207,977·86	186,778,566	528,211,775	321,146,000
1926	514,718,693·18	255,808,004	580,647,200	288,558,500
1927	938,206,000·00	274,702,186	938,206,000	274,702,186
1928	313,482,000·00	318,281,256	313,482,000	318,281,256
1929	430,939,000·00	417,534,945	430,939,000	417,534,945
1930	678,423,000·00	325,130,783	678,423,000	325,130,783
1931	291,718,000·00	192,377,912	291,718,000	192,377,912
1932	61,790,000·00	72,165,315	61,790,000	72,165,315
Total	4,067,422,095·25	2,385,958,924	5,332,620,265	3,036,088,522

[1] In stabilized Francs.

[2] *Senate Commission Report*, No. 108; 18th June, 1935, pp. 64–65.

The large increase in the total imports up to 1930 is shown in Table 72, with which the above figures should be compared. It is significant that the average imports for public works for the four years 1927–1930 formed 47% of the average of the total "special" imports for these years. The growth in imports resulted in a considerable rise, and then in the inevitable fall, of customs receipts, which (including excise) formed 26·6% of all the ordinary revenue receipts (in stabilized Francs) in 1930 but only 19·6% in 1932.[1] There was also a very considerable increase in the ordinary expenditure of the territory (see Table 74). It rose from 234 millions (actual) Francs in 1925 to 636 million Francs in 1929. On the other hand ordinary[1] revenue receipts rose from 266 million (actual) Francs in 1925 to 690 million Francs in 1929. In 1932, however, ordinary revenue receipts had fallen to the low level of 375 million Francs, which should be compared with the position in 1914, when the ordinary revenue receipts amounted to no less than 303 million *gold* Francs.

For the years 1934 and 1935 together, the deficits of the territory amounted to no less than Frs. 673 millions, or 47% of the ordinary expenditure for these years; and for these two years the Belgian subventions amounted to Frs. 330 millions and covered 49% of the deficit. In addition, it was actually found necessary to resort to a colonial lottery in the attempt to cover the remainder of the deficit.

In recent years, as is shown by the trade statistics given in Table 72, the Congo has shared in the general economic recovery in African territories as a result of the increase in exports[2] and in world prices for raw materials. The recovery in the value of

[1] Ordinary revenue in the Belgian Congo is obtained from a large number of taxes. Of the total in 1935 direct native taxation accounted for 22·4%, income and company taxation 21·8%, and customs and excise 27·9% (*cf.* pp. 13–15, Report No. 108, 1935).

[2] It is of importance when utilizing the export statistics of the Belgian Congo to note that the values for official purposes are arrived at on the basis of an official valuation. This consists in fixing the prices at which the commodities exported are to be valued for customs purposes, and the valuation takes place at the beginning of the year, after consultation with the local Chambers of Commerce. The valuation so fixed is then used in drawing up the export statistics for the whole year. The resulting values are, therefore, often either too high or too low, depending on the actual price fluctuations that occur after the official prices have been determined. The accuracy of export values is of course greatly affected by this system. (*Cf.* an article by M. Charles Morisseaux, "La Situation économique du Congo Belge en 1930", *Bulletin de l'Institut des Sciences Économiques*, Louvain, February, 1932, p. 124.)

TABLE 74.—*Belgian Congo. Finance*, 1924–36.

Year.	Debt Charge. (Millions of unstabilized Francs.)	Ordinary Revenue.(a) (Millions of unstabilized Francs.)	Ordinary Expenditure.(b) (Millions of unstabilized Francs.)	Debt Charge as percentage of Ordinary Revenue.	Domestic Exports (Millions of unstabilized Francs.)	Debt Charge as Percentage of Domestic Exports.	Imports. (Millions of unstabilized Francs.)
1924	...	188	178	...	477	...	490
1925	...	266	234	...	629	...	876
1926	...	322	325	...	729	...	1,293
1927	89	525	462	17·0	1,055	8·4	1,496
1928	122	591	564	20·6	1,288	9·5	1,624
1929	...	690	636	...	1,444	...	1,943
1930	126	634	584	19·9	1,511	8·3	1,581
1931	141	542	564	26·0	1,104	12·8	962
1932	177	375	419	47·2	668	26·5	465
1933	298	339(c)	397	87·9	658	45·3	389
1934	316	365(d)	374	86·6	843	37·5	378
1935	322	406(e)	362	79·3	1,203	26·8	525
1936	...	...	...	...	1,489	...	725

(a) Excluding subsidy from Home Government.
(b) Including pensions but excluding debt charge.
(c) Final result.
(d) Provisional estimate.
(e) Provisional result.

mineral exports (particularly copper) has been the main cause of the improved economic situation in the Congo, and this, as well as the rigid economy measures, has brought about a great improvement in the financial situation.

The changes in the economy of the Congo since the War are well illustrated by the statistics in Table 75, which show the variations in the quantities of the different products exported since 1900.[1]

From this table the manner in which mineral production has altered the economy of the country is clearly apparent. Rubber and ivory accounted for almost the whole of the value of the exports of the Congo in the early years of the century, during the era of despoliation. In 1900 they formed 96% of the value of the domestic exports, and in 1910 they still accounted for 70%. To-day, minerals take the place of these two natural products.

The growth in the export of palm kernels and palm oil, and more recently of cotton, illustrates the changes in the agricultural economy of the territory. The growth in the exports of palm oil, from 6,000 tons during the War to 58,000 tons in 1936, is in large part due to the activities of Lever Brothers and of its subsidiary, the Société des Huileries du Congo Belge, which has a large concession of some 750,000 hectares for plantation purposes. The Congo now occupies third place in the world as an exporter of palm oil; its exports in 1935 amounted to 57,000 tons, as compared with 143,000 tons from Nigeria, and roughly the same amount from the Netherlands Indies.

The Congo exported palm kernels amounting to some 65,000 tons in 1935, which can be compared with the 313,000 tons exported from Nigeria, which supplies 50% of the world's production; in the same year the French colonies exported 134,000 tons.

It has been estimated by Edmond Leplae[2] that Frs. 475 millions

---

[1] *Cf.* an article by Gaston Eyskens, "Les indices de la conjoncture économique du Congo Belge depuis la guerre de 1919 à 1933", *Bulletin de l'Institut des Sciences Économiques*, Louvain, August, 1933. The statistics up to and including the year 1932 are from a table in this article.

[2] "La Situation Economique à Congo Belge, 1935–6," *Bulletin de l'Institut des Sciences Économiques*, February, 1937.

TABLE 75.—*Belgian Congo. Principal Products Exported. Quinquennial Averages, 1901–30, and Per Annum, 1930–36.*

(Metric tons.)

Products.	1901–05.	1906–10.	1911–15.	1916–20.	1921–25.	1926–30.	1930.	1931.	1932.	1933.	1934.	1935.	1936.
Rubber	5,397	4,247	2,993	2,063	736	955	511	249	92	...	280	802	918
Palm kernels	4,807	5,426	7,788	33,110	54,281	71,744	66,356	47,172	58,526	62,069	49,296	64,996	...
Copal	538	1,110	4,370	7,834	12,788	17,336	16,680	10,331	10,094	...	17,000	16,867	21,295
Ivory	202	218	249	285	296	204	153	132	163	...	107	216	189
Palm oil	1,726	2,005	2,428	6,002	12,980	26,122	36,989	36,583	40,054	52,454	45,041	56,788	58,000
Cocoa	107	647	708	697	701	965	1,195	979	1,186	...	1,279	1,260	1,469
Cotton	...	...	...	55	943	6,904	9,977	12,541	12,410	...	...	...	...
Coffee	...	...	12	78	170	691	1,537	2,918	5,386	...	12,396	13,904	18,110
Timber	...	...	...	520	1,004	7,143	13,333	8,865	6,771	...	24,500	37,602	56,000
Hides and Skin	...	...	51	150	189	299	331	196	123	...	...	...	...
Sesame	...	...	...	300	456	1,487	775	196	247	...	...	...	...
Copper	...	...	6,701	23,066	61,242	108,249	146,749	124,004	59,630	...	131,769	107,682	100,000
Cassiterite	...	...	23	225	1,386	1,276	1,115	...	721	...	5,307	5,370	5,786
Gold(a)	45	494	1,642	3,366	3,164	4,800	5,946	7,339	8,661	...	11,600	13,200	14,000
Precious metals(b)	...	...	27	172	414	1,648	2,086	3,669	3,751	...	...	...	...

(a) Kilogrammes
(b) Thousands of carats.

of capital have been invested in the palm products industry, and that it employs 30,000 workers. There are 35 companies engaged in the industry, but the Société des Huileries du Congo Belge accounts for 80% of the palm oil production.

Cotton.—In 1936 it was estimated that 700,000 natives were occupied in growing cotton, and that the crop fetched some 83,000,000 Francs. The expansion of the industry is shown by the steady increase in cotton exports, and the fact that this continued without interruption throughout the depression.

Of the food products in the Belgian Congo the most important are manioc, bananas, maize, various root crops and rice. Coffee is grown by Europeans. In 1936 some 57,000 hectares were planted, and the output consisted of some 18,000 tons.

That Belgium has made very great efforts to develop its vast Central African Colony is shown by the amount of overseas capital that she has invested in the territory. But one gains the impression that much of this capital has been invested in relatively uneconomic directions and for purposes which, in some cases, are premature. The country appears to have suffered, on the one hand, from somewhat excessive Government interference, and, on the other, from a multiplicity of vested interests.

In recent years the need for developing native peasant production has been clearly realized, and efforts have been made to protect native institutions, to establish better hygienic conditions, to improve education, and generally to stimulate the progress of the native peoples. The crux of the problem, however, lies in the great distances of the territory from world markets, the low density of its population, the many climatic and ecological disadvantages, and the inevitable slowness of the task of developing a backward population. For a long time to come the territory's relations with the world economy must continue to depend largely on mining. It appears that every effort should be made to throw open the country to unfettered enterprise in this direction. In this way the excessive dependence of the Colony on the paternal and unavoidably expensive solicitude of the State and the disadvantages of the over-extended concession system, may be obviated, and the economy of the country thus enabled to develop in a more natural manner.

XII

RUANDA-URUNDI.

The mandate over the sultanates, Ruanda and Urundi, was given to Belgium in 1922, but not accepted formally until October 20th, 1924. Belgium controls the territory by a system resembling that of indirect administration as practised in British territories.

The European population is under 1,000 ; the non-European population was estimated to be approximately 3,300,000, and in addition there were approximately 600 Asiatics.

The territory has had to be assisted by advances from Belgium and the Belgian Congo; since 1933 most of this debt has been funded. The Public Debt at the end of December, 1934, amounted to 163,000,000 Belgian Francs. The debt charges on this were 8,325,052 francs, equivalent to some 22% of the expenditure. The expenditure from loans has been mainly on railway construction (50,000,000 Francs), and the rest has been in aid of general revenue, part going to the "Budget Ordinaire" and part to the "Budget Extraordinaire". The Budget Ordinaire and the Budget Extraordinaire contain cross-entries and cannot be clearly separated. But in order to give a general picture of the financial development of the territory the following figures[1] may be quoted:

Budget Ordinaire (in 1,000 Frs. Belg.).

			Revenue.		Expenditure.
1925	.	.	.	7,045	.	7,357
1926	.	.	.	10,548	.	11,870
1927	.	.	.	15,382	.	15,242
1928	.	.	.	23,842	.	23,484
1929	.	.	.	26,157	.	34,559
1930	.	.	.	30,947	.	34,654
1931	.	.	.	34,277	.	40,211
1932	.	.	.	28,348	.	32,851
1933	.	.	.	40,745	.	34,403
1934	.	.	.	42,905[2]	.	37,637

[1] From the Mandates Reports of the Belgian Congo to the League of Nations.
[2] Including 12,000 subventions.

The development of the trade of the territory is shown by the following figures of exports and imports:

Exports and Imports of Ruanda-Urundi from 1922 to 1934.

	Exports. (Belgian Francs.)	Imports. (Belgian Francs.)
1922 . . .	1,617,450 .	3,800,000
1923 . . .	6,019,649 .	7,828,000
1924 . . .	9,523,686 .	10,269,304
1925 . . .	9,953,199 .	14,990,164
1926 . . .	13,388,346 .	9,289,827
1927 . . .	19,575,346 .	30,087,322
1928 . . .	18,746,629 .	45,913,298
1929 . . .	14,553,581 .	58,476,384
1930 . . .	14,317,204 .	57,553,128
1931 . . .	14,985,359 .	60,533,128
1932 . . .	13,096,556 .	23,343,380
1933 . . .	15,646,005 .	27,559,396
1934 . . .	29,352,835 .	30,617,063

The quantities of the principal products exported are shown by the following figures for the five years ending 1934:

	1930. (Tons.)	1931. (Tons.)	1932. (Tons.)	1933. (Tons.)	1934. (Tons.)
Hides and skins (cattle) .	623 .	706 .	681 .	1,270 .	694
,, ,, (small) .	137 .	59 .	22 .	58 .	28
Live stock (large) .	581 .	1,794 .	3,197 .	1,418 .	620
,, ,, (small) .	645 .	802 .	1,645 .	661 .	345
Foodstuffs . . .	239 .	826 .	671 .	1,301 .	2,515
Palm kernels . . .	150 .	89 .	213 .	204 .	129
Palm oil . . .	89 .	69 .	40 .	41 .	37
Cotton	97 .	231 .	312 .	319 .	446
Coffee	17 .	88 .	109 .	121 .	256
Butter	8 .	3 .	3 .	— .	3
Tobacco . . .	10 .	5 .	33 .	7 .	16
Wax	17 .	12 .	25 .	28 .	20
Tin	144 .	129 .	384 .	430 .	995
Gold	— .	— .	— .	— .	0·289

Cattle raising is an important industry in Ruanda-Urundi, which, owing to its altitude, is the main region in the Belgian Congo suited for it. The above table shows the importance of the exports of livestock. The growth in the exports of cotton and coffee illustrates the efforts being made to develop agriculture.

Four European companies[1] have been established for the exploitation of the mineral wealth of the territory, and their efforts have led to the discovery of cassiterite occurrences, which have been yielding increasing quantities of tin, as is shown by the above figures.

So far, European economic activities, other than mining, have been limited, the principal agricultural crops being coffee, cotton, sisal, tobacco and palm products.

XIII

WEST AFRICA.

The conditions in West Africa differ in many fundamental respects from those of East African territories. The climate, like that in Central Africa, is definitely unsuitable for European settlement, and even for residence by Europeans for any prolonged period.[2]

There is the hot and humid coastal forest belt stretching from Sierra Leone to the mouth of the Congo; inland, the country gradually becomes drier until, in the extreme north, it borders on the Sahara; conditions in large parts of Northern Nigeria resemble those of the Anglo-Egyptian Sudan; the climatic conditions of the south, on the other hand, resemble the heavy rainfall areas of tropical South America or the Dutch East Indies. All the West African territories suffer from a large variety of tropical diseases.

The climate "has determined and must continue to determine British policy in West Africa, with its two essential features of

[1] The Companies are: Société des Mines d'étain du Ruanda Urandi (capital Frs. 54,250,000); Société Minière de la Kagera-Ruanda (capital 15,000,000 Frs.); Société Minière du Ruvuvu (capital Frs. 5,000,000); Compagnie du Kivu.

[2] In West Africa, with the exception of the Cameroon mountain and the small barren Bauchi plateau (4,000 feet), there are no highlands where Europeans could go for local leave to recuperate. "The man who goes to West Africa has to face greater disadvantages than in many other tropical countries, besides those inherent in life in any tropical climate. . . . Europeans, as a general rule, spend shorter periods in the country without any leave in a temperate climate than in any other of our colonial possessions." (*Report by the Hon. W. G. A. Ormsby-Gore on his Visit to West Africa in 1926*, Cmd. 2744, pp. 11–12.)

indirect rule and native agriculture", wrote Mr. Ormsby-Gore.[1] "The European can at best be only a sojourner, . . . and thus it is very difficult to achieve that degree of personal continuity essential to the effective working of direct administration, of the kind which obtains in, for example, Rhodesia and parts of East Africa. White settler farmers are out of the question, and the management of plantations such as those in the Far East would be rendered difficult by the changes of staff and interruption of work caused by frequent spells of leave out of the country."

The African peoples of West Africa have, with few exceptions, little in common with the Bantu of South and East Africa either in tribal organization or habits of life. If any generalization is possible in regard to the British West African Colonies taken together, it is, that on the whole the native peoples of these territories are, broadly speaking, the most advanced, and certainly the most commercially enterprising in Africa. But generalization is dangerous. "There is," said Sir Hugh Clifford, "a greater difference between the Hausa and the Munchi than there is between the Scandinavian and the Slav."[2]

British West Africa is in fact an Empire of its own. The area of Nigeria alone (368,000 square miles) is about one-third of that of British India, and its total population of some 19 millions forms 45% of the population in all the British African colonies, Mandates and Protectorates. Indeed, in regard to population, it is the third unit in the British Empire after India and Great Britain, and is also the most densely populated territory south of the Sahara.

The histories of the four British West African territories have been very different, and their present laws, policies and administrations vary considerably. They are, moreover, specializing in different products. All four dependencies are hemmed in completely on their land side by French territory, with the exception of Sierra Leone, which has Liberia on its south-eastern frontier. French West Africa, in contradistinction to British West Africa, is

[1] *Ibid.*, p. 12.
[2] Quoted by Allen McPhee, *The Economic Revolution in British West Africa.* (London : Routledge, 1926.)

a continuous whole, and may be spoken of as a unit more consistently than may British West Africa. The area of French West Africa, about 1,500,000 square miles, is roughly three times that of British West Africa, but its population is little more than half, and this factor has played a vital *rôle* in determining the different rate of economic development in the two regions. The contiguity of the British and French territories has led to close relations between them. The development of communications in the French has had its effect upon the adjoining British areas, and *vice versa*. The complete establishment of customs barriers between the two regions has never been possible.

Britain has been associated with West Africa for a longer period than with East or South Africa. But, from an economic point of view, the greater part of the area of British West Africa only began to occupy an important place in the world economy during the twentieth century.

At the beginning of the twentieth century the total trade of all the West African colonies, taken together, was less than £6 millions, while to-day it is nearly £40 millions.[1] The "Economic Revolution in West Africa",[2] as it has been rightly termed, has been based on three fundamental factors: (*a*) these territories possess a variety of valuable indigenous, or relatively easily cultivable products, and a population which has the aptitude, and shows increasing willingness to develop them for commercial purposes; (*b*) good administration has given them peace, on the one hand, and transport facilities on the other; and (*c*) develment has been based on the individual efforts of the population and on the uninterrupted stimulus of trade, which has been fostered and financed by powerful commercial interests.

Trade and transport have been the main features in British West Africa's economic progress, and there can be little doubt that the policy of "developing the native resources for the natives,

---

[1] *Cf.* Table 45.

[2] *Cf.* the valuable study of the development of West Africa by A. McPhee, for an excellent account of the economic history of the territories, the development of their trade, production, and transport, and the important changes in administration which have occurred during the last fifty years. An excellent summary of the economic development and transport and health problems of West Africa will also be found in the Report by Mr. Ormsby-Gore, *ibid.*

by the natives under British supervision" on which that progress is based, has been amply justified.

It is not possible, here, to describe in detail the economic development of the West African territories, or to give an account of the great changes which have taken place in them during the last forty years—a process which has not inaptly been described as the superimposition of the twentieth century after Christ on the twentieth century before Christ. But the following sections which deal with each West African territory present figures which illustrate some of the results of the conversion of West Africa from the subsistence economy of the past to the emerging money economy of the present.

XIV

NIGERIA.

Development in Nigeria has been based on the products of the palm.[1]   As is shown in Table 76, which gives the statistics of trade[2] from 1900–1936, exports of palm products as late as 1920 still formed 63% of the total value of the domestic exports of the country. In 1935 they had fallen to 39% of the total. Ground nuts, which accounted for only 6·7% of the exports in 1920, occupied second place in 1936, and formed 19% of the total. The growth in cocoa production has been equally remarkable. The exports of this commodity, which formed only 7·4% of all domestic exports in 1920, amounted to 14% in 1936.[3]

Strictly speaking, there is very little palm oil cultivation in West Africa. The industry consists mainly in collecting and

[1] Nigeria is divided into four main zones :
   (i) A belt of swamp and mangrove forest, 10 to 60 miles wide and following the coastline. It includes the delta of the Niger, and is intersected by innumerable rivers and creeks.
   (ii) A belt of dense tropical forest from 50 to 100 miles wide which is very rich in oil palms and constitutes at present the chief wealth of Nigeria. This zone merges into the next.
   (iii) A belt of more open country which gradually becomes clearer, park-like land followed by open expanses covered with high grass.
   (iv) A vast undulating plateau, generally about 2,000 feet high, but in part of the Plateau Province and to the South-West of Yola rising heights to over 6,000 feet.
[2] The trade figures of Nigeria include the trade of the British Cameroons, which territory is therefore not considered separately in this chapter.
[3] See *Annual Colonial Report of Nigeria, 1936*.

TABLE 76.—Nigeria.(e)   Trade Statistics, 1900–36(d), and Proportion per cent. of Annual Exports of Selected Commodities to Annual Value of all Domestic Produce Exported. (f)

Year.	Merchandise Imports (a) £(000).	Exports.(b) Domestic Produce (c) £(000).	Exports.(b) Re-Exports £(000).	Palm Kernels Exports £(000).	Palm Kernels Exports %.	Palm Oil Exports £(000).	Palm Oil Exports %.	Ground Nuts Exports £(000).	Ground Nuts Exports %.	Cocoa Exports £(000).	Cocoa Exports %.	Tin Exports £(000).	Tin Exports %.	All Mineral Exports £(000).	All Mineral Exports %.
1900	1,735	1,887	…	834	44·2	681	36·1	…	…	…	…	…	…	…	…
1901	1,812	2,020	…	948	46·9	813	40·2	…	…	…	…	…	…	…	…
1902	1,977	2,512	…	1,274	50·7	958	38·1	…	…	…	…	…	…	…	…
1903	2,129	2,357	…	1,094	46·4	848	36·0	…	…	…	…	…	…	…	…
1904	2,423	2,781	…	1,278	46·0	929	33·4	…	…	…	…	…	…	…	…
1905	2,710	2,672	…	1,207	45·2	858	32·1	…	…	…	…	…	…	…	…
1906	2,847	2,950	…	1,193	40·4	1,002	34·0	…	…	27	0·9	…	…	…	…
1907	3,839	3,612	252	1,658	45·9	1,314	36·4	18	0·5	48	1·3	25	0·7	25	0·7
1908	4,046	3,102	234	1,425	45·9	1,155	37·2	15	0·5	51	1·6	78	2·5	78	2·5
1909	4,530	3,829	285	1,816	47·4	1,447	37·8	15	0·4	72	1·9	38	1·0	38	1·0
1910	5,122	4,964	295	2,451	49·4	1,742	35·1	9	0·2	101	2·0	73	1·5	73	1·5
1911	5,234	5,072	282	2,574	50·7	1,697	33·5	10	0·2	165	3·3	182	3·6	182	3·6
1912	5,949	5,477	297	2,797	51·1	1,671	30·5	19	0·3	131	2·4	336	6·1	336	6·1
1913	6,324	6,779	318	3,110	45·9	1,984	29·3	175	2·6	157	2·3	568	8·4	568	8·4
1914	6,269	6,151	270	2,541	41·3	1,634	26·6	179	2·9	172	2·8	708	11·5	709	11·5
1915	4,978	4,874	72	1,693	34·7	1,463	30·0	72	1·5	314	6·4	723	14·8	729	14·9
1916	5,281	5,884	146	1,740	29·6	1,403	23·8	474	8·1	393	6·7	860	14·6	868	14·8
1917	5,931	8,482	120	2,582	30·4	1,383	22·2	710	8·4	499	5·9	1,486	17·5	1,498	17·7
1918	7,552	9,359	153	3,226	34·5	2,610	27·9	920	9·8	236	2·5	1,770	18·9	1,772	18·9
1919	10,932	14,501	175	4,948	34·1	4,373	30·2	699	4·8	1,068	7·4	1,324	9·1	1,324	9·1
1920	20,930	16,718	236	5,718	34·2	4,814	28·8	1,120	6·7	1,238	7·4	1,786	10·7	1,788	10·7
1921	10,236	8,028	230	2,832	35·3	1,671	20·8	1,112	13·9	436	5·4	915	11·4	917	11·4

1922	10,303	8,790	253	2,810	32·0	2,676	30·4	481	5·5	871	9·9	932	10·6	935	10·6
1923	10,270	10,795	82	3,741	34·7	2,982	27·6	403	3·7	922	8·5	1,190	11·0	1,194	11·0
1924	10,945	14,384	140	4,461	31·0	3,944	27·4	1,461	10·2	980	6·8	1,548	10·8	1,554	10·8
1925	14,778	16,900	57	4,937	29·2	4,166	24·7	2,394	14·2	1,484	8·8	1,738	10·3	1,742	10·3
1926	12,755	16,538	142	4,440	26·8	3,616	21·9	2,343	14·2	1,363	8·2	2,217	13·4	2,222	13·4
1927	14,432	15,470	204	4,439	28·7	3,375	21·8	1,630	10·5	1,999	12·9	2,287	14·8	2,287	14·8
1928	15,761	16,927	148	4,423	26·1	3,751	22·2	1,849	10·9	2,421	14·3	2,210	13·1	2,210	13·1
1929	13,216	17,581	176	4,265	24·3	3,767	21·4	2,466	14·0	2,306	13·1	2,299	13·1	2,300	13·1
1930	12,614	14,778	251	3,679	24·9	3,250	22·0	2,196	14·9	1,756	11·9	1,373	9·3	1,380	9·3
1931	6,509	8,552	218	2,132	24·9	1,542	18·0	1,511	17·7	1,093	12·8	906	10·6	938	11·0
1932	7,194	9,267	198	2,696	29·1	1,514	16·3	1,874	20·2	1,461	15·8	580	6·3	619	6·7
1933	6,339	8,460	167	1,899	22·4	1,384	16·4	2,064	24·4	1,144	13·5	659	7·8	766	9·1
1934	5,364	8,500	140	1,591	18·7	885	10·4	1,860	21·9	1,290	15·2	1,244	14·6	1,497	17·6
1935	7,804	11,197	142	2,245	20·1	1,656	14·8	2,093	18·7	1,584	14·1	1,457	13·0	1,753	15·7
1936	10,829	14,686	147	3,637	24·8	2,079	14·2	2,847	19·4	1,997	13·6	1,763	12·0	...	...

(a) Excluding bullion and coin; including goods subsequently re-exported.
(b) Excluding bullion and coin except for 1907 to 1921.
(c) Exports of domestic produce include re-exports prior to 1907.
(d) The figures for the pre-war years are totals for the areas subsequently amalgamated into the Colony and Protectorate of Nigeria.
(e) Including the overseas trade of the British Mandated area of the Cameroons.
(f) Extracted from the Statistical Abstracts for the British Empire, the figures for all mineral exports are from Nigeria Annual Reports.

preparing sylvan produce. The manufacture of the oil and the cracking of the kernels is still a manual and household industry. Nevertheless, while the oil palm may be said to grow wild all over Southern Nigeria, actually many of the trees have been deliberately though irregularly planted. Except in a few small plantations which have been established in recent years, no weeding or attention is given to the trees. To climb a tall palm and harvest the fruit is definitely hard work, but the extracting of the oil, though it takes a considerable time, involves little hard labour, and is largely carried out by women. The quantity of oil exported annually is now usually about 125,000 tons. Palm oil also forms a very important part of the diet of the people of Southern Nigeria, and, with the improvement of means of transport, a trade in palm oil from Southern to Northern Nigeria has sprung up and is increasing annually. The internal trade is estimated to amount to at least 100,000 tons[1] per annum, making a gross production of 225,000 tons. It is also estimated that, by 1935, some 2,500 acres had been planted or re-planted by native farmers; the export of palm oil from Nigeria has steadily increased since 1900, when it amounted to about 55,000 tons. The limiting factor is not really the amount of fruit available, but the amount of labour used in the collection of the fruit, and the preparation of the products. Indeed it is apparent that much of the fruit is never picked at all, especially in the densest palm areas. The population of the palm belt of Southern Nigeria is large, but the time occupied in climbing the trees, and in carrying the produce to market in an area where transport facilities are restricted, limits the more rapid development of the industry. Also, much palm oil is lost each year through primitive methods of extraction. All this goes to show what vast potential wealth there is in the natural palm forests of West Africa.[2]

In recent years the growing competition from the cultivated and selected oil palm grown under scientific plantation conditions in Sumatra, Malaya and the Belgian Congo has given rise to fears as to the outlook for the West African industry.

As regards the Congo, however, the limiting factor is

[1] See *Annual Colonial Report of Nigeria, 1936*.
[2] See Ormsby-Gore, "Report on West Africa", *ibid.*, p. 101.

population, and competition from this quarter is, therefore, not likely to increase as much in the future as it has done in the past. The eastern planter, on the other hand, while getting a cheaper production of fruit and, therefore, of oil, has to send his oil on a long sea voyage through a hot climate, and has also to face the heavy overhead charges incidental to the plantation system. Nevertheless, Sumatra and Malaya have become a big factor in this market.

The fact that West Africa has to face this competition in a product hitherto regarded as her natural monopoly has led to the realization that steps must be taken to rouse the West African native producer from his present easy contentment with the old ways of conducting the industry. The problem is really whether forms of compulsion and land appropriation for plantation purposes should be sanctioned, or whether the essential Nigerian policy should be retained, and native communities allowed to continue in the full and free use of their land, to which they are passionately attached. "Any attempt to alter this system fundamentally would cause the greatest unrest throughout the country. The problem is how to preserve what is good in the system, while bringing the methods of cultivation and extraction more up-to-date."[1]

The Annual Reports on Nigeria show that progress is being made in the introduction of presses for the extraction of palm oil from the fruit, but the problem of introducing modern methods is a vast one, and will require great efforts by the Government in co-operation with the people if it is to be solved.[2]

---

[1] See Ormsby-Gore, "Report on West Africa", *ibid.*, p. 101.

[2] The following figures (*An Economic Survey of the Colonial Empire* [*1935*], Colonial No. 126) show the exports of palm kernels and palm oil; the great fluctuation in prices is noteworthy (1936 figures are from the *Annual Colonial Report*):

Palm Kernels.

	Export in tons.		Average annual price per ton at Lagos.
			£ s. d.
1931	254,454	.	6 6 6
1932	309,061	.	6 17 0
1933	259,945	.	4 18 0
1934	289,477	.	3 12 10
1935	312,746	.	6 7 2
1936	386,143	.	...

[*Continued overleaf.*

Cocoa.—The cocoa tree is not indigenous to West Africa. Its cultivation is restricted to areas in which there is ample atmospheric humidity and where the soil is both good and deep. As is well known, the Gold Coast has been best suited for its production. The greater portion of the four western provinces of Nigeria and parts of certain other provinces are suitable for cocoa production. It involves thorough weeding and some cultivation during the first four or five years; thereafter this product entails remarkably little labour. The expansion of cocoa exports is shown by the following figures:

	Cocoa. Exports (in tons).	Average monthly price per ton at Lagos.
		£ s. d.
1931 . . .	52,806 .	17 11 0
1932 . . .	71,035 .	15 16 0
1933 . . .	60,737 .	14 14 0
1934 . . .	77,983 .	14 19 11
1935 . . .	88,142 .	16 15 3
1936 . . .	80,553 .	—

Ground Nuts.—The production of ground nuts for export is almost entirely confined to the light sandy soils of the extreme north of Nigeria. As the amount of local consumption is not known, it is not possible to give figures for total production, but this appears to be increasing steadily. There has been a very big increase in the quantity exported since 1928, owing to the opening up of new branch railways, which have enabled the industry to develop in new areas. The increasing production of ground

	Palm Oil.	
	Exports in tons.	Average annual price per ton at Lagos. £ s. d.
1931	188,179 .	9 13 6
1932	116,060 .	9 7 0
1933	128,696 .	7 2 0
1934	112,773 .	4 19 1
1935	142,628 .	10 11 3
1936	162,779 .	...

nuts affords another example of the economic expansion which follows upon the introduction of modern communications.[1]

Cotton.—Cotton has been grown in Nigeria for over 1,000 years and the industry has had a fascinating history[2] in recent times. In fact the British Cotton Growing Organization, formed in 1902 under the presidency of Sir Alfred Jones, the West African shipping magnate, first concentrated all its efforts on West Africa. The expansion of cotton production for export depends on the solution of two fundamental problems—the provision of transport facilities and the adoption of a system of mixed farming, which will ensure the concomitant production of adequate food crops and which will supply animals for ploughing and manure. It has been argued that, until the system of mixed farming is introduced, Northern Nigeria is not likely to export more than 75,000 bales of cotton per annum. In 1936 the exports amounted to about 62,000, as compared with 12,000 bales in 1921. There is, however, a considerable output which is consumed locally by the weaving industry. In the south cotton is grown as a catch crop only; the amounts exported have so far not exceeded 6,000 bales.

Animal Husbandry.—In Nigeria there is a very great export trade in animal products and an even greater internal trade. The majority of the livestock is in the northern provinces. It has been estimated that the total annual gross profit from the internal trade alone exceeds £2,000,000. In 1936 hides and skins to the value of £762,000 were exported.

Tin.—In recent years Nigeria has supplied approximately 10 to 13% of the tin production of the world. Tin exports, however, have not formed more than 15% of the total of Nigeria's domestic exports in post-war years. The large fluctuations in

[1] *Ground Nuts.*

	Exports in tons.	Average price at Kano 1st October to 31st March.		
		£	s.	d.
1931 · · · ·	159,739 ·	4	17	0
1932 · · · ·	188,123 ·	7	10	0
1933 · · · ·	204,606 ·	5	14	0
1934 · · · ·	244,886 ·	2	14	4
1935 · · · ·	183,993 ·	7	14	11
1936 · · · ·	218,389 ·	...		

[2] For an excellent account see McPhee, *ibid.*, pp. 44 ff.

world tin prices have led to great variations in the relative importance of tin among the annual domestic exports of the territory. There were 36 companies and firms and 39 private owners engaged in tin-mining operations in 1935, as compared with 139 companies and individuals in 1928, the peak year of the tin industry before the depression. There were less than 10 mines[1] producing 200 tons or more of ore during the year 1935 owing to the International tin restriction agreement.

The figures below show the tin ore exported for the years 1912 to 1936. Gold production from the alluvial fields increased from 192 oz., in 1929, to 33,000 oz. in 1936. The average number of Europeans employed in all mining during the year 1935 was 225, and the average number of natives was about 40,000, which was the highest figure so far recorded.

Tin Ore Exported.[2]

	Tons.			Tons.
1912	2,605	1924		8,852
1913	4,139	1925		9,294
1914	6,152	1926		10,562
1915	6,507	1927		10,926
1916	7,054	1928		13,069
1917	9,941	1929		15,129
1918	8,294	1930		12,067
1919	7,685	1931		10,794
1920	7,913	1932		5,967
1921	7,181	1933		5,216
1922	8,127	1934		7,528
1923	8,475	1935		8,948
		1936		13,100

The most important factor, in the recent economic development of the country, is the way in which it is being released from its previous dependence on monoculture for its trade and prosperity. Nigeria, moreover, is practically self-supporting as

---

[1] Of the tin mines in Nigeria, six with over £2,000,000 of capital are controlled by the Anglo-Oriental Mining Corporation which, as is well known, also controls a large number of mines in Malaya, Burma and Cornwall. Its investments were calculated to be as high as £7,270,000 by Mr. J. W. Furness, Chief, Economics Branch, Bureau of Mines, U.S. Department of the Interior (cf. "International Control in the Non-Ferrous Metals," ibid., p. 313).

[2] Cf. Nigeria: Annual Report of the Mines Department, 1935. Government Printer, Lagos, 1936. Annexe " B ".

far as the African population is concerned; its agriculture is almost entirely a peasant industry. The chief food crops are yams and maize in the south, and guinea corn and millet in the north. There is no export trade in either of these crops. Moreover, the cotton-weaving industry in the Kano and Oyo Provinces is important; there is even some export of its products to the neighbouring French territories. Indeed, the trade of Nigeria is mainly internal, however little this fact is reflected in the export statistics. The vast network of local trade is almost entirely in the hands of native middlemen.

The fundamental problem in Nigeria is that of opening up the territory by communications and public works. Although the country has a wonderful network of rivers and connecting waterways, it as yet possesses only some 1,900 miles of railway. Very considerable road building has taken place in recent years. Nevertheless, it is obvious that enormous further development of communications is needed. The problem of railway construction is, apart from local difficulties of labour supply and training native staff, again mainly a problem of finance. In recent years the operations of the Nigeria Railways, owing to the considerable railway construction since the War, have been burdened with continuous deficits, arising from the increasing debt charges which the railways had to bear. It has been recognized, after an exhaustive review,[1] that the finances of the railway should be relieved of the interest charges on what are really development lines. The Enugu-Benue Bridge-Kafanchan section of main line is to be regarded as having been constructed for colonial development purposes, and the Nigeria Railways are to be relieved of the interest charges on this section of the line, on which the losses in recent years have been particularly heavy.

From a railway point of view, this is an important reform, but, of course, it does not alter the main problem as far as the territory itself is concerned. Nigeria borrowed heavily in the years before the depression and, as has been shown above, the burden of debt charges which it now has to meet, though not anything like as high as those of certain other African territories, is such that it cannot be very greatly increased until further

---

[1] *Cf.* Nigeria Treasurer's Report, 1936.

development has taken place. The fluctuations to which Nigerian exports are subject in world markets make it particularly necessary to exercise caution as far as loan expenditure is concerned. Statistics relating to the finances of the territory are given in Table 77.

Nigeria would appear to offer a particularly good field for the investment of capital on special terms—for example, by large development loans at rates of interest which are kept low by some form of assistance from the Imperial Government. The country is one in which capital investment in communications and public works leads to a rapid growth in production, and the commercial possibilities of this wealthy region, given a rising standard of life for its large population, are unlimited.

XV

THE GOLD COAST.

The Gold Coast comprises the Gold Coast Colony, Ashanti and the Northern Territories and Togoland (under British Mandate). The area of the colony is 23,937 square miles; of Ashanti 24,379 square miles; of the Northern Territories 30,486 square miles; and of Togoland (under British Mandate), 13,041 square miles, the total being 91,843 square miles. The country may be divided up into three belts: in the centre is the forest area; the south-eastern corner consists of rolling plains covered with scrub and grass; and the north is largely " orchard " country. The population is approximately 3,500,000, of whom some 3,000 are non-Africans—mainly Europeans. The majority of the native inhabitants of the Gold Coast are peasant farmers.

By far the most important crop which is cultivated is cocoa. Its early development was largely made possible by the Botanical Station supplying plants at nominal prices and giving instruction in cultivation and preparation. Fishing is a common industry all along the coast, while in the large towns there is an abundance of African skilled labour. The educated classes are employed largely in the Government service, by the mercantile houses and in the teaching profession. Petty trading is the peculiar occupation of the women. Numbers of foreign unskilled labourers come

TABLE 77.—*Nigeria.*(b), (e)   Finance, 1900–35.(f)

Year.	Gross Revenue. (a, c)	Customs Revenue.	Percentage of Total.	Gross Expenditure. (c)	Public Debt.
	£(000).	£(000).		£(000).	£(000).
1900	639	601	94·1	735	973
1901	675	603	89·3	865	1,066
1902	868	732	84·4	1,099	1,081
1903	909	753	82·4	1,280	1,248
1904	1,047	846	80·8	1,391	1,140
1905	1,035	802	77·5	1,382	2,000
1906	1,281	771	60·2	1,555	2,000
1907	1,673	1,262	75·4	1,716	2,000
1908	1,636	1,105	67·5	1,898	5,000
1909	1,645	1,076	65·4	2,215	5,000
1910	2,278	1,536	67·4	2,158	5,000
1911	2,571	1,537	59·8	2,545	10,000
1912	2,754	1,656	60·1	2,821	8,268
1913	3,327	1,773	53·3	2,916	8,268
1914	2,948	1,506	51·1	3,596	8,268
1915	2,603	1,383	53·1	3,434	8,268
1916	2,843	1,149	40·4	3,610	8,471
1917	3,417	1,196	35·0	3,220	8,471
1918	3,964	1,382	34·9	3,460	8,471
1919	4,959	1,876	37·8	4,529	11,997
1920	6,819	3,094	45·4	6,493	10,246
1921	4,876	1,680	34·5	7,172	13,609
1922	5,562(d)	2,539(d)	45·6	6,565	13,609
1923	6,261	2,626	41·9	5,501	19,309
1924	6,944	2,935	42·3	5,769	19,309
1925	8,269	3,613	43·7	6,583	19,309
1926	7,734	2,929	37·9	7,585	23,559
1927	6,305(c)	3,541	56·1	6,724(c)	23,559
1928	5,895	3,438	58·3	6,861	23,559
1929	6,045	3,360	55·6	6,290	23,559
1030	5,622	2,981	53·0	6,330	28,351
1931	4,858	2,077	42·8	6,188	28,351
1932	4,985	2,377	47·7	4,984	27,822
1933	4,887	2,133	43·6	5,036	27,822
1934	4,961	2,069	41·7	4,837	27,964
1935	5,996	2,912	48·6	5,757	27,964

(a) Excluding grants-in-aid, which amounted to £4,872,000 between 1897 and 1919.
(b) The figures to 1913 are combined totals for the colony and protectorate of Southern Nigeria and the Protectorate of Northern Nigeria. There is a slight duplication on account of duties collected on goods for Northern Nigeria by Southern Nigeria being included in the revenues of both.
(c) As from 1927 net railway revenue only is included, instead of the gross railway revenues and expenditures as hitherto.
(d) To 31st December up to 1920. As from 1921, for the twelve months ended 31st March of the year following that stated.
(e) Includes the Mandated area of British Cameroons.
(f) Extracted from the *Statistical Abstracts for the British Empire.*

from the north into the country every year in the hope of securing employment, and traders come down with cattle for sale, and return to their homes with kola nuts.

The progress of the trade[1] and finances of the Gold Coast is shown in Tables 78 and 79. From the former, it is clearly apparent how gold and cocoa have shaped the economic history of the country, the latter replacing the wild rubber exports in the early years of the twentieth century. In 1929 cocoa formed 78% of the value of the total domestic exports, and gold accounted for 7% of the total. In 1936 the percentages were 62·6% for cocoa and 24·9% for gold.

Gold is found, generally speaking, all over the forest area, and it has recently been located in parts of the northern territories, but it is only in certain districts that it can be extracted at a profit. Nearly all the gold is won from mines of the banket or quartz reef series, but in the past few years alluvial deposits of commercial value have been found, and have been worked. Gold mining activities have more than trebled during the past three years under the stimulus of the gold premium (see Table 78), and this has afforded an opportunity for a more careful and systematic exploration of the mineral wealth of the colony.

The amount of gold exported increased steadily up to 1913. In that year gold exports were nearly 33% of the total domestic exports of the Colony. After the War, gold exports declined until the industry revived as a result of the rise in the currency price of gold in 1931.

There is no doubt that for centuries the Portuguese, Dutch, French and British obtained large quantities of gold from the Gold Coast. In fact, the earliest records of any trade at all with the West Coast of Africa are of the trade in gold dust.

It was not, however, until the beginning of the present century that gold mining began in earnest. The potentialities of the field were introduced to Europe in the usual fashion, that is, by an exaggerated, quite unwarranted, and soon exploded boom in the shares of innumerable companies whose prospectuses portrayed a new Witwatersrand. Some aspects of this boom have already been referred to. It has been estimated that 321 companies were registered up to June, 1901, with a total nominal

---

[1] The trade statistics for the Gold Coast include the trade of the Mandated area of British Togoland, which territory is therefore not considered separately in this chapter.

capital of over £25 millions, of which possibly £15 millions was issued.[1]

The exports of gold in recent years have been as follows:

						Fine oz.
1929	.	.	.	.	.	202,847[2]
1931	.	.	.	.	.	246,162[2]
1932	.	.	.	.	.	286,568[3]
1933	.	.	.	.	.	294,373[3]
1934	.	.	.	.	.	351,401[3]
1935	.	.	.	.	.	370,769[3]
1936	.	.	.	.	.	434,397[3]

The mineral wealth of the country is, however, not confined to gold. The growth in the output of manganese, which was discovered during the War, has been remarkable. In 1916 4,000 tons of manganese ore were exported. By 1929, the peak year, this had risen to no less than 419,224 tons, valued at £748,286. Manganese is produced at Ensuta in the western province of the colony by the African Manganese Company Limited. The industry was greatly affected by the world depression, and exports in 1932 declined to 50,688 tons, valued at only £123,627. But it has recovered since then, and exports reached 265,140 tons in 1933, and 411,024 tons in 1936, valued at £612,930. In recent years the Gold Coast has been the second largest producer of manganese ore in the world.

Diamonds have also contributed considerably to the wealth of the colony. The following table shows the diamond exports:

				Carats.		Value.
1929	.	.	.	660,536	.	£584,613
1931	.	.	.	880,479	.	440,924
1932	.	.	.	842,297	.	536,946
1933	.	.	.	803,985	.	518,400
1934	.	.	.	2,391,609	.	756,816
1935	.	.	.	1,349,847	.	546,094
1936	.	.	.	1,414,677	.	584,997

[1] *Cf.* E. D. Morel, *Affairs of West Africa* (London : Heinemann, 1902), which also contains an excellent account of the boom.

[2] Estimated fine ounce (90% of the bullion ounces).

[3] Actual quantity.

TABLE 78.—*Gold Coast.*(c)   *Trade Statistics, 1900-36, and Proportion per cent. of Annual Exports of Selected Commodities to Annual Value of all Domestic Produce Exported.*

Year.	Merchandise Imports.(a) £(000).	Exports. Domestic Produce.(b) £(000).	Exports. Re-Exports.(d) £(000).	Cocoa Exports. £(000).(d)	Cocoa Exports. %.	Gold Exports.(e) £(000).	Gold Exports.(e) %.	Rubber Exports. £(000).	Rubber Exports. %.	All Mineral Exports.(f) £(000).	All Mineral Exports.(f) %.
1900	1,099	852	12	27	3·2	38	4·5	328	38·5	38	4·5
1901	1,595	534	14	43	8·1	22	4·1	104	19·5	22	4·1
1902	1,833	716	12	95	13·3	97	13·5	89	12·4	97	13·5
1903	1,829	897	28	86	9·6	255	28·4	197	22·0	255	28·4
1904	1,726	1,238	9	200	16·2	346	27·9	360	29·1	346	27·9
1905	1,381	1,448	8	187	12·9	597	41·2	324	22·4	597	41·2
1906	1,631	1,863	45	336	18·0	859	46·1	334	17·9	859	46·1
1907	1,929	2,502	12	515	20·6	1,165	46·6	333	13·3	1,165	46·6
1908	1,868	2,327	6	541	23·2	1,152	49·5	168	7·2	1,152	49·5
1909	2,005	2,452	7	755	30·8	1,008	41·1	264	10·8	1,008	41·1
1910	2,783	2,608	6	867	33·2	790	30·3	359	13·8	790	30·3
1911	2,903	3,463	8	1,613	46·6	1,070	30·9	219	6·3	1,070	30·9
1912	3,452	3,996	8	1,643	41·1	1,470	36·8	169	4·2	1,470	36·8
1913	3,510	5,014	10	2,489	49·6	1,656	33·0	88	1·8	1,656	33·0
1914	3,584	4,460	10	2,194	49·2	1,687	37·8	22	0·5	1,687	37·8
1915	3,472	5,800	14	3,651	62·9	1,782	30·7	25	0·4	1,782	30·7
1916	5,007	5,561	16	3,848	69·2	1,242	22·3	79	1·4	1,248	22·3
1917	3,220	5,505	26	3,147	57·2	1,741	31·6	110	2·0	1,789	32·5
1918	2,920	3,970	57	1,797	45·3	1,384	34·9	57	1·4	1,440	36·3
1919	7,111	10,706	74	8,279	77·3	1,425	13·3	35	0·3	1,497	14·0
1920	14,141	12,225	77	10,056	82·3	901	7·4	27	0·2	970	7·9
1921	6,817	6,387	70	4,764	74·6	863	13·5	7	0·1	877	13·7
1922	5,510	7,522	69	5,841	77·7	889	11·8	(g)	…	1,002	13·3
1923	7,727	8,394	55	6,567	78·2	851	10·1	9	0·1	1,189	14·2
1924	7,207	9,590	91	7,250	75·6	875	9·1	9	3·1	1,487	15·5

Year					%					%		%
1925	8,821	10,626	29	8,222	77·4	841	7·9	34	0·3	1,621	15·3
1926	8,444	11,849	38	9,181	77·5	850	7·2	53	0·3	1,898	16·0
1927	11,703	14,186	52	11,728	82·7	727	5·1	31	0·2	1,922	13·5
1928	11,302	13,629	111	11,230	82·4	685	5·0	26	0·2	1,870	13·7
1929	9,626	12,401	96	9,704	78·3	870	7·0	28	0·2	2,203	17·8
1930	8,507	9,911	154	6,970	70·3	1,056	10·7	22	0·2	2,538	25·6
1931	4,434	7,574	118	5,493	72·5	1,070	14·1	(g)	...	1,900	25·1
1932	5,350	8,022	81	5,511	68·7	1,693	21·1	(g)	...	2,354	29·3
1933	5,096	7,800	80	4,971	63·7	1,842	23·6	(g)	...	2,717	34·8
1934	4,390	7,850	97	4,041	51·5	2,422	30·9	(g)	...	3,660	46·6
1935	7,348	9,241	74	5,204	56·3	2,635	28·5	14	0·2	3,793	41·0
1936	8,531	12,240	97	7,660	62·6	3,048	24·9	24	0·2	4,248	34·7

(a) Excluding bullion and coin ; including goods subsequently re-exported.
(b) Includes bullion and the value of the gold "premium".
(c) Including the trade of the mandated territory of British Togoland as from 1926.   Extracted from the *Statistical Abstracts for the British Empire.*
(d) Excluding bullion and coin.
(e) Including the value of gold premium.
(f) Includes precious stones.   Figures from Annual Reports.
(g) Negligible.

In 1935 minerals accounted for no less than 41% of the total domestic exports of the territory. The average daily number of

TABLE 79.—*Gold Coast.(c)   Finance, 1900–35.*

Year.(b)	Gross Revenue.(a)	Customs Revenue.	Percentage of Customs to Total Revenue.	Grant-in-Aid.	Gross Expenditure.	Public Debt.
	£(000).	£(000).		£(000).	£(000).	£(000).
1900	333	281	84·4	50	516	...
1901	471	351	74·5	25	469	1,330
1902	492	383	77·8	10	523	2,083
1903	555	370	66·7	23	594	2,253
1904	650	384	59·1	32	622	2,273
1905	572	334	58·4	14	596	2,248
1906	673	386	57·4	10	602	2,253
1907	704	415	58·9	5	602	2,207
1908	752	490	65·2	...	667	2,207
1909	779	459	58·9	...	709	2,663
1910	1,007	611	60·7	...	775	2,514
1911	1,112	663	59·6	...	890	2,489
1912	1,231	735	59·7	...	1,021	2,469
1913	1,302	780	59·9	...	1,238	2,449
1914	1,332	769	57·7	...	1,572	3,464
1915	1,456	828	56·9	...	1,470	3,444
1916	1,836	1,132	61·7	...	1,359	3,424
1917	1,624	894	55·0	...	1,361	3,409
1918	1,299	620	47·7	...	1,318	3,389
1919	2,601	1,672	64·3	...	1,643	3,364
1920	3,722	2,282	61·3	...	2,797	7,364
1921	3,017	1,777	58·9	...	3,285	7,319
1922	3,357	2,035	60·6	...	2,935	7,299
1923	3,743	2,155	57·6	...	3,155	7,279
1924	3,971	2,283	57·5	...	3,828	7,259
1925	4,116	2,439	59·2	...	4,255	11,791
1926	4,365	2,410	55·1	...	4,328	11,791
1927	4,112	3,181	77·1	...	3,619	11,791
1928	3,914	2,603	66·5	...	4,109	11,791
1929	3,397	2,490	73·3	...	3,861	11,791
1930	3,499	1,735	49·6	...	3,721	12,961
1931	2,284	1,474	64·5	...	2,824	12,961
1932	2,671	1,648	61·7	...	2,673	12,961
1933	2,685	1,823	67·9	...	2,313	12,961
1934	2,636	1,906	72·3	...	2,554	11,863
1935	3,169	2,435	76·8	...	3,128	11,435

(a) Excluding Imperial Grants.
(b) To 31st December of year stated to 1920.   To 31st March of year following that stated thereafter.
(c) Including the mandated area of British Togoland as from 1926.   Statistics are from the *Statistical Abstracts for the British Empire.*

persons employed in all mining and prospecting operations during the year amounted to 839 Europeans and 33,403 Africans.

The principal occupation of the native inhabitants, however, is agriculture. In the Colony, Ashanti and the southern section of Togoland under British Mandate, the chief agricultural industry is the cultivation of cocoa for export. In the Northern Territories, where cocoa does not thrive, food crops are grown and livestock is raised and marketed. Even in the cocoa-bearing areas, however, and in the region of the considerable fishing industry of the littoral, food farms are numerous and there is a large internal trade in foodstuffs.[1]

It is estimated[2] that there are 1,000,000 acres under cocoa in the Gold Coast, with 400 trees to the acre, and that the labour expended on its production amounts to one-sixth of the total labour potentialities of the country.

In the cocoa-growing areas almost every member of the community has his plot, the main preoccupation is the cocoa industry, and the income of the family is dependent on the price and size of the crop. An acre—the size of the average individual farm— will yield about nine loads of 60 lb. each.

Originally, the whole of this considerable industry—it is estimated that the total production for the financial year was 285,251 tons—could have been attributed to the work of personal proprietors or small holders, but to-day this is no longer the case. The increasing demand for cocoa has brought about the introduction of hired labour, and a considerable number of natives from the non cocoa growing areas of the Gold Coast and from surrounding territories find employment in the production and transport of the crop. There are no data available at present to show the proportion of the whole crop produced by the working small-holder.

The rates of wages of labourers hired by the year have been reduced as a result of the depression. Rates have now been estimated to vary from £4 to £5 per annum, as opposed to £4 to £10 paid in 1926. In some areas labourers who are employed to weed, pick and prepare the crop, and to convey it to the farmers' houses, are paid in kind, receiving one-third of the produce for their services. These wages throw some light on the standard of life and income of this class of the population, and again indicate

[1] *Annual Colonial Report on the Gold Coast, 1935/6*, Colonial No. 1785, p. 17.
[2] *Ibid.*, p. 23.

the great scope there is throughout the continent for a rise in the standard of life of the African peoples.

The cocoa exports since 1929 are shown by the following figures; they have formed about 45% of the world exports in recent years. The second largest exporter is Brazil, and Nigeria occupies third place.

Cocoa Exports.

	Tons.	Value.
1929 . . .	238,068	. . .
1931 . . .	244,097	5,493,165
1932 . . .	233,745	5,511,360
1933 . . .	236,117	4,971,478
1934 . . .	230,272	4,040,696
1935 . . .	268,891	5,204,182
1936 . . .	311,151	7,659,743

The development of the finances of the territory is shown in Table 79. It will be noted that Customs Duties represented 76·8% of the total revenue of the colony in 1935; there is no direct taxation in the territory, and this fact has contributed to the considerable fluctuations in revenue, and its marked decline during the depression. The public debt of the Colony at the 31st March, 1936 was £11,435,000. The debt per head of the population is much higher than in Nigeria and many other African territories. Yet it is noteworthy, as has been shown previously,[1] that the proportion which the debt charges of the Gold Coast form of its domestic exports and of its ordinary revenue is very low. The Gold Coast provides a good example of the inadequacy of statistics of the debt per head of the population, as an index of the borrowing capacity of a colonial territory.

A problem of importance in the Gold Coast is that of further developing the production of food crops for local consumption, and in recent years considerable progress has been made in this direction. The development of the main export crops has, in the past, been at the expense of the production of products which are a necessary part of an adequate diet for the population. The Gold

[1] *Cf.* Table 37, p. 182 above.

Coast still imports much rice and even tinned foods for native consumption. This question is one of great importance in almost all tropical colonies in which development of specialized mono-cultures has been unduly stimulated, or in which there are large areas where diversified production is not possible.[1]

The Gold Coast is quite likely to make considerable further progress in mining, and this is of great importance as offsetting the disadvantage of the country's dependence on cocoa. The probable increase in mining activity, combined with the efforts being made to increase the production of other crops, augurs well for the future progress of this wealthy area. The development of the northern provinces depends largely on the possibility of providing additional transport facilities.

XVI

THE COLONY AND PROTECTORATE OF SIERRA LEONE.

The territory comprising the Colony and Protectorate of Sierra Leone has an area of 27,925 square miles, of which the portions administered strictly as a Colony occupy 256 square miles. The estimated population of the Colony and Protectorate on the 31st December, 1935, was 1,890,000.

Till recently, the development of the territory has lagged behind that of the other West African colonies, but the discovery of minerals, the increase in gold production, and to a lesser extent in platinum and iron production, have stimulated the progress of the territory.

Tables 80 and 81 show the commercial and financial development of the territory. In 1928, 78% of the total domestic exports consisted of palm products and a further 17·5% of kola nuts. By 1936 there had been a considerable change, and palm products accounted for only 38·6% of the total domestic exports, kola nuts for only 1·9%, while mineral exports formed approximately 57% of the total.

The growth in diamond production which is carried on by

[1] *Cf.* an interesting discussion of this question in Mr. Ormsby-Gore's Report, *ibid.* It, of course, raises far-reaching economic issues, which, however, cannot be discussed here.

TABLE 80.—*Sierra Leone. Trade Statistics, 1900–36, and Proportion per cent. of Annual Exports of Selected Commodities to Annual Value of all Domestic Produce Exported.(f)*

Year.	Merchandise Imports.(a)	Exports.(e)		Palm Kernels Exports.		Other Palm Products (Fibre and Palm Oil) Exports.(d)		Kola Nut Exports.	
		Domestic Produce.(b)	Re-Exports.(g)						
	£(000).	£(000).	£(000).	£(000).	%.	£(000).	%.	£(000).	%.
1900	553	318(c)	...	172	54·1	8	2·5	79	24·8
1901	547	265(c)	...	162	61·1	10	3·8	52	19·6
1902	596	326(c)	...	201	61·7	14	4·3	61	18·7
1903	665	341(c)	...	196	57·5	14	4·1	76	22·3
1904	634	407	...	214	52·6	17	4·2	81	19·9
1905	614	436	12	269	61·7	23	5·3	76	17·4
1906	741	526	25	330	62·7	33	6·3	104	19·8
1907	865	676	59	448	66·3	57	8·4	114	16·9
1908	730	530	55	333	62·8	45	8·5	109	20·6
1909	782	760	82	483	63·2	74	9·7	154	20·3
1910	972	968	83	645	66·6	72	7·4	192	19·8
1911	1,050	1,005	105	657	65·4	82	8·2	194	19·3
1912	1,219	1,223	127	793	64·8	83	6·8	276	22·6
1913	1,438	1,376	114	921	66·9	69	5·0	328	23·8
1914	1,166	933	109	559	59·9	58	6·2	279	29·9
1915	1,079	853	90	504	59·1	73	8·6	235	27·5
1916	1,135	1,102	73	681	61·8	73	6·6	303	27·5
1917	1,333	1,276	222	843	66·1	71	5·6	321	25·2
1918	1,680	1,189	328	683	57·4	49	4·1	398	33·5
1919	2,035	1,807	241	1,192	66·0	148	8·2	417	23·1
1920	3,300	2,248	668	1,402	62·4	138	6·1	627	27·9
1921	1,576	1,042	270	685	65·7	21	2·0	314	30·1
1922	1,408	1,069	53	722	67·5	86	8·1	208	19·5
1923	1,916	1,347	43	969	71·9	123	9·1	187	13·9
1924	1,686	1,510	37	1,096	72·6	105	7·0	181	12·0

1925	1,941	1,628	34	1,152	70·8	124	7·6	216	13·3
1926	1,626	1,562	32	1,117	71·5	113	7·2	247	15·8
1927	1,881	1,527	64	1,077	70·5	129	8·4	269	17·6
1928	1,784	1,609	50	1,151	71·5	106	6·6	282	17·5
1929	1,667	1,319	109	876	66·4	92	7·0	266	20·2
1930	1,336	1,046	51	665	63·6	116	11·1	186	17·8
1931	991	616	22	450	73·1	52	8·4	48	7·8
1932	1,220	878	21	687	78·2	50	5·7	41	4·7
1933	817	754	18	473	62·7	48	6·4	44	5·8
1934	776	832	15	361	43·4	48	5·8	18	2·2
1935	1,127	1,556	14	584	37·5	67	4·3	39	2·5
1936	1,298	2,225	19	810	36·4	49	2·2	42	1·9

(a) Including goods subsequently re-exported, excluding specie.
(b) Including bullion and coin subsequent to 1930.
(c) Including re-exports.
(d) Excludes Fibre prior to 1924.
(e) The export of minerals, which was negligible prior to 1934, amounted in that year to £372,000, equivalent to 44·7% of all exports of domestic produce. For 1935 the corresponding figures were £810,000 and 52·1%. The chief minerals are diamonds and gold. In 1936 the value of the diamond exports was £723,000, that of gold £250,000, that of iron £262,000, and that of platinum £3,000; the total of all mineral exports was £1,246,000, i.e. 56% of the total domestic exports.
(f) Extracted from the *Statistical Abstracts for the British Empire*, figures for mineral exports are from *Colonial Reports*.
(g) Excluding bullion and coin.

the Sierra Leone Selection Trust, a subsidiary of the African Selection Trust, has been referred to previously.[1]

TABLE 81.—*Sierra Leone. Finance,* 1900–36.(*c*)

Year.	Gross Revenue. (*a*) (*b*)	Customs Revenue.	Percentage of Customs to Total Revenue.	Gross Expenditure. (*a*)	Public Debt.
	£ (000).	£ (000).		£ (000).	£ (000).
1900	169	103	60·9	156	...
1901	192	105	54·7	173	458
1902	206	122	59·2	185	589
1903	238	127	53·4	206	783
1904	240	133	55·4	238	1,274
1905	282	144	51·1	295	1,277
1906	305	163	53·4	286	1,279
1907	359	198	55·2	346	1,280
1908	321	164	51·1	342	1,276
1909	361	189	52·4	337	1,271
1910	424	226	53·3	361	1,262
1911	458	242	52·8	387	1,255
1912	560	301	53·8	450	1,248
1913	618	317	51·3	562	1,296
1914	497	199	40·0	680	1,731
1915	504	230	45·6	547	1,730
1916	551	274	49·7	533	1,730
1917	536	258	48·1	513	1,730
1918	583	298	51·1	544	1,730
1919	749	442	59·0	740	1,730
1920	999	630	63·1	843	1,730
1921	638	339	53·1	982	1,730
1922	787	454	57·7	817	1,730
1923	845	512	60·6	728	1,730
1924	886	481	54·3	778	1,730
1925	946	539	57·0	843	1,730
1926	855	453	53·0	957	1,730
1927(*a*)	720	534	74·2	754	1,730
1928	826	558	67·6	815	1,788
1929	741	507	68·4	871	1,788
1930	743	427	57·5	806	1,990
1931	884	339	38·3	884	2,141
1932	872	452	51·8	832	2,141
1933	656	370	56·4	692	2,141
1934	599	313	52·3	603	1,718
1935	679	441	64·9	586	1,718
1936	970	491	50·6	879(*d*)	1,718

(*a*) As from 1st January, 1927, the railway accounts were excluded from the Colony's general accounts.
(*b*) There were no grants-in-aid during the above period.
(*c*) Extracted from the *Statistical Abstracts for the British Empire.*
(*d*) Includes £187,020 transferred to Reserve Fund.

A deposit of good grade hæmatite, containing some 12,000,000 tons of ore, averaging approximately 56% iron, occurs in the

[1] See p. 74 above.

northern provinces. It is being exploited by the Sierra Leone Development Company Limited. The exports of hæmatite ore commenced in September, 1933, and have increased rapidly. Gold production, which is alluvial, has grown since 1930, when it was valued at approximately £3,000 to approximately £256,000 in 1936. Alluvial deposits of platinum occur in the Colony in the neighbourhood of York. Production since mining commenced in 1929 has been as follows:

	Ounces (Crude Platinum).	Approximate value. £.
1929/30 . . .	568	3,307
1931	594	3,093
1932	531	4,147
1933	431	2,493
1934	474	2,666
1935	750	3,933
1936	482	4,359
Total . .	3,830	£23,998

Mining has absorbed a number of unskilled native labourers. In 1935 the labour force was 9,445.

The exports of palm kernels and palm oil in recent years have been as follows:

	Palm Kernels.		Palm Oil.	
	Tons Exported.	£.	Tons Exported.	£.
Average 1920–29 .	58,150	1,024,798	2,562	81,742
1930 . . .	56,641	664,591	3,652	79,310
1931 . . .	54,463	449,742	1,359	19,830
1932 . . .	77,162	687,477	2,208	26,914
1933 . . .	64,084	472,824	1,619	16,637
1934 . . .	68,655	470,780	2,225	18,032
1935 . . .	78,019	583,645	2,892	35,814
1936 . . .	84,578	810,238	1,223	16,313

Kola nuts have declined in price, and less are being exported than a few years ago, but there was a recovery in both price and quantity in 1935 and 1936. The industry depends on the demands for kola nuts in West African markets. Certain markets, such as

Dakar, are being closed against Sierra Leone kola nuts by high preferential tariffs, while the high import duties into Nigeria and into the Gambia are having a limiting effect on the exports to those countries. The exports in recent years have been as follows:

	Tons Exported.	£.
Average 1920–9	2,932	279,678
1930	2,271	186,197
1931	1,584	47,847
1932	2,085	41,373
1933	1,812	43,656
1934	1,460	18,303
1935	1,859	39,415
1936	2,301	41,539

Other export crops of some importance are ginger and piassava. The following figures indicate the position:

	Ginger.		Piassava.	
	Tons Exported.	£.	Tons Exported.	£.
Average 1920–9	1,582	56,778	1,645	22,707
1930	1,972	57,228	2,417	36,582
1931	1,927	32,518	3,150	31,846
1932	1,382	22,877	2,877	23,290
1933	1,545	16,543	3,499	30,108
1934	1,659	23,254	3,659	30,390
1935	1,506	36,918	3,438	30,997
1936	1,642	58,673	3,558	32,777

Minor export crops comprise chillies, cocoa, coffee and benniseed. The most important food crop is rice, which is the staple food of the people. Exact statistics of its production are not available. Sierra Leone is practically self-supporting in food supplies, except for the requirements of the Europeans. There are no organized manufacturing industries, but there are several handicrafts, such as weaving.

The future economic progress of the territory depends on further mineral expansion and on the fortunes of the palm industry.

XVII

GAMBIA—COLONY AND PROTECTORATE.

The Gambia Colony has an area of only 69 square miles. The Protectorate comprises an area of about 4,000 square miles, and consists of a narrow strip of territory approximately 10 kilometres wide, and 300 miles in length, on each bank of the river Gambia. The river is tidal throughout its length in British territory, and is navigable by ocean-going steamers for nearly 150 miles up-stream. There are no railways. Gambia's population is only about 200,000.

Farming is the principal occupation of the people. The country is unsuitable for European settlers, and there are no permanent plantations or estates; production is based on a system of "shifting" cultivation.

The economic progress of this small, unhealthy territory is summed up in the trade and finance statistics given in Table 82. Its total domestic exports in 1935 were only £376,000.

Ground nuts account for 98% of the value of the exports. Nearly the whole male population is engaged in this industry for eight months of the year, and the whole economic life of the territory is bound up and varies with the fluctuations in world prices for this product. There are no minerals in Gambia, no important manufacturing or handicraft industries, nor any animal industry. Fishing the people of Gambia leave in the hands of the Senegalese natives. All these facts sufficiently account for the slow progress of the territory as compared with other West African Colonies.

XVIII

FRENCH WEST AND EQUATORIAL AFRICA.

The key to an understanding of the economic development of French West Africa and French Equatorial Africa lies in the enormous extent of these colonies and their relatively small population. They comprise 34% of the area of Africa considered

TABLE 82.—*Gambia.*(d)   *Trade Statistics, 1900–36, and Finance, 1900–36.*(e)

Year.	Gross Revenue. £(000).	Customs Revenue. £(000).	Percentage of Customs to Total Revenue.	Expenditure. £(000).	Merchandise Imports.(a) £(000).	Exports. Domestic Produce.(b) £(000).	Exports. Re-Exports. £(000).	Exports of Ground Nuts. £(000).	Exports of Ground Nuts. Percentage of Total Exports of Domestic Produce.
1900	49	39	79·6	30	194	241(c)	...	222	92·1
1901	44	33	75·0	49	185	194(c)	...	172	88·6
1902	51	39	76·5	52	188	210(c)	...	193	92·0
1903	56	42	75·0	68	215	291(c)	...	275	94·5
1904	54	40	74·1	52	197	249(c)	...	229	91·9
1905	52	35	67·3	72	182	184(c)	...	169	91·8
1906	65	51	78·5	57	280	299(c)	...	278	93·0
1907	66	52	78·8	58	296	280	11	257	91·8
1908	58	44	75·9	61	245	262	9	245	93·5
1909	73	55	75·3	56	405	341	10	323	94·7
1910	83	75	90·4	63	370	400	23	388	97·0
1911	86	68	79·1	71	422	454	12	437	96·3
1912	96	73	76·0	81	471	529	10	502	94·9
1913	125	98	78·4	95	619	655	8	622	95·0
1914	86	61	70·9	121	388	682	12	650	95·3

Year									
1915	92	66	71·7	89	302	421	9	400	95·0
1916	103	75	72·8	83	479	534	9	506	94·8
1917	118	85	72·0	95	697	940	13	870	92·6
1918	133	97	72·9	89	919	867	16	800	92·3
1919	181	137	75·7	143	1,180	1,185	45	1,154	97·4
1920	269	201	74·7	171	2,376	2,357	107	2,322	98·5
1921	183	125	68·3	225	682	629	29	620	98·6
1922	204	144	70·6	242	653	776	33	767	98·8
1923	230	162	70·4	211	790	863	21	852	98·7
1924	208	133	63·9	203	670	856	137	842	98·4
1925	189	111	58·7	272	615	684	38	667	97·5
1926	214	141	65·9	214	651	835	69	819	98·1
1927	252	173	68·7	278	863	939	59	916	97·6
1928	255	177	69·4	251	1,011	1,113	43	1,093	98·2
1929	235	124	52·8	290	597	783	58	766	97·8
1930	216	140	64·8	253	530	878	21	868	98·9
1931	185	122	65·9	227	250	517	10	506	97·9
1932	206(f)	100	48·5	196(f)	293	400	7	392	98·0
1933	232(f)	157	67·7	180(f)	436	506	9	501	99·0
1934	222	142	64·0	175	327	394	8	387	98·2
1935	245	174	71·0	195	483	376	17	369	98·1
1936	261	185	70·9	259	582	435	10	426	98·2

(a) Excludes bullion and coin; includes goods subsequently re-exported.
(b) Excludes bullion and coin.
(c) Includes re-exports.
(d) Gambia had no Public Debt prior to 1922, when it received a loan of £200,000 to meet the cost of demonetizing the franc. This loan has since been repaid.
(e) Extracted from the *Statistical Abstracts for the British Empire*
(f) Extracted from *Annual Colonial Reports.*

in this study, but they account for only 19% of its total population.

French West Africa with an area of 4,700,000 square kilometres (about 1,800,000 square miles) covers four times the area of the Union of South Africa, over five times the area of Nigeria, and more than four times the area of all the British West African colonies together. Its population of about 15,000,000, of whom less than 25,000 are Europeans, is less than three-fifths of that of British West Africa. Moreover, the population of French West Africa is unevenly distributed, as is shown by the following table of the area and population of its various colonies.

	Sq. Km. (000).	Population (1933 estimate). (000.)	Density per Sq. Km.	Population 1934 and 1936 (a) (including troops) (000.)
Dakar . . .	0·16	·063	460	·093*
Senegal . .	200	1·600	8·0	1·698*
Soudan . .	1,500	3·600	2·4	3·569*
Guinea . .	250	2·100	8·4	2·011*
Côte d'Ivoire .	475	3·900	8·0	3·872
Dahomey .	110	1·100	10·0	1·352*
Niger . .	1,300	1·800	1·4	1·764*
	850	0·350	0·4	0·410
Totals . .	4,700	14·500	3·1	14·769

(a) General Census, March 8th, 1936, quoted in *D.O.T. Report*, 1937, No. 664. Figures not marked with an asterisk are those as estimated at December 31st, 1934.

French Equatorial Africa comprises an area of 2,256,000 square kilometres (about 71,042 square miles), which is slightly less than the area of the Belgian Congo and three times the area of British West Africa, but its population is less than a third of the former, and about one-seventh of the latter.

The combined area of French West Africa and French Equatorial Africa is over twelve times the size of France, but the combined population of the colonies is less than half of the population of the mother country.

The first fact that France realized after the establishment of the Federation was that, far from being densely populated, "West Africa was a country without Negroes". Only in Guinea and the Upper Volta was the population adequate for the needs of development.

The second fact was that this vast territory, apart from all the disadvantages of climate and disease common to Western and Central Africa, was interspersed with considerable areas of little value for economic purposes, and the limited forest and agricultural lands were found to fade gradually into the great interior desert. This has made the problems usually encountered in the development of communications in tropical areas lacking mineral resources particularly difficult in this region:[1] while often when railways had been provided, and fertile areas brought into touch with the coast, the difficulties of securing an adequate labour supply for rapid development proved insuperable.

It was clear, from the outset, that development in West Africa had, of necessity, to be in native hands; "the only choice was whether there should be European *entrepreneurs* using the natives as tenants, or whether the requisite capital should be afforded by the Government, and the natives develop along the lines of a progressive peasant-proprictorship. Inclination and necessity combined to favour the second of these alternatives, to the development of which the whole of West African policy has been directed.[2] This policy, moreover, received a great fillip

---

[1] In West Africa, as elsewhere, railways were the *sine qua non* of any development.

The Niger did not go to the sea in French Territory, and the Senegal, the most obvious way to the interior, was navigable to Kayes only for $2\frac{1}{2}$ months in the year, and, at the best, was an extremely precarious passage-way. This left railways as the only medium of communication. As Governor-General Roume, the economic founder of West Africa, said in 1906, summing up the whole of the Colony's problem:

"The object is to open to civilization that vast part of the African Continent given to France in the partition, and which, by reason of its configuration, has so far been kept in primitive barbarism. The real cause of the prolonged stagnation is that this rich region was separated from the rest of the world by the Sahara on the north, an inhospitable coast on the east and south, and a dense curtain of tropical forest, all of which formed practically impassable obstacles to civilizing actions. Even in the interior, the lack or uncertainty of communications is still almost complete. Rivers encumbered by rapids allow an irregular and inadequate traffic, and it is only round the great navigable bend of the Middle Niger that relatively important centres of civilization have been possible. The resources of science and capital, however, permit us now to open these countries, hitherto hermetically sealed by Nature, by improving the few natural sea-outlets, by correcting the defects of the riverways wherever possible, and above all by *creating artificial routes—the railways*."

Roume therefore made railway-construction the pivot of his economic policy, and quoted with approval Sir Walter Egerton's pronouncement of policy for South Nigeria and Lagos: "If you ask what my policy is, I should say, '*Open means of communication*', and if you would wish for additional information, I would reply, '*Open more of them*' ! ".—Roberts : *History of French Colonial Policy*, vol. i, pp. 328–9.

[2] Roberts, *ibid.*, vol. i, p. 318.

from the success of native production in the neighbouring British Colonies.

The policy of the French Government has been to assist economic specialization within each local area; and the colonies of the Federation have tended to become areas of mono-culture.

Corresponding to the ground nut of the Senegal is the cocoa of Guinea, the timber of the Ivory Coast, and the palm production of Dahomey. The large-scale projects for the development of the natives of the Sudan form an exception.

This specialization has, of course, been mainly determined by climatic factors, and French West African development has consisted so far in the erection of a ring of coastal cultures round the Sudan-basin.

The long-discussed plans for the future involve the intense economic development of the basin itself, i. e. a move from the coastal cultures to the exploitation of the Timbuktu-Bamako river regions.

For years the means for achieving this project have been elaborated. The construction of railways and public works has been dominated by it and, in particular, by the possibility of making the Sudan-basin an irrigated cotton area, and the principal source of cotton supplies for the looms of the mother country.

The only way of producing cotton in Western Africa is by irrigating the Senegal and Niger valleys. The Niger Valley, in particular, conforms to the desired conditions, and has an enormous area of river flats available for irrigation.

The Niger river irrigation works were first started by the "Service des Textiles de l'Afrique Occidentale Française". The colonization of the irrigable lands was undertaken, as far back as 1925, at Nienébalé, Sotuba and Diré. At Sotuba an experimental canal was cut, making it possible to irrigate 23 square miles. In 1932 the "Office du Niger" was charged with the work of surveying, planning and executing the irrigation works of the Niger Valley and developing the land. The hydraulic works of the Niger basin are now being carried out.

When the works are finished it is hoped that over 5,400 square miles can be irrigated and cultivated.

The scheme was originally financed by the General Budget of the Federation, which invested 33 million Francs in the first undertaking. Out of the funds of the Colonial loan, 300 million francs were set aside for the completion of the programme.

The expenditure on the project,[1] which has been borne by the Colonial Loan up to the end of 1935, amounted to approximately Frs. 92 millions, and that covered by the General Budget to about Frs. 53 millions.

Irrigation works, however, are only one phase of the situation, and even given the necessary training of the natives, the question of transport looms in the background, here, as elsewhere, the bane of Western Africa. If the fertile Niger Valley produces cotton, it will have to be transported for over 1,200 kilometres to the coast.

So far, two decades of discussion and planning, and much effort, have not yet succeeded in making cotton an important article of export from French West Africa.

In 1930, the export of cotton reached 4,883 metric tons, but with the decline in prices exports have languished; they fell to 1,376 metric tons in 1931, were 2,944 metric tons in 1935, and 3,453 metric tons in 1936. Cotton is still extensively grown in many districts, but it is used mainly for the local needs of the natives; prices remain too low for important exports.

The trade of French West Africa still rests mainly on the production of the coastal zones, with their climatic advantages for special cultures, and particularly their ready access to important harbours.

Of the coastal cultures, the ground-nut production of the Senegal is by far the most important. Ground nuts have been exported from Senegal since the middle of the nineteenth century. The export was about 9,000 metric tons at the end of the 'fifties, and grew to 60,000 at the beginning of the 'eighties. It fell as a result of the opening of the Suez Canal and the competition of the Near East, but recovered with the opening of the famous "ground-nut railway" from Saint Louis to Dakar. At the end

[1] The construction of the Sansanding Barrage, the essential organ of the system, will take six or seven years. During this period it is hoped to put under cultivation about 115 square miles of land, of which two-thirds are in the Sahel district and one-third in the Macina district (the rice-growing region of Bokywéré).

of the nineteenth century, exports had again risen to about 50,000 metric tons per annum, and since then they have grown by leaps and bounds. They reached 200,000 metric tons during, and over 400,000 metric tons after the Great War. As is shown in Table 83, more than one-half of the value of the exports of French West Africa originated in the Senegal, while the exports of the latter consist mainly of ground nuts and ground-nut oil:

TABLE 83.[1]—*French West Africa and Senegal. Comparison of Exports,* 1930–36.

	Millions of Francs.						
	1930.	1931.	1932.	1933.	1934.	1935.	1936.
Value of ground nuts in shell, shelled and ground-nut oil exported from Senegal	...	...	...	186·2	234·0	313·4	430·9
Value of ground nuts in shell, and shelled, and ground-nut oil exported[2] from French West Africa	506	309	169	190·6	263·8	373·3	496·9
Total value of exports " special " from Senegal	601	371	198	238·1	299·8	400·9	503·7
Total value of exports " special " from French West Africa	1,102	660	447	455·4	533·3	698·2	926·8

This table also shows the catastrophic fall in the value of the ground-nut exports during the depression and the effect of this on the exports of French West Africa as a whole.

The ground-nut is grown as the staple food-stuff of the native in a wide belt, extending from latitude 8° North to 14° North, which comprises a very large portion of the agricultural area of the Federation. This belt is, in general, not well suited for other products.

The development of Senegal has been greatly favoured by its geographical position with its sea-ports of Dakar and Rufisque, and its river harbours such as Kaolack, Foundrougue and Saint Louis. Goods can be forwarded to the French Sudan by rail. There is also a certain amount of river traffic.

[1] Extracted from *D.O.T. Reports on French West Africa,* and from *Bulletin Mensuel de l'Agence Économique de l'A.O.F.*
[2] The figures for the years 1930, 1931 and 1932 exclude ground nut-oil.

The railways have played the most important part in the recent great expansion of the Senegal ground-nut exports, both in supplying means of transportation for the product, and because of the ease with which labour can, in due season, be brought from the interior to assist in the gathering of the crop. Production is now being extended to that part of the French Sudan which is served by the Thiés to Niger railway. Moreover, the development of motor transport has had a revolutionary effect on the industry; ground nuts are now produced in areas as much as fifty miles from the railway. The gradual extension of production into the interior, in place of production in the coastal zone, is largely due to the extensive and primitive methods of cultivation, and the consequent exhaustion of the soil. This disadvantageous factor is frequently overlooked when the increasing size of the crop is considered.

Exports of ground nuts from West Africa reached 510,463 metric tons in 1930, but, thereafter, greatly declined owing to the disastrous fall in prices, and also to a series of very unfavourable seasons. For the 1930/31 crop, the average price paid to the natives was about Frs. 35 per 100 kg., whereas, prior to the depression, they received as much as Frs. 125 to Frs. 150 per 100 kg. In 1934, exports reached 544,068 metric tons, but prices were still very low; in 1935, there was some recovery in prices, but the crop was smaller, the amount exported being 411,576 metric tons of ground nuts; in 1936, the exports reached 534,682 metric tons; in recent years there has also been a small, but growing, export of ground-nut oil, which reached 2,073 metric tons in 1936.

French West Africa now accounts for some 30% of the world exports of ground nuts, and other African territories (excluding Egypt[1]), mainly the British possessions, account for a further 22%.

The following table (84) shows the exports of the various colonies of the Federation. It will be seen that the Ivory Coast is second, and French Guinea third in importance after Senegal.

---

[1] *League of Nations Economic Intelligence Service: International Trade in Certain Raw Materials and Foodstuffs*, 1936, p. 90. The above percentages refer to the position in 1935.

TABLE 84.—*French West Africa.   Exports (Special),*[1] *1933–36.*

	1933.		1934.		1935.		1936.	
	Metric Tons.	Value in Thousand Francs.	Metric Tons.	Value in Thousand Francs.	Metric Tons.	Value in Thousand Francs.	Metric Tons.	Value in Thousand Francs.
Senegal and Sudan	469,945	238,126	616,967	299,894	464,873	400,922	721,658	503,720
French Guinea .	36,597	55,060	42,061	64,549	49,363	78,696	65,383	100,130
Ivory Coast .	106,512	117,932	119,373	116,704	138,319	138,111	168,505	182,347
Dahomey .	49,551	27,241	82,686	33,907	95,029	56,364	117,060	90,335
Niger Colony	48,437	16,035	47,377	17,335	59,208	23,359	79,933	49,220
Mauritania .	358	1,094	2,470	967	438	811	543	1,044
Totals . ˙ .	711,400	455,488	910,934	533,356	807,230	698,263	1,153,082	926,846

The most important exports, apart from ground nuts, are palm kernels and palm oil, cocoa, timber and, in recent years, gold. The percentages which these form of the total domestic exports are shown in Table 85.

The palm abounds in the coastal regions of French Guinea, the Ivory Coast and Dahomey.   The Ivory Coast accounts for almost the whole of the coffee exports of the Federation; the cultivation of coffee has been considerably extended in recent years, exports from the Ivory Coast amounted to 6,485 metric tons in 1936; the Colony also supplies almost the whole of the cocoa exports of the Federation; exports of cocoa from the Ivory Coast amounted to 49,766 metric tons in 1936; it is also the only exporter of ebony-wood of which its exports were 30,311 metric tons in 1936.

Exports of bananas have risen very much, owing to the encouragement given to the industry by the Government; they are produced mainly in French Guinea, and latterly also in the Ivory Coast.   In 1927, exports from the Federation were only 3,000 metric tons;   by 1936, they had reached 51,650 metric tons.

The other exports of French West Africa include shea kernels, shea oil and butter, kapok, sisal, orange essence, cattle, sheep, goats and gum arabic.   The export of rubber, very important before modern economic development took the place of mere

[1] Extracted from *D.O.T. Reports* and *Bulletin Mensuel de l'Agence Économique de l'A.O.F.*

TABLE 85.—*French West Africa. Trade Statistics(a) and Principal Products and Proportion per cent. of Total Special Exports, 1913–36 (Francs millions).*

Year.	Imports. Special.	Exports. Special.	Exports. Ground Nuts.	Percentage to Total Exports.	Palm Kernels and Palm Oil Exports.	Percentage to Total Exports.	Cocoa Exports.	Percentage to Total Exports.	Mahogany and other Timbers Exported.	Percentage to Total Exports.	Baranas Exported.	Coffee Exported.
1913	152(b)	126(b)	...	...	...	...	...	...	...	...	...	...
1920	210(b)	160(b)	...	...	...	...	...	...	...	...	...	...
1924	764(b)	654(b)	...	...	...	...	...	...	...	...	...	...
1927	...	...	630	...	188	...	59	...	115	...	9	2
1928	1,427(b)	1,154(b)	608	52·69	154	13·34	106	9·19	87	7·54	4	2
1929	1,326(b)	1,167(b)	553	47·39(b)	162	13·88(b)	98	8·40(b)	69	5·91(b)	6(b)	4(b)
1930	1,386(b)	1,098(b)	506	46·08	152	13·84	106	9·65	83	7·56	9	4
1931	708(b)	651	309	47·47	80	12·29	65	9·98	37	5·68	12	4
1932	553	446	169	37·89	53	11·88	73	16·37	20	4·48	17	6
1933	586	455	191	41·98	30	6·59	60	13·19	14	3·08	20	9
1934	546	543	264	43·62	32	5·89	59	10·87	17	3·13	25	14
1935	661	698	372	53·30	56	8·02	57	8·17	16	2·29	26	26
1936	903(b)	927(b)	491	52·96	92	9·92	72	7·76	15	1·61	41	34

(a) Extracted from *D.O.T. Reports on French West Africa,* 1926–36, and from *Year Books of Compared Colonial Documentation,* 1933–35.
(b) Estimated

exploitation, has declined to negligible proportions; the 1936 exports were only 574 metric tons.

A large part of the construction of French West African public works and railways has been financed by loans raised from 1903 onwards. The first of the four loans, all of which are guaranteed by the State, was issued in July, 1903, the amount being 65 million Francs, a 100 million loan followed in 1907, while 14 million Francs were raised in 1910. These loans bear 3% interest, and provision was made for a sinking fund. In 1913 arrangements were concluded for the fourth loan, the amount being 167 million Francs, of which 25 millions were raised in December of that year, bearing $3\frac{1}{2}\%$ interest, and a sinking fund was provided for. The next instalment, however, was not issued until after the Great War, when 25 millions were raised in 1920, and a similar sum in 1922, the rates of interest being $5\frac{1}{2}\%$. Two years later a further instalment of 50 million Francs was issued, but the rate had increased to $6\frac{1}{2}\%$. The rising rate of interest discouraged the Government from seeking the balance, and it was decided to wait until the period of dear money had run its course.

From 1903–24, therefore, the funds raised by these loans amounted to only 304 million Francs, of which 100 millions were raised during and after 1920.[1] It is interesting to note that, in the six years from 1923–28, no less than 613 million Francs were forthcoming for public works and public services from the local resources of the Federation.

In 1931 authority was given to the Federation to contract a loan of 1,570 million Francs (as West Africa's portion of the Great French Colonial Loan), and a further 120 million Francs for sanitary measures were also authorized. The loan powers of the Federation were again increased by 60 million Francs, for various purposes, in 1932.

The programme of public works and improvement schemes under these loans was estimated to cost 2,073 million Francs, of which it was intended that 503 million Francs should be borne by the Budgets of the Federation.

[1] Some of the loans authorized before the War do not appear to have been raised yet.

The loans authorized were revised again in July, 1936, and the total amount brought up to 1,837 millions (apart from the amounts to be financed by the local budgets).

Of the loans authorized since 1924, Table 86 shows the amounts actually spent to the end of 1934, the estimated expenditure for 1935, the provisional expenditure for 1936, and the estimated total to the end of 1936; the table also distinguishes between the various purposes of the expenditure.

The revenue and expenditure of the General Budget of the Federation (which bears the expenses of the General Government) from 1913 to 1936 are shown in Table 87.

For 1935 and 1936, the debt charges borne by the General Budget are estimated to amount to 63[1] and 68[1] million Francs respectively.

The service of the debt, which has been steadily rising in recent years, now amounts to approximately 40% of the ordinary expenditure included under the General Budget. The population of French West Africa is thus bearing a considerable burden of debt; in this connection it must be remembered that the public works' programme is not only financed out of the General Loan Funds, but also from the local Budgets of the Colonies, which involve a considerable contribution from revenue for expenditure on constructional activities. Unfortunately, a comparison with the position in British Territories is not possible owing to the entirely different manner in which the French accounts are drawn up.

Table 88 gives particulars of the General and Local Budgets for recent years.[2]

Notwithstanding the very large plans for future development,

---

[1] Includes approximately 5·6 million francs in 1935 and 5·7 million francs in 1936, consisting of:

" Frais accessoires des emprunts."

" Rachat d'entreprises d'intéret local."

Cf. p. 409, Year Book of Compared Colonial Documentation, 1936, from which the above figures are extracted.

[2] The finances of the Circumscription of Dakar, of the Port of Dakar, and of the railways within the Federation, are regulated by means of supplementary budgets. From the 1st of January, 1936, the name "Railways' Budget" has been changed to "Transports' Budget of French West Africa ', and has as its charge not only all the railways, but also motor and wharf transport services in Dahomey, the Cotonou Wharf, the Wharfs of the Ivory Coast and the Port of Conakry. The local budgets are those of the individual Colonies, maintained by local taxes.

TABLE 86.—*French West Africa. Loans Authorized and Actual Loan Expenditure (Francs).*

Programme prévu par la loi d'emprunt du 22 février 1931 et remainée par celle du 7 juillet 1936.	Dotations légales.	Dépenses constatées fin 1934.	Dépenses présumées des 1935.	Prévisions de 1936.	Total général des dépenses présumées.
Dépenses générales	...	3,172,320·15	1,322,000	1,555,000	6,049,320·15
Ports et rivières	447,000,000	136,335,945·01	30,135,000	34,246,000	200,716,945·01
Voies ferrées	626,000,000	158,956,898·81	28,342,000	26,739,000	214,037,898·81
Routes et ponts, outillage routier	83,000,000	8,502,706·05	4,455,000	5,720,000	18,677,706·05
Routes aériennes	10,000,000	2,813,935·38	3,635,000	4,231,000	10,679,935·38
Enseignement et particulièrement enseign. agricole	12,000,000	23,773·26	...	3,225,000	3,248,773·26
Batiments militaires	10,000,000	113,763·46	110,000	1,040,000	1,263,763·46
Irrigations du Niger, travaux et études	300,000,000	73,187,465·88	25,000,000	19,850,000	118,037,465·88
Amenagement de la production	227,000,000	1,283,575·50	8,812,000	18,073,000	28,168,575·50
Protection sanitaire démographique	120,000,000	39,719,709·72	10,938,000	12,730,000	63,387,709·72
Totaux	1,837,000,000	424,110,093·22	112,749,000	127,409,000	664,268,093·22

TABLE 87.—*French West Africa. Budget General*, 1913–36 [1]
(*million Francs*).

Year.	Recouvrements.	Paiements.
1913	34·3	31·6
1914	26·6	26·6
1915	22·7	22·7
1916	25·6	22·5
1917	25·1	22·1
1918	32·0	25·9
1919	42·3	30·1
1920	62·6	42·1
1921	64·7	60·6
1922	76·5	66·4
1923	94·0	75·4
1924	126·7	83·8
1925	159·7	100·5
1926	242·8	176·1
1927	250·8	194·3
1928	297·1	210·6
1929	282·2	235·3
1930	313·2	282·5
1931	252·4	311·2
1932	291·1	285·3
1933	212·9	200·0
1934 (a)	233·0	223·3
1935 (a)	163·8	163·8
1936 (a)	189·5	189·5

(a) These are "prévisions", which usually do *not* approximate at all closely to actual figures.

and the loans authorized to finance them, it is significant that, so far, the actual capital invested in the territory by the Government has been small. (See Table 85.)

Of the loans authorized to date, the amount raised up to the end of 1934 was 814 million Francs, the larger part of which was raised after the War in depreciated Francs.

[1] Extracted from the *Year Books of Compared Colonial Documentation, 1934–6.* The amounts are in actual Francs; it is clear that no allowance has been made for the changing value of the Franc.

TABLE 88.—*French West Africa. Revenue and Expenditure of the Ordinary Sections of the Various Budgets of the Federation,* 1932–35.(a)

REVENUE.

	1932.	1933.	1934.	1935.
		(Million Francs.)		
General Budget	131·9	150·9	153·3	177·1
Supplementary Budgets:				
Railways	75·6	64·9	97·1	103·7
Port of Dakar	5·4	5·3	5·5	6·1
Circn. of Dakar	37·9	35·9	34·9	39·2
Local Budgets:				
Senegal and Supplementary Medical Services	86·2	105·1	87·6	82·6
Mauritania	16·87	20·2	13·2	12·5
French Sudan	65·3	63·7	63·4	64·2
French Guinea	47·6	47·8	46·6	44·6
Ivory Coast	61·5	73·9	77·4	81·4
Dahomey	36·3	29·3	35·1	31·7
Upper Volta(b)	27·8	...	...	...
Niger	23·4	22·9	24·7	24·5
Totals	615·7	619·9	638·8	667·6

EXPENDITURE.

	1932.	1933.	1934.	1935.
		(Million Francs.)		
General Budget	126·1	138·0	143·6	140·2
Supplementary Budgets:				
Railways	80·8	71·4	81·4	85·0
Port of Dakar	5·4	4·9	4·8	5·1
Circn. of Dakar	37·9	35·9	34·9	37·8
Local Budgets:				
Senegal and Supplementary Medical Services	104·1	106·8	89·7	82·4
Mauritania	17·5	17·4	14·6	12·5
French Sudan	59·9	63·6	61·2	63·8
French Guinea	46·0	43·2	43·4	43·1
Ivory Coast	57·5	68·3	68·9	72·6
Dahomey	45·8	39·3	37·6	31·2
Upper Volta	31·4	...	...	...
Niger	26·0	26·0	23·3	24·3
Totals	638·4	614·8	603·4	598·0

(a) These figures have been extracted from the *Department of Overseas Trade Report on Economic and Commercial Conditions in French West Africa,* 1933–36, No. 664 (London, 1937); pp. 5 and 6. The figures do not agree with those in Table 86, and have clearly been tabulated on a different basis. They, however, illustrate the relation between the General and Supplementary Budgets. The figures for 1935 are provisional.
(b) After 1932 included in other Provinces.

The recent depression struck the finances of the territory a severe blow, and the financial difficulties of the mother country make it likely that the execution of the large projects envisaged will take a long time. At first sight, the sums which it is proposed to invest (the loans will be raised over a period of years) do not appear large if the enormous extent of the territory is taken into account, but, when the expenditure is considered in the light of the present stage of economic development of the territory, it is seen to involve a considerable debt burden on the economy. The weight of this burden is increased because a considerable part of the capital expenditure has been incurred for non-economic purposes, such as military requirements and communications built for strategic purposes.

Private capital investments in a country like French West Africa have, of necessity, been restricted mainly to commercial investments, and, as has been shown in Summary Table 48, the total capital invested to date has been small. French West Africa accounts for only 2·49% of the total capital invested in Africa as compared to 9·56%, the corresponding figure for the British West African Colonies.

As in other African territories, more rapid development than that in the past will depend on the possibility of capital's being made available at low or even nominal rates of interest. It does not seem likely that France will be able to afford much special assistance in this direction, so that development will probably be restricted to the borrowing capacity of the territory, at ruling rates of interest, and this is not likely to increase rapidly.

That French West Africa has enormous resources is undoubted, but the above considerations indicate clearly the many difficulties which will have to be overcome in furthering the economic progress of this immense and sparsely populated region.

XIX

FRENCH EQUATORIAL AFRICA.

Whereas the domestic exports of French West Africa were valued at nearly £10,000,000 in 1935, and were, therefore, roughly equal to those of the Belgian Congo, the domestic exports of French Equatorial Africa were still only £2·3 millions—less than those of South-West Africa. As late as 1924 the total trade of French Equatorial Africa was less than two-thirds of that of the Cameroons, and even smaller than that of Togo. Since then, however, as was shown in Tables 43–47, the trade of Equatorial Africa has grown very much more rapidly than that of either Togo or the Cameroons.

The historical and geographical factors which retarded the development of French Equatorial Africa, and caused it to be regarded as the Cinderella of the French Empire, have been referred to previously; the present economic situation remains to be examined.

French Equatorial Africa resolves itself into a huge coastal forest, an intermediate series of agricultural plateaux, and a pastoral steppe-zone, gradually merging into the northern desert. It has been estimated that the desertic areas cover a minimum of 800 square kilometres. This configuration has determined the direction of the country's development. "The Forest abutted on the sea and offered the easiest riches; therefore, the whole of the Colony's economic history has been limited to this belt. The agricultural zone was feebly populated, shut off from the Coast, and unhealthy; therefore, it was left alone. The innermost region, the pastoral-steppe, was left to native development." For all effective economic purposes the French Congo was limited to the forest in the two coastal provinces[1]; but, even here, development was seriously handicapped owing to the uneven distribution of the population. The following table shows, for each colony, the estimated population, and its density, on the basis of the 1926 Census. The figures for the Cameroons have been added, and illustrate the relatively more favourable situation in this territory. In 1926 the number of Europeans in French Equatorial Africa numbered approximately 2,500.

After the decline of rubber exports which, with ivory, accounted for the bulk of the exports at the beginning of the century and during the period of despoliation, the French turned to the exploitation of the timber and palm resources.

The French Congo is the most richly wooded of all the French

[1] Roberts, *ibid.*, pp. 344/5.

Colonies.	Superficies Habitées. (kms. sq.)	Population.	Densité Moyenne.
Gabon	260,000 .	465,000 .	1·79
Moyen Congo . .	410,000 .	770,000 .	1·87
Oubangui Chari .	442,000 .	1,100,000 .	2·48
Tchad	413,000 .	1,100,000 .	2·42
A.E.F. totale . . .	1,525,000 .	3,435,000 .	2·19
Cameroun . . .	390,000 .	1,950,000 .	5·0
Total General . .	1,915,000 .	5,385,000 .	2·76

Colonies. In 1935 timber exports amounted to nearly 35,000 tons, valued at 103 million Francs, *i. e.* nearly 60% of the domestic exports of the country. The export of palm products has declined in importance in recent years owing to the large fall in prices. Palm kernel and palm oil exports were valued at some 12 million Francs in 1925, as compared with 8·1 million Francs in 1935; the quantity exported amounted to approximately 18,000 metric tons in 1936. There is also a large number of minor exports, such as cotton seed, gold, coffee, cocoa, etc., but none in themselves assume noteworthy proportions. The lack of communications and shortage of labour have proved even greater obstacles to development in French Equatorial than in French West Africa. As late as 1924 the Colony did not possess a single kilometre of railway beyond a tiny mineral line to the Mindouli copper mine.

The outlet for the country's produce depended on the Matadi-Leopoldville line built by the Belgians in 1898, and until the Congo Ocean Railway was constructed in the French Congo, the whole economic history of the territory was bound up with the Belgian Railway.[1]

The construction of the Congo Ocean-Pointe Noire Railway was an immense engineering achievement, and proved extremely costly. This accounts for the fact that, up to the end of 1933, a

[1] The trouble was that goods could come down by water only as far as Brazzaville, which is 400 kilometres inland. At that point the river communicates with the sea only by a series of cascades or rapids which are perfectly useless for purposes of commerce. The interior of the Congo would have been worthless if Belgium had closed its line. Everything was dominated by the economic bottleneck of Stanley Pool. The French, therefore, concentrated on securing a railway of their own, and thus attaining economic independence, and they invested an enormous amount of capital in doing so.

TABLE 89.—*Revenue and Expenditure of French Equatorial Africa, Togo and Cameroons, 1922–34.*

REVENUE. (Million Francs.)

Year.	French Equatorial Africa.	French Togo.(a)	French Cameroons.
1922	...	4·3	...
1923	...	13·5	...
1924	...	21·3	44·1
1925	...	33·6	61·9
1926	...	37·9	116·5
1927	...	44·6	125·2
1928	...	49·7	120·9
1929	...	46·9	122·8
1930	83·2	48·8	131·2
1931	79·9	29·1	141·5
1932	74·9	24·4	86·7
1933	97·2	24·0	80·2
1934	98·4	...	66·7

EXPENDITURE. (Million Francs.)

Year.	French Equatorial Africa.	French Togo.(a)	French Cameroons.
1922	...	3·5	...
1923	...	5·0	...
1924	...	8·5	35·5
1925	...	16·5	46·1
1926	...	26·2	98·1
1927	...	35·0	113·7
1928	...	47·0	98·1
1929	...	43·5	99·5
1930	83·2	44·7	124·9
1931	79·6	30·8	137·9
1932	74·0	28·3	82·3
1933	97·2	31·0	75·4
1934	98·4	...	63·9

(a) Excluding the "Budget annexe de la santé publique".

greater loan expenditure had been incurred in French Equatorial than in French West Africa.

Up to 1933, 1,513 million Francs of loans had been authorized, most of them after 1926. Of this sum, it was intended that 1,360 million Francs should be spent on the Railway and the Pointe Noire Port. Up to the end of 1933 approximately 867 million Francs had been spent, of which about 796 million Francs represented the expenditure on the Railway and Port.[1]

TABLE 90.—*French Equatorial Africa. Trade Statistics,*[2] *1913–36 (Francs millions).*

Year.	Imports. (Special)	Exports. (Special)	Timber Exports.	% of Total Exports.(a)	Palm Kernels and Palm Oil Exports.	Cotton Exports.	Gold Exports.
1913	21(b)	37(a)	...	...	...	...	...
1920	17(b)	31(a)	...	...	...	...	...
1924	47(b)	44(a)	...	...	...	...	...
1927	172(b)	137(a)	...	...	...	...	...
1928	228(b)	151(a)	...	...	...	...	...
1929	277(b)	152(a)	...	...	...	...	...
1930	339(b)	198(a)	...	...	...	...	...
1931	272	124	84	67·74	6	8	4
1932	222	120	82	68·33	8	9	7
1933	179	141	92	65·25	11	13	11
1934	161	168	107	63·69	8	24	13
1935	169	174	103	59·20	8	27	12
1936	180	160	...	...	...	...	...

(a) Estimated.

The service of the debt in 1934 amounted to approximately 80 million Francs, which was about 81% of the ordinary expenditure under the General Budget. This fact indicates the heavy burden which the construction of the railway, though it was thought necessary for politico-economic reasons, has involved. Table 89 shows the revenue and expenditure of the territory in recent years; the relevant statistics for Togo and the Cameroons have been added for comparative purposes. Table 90 gives the trade statistics, and shows the proportion per cent. of the main products exported to the total domestic exports.

[1] These figures have been extracted from the *Report of the Gouvernement Général de l'Afrique Equatoriale Française: Budget Spéciale Annexe Sur Fonds d'Emprunt, 1934.* Rapport du Sénat No. 610 (Annexe 15). 1934. Session Extraordinaire (p. 65). The figures were tabulated by Dr. Charlotte Leubuscher.

[2] Extracted from *Year Books of Compared Colonial Documentation,* 1933–1935.

XX

CAMEROON UNDER FRENCH MANDATE.

France obtained the mandate over the largest part of the territory previously owned by Germany.[1] The population of the French mandate consists of approximately 2·2 million natives and some 2,000 Europeans, and the area of the territory is roughly 430,000 sq. kilometres, as compared with the British Mandate, which covers an area of 89,000 sq. kilometres. The acquisition of this land was greatly desired by France, because it commands the communications with the western interior. "It is a rich, though relatively sparsely peopled, colony" reported the Fourneau Mission in 1918, *"and is the key of our West Africa"*.[2]

It is essentially an agricultural country, more suitable for plantation purposes than the Congo, and better able to stand alone. Its forest zone is the continuation of the coastal belt of the French Congo ; this gives way to a transition belt of savannahs and plateaux, which opens onto the real heart of the country, the rich volcanic lands rising to Mount Cameroon.

As is shown in Table 91, the exports of the territory increased steadily from 1923–9, but thereafter, as in other West African territories, its development was seriously affected by the drastic fall in world prices for its products.[3] It is also significant that the

[1] Comparison between the progress of the French Mandate and the position under German rule is not possible because the area of the territory involved is not the same. It is interesting to note, however, that, in 1913/14, Kamerun was still receiving an annual subsidy of about £400,000 from the German Imperial Treasury. Its exports were valued at about £1,200,000, and imports at £1,700,000. It possessed 193 miles of railway, and there were 266 commercial undertakings, two oil palm plantations, one tobacco plantation and 75 general plantations.

[2] Quoted by Roberts, *ibid.*, i, p. 371.

[3] The report of the French Government to the League of Nations for the year 1934 contains the following interesting indices showing the fall in values, based on the quantities exported in 1934, of the four main products of the territory:

Products.	1930.	1931.	1932.	1933.	1934.
			1934 = 100.		
Amandes de palme	68	48	40	32	20
Huile de palme .	81	49	44	33	25
Cacao .	57	38	27	25	21
Arachides	76	62	53	51	42
Total .	70	47	38	31	22

TABLE 91.—*Cameroons under French Mandate. Trade Statistics,*
1932–36[1] *(Francs millions).*

	Togo.					Cameroon.			
Year.	Imports (General).	Exports (General).	Palm Kernels and Palm Oil Exports.	Cocoa Exports.	Year.	Imports (Special).	Exports (Special).	Palm Kernels and Palm Oil Exports.	Cocoa Exports.
1923	...	...	...	...	1923	54	42	...	...
1924	...	...	...	...	1924	24	67	...	...
1925	...	...	...	...	1925	126	113	...	...
1926	...	...	...	...	1926	192	155	...	...
1927	...	...	...	...	1927	195	163	...	...
1928	...	...	...	...	1928	206	159	...	...
1929	192	83	...	...	1929	194	170	...	...
1930	101	83	...	...	1930	173	137	...	...
1931	70	50	...	...	1931	104	82	...	...
1932	65	29	7	11	1932	73	83	...	...
1933	42	28	4	14	1933	75	78	32	23
1934	32	30	6	8	1934	59	73	19	23
1935	31	35	8	14	1935	89	98	...	...
1936	46	44	...	...	1936	126	168	...	...

total tonnage of its exports rose from some 48,000,000 metric tons
in 1923 to some 119,000,000 metric tons in 1929; by 1931 the
total tonnage exported had fallen by roughly 25% to just under
90,000,000 metric tons, but the total value of these exports had
dropped by over 50% from 170,000,000 Francs in 1929 to
82,000,000 Francs in 1931. Thereafter, the value of the exports
continued to show a small decline, although the tonnage exported
rose ; in 1934 it stood at 124,000,000 metric tons, while the value
of the exports was 72,000,000 Francs.

Cocoa, palm kernels and palm oil account for about 58% of
the total domestic exports of the territory. The value of palm
kernels and palm oil exported amounted to nearly 19 million
Francs in 1934, and the value of cocoa exports to some 22·6
million Francs. The next most important export was timber,
followed by ground nuts. The other exports consist of a considerable range of products, including coffee, tobacco, tin,
bananas and small quantities of rubber, cotton and sesame.

The public debt charges at the end of 1934 amounted to
1·8 million Francs per annum, *i. e.* only 3% of the ordinary
expenditure.

The amounts spent from loan funds have not been large. The

[1] Extracted from 1934 Report of the French Government to the League.

portion of the Colonial Loan authorized for the Cameroons was 57,000,000 Frs. Of this sum 30·6 million Francs had been borrowed up to 1934. Of the 57 million, some 24 million Francs was for alterations to the railway system, roads and harbours. Statistics of the Revenue and Expenditure of the territory for recent years are given in Table 89,[1] from which the effects of the depression are clearly discernible.

It should be noted that the trade figures relating to the British portion of the Cameroons Mandate are included in Nigeria, and that the statistics for the French Mandate are not very reliable, because they appear to include some trade which is already counted in the trade of Nigeria.

XXI
TOGO.

The area of the French Mandate over Togo covers 53,000 sq. kilometres, and its population numbers approximately 764,000. The main products of the territory are palm kernels, palm oil, cocoa, cotton seed and copra; the trade statistics for recent years are given in Table 91. It will be seen that development was seriously affected by the depression.

A larger amount of the French Colonial Loan has been authorized for Togo than for the Cameroons. In 1931 it was estimated that a sum of 118 million Francs was to be spent on public works.

The loans raised from 1931–4 amount to 75·7 million Francs. The amount spent on railway construction for the same period was 112·9 million Francs, of which about 65 million Francs was from loan funds, up to 1933, and the balance from other sources. The total debt outstanding at the end of 1934 was 75·7 million Francs, and the annual debt charge amounted to 3·5 million Francs, equivalent to 9% of the total expenditure in 1933.

XXII
ANGLO-EGYPTIAN-SUDAN.

The economic development of the Anglo-Egyptian Sudan presents certain features of particular interest. Its economic progress has been based, to a greater extent than that of

[1] p. 350 *supra.*

any other territory, on planned public investment; and it is
the only African dependency in which large irrigation works, of
the kind which have been so much discussed, but not far advanced,
in the French Sudan, have been successfully carried out. Cotton
has been installed as king of the economic development of the
Sudan, but its rule rests also on the concomitant expansion of
food production. The most significant feature in the economy of
the Sudan is the large capital investment which has been necessary to bring it about. It is doubtful whether that investment
would have been undertaken without the spur of Imperial considerations, which, owing to the fear of a shortage of cotton for
Great Britain from other sources, led to the adoption of vast
irrigation projects in this country. The public listed capital is
over 83% of the total capital invested in the territory, and most
of it has been spent on railways and irrigation.

The public debt of the territory was nearly £E 15,000,000[1] at
the end of 1935, and this involves an annual debt charge of no less
than £E 951,756[1] from 1933 to 1938, and will involve a charge of
about a million pounds in 1944.

This debt burden is very large in relation to the exports of the
territory which, at the end of 1935, amounted to £E 4·6 millions.
In 1931 the exports had fallen to £E 1·8 millions, as compared
with the highest point in 1929, when they reached £E 6·7
millions. It is obvious from Table 92, which shows the trade
statistics of the Anglo-Egyptian Sudan, what a serious problem
the debt charges present in a territory which shows such large
fluctuations in the value of its exports. In 1935, as shown in Table
93, which portrays the development of the finances of the country,
the revenue (including only the net revenue from the railways)
amounted to some £E 4 millions, but this includes an annual
subsidy of £E 750,000 from the Egyptian Government. Without
that subsidy, the Sudan would not be in a position to meet the

---

[1] These figures are quoted from *The Anglo-Egyptian Sudan* (London: Faber & Faber,
1934) by Sir Harold Macmichael, who was a member of the Governor-General's
Council, and presided over the Special Committee which investigated the financial
position of the Sudan at the end of 1931 in order to examine ways and means to bring
about retrenchment, and to reduce expenditure, owing to the depression and the
serious failure of the cotton crop. It is noteworthy that from 1930 to 1933 a reduction
in expenditure of no less than 30% was achieved—an indication of the enormous
fluctuations to which the Sudan is subject.

TABLE 92.—*Anglo-Egyptian Sudan. Trade Statistics, 1900–36, and Proportion per cent. of Annual Exports of Selected Commodities to Annual Value of all Domestic Produce Exported.(f)*

Year.(c)	Merchandise Imports.(a)	Exports.(b)		Cotton Exports.		Cotton Seed Exports.		Gum Arabic Exports.	
		Domestic Produce.	Re-exports.						
	£(000).	£(000).	£(000).	£(000).	%.	£(000).	%.	£(000).	%.
1900	...	...	...	...	...	...	...	...	...
1901	380	...	...	...	...	...	...	...	...
1902	764	407(d)	...	...	...	...	...	...	...
1903	769	408(d)	...	...	...	...	...	...	...
1904	1,128	403(d)	...	...	...	...	...	...	...
1905	1,431	338(d)	...	...	...	...	...	...	...
1906	1,253	336(d)	...	...	...	...	...	...	...
1907	1,646	461	50	45	9·8	7	1·5	159	34·5
1908	1,942	529	38	43	8·1	9	1·7	180	34·0
1909	1,822	691	63	40	5·8	9	1·3	206	29·8
1910	1,981	1,003	59	75	7·5	11	1·1	224	22·3
1911	2,333	1,413	77	200	14·2	32	2·3	447	31·6
1912	2,018	1,409	95	90	6·4	16	1·1	619	43·9
1913	2,165	1,216	96	156	12·8	22	1·8	381	31·3
1914	1,940	1,047	90	101	9·6	13	1·2	323	30·9
1915	1,749	1,619	134	243	15·0	34	2·1	321	19·8
1916	2,730	2,348	233	276	11·8	40	1·7	601	25·6
1917	3,182	3,581	245	579	16·2	47	1·3	764	21·3
1918	4,129	4,026	294	287	7·1	19	0·5	655	16·3
1919	4,931	2,812	296	370	13·2	27	1·0	563	20·3
1920	7,189	4,835	373	1,648	34·1	90	1·9	582	12·0
1921	5,059(e)	2,111	268	389	18·4	68	3·2	356	16·9
1922	4,362(e)	2,045	313	351	17·2	65	3·2	544	26·6
1923	4,789(e)	2,628	201	470	17·9	73	2·8	1,032	39·3
1924	5,579(e)	3,633	285	1,498	41·2	161	4·4	869	23·9

1925	5,577(e)	3,899	376	1,679	43·1	122	3·1	812	20·8
1926	5,717	5,001	322	2,919	58·4	263	5·3	866	17·3
1927	6,313	5,082	279	3,283	64·6	369	7·3	698	13·7
1928	6,628	5,778	318	3,698	64·0	409	7·1	743	12·9
1929	7,030	6,692	288	4,710	70·4	409	6·1	705	10·5
1930	6,325	5,079	299	3,129	61·6	211	4·2	1,006	19·8
1931	3,840	1,777	288	530	29·8	132	7·4	618	34·8
1932	3,133	3,894	372	2,129	54·9	292	7·5	473	12·1
1933	3,242	2,673	287	1,438	53·8	185	6·9	403	15·1
1934	4,046	3,947	274	2,118	53·7	116	2·9	507	12·8
1935	5,508	4,684	434	2,458	52·5	364	7·8	694	14·8
1936	5,483	5,724	850	3,443	60·2	329	5·7	661	11·5

(a) Excludes bullion and coin ; includes goods for re-export.
(b) Excludes bullion and coin to 1921, and excludes coin only thereafter.
(c) The statistics for the years prior to 1907 have been obtained from Macmichael: *The Anglo-Egyptian Sudan* (Faber & Faber, 1934), and are not strictly comparable with those for succeeding years.
(d) Total exports.
(e) These figures differ slightly in two separate editions of the *Statistical Abstracts*.
(f) Extracted from the *Statistical Abstracts for the British Empire*.

TABLE 93.—*Anglo-Egyptian Sudan. Finance*, 1900–36.

Year.(a)	Gross Revenue.(b) £(000).	Gross Expenditure.(e) £(000).	£E(000),(b) "Net"(c) Revenue.	£E(000), "Net" Expenditure.(d)	Customs Revenue. £(000).	Percentage of Customs to Total Revenue. £(000).	Public Debt.(f) £(000).
1900	157(a)	332(a)	…	…	…	…	…
1901	242(a)	407(a)	…	…	…	…	…
1902	270(a)	517(a)	…	…	…	…	…
1903	463(a)	616(a)	…	…	…	…	…
1904	579(a)	629(a)	…	…	…	…	…
1905	665(a)	682(a)	…	…	…	…	…
1906	818(a)	828	…	…	…	…	…
1907	948	986	…	…	90	9·5	…
1908	949	1,139	…	…	72	7·6	…
1909	1,008	1,129	…	…	66	6·5	…
1910	1,134	1,189	…	…	72	6·3	158
1911	1,269	1,320	…	…	103	8·1	633
1912	1,391	1,458	…	…	96	6·9	726
1913	1,609	1,572	…	…	192	11·9	744
1914	1,584	1,571	…	…	195	12·3	1,280
1915	1,534	1,502	…	…	179	11·7	1,287
1916	1,906	1,791	…	…	239	12·5	1,291
1917	2,253	1,951	…	…	226	10·0	1,286
1918	2,847	2,397	…	…	256	9·0	1,291
1919	3,071	2,791	…	…	337	11·0	4,145
1920	4,541	3,658	…	…	536	11·8	4,299
1921	4,175	4,002	…	…	500	12·0	7,180
1922	3,588	3,587	…	…	413	11·5	6,381
1923	3,863	3,479	…	…	435	11·3	9,630
1924	4,409	3,542	…	…	524	12·0	12,079

Year							
1925	4,415	4,488	3,345	2,854	561	12·7	13,473
1926	5,239	4,813(c)	4,144	3,768	569	10·9	13,473
1927	5,313	4,908(c)	4,178	3,798	595	11·2	15,783
1928	6,048	5,392(e)	4,680	4,079	687	11·4	15,783
1929	6,391	5,968(e)	4,835	4,464	748	11·7	15,692
1930	6,179	6,152(e)	4,694	4,694	681	11·0	15,569
1931	5,588	5,666(e)	4,232	4,399	467	8·8	15,410
1932	4,584	4,896(e)	3,653	3,854	395	8·6	15,242
1933	4,578	4,637(e)	3,632	3,622	401	9·4	15,021
1934	4,698	5,009(e)	3,775	3,749	504	10·7	14,787
1935	5,455	5,696(e)	4,098	3,993	623	11·4	14,543
1936	..	...	4,462	4,205	...	...	...

(a) The statistics for the years prior to 1907 have been obtained from Macmichael: *The Anglo-Egyptian Sudan* (Faber & Faber, 1934), and are not strictly comparable with those for succeeding years. They are exclusive of subsidy paid by Egypt and are in £ Egyptian.

(b) Revenue figures include contributions from the Egyptian Government.

(c) The word "Net" is used to show that the figures include only the *net* revenue and expenditure from Railways and Steamers, whereas the figures called "Gross revenue and expenditure" include the whole of the earnings and expenses of the Railways and Steamers. It is probable that the same applies to the receipts and expenditure for certain other Government undertakings.

(d) Including Military Expenditure and payments to Military Pensions Fund, also all Irrigation Expenditure, including allocations to special funds and reserves.

(e) Excludes expenditure on Sudan Defence Force in and subsequent to 1926.

(f) Excludes advances by Egypt for capital expenditure amounting to £3,484,000.

service of its debt. It will be seen that, if the Egyptian contribution is excluded, then the annual debt charges amounted to nearly 30% of the ordinary revenue in 1935.

The development of the Anglo-Egyptian Sudan is also of great interest, because it is based on the largest African experiment in peasant production with Government participation and assistance.

The large sum spent on this project—the irrigation of the Gezireh—might have been thought to excuse the expropriation of private property, but the irrigation scheme provided safeguards for native land rights, all claims being examined before any area was declared Government land. The Government took powers to acquire any native-owned land which it needed, on the basis of a forty years' lease at 2s. per acre—a price above the current rate. Natives could and did take up tenancies in the areas where they had freehold rights. As is well known, a private company, the Sudan Plantation Syndicate, was then given a concession of about 300,000 acres for ten years, later extended to twenty years, on the understanding that it would finance the settlement of peasant cultivators, and act as agricultural manager in return for a share in the cotton crop. The land rights remain with the Government and the freeholders; there is no permanent alienation to the Company. Cotton is grown as a crop, in a four-year rotation, and the acreage is divided into small holdings, let out so that they can be prepared for cultivation, in such a way as the Company determines. The Government arrange for the water supply from the Sennar Dam, and take 35% of the gross yield. The native provides the labour, and gets 40% of the gross yield, from which is deducted the actual cost of ginning and marketing; moreover, he has the benefit, free of taxes, of the other crops he may grow, and his rights in this direction have been a great inducement to him to work in wholehearted co-operation with the Company. The latter supervises the cultivation, ginning and marketing of the crop and takes 25%. It makes cash advances to the tenants, erects building and carries out minor canalization. The Kassala Cotton Company operates on a smaller scale in the same district on the same system.

As compensation to the owners of land along the river, who will be displaced by the lake to be formed south of the new Gebel

Aulia Dam, the Government have projected in the Gezireh another scheme slightly different from that of the Syndicate, in that the tenants will be encouraged to do their own ploughing. British inspectors supervise the district with the help of the native agriculturists and the sheiks, and not directly, as in the Syndicate's area, and the tenants are taught mixed farming, not merely cotton growing.

Similar schemes are in operation in the Gash Delta and Tokar, both of them flood districts, and, in the Southern Sudan, in the Nuba mountains, the Upper Nile Province and the Mongalla Province, where the people are more backward. Cotton in the latter districts is rain grown.[1]

The irrigation of the Gezireh was first studied, and the area surveyed, in 1904, under the newly formed Sudan Branch of the Egyptian Irrigation Service. After this a Government register of land ownership was taken, and the next important step, the construction of the railway, was carried out in 1909. Preliminary canalization and cotton-raising experiments were undertaken under Government auspices at Tayiba and Barakat in 1913 by the Sudan Plantations Limited, or the Sudan Plantation Syndicate as it was more commonly called, which was already interested in pump irrigation in the Zeidab Barber Province.

In 1913 the whole larger scheme of the Sennar Dam and the Gezireh irrigation was discussed and considered by Sir Murdoch Macdonald, and a Committee of Engineers in London. The profit-sharing arrangement, which later became the basis for the whole enterprise, was then decided upon. It was also settled at this time that an area of 300,000 acres should be canalized, 100,000 to be reserved for cotton, and that the dam should be located at Sennar on the Blue Nile, in order to supply irrigation by gravity instead of by pumps.

Work had been begun at the beginning of 1914, and the schedule of the Government of the Sudan Loan Act 1913, as amended in 1914, had divided the three million pounds which were to be raised as follows:

---

[1] The above details have for the most part been extracted from the description contained in the *Colonial Problem*, a report by a Study Group of members of the Royal Institute of International Affairs, Oxford University Press, 1937, pp. 160/1.

(1) Works for the purpose of irrigating the
Gezireh Plain £2,000,000
(2) Extension of Sudan railway system . . 800,000
(3) For irrigation works and contingencies . 200,000

Total . . £3,000,000

The scheme was, however, inevitably held up, except for experimental work, by the Great War, which also made it impossible to raise the loan during hostilities. By 1919, the enormous rise in the cost of materials and labour, and the need to increase the scope of the scheme to ensure its financial success, made it necessary to ask for additional guarantees. In August 1919, the British Treasury extended the scope of the Loan Act of 1913 from £3,000,000 to £6,000,000. This sum was also found to be inadequate. As a result of a further examination of the financial aspects of the scheme, the British Government felt justified in guaranteeing a further £3,500,000 under the Trade Facilities and Loans Act of 1922, and in increasing this figure again in 1924 to £7 millions under the corresponding Act of that year. The total guarantee was thus £13 million in all. The contract for the construction of the Sennar Dam was granted to a British Firm, S. Pearson & Son, in 1921. The Dam and the main irrigation canals were completed in the summer of 1925. The formal opening of the Dam on January 21st, 1926, might be said to have inaugurated a new era, and was probably the most important event in the history of the country since the recapture of Khartoum.

In 1918 the approximate areas under cotton covered 56,076 feddans, of which 13,282 were under artificial irrigation, and the balance rain land and flood land. In the season 1926/7 218,554 feddans were under cotton, of which 106,681 were artificially irrigated, and 47,131 were rain land and 30,453 flood land. In 1934/5 no less than 351,257 feddans were under cotton, of which 194,450 were under artificial irrigation, 96,916 were rain land and 57,891 were flood land.[1]

---

[1] The area under cotton in the Gezireh amounted to 175,183 feddans for the 1934/35 season, and that in the Tokar and Gash (Kassala) Deltas to 31,681 feddans and 28,210 feddans respectively.

The general results (the financial aspects are considered below) of the Gezireh undertaking appear to have been excellent, and to have established a prosperous and contented peasantry. The growers are under close supervision and have no voice in the disposal of their cotton, but they are, and feel themselves co-operators in a scheme, the benefits of which they fully realize. Their interests are partially safeguarded by the Government's being directly involved as a partner in the enterprise.

Mr. H. Martin Leake and others have argued that this type of triple partnership of the State, Landlord and Peasant, in the organization of tropical agriculture should be extended to other territories, particularly to Kenya.[1] At first sight, one is tempted to agree immediately with this suggestion, but it must be realized that the position in the Sudan presented certain special features. First, the most important factor of all, as already mentioned, was the fact that there was here a clear objective, and one not based only on economic considerations. Cotton was wanted at almost any price, and it is significant that the scheme was only seriously developed long after it had been planned, and at a time when it was thought that Empire cotton supplies had to be safeguarded. Secondly, it is clear that the project could not have been undertaken in any other way. The loans necessary were raised at very high rates of interest, and only Government could have assumed the responsibility which this involved. Thirdly, nothing else could have been done in the Sudan, while for the pacification of the country some development of this kind was absolutely essential. Private enterprise had not to be considered as a possible alternative.

In most other African territories vast schemes of this nature would conflict with other possible developments requiring labour supplies. This is not to say that, in particular regions, for example in the French Sudan, similar projects, given the necessary capital, might not prove highly beneficial, and that on a smaller scale the principles developed in the Sudan afford an important example of a type of economic organization which is likely to be found valuable in future.

[1] *Cf.* H. Martin Leake, *Land Tenure and Agricultural Production in the Tropics.* (Cambridge University Press, 1927.)

Yet, it is important to realize that the key to the situation lies in the fact that the welfare of the whole population of a large area is made to depend on one single industry. Moreover, in the case of cotton the product is subject, not only to enormous fluctuations in world prices, but also to the vagaries of nature. A project of this kind, therefore, requires the fatherly hand of a strong Government able to take upon itself full responsibility for the population should its plans fail, either owing to natural difficulties or owing to changes in world demand.

The extent to which the economic prosperity of the population of the Sudan depends on cotton is clearly shown in Table 92. In 1929 no less than 76·5% of the total domestic exports of the country consisted of cotton and cotton seed, and almost the whole of the balance of the exports was accounted for by gum arabic.

In 1935, however, the cotton and cotton seed exports had fallen to just over 60% of the total domestic exports, and those of

TABLE 94.—*Anglo-Egyptian Sudan.* *Quantities of Cotton and Cotton Seed Exported,* 1911–35.

Year.	Ginned Cotton. (Tons.)	Unginned Cotton. (Tons.)	Cotton Scarto. (Tons.)	Cotton Seed. (Tons.)
1911	3,044	2,181	65	7,105
1913	2,315	39	4	4,786
1914	1,711½	5	11	3,012
1917	4,168	83	36	7,672
1920	3,954	12	43	7,470
1921	5,023	60	203	9,291
1924	8,364	57	114	18,003
1927	28,846	39	264	57,847
1928	23,450	81	302	47,960
1929	30,456	62	176	59,800
1930	27,768	93	80	56,267
1931	9,005	60	116	47,637
1932	38,623	16	473	94,807
1933	24,395	4	222	51,068
1934	32,978	14	154	56,438
1935	37,704	4	428	90,196

gum arabic to about 15%, the balance being made up mainly by dura, sesame, dom-nuts and products, ghee, hides and skins, maize, ground nuts, salt, and gold.

The great increase in the quantity of cotton and cotton seed exported since 1911 is shown by the figures (Table 94) for selected years from 1911.[1] The failure of the crop in 1931 is particularly striking.

The finances of the country are, of course, greatly affected by the value of the cotton crop; for the season 1935/36 the estimated divisible proceeds from the Gezireh scheme amounted to £E 2,286,330, of which the estimated Government share amounted to approximately £E 874,000. The estimated divisible proceeds of the Kassala cotton scheme (Gash Board) amounted to £E 218,681, of which the estimated Government share was £E 48,110. Table 95 shows the estimated divisible proceeds and the nett Government share in each of these two schemes for recent years:

TABLE 95.—*Divisible Proceeds and Government Share in Gezireh Irrigation Scheme and Kassala Cotton Scheme*, 1929–30 *to* 1935–36.

| | Gezireh Irrigation Scheme. | | Kassala Cotton Scheme. | |
Season.	Total estimated divisible proceeds. £E(ooo).	Estimated Government shares in net proceeds. £E(ooo).	Total estimated net proceeds of cotton and cotton seed. £E(ooo).	Estimated Government shares in net proceeds. £E(ooo).
1929/30	881	336	...	...
1930/1	393	144	169	36
1931/2	2,103	820	80	16
1932/3	814	312	86	17
1933/4	993	379	206	45
1934/5	2,237	851	220	50
1935/6	2,286	873	219	48

The disastrous failure of the 1930/1 crop and the general fluctuations in the receipts from these irrigation schemes deserve special attention. Sir Harold Macmichael estimated that, by 1930, interest and sinking fund payments on capital loans for the

[1] Extracted from the *Annual Report of the Department of Economics of the Sudan Government*, 1935, No. XXIX.

Gezireh scheme alone had risen from £E 571,477 in 1926 to £E 729,009, and had then not yet reached their peak. It is, therefore, obvious how precariously balanced is the financial success of the scheme with the existing heavy debt burden.

If the loans had been raised at the low interest rates ruling in 1913, and construction carried out at the lower costs which were envisaged at the time the scheme was planned, it is clear that the results would now be much more favourable. This is a fact that must be taken into account in judging the present position. The Sudan was unfortunate in having to embark on this great project at an unfavourable time.

Another special feature of the finances of the country is the very large annual contribution to general revenue which has, for many years, been made by the Sudan Railways. The following figures show the extent to which the Government has benefited from this source in recent years:

Year.	Net Revenue from Railways and Steamers. £E(000).
1925	388
1926	402
1927	429
1928	399
1929	403
1930	506
1931	361
1932	512
1933	447
1934	606
1935	542
1936	498

The Sudan railways have achieved the most successful results of any railway system in Africa, apart from that of the Union, with which direct comparison is not possible. Their success has, in part, been due to the large population of the Sudan, numbering as it did over 5,760,000 in 1935, of which Europeans numbered less than 7,000.

This population is effectively enrolled in the modern economic activities of the country to a greater extent than in the case of most other indigenous African populations. Moreover, its income depends to an exceptional extent on trade, resulting from its great export monoculture on the one hand, and its imports of many essential necessities on the other.

A useful index of the rising income of the people of the Sudan is provided by the growth in refined sugar imports, which have grown from 13,221 tons in 1919 to 24,009 tons in 1935; the highest point reached was in 1930, when the imports were 31,250 tons.

There can be no doubt that the economic development of the Sudan in the twentieth century has been a remarkable achievement, and one which, in many respects, can be regarded as a model for other African countries.

XXIII

PORTUGUESE EAST AFRICA.

Some aspects of the capital investment in Portuguese Colonies have already been referred to, in particular the large proportion of the overseas investment which came from British sources, and the relatively small percentage which the capital invested in the Portuguese Colonies forms of the total investment in Africa from abroad. The districts of Manica and Sofala have been administered since 1892 by the Mozambique Company under a fifty-year charter. The economic importance of the Company's territory at present is mainly due to the rich hinterland served by the two main railway lines to Rhodesia and Nyasaland. British capital and enterprise have played an important part in the development of the districts of Manica and Sofala, which are mainly agricultural, concentrated on the southern banks of the Zambesi river and along the railways, and whose economic activities are based on a plantation economy. The area of the Company's territory is roughly 52,056 square miles, and it has a population of some 4,000 Europeans, 1,500 Indians, 2,000 half-castes and 344,000 natives. Of the Europeans resident in the country, about 800 are British subjects.

The remaining portion of Portuguese East Africa, with an area of about 235,700 square miles, is administered by the Government; it has a population of some 3,626,000 natives, 7,000 Indians and about 15,000 Europeans. The territory is commonly referred to as the Colony of Mozambique. Its northern area was, until 1929, administered by the Niassa Company, but, owing to the small success of the Company, the area was taken over by the Colony. The Company had been unable to provide sufficient new capital for development, and the state of inactivity into which the area had been allowed to fall resulted in the decision of the Government to take it over.

The economic development of the Colony of Mozambique has, in the past, suffered very considerably from neglect and from the disadvantages of the concession system. In recent years the Government has endeavoured to speed up the rate of development by public works and better administration, but its efforts suffered a setback owing to the world depression.

This is shown by the fact that, excluding Government stores and specie, the value of the Colony's exports in 1933 was approximately £968,000, compared with nearly double that figure in 1929. In 1934, the quantity of the Colony's exports at 189,485 tons was the highest on record, but their value at £1,014,000 was considerably less than in any year since 1929, excepting 1933. The development of the trade and finances of the Colony, and the trade in the Mozambique Company's territory, in recent years, is shown in Table 96.

A very important feature of the trade of both territories is the international transit traffic. Such traffic, through the port of Lourenço Marques, has increased considerably in recent years. In 1933, 382,109 tons valued at £6,746,792 passed through the port for the Transvaal, while 281,387 tons valued at £1,219,608 passed through it from the Transvaal. Table 96 also shows that the transit trade is of great importance in the case of the territory administered by the Mozambique Company. In fact, the imports for local consumption and the domestic exports of the territory are very small compared with its transit trade. Over 80% of the transit traffic is to and from the Rhodesias, whose exports of copper, asbestos, chrome, zinc and maize, combined with

TABLE 96.—*Portuguese East Africa, Mozambique Company and Colony. Trade Statistics,* 1926–35.(b)

In Gold Contos.

Year.	Imports.			Imports. Colony. Depreciated Escudos.	Domestic Exports.(a)			Domestic Exports. Colony. Depreciated Escudos.	Transit Trade.		Re-exports and Transhipments.		Colony.(b) Revenue in Libras.	Colony.(b) Expenditure in Libras.
	Mozambique Company.	Colony.	Total.		Mozambique Company	Colony.	Total.		Mozambique Company.	Colony.	Mozambique Company.	Colony.		
1926	4,500	9,658	14,158	207,968,563 $00	1,753	10,024	11,777	216,673,883 $00	35,985	61,897	6,131	7,123	1,732,458	1,552,849
1927	5,708	11,885	17,593	250,908,077 $00	2,295	11,530	13,825	243,399,359 $00	54,795	37,483	5,279	7,892	2,206,767	1,778,174
1928	6,336	13,308	19,644	290,824,095 $00	2,436	11,877	14,313	259,538,933 $00	56,024	36,564	7,280	8,534	2,350,077	2,194,511
1929	6,413	14,002	20,415	308,033,990 $00	2,565	11,336	13,901	249,381,374 $00	57,269	37,892	...	7,568	2,398,093	2,338,882
1930	6,717	15,956	22,673	351,032,770 $00	2,019	10,048	12,067	221,064,778 $00	67,641	31,334	...	6,806	2,485,921	2,382,701
1931	4,630	14,415	19,045	328,324,282 $00	1,466	7,485	8,951	170,494,796 $00	38,723	31,373	...	5,165	2,161,918	2,139,791
1932	2,523	9,790	12,313	235,845,257 $00	1,157	7,227	8,384	169,449,270 $00	32,517	...	...	...	2,014,736	2,206,182
1933	1,880	11,025	12,905	282,940,048 $00	1,504	6,660	8,164	161,335,272 $00	30,977	...	...	...	1,873,572	1,849,042
1934	1,888	9,941	11,829	247,799,126 $00	1,849	6,341	8,190	157,597,575 $00	34,035	...	...	...	2,267,691	1,844,948
1935	...	...	...	251,152,123 $00	...	7,916	...	196,307,164 $00	...	...	...	...	3,944,611	2,900,000
1936	...	...	...	...	...	...	...	...	...	...	...	...	...	...

(a) Apparently including specie.

(b) Extracted from D.O.T. Reports, and from Year Books of Compared Colonial Documentation; in addition, from figures supplied by official departments.

Nyasaland's exports of tobacco, tea and cotton, are particularly important. The districts of Quelimane and Mozambique continue to be the principal exporting areas. In 1933 they accounted for approximately 70% of the value of the Colony's domestic exports.

The Colony is, and for a considerable time will continue to be mainly dependent on its agricultural products. Its agricultural potentialities are considerable and varied, as regards both tropical and temperate products, but the full development of these is made difficult by the irregularity of the rainfall, especially in the southern part of the Colony, and by the fact that large areas are infested with tsetse fly and other pests. In addition, the Colony lacks capital resources for public works, and particularly for irrigation.

Agriculture is carried on in the Colony by natives, by European Colonists and by Companies, with national, foreign, or mixed capital. Generally speaking, the Companies under foreign or mixed control are chiefly interested in the cultivation of export crops and crops which require treatment by machinery; these comprise cocoanuts, sisal and sugar-cane, which together account for more than half of the area under cultivation in the Colony. Cotton, cocoanuts and ground nuts are grown by both natives and Europeans. In recent years the Government has been making considerable efforts, by supplying seed and free instruction, to bring about an improvement in native methods of production. The cultivation of ground nuts, sesame, millet, maize and rice is general throughout the Colony; other crops such as cocoanuts, sisal, tobacco, citrus and sugar-cane are cultivated only in certain areas.

The most important feature of the Colony's economy is the income it draws from its invisible exports, which are made up of freight and other charges on transit traffic to and from the Transvaal, and the earnings of the considerable labour force which the territory supplies to the Witwatersrand Gold Mines. The territory has always used the emigration of native workers to the Transvaal as a bargaining weapon for its share of the railway traffic to and from the Union. Native workers emigrate also to Southern Rhodesia. The numbers of Portuguese natives in the

Transvaal in 1934 were approximately 70,000, and those in Southern Rhodesia approximately 26,000. The Colony receives a considerable revenue from the direct taxation of these natives when they return from their contract labour. It has been realized for some time that this migration is detrimental to the further economic development of the territory's own resources, and the sociological factors involved in the question have, in recent years, also received some recognition.

Ground nuts, besides their local importance as a foodstuff, are the Colony's most important export. The area under cultivation is capable of large expansion as almost every part of the Colony is suited for their growth, and the crop is especially suited to native agriculture. Maize is also mainly grown by natives, and, before the depression, was an important article of export, but exports declined owing to the fall in world prices. Sugar-cane is cultivated in the river valleys and in the swampy country near Inhambane, and it is also one of the main exports from the territory of the Mozambique Company. The sugar exports from the latter were 36,278 tons in 1929, but fell to 14,816 tons in 1932, and have since recovered to 22,922 in 1935; allowing for cyclical fluctuations, the quantity of sugar exported from the Company's territory has not altered much in the last twenty years, but, in the Colony, there has been a steady rise in sugar production for export from 14,525 tons in 1923 to 51,035 tons in 1935, and the depression did not greatly affect the quantity exported.

Considerable efforts have been made to foster the production of cotton in the Colony, but the irregular rainfall and the insect pests have proved a great obstacle and, combined with the fall in world prices, caused many plantations to close down. Nevertheless, the tonnage of cotton exported has steadily risen from 1,124 tons in 1929 to 2,349 tons in 1935. The exports of cotton from the districts of Manica and Sofala have remained very small. Ground-nut exports from the Colony fell from 22,685 tons in 1929 to 13,423 tons in 1933, but again recovered to 30,345 tons in 1935. The export of maize from the Colony exceeded 25,000 tons in 1930, but fell to 3,436 tons in 1931, since when there has been no appreciable recovery. Sisal exports from the Colony have grown steadily from just over 5,000 tons in 1928 to 19,646 tons in 1935. The Colony exports a considerable number of other products, but none of them of appreciable importance in themselves.

XXIV

ANGOLA (PORTUGUESE WEST AFRICA).

Angola is the largest of the Portuguese Colonies, its area being about 494,000 sq. miles, and it has the largest white population, which now numbers about 58,000. The half-caste population is approximately 20,000 and the native population 3,000,000. It has a large tableland in the interior with a cool and pleasant climate.

The potential wealth of the Colony is considerable, and favours the cultivation of such products as coffee, sisal, sugar, palm oil, maize and cotton. The country has suffered from lack of capital and lack of settlers, and, like others, from the world economic crisis.

The importance of the export of diamonds has been referred to previously.[1] It is of interest to note that the diamond company at Angola has also assisted the territory by making a loan to it for development purposes. The amount advanced so far is approximately 57,000,000 Angolares.

Apart from its diamond industry, Angola is essentially an agricultural country. It produces both Arabica and Robusta coffee, and also maize; sugar is now an important crop, and sisal is being developed.

The trade and finance statistics of the Colony are unsatisfactory because they are revised from time to time, and different publications contain different figures. Approximate figures for recent years have been prepared from various sources, and are shown in Table 97. It will be seen that, after diamonds, the most important articles of export are maize, coffee and sugar. Dried fish is also an important export; but its value has dropped in recent years.

On the 31st December, 1936, the debt of Angola was given as amounting to approximately 967,356 Contos, that is, roughly £8,706,000. Early in 1936, the Government Council of Angola

---

[1] See p. 213 above.

TABLE 97.—Angola (Portuguese West Africa). Trade and Finance Statistics, and Proportion per cent. of Exports of Selected Commodities to General Exports, 1920–35. (a)

Year.	Imports. General. Contos.	Exports. General. Contos.	Coffee. Contos.	Percentage to General Exports.	Diamond Exports. Contos.	Percentage to General Exports.	Maize. Contos.	Percentage to General Exports.	Revenue. Contos.	Expenditure. Contos.
1920	24,387	19,181	...	...	...	...	...	...	...	...
1921	46,225	29,660	...	...	...	...	...	...	...	...
1922	88,653	111,394	...	...	...	...	...	...	...	...
1923	233,781	201,317	...	...	...	...	...	...	...	...
1924	333,098	275,194	...	...	...	...	...	...	...	...
1925	253,145	233,638	88,782	38·0	27,527	11·8	21,885	9·4	...	...
1926	233,917	200,041	57,847	28·9	30,926	15·5	23,092	11·5	...	...
1927	284,314	213,148	47,128	22·1	38,498	18·1	42,457	19·9	...	...
1928	269,817	272,373	61,790	22·7	53,423	19·6	50,011	18·4	...	...
1929	314,216	281,920	53,430	19·0	69,602	24·7	41,562	14·7	...	...
1930	240,544	233,941	36,094	15·4	74,640	31·9	38,754	16·6	...	...
1931	146,870	203,479	32,110	15·8	65,884	32·4	23,185	11·4	142,759	142,759
1932	191,346	199,877	47,891	24·0	37,062	18·5	34,313	17·2	142,960	142,960
1933	175,937	246,699	37,874	15·4	70,425	28·5	50,010	20·3	147,232	147,232
1934	166,994	236,444	40,800	17·3	63,784	27·0	49,575	21·0	147,975	147,989
1935	164,484	221,964	28,583	12·9	70,169	31·6	24,719	11·1	165,003	165,589

(a) Extracted from *Year Books of Colonial Documentation* and from *D.O.T. Reports.*

drew up a scheme for a development loan amounting to 200,000 Contos or about £1,800,000.

If the future economic progress of the territory is to be more rapid than that of the past, it will be necessary to attract immigrants, and also to incur much greater expenditure on public works and essential scientific and experimental services than has so far been possible.

SECTION III

AFRICAN RAILWAY FINANCE

The most important requisite for the penetration of Africa is the provision of transport and communications. It is, therefore, not surprising that, up to the present, the main direction of public overseas investment in Africa has been in the construction of railways, harbours, roads, telegraphs and the works connected therewith. Between 50% and 60% of the public listed capital invested from abroad in British territories has been spent on railways and harbours.

In Africa, railways were essential for strategic and administrative purposes, and it is quite impossible to draw a hard and fast line between railways built for economic and those constructed for other purposes.

Minerals were the magnet which drew most of the existing lines across the continent of Africa. It is probable that the main railways of South Africa, Rhodesia, Bechuanaland, Belgian Congo, Angola and Portuguese East Africa, which together now measure some 21,000 miles, i. e. roughly 66% of the total railway mileage (32,000 miles) in Africa[1] would not have been constructed without the traffic to and from the mining fields. Certainly the railway map of these territories would have developed quite differently but for the mineral discoveries.

The diamond discoveries in the Cape really inaugurated the era of railway construction. Previously there were only 58 miles of railway in the Cape Colony[2] and 5 miles in Natal. The only other railways in the Continent at that time were from Alexandria to Cairo and from Cairo to Ismailia. As late as 1872, there were no

---

[1] Africa here, as elsewhere in this study, refers to the territories listed on p. 2, Chapter I, unless otherwise stated.

[2] The Cape line was constructed by an English Company which received a Government guarantee of 6% per annum on a sum of £520,000. In 1862 private enterprise started on a small private line from Salt River to Wynberg without any guarantee or subsidy.

railways south of the Sahara, with the exception of 152 miles in the Cape and Natal.

Twenty-five years later, as a result of the mineral discoveries, there were 5,227 miles of railway in Southern Africa, of which 490 miles were in Portuguese East Africa, and 586 miles had been built in Bechuanaland as one of Rhodes's great African projects. In the other territories considered in this study, the British East Africa line of 400 miles was the most important. Senegal possessed 246 miles of railway, Angola 244, the Gold Coast 100, Lagos 100, Sierra Leone 32, and the Congo Free State 718, making a total of 1840. At the same date the railway mileage in Australia was over 13,000, in Canada over 17,500, and in India nearly 4,000.

Africa has not lent itself to the construction of railways by private enterprise. Most of them have had to be constructed by Government or with State assistance in the form of guarantees or subsidies. In the Belgian Congo, a large variety of expedients to attract capital had to be adopted; some of the lines, for example the Benguella railway, which it was intended would serve the mineral area of the Congo, were completed only owing to the initiative of British financiers. In other cases, the State had to sugar the financial pill by offering large mineral and land concessions.

Railways in other continents were built to serve flourishing urban or industrial areas, or to traverse relatively densely populated agricultural regions. Alternatively, they opened up new land, as in the United States and Canada, and soon attracted European settlers, whose activities provided the railway with traffic.

In Africa none of these attractions existed. The offer of the ownership of land as an inducement to railway companies was of limited value, because there was little likelihood of the land's being taken up by immigrants, or of its being rapidly developed by the sparse indigenous population and so ensuring sufficient traffic. In certain cases, the method of granting mineral and land concessions as an inducement to railway construction was found to be very wasteful. The concessions were often large, but, notwithstanding this, they really did not solve the basic problem, which was how to guarantee the railway companies a sufficient annual revenue to warrant the capital expenditure on construction. Indeed, mineral concessions often added to the difficulties of the concessionaires in that they had to find the capital both for the proposed railway and for the exploitation of the minerals which were to provide the traffic and the revenue. In the Belgian Congo, for example, the State in some cases was forced, not only to guarantee railway loans, or itself to become a shareholder in the proposed railway, but also to guarantee part of the capital of the mining companies floated by the concessionaires.

The difficulty once again was that the development of productive resources in these backward territories required long-term capital expenditure, which could not be made an attractive investment for private enterprise. After 1906, the French, German and Belgian Governments clearly realized this, and they endeavoured to reverse their previous policy of granting large concessions, as in many cases these had led merely to speculation, fraud, and the destruction of the indigenous resources of the areas under the control of the concessionaires. The Governments made every effort to regain control over the lands they had surrendered, and, as far as they could, to undertake the necessary long-term investment themselves. Germany was the most successful in this reversal of policy, and before 1914 had constructed nearly 3,400 miles of railway in her African Colonies (mainly for administrative and strategic purposes) at a cost of roughly £21,500,000. Belgium and France, owing to their smaller capital resources, and because the concessionaire policy had been carried far, were unable to shake off their entanglements as easily. Belgium, in particular, however, has now succeeded in establishing far-reaching measures of control over transport in the Congo.

The decision of the Government of the Cape Colony to construct and to retain the ownership of its railways was a wise one,[1] and

---

[1] Private enterprise alone could not have built the railways. The Cape and Natal, in constructing their railways, aimed at developing the traffic to the diamond and gold mines in order to levy toll on this traffic by customs duties and railway rates. A moment's consideration will show that this aim could not have sufficed to encourage private enterprise to build railways for hundreds of miles inland. Each line had to cross a series of mountain ranges, to negotiate steep gradients, to cover large tracts of

it is significant that, with the exception of those in Rhodesia and Nyasaland, all the railways in British African territories were constructed by, or on behalf of the Government concerned, and were owned and operated by it. Strategic and administrative factors were, of course, a powerful reason which led Governments to assume responsibility themselves. In fact, many lines in Africa were built because the establishment of civilized rule over vast areas would have been impossible without them. The Kenya and Uganda railway project can be partly ascribed to patriotic and philanthropic motives; but it was mainly undertaken for strategic reasons, and the Imperial Government expected to face an annual deficit for years to come, although, significantly, it has not yet been decided whether or not the territory itself shall, at some future date, repay the accumulated debt which has resulted.

In the Rhodesias, the British South Africa Company found itself in the same position in respect of the railways as any African Government. Nearly all the capital required had to be raised by debentures,[1] and it was necessary for the Chartered Company to

---

[1] Brigadier-General F. D. Hammond, in his report (1926) on the Railway System of Southern Rhodesia, vol. i, stated in regard to the Rhodesia Railways Ltd.:

"The first point which calls for comment is that practically the whole of the capital for construction was raised by debentures. The interest on the five per cent. issue was guaranteed by the British South Africa Company for twenty years from 1st November, 1895 ; that guarantee has now lapsed. The other two debenture issues are guaranteed by the same company as to principal, premium and interest, for fifty years from the 1st May, 1899. These onerous conditions explain why the debenture capital forms such a large proportion; if it had been possible to raise capital on more favourable terms from the public, it may be taken for granted that the owners, the British South Africa Company, would have done so, without saddling themselves with these severe obligations. It gains no benefit; it has a heavy liability."

---

semi-arid country, to traverse a series of plateau regions rising to 6,000 ft. above sea-level, and the lines had to be operated under most exceptional difficulties. Moreover, the goal itself was uncertain. For many years after the gold and diamond discoveries it was not known whether the gold and diamond mines could be regarded as permanently established sources of wealth. Added to this were the political circumstances which, prior to the Boer War, made it uncertain whether the maritime colonies would or would not be able to share in the wealth of the Transvaal permanently. It is significant that the attitude of the British Government towards development of railways by private enterprise in Natal throughout the decade 1860–70 (when many proposals were made by private companies willing to construct railways on the basis of guarantees or concessions) was that of protecting the colony from exploitation. *Cf.* W. J. Busschau's interesting article, "Some Aspects of Railway Development in Natal," *S.A. Journal of Economics*, vol. i, December, 1933. The article is an extract from his thesis, *The Development of the Natal Government Railways*.

guarantee the interest; and it had to make up the losses on these railways over a very long period. Indeed, from the inception of the Rhodesia Railways Ltd., and the Mashonaland Railway Co., Ltd., the British South Africa Company made advances to these two railway companies, on open account without any security, not only to enable them to meet their debenture interest, but also to provide funds for capital expenditure. Under its guarantees, the British South Africa Company was obliged to furnish the former, but was under no obligation in regard to the latter.

In the year 1911 the Rhodesia Railways Trust took over the outstanding debts due by the two railway companies at that date. It is significant that the debt amounted to no less than £1,131,888, of which Rhodesia Railways Ltd. was responsible for £570,024, and the Mashonaland Railway Co., Ltd., for

---

In regard to the Mashonaland Railway, General Hammond concluded:

"As in the case of the Rhodesia Railways, the proportion of debentures to total capital is most marked, but as the British South Africa Company guaranteed the interest on all these issues also, the reason for this must again be sought in the difficulty of raising capital otherwise."

The same applies to a somewhat smaller extent to the Beira Railway Company and the Beira Junction Railway, neither of which, however, would have been built without the help of the Rhodesia Railway Companies. In the case of the Blinkwater Railway, the authorized and issued capital consists of 200,000 Ordinary Shares of £1 each. The whole of these shares are owned by the Beit Railway Trustees. There are no debentures. In the case of the Rhodesia-Katanga Junction Railway and Mining Company, most of the capital was raised by debentures guaranteed for twenty years as to interest by the Tanganyika Concessions, Ltd.

General Hammond estimated the capital expenditure of the whole system up to 1924 as follows:

Rhodesia Railways Limited.		£8,499,304
Mashonaland Railway	£4,432,142	
Less Beira Railway Debentures.	82,500	
		4,349,642
Beira Railway		2,240,469
Beira Junction Railway	543,042	
Cost of Concession	67,415	
Wharf Construction	98,682	
		709,139
Blinkwater Railway		411,750
Rhodesia-Katanga Junction Railway		767,000
		£16,977,304

Of this the debentures issued by the Rhodesia Railways and the Mashonaland Railway alone amounted to over £12,000,000.

TABLE 98.—*Financial Results of Rhodesian Railways, 1927-36. Statement showing the Profit or Loss for each of the Years ended 30th September, 1927, to 1936 in Respect of the Rhodesia Railways Ltd. and the Mashonaland Railway Company Ltd., and of the Shabani Railway Company Ltd., and the Beira Railway Company Ltd., and also the Position of the Reserve, Dividend, Rates Stabilization and Net Revenue Accounts.*

	THE RHODESIA RAILWAYS LTD. AND THE MASHONALAND RAILWAY COMPANY LTD.					THE SHABANI RAILWAY COMPANY LTD.			THE BEIRA RAILWAY COMPANY LTD.			
	Profit or Loss for the year after meeting interest on Debentures, Depreciation and Renewals, Income Tax, etc.	Appropriated to— Reserve Account	Appropriated to— Dividend Account	Appropriated to— Rates Stabilization Account	Net Revenue Account	Profit or Loss for the year after meeting interest on Debentures, Depreciation and Renewals, Income Tax, etc.	Appropriated to— Dividend Account	Net Revenue Account	Profit or Loss for the year after meeting interest on Debentures, Depreciation and Renewals, Income Tax, etc.	Appropriated to— Reserve Account	Appropriated to— Dividend Account	Net Revenue Account
	£ s. d.	£ s. d.	£ s. d.	£ s. d.	£ s. d.	£ s. d.	£ s. d.	£ s. d.	£ s. d.	£ s. d.	£ s. d.	£ s. d.
Balance as at 30th September, 1927					906,153 12 5							
Year ended 30th September, 1927	700,661 3 5	550,661 3 5	150,000 0 0	…	…	14,037 14 4	…	14,037 14 4				
„ „ 1928	539,832 12 1	375,219 6 1	164,613 6 0	…	…	651 10 5	…	651 10 5				
Balance as at 30th September, 1929												
Year ended 30th September, 1929	804,426 13 9	607,432 0 8	196,994 13 1	…	…	15,818 11 1	…	15,818 11 1	116,379 15 2	50,000 0 0	…	123,359 1 3
„ „ 1930	542,778 4 7	349,987 4 1	192,791 0 6	…	…	3,565 8 5	…	3,565 8 5	25,277 5 7	50,000 0 0	52,500 0 0	14,379 15 2
„ „ 1931	192,697 4 3	19,688 5 4	173,008 8 11	…	…	74 18 10	…	74 18 10	107,806 2 4	25,000 0 0	65,625 0 0	115,902 5 7
„ „ 1932	948,122 14 6	948,122 14 6	…	…	…	7,215 17 0	…	7,215 17 0	…	…	…	107,866 2 4
„ „ 1933	553,427 14 6	553,427 6 6	…	…	…	4,328 7 3	6,250 0 0	1,921 12 9	37,692 14 1	125,000 0 0	…	87,307 5 11
„ „ 1934	34,305 6 6	34,305 6 6	…	…	…	4,460 4 4	6,250 0 0	1,789 15 8	91,758 7 8	…	…	91,758 7 8
„ „ 1935	416,605 9 9	349,177 9 9	…	67,428 0 0	…	6,250 0 0	6,250 0 0	…	166,335 9 5	55,000 0 0	78,750 0 0	111,335 9 5
„ „ 1936	117,174 7 3	95,658 7 3	…	21,516 0 0	…	6,250 0 0	6,250 0 0	…	160,800 3 6	95,000 0 0	…	12,949 16 6
Totals . . .	£1,778,319 19 7	811,968 1 1	877,407 8 6	88,944 0 0	906,153 12 5	£34,391 5 4	25,000 0 0	9,391 5 4	£364,997 13 9	150,000 0 0	196,875 0 0	191,481 15 0
Deduct: Dividends paid / Amount appropriated to Revenue Account in terms of Section 14 of the "Railways Act, 1935". .		…	771,100 0 0	46,200 0 0	…		25,000 0 0	…		…	196,875 0 0	…
As at 30th September, 1936, as per Balance Sheets .		£811,968 11 1	106,307 8 6	42,744 0 0	906,153 12 5		…	£9,391 5 4		…	…	£191,481 15 0

£561,864, which is a sufficient indication of the struggle they had experienced since their construction, notwithstanding the mineral resources of the territories which they traversed. Within the course of the next two years, the Rhodesia Railways Ltd. was able to liquidate in full their debt to the Trust, but the Mashonaland Railway Co., Ltd., was compelled to receive further assistance until by the 30th September, 1921, it owed no less than £1,718,584 for loan and accrued interest. This sum has been very greatly reduced in recent years, and at the 30th September, 1936, the outstanding debt amounted to £276,679, made up as follows:

Principal. . . .	£240,090
Interest	36,589
	£276,679

The finances of the Rhodesian Railway Companies are of very great interest, and their development since 1927 is shown in Table 98, which gives the detailed results, not only for the Rhodesia Railways Ltd., and the Mashonaland Railway Co., Ltd., but also for the Shabani Railway Co., Ltd., and the Beira Railway Co., Ltd.

At the 30th September, 1936, the total combined capital of the railways was as follows:

Rhodesia Railways Ltd. . .	£12,389,003	
Mashonaland Railway Co., Ltd. .	8,805,500	
		£21,194,503
Shabani Railway Co., Ltd.		304,165
Beira Railway Co., Ltd.		1,802,150
		£23,300,818

The annual debt charges for the year ended 30th September, 1936, amounted to no less than £619,029 for the Rhodesia Railways Ltd., £458,380 for the Mahonaland Railway Co., Ltd., £22,500 for the Shabani Railway Co., Ltd., and £158,500 for the Beira Railway Co., Ltd., a total of £1,235,909.

Broadly speaking, hardly a railway exists in Africa which has been managed purely on the principles which govern the policy of a private railway undertaking. In one way or another all the railways have been used as the economic instruments of Governments.

The formal separation of the railway from the General Budgets has now been carried out in one form or another in most African territories; but, although this is of the greatest importance from the point of view of efficiency, it does not alter the fact that all the railways in Africa are still used to further state policies, and that their finances, and the rates charged by them, are greatly influenced thereby.

The most extreme example of the domination of politico-economic objectives in the development and administration of a railway system is that provided by the South African Railways and Harbours. I have described and analysed this situation in my book on *The Railway Policy of South Africa*. It is not possible to enter into the question in any detail here, but there are some points of general significance which must be referred to. The history and the policy of the South African Railways and Harbours has been determined by the expansion of mining. As is well known, before Union, railway development was based on inter-colonial competition for a share in the traffic to the gold-fields. The construction of the main railway lines in South Africa resulted from this struggle to reach the Witwatersrand, on which the Union railway system pivots.

Long before the Union the rates structure had already been developed to extract the greatest possible railway revenue from the traffic to the Rand. Up to the present this policy has been continued; and the excessive revenue obtained by the railway system from the urban communities of the Interior Provinces continues to be used to subsidize agricultural export rates, and to protect various local industries.

The policy of encouraging exports at the expense of imports has been adopted in a greater or lesser degree elsewhere in Africa. It is a policy peculiarly suited to the artificial encouragement of special agricultural commodities, many of which are produced largely by Europeans, as, for example, maize, fruit, sugar, dairy produce and meat in the Union, and maize, coffee and sisal in Kenya.

The existence of these special rates, however, does not imply that the general level of rates on African railways is low. On the contrary, notwithstanding the precarious financial position of many African railways, their average level of rates is high, and retards African economic development. The special export rates, although lower than the average, are not necessarily low in themselves; but, because they are more favourable than the other rates, they lead to the investment of resources in directions which would otherwise be uneconomic to *entrepreneurs*.

In the Union the taxation, through heavy railway rates, of the wealth of the Witwatersrand area has not only enabled the railway system to bear the cost of very large subsidies in the form of unduly low railway rates for uneconomic traffic, but has also made it possible for the system to earn the whole of the interest on its capital[1] to date, and to contribute over £11,000,000 to a Betterment Fund, and £54,000,000 to a Renewals Fund, which, in the past, has also been freely used as a means of meeting new capital expenditure out of revenue. The system has also built up considerable additional reserves of one kind or another.

During periods of depression deficits have been allowed to accumulate, but, so far, these have been made good regularly in subsequent periods of prosperity. The interest charges on the borrowed capital invested in the railways (apart from harbours and other services) amounted to £5,052,155 for the year ending March, 1937, and in this year they formed 44·71% of the surplus of earnings over gross working expenditure.

The effects of the depression, and the extraordinary prosperity which has since then been experienced by the railways as a result of the boom conditions in South Africa in recent years, are shown by the following statistics (Table 99) of earnings and expenditure.

Under the guidance of the present Minister of Railways, a vigorous policy of development has been pursued ; railway, road motor services and airways have been expanded, considerable

---

[1] The total expenditure on the system as a whole, including harbours, steamships and airways, amounted to £171,903,144 on the 31st March, 1937, as compared with approximately £73,000,000 at the time of Union. The interest-bearing capital at the 31st March, 1937, amounted to £151,320,810.

TABLE 99.—*South African Railways*, 1929–37.

Year ended 31st March.	Total Ordinary Working Expenditure.	Total Earnings.	Balance, (a) being Surplus of Earnings over Expenditure.	Interest payable on Capital.	Surplus (Cr.) or Deficit (Dr.) after Payment of Interest.	Percentage of Gross Profit on Capital.		
	£	£	£	£	£	£	s.	d.
1929	20,298,664	26,090,712	5,792,048	5,120,581	Cr. 766,527	4	8	11
1930	20,878,539	26,130,549	5,252,010	5,350,036	Cr. 63,491	3	18	10
1931	19,308,444	24,321,854	5,013,410	5,547,961	Dr. 309,431	3	7	8
1932	17,604,116	22,039,659	4,435,543	5,683,168	Dr. 1,212,386	3	2	0
1933	15,591,054	20,619,878	5,028,824	5,741,581	Dr. 627,120	3	9	1
1934	16,919,521	23,707,524	6,788,003	5,337,838	Cr. 1,813,506	4	16	5
1935	18,341,222	27,021,815	8,680,593	5,161,420	Cr. 3,888,725	6	1	3
1936	19,657,616	30,049,854	10,392,238	5,120,633	Cr. 5,623,158	7	1	11
1937	20,593,860	31,892,791	11,298,931	5,052,155	Cr. 6,464,021	7	9	9

(a) Excludes other small amounts comprising miscellaneous receipts (net).

re-organization has taken place, and betterment schemes and electrification extensions have been inaugurated. What is now necessary in the Union is that the system should relinquish the exercise of excessive monopoly powers, and should at last revise its general rates policy in order to free those economic activities of the country which now suffer from uneconomic discrimination in transport charges. Moreover, private enterprise in road transport should be freed from the uneconomic restrictions which have been imposed on it, largely in order to protect the railways. If this is done, private enterprise will be able, at last, to play its necessary and important role in the transport of the country.

The extent to which the Union, owing to its mineral industries, has been able to adopt a lavish railway policy in order to stimulate sub-economic forms of production can be illustrated by the following statement laid on the table of the House of Assembly in March, 1936, by the Minister of Railways and Harbours:

"The Railway Administration has endeavoured to promote the agricultural development of *all* portions of the Union by quoting very low rates for the conveyance of *all* classes of agricultural products. This policy has had remarkable results in the character and volume of the traffic conveyed by the railways, and the revenue resulting therefrom.[1]

[1] My italics.

"For the year ended 31st March, 1933:

"Low-rated traffic, *i.e.* traffic conveyed under tariffs lower than No. 6   Amounted to 15,348,000 tons or 85·16% of the whole ;

"High-rated traffic, *i. e.* traffic conveyed under tariffs Nos. 1 to 6   Amounted to 2,673,000 tons or 14·84% of the whole.

"On the other hand when we come to revenue we find that low-rated traffic produced £5,751,000 or 41·64% of the whole, while high-rated traffic produced £8,058,000, or 58·36% of the whole.

"There is, therefore, a striking disproportion between the revenue contributed by the relatively small tonnage of high-rated traffic and that produced by the large volume of low-rated traffic, and it is not difficult to understand the sense of grievance of the industrialist.

"We are satisfied that any attempt to adjust the balance by making any material increase in the tariffs on agricultural produce would fail, because the traffic could not bear any such increase. On the other hand, any material decrease in the tariff for the higher class goods would lead to a loss of revenue, which, in present circumstances, the railways could not suffer without having to contemplate a deficit in their working."

It is only necessary to add that the largest part of the high-rated traffic is made up of imported goods railed to the Witwatersrand area. The policy of agricultural development rests almost entirely on the indirect taxation of the great mineral industries which the Union is fortunate enough to possess. Its counterpart has been the construction of hundreds of miles of non-paying branch lines into poor or even useless agricultural areas, with the intention of stimulating European settlement therein.

The mileage of the Union's railway system[1] has been almost

---

[1] Railway construction in the separate Colonies was, prior to Union:

1860–9	.	.	.	.	.	.	68
1870–9	.	.	.	.	.	.	781
1880–9	.	.	.	.	.	.	1,065
1890–9	.	.	.	.	.	.	2,046
1900–9	.	.	.	.	.	.	2,977
							6,937

doubled since Union; the total mileage operated by the Administration at the 31st March, 1936,[1] amounted to 13,869 miles.
Excluding the mileage in South-West Africa, the growth in the
system is due almost wholly to the construction of branch railway
lines, most of which have remained unpayable from the date of
opening, and it has recently been proposed by the Minister of
Railways that the only thing to do with them is to try to link
them up in such a way that they can be used to relieve the traffic
on the main lines. From 1910–34, approximately 4,235 miles of
branch lines were constructed at a cost of roughly £17 million.
The total capital invested in *unpayable* branch lines was stated,
by the Minister of Railways and Harbours, to amount to
not less than £14,000,000, as at 31st March, 1936. This sum is
equivalent to roughly two-thirds of the total capital invested in
the railways of the Rhodesias.

The fact that the railways in South Africa were, from the
beginning, used to further the politico-economic policies of the
Government in power, meant that they were never regarded by
the communities which they served as independent undertakings
with specific problems of their own. Once the tradition of
identifying the railway policy with that of the Government is
established, it is very difficult to break down.

The administration of the railways evolved by the Cape
Parliament was based on the appointment of a Minister of
Railways, as a member of the Cabinet. Everything was entrusted
to him, subject to questions and criticisms in Parliament. He was
expected to hand all railway profits[2] over to the General Revenues

---

[1] Made up as follows:

South African Railways, lines in the Union . .	11,727	miles.
„ „ „ „ South-West Africa .	1,462	„
Private Railways	680	„
	13,869	„

The private railways include the Vryburg-Bulawayo Section of the Rhodesian
Railways (597 miles).

[2] "Before Union the Railway Finances were not separated from the General
Finances of the Colonies except in the case of the Central South African Railways,
and even here the Railway and Government Finances were not entirely independent
of each other. There was little uniformity of method or principle as to the allocation
of railway expenditures to capital or revenue account. Both in the Cape and Natal,
for example, expenditure for relaying was frequently charged to capital account,
instead of to working or to depreciation fund ; on the other hand, rolling stock and

of the Colony, and no very clear definition was ever arrived at to show what was to be regarded as profit. The Ministers never arrived at a uniform practice in regard to the provision of new capital expenditure out of railway revenue or out of funds voted by the House. No system was ever successfully worked out to show which of the profits of the railway activities ought to be put at the disposal of capital account, and which were to be regarded as profit to be handed over to the general revenue of the Colony.

It is clear that the Ministers, who were anxious to get the support of the House, desired as large an amount as possible to be handed over annually by the Railway as profit for the state revenue. It was justified by the argument that it was not taxation at all, but only profit made out of one particular industry—the gold-mining industry which, it was alleged, was taxed insufficiently in other directions.

At Union, the Railway Board, under the Chairmanship of the Minister of Railways, was set up to manage the system, and the formal separation of the railway from the general finances of the country took place, but this separation has really never been complete. In the last resort, the determination of the amount of new capital expenditure which is to be incurred on the railway depends upon the policy of the Minister of Finance, and thus prevents the expansion of the system from being considered strictly on the principles suited to the economic requirements of a business undertaking.

In my book, *The Railway Policy of South Africa*, I summarized the point at issue as follows:

> "There is no half-way house between the management of railways owned by the State merely as a State department and their management on business principles. Under the

---

workshops were in some cases paid for out of earnings. Prior to Union, too, the Governments of the various Colonies did not make sufficient provision for depreciation of railway and harbour assets. As Government and railway finance were so closely interwoven, railway profits were frequently used to pay the ordinary expenses of the Government; at other times the surplus revenue of the Government was used for railway construction. However, notwithstanding that railway revenue had not in the past been charged with a sufficient sum to cover depreciation, the Auditor-General estimated that over £15,000,000 of Railway surpluses had been paid to the Colonial Treasuries." (*The Railway Policy of South Africa*, p. 79, par. 37.)

first system all matters of policy affecting questions of expenditure on new construction, of expansion or of rates are decided, not in accordance with the views of experts as to their effect on the earnings and efficiency of the system as a whole, but according to the popular views of politicians. They are decided in the same frame of mind as that in which the Minister of Finance deals with social expenditure; on the one hand, he has certain revenues from taxation; on the other, he finds himself confronted with innumerable projects for expenditure pressed upon him by the clamour of his political colleagues. The decisions of a manager of an industrial undertaking must be made on entirely different grounds. His revenue is not derived from sources independent of his expenditure; it is, on the contrary, dependent to a large extent on the efficiency with which the expenditure is distributed so as to increase the earning capacity of the undertaking. He has to be guided, not by the insistent demand for favours, but by consideration of the relative contribution each item of expenditure will make towards increasing the efficiency of the system as a whole. If he is obliged to incur expenditure which is relatively uneconomic, he will find himself forced, sooner or later, to curtail expenditure in more essential directions, e. g. expenditure which might have resulted in large economies of operation, or large developments of traffic.''

It is very significant that similar difficulties have been met with in the case of every British Government railway in Africa. On frequent occasions various Commissions of Enquiry have stressed the evils of this identification of railway finance[1] with the general finance of the territories concerned, and, as a result, during the last decade, the formal separation of the railway and general budgets has taken place in many British African territories. This has been a step in the right direction, but it must not be supposed

---

[1] Brigadier-General Hammond, in his Report in 1921 on the Kenya and Uganda Railway, expressed the view that "the finances should be divorced completely from those of the Colony, and the Railway treated as a business concern on commercial lines". In 1924 General Hammond also reported on the railway system of Nigeria, and found it necessary to make strong criticisms of the way in which the accounts of the railway were merged in the financial returns of the Colony. He stated—"the consequences of this are numerous and evil. It makes it impossible for anyone, whether connected with the railway or not, to judge from the accounts how the railway stands in its money matters. . . . The consequences to the people in charge of the railway are, however, much more serious than to outsiders".

that such a separation, in fact, necessarily results in the management of the railways as absolutely separate economic undertakings. In most of the British Colonies no loan can be raised for the construction of new railways or for additions to the capital assets of existing railways, except by the Government.

Thus, as Mr. Roger Gibb pointed out in his report on *Railway Rates and Finance in Kenya, Uganda and Tanganyika Territory* (1932), "the entire task of success or failure of the railway falls upon the Government of the Colonies as directly as though the railway accounts were merged with the Colonial Budgets," and "although the Legislative Councils do not now interfere directly in the railway management, the Railway Advisory Council certainly does, and brings non-railway influence to bear on real managerial problems, in a manner in many ways less desirable than control exercised more openly through the Legislative Councils."[1]

There is no doubt that it is very desirable that autonomous bodies should be established wherever possible so that the railways can be managed as really independent undertakings, able to expand and contract their operations as and when economic circumstances make it necessary, and without the hampering influence of political pressure; but it is necessary to realize that there is little purpose in setting up such organizations with all the trappings of autonomy, if, in fact, conditions in the territories are such that the railways will soon become financially dependent on the State, simply because they cannot pay their own way. The fact must be faced that, in most territories, only Governments could create the railways, and even now, with few exceptions, only Governments can afford to operate them. When a railway ceases to be able to operate successfully and becomes almost completely dependent financially on the Central Government, little purpose is served by keeping up the fiction that it is a separate commercial undertaking.

[1] Mr. Gibb, in order to bring about a complete separation of railway from State finances, and in order to cause the railway to be managed purely on business lines, and to avoid local pressure and influence being brought to bear upon State railway management, suggested that, in the case of the Kenya and Uganda Railway, a railway company should be formed, somewhat on the lines of the Nyasaland Railway Company, with a London Board. "Future capital requirements of the Railway should then be raised by the Railway Company and not by the Governments." This recommendation was not adopted.

The intimate association of the State with the railways has had similar results in other African territories as in the Union. In all of them rates have been influenced to some extent by politico-economic motives, but interference has not been carried as far as in South Africa, for the simple reason that the available high-rated imported traffic has not been a large enough proportion of the whole. Nevertheless, the policy of using the Railway Tariff as a means of protecting special interests has exercised a considerable influence on the direction in which the resources of the territories have been developed.

The fundamental cause of the peculiar rate structure undoubtedly consists in the inevitable difficulties which result from the construction of railways which traverse vast areas, and which involve very heavy fixed interest charges, and, therefore, force Governments to do everything in their power to stimulate exports, in order to raise the means of meeting the obligations of the territory. The policy of forcing exports at all costs has resulted in various types of uneconomic production which, in some cases, have become a burden on the territories concerned. The reason for the financial difficulties of many African railways, therefore, lies in the fact that *ab initio* many were built for non-economic reasons, and this also is why it has so far not been possible to manage them as purely business undertakings.

In relation to the economic development of most African territories, it is quite clear that the railways have been over-built, and, as a result, Governments have been brought up, time and again, against the fundamental difficulty that capital investment in itself cannot lead to economic development, but requires a concomitant expansion of the other factors of production. Capital alone cannot solve the economic problem.

On the contrary, over-investment is likely, under certain conditions, to retard rather than to stimulate economic progress. If, as a result of extensive capital expenditure, the railway is burdened with large interest obligations, this brings about excessively heavy rates on imported or local traffic; and the railway, in adopting unduly low development rates in order to build up traffic, stimulates types of production which may not be in the real interests of the future development of the territory.

Moreover, once certain export mono-cultures have been encouraged, it is very difficult to reverse the process by raising railway rates later, even if this were in the economic interests of the territory, or were necessary from the point of view of the finances of the railway. Yet the burden of debt incurred in the construction of the railway extension remains, and has to be borne by other sections of the economy, either through higher railway rates or increased taxation. Artificially stimulated traffic has to be supported 'at the expense of existing profitable activities, or of potentially sound economic development elsewhere.

These difficulties can be avoided only by obtaining capital for the extension of the railway system at very low rates of interest (by means of subsidies from the Metropolitan country), or by the issue of equity shares. Unfortunately, the latter method, which would adjust the burden of debt to the earning capacity of the railway, and has been advocated frequently, has very limited possibilities in Africa. The main lines have been extended to an extent which is, in many cases, greater than that warranted by purely business considerations; the railways, therefore, are not in a position to hold out good prospects to the ordinary investor. Moreover, the earning capacity of the railways is subject to extreme cyclical fluctuations, not only because the African territories produce raw materials and foodstuffs which are subject to large price fluctuations in world markets, but also because most of the territories depend almost entirely on a few main export crops and are, therefore, particularly vulnerable to changes in world demand.

The cyclical fluctuations in earnings are intensified by the fact that most African railways obtain the largest part of their revenue from high-rated imported traffic. This imported traffic fluctuates with the flow of investment from abroad. During periods of capital imports (which as a matter of fact usually coincide with periods of prosperity), railway earnings are abnormally inflated, and this leads to demands for further railway extensions and capital improvements. When the period of prosperity fanned by capital imports comes to an end, railway finances become particularly vulnerable; their expenditures, and often their fixed charges also, have been increased, but revenues now decrease drastically, owing to the effects of the depression on export traffic, and, especially, owing to the decline in capital investment from abroad which accentuates the general fall in imports.

It is possible to interest the private investor, on terms other than as a holder of fixed interest-bearing securities, only in cases where *nett* railway earnings have been favourable for some years, and where the territory is showing steady progress relatively free from serious cyclical interruptions.

The survey of the economic conditions in African territories, which has been conducted in this chapter, shows that these conditions are not fulfilled in most African Colonies.

Where equity capital cannot be raised and fixed interest-bearing capital cannot be borrowed on special terms, it is far better to postpone railway development than to burden the economy with heavy interest obligations abroad. Left to develop steadily, a railway will often gradually build up a sound financial position; but, if it is induced to incur heavy capital expenditure and to extend its system unduly, it may eventually fail to cover even its operating expenses.

The factors discussed so far are best illustrated by a brief examination of the main features of some of the railway systems in Africa, and by presenting relevant data from the official reports themselves.

Government Railway of Nigeria.—In the 1934 report of the Government Railways of Nigeria, the General Manager summed up the fundamental conditions under which the system operates in the following striking terms:

> "The Railway has been constructed and equipped by Government in order to enable the Colony to be developed. The longest possible view ahead has been taken. *The trade of the Colony is not yet developed to anything like the transport capacity of its railway route mileage.*
>
> "No private railway company could have constructed so much mileage, and the whole Colony has greatly benefited from the transport facilities which have been provided from the resources of the State. The present recurring deficit is due to heavy interest charges and insufficient receipts to meet them. Were the annual capital charges of the railway to be set alongside the aggregate income of the population which

it serves, it would be clear that, *short of a valuable bulk mineral discovery*, the main direction in which the annual capital charges could be met year by year from railway earnings must be the carriage by it of a very large volume of agricultural products, and the whole of that volume wherever the railway can reach it. A sufficient volume of export products does not now exist; while for the tonnage available, direct competitors by river and road parallel the railway route. Imports into Nigeria are a relatively small tonnage. Some of this is diverted from the railway by its competitors.

"For a considerable mileage the railway runs through, as yet, slowly developing country. The section between Enugu and Kafanchan, containing the bridge over the river Benue, is one of these. In the future, when the railway is extended to Maiduguri, as it must be for the extensive north-east territory to become developed, this eastern railway route should come more fully into its own. At the present time its earnings are small in relation to its interest changes.

". . . *The railway is purely a utility one; the bulk of its haulage low-rated produce; the bulk of its travel third-class passengers at one farthing per mile*. It has no tourist travel. Its first-class passengers are mostly officers travelling to and from their posts; while second-class is lightly patronized.

"*The eastern section of the line, between Kaduna and Enugu, is showing a heavy deficit and is being carried by the rest of the system*. It is submitted that *a case exists for a reduction of the capital charged against the railway* qua *railway*.

". . . In regard to the whole of the foregoing, it should be borne in mind that while a company-owned railway pays fixed interest on its debenture stock only, money paid to the shareholders being contingent upon the railway earnings, the Nigerian Railway is now charged with full interest at fixed rates on its capital cost."

After an exhaustive review, the Government, as already mentioned, decided to take the advice of the General Manager of Railways on this question, and to regard the Enugu-Benue Bridge-Kafanchan section of the main line as constructed on Colonial development principles, and to relieve the finances of the railway, qua railway, of the interest charges on this section as from the 1st April, 1936. Under this change the railway also "becomes fully commercialized and will be held responsible for meeting its operating costs, pension commitments, and the interest on all of the remaining capital; it will also be required to contribute in full towards its renewal fund in accordance with the recommendations of a Committee which reported in 1936 on the wasting assets of the railway. Moreover, the Government will no longer automatically meet railway deficits, as in the past. Should a deficit occur, the railway will be required to borrow on overdraft from Government funds at a stated rate of interest. It will, therefore, be incumbent on the railway so to adjust its earnings and expenditure as to avoid deficits. Under the new scheme the railway finances have been given further relief by the reduction of interest from 5% to 3% on existing loans from Government funds, and also by a reduction in the total value of capital assets. "These changes," says the report of the General Manager, "clear a formerly opaque outlook. . . . Hitherto the earnest efforts of the railway management and staff have frequently been nullified by the depressing effect of the recurring deficit. On the other hand, the existence of a generous Government, apparently prepared to pay any deficit, has robbed the railway personnel of that commercial incentive which should be proper to them . . ."

Under the financial rearrangement, it is also hoped gradually to build up a substantial railway reserve, in order to meet such contingencies as the failure of the main export crop, and to avoid rising railway rates when trade is declining.

In the peak year 1929/30, the railway was able to pay £75,030 into the General Revenue of the colony. For the years 1930/1 to 1934/5 there were heavy deficits, although no provision was made for renewals. The deficits totalled £956,923 by the 31st March, 1934. To meet full interest and depreciation charges the railway earnings would have had to be higher by £763,503 in 1933/4, by £507,205 in 1934/5, and by £853,724 in 1935/6 than they were. In addressing the Legislative Council in March, 1935, the Governor, referring to the General Manager's summary of the position, said:

> "It is difficult to visualize any period when strict control could be relaxed on the railway. Apart from the capital charges which have to be carried—the aggregate of which is unduly heavy in relation to the sectional earning possibilities of the railway—the bulk of railway receipts is derived

from the export of produce originating in thousands of small native holdings. Under such conditions, the country cannot afford a railway organization which is other than of a simple and relatively inexpensive nature.

"The Nigerian Railway has the heaviest capital expenditure of any Crown Colony Railway. It has received no part of its capital free of interest or subsequent repayment. Unlike company-owned railways, it has not the elastic machinery of debenture, preference and ordinary stock, but is charged with interest on every pound spent since its inception. The only course open to it is to operate at the lowest practicable cost."

The total capital expenditure, including the cost of raising loans, stood at £22,950,856 at the 31st March, 1936, on which the annual interest charges had reached £1,048,729, or the very large proportion of 53% of the gross receipts of the Railway and its ancillary undertakings.

Of the total capital expenditure, £19,993,437 was loan capital; £3,922,954 was made up of advances from the Colony at 5% interest, and £34,465 was the amount of advances at 5% for road motor services. The mileage of the system is now 1,900 route miles, and 2,184 track miles. The railways have been suffering to an increasing extent from road motor competition.

The gross expenses in 1935/6 amounted to £1,966,012, and the gross earnings to £1,045,914 (excluding £292,382 adjustment of capital).

The gross receipts of the Enugu-Benue Bridge-Kafanchan section, referred to above, were only £201,252, but the working expenses plus interest charges amounted to two and a half times this sum, and totalled £502,110, after excluding £150,000 for depreciation.

Tanganyika Railways.—The Tanganyika Railways, which cover an open mileage of 1,377 miles, have the advantage that of the total cost of the system, which at the end of 1936 was estimated to amount to £9,925,702, assets valued at £4,894,050 were obtained for about £34,000, when these were taken over from Germany on the 1st April, 1919.

Notwithstanding this, the year 1936 was the first after five years in which there was a surplus of revenue over expenditure. The surplus amounted to £52,825, and was utilized to pay off part of the outstanding debt of the territory, which had been incurred in past years, owing to the inability of the railway to earn sufficient to cover its working expenditure plus interest charges. At the same time, a further loan from the Government was necessary to finance the replacement of worn-out assets, for which it had not been possible to provide by building up a Renewals Fund in previous years. The effect of this procedure on the finances of the railway is that any surpluses which may accrue will be devoted to the liquidation of the present outstanding debt to the territory, while, at the same time, a new debt will be built up consisting only of advances made by the territory to finance the Railway's Renewals Fund.

In 1936, which was a favourable year, the nett earnings gave a return of 3·71% on the total cost of the system, a percentage which was still much below the average cost at which the capital had been borrowed since the War.

The British capital expended on the system was made up as follows:

(a)	Free Loan advanced 1919/20, 1920/1 and 1923/4	£126,462
(b)	Loan from Imperial Exchequer at 5% interest and 1% sinking fund .	1,284,123
(c)	Guaranteed Loan 1948–68 . .	1,799,393
(d)	,, ,, 1951–71 . .	2,011,928
(e)	,, ,, 1952/72 . .	77,443
		£5,299,349

The Railways' Liability to the Territory at the 31st December, 1936, was as follows:[1]

[1] In addition amounts totalling £413,049, the deficiencies during 1919/20 and 1920/1, are excluded from the accounts as these are repayable only should the Railways become a separate entity; also, further sums to the amount of £449,505 advanced from the Imperial Exchequer to meet the deficiencies for the years 1921/2 to 1925/6 are excluded as no debt charges are at present incurred, and any question of repayment is deferred until 1938.

Value of floating assets taken over at the 31st March, 1927	£151,416
Borrowings from Territory Funds for revenue purposes during 1933 to 1936 .	153,066
Borrowings from Territory Funds for revenue purposes during 1934 . .	147,649
	£452,131

The annual debt charges have grown from a total of £60,331 in 1926/7 to £295,773 on capital works, and £19,481 on capital expenditure from Government revenues, in 1936, making the total debt charges £315,254. Even in the relatively favourable year 1936, the debt charges were no less than 43% of the total gross earnings. It is highly significant that in 1936, ordinary working costs, inclusive of depreciation, but exclusive of loan charges, expressed as the average cost per public freight avoirdupois ton-mile, amounted to 8·991 cents, but that, in addition, the loan costs amounted to no less than 6·396 cents, and this notwithstanding the fact that, as has been mentioned above, so large a part of the system was taken over for practically nothing.

The Railways' deficits (after payment of debt charges) amounted to £112,635 in 1933; £124,254 in 1934; and £11,059 in 1935; while there was a surplus of £52,875, previously referred to, in 1936.

An indication of the effects of the depression on African railways is afforded by the fall in total railway earnings in Tanganyika; in 1930/31 these had reached the record figure of £798,745, but, in the next year, they had fallen to £483,216. This situation was paralleled in greater or lesser degree on all African Railways.

There is one special circumstance which has proved particularly unfortunate for the Tanganyika system. Since 1931, the bulk of the Belgian copper freight has been diverted from Dar-es-Salaam to Lobito Bay; the magnitude of this loss can be gauged by the fact that in 1930/1, a record railway year, Belgian copper freight, now negligible, accounted for more than 50% of the value of the freight carried. The dependence of the railway on mineral traffic up to this time is in itself noteworthy.

It is significant that in 1931 Sir Sidney Armitage-Smith expressed[1] the opinion that—

"It should be definitely accepted that (apart from the discovery of, *e. g.*, gold on a large scale), the era of railway construction in this territory is past. No more money should be spent on surveying for extensions, and any staff employed on such work should be disbanded.

"Communications are, it is true, lamentably deficient, but when resources become available a less expensive method of transport must be adopted.

"Something better than the existing roads must be produced if the agricultural produce of the territory is to be carried to the coast in greatly increased amounts; in Uganda it appears possible to construct good metalled roads for about £400 a mile. In any event Tanganyika cannot afford to continue railway construction, and must rely for the future on motor transport to open up new areas."

The recent expansion of gold production, if it continues, may, of course, alter the position.

Kenya and Uganda Railways and Harbours.—Of the capital expenditure on this system, amounting to £21,999,072 at the 31st December, 1936, the sum of £8,074,966 is free of interest, having been found from the following sources:

Parliamentary Grant 1895/6 and 1902/03 . .	£70,000
Parliamentary Grants Uganda Railway Acts, 1896 and 1902	5,502,592
Other sources, revenue and non-interest bearing .	2,398,269
Loans redeemed from revenue	104,105
	£8,074,966

The balance, totalling £13,924,106, consists of interest-bearing capital guaranteed by the respective Governments in the following proportions:

Kenya Government .	£13,045,343[2]
Uganda ,, . .	878,763
	£13,924,106

---

[1] *Report on a Financial Mission to Tanganyika*, 1932 ; Cmd. 4182, p. 85.

[2] Of this the Uganda Government has accepted responsibility for approximately £2,000,000, representing assets constructed in Uganda and a share of rolling stock expenditure.

It has already been mentioned that Kenya's development is being seriously affected by the large debt burden it has to bear.[1] A considerable part of Sir Alan Pim's important report[2] was devoted to discussing ways and means of remedying this state of affairs.

One of the obstacles is the fact that there is a contingent liability on account of the £5,502,592 Parliamentary Grants shown above. This £5½ million is still considered by His Majesty's Treasury, and has been admitted by the Colonial Office, to be a liability of Kenya, and it appears as a realizable asset in the reports of the Select Committee on Public Accounts in the House of Commons. "Under the present arrangements, the question of the liability of the Colony in respect of this sum will come up for consideration in 1938, and, until it has been decided, His Majesty's Treasury can hardly agree to such reductions in the Railway rates as would affect the ability of the Colony to meet the full payments in account of the interest and Sinking Funds on the various loans. The same considerations apply to the question of the rate of levy for the Renewals Fund. The additional liability on account of the original cost of construction of the railway remains as a liability of the future to be reduced to concrete figures as and when circumstances permit."[2]

Sir Alan Pim has given a detailed account of the history of this liability, which shows that the commercial prospects of the line, or the possibility of developing what is now Kenya Colony, played practically no part in the circumstances which led to the construction of the Railway, and in the circumstances which influenced the British Government at the time. He finally recommended that "in view of the present finances and economic position of the Colony . . . I trust that it may be found possible to relieve the Colony of the prospect of this heavy additional burden".[3]

[1] See p. 178.
[2] *Ibid.*, p. 239 ff.
[3] *Ibid.*, p. 243. He added: "There are, however, wider considerations, which would appear to justify a generous policy in regard to this liability. Although the Colony has succeeded in balancing its Budget and, given moderately favourable conditions, it should continue to do so, it has nevertheless suffered very severely during the last few years, and its taxable capacity is small, more especially that of the preponderating native community. At its present stage of development it required expenditure in many

"High railway rates are one of the most serious handicaps to the agricultural prosperity and to the trade of Kenya. They are partly, as in most parts of Central Africa, a result of the long haul through barren country from the productive areas of the Colony to the Coast, but they are accentuated by the necessity of providing for very heavy annual payments on account of the existing loans. If these payments are to be increased in the future by adding contributions on account of the original cost of construction the result will be to suspend development, both directly on the Railway itself, and indirectly on the other industries of the Colony, which are so largely dependent on transport rates. Even if the liability to additional payments is postponed to the dates of maturity of one or more of the existing loans, the result of such an addition will be to prevent the accrual of the benefits which should then arise from conversion, and again to postpone the substantial reduction in railway rates, which, if carried out on judicious lines, is one of the greatest needs of the Colony. Apart from other advantages it should make it possible largely to dispense with the recurring grants and loans for the assistance of special agricultural industries which a country without large mineral and industrial resources cannot afford."

The above considerations are understandable when the loan charges of the system are examined. In 1936 these amounted to £850,100, as compared with about half this sum (£434,742) ten years earlier. In 1936 the fixed interest charges formed 28·4% (26·47% in 1937) of the total revenue received, as compared with 39·58% in 1932, and 24·26% in 1929. The following table compares the percentages for recent years of the total *nett* earnings and the total loan charges to the total capital expenditure on the system. Loan charges have to be met out of nett earnings, so that the excess, or short-fall, in railways earnings is indicated by the

---

directions if either European agriculture is to be able to compete on fair terms in the markets of the world, or if the remaining communities, and more especially the three millions of the native population, are to advance in economic prosperity, in education, or in health. They labour already under a burden of debt which is very heavy in comparison with their resources, and, as much the greater part of this debt has been incurred in connection with the Railway and the Port, its service has to be mainly provided for by heavy railway rates". (*Ibid.*, p. 244.)

difference between the first and the second percentages. The effect of the depression is apparent.

Year.			Percentage of Nett Earnings to Total Capital Expenditure.		Percentage of Total Loan Charges to Total Capital Expenditure.
1930	.	.	3·00	.	...
1931	.	.	1·97	.	3·66
1932	.	.	2·91	.	3·76
1933	.	.	4·70	.	3·66
1934	.	.	5·24	.	3·70
1935	.	.	5·48	.	3·84
1936	.	.	5·75	.	3·86
1937	.	.	6·50	.	3·86

It must, however, be borne in mind that this Railway System has made regular contributions both to a Renewals Fund and to a Sinking Fund. The position of the railway is, therefore, better than would appear at first sight. It is a debatable question whether, in fact, a railway should contribute both to a Sinking Fund and to a Renewals Fund, as this involves keeping the assets of the railway intact, and, at the same time, redeeming its capital debt, and thus entails burdening the present users of the railway for the benefit of posterity. A private railway which raises most of its capital by the issue of equity shares is not required to redeem its capital; I have argued elsewhere "that it is undesirable for a Government railway to be placed in a worse position in this respect, and that heavy Sinking Funds and complete contributions to a Renewals Fund, at one and the same time, are not desirable from an economic point of view".[1]

The Kenya and Uganda railway system has made great progress in the last decade. Its excellent management deserves high credit for achieving the results shown; particularly in view of the absence of mineral resources in the territory, and the heavy debt charges. If it had not been for the latter, the rates structure would, no doubt, have been modified considerably in order to stimulate further development.

The effects of the depression, the fluctuating fortunes of the

[1] Cf. "Railway Policy of South Africa", ibid.

Railway and Harbours, and the general upward trend in recent years are shown by the following comparative figures of gross earnings, ordinary working expenditure, and deficit or surplus, after meeting debt and other charges:

Year.	Net Surplus, +, or Deficit, —	Gross Earnings.	Ordinary Working Expenditure.
	£	£	£
1928	+255,638	2,111,227	1,376,685
1929	+187,367	2,825,310	1,669,563
1930	−83,210	2,569,721	1,641,742
1931	−378,184	2,219,056	1,474,227
1932	−189,388	2,121,015	1,169,385
1933	+232,836	2,426,184	1,121,145
1934	+344,654	2,560,040	1,126,443
1935	+362,772	2,793,845	1,243,831
1936	+415,048	2,986,591	1,321,663
1937	+584,326	3,228,765	1,460,765

The General Manager has pointed out that, if the burden of interest charges is to be reduced in future through debt redemption, this implies a "pioneer" service: "It means the complete elimination of services which do not pay. If the desire of the country is for cheaper transport, that transport must be limited to essential services without any frills."

These remarks aptly summarize the conclusion reached in the analysis contained at the beginning of this section. Over-extension of railway construction and railway services (particularly when capital has to be raised at high rates of interest), defeats the possibility of sound progress.

The policy of the Administration is expressed in the following important observations of the General Manager on the rates structure, which are of far wider application than to Kenya alone:

"While it is felt that the present rates structure, taking into consideration existing and past conditions, is on the whole distributing the burden equitably and fairly, there are still a number of defects which should be eliminated as and when the opportunity arises.

"By far the most important is the unbalanced nature of our rates structure. . . . While the *average* charge to the public . . . is very reasonable for a Railway of this size, having heavy grades, sharp curvature and a low density of traffic working at a high altitude, importing all its coal and paying high rates on its loan charges, it will be noticed that certain comparatively small tonnages of high-valued imported goods pay very high rates indeed, and contribute a large proportion of the total revenue, while large tonnages of low-valued agricultural exports pay extremely low rates. The unbalanced nature of this tariff above and below the average rate introduces many consequential troubles and difficulties. On the one hand, the high rates (Classes 1, 2 and 3) render the Railway unduly vulnerable to road and air competition, and make it incumbent upon the Governments, if the policy is to be maintained, to provide adequate protection by means of legislation. Furthermore, such high rates keep up unduly the cost of the commodities concerned, tending to increase the cost of living and the cost of manufacture where imported products are used.

"On the other hand, the assistance to agriculture for bulk crops is so great as to cause considerable difficulty financially when specially large tonnages have to be dealt with. This difficulty, it is true, has been largely overcome by the introduction of the quota system for the two main bulk crops—cotton-seed and maize—but is always a possible source of anxiety to the Railway Administration and of annoyance to the farmer, who, of course, is anxious to get unrestricted movement of his crops, though not able to pay for it. . . .

"Moreover, protection through railway rates is unsound in several ways, particularly perhaps because it is hidden and the general taxpayer has no control over it, but also because it is least efficient nearer the Coast, where it is most required, and more intensive up country, where it is not required. In this way industries may be getting financial assistance at the expense of others which they do not need, and to which they are not entitled. . . .

". . . no startling or sudden changes are contemplated, but such changes as are brought about from time to time should tend to eradicate known defects, rather than to perpetuate them."

The remarks of the General Manager speak for themselves.

The Beira, Mashonaland and Rhodesia Railways.—The Rhodesian Railway System is the only private system in Africa which has been operated independently of Government assistance, but, as already mentioned, the British South Africa Company took the place of the Government in relation to the financing and operation of these railways.

The system is now under the control of a Railway Commission, which determines rates and financial policy. In recent years, thanks largely to the development of the mineral resources of the Rhodesias, the combined railways have been able to meet all debenture charges, to build up statutory reserves, and to pay dividends. As has already been shown in the financial returns relating to these railways (Table 98), the Mashonaland Railways have not been as successful as the Rhodesian Railways.

Some indication of the increase in revenue due to the expansion of mining is provided by Table 100,[1] which gives particulars of the revenue earned from mineral traffic, and from stores imported by the Northern Rhodesian and the Union Minière Copper Mines, during each of the ten years 1927–36, together with the percentage which this figure bears to the total revenue earned. Particulars are not available of the revenue from imports for the mining companies in Southern Rhodesia.[2] It must also be borne in mind that mining is important to the railway companies, not only on account of the mineral products and mining stores, but also because a large part of the traffic to the urban areas results therefrom.

It will be seen that the revenue from the mineral and stores

[1] In considering this table it should be noted that during the years 1927–30 the rates from coal and coke, copper, lead and zinc were subject to a special addition dependent on the market selling prices of these products for the years mentioned. These excess railages were considerable and amounted to the following:

Year.	Coal and Coke.	Copper.	Lead and Zinc (included under ("other minerals").
	(£.)	(£.)	(£.)
1927	...	...	5,480
1928	10,631	12,449	2,196
1929	127,106	102,653	11,315
1930	50,799	46,142	175

[2] I am greatly indebted to the management of the Rhodesian Railways and to the Railway Commission for making available the figures, and also for preparing Tables 98 and 100.

TABLE 100.—*Rhodesian Railways: Earnings from Mineral Traffic, 1927–36. Statement Giving Particulars of the Revenue Earned from Mineral Traffic and from Stores Imported by the Northern Rhodesia and Union Minière Copper Mines during each of the Ten Years, 1927–36, Together with the Percentages which such Traffic Bears to the Total Revenue Earned.*

	1927.	1928.	1929.	1930.	1931.	1932.	1933.	1934.	1935.	1936.
	£.	£.	£.	£.	£.	£.	£.	£.	£.	£.
Coal and Coke for the Public	717,295	918,702	934,865	714,907	402,702	282,946	247,446	380,980	454,629	387,363
Copper for Export	417,229	557,446	558,371	509,623	316,651	358,628	497,728	718,370	829,385	732,587
Chrome Ore	265,858	196,382	237,190	247,329	83,477	32,084	22,058	56,558	90,361	137,548
Asbestos	60,771	90,844	126,638	109,788	85,438	32,778	108,552	102,989	148,605	186,015
Other Minerals	49,542	72,162	120,870	117,355	78,583	38,199	73,201	112,241	120,231	145,509
Stores for Northern Rhodesia and Congo Copper Mines	...	208,823	300,477	399,322	425,845	45,607	57,777	250,427	284,643	110,801
£	1,510,695	2,044,359	2,278,411	2,098,324	1,392,696	799,242	1,006,762	1,621,565	1,927,854	1,699,823
Total Revenue £	4,908,519	5,105,460	5,428,232	5,297,768	4,130,837	2,634,266	2,887,677	3,895,490	4,558,632	4,450,426
Percentages of Mineral Traffic and Stores for Copper Mines to Total Revenue	30·78	40·04	41·97	39·61	33·71	30·00	34·86	41·63	42·29	38·19

traffic for the Northern Rhodesian and the Congo copper mines has been subject to considerable fluctuations. In 1929 it had reached £2,278,411, by 1932 it had dropped to £790,242, and by 1936 it had again reached £1,699,823, and, in that year, formed no less than 38·19% of the total revenue of the railway system.

The mileage owned by the various railway companies of the Rhodesian system is as follows:

The Mashonaland Railway Company　.　923 miles.
The Rhodesia Railways Limited　.　.　1,518　,,
The Beira Railway Company Limited　.　204　,,
The Shabani Railway Company Limited　.　63　,,

Giving a total mileage at 30th September,
　1936, of　.　.　.　.　.　.　2,708　,,

The fluctuating fortunes of the combined Rhodesian Railways, in particular the adverse effects of the recent depression, enhanced as they were by the great decline in mineral traffic, are shown by the following statistics of earnings and expenditure in South Africa.

Summary of Railway Operations, 1925–36.

Year ended 30th September.			Total Earnings in South Africa.	Total Operating Expenditure in South Africa.
1925	.	.	£3,977,537	£1,828,113
1926	.	.	4,248,610	2,130,761
1927	.	.	4,908,519	2,233,935
1928	.	.	5,105,460	2,513,184
1929	.	.	5,428,232	2,638,754
1930	.	.	5,297,768	3,064,193
1931	.	.	4,130,837	2,573,091
1932	.	.	2,634,266	2,009,224
1933	.	.	2,887,677	1,729,094
1934	.	.	3,895,490	1,926,548
1935	.	.	4,558,632	2,069,064
1936	.	.	4,450,426	2,218,542

It is significant that, in 1936, the interest charges and loan service for the Beira and Mashonaland and Rhodesia Railways

Limited formed 80·7% of the total nett operating income, after allowing for depreciation and renewals.

A noteworthy feature in the construction of railways in Rhodesia has been the assistance rendered by the Beit Trustees, who have built certain lines which could not be financed in the usual way, as they were purely for development purposes.

Sierra Leone and Gold Coast Railways.—It is not necessary to examine in any detail the position of the Sierra Leone and Gold Coast Railways; no new principles emerge from a study of their finances.

The capital expenditure of the Sierra Leone Railway amounted to £1,428,238, of which approximately £383,000 were free of interest. The Railway has constantly been unable to meet the debt charges on its capital, and, from 1899–1935, the Government had to pay £1,939,681, more than the whole of the capital expenditure on the railway, to make up the deficits in its earnings. The working results during 1935 were the best since 1930, but, even so, were a final deficit of £6,549. The expenditure upon renewals in 1935, and for several years previously, has been small. In the absence of a Renewals Fund, it is anticipated that the Government will be called upon to make special provision for renewals and replacements after 1940.

The railway depends upon one particular commodity, viz. palm kernels, the tonnage of which is subject to great fluctuations; a serious decline in the amount exported is apt, at a moment's notice, to curtail its earnings drastically.

In 1935 the revenue for the year amounted to £180,005, and the gross expenditure to £186,679, excluding depreciation, but including loan charges.

Gold Coast Railway.—The total capital expenditure on the Gold Coast Railway and Harbours system amounted to £9,247,333 to the end of March, 1936, of which £1,355,139 was provided from Government funds, free of interest.[1] The average rate of interest (excluding sinking fund) on the unredeemed loans was 5·12%. Debt charges (interest and sinking fund combined) which the

---

[1] For an account of the fundamental, financial and management problems of the railway, see F. D. Hammond's *Report on the Railway System of the Gold Coast*, Published by the Crown Agents for the Colonies, London, 1922.

railway has to meet on its interest-bearing capital average 5·94%, which means that, under normal conditions, the loan charges still equal over 40% of the gross annual railway expenditure.

In 1934/5 the capital and sinking fund charges were over 49% of the revenue of the railways, but, in the year 1935/6, this had been reduced to 42%, owing to this being the best year since 1929/30 and also owing to certain conversion operations which reduced the interest charges. The year 1935/6 was the first since 1929/30 in which the railway earned a surplus over and above ordinary working expenditure, including full contributions to renewals and interest and sinking fund charges.

The earnings of the railway are greatly dependent on the cocoa and manganese traffic, and the considerable fluctuations to which both the quantity and value of these commodities are subject; in 1935/36 the latter accounted for over 50% of the tonnage handled (excluding livestock).

In the year 1928/9 the gross revenue was £1,242,947, which fell to £683,103 in 1932/3, and had recovered to £1,000,336 in 1935/6. The corresponding expenditure figures were £598,381 for 1928/9, £420,800 for 1932/3, and £548,641 for 1935/6.

Sudan Railways.—As already mentioned, the Sudan railways and steamers have achieved extremely successful results for many years, and have contributed regularly to the central revenues of the country. In the year 1936, after providing fully for depreciation, and making appropriations for interest, sinking fund charges, pensions, capital and renewal adjustments, the balance accruing to the Central Government was £498,000.

The revenue and expenditure has shown considerable fluctuations, as is indicated by the following figures:

Year.	Revenue. (£E.)	Operating expenses.(a) (£E.)
1930	2,587,298	1,685,518
1931	1,868,654	1,455,446
1932	1,877,540	1,264,836
1933	1,737,142	1,216,901
1934	2,161,811	1,265,819
1935	2,511,827	1,316,633

(a) Includes the full charge for depreciation.

The statistics of the nett balances which accrued to the Central Government in every one of these years have been given previously.

A contributory factor to the prosperity of the railways, apart from the large export and import tonnage, is the considerable local traffic.

Belgian Congo.—The growth of railway construction in the Belgian Congo is shown by the following table:

Open Miles of Railways in the Belgian Congo.

Year.	Government Constructed but Private Operation and Ownership.	Private.	Government.	Total.
To 1900 . .	...	245	50	295
To 1920 . .	443	433	35	911
Total . .	443	678	85	1,206
1921 to 1935 . .	1,104	394	...	1,498
Grand total .	1,547	1,072	85	2,704

The methods of financing the establishment of this system have been complicated. In some cases the building of the railways was commenced by private enterprise, but had to be completed by the Government, which then took over; in other cases the lines were constructed by the Government on behalf of private companies, which own and operate them. In a few cases the lines were built by the State itself, and are owned and operated by it. Most of the private companies have been assisted in one form or another by the State. Since 1928 this has been mainly by Government guarantees of the interest on the capital required. The figures on p. 408 show the capital invested before and after the War.

It will be noted that the total investment prior to 1922 amounted to 483 million gold Francs, equivalent to about £19,300,000 ; from 1923 to 1932 some 3,337 million Francs (paper) were invested, equivalent to approximately £19,000,000. Thus, up to 1932, the total investment in the Belgian Congo

Approximate Capital Invested in Railways (Shares, Loans and Advances).

Year.(a)	Total.		
	Paper Fr.	Gold Fr.	£
	(000,000.)	(000,000.)	(000,000.)
1890	...	25·0	...
1891/1900	...	65·0	...
1901–10	...	83·0	...
1911–21	...	310·0	...
Total	...	483·0	19·32
1922–32	3,337	476·7	19·06
Total to 1932	...	959·7	38·38
Advances by the Colony :			
1929–32	407	58·1	2·32
Grand total	...	1,017·8	40·70

(a) The above classification as to the years in which the capital was expended is approximate.

Railways was about £38,000,000. In addition the Colony had advanced approximately £2,300,000 from revenue.

The main companies concerned in the railway development are listed in the following table, which shows the amount of the guarantees undertaken by the State in each case, and the resulting burden on the Government in 1934:

Company.	Guaranteed Capital (Shares or Debentures). (Francs.)	Financial burden on the Government in 1934. (Francs.)
Chemin de fer du Bas-Congo	925,000,000	29,000,000
„ de Leokadi	600,000,000	42,000,000
„ des Grands-Lacs	250,000,000	13,624,500
„ du Congo vicinaux	316,942,500	10,397,165
„ du Kivu	180,000,000	8,860,000
Total	2,271,942,500	103,863,665

In the case of the Chemin de fer des Grands-Lacs, whose guaranteed capital is 250,000,000 Francs, it has been estimated that, from 1914 and up to 1932, the State had to pay approximately 290,000,000 Francs (paper) under its guarantees. As a matter of fact, this company was induced to undertake railway construction as a result of the allocation to it of very considerable mineral rights. It is alleged in the report of the Belgian Senate Commission, No. 85, 1934, that the payments under the State Guarantee could have been avoided, and the Commission cites this as an example of the dangers inherent in this form of State guaranteed railway construction by private companies.[1]

It is not possible to examine the operations of the various railway companies in detail. From the reports of the Colonial Commission of the Belgian Senate, it appears that railways of the Belgian Congo have suffered greatly from the financial methods used in order to bring about their construction, and from the resulting conditions under which they were owned and operated. It appears also that the system of concessions, and Government guarantees, has led to waste and to over-investment of capital. No unified railway policy has been achieved; as a result, the systems of rates adopted by the various companies have developed in a most contradictory fashion, and, in most cases, have led to charges on traffic which are extremely high, and which have hampered the development of the resources of the territory.

The following quotation from Senate Report No. 108 (1935) Colonial Commission illustrates the position: (p. 39.)

"Tout alla à merveille aussi longtemps que les prix de vente des produits couvraient, tout en laissant une marge

---

[1] The report of the Belgian Senate No. 108, 1935, sums up this matter as follows: (p. 49.)

"Mais chaque année, depuis que le chemin de fer existe, la garantie donnée par le Gouvernement a joué. A fin 1932, les sommes payées de ce chef s'élèvent a fr. 134,086,500–18, dont une partie en francs stabilisés, cette somme s'élève à environ 290,000,000 de francs (papier). Votre rapport de l'an dernier à fait l'historique de cette Société et démontré, chiffres ' l'appui, comment par la création d'une filiale 'La Minière des Grands Lacs' elle a cédé à cette dernière de vastes concessions minières dont les revenus auraient dû servir à amortir son capital et venir en déduction des nombreux millions que l'État lui a versés annuellement au titre de garantie d'intérêt. Nous croyons inutile de revenir sur cette question malgré l'influence de cette opération sur les bilans successifs de la compagnie de Chemin de fer."

bénéficiaire, les frais des producteurs, des commerçants et des transporteurs.

"Mais la crise est venue; les prix de réalisation des produits d'exportation ont subi des chutes considérables et cette situation compromet tout le système économique de la Colonie parce que les transporteurs ne peuvent ramener leurs prix à des niveaux suffisamment bas.

"Le problème des transports se pose à nouveau au Congo, tel que l'envisageait l'honorable Ministre d'État en 1914. '*Toute entreprise de transports aux colonies doit tirer son bénéfice, ou couvrir ses charges financières, par l'accroissement du trafic en lieu et place de l'elévation des tarifs*; tout movement de hausse des tarifs conduit au ralentissement du trafic.'

"Le contraire se produit pour tout abaissement de tarif. La question des tarifs domine donc tout le problème des transports au Congo; le coût des transports des produits coloniaux doit toujours être établi sur les prix les plus bas et les tarifs doivent se calculer uniquement sur les frais d'exploitation augmentés de la rémunération des capitaux investis et des amortissements qu'ils comportent.

Si l'on considère l'avenir de la Colonie et non l'intérêt de quelques-uns, aucune autre base de tarifs n'est admissible. Pour que les transports puissent se faire économiquement, et assurer en tout temps l'exportation de la production, l'Etat doit être le maître absolu des grandes voies de communication tant par fer que par eau; quant aux transports par routes il doit éviter tout monopole et laisser jouer la libre concurrence. *Ce n'est pas ce qui s'est pratiqué cette année encore et la commission ne peut pas s'y rallier.*

Votre rapport de 1934 a démontré l'inflation des dépenses dont le gouvernement a donné un example regrettable. L'exploitation des chemins de fer n'a pas échappé à cette mégalomanie des dépenses sans compter.

"C'est cependant sur ces bases forcées de prix de revient que les dégrèvements massifs ont été accordés."

All sorts of *ad hoc* measures have been taken in order to overcome the high level of railway rates. In addition to bearing the burden of interest payments on most of the lines, the Government actually bound itself to grant direct subsidies in order to lower railway rates on some of the lines. This made confusion worse confounded, and appears to have added to the forces making for inefficiency, and to the uncertainty of the future trend of railway rates. This is indicated in the following summary from the same Report (at p. 54):

> "Une seule chose est irréductiblement anti-économique au double point de vue de la technique du budget et de la pratique des affaires, c'est le fait d'un état conditionnant l'équilibre de son budget en fonction du déséquilibre économique.

> "Comment, en premier lieu, justifier du point de vue économique, la garantie d'intérêt accordée par l'État à des Sociétés privées sans clauses de récupération possible; comment justifier le service durant des années, de ces intérêts, pendant que les bénéficiares réalisaient d'importants profits, pratiquaient de sérieux amortissements et se constituaient de notables réserves et un important portefeuille ? D'autre part, est-il admissible qu'afin d'activer la circulation des produits et de stimuler le commerce d'exportation, le Gouvernement de la Colonie impose aux Sociétés de transport des dégrèvements massifs, dont en fin de compte, il supporte les frais; dégrèvements qui eurent peut-être dans le domaine des affaires des répercussions favorables, mais qui sont totalement indéfendables du point de vue budgétaire ? "

> "Est-il admissible d'octroyer à quelques privilégiés des monopoles de droit ou de fait qui vinculent la liberté du commerce en faussant le jeu de la libre concurrence des prix ?

> "On aurait pu croire que le Gouvernement, ayant compris ce que lui avait coûté dans le passé l'octroi de ces monopoles injustifiés, se serait bien gardé de récidiver; il n'en est rien, hélas !

> "*L'octroi d'un nouveau monopole des transports automobiles définitivement accompli entre 1928 et 1934, vient de prouver que l'expérience ne lui a rien appris. La Commission le regrette, le condamne et ne désire en rien s'associer à cette mesure dangereuse qu'elle réprouve sans ménagement.*

> "Ce qui est au plus haut point anti-économique c'est de prendre comme entrepreneur de travaux publics, une société de transport, dont le rôle se borne à celui d'intermédiaire qui s'empresse de passer l'affaire à des soustraitants, moyennant les profitables contrats qui se devinent aisément, tout comme si l'État lui-même ne pouvait traiter directement avec les entrepreneurs et

épargner de ce fait les plantureux bénéfices réalisés par les
intermédiaires.

"Ne l'oublions pas, c'est à la faveur de pareils errements
que des fautes ont pu être commises dont la gravité s'impose
de plus en plus à l'évidence: les ports d'Ango-Ango et de
Matadi, le mur de quai de Coquilhatville et bien d'autres
entreprises encore, nous ont valués une expérience acquise au
prix de plus d'une leçon sévère, mais méritée.

"Ce qui est anti-économique ce sont ces concessions
immenses de terrains octroyées à des groupes de financiers
qui, contrairement à tous engagements, n'en exploitent
qu'une infime partie privant ainsi l'État de revenus qu'il
est en droit d'escompter.

"En résumé ce qui est anti-économique, ce sont les
prodigalités de l'État faites dans tous les domaines avec des
milliards qu'il ne possède pas."

Since the depression, the State has made considerable efforts to
control the situation, and to bring about greater uniformity in
railway rates. The rating system itself made much use of devices
by which rates fluctuated with the value of the products handled.
As this system was extensively applied, accurate budgeting
became very difficult, and the liability of the State was uncertain
from year to year.

It is an extraordinary fact that, from 1920–32, the whole of the
dividends and interest payments of the Railway Companies,
whose total registered capital (the capital expenditure, of course,
was greater than the registered capital) in 1932 amounted to
approximately 3,511,000,000 Francs, were only 475,000,000 Francs,
or a return of about 1·05% per annum. Of this total, approximately
239,000,000 Francs were paid out by the Katanga Railway, which
shows a return on its registered capital of nearly 4% per annum
(on the total capital expenditure the return is only a little
over 3% per annum). A further 105,000,000 Francs was paid
during the same period by the State on behalf of the Chemin
de Fer des Grands-Lacs, leaving a return of approximately
136,000,000 Francs for thirteen years on a capital of approximately 2,588,000,000 Francs on the other railways apart from
Katanga. It should be remembered, however, that approximately
1,500,000,000 of this latter sum is the capital invested in the

Leokadi railway, which was being extended and reconstructed until 1931. But even so, a return of 136,000,000 Francs on, say, 1,500,000,000 Francs in thirteen years is a sufficient indication of the unsatisfactory financial position of these railways. It should, of course, be remembered that these figures are approximate, and, owing to the depreciation of the Belgian Franc, include both gold and paper Francs. They, however, indicate the trend of the financial results of the railway as a whole.

It is highly significant that the only railway line which has been able to attain financial independence is the Chemin de Fer du Katanga. This line, as is well known, was in the first place built in order to connect the Katanga mineral area with the Rhodesian Railway System, to enable the transport of copper to the East Coast. The financing of the line was assisted by the Tanganyika Concessions, Limited. The Government also later guaranteed 100 million Francs as to interest and amortization. The total capital expenditure on the railway to 1932 was approximately 765 million Francs. The Government has never been called upon under its guarantee. It is highly significant that this, the only paying line in the Belgian Congo is concerned mainly with mineral traffic. An examination of the various traffics on this line shows that over 85% of the average annual ton kilometres for recent years consisted of mineral traffic.

In 1932 there was a drastic restriction of traffic, and a consequent large fall in receipts in the case of all the companies, as a result of the depression. This can be illustrated by the change which took place in one year, from 1931 (itself not a very prosperous year) to 1932, in the case of one company, the Chemin de Fer du Katanga. The total tonnes kilométriques fell from 203 millions to 87 millions, a decline of 56% in one year; the receipts from 113 million Francs to 49 million Francs. The decline was, of course, largely ascribable to the fall in mineral traffic. The recession in mineral traffic can also be illustrated by its effect on the Port-Franqui Bukama. In 1931, 160,024 tons were handled. In 1932 this had fallen to 75,319. Mineral traffic had fallen from 42,365 tons in 1931, to 18,863 tons in 1932.

The financial results of the railways as a whole were, of course, affected equally drastically by the depression. Indeed, in 1932 the total interest charges amounted to about 225 million Francs (paper), and the amortization charges to 115 million Francs, a total of 340 million Francs. This sum was actually equivalent to 165% of the total receipts of the railways. If working and general expenditures are added to the financial charges, the total expenditure was 503 million Francs, as compared with total receipts of only 206 million Francs. The total expenditure, therefore, was 243% of the total receipts in this year.

The comparative results for 1932 of the main railways of the Belgian Congo are shown in Table 101.[1]

French Colonies.—The capital invested in the Railway Systems of the French Colonies is shown by the following approximate figures, which also give the growth in the railway mileage:

Approximate Amounts of Capital Invested in (or Cost of Construction of) Railways in French Territories in Africa. Francs (000,000).

Year.	West Africa.(a)		Other Africa.(b)		Total. French Africa.	
	Gold Francs.	£.	Gold Francs.	£.	Gold Francs.	£.
To 1920 . .	225·64	9·02	144·00	5·76	369·64	14·78
1921–34 . .	52·00	2·08	378·20	15·12	430·20	17·20
Total . .	277·64	11·10	522·20	20·88	799·84	31·98
Add Railways in German Colonies prior to 1914 .	...	...	...	...	...	4·20
Grand total						36·18

(a) West Africa includes Senegal, Guinea, Ivory Coast, French Sudan, Dahomey.

(b) Other Africa includes Moyen Congo, Somali Coast, Madagascar, Réunion—it was not possible to separate the figures for Réunion and Madagascar from the above figures. The amounts involved are, however, relatively small.

Mileage in French Territories in Africa.

Year.	West Africa.	Other Africa.	Total. French Africa.
To 1920	1,578	360	1,938
1921–34	341	609	950
Total French . .	1,919	969	2,888
Add Railways in German Colonies prior to 1914 .	...	...	448
Grand total			3,336

[1] The information has been extracted from Report No. 108 of the Belgian Senate, June 18th, 1935.

TABLE 101.—*Comparison of Financial Results of Belgian Congo Railways*, 1932
(*Belgian Francs*).

	Matadi-Leo.	Léokadi Dilolo.	Katanga.	Grands Lacs.	Vicicongo.	Mayumbe.
Longueur exploitée	39½	1,645	861	763	466	140
„ „ par eau	...	...	...	1,870	...	...
Capital investi	984,004,987	1,326,000,000	765,484,209	454,740,695 dont une partie en or	213,934,120	76,500,000
Charges financières	50,666,628	75,000,000	...	18,938,660	12,836,047	4,590,000
Part. garantie par Colonie	35,000,000	37,500,000	5,930,400	18,938,660	2,776,350	4,590,000
Charge financière par kilometre	126,870	45,592	...	24,821	27,545	32,785
Récuperation.—Dégrèvements massifs	4,417,930	neant.	neant.	1,978,880	4,832,602	240,813 (solde)
Charge financière par T. K.	0·43	1·25	...	1·20	2·47	1·52
Dépenses d'exploitation, y compris frais généraux	63,012,022	26,244,573	39,375,781	21,059,987	7,158,916	4,528,616
Idem, par kilometre	157,727	14,579	45,732	27,575	15,352	32,348
Dépenses par T. K.	0·54	0·42	0·45	1·41	1·53	1·50
Récettes d'exploitation	87,858,368	27,587,602	49,512,655	24,362,239	10,910,694	4,528,616
Récette par kilometre	219,948	13,787	59,828	31,929	23,413	32,348
Récette par T.K.	0·75	0·38	0·56	1·55	2·33	1·50
Tonnage	490,071	103,328	888,778	41,058	20,617	29,759
Tonnes Kilometres	116,619,027	47,241,553	87,367,436	15,667,298	4,672,305	3,012,979

Note.—Il y a plus de 250,000,000 d'amortis et nous n'avons pu fixer la charge financière

The total capital investment amounts to roughly £32,000,000, and to this amount must be added approximately £4,000,000 which was invested in the German railways prior to 1914 in the territories now under French mandate. These figures are based on an investigation of the separate railway systems, but, owing to the accounting methods used, and the frequent overlapping between the accounts of the territories, and those of the railways, they must be regarded only as broad estimates. The information available as to the working results of these railways is very unsatisfactory. Practically all the railways are now administered and managed as departments of state, and no separation of railway accounts from the general accounts takes place. It is, therefore, not possible to examine the finances of the railways on the same lines as has been done in the case of British railways.

The French Colonial railways have suffered under the same difficulties as have faced the Belgian Congo railways in the non-mineral areas. Most of the railways have not been financially self-supporting at any time, and some of them show very heavy losses, greatly intensified, of course, by the depression. In addition, most of the railways have been constructed and part-operated to further various military objectives, and the systems have been burdened with non-economic extensions, and render non-economic services.

Portuguese Railways.—The capital invested in the Portuguese Railways amounts to approximately £2,000,000 in the State Railways of Angola, and approximately £13,000,000, nearly all of which is British capital, in the Benguella Railway, which traverses Angola to the Katanga. In Portuguese East Africa the Government railways are operated by an autonomous body (Concelho de Administracao dos Portos e dos Caminhos de Ferro da Colonia de Moçambique), and the capital invested now amounts to about £8,000,000. In addition, British capital has built the Beira Railway, the Beira-Junction Railway, and the Trans-Zambesi Railway, parts of which traverse the territory of the Mozambique Company.

The State railways of the Portuguese Colony of Mozambique have benefited considerably from the use of Lourenço Marques as a port of entry for the Transvaal—particularly from the high-rated traffic to the Witwatersrand. The railways cover approximately 861 miles; the line Lourenço Marques–Ressano Garcia, 89 kilometres, joins the South African railways at the Transvaal border, and is the most important line in the Colony. The line Lourenço Marques–Goba, near the frontier of Swaziland, was intended to be linked up, across Swaziland, with the contemplated line to Ermelo in the Union, but the project was not completed. Another important line is that of Lumbo (Mozambique to Eibaue); this line, about 280 kilometres of which are now completed, is gradually being extended to the Nyasaland border. Besides tapping the agricultural region of the Colony, it will eventually be a valuable asset as a speedy outlet for the produce of Nyasaland and other parts of Central Africa.

The accounts of the railway administration of the Colony for the year ended June, 1934, showed 235,687 tons of goods carried; in addition, no less than 917,400 tons were received from the South African railways. Railway earnings amounted to £623,581, and total earnings, including ports and road services, to £917,577. The total expenditure was £494,246, leaving a surplus of £423,331. A noteworthy factor in the development of the Colony is the large amount of road construction that has taken place in recent years. There are 4,766 kilometres of roads in the Colony which are classed as "first class", and the total length of roads of all classes is nearly 23,000 kilometres.

The State railways of Angola include the Loanda Railway, running 433 kilometres to Malange, with three branch lines of 30 kilometres each, and one of 94 kilometres. It taps a good maize, sisal and coffee region. Its traffic has been seriously affected owing to the depression, but it is likely to develop with the improvement in the economic position of the Colony. The State railway system also includes the Amboim railway, which runs for 106 kilometres from Port Amboim to Chindinde, and taps the coffee plantations of that region, but its traffic has fallen steadily in recent years. The Benguella railway runs 1,347 kilometres from the port of Lobito to the Belgian Congo frontier, where it connects with the line to Elizabethville. Its results, so far, have been disappointing, but, sooner or later, this line, served by an admirable harbour, will come into its own, as it is the shortest route from Europe to the Katanga region. Attempts are also being made to promote agricultural settlement with the assistance of the railways.

Conclusion.—An approximate estimate of the total capital expenditure on railways in Africa, and also of the amounts of interest-bearing capital invested in the British African railways, is presented in Table 102; the estimate is to the end of 1934, or to the year nearest to 1934 for which figures are available.

It will be seen that the total capital expenditure on British railways amounted to roughly £283,000,000.[1]

The interest-bearing loan capital, including debentures of private railways in British territories, amounted to roughly £230,000,000.[2]

In the remaining African territories, the capital expenditure amounted to about £79,000,000, excluding the Benguella Line; and to this must be added the capital invested in the ex-German Colonial railways, amounting to £21,500,000. It will, therefore, be seen that the British capital expenditure on railways has been nearly three times as much as the total foreign capital so invested.

The foregoing survey of the results of various African railways shows that, unless mineral traffic, or considerable imported traffic to mineral areas is available, great difficulty is experienced in making the railways earn sufficient to pay the interest on the capital which they have had to borrow at relatively high rates of interest. In general, African railways have been constructed on the basis of a too optimistic view of the rate of economic development in the territories they serve, and many of them have been built in areas where little economic progress can be expected. Failing the development of new mineral resources, considerable further railway construction in the near future will not be warranted from an economic point of view, unless the cost of construction does not fall upon the railways or the Colonial territories. Of course, in so far as Imperial Governments are, for any reason, prepared to bear the losses on Colonial railways, no economic limit to their extension can be laid down, and the same

[1] This includes the British-built railways in Portuguese East Africa and Angola.
[2] To this sum must be added about £12,000,000 for the Benguella line.

TABLE 102.—*Railway Systems in Africa. Approximate Capital Expenditure to* 1934.

BRITISH.

	Capital Expenditure. (£000,000.)		Interest-bearing Loans. (approximate). (£000,000.)
South African Railways and Harbours	167·3	.	150·2
Northern and Southern Rhodesia (including Beira Railway and Beira Junction Railway) .	26·0	.	25·0 (Debentures)
Nigeria Railway . . .	23·0	.	19·2
Tanganyika	5·3 (British)	.	5·3
Kenya and Uganda Railways and Harbours	22·4	.	14·0
Nyasaland	5·0	.	4·0 (Debentures)
Gold Coast	9·2	.	7·9
Sierra Leone	1·4	.	1·0
Sudan Railways . . .	11·1	.	3·6
Total British . . .	270·7		230·2

FOREIGN.

Portuguese:		
Angola State Railway . .	2·0 (Rough estimate)	
Benguella Railway (private) .	13·0 (Nearly all British capital)	
Portuguese East Africa (a) .	6·6	
French Colonies	32·0	
Belgian Congo	38·0	
	91·6	
Ex German Colonies:		
German East Africa . .	10·4	
Kamerun	3·2	
Togo	0·9	
South-West Africa . .	7·0	
Total Foreign . .	113·1	
Total British . .	270·7	
Grand total .	383·8	

(a) The Beira Railway, the Beira Junction Railways and the Trans-Zambesi Railway have been included in the Rhodesian Railways and the Nyasaland Railways respectively. They were built by them mainly with British capital.

consideration applies to the construction of railways for strategic, military or administrative purposes.

Future transport development in Africa will be bound up to an ever-increasing extent with the building of roads and the provision of road motor services, both of which have expanded enormously in recent years ; considerable expenditure in this direction took place even during the depression. At no distant time the greater part of Africa will be linked up by an excellent system of all-weather roads, which will revolutionize the economic activity in large areas of the continent. Owing to the emphasis on road, rather than further railway, construction, the external capital charges which will have to be borne by African territories in connection with the provision of communications are not likely to increase at anything like the same rate in the future as they have done since the War.

The outstanding transport problems of the next few years lie in the field of road, rail and air co-ordination, and the building up of traffic for the main railway lines. Coupled with this will be the final establishment of the vast network of airways, which has been planned already, and much of which is being operated to-day. This will greatly affect the future of economic development in Africa. It will not only link vast areas with Europe in the north, and the Union in the south, but it will inaugurate also a new era of financial, economic, and political co-operation between the different countries of the continent.

CHAPTER VI

CONCLUSION

In the foregoing chapters I have endeavoured to outline the nature and direction of some of the great economic changes which have taken place since the European powers first began to develop the resources of Africa, and awakened its peoples from the slumber of ages.

My object has been to present the facts, and to let the facts speak for themselves. These concluding remarks, therefore, will be confined to certain special matters directly arising out of the material which has already been submitted.

The positive achievements of the colonizing powers, during the brief period of contact with Africa in modern times, have been innumerable; those who belittle these achievements do not grasp the essence of the revolution which has swept over Africa, and which heralds a new era for its inhabitants.

The positive progress has been analysed in the foregoing pages, but there is also a negative measure of that progress which consists in the growing realization that many of the policies in the past were erroneous. Indeed, the most significant fact for the future lies in the still fluid state of Africa's economic relationships; no final system of economic organization has been evolved, no single pattern has yet crystallized out of the ever-changing economic factors in the African scene.

In some parts of Africa the extent of the rigidities which have been introduced in economic relationships is greater than in others, but we must beware of assuming that these are, in fact, permanent patterns or fundamental lines of economic demarcation.

Even in South Africa, where the rigidities are in many respects most marked, and in which they affect the work of the economy most seriously, the forces of change are already exerting enormous pressure. Whether or not the urgent need for new income-creating opportunities, through which alone the tide of proletarization and poverty can be stemmed, is, or is not to be met by the peaceful evolution of new means of constructive economic co-operation, will constitute the acid test, not only of South African statesmanship, but of South African, perhaps even of African civilization. The battle for a new synthesis in African economic relationship is, with certain exceptions, likely to be fought out south, and not north of the equator, for, in the north, climatic and geographical conditions make the problems different in some respects, and less urgent in others. The clash of progress in the north will not be as strident, and time will have greater scope to mellow change, and yet, even here, much more than we can now see may depend on the results of the great sociological experiments in Southern Africa.

It would be idle, in the face of the present international situation, to attempt to prophesy as to the supply of capital which will be available for Africa in the future, but it is doubtful whether the average annual amount, for the time being, will be as large as in the past.

If international trade does not revive, and if the impoverishment of Europe, owing to the existing politico-economic conditions, continues, both the supply of capital and the opportunity for its investment in Africa may be seriously retarded. On the one hand, Africa is mainly a producer of raw materials, the increased demand for which depends mainly upon a rising standard of life in Europe and America, while, on the other hand, without a rising income-level in these countries, it is unlikely that capital will continue to be available for Africa in the same quantities as previously.

To this statement there are three qualifications of importance. The first is that, if the post-war trend of British overseas investment, which has led to greater investment in the British Empire, rather than in foreign countries, continues, it is possible that British capital will be available for Africa in increasing quantities, particularly as it is probable that some of the Dominions will not borrow in London in future as heavily as they did in the past.

The Government of the Union of South Africa, also, should no serious change in the importance of gold mining occur, is not likely to borrow as much in London as previously. As opposed to this, however, mining and industrial development is likely to remain greatly dependent on overseas resources, but, in general, the Union's demand for capital will depend increasingly on its ability to re-organize its economy in order to open up new avenues for the employment of capital.

The second qualification is that, on the assumption that colonial possessions are to be developed, supplies of capital for that purpose from the metropolitan countries are absolutely essential. Various theories of curtailing the investment of capital overseas have in recent years become prevalent. These are based on such allegations as that the yield of overseas capital investment is not a sufficient indication of its desirability, judged from a national point of view, or that, taken as a whole, overseas investment does not show an economic yield greater than that which could be obtained by the investment of the same capital resources at home. In my opinion, the correctness or otherwise of these allegations, however important they may in themselves be, does not meet the real point at issue in questions concerning the provision of capital for colonial development. If colonial development is to continue, there can be no difference of opinion about the need for overseas capital investment.

In any case, the problem whether the ownership of colonial territories is desirable or not is not solely an economic one; it cannot be decided on economic principles or according to the method of striking a balance sheet of profit and loss, even if that were (in the writer's opinion an untenable assumption) statistically possible.

There is some reason to believe, therefore, that, far from restricting overseas investment in colonial territories, it may become necessary in the future, if the supply of capital available for investment abroad should decline, to divert an increased proportion to colonial territories, and away from certain foreign countries.

What is important, however, is that the extent to which capital is diverted into particular channels in the colonial territories should be subject to the most detailed scrutiny on the basis of past results and of past methods of raising and applying it. The success of capital application in particular directions can be assessed according to the special standards corresponding to its various uses, and according to its repercussions on the general economy of the areas concerned. The latter often involve the colonial territories in very serious problems and, in many cases, impose on them a heavy burden.

The third qualification is that obviously no forecast can be made as to the limits to investment on non-economic principles and for purposes other than those directly related to the yield of the capital investment. It is also not possible to take account of the many political and other considerations which may influence investment in undeveloped colonial territories by the countries owning or administering them, or of the effects of national, military or autarkic policies in the home countries.

In so far as capital is made available for non-economic purposes by metropolitan powers whose economy is subject to autarkic controls, the amounts so set aside may, for a time, be larger than would otherwise be the case. Ultimately, however, this type of artificially-stimulated investment is not likely to be as large as popular opinion is apt to believe. There is no evidence that the available resources for overseas investment by foreign powers will be larger in the forseeable future than they were previously, when, in many cases, they proved inadequate for colonial needs. Even if resources are compulsorily diverted to colonial development at the expense of more urgent tasks in the mother country itself, there is a definite limit to the amounts of capital which can be made available in this way.

However this may be, past African experience shows that the rate at which capital can be absorbed by colonial territories depends on the rate at which the other complementary factors of supply can be made available, and that the pace of African economic development cannot be forced by artificial expedients, by lavish capital expenditure, or by the use of compulsion.

Whatever the future may bring, one fact stands out clearly from the analysis presented in this book, that is, the extraordinary dependence of African development on British capital. That dependence has been due by no means only to the larger resources of Great Britain, but has resulted also from the highly developed and specialized character of British financial institutions. This intricate network of British finance, which has undoubtedly made possible the greater degree of progress attained in British African territories, is, relatively to the methods of finance generally adopted in the world to-day, an extremely efficient mechanism—perhaps the most efficient in existence. It is built on a long and varied experience of world and colonial conditions. It is this experience, personified in thousands of individuals and incorporated in hundreds of institutions by long specialization, which has made for the relatively greater financial success of British enterprise in Africa. To that success the excellent financial administration of the British colonies has greatly contributed. British methods of colonial finance, audit, and control compare extremely favourably with those in certain foreign colonies.

All these factors are bound to continue to exert an important influence on the direction of investment, and on African economic progress. It does not seem that British financial leadership in Africa will be challenged in the foreseeable future. Any suggestion for altering the methods of financing African development must take this fact into account, and, clearly, any changes contemplated must be based on the financial machinery, and the experience, of the past.

Yet that experience has also demonstrated beyond doubt that, whatever the rate of overseas investment in Africa may be in the future, it is very necessary to foster those forms of economic progress which will enable the populations of the African continent to contribute in greater measure than they have done so far to the upbuilding of capital resources themselves. Events in Europe may, in any case, force Africa to rely to an increasing extent on its own capital resources, but, quite apart from this consideration, it is obviously undesirable that the future of African countries should continue to be mortgaged, to meet fixed interest burdens abroad, at the same rate as in the past.

The capital which has been supplied to Africa up to the present, has been largely utilized in providing African territories with a skeleton structure composed of modern means of transport production and administration. It is an expensive structure, and involves the colonies in enormous overhead charges. The skeleton must now be filled in with the flesh and blood of more intensive, decentralized, individual production, and gradual capital accumulation, by the people of Africa themselves.

This involves great difficulties. A large part of the efforts of African populations must, of necessity, be devoted to the production of crops for export, and there are definite limits at present to the extent to which local production can be stimulated. When large mineral resources are available the problem becomes more difficult in some respects and easier in others. The need to divert labour to mining obviously tends to restrict local production. On the other hand, as mining capital is usually of the equity type, it does not involve fixed external debt charges, and makes it easier for the territories concerned to meet their other external burdens. Mining also provides local markets for agricultural products if the labour supply available is sufficient for this.

The greater the degree of economic development, the more pressing will the question of population and therefore of the supply of labour become. From an economic point of view, Africa is under-populated in the sense that the number of its peoples available for modern economic activities is smaller with their present educational and sociological standards, than the exploitation of its resources requires. An important advance in any one direction in economic enterprise—for example, in mining—is therefore likely to affect seriously the supply of workers available for other purposes. All territories in Africa do not suffer from this difficulty to the same extent. In those with relatively small mineral resources the rate of development is likely to depend on the rate at which cultural, sociological and administrative changes can bring about more suitable or better methods of production for the indigenous peoples. In these territories, in particular, the excessive investment of capital on fixed terms is dangerous, and the use to which such capital is put requires particularly careful and unbiased consideration.

In this connection it must not be forgotten that political frontiers do not necessarily involve the economic isolation of

African territories from one another. On the contrary, factors of supply move across national frontiers, or trade takes the place of such movements, and here the mobility of native labour assumes special importance.. The development of territories which possess considerable mineral resources will, therefore, continue to affect neighbouring countries, and the economic stimulus provided by the mineral industries themselves will extend far beyond the immediate areas concerned.

The whole problem is really a question of the rate of economic development which can be adopted. Undue capital investment from abroad causes a gap between the degree of development of the capital equipment of the territory and the degree of development of the customary means of production and consumption. Any undesirable effects resulting can be avoided only by a slower rate of capital investment, and this implies a simpler system of production and simpler means of meeting the economic wants of the population. It implies, also, a restriction of the needs of the population which can be satisfied, and particularly a restriction of the growth of administrative and other social services, and therefore in the total cost of supplying them. The problem of economic development in Africa can no longer be regarded as one to be judged only by the success of particular industries or private *entrepreneurs* exploiting particular African resources, nor can it be assumed that the diversion of capital into particular channels, owing to momentary optimistic expectations of its profitability, is necessarily in the interests of either the debtor or the creditor country.

The most extraordinary fact in the past trend of development in Africa is the influence of mining; there is every likelihood that its predominant importance in Southern and in parts of Central Africa will continue, and that in turn it will, as previously, stimulate complementary or subsidiary industries, including farming. The proportion of equity capital investment in Africa is therefore likely to increase. Moreover, in the Union, in West Africa, and in certain other areas, it is probable that there will be a further growth in the rate of such private capital investment as falls under the definition of "non-listed" capital. In part, the growth will result from the establishment of branch companies, factories and commercial undertakings. These will either be manufacturing articles previously imported, or will be engaged in processing, collecting, or refining raw materials for the parent undertakings, or for sale in world markets. There is also likely to be a growth in the registration and flotation of such undertakings, as independent companies, in colonial territories. These will probably be sponsored by overseas parent concerns which will invest considerable, though not necessarily controlling amounts of capital in the new undertakings. Developments of this kind are to be welcomed. As Sir Arthur Salter has shown in his well-known Report on China, it is desirable that local initiative and ownership should be associated with overseas capital as a solution of the problems connected with international capital movements, in order to avoid undue Government borrowing on fixed terms, and in order to increase the flexibility of the capital structure. All these activities are bound up closely with the evolution of new methods of co-operation between Government and private enterprise in the supply of capital and its control and management.

One of the striking facts which emerges from the survey conducted in this book is the preponderating importance of South Africa in the economic transformation of the Continent. The role of the Union in Africa, assuming that it can bridge its own political schisms, and ignoring other unforeseen political changes, is likely to grow further in importance. For it is in the Union that the interests which are financing a large part of the mining and exploration activities throughout Africa have established themselves. Much private investment from abroad for other African territories is taking place via the Union, and it is possible that from its own recources South Africa may eventually finance much African enterprise beyond its borders.

If the Union can succeed in increasing its national income by achieving a new unity and freedom in its economic affairs, it might look forward with confidence to the possibility of assuming the economic leadership of a large part of the African continent. For it is in the Union that Europeans have had the longest opportunity to grapple with African problems, and have been fortunate in possessing large resources with which to support a

European civilization, and to build up its social heritage in Africa.

In the last resort, however, the future of capital investment, like the future of all African economic progress, will depend on freeing the African peoples from the factors which have checked their progress in the past, and the artificial restrictions which in some territories still prevent the unfolding of their abilities. It is for this reason that, in the future, non-material capital accumulation, which consists in the spread of knowledge, education and scientific inquiry, and new adaptations to ecological conditions, will assume an ever-growing importance.

If twentieth century experience in Africa has proved anything at all, it is that the wealth of Africa has, as yet, hardly been discovered, simply because it lies deep in the soil of Africa itself. Only by the co-operant efforts of Africans and Europeans will it be unearthed; undue haste will destroy much of it. It is patient united effort that is needed. There must be an avoidance, as far as possible, of extreme fluctuations in the rate of economic progress, and uneconomic vested interests must not be allowed to retard the growth of the whole for the benefit of the part.

It may be thought that these are mere general phrases, and, indeed, they are of import not only in the continent of Africa. Yet there is perhaps some hope that their application to that continent may prove in some small measure simpler than elsewhere. The curtain has only just risen on the African scene—the drama has yet to be played.

Indeed, the twentieth century opens the era of constructive and creative activity by Western powers in Africa. In this difficult task it has at least one advantage: the path is not yet blocked by the boulders of privilege, and the opportunities are many for the development of new knowledge, the application of science and a new co-ordination of effort.

APPENDIX

NOTE ON AFRICAN STATISTICS

ONE of the most necessary developments in Africa is the establishment of machinery for the standardization of African statistics. With few exceptions, the statistical material made available by the Governments of African territories is still, as is, of course, to be expected, inadequate.

It cannot be expected that the statistical material in Africa should be better than that which is made available elsewhere at the present day, but it should be possible to bring the standard in Africa into greater conformity with the techniques of compilation and tabulation in general use. At the present time African statistics are, in general, characterized by their lack of uniformity and of sufficiently precise definition. This is due, in part, to the fact that they are made available by many different departments and compiled for different purposes in the various territories. They are not, as a rule, collected by a central statistical department. As a result, there are great differences in the methods used in obtaining or calculating them in any one territory, and little uniformity between the practices of different territories. The lack of continuity in the methods of preparing statistics frequently makes it very difficult to obtain even the most fundamental statistical series over a long period of years.

There are, moreover, often serious differences of nomenclature. For example, the exact meaning to be ascribed to such terms as "imports for home consumption", "domestic exports", "transit trade", "trans-shipment trade", "re-exports", or "ordinary" revenue and expenditure, "extraordinary" revenue and expenditure, etc., is often difficult to determine, while the meaning at one time may not be the same as that used on other occasions.

The lack of homogeneity in African statistics is well illustrated by such a publication as that on *International Trade in*

Certain Raw Materials and Foodstuffs, now prepared annually by the Economic Intelligence Service of the League of Nations,[1] which is based on questionnaires to the different countries concerned. The replies to the questionnaires and the compilation of the information show the extremely numerous qualifications with which African official statistics have to be hedged about in order to achieve some measure of comparability. It would have been quite impossible to obtain anything like even this relatively unsatisfactory measure of comparability if only the official publications of the territories concerned had been utilized.

To describe all the different methods, and the qualifications necessary for exactitude, in the use of the official statistical information, as now published by the different African territories, would require a separate volume. In this study it has been necessary to compile a considerable number of statistical series over long periods, and this has been possible only by ignoring the minor qualifications and by concentrating attention on the broader issues. My objective has been to give a general picture of the development of trade and finance in the territories considered. The difficulties of doing even this have been increased by the fact that, except for recent years, complete files of the annual reports of each territory were not available in Johannesburg, while, even when they were available, the annual reports in many cases did not enable one to obtain an accurate unbroken series.

I finally decided to base the main statistical tables relating to the trade and finance of most British African territories on the statistics given in the annual volumes of the *Statistical Abstract of the British Empire*. It must, however, be noted that the figures in this publication do not always tally with those in the official reports of the individual territories. This is not surprising because the official reports themselves do not always agree from year to year. Moreover, any particular figure may be qualified in an official report by some special explanation referring to the inclusion or exclusion of particular items. To have listed all such special qualifications would have made the information presented in this book unduly cumbersome, and would have detracted attention from the main objective.

[1] *Cf.* Reports for 1935 and 1936.

The following general notes supplement those which are given in the text of the book:

TRADE.

Except where otherwise stated, trade figures referring to British African territories have been designed to show the total imports, that is, imports including re-exports (and Government imports), but not including transit or trans-shipment trade. The export tables have been designed to show domestic exports, and therefore exclude re-exports. This is a general classification, and particular figures may be found to fall short of this standard for special reasons, or owing to the vagueness of the official nomenclature. The summary table of Total Value of Domestic Exports of Each African Territory for Selected Years (Table 43) has been compiled from the individual sheets relating to British African territories and from the figures relating to the trade of non-British territories presented elsewhere in the book. Some of the figures represent total exports because the amount of the re-exports was not known, and, in some cases, it is not clear whether the figures are total exports or domestic exports. The summary Table showing the Total Imports of Each African Territory for Selected Years (Table 44) is intended to represent imports *less* re-exports, that is, broadly speaking, imports for "home consumption". Again, it must be realized that all the figures did not achieve this object. In some cases, the imports are total imports; in other cases, it is not quite clear what the term "imports" really covers. Table 45, Total Trade of Africa for Selected Years, represents the addition of items in Tables 43 and 44, and the qualifications which apply to the first two sheets must be borne in mind in regard to it, in particular that it represents the addition of imports and exports after excluding re-exports.

The treatment of bullion and specie presented very great difficulties. There is an extraordinary amount of confusion in regard to these items in the various official reports, and inevitably therefore in the *Statistical Abstracts*. The object in the tables presented in this book has been to exclude movements of coin and bullion for currency purposes, but to include bullion in domestic exports when bullion was itself being produced by the territory concerned. In regard to some territories there is a considerable measure of confusion between re-exports and transit or trans-shipment trade.

Kenya and Uganda trade statistics are combined in the official trade returns ; only estimates are available for separating the exports of Kenya and Uganda. The trade statistics of these territories are particularly complicated, and the methods of presenting them have been varied from time to time. The table of trade statistics of Kenya and Uganda has had to be compiled from various sources, as is shown in the notes thereto.

It should finally be noted in regard to trade statistics in general that great differences exist between methods of valuing exports and imports in the different territories. Information on this is contained in the *Statistical Abstracts* and in the official trade reports themselves. It is in this field, in particular, that efforts should be made to bring about standardization.

The trade statistics of the non-British territories in Africa are in general less satisfactory than those of the British territories. Reference has already been made in the text (see p. 297) to the somewhat peculiar method of valuation utilized in the Belgian Congo in order to arrive at the value of the export trade. In many cases foreign trade statistics do not distinguish clearly between domestic and total exports or between total imports and imports for home consumption, or between different classes of imports, *e. g.* government imports and merchandise imports. Sometimes the figures refer to one, and sometimes to another category. The difficulty of compiling foreign trade statistics has been very generally enhanced by the fluctuations of the French, Belgian and Portuguese currencies.

FINANCE STATISTICS.

The finance statistics of British territories are, except where otherwise stated, mainly based on those given in the *Statistical Abstracts*, supplemented by official reports.

The terms "revenue" and "expenditure" in general refer to the *gross*[1] revenue and *gross* expenditure of the territories concerned. It was found quite impossible to attempt to make allowance for

[1] This is the term used in the *Statistical Abstracts*.

the extraordinary differences in the meaning attached to such terms as "extraordinary expenditure" and "extraordinary revenue". Items which may be classified as extraordinary revenue in one year in one territory will be found to be classed differently in other years or in other territories. For this reason the procedure adopted in the *Statistical Abstracts* has been followed. Gross revenue in general excludes revenue from loan funds, but there are cases where no exact line between the two could be drawn. Public Debt figures are gross public debt, and do not make allowance for the amounts standing to the credit of Sinking Funds where these exist. Customs revenue in general refers to the revenue from customs duties, but in some cases it includes excise, and in other cases export duties as well. The most important point to be stressed in regard to the financial statistics is that their exact meaning is necessarily crude owing to the variety of accounting methods used in the local budgets. The figures must therefore be used with caution; both in the case of the financial and the trade statistics for any particular year, and in any particular territory, figures, if used out of their context, (in which they are intended to give a general picture only) should be checked with official documents, in order that any special qualifications may be taken into account by the reader.

BIBLIOGRAPHY

THIS Bibliography, with few exceptions, contains only those books which have a direct bearing on the subject-matter of this study. If all books which have been consulted on general colonial or economic questions (*e. g.* investment) had been included, the Bibliography would have become unduly cumbersome.

In the first section books, pamphlets and articles have been listed according to the chapters in which reference is first made to them, or to whose subject-matter they most closely approximate. Many of the books, however, deal with questions which are discussed in more than one chapter, but they have not been listed more than once.

In the second section the special literature on each African territory has been listed under the name of the territory, but books, pamphlets or articles listed previously have not been repeated.

SECTION I

CHAPTER I

BOOKS

BEER, G. L. *The Old Colonial System.* New York : Macmillan, 1912.
BUCHANAN, D. H. *The Development of Capitalist Enterprise in India.* London : Macmillan & Co., 1934.
CLARK, COLIN. *National Income and Outlay.* London : Macmillan & Co., 1934.
CONDLIFFE, J. B. *New Zealand in the Making.* London : Allen & Unwin, 1930.
COPLAND, D. B. *W. E. Hearn : First Australian Economist.* Melbourne and Oxford University Press, 1935.
CURTIS, LIONEL. *Civitas Dei.* New edition, 3 vols. in one. London : Macmillan & Co., 1938.
—————— *The Commonwealth of Nations.* London : Macmillan & Co., 1916.
DE KAT, ANGELINO. *Colonial Policy,* Vols. I and II. The Hague : Martinus Nyhoff, 1931.
DE KIEWIET, C. W. *The Imperial Factor in South Africa— A Study in Politics and Economics.* Cambridge University Press, 1937.
EGERTON, H. E. *British Colonial Policy in the Twentieth Century.* London : Methuen & Co., 1922.
FEIS, H. *Europe: The World's Banker,* 1870–1914. Yale University Press, 1930.
FISHER, ALLAN G. B. *The Clash of Progress and Security.* London: Macmillan & Co., 1935.
GIBBONS, H. A. *The New Map of Africa.* New York: The Century Company, 1916.
GREAVES, I. E. *Modern Production among Backward Peoples.* London: Allen and Unwin, 1935.
HANCOCK, W. K. *Problems of Nationality,* 1918–1936. *Survey of British Commonwealth Affairs,* Vol. I. London: Oxford University Press, 1937.
HOBSON, J. A. *Imperialism.* New York: James Pott & Co., 1902. (Third and revised edition. London: Allen and Unwin, 1938.)
HUTT, W. H. *Economists and the Public.* London : Jonathan Cape, 1936.
JOHNSTON, H. H. *The Opening up of Africa.* London: Butterworth & Co., 1928.
—————— *History of the Colonization of Africa by Alien Races: In Cambridge Historical Studies,* edited by G. W. Prothero. Cambridge University Press, 1913.
KUCZINSKI, R. R. *Colonial Population.* London: Oxford University Press, 1937.
—————— *Population Movements.* London: Oxford University Press, 1936.
LEAKE, H. M. *Unity: National and Imperial.* London: Allen and Unwin, 1935.
MARSHALL, ALFRED. *Principles of Economics,* 8th edition. London: Macmillan & Co., 1927.
PAGE, WILLIAM (Editor). *A Historical Review of the Economic Conditions of the British Empire from the Peace of Paris in 1815 to the Declaration of War in 1914, based on Parliamentary Debates.* London: Constable & Co., 1919.
REMER, C. F. *Foreign Investments in China.* London: Macmillan, 1933.
ROYAL INSTITUTE OF INTERNATIONAL AFFAIRS. *The British Empire : A Report on its Structure and Problems by a Study Group of Members.* London: Oxford University Press, 1937.
STALEY, E. *War and the Private Investor.* University of Chicago Press, 1935.
TOWNSEND, M. E. *The Rise and Fall of Germany's Colonial Empire.* New York: Macmillan, 1930.
TOYNBEE, A. J. *A Study of History,* Vols. I–III. London: Oxford University Press, 1934.
TOYNBEE, A. J. *Survey of International Affairs.* London: Oxford University Press. Royal Institute of International Affairs, Annual Volumes.

ARTICLES AND PAMPHLETS

CANNAN, E. Capital and the Heritage of Improvement. *Economica*, November, 1934.

DUFFIELD, W. B. The Chartered Companies. *Encyclopædia Britannica*, 10th edition, Vol. XXVI.

FRANKEL, S. H. Professor A. G. B. Fisher on the Clash of Progress and Security. *South African Journal of Economics*, September, 1936.

FISHER, A. G. B. International Problems of Economic Change, *International Affairs*, March–April, 1938.

HUTT, W. H. Logical Issues in the Study of Industrial Legislation in the Union of South Africa. *South African Journal of Economics*, March, 1935.

KINDERSLEY, R. British Overseas Investments. *The Economic Journal*, London, March, 1929 ; June, 1930 ; September, 1931; June, 1932; June, 1933; September, 1934; September, 1935; December, 1936.

SERTON, P. The Geographical Environment, chap. i. *The Cambridge History of the British Empire*, Vol. VIII, South Africa (1936).

WARMINGTON, E. H. Africa in Ancient and Modern Times, chap. iii. *The Cambridge History of the British Empire*, Vol. VIII, South Africa (1936).

CHAPTER II

BOOKS

ARNDT, E. H. D. *Banking and Currency Development in South Africa*. Capetown: Juta & Co., 1928.

BEER, G. L. *African Questions at the Paris Peace Conference*, edited by L. H. Gray. New York: Macmillan, 1923.

BIXLER, R. W. *Anglo-German Imperialism in South Africa*, 1880–1900. Baltimore: Warwick & York, 1932.

BUELL, R. L. *The Native Problem in Africa*, Vols. I and II. New York: Macmillan, 1928.

CALVERT, A. F. *The German African Empire*. London: T. Werner Laurie, 1916.

DE KIEWIET, C. W. *British Colonial Policy and the South African Republics*, 1848–1872. Published as No. 3 in Imperial Studies. London: Longmans, Green & Co., 1929.

DE KOCK, M. H. *Selected Studies in the Economic History of South Africa*. Capetown: Juta & Co., 1924.

EDWARDS, I. E. *The 1820 Settlers in South Africa*. No 9 in Imperial Studies. London: Longmans, Green & Co., 1924.

GOODFELLOW, D. M. *A Modern Economic History of South Africa*. London: James Nisbet & Co., 1902.

HALLBERG, C. W. *The Suez Canal: Its History and Diplomatic Importance*. London: George Routledge & Sons, 1931.

HAWTREY, R. G. *Economic Aspects of Sovereignty*. London: Longmans Green & Co., 1930.

HOLMSTROM, J. E. *Railways and Roads in Pioneer Development Overseas*. London: P. S. King & Son, 1934.

HUXLEY, E. *White Man's Country*. London: Macmillan, 1935.

JOHNSTON, H. H. *The Backward Peoples and Our Relations with them*. London: Oxford University Press, 1920.

KING, W. T. C. *History of the London Discount Market*. London: George Routledge & Sons, 1936.

KNOWLES, L. C. A., and KNOWLES, C. M. *The Economic Development of the British Overseas Empire*, Vol. III, South Africa. London: George Routledge & Sons, Ltd., 1936.

KNOWLES, L. C. A. *Economic Development in the Nineteenth Century*. London: George Routledge & Sons, Ltd., 1932.

LOVELL, R. I. *The Struggle for South Africa*, 1875–1899. New York : Macmillan, 1934.

MACGREGOR, D. H. *Enterprise, Purpose and Profit.* Oxford: Clarendon Press, 1934.

MARTIN, L. *The Treaties of Peace,* 1919–1923, Vols. I and II. The Carnegie Endowment for International Peace, New York, 1924.

MOON, P. T. *Imperialism and World Politics.* New York: Macmillan, 1926.

MOREL, E. D. *Affairs of West Africa.* London: William Heinemann, 1902.

ROBERTS, S. H. *History of French Colonial Policy,* 1870–1925, Vol. I. London: P. S. King & Son, 1929.

ROYAL INSTITUTE OF INTERNATIONAL AFFAIRS. *The Colonial Problem: A Report by a Study Group of Members.* London: Oxford University Press, 1937.

THOM, H. B. *Die Geskiedenis van die Skaapboerdery in Suid Afrika.* Amsterdam: Swetz & Zeitlinger, 1936.

VILJOEN, S. *The Economics of Primitive Peoples.* London: P. S. King & Son, 1936.

WHITE, F. *Mandates.* London: Jonathan Cape, Ltd., 1926.

WOOLF, L. *Empire and Commerce in Africa.* London: Allen & Unwin, 1920.

WRIGHT, P. Q. *Mandates under the League of Nations.* University of Chicago Press, 1930.

WYNDHAM, H. A. *The Atlantic and Slavery. Problems of Imperial Trusteeship. Report in the Study Group Series of the Royal Institute of International Affairs.* London: Oxford University Press, 1935.

ZIMMERMANN, A. *Geschichte der Deutschen Kolonialpolitik.* Berlin, 1914.

La Crise et les Colonies. Colonial International Library, Brussels, 1933.

ARTICLES AND PAMPHLETS

FRANKEL, S. H. *Africa in the Re-making. Our Changing World View,* by J. C. Smuts and others. Johannesburg: University of the Witwatersrand Press, 1932.

PLANT, A. *South Africa's Economic Development,* chap. xxix. *The Cambridge History of the British Empire,* Vol. VIII, South Africa.

ROBERTSON, H. M. *Effective Colonization. South African Journal of Economics,* December, 1937.

SCHUMANN, C. G. W. *Business Cycles in South Africa,* 1910–1933. *South African Journal of Economics,* June, 1934.

WELLINGTON, J. H. *Possibilities of Settlement in Africa,* reprinted from *Limits of Land Settlement.* (Edited by I. Bowman. New York: Council of Foreign Relations, 1937.) *Report to the Tenth International Studies Conference, Paris,* 1937.

WELLINGTON, J. H. *Some Geographical Aspects of the Peopling of Africa. Presidential Address. South African Journal of Science,* July, 1937.

CHAPTER III

BOOKS

AMPHLETT, G. T. *History of the Standard Bank of South Africa Limited,* 1862–1913. Glasgow University Press, 1914.

ARNDT, E. H. D., and RICHARDS, C. S. The Banking System of South Africa, *in Foreign Banking Systems,* edited by Willis and Beckhart, London, 1929.

ASHMEAD, E. *Twenty-five Years of Mining,* reprinted from *The Mining Journal.* London, 1909.

AUSTIN, A. C., and MERCER, M. *The Story of Diamonds.* Chicago, 1935.

BALLINGER, W. G. *Race and Economics in South Africa.* London: Hogarth Press, 1934.

BASTER, A. S. J. *The Imperial Banks.* London: P. S. King & Son, 1929.

BEET, G. *The Grand Old Days of the Diamond Fields.* Capetown: Maskew Miller Limited, 1931.

BUSSCHAU, W. J. *The Theory of Gold Supply.* London: Oxford University Press, 1936.

CAMPBELL, P. C. *Chinese Coolie Emigration to Countries within the British Empire.* London: P. S. King & Son, 1923.

CASSEL, G., GREGORY, T. E., KUCZINSKI, R. R., and NORTON, K. *Foreign Investments.* University of Chicago Press, 1928.

CULBERTSON, W. S.   *International Economic Policies*.   London: Appleton & Co., 1931.

DAVIES, A. E.   *Investments Abroad*.   McGraw Hill Book Company, 1927.

DEMUTH, J.   *Der Diamentenmarkt*.   Volkwirtschaftliche Abhandlungen der Badischen Hochsculen.   No. 13.   Karlsruhe, 1913.

EMDEN, P. H.   *Randlords*.   London : Hodder & Stoughton, 1935.

EVANS, M. S.   *Black and White in South-East Africa*.   London: Longmans, Green & Co., 1916.

FORT, G. SEYMOUR.   *Alfred Beit—A Study of the Man and His Work*.   London: Ivor Nicholson & Watson, 1932.

FOWLER, R. F.   *The Depreciation of Capital*.   London: P. S. King & Son, 1934.

FRANKEL, S. H.   *The Railway Policy of South Africa*.   Johannesburg: Hortors Limited, 1928.

GIFFEN, R.   *Essays in Finance*.   London: G. Bell & Sons, 1886.

GOLDMANN, C. S.   *South African Mines—Their Position, Results and Developments*.   London: Effingham Wilson & Co., 1895.

GOLDSCHMIDT, R. W.   *Kapitalpolitik*.   Berlin: Junker und Dunnhaupt Verlag, 1933.

GRANT, A. T. K.   *A Study of the Capital Market in Post-War Britain*.   London: Macmillan & Co., 1937.

GRAY, J.   *Payable Gold*.   Johannesburg: Central News Agency, 1937.

HARROD, R. F.   *International Economics*.   London: Nisbet & Co., 1933.

HATCH, F. H., and CHALMERS, J. A.   *The Goldmines of the Rand*.   London: Macmillan & Co., 1895.

HOBSON, C. K.   *The Export of Capital*.   London: Constable & Co., 1914.

HOBSON, J. A.   *International Trade: An Application of Economic Theory*.   London: Methuen & Co., 1904.

HOFMEYR, J. H.   *The History and Control of National Debts*.   Capetown: Townshend, Taylor & Snashall, 1918.

IVERSEN, C.   *Aspects of the Theory of International Capital Movements*.   London: Oxford University Press, 1935.

JACOBSON, D.   *Fifty Golden Years of the Rand*.   London: Faber & Faber, 1936.

KEYNES, J. M.   *The General Theory of Employment, Interest and Money*.   London: Macmillan & Co., 1936.

KEYNES, J. M.   *A Treatise on Money*.   London: Macmillan & Co., 1930.

——— *The End of Laissez-faire*.   London: Hogarth Press, 1927.

LEHFELDT, R. A.   *Restoration of the World's Currencies*.   London: P. S. King & Son, 1923.

LEHFELDT, R. A.   *Gold Prices and the Witwatersrand*.   London: P. S. King & Son, 1919.

LEWIS, C.   *The International Accounts*.   London: Allen & Unwin, 1927.

LIEFMANN, R. R.   *Beteiligungs und Finanzierungsgesellschaften*.   Jena, 1909.

LOVELL, R. I.   *The Struggle for South Africa, 1875–1899: A Study in Economic Imperialism*.   New York: Macmillan & Co., 1934.

MABSON, R. R.   *Mines of the Transvaal*.   Published annually at the offices of the *Statist*, London.

MARRIOT, H. F.   *Money and Mines*.   London: Ernest Benn, Limited, 1925.

MARSCHAK, J., and LEDERER, W.   *Kapitalbildung*.   London: William Hodge & Co., Ltd., 1936.

MARSHALL, H., SOUTHARD, F. A., and TAYLOR, K. W.   *Canadian American Industry: A Study in International Investment*.   Published for the Carnegie Endowment for International Peace.   New Haven: Yale University Press, 1936.

MATTHEWS, J. W.   *Twenty Years of Personal Experience in South Africa (Incwadi Yami)*.   London: Sampson Low, etc., 1887.

OHLIN, B.   *International and Inter-regional Trade*.   Cambridge : Harvard University Press, 1933.

REUNERT, T.   *Gold and Diamonds in South Africa*.   London: Edward Stanford; Cape Town: J. C. Juta & Co., 1893.

ROYAL INSTITUTE OF INTERNATIONAL AFFAIRS.   *The International Gold Problem*, by a Study Group of Members.   London: Oxford University Press, 1931.

SALTER, A.   *China and the Depression*.   Published by the National Economic Council.   National Government of the Republic of China.   Special Series, No 3, 1934.

SAYERS, R. S.   *Bank of England Operations, 1890–1914*.   London: P. S. King & Son, 1936.

SCHACHT, H. *Die Südafrikanische Diamantindustrie.*
SOMARY, F. *Wandlungen der Weltwirtschaft seit dem Kriege.* London: P. S. King & Son, 1931.
STAMP, J. C. *Double Taxation and the Freedom of International Investment. Studies in Current Problems in Finance and Government.* 1925.
STOKES, R. S. G. *Mines and Minerals of the British Empire.* London: Edward Arnold, 1908.
VINDEX. *Cecil Rhodes: His Political Life and Speeches.* London: Chapman & Hall, 1900.
WILLIAMS, B. *Cecil Rhodes.* London: Constable & Co., 1926.
WILLIAMS, G. F. *Diamond Mines of South Africa.* New York: Macmillan, 1902.
WILSON, J. *Twentieth Century Impressions of Natal.* 1906.
WILSON, R. *Capital Imports and the Terms of Trade in the Light of Sixty Years of Australian Borrowing.* Melbourne University Press, 1931.
WORSFOLD, W. B. *South Africa: A Study in Colonial Administration and Development.* London: Methuen, 1897.

The Gold Fields, 1887–1937. A Brief History of the Consolidated Gold Fields of South Africa Limited. Published by the Company, London, 1937.
The Mineral Resources of the Union of South Africa. Compiled in the Office of the Geological Survey, and published by the Government Printer, Pretoria, 1936.

ARTICLES AND PAMPHLETS

ANGELL, J. W. Review of Viner's *Canada's Balance of International Indebtedness. Political Science Quarterly,* 1925.
BLACK, D. The Incidence of the Tax on Gold Mining in South Africa. *South African Journal of Economics,* March, 1937.
BUSSCHAU, W. J. Rand Mining Economics. Paper read to the Chemical, Metallurgical and Mining Society of South Africa, November, 1937.
BUSSCHAU, W. J. Gold Mining Investment. *South African Journal of Economics,* March, 1937.
BUSSCHAU, W. J. Gold Mining Taxation: A Method of Analysis. *South African Journal of Economics,* September, 1935.
CLAY, HENRY. *Preface to Group Administration in the Gold Mining Industry of the Witwatersrand,* by John Martin.
DALTON, J. P. Taxation and Grade in Gold Mining: A Study in Equalities. *South African Journal of Economics,* September, 1937.
DAVID, H. Das Deutsche Auslandskapital und seine Wiederherstellung nach dem Kriege. *Weltwirtschaftliche Archiv,* 1919.
EDGEWORTH, F. The Theory of International Values. Papers relating to Political Economy, II. London, 1925.
EDWARDS, G. W. Government Control of Foreign Investments. *American Economic Review,* 1928.
EDWARDS, G. W. American Policy with Reference to Foreign Investments. *American Economic Review,* Supplement, 1924.
EMDON, M. H. Credit Facilities on the Johannesburg Stock Exchange. *South African Journal of Economics,* March, 1935.
EWING, J. M. M. Witwatersrand Mining Policy. *South African Journal of Economics,* June, 1934.
FISHER, A. G. B. Capital and the Growth of Knowledge. *Economic Journal.* London, 1933.
FLUX, W. A. The Yield of High-Class Investments. *Transactions of the Manchester Statistical Society,* 1910/11.
FRANKEL, S. H. The Return to Capital Invested in the Witwatersrand Gold Mining Industry, 1887–1932. *Economic Journal,* March, 1935.
FRANKEL, S. H. The Situation in South Africa, 1929–1932. *Economic Journal,* March, 1933. London.
FRANKEL, S. H. South African Monetary Policy. *South African Journal of Economics,* March, 1933.
HELFFERICH, K. Auslandwerte. *Bank Archiv,* 1910/11.

KEYNES, J. M. Some Tests for Loans to Foreign and Colonial Governments. *The Nation*, 1925.

KEYNES, J. M. Foreign Loans and Public Advantage. *The Nation*, 1924.

KOTZE, Sir ROBERT N. Notes on the Theory of Gold Supply. *South African Journal of Economics*, March, 1937.

KOTZE, Sir R. N. The Excess Profits Tax on Gold and Some of its Implications. *South African Journal of Economics*, September, 1933.

KOTZE, Sir R. N. The Gold Mining Position. *South African Journal of Economics*, June, 1933.

LASSWELL, H. Political Policies and the International Investment Market. *Journal of Political Economy*, 1923.

LIMEBEER, A. J. The Gold Mining Industry and the Gold Standard. *South African Journal of Economics*, June, 1935.

MILLS, R. C. The Lesson of Australia. *Index*, July, 1934.

PELKOWITZ, M. The Platinum Boom of 1925. *South African Journal of Economics*, December, 1936.

READ, C. L. The Union Native and the Witwatersrand Gold Mines. *South African Journal of Economics*, December, 1933.

RICHARDS, C. S. The Boom in Kaffirs: An Analysis. *South African Journal of Economics*, September, 1933.

STOKES, R. S. G. The Economics of Rand Mining. *South African Mining and Engineering Journal*, 28th August, 1937.

SMITH, F. B. Some Observations upon the Probable Effect of Closer Union of South Africa upon Agriculture. 1908. *S.A. Pamphlets*, Vol. 3, No. 60 in C.D. & O. Library, London.)

VINER, J. International Finance and Balance of Power Diplomacy, 1880–1914. *The South-Western Political and Social Science Quarterly*, 1929/30.

VINER, J. Political Aspects of International Finance. *Journal of Business of the University of Chicago*, 1928.

VINER, J. International Free Trade in Capital. *Scientia*, 1926.

WARD, R. L. Are the Gold Mines Overtaxed? A Commentary. *South African Journal of Economics*, March, 1936.

OFFICIAL REPORTS

Report of the Commission of Inquiry upon the Finances of the Cape of Good Hope. Parliamentary Papers, 1827, xxi.

Report of the Commission of Inquiry upon the Trade of the Cape of Good Hope. Parliamentary Papers, 1829, v.

Report of the South African Native Affairs Commission, 1903–5. Cmd. 2399.

Report of the Transvaal Labour Commission. Cmd. 1896, 1904.

Report of the Customs and Industries Commission. T.G. 6–1908. (Annexures to Votes and Proceedings of Transvaal Legislative Assembly, 1908, Vol. II.)

Report of the Mining Industry Commission, and Minutes of Evidence with Appendices and Index, 1908.

Report of the Commission on Conditions of Trade and Industries. U.G. 10–1912. Annexures to Votes and Proceedings of House of Assembly, 1912, Vol. III.

Report of the Economic Commission. U.G. 12–1914.

Report of the State Mining Commission, 1916–17.

Report of the Low Grade Mines Commission, 1919.

Report of the Mining Industry Board. Capetown, 1922. U.G. 39–1922.

Report of the Kemmerer and Vissering Commission. U.G. 13–1925.

Report of the Mining Regulations Commission. U.G. 36–1925.

Transvaal Chamber of Mines—Gold Producers' Committee—Mining Industry Arbitration Board, 1926–27: *Argument of Employers, Statements of Evidence, Memoranda and Statistics, Arbitrators' Report.*

Report of the Miners' Phthisis Commission. U.G. 38–1930.

Report of the Low Grade Mines Commission. U.G. 16–1932.

Report of the Select Committee on the Gold Standard. S.C. 9–1932

Report of the Committee of Investigation into the Conditions on the Alluvial Diamond Diggings. 1937. Published Departmentally.
Annual Reports of the Transvaal Mines Department.
Annual Reports of the Transvaal Chamber of Mines.
Annual Reports of the De Beers Consolidated Mines.
Annual Reports of the Government Mining Engineer.
Annual Stock Exchange Year Book.
Transvaal Chamber of Mines—Statements presented to the Economic Commission, 1913.

CHAPTER IV

BOOKS

BOTHA, J. H. *Unie-Finansies.* Capetown: Stewart Drukkersmaatskappy, 1936.
BROOKES, E. H. *The History of Native Policy in South Africa from 1830 to the Present Day.* Pretoria : Van Schaik, 1927 (2nd edition).
CORY, Sir G. E. *The Rise of South Africa.* London: Longmans, Green & Co., Vol. I, 1910 ; Vol. II, 1913 ; Vol. III, 1919; Vol. IV, 1926; Vol. V, 1930.
DIETZEL, K. H. *Die Südafrikanische Union.* Berlin, 1936.
EVANS, IFOR L. *Native Policy in Southern Africa: An Outline.* Cambridge University Press, 1934.
FRANKEL, S. H. *Co-operation and Competition in the Marketing of Maize in South Africa.* London: P. S. King & Son, 1926.
HOFMEYR, J. H. *South Africa.* London: Ernest Benn, 1932.
—— and others. *Coming of Age—Studies in South African Citizenship and Politics.* Capetown: Maskew Miller, Limited, 1930.
LEHFELDT, R. A. *The National Resources of South Africa.* Johannesburg: University of the Witwatersrand Press. London: Longmans, Green & Co., 1922.
LEPPAN, H. D. *Agricultural Policy in South Africa.* Johannesburg: Central News Agency, 1931.
MACCRONE, I. D. *Race Attitudes in South Africa: Historical, Experimental and Psychological Studies.* London: Oxford University Press, 1937.
MACMILLAN, W. M. *The South African Agrarian Problem and its Historical Development.* Johannesburg, 1919.
ROSS, G. E. N. *Landbou-krediet. 'n Inleiding tot die Studie van die probleem van Kredietverskaffing vir die Boer in Suid Afrika.* Amsterdam: H. J. Paris, 1927.
SCHAPERA, I. (Editor). *Western Civilisation and the Natives of South Africa.* London: George Routledge & Sons, 1934.
SCHUMANN, C. G. W. *Structural Changes and Business Cycles in South Africa, 1806–1936.* London: P. S. King & Son, 1938.
SCHUMANN, C. G. W. *The World Depression: South Africa and the Gold Standard.* Capetown : Maskew Miller Limited, 1932.
SCHUMANN, C. G. W. *Die Kredietmark in Suid Afrika.* Rotterdam: De Wester, 1928.
VAN DER POEL, J. *Railway and Customs Policies in South Africa, 1885–1910.* No. 8 in Imperial Studies. London: Longmans, Green & Co., 1933.
VAN DER POST, A. P. *Economics of Agriculture.* Johannesburg: Central News Agency, 1937.
WALKER, E. *The Great Trek.* London: Macmillan & Co., 1934.
—— *A History of South Africa.* London: Longmans, Green & Co., 1935.
—— *Lord De Villiers and His Times, 1842–1914.* London: Constable & Co., 1925.

ARTICLES AND PAMPHLETS

ARNDT, E. H. D. Die Landboukrediet—'n Landbouskuldvraagstuk. *South African Journal of Economics,* June, 1933.
BOTHA, J. H. Financial Problems of Provincial Government in South Africa. *South African Journal of Economics,* June, 1933.

FRANKEL, S. H.   Some Comments on Price and Marketing Control in South African Agriculture.   *South African Journal of Economics*, September, 1934.

FRANKEL, S. H.   Economic and Racial Problems of South Africa.   *Journal of the Royal Institute of International Affairs*, May, 1932.

FRANKEL, S. H.   A National Economic Policy in *Coming of Age*.   Edited by J. H. Hofmeyr.   Capetown: Maskew Miller Limited, 1930.

FRANKEL, S. H.   An Investigation into the Importance of the Gold Mining Industry of the Witwatersrand in Relation to the Finances of the Union of South Africa.   *Low Grade Mines Commission.*

FRANKEL, S. H.   Road and Rail Transport in *Coming of Age*.   Edited by J. H. Hofmeyr.   Capetown: Maskew Miller Limited, 1930.

FRANKEL, S. H., and BROOKES, E. H.   Problems of Economic Inequality: The Poor White and the Native, in *Coming of Age*.   Edited by J. H. Holmeyr.   Capetown: Maskew Miller Limited, 1930.

GILBERT, D. W.   Economic Effects of the Gold Discoveries upon South Africa, 1886–1910.   *Quarterly Journal of Economics*, August, 1933.

GRAY, J. L.   The Comparative Sociology of South Africa.   *South African Journal of Economics*, September, 1937.

GROSSKOPF, J. F. W.   Vestiging en Trek van die Suid-Afrikaanse Naturelle-Bevolking onder Nuwere Ekonomiese Voorwaardes.   *South African Journal of Economics*, September, 1933.

GROSSKOPF, J. F. W.   Die Plek van die Bantoe-Bevolking in die Suid-Afrikaanse Volkshuishouding.   *South African Journal of Economics*, December, 1933.

HAINES, E. S.   The Economic Status of the Cape Province Farm Native.   *South African Journal of Economics*, March, 1935.

HOLLOWAY, J. E.   The American Negro and the South African Abantu: A Study in Assimilation.   *South African Journal of Economics*, December, 1933.

HUTT, W. H.   Economic Aspects of the Report of the Poor White Commission.   *South African Journal of Economics*, September, 1933.

HUTT, W. H.   Natural and Contrived Scarcities.   *South African Journal of Economics*, September, 1935.

HUTT, W. H.   Logical Issues in the Study of Industrial Legislation in the Union.   *South African Journal of Economics*, March, 1935.

HUTT, W. H.   The Price Mechanism and Economic Immobility.   *South African Journal of Economics*, September, 1936.

HUTT, W. H.   The Economic Position of the Bantu in South Africa, in *Western Civilization and the Natives of South Africa*.   Edited by I. Schapera.   London: Routledge, 1934.

JACOBSSON, P.   Some Foreign Trade Problems of To-day.   *Index*, September, 1930.

LANDSBERG, E.   South Africa's Imports of Capital and the Balance of Payments.   *South African Journal of Economics*, September, 1937.

LANSDBERG, E.   The Present Position of Investment Funds and Government Loan Expenditure in South Africa.   *South African Journal of Economics*, September, 1936.

LESLIE, R.   Economics in South Africa.   *South African Journal of Economics*, September, 1936.

LESTRADE, G. P.   Some Aspects of the Economic Life of the South African Bantu.   *South African Journal of Economics*, December, 1934.

LIMEBEER, A. J.   Notes on the Union's Imports, Exports and Overseas Balances.   *South African Journal of Economics*, March, 1937.

MIDDLETON, J. J. I.   Building Society Finance. A Review with Comments upon some Features of Proposed Union Legislation.   *South African Journal of Economics*, March, 1934.

PEARSALL, C. W.   Some Aspects of the Development of Secondary Industry in the Union of South Africa.   *South African Journal of Economics*, December, 1937.

PEARSALL, C. W.   Industrial Fluctuations in South Africa.   *Commercial Bulletin of South Africa*, March–April, 1929.

POLLAK, H. P.   European Population Growth since Union. An Analysis of the Birth, Fertility and Death-Rates with Reference to the Future Increase of Population.   *South African Journal of Economics*, March, 1936.

RICHARDS, C. S.   Subsidies, Quotas, Tariffs and the Excess Cost of Agriculture in South Africa.   *South African Journal of Economics*, December, 1935.

ROBERTSON, H. M.   150 Years of Economic Contact between Black and White.   *South African Journal of Economics*, December, 1935.

SCHUMANN, C. G. W.   Die Abwertung des Südafrikanischen Pfundes.   *Weltwirtschaftliches Archiv*, January, 1936.

SHANNON, H. A.   Urbanization, 1904–1936.   *South African Journal of Economics*, June, 1937.

SHANNON, H. A.   A Survey of the Financial Administration of the Union, 1920–1935.   *South African Journal of Economics*, September, 1936.

VAN DER HORST, J. G.   Two Conferences.   *South African Journal of Economics*, March, 1933.

VAN DER HORST, S. T.   Some Effects of Industrial Legislation on the Market for Native Labour in South Africa.   *South African Journal of Economics*, December, 1935.

VILJOEN, S.   Are the Gold Mines Overtaxed ?   *South African Journal of Economics*, December, 1935.

OFFICIAL AND OTHER PUBLICATIONS

Papers Relating to the Finances of the Transvaal and Orange River Colony.   Cd. 1551, 1903.

Papers relating to the Progress of Administration in the Transvaal and Orange River Colony.   Cd. 1552, 1903.

Reports of the Transvaal Labour Commission.   Cd. 1896, 1904.

Report of the Transvaal Indigency Commission.   T.G. 13–1908.

Dominions Royal Commission Reports.   Cd. 7505, 1914; Cd. 7706–7, 1914; Cd. 8462, 1917.

Report of the Sugar Inquiry Commission.   U.G. 22–1922.

Report of the Drought Investigation Commission.   U.G. 49–1923.

Report of the Economic and Wage Commission.   U.G. 14–1926.

Report of the Native Economic Commission.   U.G. 22–1932.

Report of the Commission on Co-operation and Agricultural Credit.   U.G. 16 1934.

Report of the Railways and Harbours Affairs Commission.   U.G. 36–1934.

Report of the Industrial Legislation Commission.   U.G. 37–1935.

Report of the Customs Tariff Commission.   U.G. 5–1936.

Report of the Carnegie Commission on the Poor White Problem.   (Stellenbosch, 1932.)

Official Year Book of the Union of South Africa.

Monthly Bulletin of Union Statistics.

South African Municipal Year Book.

Federation of British Industries—Annual Reports on British South Africa.

Annual Statistics of Production—Agricultural and Industrial.

Trade of the Union of South Africa, Southern and Northern Rhodesia, the Territory of South-West Africa, and British South Africa (Monthly and Annually).

Summaries of Insurance Returns.   Annual.

Irrigation Department.   Annual Reports.

Irrigation Commission.   Annual Reports.

Irrigation Finance Commission, 1925 and 1926.

Land and Agricultural Bank.   Annual Reports.

Registrar of Building Societies.   Annual Reports.

Electricity Supply Commission.   Annual Reports.

Trade Reports—Customs and Excise.   Annual and Quarterly

Shipping Board Reports.   Annual.

Controller and Auditor-General's Reports.   Annual.

Commissioner for Inland Revenue.   Annual Reports.

Provincial Auditors.   Annual Reports.

Estimates of Expenditure from Revenue and Loan Funds.

Estimates of Revenue and Expenditure of Cape, Natal, Transvaal and Orange Free State.

Estimates of Capital Expenditure of Cape, Natal, Transvaal and Orange Free State.

Public Debt Commissioners.   Annual Reports.

Census of Agricultural and Pastoral Production.   Annual.

Census of Manufacturing Industries.   Annual.

Reports of the Native Affairs Commission. Annual.
Report of the Natives Land Commission—Native Grievances Inquiry (1913–14).
Reports of the General Manager of Railways and Harbours.
Reports of the Railways and Harbours Board.
Controller and Auditor-General's Statements of Accounts.
Estimates of Revenue and Expenditure. Railways.
Report of Departmental Railway Tariffs Inquiry. U.G. 56–1930.
Road Transportation Board Reports.
Report of the Financial Relations Commission. U.G. 16–1935.
Report of the Inter-Departmental Committee on the Labour Resources of the Union. Government Printer, Pretoria, 1930.
List of Official Union Publications issued by the Government Printing and Stationery Department, Pretoria, 1935.
Farming in South Africa. Official.
Journal of the Institute of Bankers.
S.A. Mining and Engineering Journal.
S.A. Mining Review.
Standard Bank of South Africa Monthly Review.
Proceedings of the Economic Society of South Africa.
Journal of the Union Department of Agriculture.

CHAPTER V

BOOKS

ANGELL, J. W. *The Theory of International Prices.* Cambridge: Harvard University Press, 1926.
BALTZER, F. A. W. *Die Kolonialbahnen mit Besonderer Berücksichtigung Afrikas.* Berlin: G. J. Goschen Verlagshaundlung, 1916.
BALTZER, F. A. W. *Die Erschliessung Afrikas durch Eisenbahnen.* Berlin: Dietrich Rimer, 1913.
BODELSEN, C. A. *Studies in Mid-Victorian Imperialism.* New York, 1925.
BOURRAT, C. *Les Chemins de fer en Afrique et Leur rôle dans l'expansion Coloniale.* Perpignan: J. Martz, 1910.
BOWMAN, I. *The Pioneering Fringe.* American Geographical Society, New York, 1931.
CLARK, G. *A Place in the Sun.* New York: Macmillan & Co., 1936.
———— *The Balance Sheets of Imperialism.* New York: Columbia University Press, 1936.
DAVIS, J. M. *Modern Industry and the African.* London: Macmillan & Co., 1933.
DIETZEL, K. H., and RUDOLPHI, H. *Koloniale Studien.* Berlin: D. Reimer, 1928.
ELLIOT, W. Y., MAY, E. S., ROWE, J. W. F., and others. *International Control in the Non-Ferrous Metals.* New York: Macmillan, 1937.
FERDINAND-LOP, S. *Les Colonies Françaises.* Paris: E. Molfère, 1931.
GIRAULT, A. *The Colonial Tariff Policy of France.* Oxford: Clarendon Press, 1916.
HARRIS, J. H. *The Chartered Millions.* London: The Swarthmore Press, Ltd., 1920.
HOFFHERR, R., and MAUCHAUSSE, P. *Formules Modernes d'Organisation Minière Africaine.* Paris, 1933.
HYATT, S. P. *The Old Transport Road.* London: Melrose & Co., 1914.
KRANOLD, H. *The International Distribution of Raw Materials.* London: George Routledge & Sons, 1938.
LEITH, C. K. *Minerals and World Politics.* New York: The McGraw Hill Book Company, 1931.
MARTIN, G. *La Situation Financière de la France, 1914-1924.* Les Cours De Droit, Paris.
MEYER, H. *Die Eisenbahnen in tropischen Afrika.* Leipzig, 1902.
MOULTON, H. G., and LEWIS, C. *The French Debt Problem.* Brookings Institute, New York, 1925.
PAGE, W. (Editor). *Commerce and Industry—Statistical Tables.* London: Constable & Co., Ltd., 1919.

PERHAM, M., and CURTIS, L. *The Protectorates of South Africa*. London: Oxford University Press, 1935.

RAPHAEL, L. A. C. *The Cape-to-Cairo Dream*. New York: Columbia University Press, 1936.

RENTY, E. A. *Les Chemins de fer Coloniaux en Afrique*. Paris, 1904.

ROBBINS, L. *Economic Planning and the International Order*. London: Macmillan & Co., 1937.

————— *The Great Depression*. London: Macmillan & Co., 1934.

ROUMENS. *L'Imperialisme français et les Chemins de fer trans-Africains*. Paris : Plon-Nourrit et Cie, 1914.

ROWE, J. W. F. *Markets and Men*. Cambridge University Press, 1936.

ROYAL EMPIRE SOCIETY. *The Crucial Problem of Imperial Development*. No. 15 in Imperial Studies. London: Longmans, Green & Co., 1938.

SHEPHERD, H. L. *The Monetary Experieuce of Belgium, 1914–1936*. London: Oxford University Press, 1936.

STALEY, E. *Raw Materials in Peace and War*. Council on Foreign Relations. New York, 1937.

SOUTHWORTH, C. *The French Colonial Venture*. London: P. S. King & Sons, 1931.

TOWNSEND, M. E. *Origins of Modern German Colonialism*. New York: Columbia University Press, 1921.

TROLL, C. L. *Das Deutsche Kolonialproblem*. Berlin: Andrews & Steiner, 1935.

TRUPTIL, R. J. *British Banks and the London Money Market*. London: Jonathan Cape, 1936.

VAN DER VELDE, M. W. *Economie Belge et Congo Belge*. Antwerp: Editions Lloyd Aversois, 1936.

VANDERVELDE, E. *La Belgique et Le Congo*. Paris, 1911.

VINER, J. *Studies in the Theory of International Trade*. London and New York: Harper & Brothers, 1937.

VINER, J. *Canada's Balance of International Indebtedness, 1900–1913*. Cambridge University Press, 1924.

WAIBEL, L. *Die Rohstoffgebiete Des tropischen Afrika*. Leipzig, 1936.

WEINER, L. *Les Chemins de Fer Coloniaux de l'Afrique*. Paris, 1931.

WEINTHAL, L. *The Story of the Cape to Cairo Railway and River Route*. London: Pioneer Publishing Co., 1923. 5 volumes.

WHITFORD, H. N., and ANTHONY, A. *Rubber Production in Africa*. United States Department of Commerce: Government Printing Office, Washington, 1926.

WHITE, H. D. *The French International Accounts, 1880–1913*. Cambridge: Harvard University Press, 1933.

WOOLF, L. *Imperialism and Civilization*. London: Hogarth Press, 1928.

WOHL, P., and ALBITRECCIA, A. *Road and Rail in Forty Countries*. London: Oxford University Press, 1935.

WOYTINSKY, W. *Die Welt in Zahlen*. Berlin: Mosse, 1927. 7 volumes.

ZIMMERMAN, E. W. *World Resources and Industries*. New York: Harper and Brothers, 1933.

Raw Materials and Colonies. Royal Institute of International Affairs, Information Department, Paper No. 18.

Pioneer Settlement: Co-operative Studies. American Geographical Society, Special Publication, No. 14. New York, 1932.

Raw Materials and Foodstuffs in the Commercial Policy of Nations. *Annals of the American Academy of Political and Social Science*. March, 1924.

ARTICLES AND PAMPHLETS

BUSSCHAU, W. J. Some Aspects of Railway Development in Natal. *South African Journal of Economics*, December, 1933.

EYSKENS, GASTON. Series of Articles on the Belgian Congo in the *Bulletin de l'Institut des Sciences Economiques, Université Catholique de Louvain*.

GIFFEN, R. The Use of Import and Export Statistics. *Economic Inquiries and Studies*. London, 1904.

GUYOT, Y. The Amount, Direction and Nature of French Investments. *Annals of the American Academy of Political and Social Sciences*, 1916.

KEMMERER, E. W. Theory of Foreign Investments. *Annals of the American Academy of Political and Social Sciences*, 1916.

MICHELL, L. The Cape to Cairo Railway. *Journal of the Society of Arts*, November, 1906.

ORMSBY-GORE, W. The Economic Development of Tropical Africa and its Effects on the Native Population. *Geographical Journal*, LXVIII.

PAISH, Sir G. Great Britain's Capital Investment in other Lands. *Journal of the Royal Statistical Society*, 1909 and 1911, and the *Statist*, 1914.

OHLIN, B. Das Verhältnis zwischen dem internationalen Handel und den internationalen Bewegungen von Kapital und Arbeit. *Zeitschrift für Nationalökonomie*, Bd. II, 1930.

RAFFOLOVICH, A. L'Exportation des capitaux. *Journal d'Economistes*, 1911.

SPEARPOINT, F. The African Native and the Rhodesian Copper Mines. *Journal of the Royal African Society*, July, 1937.

WILLIAMS, Sir R. Milestones of African Civilization. *United Empire*, 1917.
——— The Cape to Cairo Railway. Royal Empire Society, 1921. Address.
——— An African Romance, 1918.
——— The Cape to Cairo Railway from the Point of View of African Development. *Journal of the Central Asian Society*, 1922.

WILSON, R. Australian Capital Imports, 1871–1930. *The Economic Record*, 1931.

ZWEIG, K. Strukturwandlungen und Konjunkturschwankungen im Englischen Aussenhandel der Vorkriegszeit. *Weltwirtschaftliches Archiv*, 1929.

BRITISH GOVERNMENT AND OTHER PUBLICATIONS

Reports of His Majesty's Trade Commissioners published by the Department of Overseas Trade.

Empire Marketing Board Publications prepared in the Statistics and Intelligence Branch of the Empire Marketing Board on Production and Trade.

Survey of the Mineral Industry of the British Empire and Foreign Countries, 1930–1932.

Customs Tariffs of the Colonial Empire.

Annual Report on African Affairs, edited by Owen Clough.

An Economic Survey of the Colonial Empire, 1933, 1934, 1935. H.M. Stationery Office.

Dominions Office and Colonial Office List. Published annually.

Statesman's Year Book.

Annual Reports of the Colonies. Colonial Office. Published annually for each principal Colony, and for some of the lesser Colonies grouped together.

Annual Reports of the Mandated Territories. Published annually for each mandated area.

Colonial and Imperial Conferences, Series of Documents on, 1897 and later years. His Majesty's Stationery Office.

Department of Overseas Trade. Various publications, particularly those dealing with economic conditions in British and other Colonial territories.

Statistical Abstract of the Several Overseas Dominions and Protectorates in each year. Statistical Department, His Majesty's Stationery Office. Annual. Earlier issues entitled *Statistical Abstracts of the British Empire.*

Statistical Abstract of the United Kingdom. Statistical Department, His Majesty's Stationery Office. Annual.

Proceedings of the Royal Empire Society.

LEAGUE OF NATIONS PUBLICATIONS

International Trade Statistics. Annual.

Memorandum on Production and Trade, 1926.

Report on Certain Aspects of the Raw Materials Problem by the Provisional Economic and Financial Committee, 1921.

Report on the Problem of Raw Materials and Foodstuffs, 1921.

Review of World Trade. Annual.

Statistical Year Book. Annual.
World Production and Prices. Annual.
List of Works Relating to the Mandates System and the Territories under Mandate Catalogued in the Library of the League of Nations, 1930.
Balances of Payments. Annual.
Public Finance. Annual.
International Trade Statistics. Annual.
Money and Banking. Vol. I, *Monetary Review*; Vol. II, *Commercial Banks.* Annual.
World Economic Survey. Annual.
International Trade in Certain Raw Materials and Foodstuffs by Countries of Origin and Consumption, 1935 and 1936.
Economic Committee. Draft Customs Nomenclature, 1937.

INTERNATIONAL LABOUR OFFICE

Migration Movements, 1920–1924, 1925–1927.

INTERNATIONAL INSTITUTE OF AGRICULTURE

International Yearbook of Agricultural Statistics. Annual.
Annuaire de Documentation Coloniale Comparée.

FRENCH GOVERNMENT AND OTHER PUBLICATIONS

Annales du commerce extérieur; commerce et navigation des principaux pays étrangers. Annual.
Annuaire colonial, administratif. Ministère des Colonies.
Annuaire statistique de la France.
Bulletin Officiel du Ministère des Colonies.
L'Afrique Française—Bulletin Mensuel du Comité de L'Afrique Française et du Comité du Maroc.
Rapport fait au nom de la Commission des Finances chargie d'examiner le projet de loi, adopté par la chambre des Députés portant fixation du budget générale de l'exercice. Annual.

SECTION II

ANGLO-EGYPTIAN SUDAN

CRABITES, PIERRE. *The Winning of the Sudan.* London: George Routledge & Sons, 1934.

MACMICHAEL, H. *The Anglo-Egyptian Sudan.* London: Faber & Faber, 1934.

Peace Handbook—The Anglo-Egyptian Soudan, No. 98. H.M. Stationery Office, 1920.

The Anglo-Egyptian Sudan. A Commercial Handbook by North Winship. United States Government Printing Office, 1927.

Sudan Government—Monthly Report and Statistical Return of Foreign Trade, Khartoum.

Annual Reports on the Administration, Finances and Conditions of the Sudan. Presented by the Secretary of State for Foreign Affairs and published by His Majesty's Stationery Office.

Annual Reports of the Department of Economics and Trade.

ANGOLA AND MOZAMBIQUE

BOHM, E. *La Mise en Valeur des Colonies Portugaises—Les Presses Universitaires de France.*

JESSEN, O. *Reisen und Forschungen in Angola.* Berlin: Reimer, 1936.

DE PENHA-GARCIA, J. *Organisation Politique et administrative de l'Empire Colonial Portugais.* International Colonial Institute, 1936.

MARQUARDSEN, H., and STAHL, A. *Angola.* Berlin: Dietrich Reimer, 1928.

A Manual of Portuguese East Africa. His Majesty's Stationery Office, 1920.

Colonie de Mozambique—Finances et Credit.

Boletim Economico e Estatistico.

Economic Conditions in Portuguese East Africa—Reports of the Department of Overseas Trade.

Peace Handbooks issued by the Historical Section of the Foreign Office. Nos. 120 and 121. His Majesty's Stationery Office, 1920.

Colonie de Mozambique—Exposition Coloniale Internationale Bulletins. Paris, 1931.

Boletim de Agencia Gerol das Colonias. Monthly.

Annuario Estatistico de Portugal.

Annuario Estatistico published by the Statistical Department, Mozambique.

Report on Employment of Native Labour in Portuguese East Africa.

Reports of the Railway Companies of Angola and Mozambique.

Economic Conditions in Angola. Reports of the Department of Overseas Trade.

BASUTOLAND

HODGSON, M. L., and BALLINGER, W. G. *Indirect Rule in Southern Africa: Basutoland.* Lovedale Press, 1931.

Annual and Departmental Reports.

Financial and Economic Position of Basutoland. Report of the Commission appointed by the Secretary of State for Dominion Affairs. Cmd. 4907, 1935.

SWAZILAND

Annual and Departmental Reports.

Financial and Economic Position of Swaziland. Report of the Commission appointed by the Secretary of State for Dominion Affairs. Cmd. 4114, 1932.

BECHUANALAND

HODGSON, M. L., and BALLINGER, W. G. *Britain in Southern Africa—Bechuanaland Protectorate.* Lovedale Press.
Annual and Departmental Reports.
Financial and Economic Position of the Bechuanaland Protectorate. Report of the Commission appointed by the Secretary of State for Dominion Affairs. Cmd. 4368, 1933.

BELGIAN CONGO

GIDE, A. *Voyage au Congo.* Nouvelle Revue Française, Paris, 1927.
LEPLAE, E. Méthode suivie pour le Développement de l'agriculture au Congo Belge. *Congo*, October, 1930.
TOGUE, G. *Les Massacres du Congo.* 1907.

Chambre des Représentants—Annual Reports.
Rapports du Budget Général Ministère de Colonies, Chambre des Députés.
Banque Belge d'Afrique—Rapport du Conseil d'Administration.
Rapport Annuel sur l'Administration de la Colonie du Congo Belge.
Peace Handbook issued by the Historical Section of the Foreign Office. No. 99. *Belgian Congo.* His Majesty's Stationery Office, 1920.
Department of Overseas Trade—Annual Reports on the Belgian Congo.
L'Essor Economique Belge. Edited by · F. Passelecq. Brussels: Louis Desmet-Verteneuil, 1932.
Compagnie des Chemins de Fer du Congo Supérieur aux Grands Lacs Africains. Rapports bilan et Compte de Profits et Pertes.
Compagnie des Chemins de Fer du Congo Supérieur aux Grands Lacs Africains. Assemblée Générale Ordinaire.
Société Internationale Forestière et Minière du Congo. Rapports du Conseil d'Administration, et du Collège des commissaires présentés à l'Assemblée générale ordinaire.
Compagnie du Chemin de Fer du Bas-Congo au Katanga. Rapports du Conseil d'Administration et du Collège des Commissaires à l'Assemblée Générale des actionnaires.
Codes et Lois du Congo Belge.
Le Problème de la Main-d'oeuvre au Congo Belge. Brussels, 1931.

RUANDA URUNDI

Rapports présente par le Gouvernement Belge au Conseil de la Société des Nations au sujet de l'Administration du Ruanda-Urundi.

CAMEROONS (British)

Report presented to the League of Nations on the Administration of the Cameroons under British Mandate. Annual.
Annual and Departmental Reports.

EAST AFRICA

BRODE, H. *British and German East Africa. Their Economic and Commercial Relations.* London, 1911.
CHURCH, A. G. *East Africa: A New Dominion.* London: H. G. & G. Witherby, 1927.
ELIOT, Sir C. N. E. *The East Africa Protectorate.* London: Edward Arnold, 1905.
JOHNSTON, H. H. *East Africa, Uganda and Zanzibar Protectorates.* London, 1905.
KOCH, L. *Ostafrika in der Geschichte der Weltwirtschaft.* Berlin, 1930.
LUDGARD F. D. *The Dual Mandate in British Tropical Africa.* London: Blackwood, 1926.
McDERMOTT, P. L. *British East Africa or Ibea. A History of the Formation and Work of the Imperial East Africa Company.* London: Chapman & Hall, 1895.
WARD, H. F., and MILLIGAN, J. W. *Handbook of British East Africa, 1912/13.* London: Sifton Praed & Co., 1912.
ZIMMERMANN, E. W. *The German Empire of Central Africa.* London: Longmans, 1918.
MELLAND, E. East Africa: Our Opportunity. *Fortnightly Review*, April, 1929.

JOHNSTON, A. The Colonization of British East Africa. *Journal of the African Society,* Vol. 5, 1904/5.

WEDGWOOD, H. C. Land Settlement in East Africa. *Nineteenth Century,* Vol. 77 April, 1915.

East Africa Protectorate Blue Book. Annual.

East Africa Protectorate Agricultural Department. Annual Census.

East Africa Protectorate Native Affairs Department. Annual Report.

East Africa Protectorate Native Labour Commission, 1912/13.

East Africa Protectorate, Report of the Labour Bureau Commission, 1921.

East Africa Protectorate, Report of the Economic and Finance Committee on the Native Labour Problem, 1925.

East Africa Red Book, 1922, 1923, 1925, 1926, 1930.

East African Manual—Agriculture, Industry, Mining, 1929/30.

Report by F. D. Hammond on the Railway Systems of Kenya, Uganda and Tanganyika, 1921.

Memorandum on Transport Development and Cotton-growing in East Africa. Cmd. 2463, 1925.

East African Currency Board Reports.

Reports on East Africa—Department of Overseas Trade.

Annual Reports of the Joint East African Board.

Report of Joint Select Committee on Closer Union of East Africa, Vols. I, II and III.

Statement of Conclusions of H.M. Government in the United Kingdom as regards Closer Union in East Africa.

Report on Co-ordination of Transport in Kenya, Uganda and the Tanganyika Territory, by Brigadier-General Sir H. Osborne Mance.

Future Policy in regard to Eastern Africa. Cmd. 2904, 1927.

Report of the East Africa Commission. Cmd. 2387, 1925.

Report of the Commission on the Closer Union of the Dependencies in Eastern and Central Africa. Cmd. 3234, 1929.

Railway Rates and Finance in Kenya, Uganda and Tanganyika Territory. Cmd. 4235, 1933.

Higher Education in East Africa. Report of the Commission appointed by the Secretary of State for the Colonies, September, 1937. Colonial No. 142.

Memorandum on Native Policy in East Africa. Cmd. 3573, 1930.

Tenure of Land in the East Africa Protectorate. Cmd. 4117, 1906.

FRENCH TERRITORIES

SARRAUT, A. *La Mise en Valeur des Colonies Françaises.* Paris: Payot, 1923.

TRAILLON, J. L. *Bibliographie Critique de l'Afrique Française.* Paris: Charles Lavauzelle & Co., 1936.

Peace Handbooks issued by the Historical Section of the Foreign Office. Vol. XVII, French African Possessions. H.M. Stationery Office, 1920.

Economic Conditions in French West Africa—Reports of the Department of Overseas Trade.

Republique Française. Bulletin Officiel du Ministère des Colonies. Paris: Imprimerie Nationale.

Gouvernement Général du l'Afrique Equatoriale Française. A.E.F. Bulletin Économique de l'Afrique Equatoriale Française.

Bulletin Mensuel de l'Agence Economique Afrique Occidentale Française.

Reports on Togo and Cameroons to the League of Nations.

Statistiques Commerciales de l'A.O.F. Statistiques Mensuelles du commerce Extérieur de la France.

Bulletin du Comité de l'Afrique Française et du Comit' du Maroc.

Supplement Colonial de Economiste Europeen.

Revue Internationale des Produits Coloniaux.

Bulletin Mensuel de l'Institut d'Agronomie Coloniale, Nogent-sur-Marne.

Outre-Mer, Revue général de colonisation.

GOLD COAST

CARDINALL, A. W. *The Gold Coast.* Accra: Government Printer, 1931.

Report on the Railway System of the Gold Coast, by Lt.-Col. F. D. Hammond, 1922.

Gold Coast Handbook.
Annual Blue Book.
Annual Administration Report of the Gold Coast Railway and Takoradi Harbour.
Annual Trade Report.
Annual Report on the Social and Economic Progress of the People of the Gold Coast.
Annual Report of the Department of Agriculture.
Annual Report of the Audit Department.
Annual Report of the Mines Department.
Annual Report of the Treasurer.

KENYA COLONY AND PROTECTORATE

HOBLEY, C. M.   *Kenya from Chartered Company to Crown Colony.*   London, 1929.
LEAKEY, L. S. B.   *Kenya: Contrasts and Problems.*   London: Methuen & Co., 1936.
LEYS, N.   *Kenya.*   London: Hogarth Press, 1926.
McGREGOR ROSS, W.   *Kenya from Within.*   London: Allen & Unwin, 1927.
WEIGT, E.   *Die Kolonisation Kenias.*   Mitteilungen der Gesellschaft für Erdkunde zu
      Leipzig, 1930–31.
CASE, C.   The Pastoral and Agricultural Industries of Kenya Colony and Protec-
      torate.   *Economic Geography*, 1930.
SALVADORI, M.   *An Approximate Evaluation of the Amount of Capital required for the Mise
      en Valeur of the European Farms in Kenya* (unpublished).

*Report of a Committee appointed to Investigate and consider the Desirability of Co-ordinating
      and Regulating all Forms of Transport in the Colony.*
The Indian Problem in Kenya.   Cd. 1922.
Compulsory Labour for Public Purposes.   Cmd. 2464, 1925.
Report on Certain Questions in Kenya, by Lord Moyne, 1932.   Cmd. 4093.
Report of the Kenya Land Commission.   Cmd. 4556.
Report on Native Taxation, by G. Walsh and H. R. Montgomery, 1936,
*Report of the Commission appointed to Inquire and Report upon Allegations of Abuse and Hardship
      in the Collection of Non-native Graduated Poll Tax and of Native Hut and Poll Tax*, 1936.
Memorandum on Indians.   Cmd. 1922, 1923.
Report on Status of Indians.   H.C. 177, 1921.
Report of the Schuster Committee.   Cmd. 2701, 1926.
*Report of the Commission appointed to Inquire into and Report on the Financial Position and
      System of Taxation of Kenya.*   Colonial No. 116, 1936.
Report of the Economic Development Committee.   Nairobi: Government Printer, 1935.
Report of the Select Committee on Economy.   Nairobi: Government Printer, 1935.
Annual Blue Book.
Annual Financial Report and Statement.
Annual Report of the Mining and Geological Department.
Annual Reports on Native Affairs.
Annual Colonial Reports.
*Annual Reports of the General Manager of the Kenya and Uganda Railways and Harbours on
      the Administration of the Railways and Harbours.*
Annual Trade Report of Kenya and Uganda.

NIGERIA

BURNS, A. C.   *A History of Nigeria.*   London: Allen & Unwin, 1936.
CALVERT, A. F.   *Nigeria and its Tin Fields.*   London: Edward Stanford, 1912.
WELLESLEY, DOROTHY.   *Sir George Goldie—Founder of Nigeria.*   London: Macmillan
      & Co., 1934.

*Report by Sir F. D. Lugard on the Amalgamation and Administration of Northern and Southern
      Nigeria.*   Cmd. 468, 1920.
Report of the Railway System of Nigeria, by Lt.-Col. F. D. Hammond, 1924.   (Crown
      Agents for the Colonies.)
Annual Blue Book.
Annual Trade Report.
Monthly Trade Summary.

Annual Reports of the Customs Department.
Annual Reports of the Audit Department.
Annual Reports of the Agricultural Department.
Annual Reports of the Harbour Department.
Annual Reports of the Marine Department.
Annual Reports of the Public Works Department.
Annual Reports of the Mines Department.
Annual Reports on the Accounts and Finances.
Annual Reports of the Northern Provinces.
Annual Reports of the Southern Provinces.
Annual Reports of the Government Railway and Colliery of Nigeria.

NORTHERN RHODESIA

Evans, I. L. *The British in Tropical Africa.* Cambridge University Press, 1928.
Hole, M. H. *The Making of Rhodesia.* London: Macmillan & Co., 1926.

Agreement for Settlement of Outstanding Questions with the British South Africa Company. Cmd. 1984, 1923.
British South Africa Company's Reports on the Administration of Rhodesia.
Report of the Trade Mission to Northern Rhodesia. N.P.P. 261, 1931.
North Charterland Concession Inquiry. N.P.P. 308, 1932.
Present Position of the Agricultural Industry, and the Necessity or otherwise of Encouraging Further European Settlement in Agricultural Areas. Report by S. Milligan. Livingstone: Government Printer, 1931.
Report of the Finance Commission, 1932.
Report of the Agricultural Survey Commission, 1930–1932.
Report of the Commission of Enquiry into the Copperbelt Disturbances. Cmd. 5009, 1935.
Economics of the Cattle Industry in Northern Rhodesia, 1935.
Annual Blue Book.
Annual Reports of the Several Government Departments.

NYASALAND

Annual Blue Book.
Annual Report of the Department of Agriculture.
Annual Report of the Department of External Trade.
Annual Financial Report.
Annual Report of the Provincial Commissioners.
Annual Report of the Native Affairs Department.
Annual Report of the Audit Department.
Report on Tea Cultivation and its Development in Nyasaland.
Native Agricultural Committee Report.
Report of the Committee appointed by His Excellency the Governor to Enquire into Emigrant Labour, 1935. Zomba: Government Printer.

SIERRA LEONE

Report on the Sierra Leone Government Railway, by Lt.-Col. F. D. Hammond, 1922.
Annual Blue Book.
Annual Trade Report.
Annual Customs Report.
Annual Administration Report of the Sierra Leone Railway.
Report on Potential Rice Lands, by R. R. Glanville. Freetown: Sierra Leone, 1931.
Bibliography of Sierra Leone, by Sir H. C. Luke. London: Oxford University Press, 1925.

SOMALILAND

Annual Reports on the Social and Economic Progress of the People of Somaliland.
Report of the Somaliland Agricultural and Geological Department. Annual.

SOUTHERN RHODESIA

MALCOLM, D.   The British South Africa Company.   *Quarterly Review*, January, 1924.
WILSON, N. H.   *Notes on the Mining Industry of Southern Rhodesia*, 1930.   Southern Rhodesia Government Printer.

British South Africa Company—Financial Statements and Estimates.
Minutes of Proceedings of the Commission appointed to take an Account of what would have been due to the British South Africa Company if the Administration of Southern Rhodesia by the Company had been determined on the 31st March, 1918.   His Majesty's Stationery Office, May, 1921.
Records of the British South Africa Company.
Southern Rhodesia—Administrative Expenditure Commission.   Cmd. 1129, 1921.
Report of the Commission appointed to Enquire into the Cost of Administration of the Colony of Southern Rhodesia.   C.S.R. 20–1924.
Report by Brigadier-General F. D. Hammond on the Railway System of Southern Rhodesia.   C.S.R. 2–1926.
Interim Report of the Commission appointed to Enquire into and Report on Certain Matters in Dispute between the Beira and Mashonaland and Rhodesia Railways and the Employees of the said Railways.   C.S.R. 4–1928.
Report of the Railway Court of Enquiry.   C.S.R. 17–1929.
Report on a Trade Mission to Southern Rhodesia.   N.P.P. 261, 1931.
Ottawa Conference Report of the Committee appointed to Investigate and Report to the Government on Certain Matters relating to the Natural Resources and Industries of Southern Rhodesia, their Present Position and Future Prospects and their Relation to Empire and World Trade.   C.S.R. 1–1933.
Report of the Committee of Enquiry into the Economic Position of the Agricultural Industry of Southern Rhodesia.   C.S.R. 16–1934.
Report of the Committee of Enquiry into Certain Aspects of the Dairy and Pig Industries.   C.S.R. 4–1936.
Report of the Southern Rhodesia Land Commission.
Report of the Southern Rhodesia Agricultural Commission.
Report on Industrial Relations in Southern Rhodesia, by Professor Henry Clay.   C.S.R. 3–1930.
Annual Reports of the General Manager of the Beira and Mashonaland and Rhodesia Railways.
Annual Reports of the Auditor-General.
Annual Reports of the Land and Agricultural Bank.
Annual Reports of the Controller of Customs and Excise.
Annual Reports of the Maize Control Board.
Annual Reports of the Secretary, Department of Mines and Public Works.
Annual Reports of the Railway Commission.
Annual Statements of the Trade of Southern Rhodesia with British Countries and Foreign Countries.
Annual Reports of the Chief Native Commissioner and Secretary for Native Affairs.
Official Year Book of Southern Rhodesia.
Debates of the Legislative Assembly.

SOUTH-WEST AFRICA

CALVERT, A. F.   *South-West Africa*, 1884–1914.   London: T. Werner Laurie, Ltd., 1915.
SANDER, L.   *Geschichte der Deutschen Kolonial-Gesellschaft für Sudwest Afrika*.   Berlin, 1912.

Memorandum on the Country known as German South-West Africa.   Pretoria: Government Printer, 1915.
Report of the South-West Africa Commission.   U.G. 26–1936.
Report of the Commission on the Economic and Financial Relations between the Union of South Africa and the Mandated Territory of South-West Africa.   U.G. 16–1935.

Annual Reports presented by the Government of the Union of South Africa to the Council of the League of Nations concerning the Administration of South-West Africa.
Administrator's Reports. Annual.
Estimates of Revenue and Expenditure. Annual.

TANGANYIKA TERRITORY

GILLMAN, C. The South-West Tanganyika Territory. *Geographical Journal*, February 1927.
JENKINS, E. C. Economic Equality and the Mandates Commission. *Journal of Political Economy*, October, 1929.

Report by Sir Sidney Armitage Smith on a Financial Mission to Tanganyika. Cmd. 4182, 1932.
Report on Conditions and Cost of Living in the Colonial Empire. H.M. Stationery Office, 1937.
Report of the Customs Tariff Committee, 1930.
Report on the Railway System in Tanganyika, by Col. F. D. Hammond. London, 1930.
Report of the Tanganyika Railway Commission, 1930.
Interim Report of a Committee appointed to Inquire into the Question of Competition between Road Transport and Railways in the Tanganyika Territory. 1936.
Report on Tea Cultivation in the Tanganyika Territory and its Development, by H. H. Mann, 1937.
Annual Blue Book.
Annual Trade Reports.
Annual Reports of the Department of Agriculture.
Annual Reports of the Department of Lands and Mines.
Annual Reports of the Public Works Department.
Annual Reports of the General Manager on the Administration of the Railways and Port Services.
Annual Reports by the Treasurer.
Annual Reports on the Administration of Tanganyika Territory by H.M. Government to the League of Nations.

TOGOLAND (under British Mandate).

Annual Report on the Social and Economic Progress of the People of Togoland.
Annual and Departmental Reports.

UGANDA

BRENDEL, H. *Die Kolonisation Ugandas.* Verlagsdruckerei, George Weigel, Grobenhain, 1934.
JOHNSTON, Sir H. *The Uganda Protectorate.* London: Hutchinson & Co., 1902.
THOMAS, H. B., and SCOTT, R. *Uganda.* London : Oxford University Press, 1935.

Cotton Industry Report. Cd. 4910, 1909.
Report of the Commission of Inquiry into the Cotton Industry of Uganda, 1929.
Report on the Agricultural Prospects of the Plateau of the Uganda Railway. Cd. 787, 1902.
Annual Reports of the Agricultural Department.
Annual Reports of the Treasury.
Annual Blue Book.
Report on an Investigation into Industrial Conditions affecting Unskilled Labour in Uganda, 1937.

WEST AFRICA

FAULKNER, O. T., and MACKIE, J. R. *West African Agriculture.* Cambridge University Press, 1933.
KINGSLEY, M. H. *West African Studies.* London: Macmillan & Co., 1901.
McPHEE, A. *The Economic Revolution in British West Africa.* London: George Routledge & Sons, 1926.

Ormsby-Gore, W. G. A.   The Economic Development of Tropical Africa and its Effect upon the Native Population.   *Geographical Journal*, Vol. LXVIII, September, 1926.

Report of the Committee on Nuts and Seeds, Edible and Oil Producing.   Cd. 8247, 1916.
Report of the Private Enterprise Committee.   Cmd. 2016, 1924.
Report on Palm Oil and Palm Kernels.   N.P.P. 99, 1925.
Report by W. G. A. Ormsby-Gore on his Visit to West Africa.   Cmd. 2744, 1926.
West African Currency Board Reports.

ZANZIBAR

Report on the Zanzibar Clove Industry, by B. H. Binder.   Zanzibar: Government Printer, 1936.
Report on the Clove Industry of Zanzibar, by C. F. Strickland, 1932.
Report on Clove Cultivation in the Zanzibar Protectorate, by S. R. Troup.
Annual Reports on the Social and Economic Progress of the People of Zanzibar.
Report of the Commission on Agricultural Indebtedness and Memorandum thereon by the Government of Zanzibar, 1932.
Statistics of the Zanzibar Protectorate, 1935.
Report of the Commission appointed by the Secretary of State for the Colonies to consider and report on the Financial Position and Policy of the Zanzibar Government in relation to its Economic Resources, by Sir Alan Pim, 1932.
Report on Co-operation and Certain Aspects of the Economic Condition of Agriculture in Zanzibar, by C. F. Strickland.   Crown Agents for the Colonies, 1932.
Report on the Indebtedness of the Agricultural Classes, 1933, by C. A. Bartlett and J. S. Last.   Zanzibar: Government Printer.
Zanzibar—Its History and its Peoples, by W. H. Ingrams.   Witherby & Co., High Holborn, 1931.

INDEX

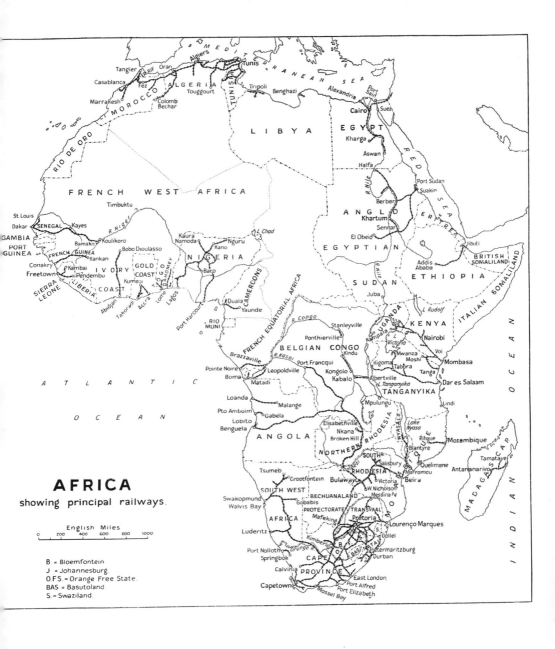

AFRICA
showing principal railways.

English Miles
0   200   400   600   800   1000

B. = Bloemfontein
J. = Johannesburg
O.F.S. = Orange Free State
BAS. = Basutoland
S. = Swaziland